THE HISTORY

OF

AMERICAN SCULPTURE

LOREDO TAFT

ARNO PRESS · NEW YORK · 1969

A PUBLISHING AND LIBRARY SERVICE OF THE NEW YORK TIMES

THE HISTORY OF

AMERICAN SCULPTURE

PLATE 1. — SAINT GAUDENS: ABRAHAM LINCOLN, CHICAGO.

THE HISTORY OF

AMERICAN SCULPTURE

BY

LORADO TAFT

MEMBER OF THE NATIONAL SCULPTURE SOCIETY

New Edition

REVISED AND WITH NEW MATTER

New York

THE MACMILLAN COMPANY

1924

Norwood Press
J. S. Cushing Co. — Berwick & Smith Co.
Norwood, Mass., U.S.A.

EDITOR'S NOTE

THIS series of books brings together for the first time the materials for a history of American Art. Heretofore there have been attempts to narrate some special period or feature of our artistic development, but the narrative has never been consecutive or conclusive. The present volumes begin with the founding of the nation, and carry the record down to the year 1904. They are intended to cover the graphic, the plastic, the illustrative, the architectural, the musical, and the dramatic arts, and to sum up the results in each department historically and critically. That the critical summary should be authoritative, the preparation of each volume has been placed in the hands of an expert — one who practises the craft whereof he writes. The series is therefore a history of American Art written from the artist's point of view, and should have special value for that reason.

The " History of American Sculpture " is the initial volume of the series. The writer of it makes acknowledgment for help received from many sources; but the editor of the series thinks it proper to say that the great bulk of the volume is original material gathered at first hand and here presented for the first time.

NOVEMBER, 1903.

CONTENTS

PART I

THE BEGINNINGS

PART II

MIDDLE PERIOD

PART III

CONTEMPORARY MEN

LIST OF PLATES

ILLUSTRATIONS IN TEXT

xi

INTRODUCTION

THE HISTORY OF AMERICAN SCULPTURE

INTRODUCTION

No more composite nation than the United States has existed in modern times. The influx of foreign elements has been enormous; yet, despite the varied antecedents and the wide affinities of the American people, our language remains English and our traditions (such as exist) are and always have been English. In matters of religion and law, the inheritance was adequate, and familiar principles were readily harmonized with a new environment. In our literature, likewise, the ancestral traditions have been positive and potent; but in regard to the other fine arts they have been negative, though not less significant, since they explain, in large measure, the unpromising conditions amid which our national art was cradled.

England's patronage of foreign artists has always been liberal, but until comparatively recent times her native production has been exceedingly meagre. If British painting was unimportant in England at the time when the American colonies were in process of making, it may be said that British sculpture did not exist at all. And thus it came about that our ancestors here in America were without sculptural tradition. Not only this, but in large measure they were of a humble class — working people unacquainted with even the allied arts — and often, with the prejudice of ignorance, attributing the arts one and all to the invention of the devil. The Pilgrim Fathers were the elder brothers of those men who decapitated the cathedral statuary, who burned paintings and tabooed the drama. Even their music was of an unhappy sort. This world was to them a vale of tears, and art was a temptation to be strenuously resisted.

3

It is not surprising, then, that stock of this character transplanted to an unsettled and inhospitable shore should have been practically immune from artistic inspirations; that painting should not have come into vogue for many a long year, and that two whole centuries were to elapse before sculpture should make a shy appearance. It may be urged that the Virginian colonies were made up of different material; that the cavaliers and adventurers who founded Jamestown were to some extent men of culture and luxury. To this fact may be attributed the earliest patronage of sculpture in America — the commissions given by Virginia to Houdon in 1781 and 1785 for representations of Lafayette and of Washington; but beyond this we find no appreciable results, since native production in the South came even later than in the North.

The Quakers who followed in Pennsylvania were hardly more favorable to the fine arts than were their brothers of New England, and although some of our best artists are of Quaker descent, there was nothing to encourage plastic expression in Philadelphia until recent times. The early Dutch settlers of New Amsterdam came direct from the land where Rembrandt and Franz Hals were even then producing their masterpieces; but there was neither a Rembrandt nor a Hals among them, nor by any possibility a sculptor, since the artistic expression of the Hollanders has always been pictorial rather than plastic.

So this broad land lay in the sun and waited — waited without knowing it for the day of art to appear. Meanwhile, to be sure, there was something else to be done. Six days of arduous toil every week, grubbing and ploughing and building; weaving and baking and brewing; and then the abrupt pause of the Sabbath, bringing with its inevitable recurrence a sort of rhythm into the patient lives of these plain men and women. The preachers did their share of work, like the others, and despite their long-drawn-out sermons, found time for writing chronicles and tracts, and even hymns of questionable rhyme and metre. By the time these had given way in part to political pamphlets, painting had made its appearance here and there. Benjamin West's triumphs in England lent a glamour to the craft, and Copley and Gilbert Stuart successively produced their admirable portraits in Boston and elsewhere. But as yet no sculpture appeared.

A few works of art had been imported into the country during this period, and some of the more elegant homes, like Mount Vernon, even boasted of marble reliefs brought from Italy. Houdon and other foreign sculptors came and went; but until the third decade of the nineteenth century there was no native sculpture other than the wax reliefs of Patience Wright, the wood-carvings of William Rush, and the unrelated efforts of Hezekiah Augur. Our first professional sculptor was born in 1805. Thus the record of the glyptic art in the United States is practically bounded by the short span of a single century. In other countries the chronicle of the last hundred years is but a fragment, a brief sequel to the story of ages of endeavor. It is difficult to realize that our actual achievement from the very kindergarten stage of an unknown art to the proud position held by American sculpture in the Paris Exposition of 1900 has been the work of threescore years and ten — has been seen in its entirety by not a few men now living.

As beginners seldom attempt groups, but work timidly on single figures, so the beginnings of American sculpture are discovered in isolated workers appearing here and there in most unexpected localities: Rush in Philadelphia; Augur in New Haven; Frazee in New Jersey. Then, with the opening years of the last century, came the first Americans destined to make sculpture a profession: Greenough in Boston, Crawford in New York, Powers in Cincinnati. One is reminded of the first adventurous flowers of early spring peeping out inquiringly from sheltered nooks, but soon to be reënforced by a host of companions. To-day our sculptors thrive in groups; the isolated practitioners of the art are few.

Almost without exception these sculptors of the first half of the century were animated by a single desire, — to get to Italy as soon as possible. The reasons for this are not far to seek. Their own country afforded neither sculptural instruction nor examples. Those who went abroad remained there; hence no returning current of helpful knowledge and counsel came to aid those left behind. Nor was there even the privilege of study from nature. The Puritan horror of the "flesh" made the introduction of life classes very difficult. As late as 1870 a sculptor's opportunity for study in Boston was limited to Dr. Rimmer's lectures on anatomy; in

1876 a model posed one evening in the week at the Lowell
Institute.

While paintings were to be met with in the homes of wealth and
in the growing art collections, works of sculpture were still extremely
rare.   A few casts from the antique, brought over from Paris and
exhibited in Philadelphia about 1845, are said to have caused a
grave scandal.   The initial collection of the National Academy of
Design remained boxed for several years, but was on view in 1820
and thereafter.   The condition, so far as concerned sculpture, was
in most cities what it is to-day in the smaller towns of the West
and the South, excepting for the important difference that seventy-
five years ago there were no photographs and no popular illustrated
magazines to familiarize the public with current works of art.   Steel
engravings were to be found in rare and expensive volumes, and
rude woodcuts in cheaper works; but beyond these there was
nothing to suggest sculpture in any form.   The old-time prejudice
had weakened somewhat, but a dense ignorance of the art still
persisted.   Can there be much wonder, then, that all sculptors' eyes
turned eagerly toward that almost fabled land beyond the sea where
art was known and appreciated ?

Another sufficient reason for the unanimous hegira of this time
lay in the dearth of good materials in this country.   Our early
sculptors were as a rule expert carvers according to the standard of
the day, but America offered them no fine marble.   What little they
used was imported at great expense and with exasperating delays
from Italy.   As for bronze casting, the case was still more hopeless.
Suitable sand was not to be had, and the experts who knew the
caster's art guarded their secret well in Munich and in Paris.   It
was not until 1847 that the first bronze statue was cast in the United
States, and this attempt was not a brilliant success.

With these conditions in mind, it may seem strange that so
many aspirants should have suddenly turned to sculpture as a profession.   When it is recalled, however, that the discovery of the
daguerreotype was not announced until 1839, and that up to that time
almost the only available reproductions of the human countenance
had been paintings and silhouettes, it is not surprising that portrait
sculpture should have been favored by the well-to-do, nor that Yankee

ingenuity should have come to discover its resources in this direction. Almost all of these early sculptors were intelligent but uncultivated men who had come to their craft by way of the marble yard, and who troubled themselves little with politics, philosophy, or poetry. Greenough was exceptional in his education; Powers and Crawford in their later mental development; but the rank and file were largely of the character described. They had nothing in particular to say, but had early discovered an aptitude for the chisel and the modelling tool, as the next one might for music or rhyming. Opportunity came — or was made — and the modest talent was cultivated, often through hardships which were silently borne or perhaps quite overlooked in the radiant vision of a career as distinguished and as profitable as that of the sculptor then promised to be.

With one accord these early men hastened to Italy, where in Florence or Rome they carved portrait busts for a living, and modelled figures as nearly in the style of Canova and Thorwaldsen as their unschooled hands and minds would permit. There were no masters among them, for masters come only with the high tides of art. The great artist is rarely found in a season of mediocrity. He comes usually as a culmination; hardly ever by way of antithesis. Hence it was impossible that there should be a great American sculptor in the first half of the nineteenth century, just as it was impossible that there should have been any at all during the two preceding centuries of colonial life. There was nothing to make sculptors out of, and even had there been a latent sense of form, there was nothing to bring it to fruition.

It has been well said of the Late Renaissance that "it did not think, it merely adapted thought; it did not feel, it appropriated the masks of classic feeling." How much more true is this of that later classic revival in Italy which followed with such servility the letter, but failed so completely to catch the spirit, of Greek art! We have grown so far away from its "classic" formula, which our primitives were reared upon, that we are scarcely able to do these men justice to-day. In the presence of their uninspired works we can sympathize with Emerson, who thought, back in the thirties, that "the art of sculpture has long ago perished to any real effect." We can understand, too, Hawthorne's petulance toward the succeeding phase of Italo-American art, — "this universal prettiness, which seems to be the highest conception of the crowd of modern sculptors." No doubt it was the reaction from such irresponsibility and childishness on the part of our sculptors which led Sidney Lanier to make the surprising claim for John Rogers' war groups that they revealed "the brightest examples of genius in the art yet afforded by our country." For it must be acknowledged that up to the time of the Centennial but little significance had crept into American sculpture. It was alien and impersonal, expressing in no way the spirit of the people nor even the emotions of its authors. The lyric strain was almost unknown; our sculptors were executants, not composers. They thought that they were doing original work, but with most of them it was mere rearrangement and recitation by rote.

Since that time the evolution of taste has been so rapid that many a worthy craftsman has been left stranded and bewildered by the receding tide of popularity. A few bridged over the period of artistic revolution and adjusted themselves to a new environment; a few — a very few — escaped the levelling influence of Italy. Generally this was the result of failure to go abroad; sometimes it was the price of ignorance; but in more than one case it was the protest of a natural independence which disdained to follow the beaten path and proposed by its own unaided efforts to blaze new trails to fame. Such men are indeed exceptional and stand out, rugged and distinct, in the history of our art. Their works speak for themselves and demand attention. Other men of less note must be mentioned in the early annals because they were first, or because of special achievement, or of the influence which they exerted, or for some other reason; but there must necessarily remain a colorless and nameless multitude, the now silenced "Greek chorus" of endeavor. These are as necessary in all periods as are the master performers, — without them are no masters, — but they leave slight record. For their unheralded efforts and their forgotten contributions we should be thankful. They had their value in the sequence of progress.

With the Centennial Exposition of 1876 came an artistic quickening such as our country never had known before. A new and growing appreciation dates from that year. It began with the recognition of our own shortcomings as compared with other lands. France in particular made strong appeal to our newly awakened tastes, and the work of one or two Americans who had studied in Paris had great influence. The demand for a better and more forceful art was not long to remain unanswered. With the advent of Saint Gaudens there came a notable change in the spirit of American sculpture, while the rapid transformation of its technic was no less marked and significant. Though we owe this change largely to Paris, the result has not been French sculpture. Paris has vitalized the dormant tastes and energies of America — that is all. A pronounced and helpful feature of the new order is the fact that as a rule the Parisian-trained sculptors do not remain abroad; they return to live with their own people and, like their French masters, they delight in teaching. The influence of such a man as Saint Gaudens, for instance, becomes incalculable when multiplied through the pupils whom he has brought up to share his labors and his triumphs. Thus the art schools of America are at the present time in a flourishing condition, and the opportunity for study from nature is so abundant in all of our large cities that it is no longer necessary for a student of sculpture to go abroad excepting for travel and observation. Hands have grown skilful and eyes discerning here in America, while not a few of our sculptors have learned the art of thinking and expressing themselves in truly sculptural terms — something which is quite distinct, it may be said in passing, from realistic imitation, and which presupposes a motive very different from one of either a picturesque or a literary character.

But while the men of the new generation have acquired such mastery of the "mechanics" of the profession as wins the praise of their foreign instructors and fellow-workers, their language is not always understood at home. Our people have no intuitive grasp of its meaning. In spite of the oft-repeated assurance that we know what we like, we do not even know what we are saying when we say it. It is true that we recognize what we like, and that we like it well, for the time at least. On the other hand, we do not have a "grand passion" for sculpture, taking it to heart like the modern French. Our feelings are not outraged by bad work, nor by transgressions of venerated laws of style, of balance, of movement, and of other sacred traditions. Likewise are we insensible, in large measure, to the charm of these fundamental virtues.   Unless a work of sculpture shows something more; unless it makes special appeal by its significance, its emotion, or its insistent beauty of face or form, we are as indifferent to it as though it were not; we do not, perhaps, even see it.

We lose much, of course, but there is after all something rather fine in this sturdy independence. It may, indeed it must, result in an art of greater meaning and intensity than we have heretofore known.   We say to the artist, as it were, " Put in all the 'composition,' all the 'technic' you please ; we have nothing against them; but first of all give us something that we can understand and sympathize with."   Hence it follows that the mere " Beaux-Arts figure " so closely allied to the *objet de Paris*, has already had its day with a considerable portion of our community.   It has followed the Graces and the Cupids of our Italian age.

Perhaps, however, we underestimate our own development in the appreciation of form for its own sake.   Unconsciously the better technic has made itself a necessity; the Parisian bronze, the Paris-trained sculptor, and — let it not be forgotten — increasing familiarity with the real masterpieces of the past have raised the standard all along the line.   While we may not be able to formulate an artistic creed, innumerably more people enjoy good art in this country at present than was the case a generation ago.   In monumental sculpture the change is particularly noticeable.   Fully one-half of our existing public monuments would fail to pass muster to-day with the municipal art commissions which have recently been created to protect the parks and avenues of our great cities.

Although any attempt at classification must be more or less arbitrary, the space of time covered in this history may be divided in a general way into three sections : —

I. The Beginnings of American Sculpture, 1750–1850.
II. Middle Period, 1850–1876.
III. Contemporary Sculpture, 1876–1903.

The first of these periods goes far back in order to bring to view the faint foreshadowings of our coming achievements, but its latter

half is a story of fascinating interest — a story of struggles and successes of the deepest significance to American art.

The second period, though including the years of the Civil War,
was largely one of commercial activity, — a time of opulence rather
than of enthusiasm, — and its achievements were by so much less
distinctive, excepting in the case of a few sturdy men who were
too strong in their own individualities to bow to the fashion of the
hour.   These men made the succeeding period possible.

The third period has brought a new revelation of the beautiful
in nature and is showing to the people of this country the possibilities of sculpture.   In this period it has reached for the first time the
dignity of a national expression, something neither Anglo-Saxon
nor Italian nor French; but a fusing of all these elements into an
art which is vital and significant — the true product of the country
and the age which have given it birth.

PART I

AMERICAN SCULPTURE

THE BEGINNINGS, 1750–1850

CHAPTER I

EARLY EFFORTS IN SCULPTURE

THE earliest sculptural expression of which we find record in the American colonies is the work of Mrs. Patience Wright of Bordentown, New Jersey. Her miniature heads in wax were celebrated by the elder chroniclers, but in the absence of ocular proof we must needs be a trifle sceptical regarding their superlative merits.

Patience Lovell was born at Bordentown in 1725. Of her parents nothing is known excepting that they had become Quakers, and as little is known of the childhood of the future artist. In 1748 she married Joseph Wright. Although there was not a statue or a cast in that part of the country, Mrs. Wright's talent revealed itself early, and long before the Revolution she had acquired a wide reputation for clever portraits in wax. Upon the death of her husband, in 1772, she removed with her three children to London, where she had a remarkable success in her art, the English periodicals of the time giving her high praise and styling her the " Promethean modeller." We are told that at one time she was freely admitted into the presence of the king, but that she lost his favor by scolding him for sanctioning the American war. It is a well-known fact that she rendered valuable service to the American cause during that trying period. Whenever a squadron was being fitted out or a general appointed, this keen-witted Quaker woman would transmit the number of troops and the place of their destination to the leaders of the Revolution. She corresponded a great deal with Benjamin Franklin, who at that time resided in Paris.

The *London Magazine* for 1775 contains a curious portrait of Mrs. Wright, showing her seated and holding a miniature bust of a man which she has apparently just modelled. The cut is accompanied by the following notice : —

" Her likenesses of the king, queen, Lords Chatham and Temple, Messrs. Barre, Wilkes, and others, attracted universal admiration. Her natural abilities are surpassing, and had a liberal and extensive education been added to her intimate qualities, she would have been a prodigy. She has an eye of that quick and brilliant water that it penetrates and darts through the person it looks on, and practice has made her so capable of distinguishing the character and dispositions of her visitors that she is very rarely mistaken, even in a minute point of manners; much more so in the general cast of character."

The " likeness " of Lord Chatham was a full-length portrait in wax, to which was accorded the high honor of a position in Westminster Abbey, where, protected by a glass case, it stood for many years.

Mrs. Wright died in London in 1785. Her younger daughter married John Hoppner, the English portrait painter; while her son Joseph Wright, after studying with Benjamin West, returned to the United States to play a modest but interesting rôle in the history of American painting.

It was in 1785, also, that Houdon, the great French sculptor, was commissioned by the state of Virginia to execute a marble statue of George Washington. For this purpose he crossed the ocean and for a fortnight remained a guest at Mount Vernon, making studies and a life mask of the future president. It is said that he even made a plaster cast of his entire person. An interesting glimpse of the facilities of ocean travel at that time is afforded by the following note in Louis Gonse's "La Sculpture Française": "Houdon sailed with Franklin from Havre on the 22nd of July, 1785. He was with Washington for fifteen days in Philadelphia, made his models, and returned to France, reaching home on January 4th, 1786."

The modelling and carving of the statue occupied two years, and the completed work, arriving at Richmond in 1788, was installed eight years later in the rotunda of the state Capitol, where it still remains. The little cistern-like room, connecting two legislative halls where history has been made, is dingy and without decoration other than a few busts and a typewriter's conspicuous card; but it has a fine top light which is worth more than upholstery and gilding. The head and shoulders of the figure are superbly illuminated, and the effect is noble beyond any impression given by replicas of the statue in other locations. The workmanship is exceedingly skilful and grows upon one with study; but there is, it must be confessed, a feeling of leanness and angularity in the lower portion of the statue. It may be that it was inherent in the subject, and it is doubtless accentuated by the costume — the uniform of a Revolutionary officer. Whatever may be the cause, there is, in spite of irreproachable drawing, an effect as of pasteboard or tinware about the lower limbs. This is further enhanced by the wide angle of the feet, which gives the figure from one view the look of having been cut out of a folded paper and then spread open. The close-fitting nether garments combined with their "tightness" of treatment, and the unheroic but doubtless circumstantial swell of the abdomen, produce a result more curiously individual than majestic, until the eye returns to the noble head, which is one of the finest examples of simplification to be found in modern art. It has in it the serenity and greatness of all time. Nearer approach discovers the perfection of drawing and of marble-cutting in the gloved right hand, which rests upon a long cane, and in the bared left, which lies upon a cloak thrown over the fasces — a bundle large, tall, and insistently prominent. This strange accessory rests in turn upon a ploughshare. The sharp lines of cane and plough and fasces are unpleasant and unsculptural, but the transfigured head welcomes the gaze after each bewildering excursion.

The base bears the inscription, " Par Houdon, Citoyen Français, 1788," and the front of the pedestal is covered with the following legend :—

> "The General Assembly of the Commonwealth of Virginia has caused this statue to be erected as a monument of appreciation and gratitude to GEORGE WASHINGTON, who, uniting to the endowments of the *Hero* the virtues of the *Patriot*, and exerting both in establishing the Liberties of his Country has rendered his name dear to his Fellow Citizens and given the world an immortal example of true glory.
>
> "Done in the year of CHRIST one thousand seven hundred and eighty-eight and in the year of the Commonwealth the twelfth."

c

Several reproductions of the figure exist, among them bronzes in the Capitol at Washington, the Museum of Fine Arts of Cincinnati, and Lafayette Park, St. Louis, and plaster casts in the Boston Athenæum and elsewhere.

The "Washington" was not M. Houdon's first contribution to the art treasures of the New World, however, for in an elevated niche of that same rotunda in the Virginian Capitol is a remarkable bust of Lafayette of earlier date, from the same fluent hand. One recognizes the strange sloping forehead and the similarly retreating hair, but the face is that of a youthful hero. The epauletted shoulders emerge from a voluminous drapery which is wound about the base and gives to the bust the air of a work of Coysevox. The inscription announces that this commission was voted Dec. 17, 1781, that is, in the same year in which Houdon exposed at the Salon his masterpiece, the "Voltaire" of the Comédie Française.

The next sculptor to visit us was an imaginative but unbalanced Italian, whose erratic career led him to the United States in 1791. Giuseppe Ceracchi was in this country for some months, and left a number of works of historic interest. He was born in Rome, July 4th, 1751, and was employed as a young man with Canova upon sculptures for the Pantheon, but journeyed in 1773 to England, where his ability was recognized by Sir Joshua Reynolds and other artists of influence. From England he went to Paris, where he was intimate with David and became affected by the revolutionary spirit then in the air. Filled with enthusiasm for "Liberty" and the new Republic, he came to America with a most preposterous scheme for Congress to erect a monument to Liberty, —a colossal group a hundred feet high, in marble, and including a score of figures, a chariot and horses, and marble clouds *ad libitum*. In the words of the "prospectus": "The Goddess of Liberty is represented descending in a car drawn by four horses, darting through a volume of clouds which conceals the summit of a rainbow. Her form is at once expressive of dignity and peace. In her right hand she brandishes a flaming dart, which by dispelling the mists of error, illuminates the universe; her left is extended in the attitude of calling upon the people of America to listen to her voice." This is but the beginning, however; a whole page of fine print is required to describe the various groups in which appear Saturn, Apollo, Clio, Philosophy, Policy, National Valor, Neptune, Mercury, and many other old friends. Probably our people were not very different then from what they are now, and it is easy to imagine their appreciation of the fanciful project. As might have been foretold, the money was not voted, — though the price was only $30,000, — and President Washington good-naturedly suggested private subscriptions, heading the list himself with a circumspect amount. As other names did not follow rapidly, the sculptor, quite disheartened, returned to France, but not until he had made a number of portrait busts which are reputed to be good, and some of which have found their way into marble. Ceracchi reached Paris just in time to have his head taken off for conspiracy against Napoleon. This happened on January 31st, 1801. His portrait is still to be seen at the Yale Museum, done in miniature by Trumbull, and is noticeable for the large, domelike forehead. The hair is in a queue, but loose and abundant over the head. The intelligent face wears a look of suffering, and the lips are tight pressed. The gray coat disappears under a foam of lace.[1]

Ceracchi's bust of Washington is erroneously said to have been placed in the Boston Athenæum. It is now in the Metropolitan Museum in New York. The sculptor also did portraits of Jefferson, Clinton, Hamilton, Benson, Jay, and Paul Jones. His marble bust of Hamilton may be seen in the New York Public Library. Two unhappy marble busts in the Pennsylvania Academy were long attributed to him. The first, a " Hamilton," is a copy by John Dixey, and the second, a " Franklin," may have been carved by the same hand from the bust by Caffieri. It has been conclusively established by Messrs. Hart and Biddle in their fine study of Jean Antoine Houdon that Ceracchi never modelled a portrait of Franklin. Ceracchi and Caffieri sounded alike to our ancestors.

A page in passing should be devoted to this same John Dixey, whose quiet personality strolls upon the scene in a manner very different from the tempestuous entry and exit of Ceracchi. Born in

[1] Dunlap, in his " Arts of Design," recites, at great length, the story of Ceracchi's tragic end.

Dublin, he spent most of his youth in London, where as a student in the Royal Academy he showed exceptional promise. Circumstances led him in 1789 to America. Transplanted to this new atmosphere, he seems to have become merely a workman of modest attainments and industrious habits, who built up a good business in house decoration. His most important contribution to a "national art" was a "Hercules and the Hydra" in bas-relief, which did not seem to be greatly needed, and finally disappeared entirely.

Dunlap, the historian of early American art, says of Dixey: "The models he executed were the fruits of his leisure hours, made at such intervals as he could spare from the pursuits which the state of the arts in this country, at that time, compelled him to resort to. He wished to revive the too much neglected art of sculpture, and his models were generally done at a considerable pecuniary sacrifice. His death occurred in 1820. Besides 'Hercules and the Hydra,' Mr. Dixey executed in 1818 a model of 'Ganymede,' and the next year he carved in wood the 'Adoration of the Wise Men of the East.' The Cherub's head in marble, on the Hamilton monument, is from his chisel, and the figures of Justice on the City Hall of New York, and the State House at Albany, are his design and execution.

"The talents and acquirements of Mr. Dixey, for many years previous to his death, were principally directed to the ornamental and decorative embellishment of public and private edifices. In the graceful and almost endless variety in which flowers are susceptible of being grouped, intermingled with the fanciful heads of men and animals, his chisel ever displayed both taste and ability." [1]

Meanwhile a certain William Rush of Philadelphia, an intelligent wood-carver of artistic temperament, had gradually perfected himself in the details of his profession. Born in Philadelphia on July 4, 1756, he had been apprenticed early to one Edward Cutbush, a carver, and his skill was presently rewarded by a large and lucrative business in the designing of figure-heads for ships. Notable among them were those for the United States frigates, *United States* and *Constellation*, representing respectively "The Genius of the United States" and "Nature." His figure of the "Indian Trader," on the ship *William Penn*, was copied by several London

[1] "Arts of Design," Vol. I, p. 329.

artists, who made casts and sketches of the head, while his " River God " for the ship *Ganges* is said to have been reverenced by the Hindus, who came in boat loads to see it.

Dunlap refers to " this intelligent and very pleasant old gentleman," and tells us that " his performances are all in wood and clay. . . . His time would never permit, or he would have attempted marble. He used to say it was immaterial what the substance was, the artist must see distinctly the figure in the block, and removing the surface was merely mechanical. When in a hurry he used to hire a wood-chopper, and stand by and give directions where to cut. By this means he facilitated work with little labor to himself. The crucifixes in the St. Augustine and St. Mary's Catholic churches, the 'Water Nymph' at Fair Mount, the figures in front of the theatre, with the statue of Washington in the State House [1] [1812], are his works in Philadelphia. It was always a source of regret that he had so little time spared him from his occupation in ship-carving, where he succeeded so admirably, especially in his Indian figures." [2]

FIG. I. — RUSH: NYMPH OF THE SCHUYLKILL.

Most of these examples of our earliest sculpture have disappeared from view, the figure-heads having "gone the way of the old-time specimens of marine architecture to which they were attached." From what remains we may well believe them to have been far more interesting artistically than the work of not a few of our professional sculptors. Mr. Rush had

[1] A life-size figure still standing in Independence Hall, Philadelphia.
[2] " Arts of Design," Vol. I, p. 315.

ideas in abundance, a sense of grace, and much facility; and in style, the resultant of all these elements, he was not lacking. When to such qualities are added enthusiasm and industry, the endowment of a good artist becomes unusually complete. An artist William Rush certainly was in his own field. The "Nymph of the Schuylkill" (Fig. 1) proves this as it stands to-day in the form of a bronze replica, near the waterworks in Fairmount Park. This ingenious work, for which, it is said, "a celebrated belle of the time consented to pose," represents a young woman holding a bittern upon her right shoulder. The plump arms are most gracefully disposed, the left hand grasping one of the feet of the bird, the right steadying a half-lifted wing. The bill threw a vertical stream of water which must have frequently deluged the maiden's abundant chignon, but otherwise her clinging attire is not ill suited to such mishaps. The waist is girdled with rushes, and the escaping drapery is skilfully handled, though the fulness of the skirt is in ridges rather than folds, betraying the wood-carver's treatment. Altogether, in spite of obvious crudities, the effect of the figure is one of lightness and grace — it may almost be said, of elegance. The original figure was carved in wood, and stood for many years in Centre Square, later called Penn Square. It was afterward removed to Fairmount Park, where it remained until it began to decay and its beauties to be threatened with as complete obliteration as had long since befallen the fair body which had inspired them. Fortunately a bronze cast was then made from the wood, preserving its every detail. Instead, however, of being placed in a museum, the original was again exposed to the weather until it all but fell to pieces, when the fragments were finally removed to the attic of a neighboring engine-house, where they are inaccessible.

Mr. Rush was one of the founders of the Pennsylvania Academy of Fine Arts. As early as 1789 he had sought with Charles Wilson Peale and others to establish such an institution, and when in 1805 it was finally inaugurated, he became a director, a position which he held actively until the time of his death. In 1812 he made a notable exhibit at this Academy of six of his later works; these, according to Dunlap, were busts of Linnæus, William Bartram, and the Rev. H. Muhlenburg, and figures of a cherub and of

"Exhortation" and "Praise." The "figures in front of the theatre," to which the historian referred, were "Tragedy" and "Comedy," and are still preserved at the Actors' Home, in the suburbs of Philadelphia. There is also mention of ideal figures of "Winter" and "Agriculture."

The only memento which the Pennsylvania Academy possesses of this remarkable man is his portrait (Fig. 2), "carved in a pine knot" by his own hands, — or rather, a plaster cast of the same, the original having long since disappeared. This bust is a unique and curious work. The shaggy shoulders are in appearance but a rough, knotty log over which a pine sprig has fallen, its needles mingling with the artist's long, thin locks. The effect of the formless mass is to suggest arms uplifted. Out of it emerges a strong and precisely characterized head of true Revolutionary type. Though the modelling is dry and literal, the ears in particular being crudely done, there is no question of its veracity; it shows us exactly what manner of man was William Rush. A whole generation of Italianate Americans produced nothing so trustworthy. The fine old head is turned vigorously to the right, the pose is strong but contained, and despite the unconventionality, not to say grotesqueness, of the wood-carver's fancy, the whole effect is one of power. The drawing of the nose, the modelling of the sensitive mouth and the fine chin, and particularly the expression of the seeing eyes are all admirable. This is one of those portraits which bind the generations of men together, which make us feel acquainted one with another. It has the same kind of authenticity that we recognize in Saint Gaudens's bust of Sherman, which stands close at hand.

In noting the resemblance of this face to certain military types, it is interesting to find that Mr. Rush actually served in his youth in the Revolutionary army. He was a member of the Council of Philadelphia for more than a quarter of a century, and made his influence felt in the political and intellectual life of his city until the time of his death, which occurred Jan. 17, 1833. It is probable that, coming at the time he did, he accomplished more for sculpture in Philadelphia than has any other one man since his day. His talent, remarkable as it was, counts for less than his personal influence. Though his own sculpture was wrought largely in perishable materials, his service to American art is enduring, for in uniting and crystallizing the floating elements of culture, in rendering them available, he made a contribution of permanent and ever-increasing value.

There was another wood-carver of those early times — though born considerably later than Rush — whose modest achievement deserves mention. Hezekiah Augur of New Haven, Connecticut, had no such influence as had William Rush, and produced little that comes within the scope of this work, but that little is exceedingly precious. The circumstances were extraordinary and will excuse some quotations from H. W. French's " Arts and Artists of Connecticut."

" The first Connecticut sculptor," says French, " was Hezekiah Augur, born in New Haven, February, 1791, the son of a carpenter. Augur, as a boy, enjoyed his father's trade; he enjoyed it more than his father did. At eight years old he ' preferred the confines of the shop to fighting schoolfellows,' to quote from a letter of his writing. This mildness of temper was to some extent unfortunate, preventing him from fighting his way into art till over thirty-four years old, though from childhood he was an artist. He had better have left carving wood with his father's tools now and then and gone out and fought his schoolfellows. The experience would have been good for him.

" His father did not like this carving and cutting, having that objection to his own business so common to the paternal mind. He put the boy under a grocer, when nine years old, to ' learn a trade.' Hezekiah did learn a trade. The grocer could mend and make shoes ; and counting it better to be a doorkeeper in art than a nabob in merchandise, Hezekiah applied himself to the awl. When the time for which he was bound expired, he issued an abominably poor grocer, but a proficient cobbler. Shoemaking was not in his father's programme for his son. He presented him with two thousand dollars and a position in a firm of reputedly honorable men as partner in a dry-goods business. This was a mistake on the part of all concerned. It was the great blunder of Hezekiah Augur's life. He knew his desires and ambition, and instead of passing unobjectingly, as he admits, into one plan or another, he should have asserted himself and let Art claim her own. His partnership continued but three years; when, he never knew precisely how, it was demonstrated to him that his two thousand dollars were not only disposed of, but that he stood indebted to the rest of the firm to the amount of seven thousand dollars more. By nature keenly sensitive, the sudden fall, after having lived upon the most social terms in the best society of New Haven, was a bitter blow, from which he did not easily recover. He found the truth of the old adage, that wealth makes honorable men at a cost of much suffering; and, wholly dropped and forgotten by his old associates, he opened a little fruit stand, where, in a sense, he succeeded."

The annals of American art present nothing more ludicrously tragic than this picture of the dazed young merchant sitting humbly amid his apples and oranges and vainly trying to make out "how it happened." But these dark hours ushered in a most unexpected dawn. For solace he resumed his old-time diversion of wood-carving, and decorated elaborately a mahogany case for a musical instrument which he had made. He chanced to take it to a cabinet-maker to varnish, and the beauty of the workmanship being recognized, he was at once offered employment at good pay. For two years he carved the legs of mahogany chairs and various ornaments in the intervals of "business." His biographer continues with worldly wisdom: "At the end of that time, having saved a considerable sum, he committed another blunder in paying up as much as he could of his indebtedness to the dry-goods firm. Encouraged by this, they began a system of dunning that so alarmed Mr. Augur that he sold out his fruit stand and carving business. The short, thin man, with light brown hair, an exceptionally fair, almost florid complexion, who was forever carving behind the counter, was missed from the fruit stand; but the general opinion among his former friends was that it was only another failure, for which the first had made him famous."

Fame was destined to come, however, in a very different guise — in a manner as unforeseen by the modest carver as by the carping neighbors. Like a romance is the next step in his progress.

"In the seclusion into which his sensitiveness and timidity forced him, he completed an invention for making worsted lace, which brought him a large price, and at once enabled him to free himself from debt.   At almost the same time his father died; and, all constraint being removed at the eleventh hour, he turned his whole soul toward art, though he said for himself of this final devotion, 'With a life-blot behind me, my only ambition is to drown memory and reflection in a pleasant pastime.'   In 1847 he also brought out a

carving machine, which is still used in several factories for carving piano legs. He originated many inventions in the course of his life, one of the more prominent being one rarely credited to him — that of producing the first bracket-saw.

"He carved so finely in wood, that Professor Morse urged him to attempt a work in marble. His first endeavor was upon the head of Apollo. He went at his marble as he had his wood, with no more of a model than his own fancy furnished him.   This, of course, necessitated exceedingly

FIG. 2. — PORTRAIT OF WILLIAM RUSH BY HIMSELF,
PENNSYLVANIA ACADEMY.

slow work, and increased the timidity of expression; but the result was exciting and encouraging.   He then produced a head of Washington and a figure of Sappho; and his fame was secure, so far as purely native talent, with no education whatever, could win it."

Mention is made of orders from New Haven and Hartford; but we can readily believe that in those days "his skill, though so remarkable, was not such as was calculated to yield a large income, except as works of his fancy might sell."   He did receive one commission from Congress to make a bust of Chief Justice Ellsworth, which still stands in the United States Supreme Court room in Washington. Mr. French then turns to " Mr. Augur's great work, . . . one that merits all the fame it achieved for its author, . . . the often-quoted pair of marble statuettes, ' Jephthah and his Daughter.' " It seems that they were carved without models. " But in themselves," he observes, with discrimination, " though expressing the faults natural to such a course, they possess much that is indicative of an exceptionally high rank of ability. In each the expression of face and limb, and the characteristic unity throughout, are worthy of great commendation. The head of the ' Daughter ' is particularly fine in the arrangement of the hair. He invited Washington Allston to criticise the work. Relating the fact to a friend, he said, ' Mr. Allston walked about them for thirty minutes without speaking, and the perspiration poured from me like rain during the whole half-hour.'

" Both in character and ability he was a man well fitted to hold a much higher position than circumstances ever allowed him to occupy. In 1833 he was made an honorary member of the alumni of Yale College. He died in January, 1858, with much, yet little, left behind as the result of his life's labor."

The so-called " group," as it is generally termed, is now in the Yale Art School and shows two detached figures in marble, intended as pendants, though unfortunately placed at some distance apart. They are about one-half life size and have a very professional look, showing no little beauty of pose and expression. Especially noticeable is the handling of the drapery, so often a stumbling-block to novices. Hezekiah Augur must have had his eyes open in those days ; he must have been familiar with good paintings, or at least engravings ; for such amplitude and richness as he has given to the garments is not the result of taste and ingenuity alone, but betokens experience — either his own or that of some one else.

" Jephthah's Daughter " stands in a dainty, timid position, the right foot advanced, the lithe body bending forward ; and to the right, the graceful arms, seemingly advanced for the father's embrace, have fallen abashed, the hands still clinging to the silenced cymbals. The little face alone shows the unskilled touch, but with all its crudity it is very sweet and very refined in intention. Its pose of frightened inquiry, with the incline of the figure and the droop of the arms, is as beautifully conceived as anything that one recalls in modern sculpture.   It has more pathos, more felt emotion, than has the whole life-work of many a more famous artist.   The thin little man of the fruit stand was a true poet!

"Jephthah" is less interesting, but he has a mighty swing as he writhes in his agony.   His Roman armor — never mind the anachronism! — is beautifully carved.   He leans on a magnificent shield introduced very boldly, and with his right hand pressed to his head he raises also the voluminous cloak, making deep shadows on both sides of a powerful torso.   The only suggestion of ineffectual workmanship here is again in the head, the sculptor's formula for the beard being especially unfortunate.   Otherwise this most elaborate figure might well be taken for the product of a French studio of the early eighteenth century — for the clever, florid work of a pupil of Pierre Puget.   Such amplitude is unique in early American sculpture, being as different as possible from the meagreness and poverty of style shown in those first-fruits of our national art which resulted from its Italian transplanting.   The wonder of it all is, however, that an artistic nature should have been evolved seemingly out of nothing; for there is no trace of the artistic in Augur's ancestry or education or surroundings.   Carpenter's son, grocer's clerk, cobbler, keeper of a fruit stand — and nevertheless a true artist!   Such things have their significance in the history of our national development.   Born fifty or sixty years later, with his native cleverness encouraged by opportunity for study, Hezekiah Augur might haply have become one of our greatest sculptors — and then again he might not!   Like scores of our own time, surrounded by advantages, he might have accomplished far less than he actually did when encouraged by every obstacle and strengthened by all ignorance.   Who shall say?

In strictly chronological sequence, Augur should have been preceded by John Frazee, who was born in 1790; but although the New Haven carver outlived Frazee by six years, the public work of the latter extends over a much longer period and a much larger territory. Augur's fame was purely local and his influence slight; Frazee's efforts were a connecting link between the early sporadic manifestations of sculptural art and the modern profession. Indeed, many overlooking the achievements of William Rush have pronounced John Frazee our first American sculptor. But despite his industry and the fact that Dunlap was able to write of him in 1833 that "he has progressed to a perfection which leaves him without a rival in this country," Frazee seems to have been singularly unpretentious and to have considered his marble business paramount to the end. He never attempted the figure seriously, though always hoping to; but many of his busts are, in both modelling and carving, good professional works of dignity and value.

Dunlap tells us[1] that the ancestors of John Frazee were emigrants from Scotland who landed at Perth Amboy among the early settlers of that place, and that the family name was Frazer, which was changed to Frazee by the grandfather of John. The historian continues: "Our subject was born on the 18th of July, 1790, in the upper village of Rahway. His mother's name was Brookfield, and he was her tenth child. Shortly after his birth she was deserted by an unworthy husband, and left to struggle with the ills of poverty. At the age of five John was taken to the protection of his grandmother Brookfield, whose character was similar to that of her daughter; and from these worthy women the child derived the basis of his moral and religious education. The boy was the household drudge as well as the outdoor laborer, but cheerfully assisted his aged relatives — even milking the cow, churning and working for his grandmother, and doing the field work. Neither the schoolboy instruction nor the schoolboy sport fell in due degree to John; and his principal amusement, when not at work, was to cut the forms of familiar objects out of boards or shingles, and to chalk figures upon the doors. His reward for these efforts was to have his ears boxed and the prediction that he would be a *limner*."

For some unknown reason the boy was removed from his grandmother, and placed with a farmer of the name of De Camp, "whose character and conduct were of the most deplorable kind. The boy remained in this habitation of vice, a slave to a brutal family, for two years." Escaping from this bondage at the age of thirteen, he returned to his passive mother and grandparents, "who joyfully

[1] "Arts of Design," Vol. II, p. 266.

received and protected him," incidentally setting him to work with responsibilities sufficient to bring out the manly virtues.

"He was not strong enough to manage and work the little farm of old Brookfield, and his mother procured him the advantage of a little more schooling. Circumstances, however, removed him from the occupation of an agriculturist, and he was bound apprentice to a country bricklayer, of the name of Lawrence. Another trial awaited young Frazee. The bricklayer took out a license for tavern-keeping; and John, in addition to working on the farm and laying bricks, had to become a tavern waiter. In the winter, when sleighing parties were frequent, many a night was spent in attending upon and supplying the reveller and the drunkard. But even here, with every temptation and example around him, the precepts of his mother and her mother preserved him. Besides, he had seen the evils of intemperance and gambling; and, at an early age, he resolved to eschew those vices, and kept his resolve firmly. Sundays were his own and he devoted them to teaching himself penmanship, and attempting to draw with his pen."

Now comes the little incident which was destined to be the momentous turning-point in his progress. "So far Frazee had proceeded in life's career without a knowledge of the instrument which was destined to open a brighter career for him — the chisel; but in the summer of 1808, Lawrence, having contracted to build a bridge over Rahway River at Bridgetown, was ambitious enough to wish his name chiselled in a neat tablet of stone, with the date of the year the work was finished. Upwards of forty men were employed on the bridge, two or three of whom were stone-cutters from New York, but none would undertake to immortalize the bridge builder. John asked permission to try his hand with the chisel, and the master consenting, he prepared the tablet and engraved on it, "Built by William Lawrence, A.D. 1808." This was the first work with the chisel by the future sculptor. He was now eighteen years of age, active, strong, and vigorous, and acknowledged as a skilful workman. From this period the chisel and mallet appeared to him the tools of his choice, and he aimed at becoming a stone-cutter instead of a bricklayer."

With such a childhood as had been his, it is not strange that the young man felt the lack of education. "Reading, writing, and the first rules of arithmetic were the whole of his learning." Despite the fatigue of his daily work as a mason and sometimes now as a stone-cutter, he set resolutely to "improve himself in useful knowledge." In this praiseworthy pursuit he was aided by a kind gentleman of culture, to whom he ever remained "unalterably attached." His position as pupil seems to have been exchanged subsequently for that of instructor, for we read farther on that, "The first years of freedom passed in bricklaying in summer, making headstones in winter, and in the evenings teaching psalmody."

Married in 1813, he entered the next year into partnership with a former fellow-apprentice, and they established themselves as stone-cutters at New Brunswick. This latter partnership appears to have been short-lived, for in the appendix of his book Dunlap informs us abruptly that "Frazee got rid of his partner, but incurred debt which induced hard work among the tomb-stones, his only employ-

FIG. 3. — BUST OF JOHN FRAZEE BY HIMSELF, PENNSYLVANIA ACADEMY.

ment, and strict economy. So ignorant was he at this time, that he had never heard of the American Academy of Fine Arts at New York, and when told that it was an exhibition of pictures and statues, he was puzzled to know how that could constitute an academy. Conscious of ignorance and thirsting for knowledge, he applied himself assiduously to books for instruction." In 1815 he lost his oldest child, a son, and on his tombstone made his first attempt at the human figure — a representation of "Grief." There is also record of a head of Franklin copied from a bust, and a loving study of one of his children eating a pie — a hint for other artists who have trouble in making young America pose. In his busy life there was little enough leisure, however, for such diversions, since the growing family — or it might be a foretaste of prosperity — incited to redoubled efforts. The evenings were now devoted to wood-carving for cabinet-makers, and the cutting of letters in steel for brands.

"Removing to New York, Frazee, in conjunction with his brother William, opened a marble shop in Greenwich Street, the first of May, 1818. Mantelpieces and tombstones occupied him for some years, and from 1819 to 1823 his principal study was lettering, which he carried to high perfection. To this was united monumental memorials in marble, which our churches may long be proud of. It was not until the year 1820 that Frazee saw the casts in the old Academy. His child's model caused an introduction to Trumbull, who told him that nothing in sculpture 'would be wanted in this country for yet a hundred years.' Frazee says in all his conversation he was 'cold and discouraging respecting the arts,' and exclaims, 'Is such a man fit for a president of an Academy of Fine Arts?'"

In spite of Trumbull's chilling rebuff, now become historic, the ardent stone-cutter became a student and member of the National Academy, and exhibited there at one time a bust of his aged mother, which Dunlap tells us he had seen with admiration.

Mr. Frazee's first marble bust was carved in either 1824 or 1825; Dunlap gives both dates in different places. The matter would be unimportant were it not for the fact that this was probably the first marble bust chiselled in this country, undoubtedly the first carved by a native American. The subject was a certain John Wells, a prominent lawyer of New York, and the monument stands in old St. Paul's Church on Broadway — not in Grace Church, as Dunlap tells us. He states further that, "It was executed from imperfect profiles after death," and that Frazee modelled it and put it in marble "without teacher or instruction." When one considers the difficulties of working from mere silhouettes, the success of this bust is extraordinary. It is very personal: the face is smooth, somewhat resembling the portraits of Hamilton; the head is well turned on the shoulders, and is alert, keen, amiable; the hair is marked by pleasing contrasts of light and shade; and the drapery is "classic," with many restless folds. The bust rests upon a projecting tablet which bears a long inscription; and the shelf-like cornice is encumbered, after the fashion of the time, with various articles of monumental bric-a-brac strewn about the base of the bust—noticeably a Greek lamp of learning on a pile of books, then, wherever convenient, marble scrolls and more books. For the Wells memorial — bust, tablet, and household goods — the sculptor received $1000. What labors intervened we do not know; but in 1831, "at the instance of the Hon. G. C. Verplanck, Congress appropriated $500 for a bust of John Jay, and Frazee executed it much to the satisfaction of his employers and his own fame." A bust of Nathaniel Prime of New York opened the way to orders from Boston; for Thomas W. Ward of the latter city, seeing this work in 1833, induced his friends to order busts of Daniel Webster and Dr. Bowditch. Dunlap adds with much sympathy: "It grieves me that I cannot relate the anecdotes of Frazee respecting the sittings of these eminent men. Webster, at the request of the sculptor, delivered a congressional speech while Frazee modelled." Elsewhere — in an appendix — he says: "I have seen with admiration his bust of Daniel Webster, and with more that of Dr. Bowditch: both chiselled in marble with skill and taste. . . . He has seven busts engaged for the Athenæum in Boston, to which city he has recently been to model the likenesses."

Dunlap's final paragraph in regard to his friend is in part as follows: "In 1831 Frazee entered into a partnership with Robert E. Launitz, who had for two years before worked with him as a journeyman at ornamental sculpture. Mr. Frazee is determined to execute the 'whole figure,' as he says, without visiting Italy. I conclude this brief notice of my very ingenious countryman of New Jersey by mentioning his family. His first wife died in 1832, leaving him with five children (having lost five), and he is married to a second, Lydia, daughter of Thomas Place of New York. Notwithstanding the prophecy of Mr. Trumbull, Mr. Frazee is in full employment, and the demand for sculpture in our happy country is daily increasing."

The "seven busts engaged for the Athenæum in Boston" are there to-day, affording an excellent notion of the workmanship of this clever man. Most of these portraits are dated 1834, and indicate a

D

very profitable visit to Boston, or at least a period of great industry. The results are not merely the product of hard work, however, but show a decided talent and always a serious and respectful approach to the subject. If the marble-cutter has not always risen to the height of his theme, and met his subjects on their own level, with a grasp equal to their importance, it is not to be wondered at. Even the scholarly Greenough and the brilliant Story missed often the *meaning* of their sitters, if it may be so expressed, and many others of greater skill have been singularly inadequate in this respect. Frazee's busts, carved by his own hands, rank well with the best efforts of Powers and Hart, supplemented by the cunning of their Florentine assistants.

The earliest of these busts is dated 1833, and is a curious effigy of Daniel Webster, perhaps the first of the long series of portraits for which the great statesman was compelled to pose. Every sculptor and portrait-painter of the North had to try his more or less 'prentice hand on Webster's Jove-like features, as those of the South must needs practise on Jackson, Clay, and Calhoun. One infers, from the variety of recognizable portraits, that not a few of these were founded upon scanty data. Frazee's bust we know to have been done from life, and it may be more accurate than our mental images of Webster. It is certainly different, and one ranks it, therefore, perhaps a little unfairly, as the least satisfying of Frazee's works in this collection. Webster's shoulders are draped in an ample and impressive Roman toga, as was the custom of those days — in sculpture. He wears also a very surprised look, due to much elevated eyebrows. One resents the pinched, weak expression about the mouth, occasioned by lips strangely thin. The forehead and cheeks are admirably modelled, however, and, like the drapery, well carved, so that the bust is on the whole above the average in excellence. It would still be considered good professional work.

Conspicuous among these portraits is a curiously rigid bust of John Marshall, which with all its drapery offers a naked bosom to the executioner, as well as an odd, wrinkled neck into which the small head seems to be withdrawn, turtle-fashion. The marble is signed 1834, but the modelling was evidently of an earlier date. Dunlap tells us that the sculptor went to Virginia to do the work.

Casts of the bust are to be seen in the Pennsylvania Academy, in Richmond, and doubtless elsewhere.

Four other busts by Frazee may be found in the Athenæum collection: William Prescott (1834), straight and stiff as Marshall; John Lovell (1834), with the head turned to one side, and showing good modelling; Dr. Bowditch, with Webster-like forehead but weak lower face, emaciated and amiable — a distinct corroboration of Ball Hughes's portrait; and finally, and best of all, the handsome bust of Colonel Thomas H. Perkins, with its strong physiognomy.

There is mention also of marble busts of General Jackson, John Jay, Judge Story, Lafayette, De Witt Clinton, and Bishop Hobart. But more interesting than any of these is the record which this true artist has left of his own manly face (Fig. 3). Whether the bust was ever put in marble is uncertain, but the Pennsylvania Academy possesses in the original plaster cast a relic of great value. It is a good bust, vigorous in pose and full of character. The shoulders are cut away, and the expanse of bare breast is ingeniously diminished without detriment to the solid sculptural mass from which the well-modelled neck rises like a tower of strength. The head is turned to the right; the eyes, though blank, follow its direction and are admirably set in their orbits; the sensitive lips are parted a little, the total effect being singularly expressive, earnest, and frank, as of a poet nature in a powerful body. The ear is summary but "right." The short, serrated side-whiskers show the too professional touch of the stone-cutter; but the curly hair, with all its conventionality, is full of color and far more artistic than the work of certain famous men who shipped busts home from Italy a few years later. Although this head represents Frazee in his thirty-ninth year, according to his own statement, it gives the impression of a much younger man. Did he consciously flatter himself? Doubtless in the interest of sculptural simplification he omitted certain marks of coming age; but the key to the personality is in that brave, virile pose. A man who carries himself in that way, who thinks of himself in that way, keeps young; and we may well believe that this is the very John Frazee of that time. One feels that it would have been a pleasure to know this admirable man.

At this distance an estimate of Frazee's influence is of necessity largely surmise.   He was not a leader, but a gifted plodder.   Unlike William Rush, he was no organizer: he founded nothing, and appears to have had no pupils.   Nor was his social position such as to cast much glamour on the art which he personally graced so well.   His wide-scattered works have had their powerful appeal in the direction of dignity and honest workmanship.   They were always striking, and in that day must have appeared strangely impressive.   Of John Frazee, as much as of any sculptor, it may be said that he lived up to the measure of his capability: he did his best.

Although not exactly sculpture, in the strictest sense of the term, the busts which were produced by John Henri Isaac Browere, in 1825 and succeeding years, were more than clever life masks. Browere, who was born in New York in 1792, had decidedly artistic leanings, and even visited Europe with the intention of preparing for a sculptor's career.   However, his professional education seems to have consisted largely in "tramping" for two years over the Continent, and when, in 1820, he returned to the United States, his talent developed — perhaps fortunately — upon the inventive side. His busts of distinguished Americans, made by a process of his own, are not only precious as human documents, but are often admirable in pose and in expression, — results, to some degree, of sculptural knowledge.

PLATE 2.—GREENOUGH: WASHINGTON.

CHAPTER II

A STUDY of the early records of American art introduces one to many winning personalities, men of exalted ideals and beautiful lives, whom we would fain know better. Sometimes, we must acknowledge, it seems as if these were the very qualities which give them remoteness, which make their illusive features so unfamiliar; but this view is doubtless a mistaken one. Certain it is, at any rate, that there is a strange courtliness and sweetness in some of the faces which have receded so far into the shadows of history's tarnished frames; and though many, like the silhouettes of their day, offer us but the barest outlines, we can detect a great distinction in their summary contours. We are drawn to them, and prize every detail which develops the picture.

When Dunlap published, in 1834, his " Arts of Design," the most successful representative of the sculptor's art in the United States was John Frazee; but the rising luminary was Horatio Greenough, who had gone abroad some eight years before, and now, at the age of twenty-nine, was just beginning his gigantic statue of Washington. These, with William Rush, were the only American sculptors whom Mr. Dunlap seems to have known, or at least to have considered worthy of mention. It was in that same year that young Crawford, a boy of twenty, sailed for Rome. Hiram Powers had just begun to " find himself," and was busy with portrait busts in the West, but was not able to embark for Italy until three years later. Ball Hughes was at work upon his short-lived statue of Hamilton, and H. K. Brown was a student of painting in Boston; while several bright-eyed, barefooted boys, in various parts of the country, were bird-nesting and playing " shinney " quite unconscious of the destiny which should write their names as leaders of American art.

The fullest and most sympathetic account of Greenough will be found in Tuckerman's "Book of the Artists." [1]   The critical estimates of the author awaken a smile to-day, for his friendship sees no faults; but while very often he "enters into a poetical enthusiasm from which he cannot stoop to commonplace details," yet his moral standard is always so high, his enthusiasm so genuine, and his pleasure in spinning out sonorous eulogies so boyishly frank, that one dips into his book with relish and comes to love his heroes regardless of their significance in the development of our national art.   Greenough's contribution was significant, however, and of vast consequence, though in a way very different from that in which Tuckerman apprehended it.   The first American deliberately choosing sculpture as a profession, and going abroad for serious study, he gave the art an importance in the eyes of his countrymen which it never had before — an importance greatly strengthened by the fortunate circumstances of his own attractions and social position. Greenough was not only a man of fair ability as a sculptor, but a ready writer who could take up the cudgels most effectively, though sometimes, it must be confessed, with a trifle too much vehemence for the best results.   His art was with him a passion, a religion; and while his distance from home clothed his work with mystery, — a mystery not often illuminated by intelligible utterances in what might be called sculptural vernacular, — he never did aught which could lower the profession in the eyes of the world.   To the end he felt himself its high priest in a new land, and kept his hieratic vestments as unsullied as the marble which he carved.   Art had an awesome, if factitious, exaltation in those days.   Its exemplars were men of distinction, who took themselves most seriously, who looked for and received extreme consideration.   There was much about them which we might call "pose" to-day, but which was sincerity and even simplicity itself in that age of ponderous elegance.   Greenough and Crawford upheld the dignity of their art, as did Bryant and Longfellow that of the poetic muse.

Genius has very promiscuous tastes, insisting more often than not in making its cradle in humble cottages, while perversely neglecting long city blocks of the "best families"!   In this first

[1] "Book of the Artists," by Henry T. Tuckerman, New York, 1867.

instance, however, Providence made no mistake; for as soon after Sept. 6, 1805, as the newly born Horatio was able to recognize his surroundings, he must have observed with satisfaction that he was in a well-to-do household. Later — considerably later — he found himself in pleasant relations with the most cultivated people of Boston. "His father," wrote Mr. Tuckerman in 1853, "belonged to that respected class of merchants whose integrity, enterprise, and intelligence, half a century ago, justly gave them a degree of consideration which is almost unknown at the present day. Comparatively few in number, and active in the political and social life of the town, they almost created public opinion, and were remarkable for individuality of character, not less than a tone of mind above and beyond the mere spirit of trade. This was evinced in the careful manner in which their children were brought up, and the intellectual privileges afforded them, the sacred interest attached to home, and the superiority of the local schools. The mother of Greenough was a native of Massachusetts, endowed with the conscientious affection and vigorous intellect that are so honorable a distinction of the genuine New England matron. He was one of several children, and shared with them the education both of public and private seminaries and of the domestic circle." [1] But such advantages can hardly explain the genesis of our first sculptor. If there was much refinement in the life and manners of Boston at this time, and a sufficient familiarity with good paintings, as well as with literature and music, there was almost nothing to suggest the unfamiliar profession. As our author observes, "Only a strong, natural bias could have so early directed Greenough's aspirations toward art."

At this point in his account a large portion of Mr. Tuckerman's material is evidently borrowed from a letter written to Mr. Dunlap in 1833 or 1834, by Henry Greenough, a brother of the sculptor. [2] To work over this authentic document yet again in paraphrase seems unnecessary and by no means advantageous, when the original words are so directly to the point. Dunlap's book is not within reach of every hand, and the reader will be pleased to gain so intimate an impression of the then promising young artist who has now lain for half a century in his grave. There is something infinitely pathetic

---

[1] "Book of the Artists," p. 248.   [2] "Arts of Design," Vol. II, p. 412.

in these personal portrayals of the ambitions and affections of a day long dead.

The first part of the letter begins with the request to the editor to "prune with an unsparing hand," since the sculptor would wish that the notice "might be confined as far as possible to a few facts and dates." Greenough is also quoted as having written deprecatingly: "A note to Allston's life might tell all of me which is essential. What is the use of blowing up bladders for posterity to jump upon, for the mere pleasure of hearing them crack?" Much is said in description of the early childish carvings; of swords and pistols, of tiny horses and carriages, "with wheels no larger than a cent," and also of an extraordinary memory compassing thousands of lines of poetry; but the real interest begins with the youth's first inspiration toward sculpture.

The letter proceeds: "I have often heard him attribute his first wish to attempt something like sculpture to having constantly before his eyes a marble statue of Phocion, a copy of the antique, which my father caused to be placed, with its pedestal, as an ornament to a mound in the garden. His first attempts were made in chalk on account of its whiteness and softness. He soon attempted alabaster, or rather rock plaster of Paris (unburnt), with equal success; and within a few weeks of his first attempt he had been so assiduous as to transform his chamber to a regular museum, where rows of miniature busts, carved from engravings, were ranged on little pine shelves. I recollect, in particular, a little chalk statue of William Penn, which he copied from an engraving in the *Portfolio* from the bronze statue in Philadelphia.[1] A gentleman who saw him copying, in chalk, the bust of John Adams by Binon, was so pleased with his success, that he carried him to the Athenæum and presented him to Mr. Shaw, I believe the first founder of the institution, and at that time the sole director. My brother was then about

---

[1] The *Portfolio* for October, 1816. The figure is not of bronze, but of lead. The article accompanying the engraving says: "The statue was originally erected at the seat of the late Lord Le Despencer, near High Wycomb, in England. The statue was alienated, and the pedestal was suffered to decay. It was afterward purchased by one of the proprietor's grandsons and presented to the Pennsylvania Hospital." The grandson in question was John Penn, who presented the statue to the Pennsylvania Hospital in Philadelphia, in 1804. This curious work still stands in front of the Hospital, at Eighth and Pine streets. The author is unknown.

twelve years old, and of course was much edified by Mr. Shaw's conversation, who assured him, as he held the chalk in his hand, that there were the germs of a great and noble art. He then showed him the casts there, and promising him he should always find a bit of carpet to cut his chalk upon whenever he wished to copy anything, gave him a *carte blanche* to the 'fine arts' room, with its valuable collection of engravings, etc. He may be considered from this time as studying with something like a definite purpose and with some system. The friendship of Mr. Solomon Willard of Boston soon initiated him into the mysteries of modelling in clay, which he had unsuccessfully endeavored to acquire from directions in the 'Edinburgh Cyclopedia'; and Mr. Alpheus Cary, a stone-cutter of Boston, gave him a similar insight into the manner of carving marble, so as soon to enable him to realize his wishes in the shape of a bust of Bacchus. He profited much also by the friendship of Mr. Binon, a French artist then in Boston, going daily to his rooms and modelling in his company.

"His progress was so rapid that his father no longer opposed his devoting most of his time to these pursuits, insisting only on his graduating at Harvard University, Cambridge, on the ground that if he continued in his determination, a college education would only the better fit him for an artist's life. He accordingly entered college at the age of sixteen, A.D. 1821. His time was now almost exclusively devoted to reading works of art, and in drawing and modelling, and the study of anatomy. Professor Cogswell, the librarian of the university, assisted him in the former by a loan of a valuable collection of original drawings, as well as by his counsel and criticisms; and to Dr. George Parkman of Boston he was indebted for most of his anatomical knowledge learned from his books, skeletons, and preparations. . . . Notwithstanding the benefit he must be sensible of having derived from his studies at Cambridge, I have heard him say he estimated them little in comparison to what he obtained from the friendship of Mr. W. Allston, whose acquaintance he made at the house of Mr. Edmund Dana, the brother of Mr. R. Dana, the poet. With Mr. Allston much of his time during his junior and senior years was spent. By him his ideas of his art were elevated, and his endeavors directed to a proper path.

"Toward the close of the senior year, a vessel being about to sail for Marseilles, he obtained permission from the government of the college to leave before the usual time, and his diploma was forwarded to him afterwards.   He arrived at Marseilles in the first of the autumn, and proceeded directly by land to Rome.   This was in 1825.   The unbounded facilities afforded by Rome to a young artist enabled him to carry into effect the plans of study he had formed under Mr. Allston's advice.   His mornings were devoted to making careful drawings of the antique; his afternoons to modelling from the life some subject of his own composition, which enabled him to exert his invention, and bring into play the practice of the morning; and his evenings to drawing from the Nudo at the Academy.   Having letters to Thorwaldsen, he was enabled to profit by the visits which he so readily pays to young artists, to improve them by his criticism, or encourage by approbation.   My brother often says, however, that in the mechanical part of the art he learnt most from young fellow-students. . . .

"He had made many studies in chalks, i.e. crayons and clays, and besides several busts of the size of life had finished a model of a statue of Abel in Rome (1825–1826), when his studies were unfortunately suspended for a year or more by his taking the malaria a little before the termination of his first year (1826).

"The effects of this illness were so severe as to oblige him to return to America, after having made an excursion to Naples in company with some friends, who had kindly taken charge of him, but without any benefit to his health.   He accordingly sailed from Leghorn for Boston, where he arrived in perfect health, his seasickness and consequent benefit of the sea air having done for him what medicine had been unable to effect.

"About a year was now passed by him in America, the first five or six months at home with his father's family, where his time was spent in drawing and modelling.   At the beginning of the winter he left home for the purpose of modelling the bust of President J. Q. Adams at Washington; besides the bust of Adams, he also modelled a likeness of Chief Justice Marshall, and on his way home modelled one or two busts in Baltimore.

"Soon after returning from Washington, he made arrangements for returning to Italy, for the purpose of executing in marble the several models for which he had commissions, and accordingly left us in the month of March, 1827. From Gibraltar and Marseilles he proceeded directly to Carrara, where he remained three months or more, during which time he finished two busts and saw others prepared. His design in thus settling at Carrara was, I believe, for the purpose of making himself thoroughly acquainted with all the details of preparing and finishing works of sculpture; for which Carrara, being the grand workshop of the Italian sculptors, gave him every opportunity.

"His next remove was to Florence, which he had fixed upon as his headquarters, on account of the advantages in the study of his art and its healthiness. During his first year there he became in a manner the pupil of Bartolini, whom he still considers the first portrait sculptor in existence. A marble Venus in the possession of Lord Londonderry has made the name of Bartolini deservedly honored in England. His time, since then, has been fully occupied in the execution of commissions from his countrymen. These works are nearly all in America, and two of them are more generally known, having been exhibited, namely, the group of the 'Chanting Cherubs,' belonging to J. Fenimore Cooper, and the 'Medora,' belonging to Mr. R. Gilmor of Baltimore. With the exception of one winter spent in Paris, where he modelled busts of General Lafayette, Mr. Cooper, and one or two other individuals, his time has been spent altogether in Florence.

"He is now almost exclusively occupied in the execution of the statue of Washington for Congress, only recreating himself occasionally by attending to smaller works."

The story of the "Chanting Cherubs" is interesting because it ushers in the first marble group by an American sculptor. We must allow Mr. Dunlap to tell about it:—

"Some of the young ladies of Mr. Cooper's family, in the course of their studies, were copying a print from a picture of Raphael, in which were two cherubs singing. Fenimore saw with regret the neglect Greenough experienced, and was convinced that if he had an opportunity of executing a figure, or, still more to show his

powers, a group, it would bring him into notice; and the thought
of the chanting cherubs struck him as a group of great beauty
and suited to Greenough's taste.   He gave him the order, and
the young sculptor, only having the print before him, which the
young ladies had been copying, produced the lovely group which
we have seen.   The effect of raising a name for Horatio Greenough
was produced; and to produce a greater effect, by convincing
Americans that they had a countryman superior in talent and skill
to the Italians they were employing, Cooper sent the group home
to be exhibited.   This is the first group from the chisel of an
American artist." [1]

This glimpse of the pioneer novelist is far more gracious than
certain others in his ruffled career.   He followed up his kindness
by publishing a letter upon Greenough and the group in the *New
York American* of Apr. 30, 1831, in which we are told, in an
earnest plea for an original and national art, that the group was
taken from Raphael's " Madonna del Trono," in the Pitti Palace;
but Mr. Cooper explains that the artist changed things so much
as to make the group practically his own, having " little more aid
from the original than he derived from the idea," and adding,
with far-sighted discernment, " Perhaps the authority of Raphael
was necessary to render such a representation of the subject pala-
table in our day."   Dunlap's quotation from the letter concludes
with these words, " I hope that the peculiarity of its being the
first work of the kind which has come from an American chisel,
as well as the rare merit of the artist, will be found to interest
the public at home."

The story of the storm which broke over the defenceless heads
of the little undraped cherubs is one of the amusing traditions of
American art.   Puritan decency was shocked by their nude baby
forms, and ominous mutterings were heard on every side.   Although
we have no record of Cooper's instituting a lawsuit, as was his
genial custom, the bitterness of the controversy is proved by
Greenough's truculent reply to his critics.   The group has disappeared from view, but a later work, somewhat similar in conception,
and doubtless suggested by the "Cherubs," is the "Angel and Child"

[1] " Arts of Design," Vol. II, p. 419.

FIG. 4.— GREENOUGH: THE RESCUE, WASHINGTON.

in the Boston Museum of Fine Arts, described by Mr. Tuckerman
with misplaced eloquence as follows: "Its conception is singularly
beautiful, and it is realized to the life.   The artist's idea was to represent a child received and guided by its angel companion into the
mysterious glories of heaven.   The difference between the human
and the spiritual is exhibited in the baby outline of the child, rounded,
natural, and real, — and the mature celestial grace of the angel, — his
look of holy courage and his attitude of cheer, while the reverence
and timidity of his newly arrived brother are equally obvious."[1]   At
which point the writer's enthusiasm becomes metrical.   But the
work is hardly so important as one might think from the description.   In the presence of the group to-day one might imagine it
merely an illustration of two babes, — for both figures are of the
same size, — one helping the other to walk.

In the same upper hall of the Boston Museum is a bust of Napoleon signed by Greenough; also his Flaxman-like relief of "Castor
and Pollux" with its curiously conventional horse.   Downstairs one
sees his bust of Hamilton, which is not strong, though probably a
good portrait.   The monotonous hair seems to have been ploughed
by machinery.   Most singular of all, to modern taste, is a small
"Cupid Bound," of inflated physique.   The little god is secured
by a chain of costly workmanship.   His confinement is solaced by
the presence of a tiny but elaborate owl, and his head is crowned
with a profusion of curls like marble watchsprings.

But if many of Greenough's perfunctory works are amusing
to us to-day rather than impressive, the sculptor disarms our criticism by his frank modesty.   He writes under date of Dec. 1, 1833,
to Dunlap, the story of his struggles: "I thank you for the
opinion you express of what little I have done in the art of sculpture; I have not yet had the time to do much.   I fear that the
circumstances under which I began my career will ever prevent
me realizing my idea of what sculpture should be.   Still, the
effort may be useful to future artists, and yield some works of
a relative and special value.   I cannot pretend to occupy any space
in a work consecrated to American art.   Sculpture, when I left
home, was practised nowhere, to my knowledge, in the United

[1] "Book of the Artists," p. 258.

States.   I learned the first rudiments of modelling from a Frenchman, named Binon, who resided long in Boston.   My friends opposed my studying the art, but gently, reasonably, and kindly.
It would require more time than you would find it profitable to
spend to listen to the thousand accidents that shaped my inclination to the study of this art.   I might perhaps interest you more by
mentioning the many instances in which I have been comforted,
assisted, advised, induced, in short, to persevere in it, by acquaintances and friends.   I could tell you of the most generous efforts to
assist me, on the part of men who scarcely knew me, of the most
flattering and encouraging notice by elegant and accomplished
women ; but I might hurt or offend those who have so kindly
helped me, and (what I shrink from also for myself) I fear there
would be a fearful disproportion between the seed and the fruit.

"Mr. Cogswell, who now keeps an academy at Northampton, contributed perhaps more than any one to fix my purpose, and supplied
me with casts, etc., to nurse my fondness of statuary.   Allston, in
the sequel, was to me a father, in what concerned my progress of
every kind.   He taught me first how to discriminate — how to
think — how to feel.   Before I knew him I felt strongly but blindly,
as it were ; and if I should never pass mediocrity, I should attribute
it to my absence from him.   So adapted did he seem to kindle and
enlighten me, making me no longer myself, but, as it were, an
emanation of his own soul.

"Dr. J. Parkman, during my sophomore year, proposed to assist
me in obtaining some knowledge of anatomy.   He supplied me with
bones, preparations, etc., every week ; as also with such books as I
could not get from the college library.   He not only continued this
kindness during the three years of my remaining college life, but lent
me generous assistance in forwarding my studies by travel.   I began
to *study* art in Rome in 1826.   Until then I had rather amused
myself with clay and marble than studied.   When I say that those
materials were familiar to my touch, I say all that I profited by my
boyish efforts.   They were rude.   I lived with poets and poetry, and
could not then see that my art was to be studied from folk who eat
their three meals every day.   I *gazed* at the 'Apollo' and the 'Venus,'
and *learned* very little by it.   It was not till I ran through all the

galleries and studios of Rome, and had had under my eye the genial forms of Italy, that I began to feel nature's value. I had before adored her, but as a Persian does the sun, with my face to the earth. I then began to examine her, and entered on that course of study in which I am still toiling.

"Fenimore Cooper saved me from despair after my second return to Italy. He employed me as I wished to be employed; and has, up to this moment, been a father to me in kindness. That I ever shall answer all the expectations of my friends is impossible; but no duty, thank God! extends beyond his means. I sigh for a little intercourse with you, gentlemen, at home. I long to be among you, but I am anchored here for the next four years. I will not risk a voyage before my statue is done. I think it my duty not to run away at the first sight of the enemy.

"When I went, the other morning, into the huge room in which I propose to execute my statue, I felt like a spoilt boy, who, after insisting upon riding on horseback, bawls aloud with fright at find-ing himself in the saddle, so far from the ground! I hope, however, that this will wear off."[1]

Incidents in the progress of the Lafayette bust, elsewhere re-ferred to, are given in considerable detail by Mr. Cooper himself in a long letter in Dunlap's book. His comparison of Greenough's "Lafayette" with a portrait by David d'Angers is entertaining. "The bust of David is like, it cannot be mistaken, but it is in his ordinary manner, heroic or poetical. The artist has aimed more at a senti-ment than at fidelity of portraiture or nature. On the other hand, the bust of Greenough is the very man, and should be dear to us in proportion as it is faithful. As Lafayette himself expressed it, one is a French bust, the other an American."[2]

Greenough's timidity in beginning the "Washington," which through the efforts of Cooper had been ordered by Congress, was but too well justified. His fright did "wear off" in time; but had the sensitive young man foreseen the lack of sympathy which was to be his reward, the derision which was to be heaped upon the results of his consecrated toil, he might well have withdrawn from the struggle and died of chagrin. How sensitive he really was

[1] "Arts of Design," Vol. II, p. 421.   [2] Ibid., p. 424.

E

and how conscious of his own deficiencies is illustrated by an
incident of his first journey.   Arriving in Genoa, he entered a
church where amid a wealth of sculptures he saw a statue more
beautiful than any he had ever looked upon.   Lost in admiration,
it was some time before he finally noticed that the crowds hurried
by without a glance.   The thought that such unattainable perfection was an everyday affair in Italy convinced him that he was
presumptuous in aspiring to accomplish anything worthy of the
art.   " He was deeply moved as the distance between himself and
the goal he had fondly hoped to reach widened to his view; and
concealing himself among the rubbish of a palace yard, the young
and ardent exile sought relief in tears." [1]

The history of Greenough's " Washington " is one of bitter disappointments, and it ended — so far as the artist was concerned —
in tragedy.   This final blow was not the rejection nor the destruction of the work, but its sentence to stand forever in the pillory
of public ridicule.   It was and is worthy of a better fate.   The city
of Washington has many worse figures which escape censure
through their mediocrity.   Few, indeed, of the sculptures of the
Capitol reveal so noble an intention as does this much maligned
work (Pl. II).   Greenough conceived it on a very high plane;
he labored on it for nearly eight years, and the execution is dignified and workmanlike, if not masterful.   Of it the artist wrote in
words freighted with an emotion which to-day seems deeply pathetic: " It is the birth of my thought.   I have sacrificed to it the
flower of my days and the freshness of my strength; its every
lineament has been moistened by the sweat of my toil and the tears
of my exile.   I would not barter away its association with my name
for the proudest fortune that avarice ever dreamed." [2]

Alas for human foresight!   Fashion has changed in regard to
portrait statues since those days.   Warriors and heroes are now pictured in their own clothes like other people.   Canova's nude " Napoleon " and Greenough's half-draped " Washington " are curiosities,
the sculptor's reverent ideal is forgotten in our sense of the incongruous.   Greenough felt that America's greatest citizen, the Father
of his Country, was worthy of apotheosis, and with dim vision of the

[1] " Book of the Artists," p. 254.   [2] Ibid., p. 262.

Olympian Zeus regnant in his pillared sanctuary, he conceived his " Washington " as a majestic, godlike figure enthroned beneath the vaulted arch of the Capitol and gilded by the filtered rays of far-falling sunlight. The conception was exalted, grandiose, and in another time or with a more imaginative people might have succeeded. But the sculptor was not adequate for the work which he had dreamed, nor had he control of certain essential details of his *mise en scene.*

The ponderous figure reached this country in 1843, after many perils by sea and by land, and had attained the very gates of the Capitol when it was found to be too large for passage. The doorway was temporarily widened, and the figure entered its haven of rest. Now came the crowning difficulty and final defeat. It was found that the immense mass of stone was too heavy for the floor, which trembled and settled at its approach. The statue was hastily withdrawn, and, although a sufficient foundation in the lower story would not seem a difficult problem of engineering, it was apparently

FIG. 5. — GREENOUGH: ANGEL ABDIEL, ART INSTITUTE, CHICAGO.

never attempted. The evicted giant was set up outside, opposite the eastern front of the Capitol, to view like another Moses the promised land from afar. And there he stands to-day, exposed to the elements, and, still worse, to the newspaper paragraphers. They are pitiless. One of them wrote one day that Washington was supposed to be saying, as he pointed in two directions, "My body is at Mount Vernon, my clothes are in the Patent Office." Whoever looks at the figure repeats the legend to his neighbor, and they laugh together. Poor Greenough; how little did he understand the generation to come, or even his own!

However, the statue was not by any means without friends. Edward Everett wrote of it from Italy in 1841 : —

" I regard Greenough's ' Washington ' as one of the greatest works of sculpture of modern times. I do not know the work which can justly be preferred to it, whether we consider the purity of the taste, the loftiness of the conception, the truth of the character, or, what we must own we feel less able to judge of, the accuracy of anatomical study and mechanical skill."

That the sculptor was grievously disappointed at its final location is shown by the following extract from a letter written while the question of site was pending : —

" Had I been ordered to make a statue for any square or similar situation at the metropolis, I should have represented Washington on horseback and in his actual dress. I would have made my work purely an historical one. I have treated my subject poetically, and confess I should feel pain at seeing it placed in direct and flagrant contrast with everyday life. Moreover, I modelled the figure without reference to an exposure to rain and frost, so that there are many parts of the statue where the water would collect and soon disintegrate and rot the stone, if it did not by freezing split off large fragments of the drapery." [1]

Speaking of its reception, he remarks : —

" Allow me to exult a little that, during the months I spent at Washington, while my statue was the butt of wiseacres and witlings, I never in word or thought swerved from my principle — that the general mind is alone a quorum to judge a great work. When in future time the true sculptors of America have filled the metropolis with beauty and grandeur, will it not be worth $30,000 to be able to point to the figure and say, ' There was the first struggle of our infant art ' ? " [2]

The " Washington " is of colossal size, being a figure which would stand nearly or quite twelve feet high if erect. Its lower limbs are covered with a loose drapery, which is carried up over the horizontal right arm, and hangs in rigid folds. The forearm is

[1] " Book of the Artists," p. 261.   [2] Ibid., p. 262.

lifted squarely, and a finger points upward. The left hand is extended, holding a Roman sword reversed. The surface treatment is generally hard, and, in the face and other details, somewhat meagre. The gesture of the left arm is ample and dignified, while that of the right is angular. The equal emphasis of the two is unfortunate.

The seat is a massive arm-chair of antique form, the sides of which are decorated with bas-reliefs. The subject of one is the infant Hercules strangling the serpent in his cradle; that of the other, Apollo guiding the four steeds that draw the chariot of the sun. The back of the chair is of open work. At the left corner is placed a small statue of Columbus, holding in his hand a sphere, which he studies; at the right corner is a similar small statue of an Indian chief.

True to its time, the monument bears a Latin inscription : —

> " Simulacrum istud
> Ad magnum Libertatis exemplum
> Nec sine ipsa duraturum
> Horatius Greenough
> Faciebat."

No one to-day calls the figure "truly sublime," as did its first partisans; but the nobility of the subject and the reverence of the artist are attested by every faithful chisel stroke. Properly elevated within the rotunda of the Capitol, in the temple for which it was designed, the statue would doubtless regain much of the majesty of Greenough's vision.

As now situated, the "Washington" confronts another of Greenough's audacious efforts. Upon the two buttresses which project from the portico on either side of the main stairway of the Capitol are two large groups in marble. Perhaps it is by courtesy alone that one of these extraordinary relics of our early art may be called a group; the absurd "Columbus," by Signor Persico, with its attendant Indian maid, is hardly to be thus classified. Of Persico we know little, except that it was in 1846 that he commemorated his great countryman for the sum of $24,000; and that he also embellished the pediment above with a lonesome "Genius of America," designed by John Quincy Adams, whose inspiration failed him at the third figure, leaving America "surrounded" by Hope and Justice and emptiness.

The decoration of the other buttress was awarded to Greenough; and while his success was not brilliant, viewed by the standard of to-day, he had at least a sculptural motive and produced a work which one regards with respectful curiosity. As the "Columbus" is supposed to personify Discovery, this group, called "The Rescue" (Fig. 4), typifies Civilization, or Settlement. It was designed in 1837, and completed in the marble in 1857. It shows a pioneer hunter in a strange, half-classic costume, rescuing his wife and child from a savage who has just raised his tomahawk to murder them. The hunter has seized his enemy from behind, and holds his arms in a powerful grip. The nude form of the Indian, bent backward, is well conceived, and combines admirably with the forward movement of his antagonist. The crouching woman and child really form a second group, but are effectively handled in a broad, simple way, and are far from uninteresting. A large dog on the opposite side shows a singular impartiality, watching the struggle quietly and without prejudice. While on the whole more ambitious than successful, this work shows an artistic intention and no little ability, united with much courage. For it took courage to do such things in those days. The "Washington" was the first colossal marble carved by an American, "The Rescue" the second.

Among Greenough's ideal works were the "Medora," already mentioned, a "Venus Victrix," and an "Abel," also an "Angel Abdiel" (Fig. 5). We are assured on better authority than Tuckerman that his busts of Washington, Lafayette, John Quincy Adams, and Fenimore Cooper were "refined and excellent." The "Adams" is in the rooms of the New York Historical Society. It is a bust which conveys at a distance a certain impression of nobility, enhanced rather than diminished by the display of unclothed shoulders. Upon closer examination the work seems lacking in individuality. One feels that with a generalization so broad it must have been very easy to make busts. Yet it is a strong, fine mask, all ready for eyes and life. The hair is of course the product of an inexorable chisel.

In summing up the contribution of this admirable man it must be acknowledged that he is more interesting than is his work, and the fact *that* he did is more important than *what* he did. He was sympathetic and delighted in the discovery of talent, and an indefatigable "promoter" for others as well as for himself. But he was also the first of our sculptors to lay himself upon the Procrustean couch of a dead classicism. Whether he was too big or too little for the uncomfortable bed, matters not to-day. Perhaps his New England inheritance, so scantily nourished on the plastic side, was stretched to ineffectual attenuation in order to fill it; perhaps, on the other hand, the most precious and vital qualities of his artistic nature were lopped off to conform to the standard which Canova and Thorwaldsen had imposed upon the world. At any rate, he did conform, and so thoroughly, — like the many who came after him, — that one scans his work in vain for a personal note.

Passionately fond of his country, a thinker, a lover of freedom, — not only political, but mental and spiritual, — a friend and disciple of Emerson, "demanding the genuine, independent, individual *man* in exchange for the disguised and dependent puppet of the world, . . . defending American art, . . . opposing academies as positive hindrances to advancement," ardent and fertile of fancy, he nevertheless presents the paradox of an artist without artistic personality; a sculptor who left behind him not one work tinged with emotion, not one marble stanza vibrant with poetic fire. There is perhaps a deeper significance than was intended in his biographer's kindly comment on his habitual generosity: "His recognition was not limited to achievement, but extended to latent powers. He was one of that invaluable minority whose perception goes beneath the surface of character and the accidents of expression; and perhaps of all his friends he valued chiefly 'the poet who never wrote.'" [1]

Even less need we look in Greenough's fettered art for a hint of a national expression, excepting as in its absence we find the very strongest expression of conditions. Greenough produced nothing that might not have been done, better or worse, but in exactly the same spirit, by any sculptor of whatsoever nationality then living in Italy. In sculpture and painting, as well as in literature, our awaken-

[1] " Book of the Artists," p. 274.

ing national consciousness " strove to prove our country civilized by conscientious obedience to eldest civilized tradition."

Greenough died — all too early — Dec. 18, 1852, having removed to this country the year before on account of political troubles in Florence.   It is pleasant to record that in spite of the disappointments of his life, one of his last letters contained this passage : " I would not pass away and not leave a sign that I, for one, born by the grace of God in this land, found life a cheerful thing, and not that sad and dreadful task with whose prospect they scared my youth."

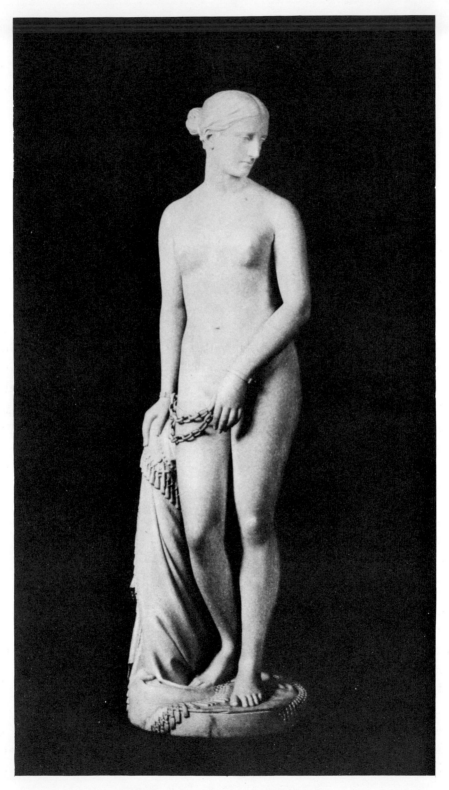

PLATE 3.—POWERS: GREEK SLAVE.

CHAPTER III

HIRAM POWERS AND THE "GREEK SLAVE"

THE second name on the list of our native professional sculptors is that of Hiram Powers. (Born in the same year with Greenough, and even some months earlier, — July 29, 1805, — he cedes primacy to his brother-artist, who began the study of sculpture long before Powers had guessed his own proper vocation.

The contrasts of the early surroundings of the two were as striking as the resultant personalities. Powers was born in no home of affluence, in no centre of culture and refinement. There was no statue of Phocion in front of the modest farmhouse on the outskirts of Woodstock, Vermont. But if art was lacking, (nature was generously abundant.) Throughout his long life the beauty of those early scenes never forsook the artist. Even the grace of Italian gardens, the historic splendor of Old World landscapes, left him hungry for a vision of the mountains of his native state.

We are told that he was "one of a large family, frugal, laborious, and affectionate," and that he "accounted it a special blessing of his childhood to have been reared by honest and harmonious parents." While Powers was still a boy the family emigrated westward, first to New York state, and ultimately to Cincinnati. The youth found employment of various sorts — in a reading room, as a collector, and finally in a clock factory. For the latter work he showed a special aptitude, but it gave way before another talent which was soon discovered — no one to-day knows just how. This was the ability to model faces.)

It will surprise many to learn that there were dime museums in those times, — those early years which we imagine to have been so deficient in the privileges of a ripe civilization, — but such an institution, or its equivalent, existed even in the almost frontier city of

Cincinnati.   Its enterprising proprietor learned of the lad's remarkable gift, and for benefits mutual offered him steady employment in
the "property room." His particular function was to model wax
images and to breathe the breath of life into them by means of ingenious clock-work devices.   The immediate success of these jerky
figures beckoned to higher flights, and soon young Powers was engaged upon a comprehensive "Inferno," with more or less of an apology
to Dante. This "great moral exhibition," while not exactly on the
lines of, say, M. Rodin's later work, was admirably suited to the public
demand.   It must have been something fearful, for we read that it
was immensely popular, and had to be closed finally because of its
very success, the impressionable ladies of Cincinnati flocking thither
and swooning, apparently in windrows, before its realistic terrors.

    But there were other objects of interest besides these imaginative
excursions.   A more temperate art was exemplified in the portraits
of celebrities; and here, in "catching a likeness," the young man
showed himself even more clever.   Henceforth his path of development was obvious.   "The manifest ability of Powers in these waxen
models led by a natural and almost necessary transition to his
experiments in a more durable material, and for a higher end."   As
for training, there was a short period when he and H. K. Brown and
Clevenger all worked together in Cincinnati, aiding each other and
gathering such instruction as they could from a German modeller
then living in that city.   Powers made rapid and sure progress,
and commissions began to come to him.   He was advised and
finally enabled to go to Washington, where he was profitably employed for two years.   Of this period Tuckerman wrote:—

    "Cheered by domestic ties, encouraged by many friends, one of
the earliest and most efficient of whom was Mr. Longworth, the life
of the farmer's son and the western emigrant gradually emerged
from casual and adroit to regular and aspiring development.   His
chosen pursuit soon gained him the best social privileges.   While
modelling the remarkable heads of General Jackson and Daniel
Webster, of John C. Calhoun, Chief-Justice Marshall, and Colonels
Johnson and Preston,—rare and emphatic types of the American
character and physiognomy, such as modern sculptors seldom enjoy,—
his frank and original nature won the confidence of his illustrious

sitters; and some of the most pleasant and most profitable hours of his life were thus occupied, affording many genial subjects of patriotic recollection." [1]

There was an encouraging harvest, too, of another sort. In 1837 Mr. Powers packed up a large number of casts for reproduction in marble, — several of these commissions having been paid for in advance, — and set sail for Italy. Florence was destined to be his home henceforth to the day of his death, June 27, 1873. Such exile seemed absolutely necessary in those days, if only for the economy of marble work. The United States offered no good marble for fine carving. Skilled workmen were lacking also, and inferior ones were far more expensive than Europe's best. In Italy the sculptor could put out and superintend the reproduction of his work, accomplishing in a year, possibly, what might require a lifetime of his own unaided efforts. These considerations, added to the necessity for professional models in other branches of the work, as well as the allurements of ancient art, made the call irresistible.

Powers and Greenough were now each thirty-two years of age. The latter had already been abroad nearly twelve years, most of which time he had been established in Florence. He had sent home his "Chanting Cherubs," and had heard from them. He was at this time engaged upon his "Washington," which had already occupied his time and thought for four years, and was destined to require as many more. Thomas Crawford had been in Rome three years, but had not yet produced anything of importance. Powers was therefore the third to go abroad. Greenough's welcome was fraternal, and aided him much. " Thorwaldsen visited his studio, and pronounced his bust of Webster the best work of the kind executed in modern times; orders flowed in upon him from the English and Italians, as well as Americans." [2]

Nathaniel Hawthorne was greatly attracted by Powers, and his " Italian Notes " are full of kindly references to the sculptor. Some of these comments are amusing, and all are illuminating. The first impression was favorable, and not to be altered : —

" Mr. Powers called in the evening — a plain personage characterized by strong simplicity and warm kindliness, with an impending

[1] " Book of the Artists," p. 278.　　　[2] Ibid., p. 279.

brow and large eyes, which kindle as he speaks. He is gray, and slightly bald, but does not seem elderly, nor past his prime. I accept him at once as an honest and trustworthy man, and shall not vary from this judgment." [1]

Elsewhere he says: " I have hardly ever felt an impulse to write down a man's conversation as I do that of Mr. Powers. The chief reason is, probably, that it is so possible to do it, his ideas being square, solid, and tangible, and therefore readily grasped and retained. He is a very instructive man, and sweeps one's empty and dead notions out of the way with exceeding vigor; but when you have his ultimate thought and perception, you feel inclined to think and see a little further for yourself. He sees too clearly what is within his range to be aware of any region of mystery beyond. Probably, however, this latter remark does him injustice. I like the man, and am always glad to encounter the mill-stream of his talk." [2]

An account of one of Mr. Powers's impromptu discourses — this time on the Venus de' Medici — is interesting, and throws a brilliant sidelight on the " orator of the day." It concludes as follows : —

" After annihilating the poor visage, Powers showed us his two busts of ' Proserpine ' (Fig. 6) and ' Psyche,' and continued his lecture by showing the truth to nature with which these are modelled. . . . Still insisting upon the eye, and hitting the poor ' Venus ' another and another and still another blow on that unhappy feature, Mr. Powers turned up and turned inward and turned outward his own Titanic orb — the biggest by far that I ever saw in mortal head — and made us see and confess that there was nothing right in the ' Venus ' and everything right in ' Psyche ' and ' Proserpine.' . . . Powers is a great man and also a tender and delicate one, massive and rude of surface as he looks; and it is rather absurd to feel how he impressed his auditor, for the time being, with his own evident idea that nobody else is worthy to touch marble. Mr. B—— told me that Powers has had many difficulties on professional grounds, as I understood him, and with his brother-artists. No wonder! he has said enough in my hearing to put him at swords' points with sculptors of every epoch and every degree between the two inclusive extremes of Phidias and Clark Mills.[3] . . .

[1] " Italian Note-Book," Vol. I, p. 290.   [2] Ibid., Vol. II, p. 55.
[3] Ibid., Vol. II, p. 22.

"I had no idea of filling so many pages of this journal with the sayings and characteristics of Mr. Powers; but the man and his talk are fresh, original, and full of bone and muscle, and I enjoy him much."[1]

Although Tuckerman gives the impression that the "Greek Slave" (Pl. III) was Powers's first figure, we are told by others that the "Eve before the Fall" preceded it, having been completed in 1839 or 1840. The "Fisher Boy" followed a little later. The "Greek Slave," the work upon which Powers's fame largely rests, was finished in 1843. The first reproduction in marble went to England, and it was not until 1847 that the sculptor's countrymen were allowed to behold this "white vision" in New York and other cities. It made a sensation wherever shown, and was fondly believed to be the greatest work of sculpture known to history. Nude art could hardly have presented itself in a more insinuating way; the subject and the treatment were such as to awaken sympathy rather than antagonism. In Cincinnati

FIG. 6. — POWERS: PROSERPINE.

the fair captive received a public vindication. A committee of clergymen made, in the interests of public morals, a critical examination of the figure, and joined unanimously in giving her a "character."

The "Greek Slave" was intended to represent a gentle prisoner, taken by the Turks from one of the islands of the Archipelago in the time of the Greek revolution. She stands stripped and manacled, offered perhaps for sale in a public place. Her right hand

[1] "Italian Note-Book," Vol. II, p. 27.

resting upon a convenient pillar supports her weary frame; the left repeats the gesture of the Venus de' Medici.   The head is turned abruptly to the left and bowed.   The face is tinged with sadness.

In spite of the fact that so many copies were made of this statue, only one is accessible to the public to-day in the United States — that being in the Corcoran Gallery in Washington.   Comparatively few have had opportunity, therefore, to see and judge this famous example of our early art, and it is perhaps good service to quote "authorities," who will settle once for all the standing of the "Greek Slave."

We turn first to Tuckerman and rejoice to find him throbbing with emotion before the beauteous creature, "until," as he says, "admiration melts into sympathy"; and, unable to restrain himself longer, he breaks forth into ecstatic verse — six stanzas — in which gyves and lives, chains, limbs and fetters, are mingled with discreet references to "the bosom's patient swell" and the "soft, relying breast."   The last verse is as follows: —

> "With thy dimpled arm depending, and thy pure averted brow,
> Earnest words I hear thee breathing to thy distant lover now :
> Words of triumph, not of wailing, for the cheer of Hope is thine,
> And, immortal in thy beauty, sorrow grows with thee divine." [1]

This seems a final verdict until we stray upon Jarves,[2] who is in a less palpitant mood: "Hiram Powers fully represents the mechanical proclivities of the nation.   His female statues are simply tolerably well-modelled figures, borrowed in conception from the second-rate antiques, and somewhat arbitrarily named."

But did not the "Greek Slave" move Mrs. Browning to fervid apostrophe ?

> "Appeal, fair stone,
> From God's pure height of beauty against man's wrong :
> Catch up in thy divine face not alone
> East's griefs, but West's, and strike and shame the strong
> By thunder of white silence overthrown."

After this how could the *London Art Journal* (of July, 1873) say that " Hiram Powers cannot be ranked among the great sculptors of our time "?

---

[1] " Book of the Artists," p. 286.   [2] " The Art-Idea," p. 265.

Another art journal,[1] however, published as recently as 1900, an article on Powers, in which we read the following extraordinary statement : —

"The name of Hiram Powers is inscribed on the highest pinnacle of the temple of art among the world's greatest sculptors; but like many another one his pathway was not strewn with roses, particularly in his early life. But his wonderful creation of the 'Greek Slave' brought him both fame and fortune, and stands to-day, and will for centuries, as one of the most beautiful and perfect representations of the female form executed by modern art."

In the average of these dicta lies the truth. The "Greek Slave" is not as good sculpture as Tuckerman would have us believe; it is not as bad as some others have hastily pronounced it. It is a sculptural conception, however timidly expressed. The artist had a glimpse, that time if never again, of something fine and poetic. If his work was not warmed by the glow of inspiration, it avoided on the other hand the turgid bombast, the exaggerated emotion of much modern Italian and French art. The "serenity" and "repose" of the old-school sculptors were not merely negative virtues.

The artist's ideal, conceived with dignified moderation, was wrought out with infinite pains. Ignorant and unskilful in the modelling of the body, Powers turned with zest to the things which he felt he could do well. The fringe and embroidery on the mantle, with the chain, are very prominent features. The latter is a marvel of patient detail, like the chains which boys whittle out of a single stick. A locket and cross are conspicuously displayed, while the clothes are hung up with amusing tidiness on the post, seemingly every article accounted for. If the effort expended upon these accessories had been intelligently applied to the figure itself, the result might have been more pleasing to the cultivated taste of to-day ; but it was admirable for its time, and wins our respect even now. Beside his " Eve Repentant " the figure seems positively good, despite this naïveté of treatment. The main lines are fair, and the work expresses a sculptural idea. Powers's female faces are always lacking in personality ; but the touch of melancholy here almost hints at

[1] *Arts for America*, Chicago.

character, while the total effect is unquestionably one of purity and sweetness.

The "Greek Slave" attained to a popularity which would scarcely be possible for any work of sculpture to-day, however good or bad it might be. Hiram Powers, the unknown carver of busts, became instantly famous, not only in his native land, but abroad, particularly in England, where he remained a favorite until his death. Thus he was the first of American sculptors to win a European reputation. The "Greek Slave" was already celebrated before the opening of the great International Exhibition of 1851 in London. At that exhibition it is said to have been the one work of art by an American that did credit to America; its success was overwhelming. It was the centre of interest at the first World's Fair in New York in 1853, and was reproduced over and over again.[1] Its fame in the United States was largely due to the fact that it was one of the first nude figures created by an American, and to its blissful heritage of a good, "taking" name. Those were the days of the Greek struggle for independence; Missolonghi and Byron and the Turk, "in his guarded tent," were still fresh in memory. American sympathies were in full flower, and only wanted some kind of a symbol to cling to. This chaste white figure of the bowed head, with its conspicuous chain and pitiful deprivation in matter of attire, was sufficient, and a whole flood of emotion, a nation's offering, rolled at her highly polished feet. There was a nation's pride in it, too, for was not this a real statue, just like the old ones in the museums — all spotless and smooth and naked? Only a few knew that she was stupid and wooden, the work of a beginner — a mechanic. Let us hope that those who did know this never breathed a word of it. It was not the moment. The infant industries of our young nation required encouragement. The clock-maker of Cincinnati had done his best, and if his ambitious work was not so complete a success as his justly famous "Inferno,"

---

[1] "Of this figure some six or eight copies came from Powers's studio: the first, sold to Captain Grant for $4000, was taken to England, and is now in the gallery of the Duke of Cleveland; the second, brought to America in 1847, attracted great attention when exhibited in New York, and is now at the Corcoran Gallery in Washington; the third copy belongs to Earl Dudley; the fourth, purchased by Prince Demidoff for $4000, was sold at that nobleman's death for $11,000 to A. T. Stewart of New York. The fifth copy is in the possession of Hon. E. W. Stoughton." — CLEMENT AND HUTTON, "Artists of the Nineteenth Century."

with its cheery waxwork devils, it was at least a step upward.   It prepared the way for better things, turning a nation's thoughts toward the ideal.   When the better things came, our people were somewhat better able to appreciate them, thanks to the efforts of the sturdy pioneers who had had their reward in the exhilaration of discovery, in the zest of doing.

But the sculptor had a teeming fancy, as he believed, and many works were to follow.   One of these has already been referred to, a possession now of the Metropolitan Museum of New York.   "Then comes a lithe, graceful, immature figure of the Fisher Boy, holding a shell to his ear, the attitude, the expression, the whole air and aspect suggestive of the mystery of life that connects its outset with eternity; as we muse with the absorbed, unconscious, and beautiful youth, as intent he listens to the mourning shell, — we seem to hear the sound of —

> " that immortal sea
> That brought us hither, which neither man nor boy,
> Nor all that is at enmity with joy,
> Can utterly abolish or destroy."

It is scarcely necessary to say who is being quoted; none but Tuckerman is so appreciative.   It makes one feel very poor and mean and envious to think that another finds so much where one's own emotions are compassed by a museum note like this: —

"Powers's 'Fisher Boy,' 1844.   Net in right hand; sea-shell at ear.   Lean little figure, straight and uninteresting."

There was a figure of " America " which comes in here somewhere, a figure whose stiff outlines are revealed even through the fulsome praise of the time.   One can imagine it to have been the worthy prototype of the army of conventional " Americas," " Libertys," and " Republics " which have followed.   It was unfortunately destroyed by fire in Brooklyn many years ago.   Powers's " Calhoun " also suffered the same fate in Columbia, South Carolina, during the Civil War, after being removed from Charleston for safety, while the first cast of the " Webster " was lost at sea.

The " California," now in the Metropolitan Museum of New York, was carved in 1858.   It is a female figure, entirely nude, and standing with one leg advanced in an easy posture.   The position

F

of the arms is unusual, one being held in front and the other behind the body. In the left hand is held a divining-rod. The figure is carefully modelled and simple in line, but uninteresting. The head looks bald at a little distance, so smoothly has the hair been patted down; but it is well poised in a thoughtful attitude, and the face, which is rather better than usual with Powers, wears a serious expression. It is hard to understand how an early critic could call it "repulsive" and "sinister," but perhaps at a time when sculptured faces untouched by the slightest shade of expression were the vogue, the look of incipient intelligence in these features was too revolutionary and shocked the connoisseurs. The criticism of another is even more difficult to understand when he says: "The dignity of some of his allegorical statues, such as 'California,' and of some of the portrait statues, as that of 'Washington,' is greatly impaired by the too lavish introduction of accessories or by peculiarities of costume."[1] All of which is true elsewhere; but as "California" has no vestige of costume, and no accessory with the exception of the divining-rod, one wonders.

FIG. 7. — POWERS: DANIEL WEBSTER, CHICAGO.

Tuckerman describes the "Eve Disconsolate," one of Powers's most celebrated works, as she "stands clasping her bosom with one hand, while the other indicates the serpent; her tall, majestic form, her luxurious floating hair, her lovely face remorsefully turned to heaven, at a glance tell with silent eloquence the story

[1] *London Art Journal*, July, 1873.

of penitence, in the Christian and highest sense thereof, while the grand proportions of the form are full of poetic dignity, of matronly and maternal grace." [1]

In reality this statue, which may be seen in the Cincinnati Museum of Art, is one of the weakest products of the time. While acknowledging the truth of Jarves's observation that all of Powers's female figures "are the same woman and might be called something else with equal felicity of baptism," it would be easy to show that this "Eve" is distinctly inferior in every way to the "Greek Slave." Through its lean modelling the sculptor has unconsciously made it one of the most naked of nude figures. Whatever may be said of the characterless face, the body has personality. It is the realism of the beginner — a truth without selection. The figure, while deficient in construction, is superficially faithful, and presents a frightened and awkward model whose physical peculiarities are far more in evidence than her beauty. The "Eve before the Fall," on the other hand, as pictured in Benjamin's "Art in America," is admirably statuesque in line, and suggests a generous plastic handling, an effect which one feels only too sure is due to the gauze which the engraver's burin has thrown over it. If it were as good as it looks in the little woodcut, it might well merit the praise which the author applies indiscriminately to the two Eves: "By these noble works, inspired by true untram- melled artistic feeling, — which we must consider his best ideal compositions, — he earned a rank very near to that of Gibson and Canova, and rendered his art worthy of lasting remembrance." [2]

There are few American museums which are not well supplied with busts by Powers. Most frequent is that head which he used to produce incessantly under the title of "Ginevra," "Evangeline," "Faith," "Proserpine" (Fig. 6), "Psyche." The face is rather pretty in outline, but insipid and expressionless. There is "no guile" in it; neither is there much of anything else. The bosom of this pure- minded lady is generally uncovered and very smooth. It is always cut .squarely just below the mathematically rounded breasts. These essential features of Powers's ideal busts are, like the shoulders, always exactly on a level. Below them an irrelevant border of snaky ornament or of sharp acanthus leaves gives what the old sculptor

[1] "Book of the Artists," p. 287.   [2] "Art in America," p. 141.

evidently considered a "neat finish." In the Pennsylvania Academy of Fine Arts, the bust of "Proserpine," of this description, touches shoulders, whether by accident or intention, with Saint Gaudens's "Sherman." They seem to be miles apart.

But if Powers's "ideal" heads have little to recommend them to modern taste, his busts of men, on the other hand, are often admirable. When he pronounced Joel T. Hart the best bust-maker of his time, he might well have excepted himself. More accomplished sculptors followed Powers—men who knew the human body and could compel it into other than stiff erect poses, artists versed in composition and able to combine figures into groups; but few, indeed, down to our own day have produced more faithful, vivid portraits of men than did this primitive carver. With the female countenance he always seemed to lose himself in a vague ideal, but with men he was unerring and unflinching. He characterized with a firm, direct stroke. He even suggested planes, and his finish, if not varied, was agreeable in flow of surface. A good example is his bust of Webster (Fig. 7), now in Chicago. One may also instance his bust of William J. Stone in the Corcoran Gallery. The subject was not a handsome man, but the artist produced an excellent work. The room contains heads by various sculptors, some of them men of note, but among them all this one is easily the best. Powers's statues of Franklin and Jefferson in the Capitol, — in the corridor of the Senate and of the House, respectively, — with all their stiffness and dreariness of authentic costuming and merciless carving, show something of the same qualities in their faces.

The head of the "Franklin" under its three-cornered hat is curiously remote in its rustic look of benignity and innocence. With his left hand lifted to his chin, the great philosopher seems absorbed in thought, an expression which fades away in the side view, giving place to an air of amiable senility, the while the pose suggests that "Poor Richard" has just perpetrated a mild joke and awaits the hearer's response. His left elbow rests upon a great stump, thick and high, the elaborate bark of which has been freshly and profoundly furrowed by devastating lightning.

The "Jefferson," like the "Franklin," has somewhat cylindrical limbs, while the attire is equally smooth and characterless. The attitude is easy and, for Thomas Jefferson, notably unaggressive. The weight rests upon the right leg; the right hand grasps the coat lapel, while the left holds a scroll — beyond peradventure the immortal Declaration of Independence. Altogether he impresses one, as a very gentle and harmless individual.

Powers's famous " Webster " stands in front of the State House in Boston, a pendant to Miss Stebbins's " Horace Mann." Like the latter it has a sufficient resemblance to a statue from a distance, and remains comparatively effective upon nearer view when approached from the front. The head is strong and impressive, the figure seems to stand fairly well. The left hand rests upon the fasces; the right points to the symbol of state with a gesture of unfortunate weakness. It is not until the spectator has mounted the stairs to a position directly oppo- site the figure that he realizes the sculptor's helplessness with the body. Here the pose becomes absurd, almost imbecile, and even the face changes with it. Surely the great orator could not have looked like this, even in his moments of abnormal exaltation. It was in answer to criticisms upon this figure that Powers wrote: " If statues of our great men are wanted, expressing fancy rather than fact, other sculptors must be employed to execute them." [1]

Many a well-modelled head has missed appreciation because it chanced to be set upon a queer body. Powers's treatment of the figure is obviously strange to modern eyes; to enjoy his sturdy strength and the very real grace of his chisel one must return to his busts of men. Here the classical traditions of his time admitted of no foolish accessories, of nothing whimsical; the bare breast and quiet pose, then *de rigueur*, were in perfect accord with Powers's

[1] The following antagonistic estimates of the "Webster" illustrate the divergence of opin- ion, even among men of culture. It should be remembered, however, that twenty years separate these verdicts.

"There is an expression of quiet, solid, massive strength in the whole figure; a deep, pervading energy, in which any exaggeration of gesture would lessen and lower the effect. He looks really like a pillar of the state. The face is very grand, very Webster; stern and awful, because he is in the act of meeting a great crisis, and yet with the warmth of a great heart through it." — HAWTHORNE, "Italian Note-Book," Vol. II, p. 158.

"'Webster,' built up after an intense study of his last suit of clothes." — JARVES, " Art Thoughts," p. 302.

"The 'Webster' of Powers is by universal criticism considered to be as indifferent a representation of that statesman as could be fashioned, and without any redeeming æsthetic feature." — Ibid., p. 305.

native simplicity and directness. (In such work he was unconsciously but conspicuously at his best.

These things which he did so admirably he held of little moment compared with his ideal creations. He was right in believing that realistic portraiture, however faithful, is not the highest expression of art. But he did not understand, apparently, that there is a portraiture which is interpretative as well. [Aiming at distinction in a field for which he was little fitted, that of imaginative sculpture, he may well have deceived himself as to his success.] So low was the standard of the time, so great his popularity, that he could scarcely have suspected anything lacking, least of all that he was deficient in originality. Some of the panegyrics of his contemporaries astonish us, not because they praise, but on account of what they praise: —

" He instinctively sought character and ignored the conventional; he had been too long near the heart of nature, he had lived too much in an atmosphere of freedom and faith, he had been too well accustomed to depend on himself, to be blinded by authority or awed by precedent." This is good doctrine. One would like to borrow these words of Tuckerman's to apply to certain of our favorites of to-day; but how strange the thought that they could ever have been written of Hiram Powers — of Powers the sculptor of the conventional, the timid, the characterless! Are our judgments of our contemporaries liable to so serious a discount thirty years from now? Doubtless Tuckerman believed this eulogy when he wrote it of Powers, and without question Powers believed it of himself. Perhaps it was the sculptor who said it first. It was the way he felt. Though the most abject of imitators, he fancied himself free. [Personally a man of character; honest, direct, original, and by no means averse to expressing himself, he probably never realized that in his art he was anything but this, that he was as hampered and controlled by the dominant traditions of Italian sculpture] as was the most colorless personality beside him — as " the McDowells, the Joneses, the Dunhams, the Nobles," of England. While his hands were tied by his lack of skill, his New England imagination was limited by the sombre and resourceless background of inarticulate generations. For our early American sculptors were anomalies, sports of nature. They represented no culmination of natural tastes, nor of inherited aptitudes. The race from which they sprang has never been artistic. Theirs was a grim, hard-working ancestry. They brought to their task no inward monitor, no intuitive sense of the harmonious, the tasteful. They escaped the ridiculous by doing the commonplace, never suspecting their own limitations. The puppets of fate, the victims of predestination, they believed themselves "free moral agents."

The wonder, then, is not that they did so poorly, but that they accomplished so much and kept so well up to the general average of the times. America owes a perpetual tribute of gratitude to these men for opening the way, for preparing the soil. Art does not flourish without such preparation; great art comes only after a weed-like crop of mediocre artists. Powers and Greenough and Crawford, like Rush and Frazee, were indispensable in the sequence which leads to the masters of the present hour, and to the yet greater men of the generations to come.

CHAPTER IV

CRAWFORD AND SCULPTURE AT THE CAPITOL

THE third man among the early sculptors of importance was Thomas Crawford, who was born in New York City in 1813, and died in London in 1857. A short life — only forty-four years; yet he crowded it remarkably full of joyous labor, and left behind him a long series of achievements. It has been said of him: "One would imagine from the eagerness and intensity exhibited by Crawford that he anticipated a brief career. Work seemed as essential to his nature as rest to less determined natures."

Crawford's attractive personality is insisted upon by the writers of his generation. He is described by Tuckerman as being "above middle height, with remarkably regular features and strongly marked, very clear eye, high forehead and straight nose."[1] He seems to have been no less amiable than handsome, and to have drawn to himself during his twenty odd years in Rome the very choicest spirits of the world of art and literature. His loyal biographer tells us that when Crawford went abroad in 1834: "He carried to Rome the ardor of Irish temperament and the vigor of an American character. . . . His lineage, school education, and early facilities indicate no remarkable means or motive for artistic development. . . . At first, contented to experiment as a juvenile draughtsman, to gaze into the windows of print-shops, to collect what he could obtain in the shape of casts, to carve flowers, leaves, and monumental designs in the marble-yard of Launitz, — then adventuring in wood-sculptures and portraits, until the encouragement of Thorwaldsen, the nude models of the French Academy at Rome, and copies from the 'Demosthenes' and other antiques in the Vatican, disciplined his eye and touch, — thus by a healthful, rigorous process attaining

[1] "Book of the Artists," p. 319.

PLATE 4.—CRAWFORD: ORPHEUS.

the manual skill and the mature judgment which equipped him to venture wisely in the realm of original conception, — there was a thoroughness and a progressive application in his whole initiatory course, prophetic, to those versed in the history of art, of the ultimate and secure success so legitimately earned."[1]

In spite of Tuckerman's enthusiasm, but little of Crawford's work may be said to have been of truly sculptural inspiration. It seldom fails, however, to show a certain poetic or at least literary flavor, which betokens the essential refinement of his nature. Somebody once called him "the Allston of American sculpture," and those who like ready-made characterizations have used the phrase ever since. One finds difficulty in tracing the resemblance. The "classic majesty and mediæval grandeur" which have been attributed to the painter are quite lacking in Crawford. The sculptor's imagination circled in a very limited field. It never soared. In practice he was unable to combine two figures into a good composition. Almost all that he did was cast in the conventional mould of the time. In the "Armed Liberty" alone did he produce a work of notable originality and unassailable strength.

Crawford had been in Rome for several years making a bare subsistence by means of portrait busts and copies of antique statuary in the Vatican, when, through the efforts of Charles Sumner, he was enabled, in 1839, to put in marble his first important work, the "Orpheus and Cerberus," now in the Boston Museum (Pl. IV). He pictures the distraught husband shading his eyes as he peers eager and intent into the gloom of Hades in search of the lost one. This graceful nude was evidently a serious effort, but, despite its sculptural conception, it seems to-day very weak. The head is effeminate and characterless, and the figure, though well-proportioned, is more suggestive of sandpaper finish than of modelling. This is especially noticeable in the arms, which are merely smoothed over, with slight regard for anatomy. The hair is extremely monotonous, with the true Thorwaldsen touch; the drapery tinlike. Even when they did the nude fairly well, those early men were almost invariably insistent in their treatment of accessories. They had no notion of subordinating anything, of relegating non-essentials

---

[1] " Book of the Artists," p. 307.

to the second place.   Every detail was emphasized and underscored. When the accessory was in itself something absurd, as in the case of the monster Cerberus, the result was grotesque.   The unfortunate creature is in no wise ferocious, but seems pained and humiliated at his own appearance.   The shapeless heads are quite without construction.   The necks are gathered together apologetically into a nondescript contrivance on legs, which looks for all the world like a clumsy piece of furniture.   Such an anticlimax brings an irreverent smile to modern eyes, and the real elevation of the artist's thought is forgotten.   We do not give it a chance.   It is not quite possible for us to do so.   Yet this group marked, if it did not make, an epoch in American sculpture, and was justly welcomed as a notable achievement.   Hawthorne held that Crawford never surpassed it, and Benjamin, as late as 1880, says: " It seems on the whole to be the most symmetrical and justly representative work of this great sculptor." [1]

It is not, then, in Crawford's minor works that we shall find great satisfaction.   The three figures in the Metropolitan Museum give a fair idea of them.   The " Dancing Girl," done in 1844, is a child's figure inspired no doubt by Donatello's little dancers and is a charming creation for its day.   The " Dying Indian Maiden," dated 1848, is much less attractive.   It is a small, recumbent figure, with a gaping wound, which the carefully arranged hands make no attempt to protect.   The work has neither sentimental appeal nor lines of beauty. The " Flora " of 1853 is likewise without sculptural import.   The casual limbs extend apparently haphazard, and the face is inane; but the abundant flowers are marvellously detached.   The total effect is not inspiring.

In the Corcoran Gallery is Crawford's once much admired " Peri," a life-size standing figure.   The pose is despondent and the face, weary and dejected, is of the Crawford " ideal " type, so unsatisfactory to modern taste — the type from which the sculptor emancipated himself successfully for once in the countenance of his girlish " Armed Liberty " of the Capitol.   The drapery is of course that of the time, hard and much corrugated, with little artificial touches, and with the general hang of a garment that could never be worn.

[1] " Art in America," p. 146.

The wings are conscientiously labored, without an inch of restful surface, and the sum total is a sufficiently pathetic creature which looks well the part of a bedraggled, outcast angel.

Among other early works of which we find record, but which do not demand extended notice, may be mentioned an "Adam and Eve," a "Shepherdess," "Children in the Woods," a "Boy playing Marbles," a "Pandora," "Dancing Jenny," modelled from the sculptor's little daughter, a "Cupid," a "Genius of Mirth," a "Hebe and Ganymede," a "Mercury and Psyche," the "Daughter of Herodias," and "Aurora." In addition to these statues and the important works now to be described, Crawford modelled more than twenty bas-reliefs of scriptural, classical, and other subjects. Neither his invention nor his industry ever seemed to flag, and the list of his designs is an almost incredibly long one. It is much to be regretted that the eighty-seven casts presented to Central Park, New York, by his widow, should have been lost through fire. Collectively, they would have formed a most interesting monument to the indefatigable man who created them.

The once famous "Beethoven," by Crawford, which stood for so many years in front of the great organ in Music Hall, Boston, has since been removed to the new Symphony Hall, Back Bay. A photograph shows this figure to be a work of dignified conception without unpleasant novelty or striking characteristics of any kind. It is imaginable that at the proper moment, at the height of some noble climax of the orchestra, or when the mighty organ is pouring forth billows of melody, this great bronze with its bowed head and quiet folded hands, its all-enveloping mantle, and its waiting roll, might seem the very personification of genius. It can be imagined, thus illuminated by the emotion of the hour, becoming the concrete symbol of Music and acquiring for the time an impressiveness denied to works of even greater artistic value. Its very lack of definite expression, its in-foldedness, permit the fancy to clothe it with significance and power. One sympathizes with the enthusiasm which prompted the Bavarians to celebrate its casting in Munich with an impromptu concert and a torchlight procession, and yet we cannot help wondering what the joyous Germans might have thought of it had they visited the foundry again the next morning.   Perhaps to eyes and tastes grown accustomed to Schwanthaler's hasty, ill-studied works this statue would always seem admirable, but with our different standards it would be hard to-day to achieve " that free and generous surrender of ourselves " to its appeal, save when under the spell of music and at a mitigating distance.

The " James Otis," in Mount Auburn Cemetery, Cambridge, is a worthy figure which may be praised almost without reservation.

FIG. 8. — CRAWFORD : FREEDOM, WASHINGTON.

The inevitable defects of its time are obvious here and there in leanness of drapery and emphasis of accessories, but these minor features are quite overshadowed by the beauty of the conception and the convincing worth of the man whom the artist has so vividly presented to us.   The happy use of a large cloak gives a sculptural motive gratifying to the eye at the very first glance.   The left hand, concealed, but felt through this drapery, rests upon the hip; the right hand holds a pen and a roll inscribed, " Speech against Writs of Assistance."   The right foot is advanced.   Behind it, upon the floor, lies the Stamp Act.   The legs are well drawn; the mantle is treated in a large, simple way; the hand is good; and, finally, the countenance is noble and serene.   The buttons and the lace of the sleeves and bosom are a little over-emphasized; but, as has been said, all details, good or unfortunate alike, are dominated by the graceful carriage, the quiet dignity of the subject.   The little sky-lighted vestibule in which this figure stands is shared by three other marble effigies of men of distinction.   In the presence of this admirable work these three look harmoniously insignificant in their three respective ways, " each according to his gift."

Crawford returned to the United States but once after taking up his residence in Rome.   This was in 1849, and while here he was commissioned by the state of Virginia to execute a monument for the city of Richmond (Fig. 10). We are told that he made the accepted sketch in a single night in New York. This appears by no means improbable, since there is nothing in the general scheme of the monument which would suggest protracted thought. The central figure is an equestrian statue of Washington; the plinth on which it stands has six protuberances in the form of attached pedestals for as many standing figures of noted sons of Virginia. The originals of two of these — Patrick Henry and Thomas Jefferson — were modelled by Crawford; the others — Marshall, Mason, Nelson, and Lewis — were done by Randolph Rogers, who on Crawford's death was commissioned to finish the monument. Six diminutive allegorical figures were placed on separate pedestals directly in front of the portrait statues. These are also the work of Rogers.

The monument was doubtless intended to be a magnificent affair, and is still supposed to be such by many who have not seen it, since little by way of disparagement has been written about it, except by Hawthorne and Jarves. It is constantly referred to as Crawford's most important work, but it is certainly not the one upon which his legitimate fame will rest most securely. The crowning group is a natural expression of those early and untoward times which gave it birth, being little if any better than Clark Mills's efforts in Washington. Indeed, so bad is it that the approaching traveller can scarcely trust his eyes when, up against the heavens, this extraordinary apparition first meets his view. If the day chances to be sunless, the bronze horse and rider upon their lofty and narrow pedestal appear flat, without modelling, and the effect is that of a silhouette — apparently a horse of pasteboard, struck by a squall and nearly blown from its moorings. To this illusion the harmonious collapse of the creature's legs contributes not a little. There may be worse horses in American sculpture; there is certainly none more amusing than this "Arabian steed" eulogized by Tuckerman, whose arched neck, distended nostrils, and expressively human countenance we shall meet again upon the bronze doors of the Senate. The last touch of absurdity is given to the brave group by that backward push, right over the edge of the thriftily inadequate pedestal. The elision of the whole upper member of the pile would help somewhat by bringing the statue down to a larger platform; but the dimensions of the bronze base, upon which two of the horse's feet rest, show that the artist was himself responsible. It is very likely that he never knew his blunder, since the statue was not set in place until after his death. Indeed, the news of Crawford's death was brought by the very ship which transported the " Washington " to this country in October, 1857.

But if Thomas Crawford was entirely beyond his depth in the problems of equestrian statuary, we find him more than adequate in his other contributions to the monument. It is much to be regretted that pressing orders led him to neglect the Richmond commission until it had finally to be completed, like so many of his undertakings, by other hands. For with all respect for the talent and sincerity of Randolph Rogers, — and his figures here are among his best, — the " Patrick Henry " and the " Jefferson " are by far the most interesting characterizations of the six. The former is indeed a noble figure, worthy to stand with its author's " James Otis." Surely the enthusiastic sculptor had a thrill of emotion the day he conceived it. He shows the patriot with arms and face uplifted. We seem to hear that impassioned utterance, " But as for me, give me liberty or give me death." The beautiful head is exalted in expression as in pose. Its very features are eloquent, while the attitude throughout is lithe, graceful, and strikingly animated. The artist could not have chosen better had he tried a hundred times; a hundred others have tried and done far worse. The cloak which adds to the volume of the figure is well placed and does not seem superfluous. Its treatment is of course hard and lean, like many other inevitable details; but, overlooking such minor things, the general air of the statue is strongly suggestive of David d'Angers at his best.

This resemblance is even more pronounced in the " Jefferson," which, while not recalling in any way the French sculptor's sprightly and powerfully modelled " Jefferson " in the rotunda of the Capitol, does evoke a memory of his curiously compact " Bichât " with folded arms, in the court of the École de Médecine in Paris. Crawford's " Jefferson " wraps a voluminous mantle about himself, and with pen uplifted appears lost in thought. In his left hand he holds the Declaration of Independence in a roll, very conspicuously inscribed " 1776."

Hawthorne tells of a visit to Crawford's studio, soon after the sculptor's death. His comments on the Richmond monument display his usual sagacity : —

" In one of the rooms was a model of the monument itself on a scale, I should think, of about an inch to a foot. It did not impress me as having grown out of any great and genuine idea in the artist's mind, but as being merely an ingenious contrivance enough. . . . When finished it will probably make a very splendid appearance, by its height, its mass, its skilful execution; and will produce a moral effect through its images of illustrious men, and the associations that connect it with our Revolutionary history; but I do not think it will owe much to artistic force of thought or depth of feeling. It is certainly, in one sense, a very foolish and illogical piece of work, — Washington, mounted on a very uneasy steed, on a very narrow space, aloft in the air, when a single step of the horse backward, forward, or on either side, must precipitate him; and several of his contemporaries standing beneath him, not looking up to wonder at his predicament, but each intent on manifesting his own personality to the world around. They have nothing to do with one another, nor with Washington, nor with any great purpose which all are to work out together."[1]

Apparently the novelist was not more favorably impressed by other examples of Crawford's art, since he pronounced them " commonplaces in marble and plaster such as we would not tolerate on a printed page," and continues: " He appears to have considered all his life and labor, heretofore, as only preparatory to the great things that he was to achieve hereafter. I should say, on the contrary, that he was a man who had done his best, and had done it early; for his 'Orpheus' is quite as good as anything else we saw in the studio."[2] It is more than likely that if Hawthorne had known Thomas Crawford as well as he did Hiram Powers, his estimate might have been different.

It was a grievance with Powers, to the end of his long life, that he had not been commissioned, *carte blanche*, to make sculptures

[1] "Italian Note-Book," Vol. I, pp. 128–130.   [2] Ibid., Vol. I, p. 128.

for the national Capitol; Crawford, on the other hand, accepted with alacrity the invitation to compete for the work. Through the aid of his old-time friend, Charles Sumner, he received what was and remained for many years "the most extensive and important commission ever given by the government to an artist." In spite of the manifest imperfections of the result, one must agree with the author of "Great American Sculptures" that "the selection of Crawford to make the group for the north pediment, the colossal statue for the dome, and the bronze doors for the north entrance was fortunate, for it is exceedingly doubtful whether any other American artist of the day — excellent as some of them might have been — could have executed the work in such a satisfactory manner as he did; for Crawford's work undoubtedly is satisfactory, even if it fails in some particulars to realize the ideal of what such work should be." [1]

The pedimental group in particular (Fig. 9), the chief decoration of the Senate wing of the Capitol, illustrates well the audacity of youth in an untried field. Probably no American sculptor of the time could have done it better, for the fundamental requirements of such a decoration were universally unknown; our designers in the gropings of their inexperience could not possibly have guessed them.

In this case the grandiloquent theme, "The Past and Present of America," interdicted any good fortune which might have come by accident. Choosing for his *motif* a "tableau" of disconnected figures, it was not possible that the sculptor should stumble upon that unity of treatment which now and then surprises us even in the work of a tyro who has sought to give expression to a single momentous thought. Moreover, the other essentials of great decorative art were to Crawford a sealed book. How could he know that even in treating the "Past and Present of America" there should be an interdependence of parts leading the eye inevitably but agreeably to a worthy culmination, and that such visible arrangement presupposes a dramatic climax in the thought? His poetic nature seems never to have suggested the possibilities of rhythm, the march of a great poem in stone with its successive strophes like the waves of the sea, interrupted but mounting higher

[1] "Great American Sculptures," by William J. Clark, Jr., p. 67.

and higher in an irresistible crescendo. Of the just measure of elaboration of these individual masses, each complete within itself, varied in detail when viewed near at hand, and effective in broad lights and shadows, as well as in the leading lines when seen from afar; of the cumulative beauty of parts closely united in the grasp of a mighty whole — in short, of the lesson of the Parthenon, Crawford seems to have been blithely unconscious. He must have known the Elgin marbles; he evidently did not grasp their significance. For him and for his colleagues the greater achievements of the past did not exist.

The official interpretation of the group as offered to the tourist may be quoted from a convenient guide-book : —

FIG. 9. — CRAWFORD: PEDIMENT OF SENATE, WASHINGTON.

"Out on the tympanum, or gable end of the portico, is a sculpture by the same artist, which by many is thought to be his greatest work and one of the chief adornments of the Capitol. In this Crawford has attempted to portray in a single group the 'Past and Present of America.' In the centre, America offers the laurel wreaths of merit to her deserving citizens; the rising sun and the eagle portray her youth and her strength; at her left the pioneer levels the forest, the youthful hunter stands near; and, beyond, the Indian warrior and his family, in deepest gloom, watch the inroads of the coming race, while only the inevitable grave is back of them. To the right stand the soldiers, ready for defence, the educated youths and their teacher, ready for good citizenship in any walk of life, and the mechanic and the merchant are here with the emblems of Agriculture and Commerce, the bulwarks of the Nation."

G

"America" stands conspicuous in the midst of the assembly, dominating her companions by her size. The figure is not weakly conceived. While in no sense distinguished, this personification of our country has dignity and grace, and withal a certain sculptural amplitude of mass which is unfortunately lacking in the composition as a whole. In her right hand she holds some wreaths; the left is extended above an eagle. The bird of freedom is balanced by the rising sun, which looks near at hand like a mechanical contrivance made of wooden slats radiating from a common centre. "America's" nearest neighbor on her right is a brave soldier, — perhaps Washington, — who draws his sword with energy, a vigorous and interesting figure. Next, without pretence of sculptural relationship, is a thoughtful individual seated upon a bale of merchandise. Then follow two youthful figures, who seem to acclaim some one, but whether "America," or the pensive gentleman on the bundle, is not clear. Beyond these two we discover a teacher and child, then a recumbent mechanic with hammer and cogwheel, and finally an anchor and sheaves of wheat.

On the other side one sees, first, the representation of a man chopping a tree. The swing of his axe is so untrammelled as to threaten the safety of the Republic; that she does not wince in the face of so great peril is an evidence of her imperturbability and strength. The general effect of the composition does not escape so lightly. The realistic action of this figure is an inharmonious note, and produces the impression of a living workman up there among the statues. Another unpleasant feature is the bulk of the enormous tree-trunk which the conscientious artist has felt it necessary to introduce — a logical adjunct of the woodman's sincere endeavor. Given the effort, there must be something to chop, and this object must seem adequate. Reason is satisfied, but the æsthetic sense protests, only to become hopelessly entangled in the next feature, a confused mass of reeds, perhaps, of mammoth growth, something entirely incongruous and unintelligible unless intended for a bit of landscape as a natural setting for the hunter who comes next, laden with game, — or is he a fisher burdened with his successful catch? At any rate, the youth bows cheerfully under his load and advances upon the scene unmindful of marble thickets and serpents, falling branches, and the threatening Thor-like swing of the woodman. Recurring to the man with the axe, one asks himself if the artist had in mind the eastern pediment of the Parthenon, and imagined that Phidias had thus shown Hephæstus with hammer still uplifted, in the presence of Zeus and his wonder-born daughter. We cannot believe to-day that Grecian taste of the Periclean age would permit so naïf a rendering of the great theme.

We come now to an element of especial interest in this "America" group — the once celebrated " Indian Chief," a replica of which may be studied, detached and at short range, in the collection of the Historical Society of New York City. Of this figure Tuckerman wrote: "No American subject has been treated in marble with such profound local significance as the ' Indian Chief,' — a statue by Crawford now most appropriately occupying the entrance hall of the New York Historical Society ; and no more judicious compliment to the artist's fame can be imagined than the English sculptor Gibson's proposal at the meeting of artists at Rome, called to pay a last tribute to Crawford's memory, that this statue should be cast in bronze, and set up as a permanent memorial of his national fame in one of the squares of the Eternal City. The attitude, air and expression, the grand proportions, the aboriginal type of form and feature, the bowed head, the clenched hand, the stoical despair of this majestic figure, adequately and eloquently symbolize the destruction of a race, and mark the advent of civilization on this continent." [1]

A correspondent of the *London Art Journal* of those days likewise found the figure full of poetic meaning : —

" Resting on a low mound is seated the Indian Chief, a nude figure excellently modelled. His head crowned with tufted feathers rests sadly upon his hand ; the weary chase of life is over, he is dying — the Great Spirit waits to conduct him to the far-off hunting grounds, that dreamy land where souls repose in boundless prairies. His tribe has disappeared, he is left alone, the solitary offshoot of a mighty race ; already the axe of the backwoodsman disturbs his last hours ; civilization and art and agriculture — all mysteries to him incomprehensible — have desecrated his home, and the dark shadows of the past gather him into their bosom ! "

[1] " Book of the Artists," p. 310.

Though apparently crushed by the cornice, this figure, taken by itself, is in many ways admirable. It is sculpturally conceived; the pose is natural and well imagined, the construction reasonably good. If it does not show the mastery of a Michael Angelo, it will at least rank well with its prototypes from the hands of Thorwaldsen and Canova. The wiping out of certain insistent and tiresome details here and there, as the joints in the rubble pier on which the figure is seated, the sharp edges of the hairy skin which serves as drapery, and the severely detached tomahawk, would go far toward making it a truly artistic work. Examination of the replica shows the head to be weak and the hair very crudely carved; but the modelling of the nude is almost good; a little hard doubtless in the softer parts, and a little flabby where it should be hard, but well drawn and treated with a pleasing *mât* finish. It is not difficult to pick flaws in it; the intercostal muscles are uncertain because not understood, but their vagueness is offset by the firm modelling of the thighs, legs, and arms. The latter are a trifle over-accentuated about the elbow, and the fingers are consistently monotonous and sharply defined. They were well done, though, for the time. Their faults were inevitable; no one was doing differently in Rome. The head, however, is unpardonably lacking in construction, and is quite without Indian character other than the conventional Roman nose, which was employed in those days as a symbol and saved a vast amount of research. The ears are unpleasantly isolated and the eyes are amateurish in treatment; but then one need not look at the eyes unless curious to see how they are done — the bowed head sufficiently conveys the impression of melancholy.

It might be difficult for the average mind to find presage of prompt death in this well-knit figure which bears no mark of violence, and is neither emaciated by illness nor blighted by age, and to-day the " profound local significance " of the statue would be much questioned. Its historic significance, however, is great. While the audacious scheme of the early enthusiast — the pediment as a whole — cannot be pronounced in any sense successful, this fragment must be viewed with respect.

The " tableau " is closed in the low north angle of the tympanum with a figure of a mother — Indian ? — clasping a babe to her bosom, and beyond her a grave.   The "detachment" continues to the end.   There is no bond of common interest uniting these figures, nor are the antagonisms, even, expressed by the composition.   Structural unity is lacking because the artist had no great and compelling idea to start with.   Spaces are poorly filled.   Lines wander aimlessly in all directions.   The sculptor is not only impotent in their regard, but quite unaware of their possibilities.   Of light and shade he knows nothing.   His figures, though robust, present lean masses to the eye. Certain accessories, like the stump, the reeds, and the mechanical sun, are almost ludicrous.   And yet, and yet — there are not a few pedimental sculptures in the capitals of Europe, with their centuries of artistic example behind them, in which all of these faults are glaring, and which are far less interesting to-day than this early American work.

A writer who recently referred to Crawford's "stately and grace- ful figure of Liberty on the dome of the Capitol" (Fig. 8) as being "far too beautiful to be placed out of sight," might possibly have re- adjusted his sentence had he visited the National Museum, where stands the original plaster cast of this enormous statue.   Here the feet are brought down to the level of the spectator's eye, and one sees the details but too well.   From near by "Liberty" (properly " Freedom ") appears devoid of grace and even character; nothing but curiosity would impel one to give her a second glance; but, thanks to the fortunate intuition of the artist, the " blocky " unmodelled figure, translated into bronze and lifted on high, crowns the noble dome fittingly and not without a certain majesty.   One questions whether a more experienced sculptor were likely to hit, even after many attempts, upon a happier design, or whether more agreeable modelling would have been as effective as those rude folds and bulky masses.   Certainly, Rogers's insignificant " Genius of Con- necticut," with her weary gesture, is not to be placed in the same category with this work.   Crawford had the good taste to give his " Freedom " a very simple, concentrated pose with plenty to occupy her hands — they were full enough in those days!   The sword and shield not only support the hands in turn, but contribute their straight lines to the architectural effectiveness of the mass.   The head is well poised and has, from a distance, an airy grace, coupled with much strength. Near approach brings surprise: the face is blankly sweet with its big, deep-set eyes and its parted lips — an expression oddly suggestive of national inexperience, or, if we adhere to the exact title of the work, of Freedom's extreme youthfulness. The stars which adorn the " Jeff. Davis helmet" (see Tuckerman) were apparently sawed from a plank, and the clumsy border of the mantle is decorated with a row of balls like sleigh-bells. The

FIG. 10. — CRAWFORD: WASHINGTON MONUMENT, RICHMOND.

hands are unmodelled, and the drapery of even the lighter garment is monotonous throughout.

But the interesting and important fact remains — the only thing which is important — that the bronze figure, in place, is successful. We have no right to go behind the record and examine the plaster cast with a microscope, though a telescope might be helpful in contemplating the bronze. It is the merest chance which offers us the model for close scrutiny, and we are reconciled to the distance of the triumphant maiden on her "mountain height" of cast iron. Few, indeed, would be willing to banish that image from the dome of the Capitol, even in exchange for a better. Whether seen or merely guessed at; whether prized for what it says to us, or for what it considerately does not say, but allows us to read into it, this figure has come to embody a national ideal. It has acquired significance as well as beauty in our eyes. It is dear to every American heart as the official, the authorized symbol of Freedom — a Freedom which has to-day a meaning that was unknown when, in 1860, Clark Mills cast this enormous statue, and when, to the booming of cannon and the shouts of a city full of soldiers, the fragments were lifted one by one to that aery height. One cannot repress the fancy that if we could scrutinize the bronze face to-day, its virgin features would show a very different expression from that of the cloistered model.   Think of the scenes which she looked down upon during those tempestuous years following her fiery birth !   Would it be strange if the face up there in the clouds had lost its unsophisticated wide-eyed stare?   At any rate, the kindly years which have laid a whole generation of men to rest since those harsh times have touched her gently, clothing her in a beautiful patina of green, which softens and elaborates her drapery until she seems now to be enveloped in a veil — a veil rich and filmy and of the color of distant forests draped in mist.

Few American sculptures have had greater fame than the bronze doors of the national Capitol.   Admired from the beginning, they have the advantages of narrative form and abundant detail, and their renown has gained momentum with the years. Crawford and Rogers were engaged upon the two portals at about the same time; but the death of Crawford in 1857 arrested work upon the doors of the Senate, and they were finished several years later by the hands of another.[1]   They did not reach their final destination until November, 1868, or seven years after the Rogers doors were hung.

Less elaborate than 'their pendants, and lacking the advantage of priority, the Crawford doors have received a smaller share of attention.   The subjects chosen by the sculptor are illustrations of Revolutionary and Federal history.   The right-hand door commemorates " War and its Terrors "; the left, " Peace and its Blessings." The period illustrated comprises eighteen years, and begins chronologically at the top on the right hand, where is portrayed the " Battle of Bunker Hill and Death of General Warren," 1775. Below is the " Battle of Monmouth and Rebuke of the Traitor, General Charles Lee," 1778; next " Yorktown and the Gallant Hamilton," 1781, with "A Hessian Soldier attacking a Colonial House " at the bottom.   Opposite, and in contrast to this last study, is an allegorical representation of " Peace"; above, " Washington's Reception at Trenton," as he was on his way to New York to assume the Presidency; next, " Inauguration of Washington," 1789; and in the upper

[1] William H. Rinehart.

panel, "Laying of the Corner-stone of the Capitol," 1793, by Washington.

"Peace and its Blessings" is particularly Thorwaldsen-like. It is a dignified little group, showing a happy family in nondescript, semiclassic costume. The father rests his hand very gently upon a plough handle, and turns with an appreciative look to his loving spouse, who seems to say, "I, too, have not been idle." Their three hopeful olive branches serve admirably for chinking in the composition. One recalls that, despite the size of the household, contemporary writers persisted in recognizing in the scene no other than George Washington and his family.

The companion relief to the "Peace," — "War and its Terrors," — is far from impressive, while "Washington at Trenton" and "Monmouth" are made laughable by the knowing expressions of the undersized ponies. These are the typical horses of art of half a century ago — just such as one finds in the old engravings. They bear the sympathetic touch of a Landseer. In the Trenton ovation, Washington's centaur-like steed carries himself with proud humility, but looks the appreciation which it would ill become him to express in words. It is in "The Rebuke of General Lee at Monmouth," however, that the equine companions rise to the greatest height of human feeling. An old description tells us — awkwardly enough — that "Washington is seen as having ridden rapidly to where he meets Lee under a tree, and rising in the stirrups of his saddle, administers a rebuke that droops the traitor's head as much as Lee's military salute to his chieftain has his sword."

Washington's pose is commanding, but the war-time writer drew on his imagination regarding the attitude of the early General Lee. In reality he neglects to lower his head at all, and also neglects to wear any particular expression. However, his deficiencies are more than atoned for by the eloquent looks of the two horses. Washington's diminutive charger holds up his head with all the rigidity of conscious worth, and snorts defiance at the four-footed traitor opposite. The latter recoils into himself, rolling agonized eyes at thought of his own degradation.

"The Death of Warren" is not fortunately chosen. The "Hamilton" is better; the "Inauguration" dignified. The quiet

" Laying of the Corner-stone " is the best of all—a simple, direct
rendering of an impressive scene.

The relief is high, some of the figures being almost in the
round; the general scheme, like that of Rogers, is evidently inspired by the gates of the Florentine baptistery.   Let us rather
say "suggested," since inspiration is a quality of which even the
chemist's ultimate analysis would discover but slight traces in
either of these painstaking works.   No doubt Crawford's designs
were produced with much spontaneity.   We are told that "his
mind teemed with so many panoramic and single conceptions —
historical, allegorical, ideal, and illustrative of standard literature
or classical fable — that only time and expense presented obstacles
to unlimited invention."   The trouble is that as a rule these
imaginings were not legitimately sculptural conceptions.   Some
were pictorial, others not even that.   The approach was almost
always literary, — a story, a sentiment; but seldom is the result an
impressive mass or an effective combination of lines.   Even this
lack might have been atoned for in part if some miracle had
endowed the ardent dreamer with a felicitous touch.   But here,
too, he was notably deficient.   He seems never to have guessed
the real merit of the Ghiberti Gates: their charm of handling,
their wealth of sculptural color, the rhythm of their grouped
figures.   How could he?   In those days such qualities received
no recognition.   Our country was as unconscious of them as it
had been of poetic melody a hundred, yes, fifty years before.   The
sense had become atrophied, if ever it had existed.   It is more
than likely that through all the generations of our ancestry it had
never been awakened.

Among the famous examples of bronze doors — the Ghiberti
Gates, the Pisano portal, the Rodin " Inferno " — there is no question, from a decorative standpoint, of the humble rank of the
American contributions.   In them neither Rogers nor Crawford
added anything to the world's sum total of beauty.   Crawford's
design possesses rather more of spontaneity and vigor than Rogers's;
but the latter is better done — as cabinet-work.   Crawford's
imagination leads him into difficulties where he is helpless;
Rogers's, distinctly more commonplace, avoids absurdities.   Neither

work shows one hint of plastic charm; the compositions are as lean in *ensemble* as they are dry in detail. Their chief value lies in their sincerity, which, as Mr. Brownell observes, is in art a very elementary virtue. They are as straightforward and brusque as a backwoodsman's story, as unadorned as a market report.

Even in a photograph the Ghiberti Gates sparkle and gleam with myriads of accents. Broad strokes reflect the light like the valleys of waves; again these are beaten into a very foam of subtle forms silhouetted against creeping shadows. Veiled distances add their mysterious charm, and the borders are like spent ripples upon a smooth beach, where at every step one catches the gleam of a pearly shell half imbedded in the sand, and where seaweeds and *algæ* reach out tremulous fingers to the faithless tide. To call those little enshrined men and women of the borders, "pearls," is no exaggeration of their value. Ghiberti's doors have been a mine of jewels for all the artists who have followed. Michael Angelo did not disdain to borrow from them. Each of those tiny figures is potentially a great statue. As has been said by the author of " Italian Sculpture of the Renaissance ": " So gracefully posed are they, so elegantly draped, so exquisitely wrought, that one longs to take them in one's hands, to finger them, examine each perfect little whole on all sides." It may be safely ventured that no one has ever desired to handle the Washington bronzes for the mere sensuous pleasure of touch. The sculptors of the Capitol have succeeded in eliminating all charm of flowing forms and of delicate gradations. Every figure is sharp cut and strikes the inexorable background with a bump. Over all is the harsh finish of the foundry instead of the loving caress of the sculptor's hand.

What right, one may ask, have we to compare these examples of primitive American art with the acknowledged masterpieces of the past — the life-works of great artists ? Why should we wish to make such comparison, to the injury of our national pride ? And the question may be answered: Merely as we would refer a pupil back now and then to his early imperfect studies. It is not American sculptors as much as American sculpture which we have under consideration. Its advance has been marvellous during the last fifty years. To measure this progress we must use some standard, and nothing is more certain than the *best*. Even the individual need not suffer through such test, unless his fame is founded upon error. It behooves us to speak wittingly of those whom we exalt as heroes, lest we be sometime discomfited.

It may be urged that the subjects treated by Crawford were ungrateful ones as compared with those which flowered under Ghiberti's touch. Our American sculptor was debarred all beautiful staging of his theme. He was handicapped by actualities, foremost among them being the costume of the eighteenth century — not so bad as our own, to be sure, but lacking the colorful possibilities of flowing draperies. For him were no angel choirs and figures which "seem to be moving to melodies unheard."

Such a plea carries much weight, and should not be overlooked. But in art criticism, as in judgments on life in general, we should remember that it is the solution of the particular problem that counts, not what might have been done under other hypothetical circumstances. We esteem a man for what he does with his individual talents. We gauge an artist by the success or failure of the thing accomplished, not by what he has dreamed of doing, or thinks he could do, or might have done in another century.

Clark's comment is doubtless justified, that " Crawford's artistic education was much more complete than that of any previous American sculptor had been;" but it is equally true that "he, however, attempted too much, and did too much, for the work to be thoroughly well done."[1] Whether he had higher ideals of execution is perhaps doubtful, but we may say that he was the first American who really tasted the joys of unhampered sculptural invention; who was completely wrapped up in his art; who let it fairly "go to his head." The result was not always good sculpture, and he never produced great sculpture; but it is of such natures as his, of such ardor, that artistic traditions are born. We must concur with Mrs. Radcliffe[2] in pronouncing Thomas Crawford "the most notable pioneer of our native sculpture."

[1] "Great American Sculptures," p. 64.
[2] A. G. Radcliffe, " Schools and Masters of Sculpture," p. 483.

CHAPTER V

SOME MINOR SCULPTORS OF THE EARLY DAYS

In this formative period of American art there lived a number of sculptors, contemporaries of Crawford, who, though not of the first rank, are nevertheless worthy of mention: Henry Dexter, John King, and Ball Hughes, who were born in 1806; Joel T. Hart, dating from 1810; and Shobal Vail Clevenger, Joseph Mozier, and Chauncey B. Ives, who came into the world during the storms of 1812.

Dexter, although an enthusiastic devotee of his profession, can scarcely be considered an important factor in American art. When it is said that he was a " self-taught genius," his standing is more or less defined, since it is an impossibility for any one to teach himself the whole of the technic of a great art. With all the good-will in the world, with the best of taste and the most perfect of aptitudes, the sculptor, like the painter, requires a guide who is able to abridge the years of groping, and to reduce the tribute which inexperience must ever pay where attainment stands for anything of value. Yet the story of this man is interesting — as is perhaps every man's when we get to the heart of things — and so typical that it must be given some space.

Born on a farm, in New York State, in the midst of an unsettled wilderness, the boy seems to have been as nearly quarantined against artistic influences as it is possible for one to be. Nevertheless, he found a way to gratify his desires: being without paper, he drew his pictures on cloth, and his colors he made for himself from the juices of fruits. Losing his father when only eleven years of age, he worked for a time on a Connecticut farm, and was later apprenticed, much against his will, to a blacksmith. He had hardly learned the trade when he married a niece of the painter, Francis Alexander. He made his first attempt at portrait-painting about this time; but Alexander himself expostulated with him for even dreaming of giving up his trade, and he reluctantly continued it for seven years.   In 1835 he went to Boston, resolved that, whether successful or not, he would at least try to become an artist, and with the assistance of Alexander he soon made a certain reputation as a portrait painter.   He practised his crude art for a few months until his friend, perhaps somewhat perplexed by the results, advised him to attempt modelling.   We are told that "he at once achieved re-markable success in making portrait busts," and that his first order was for a marble bust of the mayor of Boston, Hon. Samuel A. Eliot, after which many of the most distinguished gentlemen of Boston made requests for similar works.   "He made busts of Long-fellow, Agassiz, Henry Wilson, Cornelius C. Felton, president of Harvard College, Anson Burlingame, and of Charles Dickens, when that novelist visited Boston, as well as of several hundred others; and the work executed entirely by his own hands was frequently of surpassing merit." [1]

The latter remark must needs be qualified if we keep in view the men who are to follow; but it may be said that Mr. Dexter's busts show good, honest work and often a large simplicity.   They can hardly be called either intimate or profound; but their superficial resemblance is at least as free from petty details as it is from signifi-cance of pose and complexity of analysis.   Even so moderate a recom-mendation is impossible in the case of Dexter's half-dozen figures, if his statue of General Warren, at Bunker Hill, is a fair example.   The commander's eloquent appeal to his troops, "Stand! the ground's your own!" would have carried little weight from a man of so unmartial an air.   He himself must needs learn to stand before he could command others.

The imagination of the sculptor is better illustrated by his some-what fanciful idea of making portrait busts of all the governors of the United States.   This he actually accomplished in 1860, travelling over every state excepting California and Oregon.   He returned to Boston with his unique collection of casts; and after exhibiting them in the rotunda of the State House, set himself to the thankless toil of reproducing them in marble.   It is needless to say that the

[1] "Encyclopædia of American Biography."

patriotic project was frustrated by the Civil War, and that most of the heads were doomed to reach no such immortality. On the contrary, — and it is not a pleasure to record the fact, — these works, born of so great an enthusiasm and recorded vaguely as forming " a valuable portion of the art collection at Washington," are practically lost. In the storerooms of the National Museum, these and scores of other portrait busts are ranged in double rows upon the loftiest shelves. The dust of many years has drawn its compassionate veil over them all, as over the hopes and ambitions of those who gave them form.

John King, a Scotchman, is interesting, likewise, because of his wanderings, and because of his relations with Hiram Powers. He came to this country in 1829 and found employment as a mechanic, successively in New Orleans, Cincinnati, and Louisville. In 1832, while working in Cincinnati, he met Powers, who recognized his talent and encouraged his first attempts in modelling. By the year 1836 he was a professional sculptor, and in 1840 he made busts of several prominent citizens of New Orleans, as well as a number of likenesses in cameo. He settled in the same year in Boston, where he made marble busts of Daniel Webster, John Quincy Adams, Dr. Woodward, Agassiz, and Emerson. A bust of Commodore Morris, in the Corcoran Gallery, signed J. C. King, is conspicuous for its wrinkles and for its lack of other attributes. It is the product of an unskilled hand.

Much more distinctive is the contribution of Ball Hughes, an Englishman, who had enjoyed in London the privileges of the Royal Academy and of the studio of the sculptor Bailey, with whom he worked for some years. He had already attained to some little reputation, particularly for his statuettes and busts of George IV, when, likewise in 1829, he too decided to try his fortunes in the new country. Landing at New York, he remained for a time in that city, but finally settled at Dorchester, Massachusetts, in which neighborhood he made his home until his death in 1868. His most important work for New York City was a statue of Alexander Hamilton in marble, erected in 1835, in the rotunda of the New York Merchants' Exchange, which was destroyed eight months later by fire. This is said to have been the first portrait figure sculptured in marble in this

FIG. 11.—HART: HENRY CLAY, RICHMOND.

country.   Among the prized relics of the Boston Athenæum — safely guarded in the attic storeroom — is the little model of this historic work.   It is a slender figure, but has a very professional look, with much hip action, and the right arm raised in a heroic gesture, the whole showing a more vigorous and fluent treatment than might be expected from the author of the mild " Little Nell " on the deserted landing outside, or the " Dr. Bowditch," who occupies a more conspicuous place in the lower vestibule.

But, for all his training, Ball Hughes's significance in American sculpture is historical rather than artistic.   Not only did he carve what may have been the first marble statue made in this country, but he certainly modelled the first statue to be cast in bronze. This was the above-mentioned portrait of Dr. Bowditch, the astronomer, whose effigy is conspicuous at Mount Auburn Cemetery.   It is a seated figure, upon a massive granite pedestal of Egyptian tendencies, surrounded by an iron fence.   One approaches the "first bronze statue cast in America" with curiosity not unmingled with reverence.   It is not an insignificant work.   The scholarly doctor has a fine, intellectual head, in which the physical has small share.   His face is kindly, dreamy, almost smiling. He is attired in knee breeches and what looks like a quilted dressing-gown of ample folds, and is seated in a small but heavy chair, the sculptural solidity of ' which is cleverly enhanced by a curious fringed valance filling the spaces between its square legs.   On the right knee the amiable student supports a large volume in a vertical position, his hand resting upon it.   The left hand reposes in a somewhat deathlike fashion on its edge upon the other knee.   Beside the chair is a large globe and a sextant; the base bears the inscription, " Executed by Ball Hughes, 1847."   On the other side are more books and — a discovery !   After all our emotions we read here in impudently large letters, " Recast by Gruet Jne., Fondeur, Paris, 1886."   So this is not the original bronze, after all, and we might better have contented ourselves with examining the original plaster cast in the Athenæum.   Inquiry at the office of the cemetery brings out the fact that the family had felt that the old cast was not good enough, so had boxed it up and sent it over to Paris to be translated into worthier form.   Let us hope that they

H

were satisfied, while we mourn the loss of that precious relic which was doubtless broken into fragments after serving as a model, and disappeared forever in the insatiable melting-pots.

Among this sculptor's other works mentioned by historians is an "Uncle Toby and Widow Wadman" which is said to be in the Boston Athenæum also, but which must be on the retired list; a model of an equestrian statue of Washington, a statuette of Washington Irving, and a "Mary Magdalen." His bust of Irving is well known, but does not compare in distinction with Palmer's rendering of the same subject. Probably his most noted bust is the portrait of John Trumbull in the Yale Art Gallery, which shows good construction and capable work throughout. It is draped in the customary toga, very simply handled but with the unusual and rather incongruous feature of a decoration of some kind hanging on a ribbon which emerges from the neck opening. The hair is very hard and conventional, like wood-carving; the face not less hard, with an unrelenting look which the slightly parted lips are unable to mitigate. The only flagrant faults of execution are the deep, concave furrows of the chisel above the eyes; but despite these and the unwinning expression, the total effect is distinguished. The bust may almost be said to have style.

It is remarkable that a man of Mr. Hughes's facility should have produced so little. Perhaps he realized early that he had no great revelation to make, and resolved to hold his peace. This is not literally true, however, for tradition has not suppressed the fact that in his later years Mr. Hughes was wont to deliver lectures on art, thus making himself honorary founder of the formidable line of "talking sculptors" in this country. Whatever may be the verdict of posterity regarding his work, — and posterity may not even take the trouble to consider it at all, — it is certain that the name of Ball Hughes will be remembered. However uninspired, he chanced to be the first to do certain things important in the physical evolution of his art, and no history of American sculpture can omit him.

Of greater interest is the story of gentle Joel Hart of Kentucky, for whom a writer of his native state has recently made the following claim: " Born and reared in the primitive days of his state, and not many years after it had emerged from its swaddling-clothes, his native genius began to assert itself, and without instruction and without art surroundings he overcame all obstacles, reaching the highest prominence in his profession, not surpassed by the Grecian or the Roman sculptors of the ancient, the mediæval, or the modern age." [1]   No doubt the venerable author of " The Old Masters of the Blue Grass " believed what he was writing, and felt that no eulogy was too exalted ; but the sentence expresses even more than he intended, for it gives a glimpse of a point of view and a standard of criticism not unlike that which prevailed some fifty years ago in the east, where local enthusiasms ran high, and where budding geniuses of poetry, painting, and sculpture were endlessly coddled.

Mr. Hart was born in Clark County, Kentucky, not far from Winchester, on the tenth day of February, 1810.   His parents were people of character, intelligence, and wealth.   The family possessions were lost through the dishonesty of an agent about the time that the young Joel was ready to begin his education.   A period of three months in the local school was all that was permitted him ; but thanks to studious habits and the aid of elder brothers, the boy equipped himself for teaching before he had emerged from his teens.   This education he gained by reading at night by the light of a wood fire, for his days were spent in rough mason-work, especially in chimney-building.   In 1830 he found employment in a stone-cutter's yard in Lexington, whither came shortly young Clevenger of Cincinnati, whose mission in Lexington was to model a bust of Henry Clay.   The intelligent stone-cutter was privileged to watch the progress of the work and became convinced that he could do it also. Materials and subject were not lacking, and the ambitious youth was soon engaged in portraying another of the Kentucky Clays ; in this case the future general, Cassius M. Clay.

The bust had a great success, " proving an epoch in the art circle of Lexington," and displaying " a high degree of excellence which is attained by others only after years of experience."   Mr. Hart essayed next a bust of Andrew Jackson, which he modelled from life at the Hermitage, and this proved so satisfactory that the aged general ordered a copy in marble.   Other commissions followed from all sides.

[1] " The Old Masters of the Blue Grass," by General Samuel Woodson Price, p. 149.

A trip to Philadelphia, New York, Washington, and other places of interest, including Richmond, Virginia, gave the sculptor his first acquaintance with statuary. He took with him his bust of General Clay, and had a flattering reception everywhere. In a letter to his brother he mentions having met a host of distinguished men, and having "received attention enough for a lifetime." More important, however, is the fact that while in Richmond he was commissioned by an association of ladies to execute a statue of Henry Clay. This he began in 1846 from life. It took him three years to complete his model, which, except in the matter of likeness, was hopelessly bad when finished. The figure was finally cast and shipped to Italy, whither Mr. Hart followed, reaching Florence in the autumn of 1849. He waited long for the expected model, even journeying to Paris and London to while away the time. In London he studied anatomy at a medical school —

FIG. 12. — CLEVENGER: WASHINGTON ALLSTON, PENNSYLVANIA ACADEMY.

so we are told — for fourteen months. Returning to Florence, his forebodings were confirmed; his model (and presumably the vessel which bore it) had been lost at sea. Fortunately a duplicate cast had been made, and this was ordered, arriving just one year later. Severe attacks of cholera and typhoid fever filled this period amply, but the would-be artist found time to devise a pointing instrument to be used in transferring measurements directly from the human face to the clay. He believed that he had invented an instrument of great value, but it was never put to practical use except by himself.   One of its greatest services to its inventor was the advertisement which it gave him, a single notice in the London press bringing him orders for marble busts from "ten of the most prominent citizens," attracted apparently by the idea of "being done by machinery."[1]

The Clay statue (Fig. 11) was finally accomplished, though not until 1859.   A matter of thirteen years seems to have been nothing to this ineffectual dreamer.   In spite of his eulogists, it is evident that the lack of early training, particularly in drawing, proved a handicap throughout his life.   Of course the length of time occupied upon a work really does not matter if the result be of permanent value; but in this case the absolute nullity of the figure is so obvious, that one can but ask what the sculptor was about all those years.   It is hardly necessary to say that the figure when unveiled in Richmond met with tumultuous applause.   The only criticisms recorded were in regard to the modern attire, which evidently should have been Greek or Roman; but the art authorities allowed this to pass.

The marble orator still stands in the little summer-house which decorates a corner of the beautiful grounds of Virginia's capital. Here, while the tame squirrels scamper over his feet, the traveller may study the timid realism of the statue and muse over its misleading inscription, " J. T. Hart, 1847."   From certain views the figure, which is apparently of not more than life-size, has a look of preternatural gravity coupled with unstable equilibrium.   The position of one of the hands, just touching an opportune table, adds to the illusion of precarious balance.   While Houdon's "Washington" in the Capitol, a few hundred feet away, wears clothing so smooth and tight that he looks positively froglike as to his lower half, Mr. Clay rejoices in a suit which is "fulled up," as though by exposure to sun and storm.   Coat-sleeves and trousers alike are composed of welts and sags.   But there is no getting away from the admirably ugly head.   It is modelled with great sincerity and well carved; likewise

---

[1] Thomas Ball refers to this instrument in his autobiography as follows, "It was ingenious ; but no other mortal would ever make use of it, and he [Hart] never would have used it had any other mortal invented it."

it is full of life.   The excellent bust of Clay in the Corcoran Gallery is doubtless from the same model.

The sculptor came home with his work and met with ovations everywhere, the reception at Louisville being most agreeably accentuated by an order for a duplicate of the statue.   Then New Orleans, always prompt in following up artistic successes, ordered yet another.   Good times were now fully come to the gratified artist, and after providing for the reproduction of the figure he turned to more attractive fields.   " Conscious," as his biographer suggests, " that he had not reached the highest niche of fame that had been attained by sculptors of previous ages, he realized that he must give full scope to his artistic powers."   He had long been pursued by a dream of a fair nude figure, a woman holding an arrow out of the reach of an imploring Cupid.   It was not his idea to show her in a playful, teasing mood, which might perchance justify the *motif* as a work of fancy, but in sober earnest.   This most beautiful of all figures was to have a profound significance and an intelligible moral worth.   The group's first title was " The Triumph of Chastity," but afterward with better taste, if not better sense, it was called "Woman Triumphant."   Under one name and another it was a cherished ideal with the artist for thirty years or more.   Doubtless they were happy years.   The amiable sculptor lived in a state of soothing hallucination.   These were wife and child to him — his all.   He could never bring himself to part with them.   They were never quite finished.   To the remonstrances of acquaintances, Mr. Hart was wont to reply,   " Why, my friend, it takes God Almighty eighteen or twenty years to make a perfect woman; then why should you expect me to finish one in less time? "

The group received amazing compliments in its day.   " The art correspondent, at Florence, of the *London Athenæum*, a paper of recognized authority in art matters, said in 1871 that he 'considered it the *finest work in existence*, and that in 1868 he had begged Mr. Hart to finish it at once, but he would not; each year it grew more beautiful, and he now feared to urge its completion against the artist's better judgment.' Other art correspondents of London journals years ago pronounced it *the* work of modern times, and other writers all agree as to its perfection."

In reality the principal figure, as shown by good representations, is that of a well-proportioned and rather graceful woman, with a conventional head, the left hand raised high, holding the arrow out of reach of the child, and the right arm and hand hanging limp and expressionless.   The Cupid is indistinguishable from thousands of others, ancient and modern.   The group suggests a French clock ornament, though lacking, of course, the swing and the modelling of the best of these, *i. e.* the mastery of the skilled workman.   We have scores of sculptors to-day who could do as good a figure in a single year.   We have several who could model a vastly better one in a month.

But it does not follow that these experts are any happier than was gentle, admirable old Joel Hart with his vision.   Perhaps they are no truer artists.   To love one's work as he did, to have faith in it to the end, seems about the finest thing imaginable.   Attractive in personality and refined in taste, Mr. Hart won to himself a large group of friends, whose appreciation filled his later years with joy.   His blameless life closed Mar. 2, 1877, in Florence.   He was buried in that city, but his remains were brought in 1887 to this country and reinterred at Frankfort, Kentucky.

Though helpless with the human figure, Mr. Hart made some interesting busts.   His " Crittenden " in the Corcoran Gallery has a strange, long, and unhappy face, most carefully modelled and polished.   It is conscientious work, and compels our respect.   His head of Henry Clay in the same collection is unquestionably good. Powers pronounced Hart the " best bust-maker in the world at this time," which shows that the two men had reached " at this time " a better understanding than when, in 1857, Hart wrote, apropos of his pointing machine, " The sculptor, Powers, and the rest of them in general, hate it like the devil, however friendly they would appear toward myself."   Of the sculptor's two or three other figures, slight record remains.   Tuckerman says, " Hart's ' Angelina ' is beautiful " — and stops.   Another was " Il Penseroso," and a third represented a child with an apron full of flowers.

The sequel of the story of " Woman Triumphant " is unique in the art annals of our country.   A few years after Mr. Hart's death the women of Lexington succeeded in raising a sum sufficient for the purchase of a marble copy of the group. It was brought from far-away Florence to the Kentucky town, and for especial safety enshrined in the courthouse, a supposedly fireproof building. There it stood for some years, the pride of the city, and a subject of much discussion by the country folk and strangers generally. One day the fireproof courthouse started to burn down. It was saved after heroic efforts, but the timbers of the cupola had fallen within and crushed the poor marble lady and her mischievous companion into a thousand fragments. These were eagerly seized by the citizens as keepsakes and carried to many happy homes. Not a chip was left. A clever workman could have patched them all together again and made the figure almost as good as new; but the prized bits could never be traced. Like the pet kittens of our childhood, Lexington's glory had been literally "loved to death."

Vividly contrasting with Hart's somnolent existence was the brief, strenuous career of that same "young Clevenger" who gave the elder man his first glimpse of the sculptor's art. Shobal Vail Clevenger was the son of a New Jersey weaver, who emigrated in 1808 and settled on a farm near Middleton, Ohio. Here the son was born in 1812. He grew up in this primitive environment without display of special artistic gifts, until upon a visit to Cincinnati he chanced to see some bas-reliefs used as decorations on a building. They fascinated him and with the confidence of youth he asserted that he could do such work. As in so many cases, the way to immortality seemed to lie through the graveyard, and Mr. Clevenger was soon apprenticed to David Guion, a monument-maker of Cincinnati. He remained in his employ for four years, and returned to him after various independent ventures. It chanced one day that there was an angel to be carved on a tombstone. Mr. Clevenger essayed it, and succeeded to the admiration of his companions. A word of encouragement spoken to him in the marble yard, an introduction to Mr. Nicholas Longworth, and a very different horizon opened about the poor marble-cutter. The munificent patron of Hiram Powers, and of so many other men of talent, gave Mr. Clevenger a commission which he executed satisfactorily, and others followed, among them busts of William H. Harrison, and Henry Clay.

Through Mr. Longworth's aid Mr. Clevenger was enabled to go to Italy, but following the practical advice of his patron, visited first the various large cities of the East, where he secured a number of valuable orders. As a result the public art collections of Boston, New York, and Philadelphia have examples of his work, which was limited almost exclusively to busts. There is record of a " North American Indian," carved in Rome in 1840; but whether this was more than a head, or whether still in existence, is unknown, although the work is said to have created much interest in its day as being " the first distinctively American sculpture."

Clevenger died in 1843 at the untimely age of thirty-one. His death was particularly pathetic, occurring as it did at sea upon a homeward voyage. He had embarked because of a threatening disorder of the lungs, but the end came unexpectedly and his body was consigned to the ocean within a day's sail of Gibraltar. No biography of him is complete without Tuckerman's felicitous and kindly comment that the young sculptor's life " was for the most part happy and altogether honorable." He had scarcely begun his work when it was done, and we have no data for estimating his imaginative force. What impresses one in his art is its fidelity to nature and his skill with the chisel. In the Boston Athenæum are three of his busts which illustrate these qualities: Judge John Davis (1839), an ugly face most lovingly detailed; Lemuel Perkins (also of 1839), with broad expanse of manly bosom, sleepy eyes, and good large modelling, though rather puffy in effect, and hair treated in a softer and more truthful way than was usual; and a bust of Allston (Fig. 12) which looks surprisingly like the one by Brackett in the New York Historical Society.

The Metropolitan Museum has Clevenger's excellent bust of Henry Clay; and his " Webster " will be found in many collections and libraries. His " Edward Everett " is said to be an admirable work, which resulted in a warm friendship between the two — as, indeed, was the case whenever the young sculptor had similar opportunity to meet men of refinement and distinction. Tuckerman observes sympathetically: " It was interesting to watch the seeds of this high intercourse germinate in the virgin soil of an unsophisticated mind. Clevenger, with the instinct of honest admiration, rejoiced in the new world of thought and humanity to which his talents had introduced him. It was his privilege, day by day for three years, to commune freely in his studio with men of varied culture and experience. The effect was visible in the high standard which at last became the goal of his desires. The free, social habits of his native region prevented any blind reverence or timid reserve from nipping these advantages in the bud. He frankly exposed his need of information, and, in the spirit of genuine improvement, gratefully availed himself of the conversation and suggestions of those he respected. This unpretending and assiduous bearing made him emphatically a favorite." [1]

While Clevenger's actual contribution was slight, he had a greater influence than many who lived longer and produced more. His character, his personal worth and his winning manner; his delight in his work and his devotion to it, made a profound impression upon all who knew him. If they had entertained doubts as to the value of this alien art, these must needs have been dispelled under the warmth of such heaven-born enthusiasm as his. There was no question in his mind whether sculpture was "worth while." Is it to be wondered, then, that the name and fame of Clevenger have been enshrined by the brotherhood, and that he is honored to this day for the promise that was in him? He represents integrity in sculpture; humility, if you will, before nature. Says Tuckerman with unusual grasp: "There was an exactitude in his busts that gave assurance of skill founded upon solid principles. The majority of our young artists essay the ideal before they have any just appreciation of reality; and with the presumption, not of genius, but of audacity, illustrate imaginary beings while incompetent to exhibit faithfully the tree that overshades their window, or the friend who praises their talent. Clevenger began in art where all noble characters begin in action — at truth." [2]

Clevenger had been dead several years before Hart sailed for Italy; but the tide was already setting in that direction, and the new arrivals of the later forties found established there not only the original three, — Greenough, Crawford, and Powers, — now attained to great prominence, but several other aspirants for fame. Most

[1] "Book of the Artists," p. 608.   [2] Ibid., p. 607.

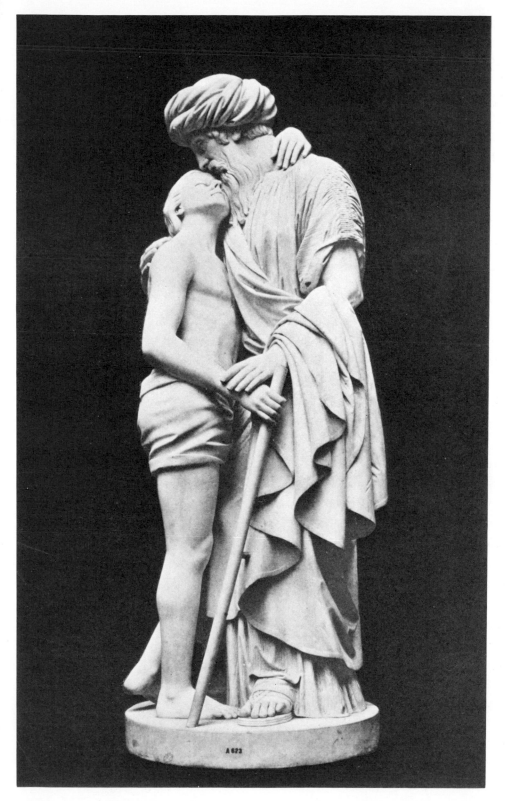

FIG. 13.—MOZIER: PRODIGAL SON, PENNSYLVANIA ACADEMY OF FINE ARTS.

of these men were doomed to disappointment; but Joseph Mozier was more successful. He was born at Burlington, Vermont, and, like Clevenger, in the year 1812. At one time a merchant in New York, his artistic tastes led him finally to abandon his business and to devote himself to sculpture. He sailed for Europe in 1845, and though at first quite untrained, opened a studio in Rome, practising his profession there until his death in 1870. In those twenty-five years he produced a long series of figures, among the better known of which are: "Pocahontas," "The Wept of Wish-ton-Wish," "Rizpah," "Peri," "Rebecca at the Well," "Jephthah's Daughter," "White Lady of Avenal," "Undine," "Queen Esther," "Truth," and "Silence" (the last two belonging to the Astor Library, New York). The "Prodigal Son" (Fig. 13), his most ambitious work, is in the Pennsylvania Academy of Fine Arts, "Il Penseroso" in Horticultural Hall, Fairmount Park, and "Peri" in the Mount Olivet Cemetery at Nashville, Tennessee.

The "Rizpah" in the Metropolitan Museum was carved in 1869, and is so bad that the curators apparently do not know what to do with it. Inanity could hardly go farther. Knowing nothing else of the author, one would pronounce his art hopeless. In a nondescript costume the queer squat creature presents herself holding a torch above her head. She lifts it languidly in her left hand, while clutching in the right a staff terminated by a great horn. With an all too vivid impression of this inept figure, one is agreeably surprised to find in New Haven a marble of at least respectable workmanship from the same hands, a life-size representation of Cooper's heroine, "The Wept of Wish-ton-Wish." Of course it is hard in treatment, — marble was not handled otherwise at that time, — but the action is good and the comely face expressive in a conventional way of hesitation or alarm, a look effectively enhanced by the lifted right hand and finger on chin. The distinctively Indian features of the costume are limited to the moccasins and to a chaplet of small shells around the head, the short skirt giving to the figure the look of a page. However, the curtailment of this portion of the costume is atoned for in part by the amplitude of the cloak which descends to the ground in many ripples and is caught up in the left hand with a graceful gesture. The hair is sharply grooved, and the hands are amateurish.

The bare arms and legs can scarcely be called shapely, for their lack of modelling is obvious; but they are "well begun," and their proportions as well as their lines are good. Though evidently beyond his depth in anatomical subtleties, the sculptor demonstrates his conscience and his joy in the work by a triumphant display of the seamstress's art; there is a "masterly" hem which is carried without faltering around the entire border of the mantle, and in which the stone stitches are as accurate as though done by the sewing-machine. Despite such puerilities the figure is much more modern and interesting than the average of the time. Although appearing to us so nearly akin to other products of the day, it must have seemed to contemporaries a work of daring originality both in subject and in treatment.

The "Prodigal Son" is a group of considerable importance. The odd costume of the father and a certain atmosphere of indecision attract notice before better qualities are revealed, but these are easily discoverable, and the final impression is of a worthy theme very adequately conveyed in sculptural terms. That it is not lacking in emotional power is suggested by the following words: "There is much pathos in this composition, which appeals with directness and force to the hearts of those who pause in their rambles through the gallery to gaze on it. The benignity and fatherly tenderness of the old man are expressed in a language that all may read, and that requires no explanation or commentary."[1]

Hawthorne visited Mr. Mozier's studio in 1858, and seems to have been indifferently impressed by the sculptor's serious efforts; but his description of the man is striking. It brings back, as it were, light and shade into a faded photograph, and develops the guessed-at outlines into a vivid presentment of a personality. "April 3d [1858] . . . A few days ago we visited the studio of Mr. ——, an American, who seems to have a good deal of vogue as a sculptor. We found a figure of Pocahontas, which he has repeated several times; another, which he calls 'The Wept of Wish-ton-Wish,' a figure of a smiling girl playing with a cat and dog, and a schoolboy mending a pen. These two last were the only ones that gave me any pleasure, or that really had any merit; for his cleverness and

[1] Clark, "Great American Sculptures," p. 121.

ingenuity appear in homely subjects, but are quite lost in attempts at a higher ideality. Nevertheless he has a group of the 'Prodigal Son' possessing more merit than I should have expected from Mr. ——, the son reclining his head on his father's breast, with an expression of utter weariness, at length finding perfect rest, while the father bends his benign countenance over him, and seems to receive him calmly into himself. This group (the plaster-cast standing beside it) is now taking shape out of an immense block of marble, and will be as indestructible as the Laocoön, an idea at once awful and ludicrous when we consider that it is at best but a respectable production. I have since been told that Mr. —— had stolen, adopted, we will rather say, the attitude and idea of the group from one executed by a student of the French Academy, and to be seen there in plaster.

"Mr. —— has now been ten years in Italy, and, after all this time, he is still entirely American in everything but the most external surface of his manners; scarcely Europeanized, or much modified, even in that. He is a native of ——, but had his early breeding in New York, and might, for any polish or refinement that I can discern in him, still be a country shopkeeper in the interior of New York State or New England. How strange! For one expects to find the polish, the close grain, and white purity of marble in the artist who works in that noble material; but, after all, he handles clay, and, judging from the specimens I have seen here, is apt to be clay, not of the finest, himself. Mr. —— is sensible, shrewd, keen, clever; an ingenious workman, no doubt; with tact enough, and not destitute of taste; very agreeable and lively in his conversation, talking as fast and as naturally as a brook runs, without the slightest affectation. His naturalness is, in fact, a rather striking characteristic, in view of his lack of culture; while yet his life has been concerned with idealities and a beautiful art. What degree of taste he pretends to, he seems really to possess, nor did I hear a single idea from him that struck me as otherwise than sensible.

"He called to see us last evening, and talked for about two hours in a very amusing and interesting style, his topics being taken from his own personal experience, and shrewdly treated. He spoke much of Greenough, whom he described as an excellent critic of art, but possessed of not the slightest inventive genius. His statue of

Washington, at the Capitol, is taken precisely from the Phidian Jupiter; his 'Chanting Cherubs' are copied in marble from two figures in a picture by Raphael. He did nothing that was original with himself." [1]

The fateful year of 1812 saw the birth of yet a third, who was destined to become a sculptor and to enjoy a considerable popularity in his day. Chauncey B. Ives was one of the earliest as well as one of the most persistent of these voluntary exiles. The son of a farmer, he was born in Hampden, Connecticut. At the age of sixteen he apprenticed himself to a wood-carver, and later studied for a short time with Hezekiah Augur. In Boston he found the vocation which he was to follow with great industry and at least commercial success throughout a long life. His stay in southern Europe was rendered desirable by reason of weak lungs, but it was also inevitable with a sculptor of Mr. Ives's ideals. He possessed the true Italian instinct for pretty, merchantable wares, and concocted any number of easily born fancies like " Cupid with his Net," "Sans Souci," " Pandora," " Bacchante," and " Shepherd Boy." Returning to New York in 1855 for a short stay, — and harvest time, — he fitted up a " studio" so attractively that he was able to sell his entire collection and return to Italy within two months, laden with numerous orders for replicas of his innocent works.

Mr. Ives may have done some fine things, or at least dreamed them, but he is exceedingly unfortunate in his public representations. Several museums contain figures bearing his signature, and they are invariably trifling and weak in their conception — not even good sculpture in intention. His one idea seems to have been to make something "taking" and salable. In the Metropolitan Museum is his " Flower Girl," a graceful figure seated on the ground and lifting a garland over its head. The lines are not bad, but they lose all value through the fussy and unsculptural elaboration of details. The garland in particular is a miracle of misapplied patience, and around the base is scattered other equally painful vegetation. Probably it was the minute whittling of these flowers which insured the sale of the work; the conscientious carver has given good measure. It is preëminently Italian commercial sculpture, though in this case of

[1] Hawthorne, " Italian Note-Book," Vol. I, pp. 154–156.

the higher grade.   As much cannot be said of his "Rebecca at the Well" in the same collection.   This little figure is so absurd that one feels its size a great merit.   If it were of life-size, it would be intolerable.   It might be difficult, however, to say what "life-size" would be, since the figure has the appearance of an overgrown child. There are only two or three other things in the museum which approach it in helpless ineptitude.

In the Corcoran Gallery at Washington, Mr. Ives is represented by a figure of similarly slight import, though of better workmanship, "The Scholar," a pretty schoolboy "with shining face," holding a bunch of papers and apparently slipping from a stump.   In the Capitol we find other unfortunate evidence of this sculptor's limitations.   Connecticut, with misplaced loyalty to an aspiring son, gave him the commission for the two figures which represent the state in the National Hall of Statuary.   The result may be seen in the two marble images labelled, respectively, "Trumbull" and "Sherman," which were introduced to that very promiscuous gathering in 1872. Description of these curious works would be unprofitable.   They fit in nicely with the majority of their companions, but of all the dead men there they seem the most conscious of being dead, the most solicitous to appear alive.   The "Trumbull" on the façade of the Capitol at Hartford and the much vaunted bust of Lemuel Towne in the Yale Art School at New Haven are both insignificant works of no artistic value.

It may be asked, Why, then, spend time upon this commercial sculptor if his art is so unworthy?   The answer is in the fact that while Ives was denied all the other artistic graces he possessed the prime one of adaptability.   He made the kind of sculpture that the people liked.   Almost more than any other he stands for the taste of our wealthy class during the last generation.   In this respect he becomes important in the history of our progress.   His sculpture did no harm, and on the other hand probably afforded a world of pleasure to wealthy ignorance — yes, and through the faithful stereoscope to humbler ignorance as well!   There is no use in calling names, or in having any feeling about such art; it came because it was precisely suited to its day.

I

CHAPTER VI

THE NATIVE ELEMENT IN EARLY AMERICAN SCULPTURE

OF very different fibre from Ives and Mozier was Henry Kirke Brown, who made contributions of great value to the development of what had remained thus far an essentially alien art. With some shadow of justice might the title of "the first American sculptor" be claimed for him also, if the emphasis be transferred to the word *American*. Brown owed less to Europe — that is to say, directly — than did any of his predecessors and colleagues who modelled figures, and some of his productions stand in the front rank of all our monuments excepting the very latest. Indeed, a foreigner, seeing for the first time his "Washington" (Pl. V), which towers so majestically in Union Square, New York, would pronounce it the work of one of our greatest masters. If, however, his introduction to the artist should be by way of the "Ruth" or the "Boy and Dog" in the rooms of the New York Historical Society, he would infer that the author of these insignificant figures was absolutely without capacity, a conviction which Mr. Brown's "William Cullen Bryant," of prehistoric date, in the same building, would do little to dispel.

The "Ruth," standing "amid the alien corn," is conventional and characterless as the veriest "Christian grace" of the graveyard, while the "Boy and Dog" (and bowl of milk on floor) is undeniably absurd. The child with inflated legs twists and tugs at the real chain which is all that keeps the dog and the supper apart. The emblazoned title, "Chi Vinci Mangia," is as unsatisfactory as a modern story, leaving the spectator in complete suspense. Mr. J. Q. A. Ward's kindly characterization of Mr. Brown as "a good deal better man than sculptor" does not sound so strange in the presence of this puerile work. One's strongest impression is the thought that for their own future fame many artists would do well to look up and

PLATE 5. — BROWN: WASHINGTON.

destroy certain of their minor productions before leaving this world, since they can never be sure of keeping even the most insignificant of them out of museums, where, as in the present instance, they may do a man's memory a great injustice. Is an artist or author as great as his highest flight, or should he be rated according to his average production? In other words, is he greatest who does nothing but great things, or shall we rank still higher the man who often makes mistakes, but now and then reaches altitudes of surpassing distinction? One hesitates to say, but the decision might influence our estimate of Henry Kirke Brown.

Mr. Brown was born at Leyden, Massachusetts, in 1814, and showed early an aptitude for portrait painting. At eighteen he went to Boston to study that art with Chester Harding, but chance led him to attempt the modelling of the head of a friend. The new work proved so interesting, and the result was so satisfactory, that the young man impetuously renounced the brush for the modelling tool, and devoted himself henceforth to sculpture. Of course there was nothing to do but to go to Italy, and the misfortunes which thwarted for several years this cherished project were real tragedies at the time. In order to earn money, Mr. Brown practised civil engineering for a while in the West, — helping to lay out the first railroad in Illinois, — and later he went to Cincinnati, where, in 1837, at the age of twenty-three, he produced his first marble bust. In 1840 he settled in Albany, whither Palmer was to follow him six years later. His own stay in that pleasant city was destined to be brief, for in 1842 good friends who had watched his struggle with poverty and bad health came to the rescue and supplied means for the long-deferred trip to Italy. The two years in Albany, with frequent visits to Troy, had been sufficient for the production of forty busts, as we are assured by the chroniclers. One is in doubt which most to admire, — the industry of the artist, or the powers of persuasion that inveigled so many into posing. Probably the persuasion resulted in large part from the kind offices of the "good friends." The measure of the young sculptor's achievement during those strenuous years becomes almost incredible when we read that he also modelled at this time figures of the "Four Seasons" for a citizen of Mount Hope.

In Italy these habits of industry continued, and during the sojourn there of four years the artist produced the usual series of marble statuettes and reliefs for home consumption, among them the " Ruth " and " Boy and Dog " already noted, a " Rebecca," an " Adonis," and a " David." But the young sculptor did not seem to fit into the Old World environment so readily as had his three famous countrymen whom he found over there. We may imagine, too, that he had a suspicion that his talents were not at their best in these traditional themes; at least one would infer as much from the fact that his very first undertaking upon his return in 1846 was to model and cast in bronze an " Indian and Panther," which has been pronounced one of his best efforts. Evidently there was no use in trying to make a classicist of him. As a sort of joyous celebration of his return to freedom, Mr. Brown, though ostensibly settled in New York and later in Brooklyn, made a series of visits and numerous studies among the Indians. His " Aboriginal Hunter " is said to have been a great favorite in its day. As the orders began to come in there was, of course, work of a more conventional nature: a large bas-relief in the Church of the Annunciation, New York, and a statue of DeWitt Clinton in Greenwood Cemetery, where also is his " Angel of the Resurrection." In 1851 Mr. Brown was elected full member of the National Academy of Design, New York. His first studio was in the old " Rotunda " on Broadway, long the home of the Academy.

The practical work of bronze-casting should not be passed over lightly. Up to this point we have had no mention of artistic founding except the production of Ball Hughes's " Dr. Bowditch," the first bronze statue created in this country, which was perhaps actually antedated by the smaller " Indian and Panther." That Mr. Brown installed a miniature foundry in his studio, and successfully carried into the ultimate metal many small works, speaks volumes for his courage and his ingenuity. It is Mr. Ward's recollection, however, that, on account of its size, the group of the " Indian and Panther" was cast outside, by a Frenchman, but that the finishing was done in the studio.

It was in February, 1853, one month after the unveiling of Clark Mills's " General Jackson," that Mr. Brown began the " Washington " of Union Square, New York, a work which erring tradition has de-nominated the first equestrian statue, in point of time, in the United States. Even Mr. Tuckerman makes this mistake, — perhaps it origi-nated with him, — though elsewhere giving correctly the two dates which disprove his assertion. His account of the work and its origin is interesting and authentic. Washington is represented " in the act of recalling his troops to repose; the figure is bareheaded, the hat resting on his bridle arm, the sword sheathed, the right arm ex-tended as if commanding quiet; the drapery is the simple Continen-tal uniform; the face slightly upturned. . . .   The subscriptions for this work were chiefly derived from the merchants of New York, through the earnest efforts of Colonel Lee; they were paid in sums of $400 each. It was projected by Horatio Greenough, who was to have undertaken it with Brown, but finally abandoned the enterprise, after having efficiently promoted the subscription." [1]

The " Washington " was unveiled in Union Square, New York, on July 4, 1856. To say that it is Mr. Brown's masterpiece, is not sufficient praise. Though but second in point of time among the equestrian statues of this country, it still remains one of the best of many, and, whatever our progress, will always be good sculpture. Mr. Frank Edwin Elwell, of the Metropolitan Museum, stated the case none too strongly when he wrote of the sculptor and his work in a New York journal : —

" The sum of all his mental powers seems to have been expended in this one glorious effort, which will be a pattern and guide to the profession for all time, for in it are honesty, truth, and dignity, and none of the straining after effect that eats up the soul of the artist and destroys his love of the noble and the true. Standing in front of this statue one appreciates the dignity and grandeur of the man that it represents. The statue tells of the sincerity and honor of the artist."

The silhouette of the horse is simple and compact, yet full of animation. The great creature is adequate but well subordinated to the commanding rider. It is the character of the man and the reality of the moment that impress us. That noble gesture bespeaks the born leader of men. It awakens the imagination, summoning visions

[1] " Book of the Artists," p. 575.

of tented fields and the glitter of arms; the figure stands no longer alone upon its narrow pedestal amid the rattle and roar of the busy highway, but is supported by an army of patriots invincible yet obedient.   There is potency in such art.

A negative character is not in itself worthy of esteem, and there is nothing negative about this splendid conception, yet it may be pointed out that the impression of serene dignity which the statue wears like an enveloping mantle is due in no small measure to the fact that, like the hero's legendary character, it has no glaring defects to catch and annoy the attention.   In it is no artificial vehemence, no attempt at picturesqueness.   We find, instead, composure and equilib- rium.   The horse is solid on its feet, and the total mass is in good relation to the simple pedestal.   There is a majestic moderation in the lifted arm.   In its compelling sweep and in the eyes that look afield is an actual protection of the figure from too curious scrutiny.   Nowhere is there harshness or meagreness of handling to attract the gaze. By both what he has put in and what he has had the good sense to leave out, the artist has succeeded in giving us here "the power and poetry of the realized ideal," of conveying to us the impression of a *great* man.

How it all happened is a mystery.   That this amiable and intellectual but generally commonplace sculptor should have done the " Washington " of Union Square seems marvellous.   Perhaps his subject exalted him for the time being above himself ; perhaps it introduced him for a brief period to his own true potential self.   At any rate, he came down again gently but securely and never did anything further that could possibly be termed great.

Two other equestrian statues from his studio must engage our attention for a moment, for, while they lack the masterly qualities of the " Washington," they are by no means insignificant.   One is the well-known and much liked " General Winfield Scott," erected in 1874 in Washington, D.C., a dignified figure well seated upon a quiet and very realistic steed.   The latter has all four feet upon the ground, and is an admirable, well-behaved horse, if not a distinctly sculptural conception.   Although the quadruped is considerably more alive than its rider, and correspondingly more interesting, this must be counted one of the best equestrian groups in Washington.   The other

FIG. 14. — BROWN: GENERAL GREENE, WASHINGTON.

work referred to above is in the same city, the curious " Nathanael Greene " in Stanton Place, which was erected in 1877 in fulfilment of a vote of the Continental Congress of nearly a century before. The horse is carefully constructed and faithfully modelled, but the silhouette of the rather undignified pose offers a surprising contrast to the stately work in Union Square. The contrast is all the more notable for the reason that the general *motif* is the same in both — a commander with uplifted right arm. But in the latter work the open-mouthed " charger " jogs along like a weary draught-horse, and the rider looks around to see what we are thinking of him. The effect is far more striking than noble.

Mr. Brown is well, or at least abundantly, represented in the National Statuary Hall in Washington, where no fewer than four figures bear his signature: General Nathanael Greene of Rhode Island (Fig. 14); Vice-President George Clinton of New York; Richard Stockton, and General Philip Kearney, the two latter of New Jersey. The first is a respectable, ineffectual kind of a figure, showing considerable skill, but awakening no interest. The costume is that of the Continental army and is very well handled, though with almost Italian insistence. The left hand presses the marble sword firmly against the breast; the right clutches the hip just as firmly, but without apparent reason. A trailing cloak helps to hold things together. The "Clinton" is a dapper little bronze gentleman, looking in various directions, and making much display of sword and gloves. The upper and lower parts have a queer look of belonging to different figures, the head and shoulders being out of proportion and out of place. The " Kearney " has a much more manly appearance than the "Stockton," and shows a good strong profile. The body has the same dislocation observed in the "Clinton," the shoulder drooping on the side where it should be raised. Altogether these figures, like many of Mr. Brown's carefully finished busts, give the effect of topographical maps of the individuals rather than of distinctive personalities. All men, according to Napoleon, lose upon nearer view, and one feels the truth of this observation when, in the gallery of notables, he studies their wrinkles and the shapes of their ears as if they were stuffed creatures in a museum. It is particularly unfortunate for those great men whose sculptors have seen nothing but wrinkles and earmarks, modelling faithful masks, but putting nothing behind them. These superficial portraits confirm the belief that Mr. Brown was at his best in equestrian subjects. In his " Washington," despite its archaic handling, he rose almost to the first rank.

To retrace, for a moment, our steps: Mr. Brown had, at the beginning of the Civil War, an interesting and costly experience, which we shall allow Mr. Tuckerman to recapitulate. " In 1858 Brown was commissioned by the state of South Carolina to execute a large group of thirteen figures for the new State House at Columbia. His design represented Hope bearing the olive branch, figures of Justice and Liberty, and laborers in the rice and cotton fields; when nearly completed this work was abandoned by the artist, in consequence of the outbreak of the Slaveholders' Rebellion, and was subsequently destroyed by the fire which consumed so large a portion of the city, and with it several studies and a collection of casts in his studio." [1]   Returning to the North, Mr. Brown settled at Newburgh, New York, where, in a pleasant rural home, he made his residence until the time of his death in 1886. Among other works of his not previously mentioned are a statue of Dr. George W. Bethune, said to have been made for the New York Historical Society, a statue of Lincoln in Union Square, New York, and another of the same subject for the city of Brooklyn.

Mr. Ward, who was a pupil of Brown, describes his early teacher as a fine-looking man, tall and athletic. He was of rather a solemn mien, as befitted in those days the high priest of a mysterious art, and his speech was enriched with much philosophy. Despite his air of distinction, he was full of genial humor — a humor which would crop out most unexpectedly, and then be as promptly withdrawn into itself. His kind interest in his pupils is remembered gratefully by his one-time "boys" after the lapse of a half-century. An enlightened privilege of his studio was an evening drawing-class, where master and pupils worked together from the living model. Mr. Brown was a skilful draughtsman, and his instruction and example alike were of the greatest value to the aspiring geniuses

1 " Book of the Artists," p. 576.

grouped about him. Intentionally or not, his whole career was a protest against the influence of Italy on American art. As said before, he is the first strongly native factor in the development of our sculpture.

The maker of the first equestrian statue in the history of American sculpture happened to be born one year later than Henry K. Brown. His name, Clark Mills, has already been mentioned; his story, given at considerable length by Tuckerman, may be summarized. He was born in New York State in 1815. He lost his father early and lived with an uncle up to the age of thirteen, when he was driven by harsh treatment to run away. Henceforth he took care of himself, working as a farm hand, with some slight schooling in winter. Later he did hauling, worked on a canal, and cut cedar posts in a swamp. Then he concluded to try employment on a higher plane and learned the trade of a cabinet-maker. He next became a millwright and followed this calling for two years, when chance led to his engagement as an overseer in a plaster and cement mill. He drifted to New Orleans and thence to Charleston, South Carolina, where he learned to do stucco work, which business he followed until 1835, when he began modelling busts in clay. Art education seems to have been entirely unnecessary, for he had his Yankee wits with him.

He discovered a new method of taking a cast from the living face, which enabled him to make busts so cheaply that he soon had as much work as he could do. He then resolved to try cutting in marble, and after procuring a block of native Carolina stone, he commenced the bust of John C. Calhoun. Quite unfamiliar with the professional methods, he was compelled to invent a system of his own, which was a very tedious process, requiring extraordinary care. He soon, however, succeeded in producing what was then considered the best likeness ever taken of Mr. Calhoun. The bust was purchased by the city council of Charleston, and he was rewarded with a gold medal, bearing on one side the following inscription : —

"Ædes Mores Juraque Curat Artesque Fovit.
Ingenii premium virtuti calcar.
Id. Apr. MDCCCXLVI."

On the other side : —

"To Clark Mills as a mark of respect for his genius for sculpture in his bust of the favorite son of Carolina, John C. Calhoun, and as an incentive to further exertions, this medal is presented by the City Council of Charleston."

This was only the beginning of his good fortune. Presently means were afforded him for study in Europe, and this circumstance, finding its way into the newspapers, attracted the attention of John Preston, a wealthy gentleman who had befriended Powers, who wrote him inviting him to come to Columbia, South Carolina, to make busts of himself and wife, stating, also, that Colonel Wade Hampton desired busts of himself and daughters, and that he might cut them in marble when he had further advanced in the art. He went to Columbia and made ten busts. An incident occurred at this time which seemed to change his whole course. A friend remarked to the artist that he ought to see the statuary at Washington before visiting Europe.

"He replied that 'if he should spend his means in travelling about, he would not be able to accomplish his main object.' — 'As for the expense,' said Mr. P., 'if you will go to Washington and take the busts of my friends Webster and Crittenden, I will pay your expenses there and back, and pay you for the busts also.' He readily accepted the offer, started for Washington, stopping at Richmond, Virginia, to see the statue of Houdon, which was the first statue he had ever seen. The first thing he did after his arrival in Washington was to visit the Capitol, that he might feast his eager eyes on the statuary there. He saw much to admire, and much which, even to his unpractised eye, appeared imperfect. The drapery on the 'Statue of Peace' seemed to surpass human skill, and the 'Muse of History,' recording the events of time, he thought was the grandest and most sublime idea ever conceived. Of the statue of Washington, by Greenough, he thought the anatomy perfect, though he could not associate Washington with the statue. The crowd of visitors, so far as he could learn, invariably condemned it for want of historical truth. He came to the conclusion while standing there that, should he ever have an order for a statue, the world should find fault for his giving too much truth, and not for the want of it."[1]

[1] "Book of the Artists," p. 584.

Now comes the important event of his life, an incident probably unparalleled in the history of sculpture: "An accidental circumstance here gave rise to the order for the Jackson statue (Fig. 15). He was introduced to the Hon. Cave Johnson, then Postmaster-General and President of the Jackson Monument Committee, who, on learning his intention to visit Europe, proposed that he should give a design for a bronze equestrian statue of General Jackson. Never having seen

FIG. 15. — MILLS: JACKSON MONUMENT, WASHINGTON.

General Jackson or an equestrian statue, he felt himself incompetent to execute a work of such magnitude, and positively refused. The incident, however, made an impression upon his mind, and he reflected sufficiently to produce a design, which was the very one subsequently executed, and which now adorns the public square in front of the White House. He concluded to accept Mr. Johnson's offer, and, after nine months of patient labor, he succeeded in bringing out a miniature model on a new principle, which was to bring the hind legs of the horse exactly under the centre of his body, which of course produced a perfect balance, thereby giving the horse more the appearance of life. The model was adopted by the committee. A contract was made for the sum of $12,000, the bronze to be furnished by the committee. After two years' labor and hard study, he finished the plaster model. After waiting nearly nine months, Congress appropriated the old cannon captured by General Andrew Jackson, and, under various disheartening circumstances, the breaking of cranes, the bursting of furnaces, after six failures in the body of the horse, he finally triumphed. On the eighth day of January, 1853, the statue was dedicated." [1]

Other orders following rapidly, larger accommodations were required, and Mr. Mills purchased a farm about three miles from Washington for the purpose of erecting the necessary buildings, studio and foundry. Mr. Tuckerman continues: " Having completed the buildings, he was about to commence work, when a gale destroyed the studio. Before it was rebuilt the foundry was destroyed by fire, but it was rebuilt as soon as possible. After finishing the statue for New Orleans, he commenced the statue of Washington, which was completed and dedicated on the 22d of February, 1860. In June, 1860, Mr. Mills commenced the work of casting the statue of ' Freedom,' after Crawford's design, which was completed in 1863, and now stands above the dome of the Capitol."

Who begrudges to-day to this brave pioneer his little meed of success? Let us hope that he never became conscious of his defects. No one of that first generation is more completely the machinist. His grasp of his subject is a purely mechanical one; his *motif* in the Jackson statue, a problem in equilibrium. He never had seen an equestrian statue; there was none in the country to see. It seems at first thought strange that America's initial performance in this line should be an attempt of surpassing audacity, but it is the story of all beginnings: the intrepidity of ignorance, the inevitable approach in the most roundabout way, and, equally important, the lack of a genuinely artistic inspiration. Having no notion, nor even suspicion, of dignified sculptural treatment of a theme, the clever carpenter felt nevertheless the need of a " feature."

[1] " Book of the Artists," p. 585.

Perhaps he had heard of "action." Possibly he had seen an engraving of Falconet's " Peter the Great." At any rate, he built a colossal horse, adroitly balanced on the hind legs; and America gazed with bated breath. Nobody knows or cares whether the rider looks like Jackson or not; the extraordinary pose of the horse absorbs all attention, all admiration. There may be some subconscious feeling of respect for the rider who holds on so well, but in spite of his frank efforts to call attention to himself, the appeal is as meagre as his personal charm, as precarious as his seat.

The committee had expected something original and American, and they got it. The statue was so much more original than they had dared to expect that a delighted and grateful Congress insisted upon adding $20,000 to the $12,000 already paid. That it was well earned in hard work there is no doubt, and that the statue "filled a long-felt want" is evidenced by the order from New Orleans for a duplicate at an advanced price. The model being already made, this was profitable. But the day of great things had come; Mills was in the full tide of prosperity, for Congress had again shown its appreciation by voting him a much larger sum — $50,000 — for a mounted " Washington."

Such is the story of the first equestrian statue of the United States, erected in 1853. As we compare this "prodigious Congressional joke" with Saint Gaudens's " Logan " and " Sherman," with Messrs. French and Potter's " Washington " and " Grant," with Ward's " General Thomas," we realize how far we have come. It is interesting, however, to note that a large part of this progress was made at a single leap. The very next equestrian sculpture, Brown's " General Washington " of Union Square, dedicated in 1856, was, and remains, as we have already seen, one of our best statues, and has a close second in Ball's dignified rendering of the same subject in the Boston Public Gardens.

In comparison with these, Mills's second effort, his " Washington," has only historic interest. It does not appeal to our curiosity even, as does the " Jackson," for with prosperity the artist seems to have lost his hardihood. Instead of making the brazen steed balance on a single hoof, as logical sequence would seem to demand, he gave his admirers a Napoleon-crossing-the-Alps effect. The horse is a nervous, springy steed, whose flying mane and lashing tail are in singular contrast to the general, sitting so calm and collected above all this agitation.

Busts in the Corcoran Gallery of Calhoun and Washington, by Mills, give us a more intimate notion of the sculptor's manner of working. The "Calhoun" head is strong and repellant, without grace of either handicraft or of personality; the "Washington" is a diligent study of Houdon's mask.

Little as we may find to-day in the sculpture of Clark Mills, we must feel grateful to him for his contribution, for doing what he could — yes, even for doing things so sensational that our hard-working grandfathers lifted amazed eyes upon them, and learned for the first time the meaning of the words *equestrian statue*. While ignorant enthusiasm is not the most favorable environment for sensitive creative powers, it is so much better than apathy that Mills may be thanked for positively helping the cause through a period when it needed to justify itself with a larger public than the cultured circles of Boston and New York and Philadelphia.

And let us not forget that this home-made sculptor not only designed and modelled those enormous creatures, but actually built his own foundry and moulded and cast the statues himself. To one who knows the difficulties of bronze-casting, this seems incredible. Verily, there were giants in those days! Whatever we may think of Clark Mills the sculptor, we owe a debt of gratitude to Clark Mills, our first professional founder of statuary.[1]

[1] Mr. Mills's last undertaking is briefly described in the *American Art Review* of 1881, p. 131. At this time he had prepared a design for an elaborate National Lincoln Monument, several "stories" in height, and including no less than thirty-six heroic statues, beginning with six equestrian figures of generals. "On the first story will stand figures emblematic of the war and its results, with historic bas-reliefs between them; next above these the standing figures of Lincoln's cabinet and of other prominent supporters of the cause of freedom; still higher up, the statues of Liberty, Justice, and Time are to find a place, and the whole is to be crowned by the seated figure of President Lincoln." It was announced that $100,000 had already been contributed, and the work was actually begun by the making and casting of the figure of Chief Justice Chase at Mr. Mills's foundry. No further mention is to be found of this project, nor even of the one completed statue. Mr. Mills died in Washington in 1883.

PART II

AMERICAN SCULPTURE

THE MIDDLE PERIOD, 1850–1876

CHAPTER VII

PALMER AND BALL

ANY attempt to divide a history of American sculpture into periods must be more or less arbitrary, but at this distance the progress of the early art in the United States shows certain well-defined phases. From about the year 1850 it takes on a new tone. Insensibly the naïvetés of primitive effort have given way to good, competent workmanship, and it is no longer necessary to name the unskilled and the modellers of busts as representative sculptors. It was during this second period — 1850 to 1876 — that our country experienced its most tragic ordeal : the Civil War swept the land, and was followed by an aftermath of desolation almost as sombre and quite as antagonistic to art as was the war itself. Yet through all this time sculpture grew — because it must — and even began to show signs of a national character. Aroused from their dreams by the drama in which they lived, our sculptors felt emotions that they had not known before, and a few of them ventured to seek expression for these feelings in their art. Timidly but hopefully American sculpture began to grow contemporaneous in spirit; the "actual" crept at last upon the stage, while classic themes gradually receded into pale obscurity. To be sure, a large proportion of our sculptors continued to go abroad, dwelling far removed from the life and thought of their country ; but an increasing number tarried at home from choice, or returned promptly with the training acquired in other lands. While their self-exiled brothers over the sea exacted tribute of all ancient history and mythology in their objective search for themes, these men struggled to express what was within their own souls. Certain of them, too, performed the wonder of reaching worthy eminence without the schooling which is to-day esteemed so essential.

The years 1817 and 1819 are noteworthy in the history of American sculpture, since they gave birth to Erastus D. Palmer and Thomas Ball, two of the most eminent artists among the remarkable men who loved sculpture instinctively and wrought it without instruction. It seems very strange that these two men, who are still living to-day, saw the very beginnings of American sculpture; that the span of their lives covers the entire development of the art upon these shores. They were respectively eight and six years of age when Greenough went abroad in 1825. As boys of fourteen or fifteen, they may have read of the arrival of those "shameless" figures, the "Chanting Cherubs," and might even have seen William Rush, had chance taken them to Philadelphia. John Frazee and Augur they might have known for thirty years or more. They were almost young men when Crawford sailed for Italy in 1834, and quite grown up when Powers followed in 1837. They have seen it all and remain to-day not only to wonder and rejoice at the marvellous progress of the century, but to receive the homage of an army of cadets who look upon them as personal friends and benefactors. For these, far more than Greenough and Crawford and Powers, are the men who have shaped the pathway of American sculpture, who have made its present development possible. Even more than Brown is Erastus D. Palmer identified with a strictly national art, for Mr. Palmer had absolutely no study abroad, and only visited Europe for a short time in middle life.

Tuckerman gives at great length the story of Mr. Palmer's early life, and pictures with sympathetic touch the scenes of his labors. We must content ourselves here with the barest outline. In 1845 an intelligent young carpenter of Utica, New York, made in his moments of leisure a cameo portrait of his wife, which was recognized by one acquainted with such work as an admirable effort. Further experiments followed with so great success that in 1846 the joiner abandoned forever his saws and planes and, removing to Albany, devoted himself to this delicate art. In the space of two years the untrained artist executed over two hundred portraits, which were pronounced "perfect gems" by his enthusiastic clients. It must be noted in this connection that while the artist was untrained, the artisan was not. All his life he had handled tools, so that his muscles

FIG. 16.—PALMER: WHITE CAPTIVE, METROPOLITAN MUSEUM.

responded to his commands. With a natural sense of form and a manual skill that had already compassed wood-carving and fine cabinet work, he was far better prepared for achievement than is the most gifted of college graduates, who may indeed be " full of knowledge and enamoured of beauty," but whose hands are unresponsive.

A seeming misfortune drove Mr. Palmer to take the next step forward. His eyes were weakened by the unremitting strain, and he feared that he might be compelled to return to his former employment, when he was advised to try larger work in clay. The little bust of the " Infant Ceres," in which he pictured one of his children, has become almost historic. It was put in marble and exhibited at the National Academy of Design in 1850, marking the beginning of Mr. Palmer's career as a sculptor. Next followed two pretty reliefs, the " Morning Star " and " Evening Star," and then the " Spirit's Flight." Other bas-reliefs of the time are " Faith" and " Mercy," the former being that representation of a female figure, standing with clasped hands contemplating a slender cross, which was once so popular. Faded photographs of this work still hang in many old-fashioned homes, but few of its admirers know that it represents one of the earliest productions of the sculptor Palmer. The original is a large relief which he modelled in 1852 for Saint Peter's Church in Albany.

His reliefs and ideal heads, like " Resignation," " Spring," " June," " Infant Flora," were in such demand that it was not until 1856 that he essayed the full-length figure in the round. This first attempt was the " Indian Girl," a marble copy of which stands in the Metropolitan Museum. It is a modest little maid who hides quietly in a nook, content to let more strident works like MacMonnies's " Bacchante " hold the centre of the stage. The mild little allegory, too, — the tiny cross on the ground and its imagined significance to the groping intellect, — seems to modern taste very childlike, but it was the poetry of the time, and the figure is astonishingly well done for a first attempt. It must be remembered that Palmer had not had the privileges of the Academy at Rome nor of the Beaux-Arts. He had not done his *bonhomme* every week for years, as the modern sculptor is obliged to do in the training of to-day. He was in a new field. This was almost his first glimpse of the marvellously complex human form, and yet he produced a figure worthy of the marble and of preservation in our greatest museum. Tuckerman says, " Perhaps a better torso was never modelled in this country," and this was probably true when written, for the " Indian Girl " remains creditable work to-day.

Meantime the artist within him was young, and Palmer, delighted to find that he could make a figure, allowed his ambition to take higher flights and even to flutter about that empty pediment of the south wing of the national Capitol. It was in 1857 that the sculptor of a single statue had the audacity to design and model a group for this tympanum, representing " The Landing of the Pilgrims." It was small, to be sure, but very elaborate, consisting of sixteen figures about fifteen inches in height, and it is safe to presume that the composition was equal to that of Crawford's " Past and Future of the Republic," on the Senate front. The sculptor met with considerable encouragement, and was, indeed, persuaded that he was to have a commission for this enormous undertaking, but his project was opposed by the then Secretary of War, John B. Floyd, on the ground, apparently, that the Pilgrims were not the only founders of the nation, and the plan was ultimately abandoned. Very fortunate it was for the sculptor that he and the country were spared such an exhibition of his immature art.

Mr. Palmer returned to more modest themes, and by doing them as well as he knew how won a far more lasting triumph than would have been his had his storm-tossed Pilgrims made harbor in the gable end of the House of Representatives, for the next year (1858) saw the birth of the delightful little figure, the " White Captive " (Fig. 16), one of the most charming things yet done by an American sculptor, and one of the earliest to show the quality of expressiveness. No photograph gives an idea of the grace of this virginal form. A slight stiffness in the finely proportioned leg which bears the weight, a vague suggestion of rigidity in the body, the face and head a trifle large — these are the most obvious defects in the reproduction, but they disappear when one contemplates the original. The lower limbs are seen to be exquisite, the movement of the torso is grace itself as one circulates about the figure, and the disproportion of head and body is merely that of youth when the maturing frame has not yet "caught up." One might well indeed be captivated by this poetic translation of the simple-hearted girl who posed for the statue. To think that anything so refined and sympathetic should have been carved in this country in 1858! It is not strange that we should have poets who could imagine radiant beauty; but that an un-schooled hand should model with such a combination of tenderness and firmness, that it should create at the same time elegance of pose and eloquence of appeal in a work of rare perfection is indeed a mar-vel. In all those years nothing so fine had come over the seas from Italy; nothing so original, so dramatic, so human; nothing that could approach it even in charm of workmanship. The carving of the head, the chiselling of the hair, the modelling of the beautiful right hand, would be complimented in the very home of sculpture.

It might be said of our early sculptors, as it was of our early poets, led by Longfellow, that they "ransacked the world for the rough jewels which they polished to the taste of the American pub-lic." The inspired workman of Albany, instead of joining this rest-less procession of seekers, found jewels enough in his own rapt fancies, and his model in the next street. No "classic" conventionalities for him! "What is done, is done; why should we do it over again?" he seemed to say as he turned impatiently from the flood of Ameri-can imitations of Canova's art — an art which consisted largely in turn of weak imitation of Roman imitations of Greek statues. There was beauty enough around him, even there in Albany; why, then, should he wander, and why should he borrow from the past? Palmer had within him somewhat of the "gift of second sight" of which Lowell spoke as "transfiguring matter of fact into matter of mean-ing"; at least, he gave to the individual something akin to the large-ness of a type, and in his best works there entered a quality of ideality as precious as it is rare. Above all, he bestowed upon them charm. There is scarcely a creation of his, however naïf, however primitive, that does not possess this quality. They never fail to give a positive pleasure.

All this while there were notable portrait busts coming from the studio in Albany — busts more intensely individual and yet more typical than America had been accustomed to; their workmanship, as well, was a revelation to a public acquainted only with the unskilful products of an earlier day. Such modelling and carving of hair and flesh, such dreaminess of eyes and grace of drapery, seemed too beautiful to be true. We have had greater artists since, and other " revelations," but the work of Mr. Palmer remains good sculpture still. Among those early busts are portraits of Hamilton, Commodore Perry, Washington Irving, Governor Morgan, Moses Taylor, Erastus Corning, Henry Burden of Troy, and a bronze of Dr. Armsby in Washington Park, Albany.

The bust of Irving stands in the vestibule of the New York Historical Society's building, where it is conspicuous for its admirable carving. The expression is the well-known kindly smile, a trifle sleepy, but full of amiability. The caressing touches and accents of the chisel have been so tastefully administered as to make this bust a work of art quite irrespective of the likeness. Its ghostly comrades look very crude or characterless beside it; one almost expects to hear them clamoring to be "done over." The bust of Henry Burden is an even finer work — a Calhoun-like head with long hair swept back in waving masses and falling below the ears. But the face itself is far from being that dreary mask which the great Southerner habitually wore in the eyes of the world. Quite as picturesque and as full of character as his, it is also animated, kindly, and responsive. The deep-set eyes seem to glow under the heavy brows; the finely characterized nose is strong; the mouth is good-humored, but with a look of the inevitable in its corners and in the massive chin beneath. The sinewy neck is bare, and rises from shoulders covered with broad drapery. It is difficult to conceive a finer bust. While the subject could hardly be surpassed, the workmanship is worthy of the theme, and shows conclusively that in the year 1862 Mr. Palmer was already a master in his art.

The following year, one of the most tragic in the history of the country, gave birth to Palmer's " Peace in Bondage " (Fig. 17), a relief showing the head and winged torso of a beautiful female figure leaning, weary and hopeless, against the trunk of a tree, to which she is presumably bound. The modelling of the body is large and distinctly sculptural, without offensive realism, the expression of the fine profile very subtle and appealing; the arrangement of the hair and of the wilted olive wreath, and particularly the treatment of the wing, are worthy of the highest praise. Both in conception and in work-manship this relief marks the great strides which the sculptor had made since the production of his amateurish "Faith" eleven years before. "Peace in Bondage" is a poetic thought, poetically ex-pressed. Such art well merits the characterization of "lyric," which has been applied to Mr. Palmer's work by Marquand and Frothing-ham.[1] How little there is in our sculpture which can be called lyric, or poetic in any sense! Works such as this are precious, even though some, in their sophistication, may consider them scarcely "up to date."

There were other figures of minor importance, like the "Emi-grant's Children," the "Ambush Chief," the "Sleeping Peri," the "Little Peasant," "Pleasures of Memory"; but the next production of note was the great figure of the seated "Angel at the Sepulchre" (1865), a monument in Albany cemetery, which is conceived in simple sculptural fashion, and possesses the double charm of beauty and of fitness. The drapery is handled in a large way, yet is admirably true; the earnest face is full of power. How Clark[2] could see in it a "fleshy and unangelic type" it is hard to understand. Perhaps the charge would be more comprehensible if one could project himself back to the centennial year, and remember that up to that time sculp-tured angels seldom had bodies in their flowing garments, and that anything more than a conventional face was counted revolutionary.

It was not until 1873 that Mr. Palmer saw Europe. He remained abroad nearly two years visiting the various capitals, finally taking a studio in Paris for a few months while he executed his statue of Chancellor Robert R. Livingston of New York for the national Capitol. This bronze, although rather smaller than the average in Statuary Hall, and less conspicuous in gesture, is one of the few worthy figures there. To ask that a modern portrait of a man should possess grace and beauty, is almost unreasonable; but both of these attributes are found in Mr. Palmer's "Livingston." The sculptor was fortunate in his subject; the subject fortunate in falling into the hands of a true artist with an appreciation of refinement. This quality he has expressed with great delicacy, not only in the face, but

[1] "A Text-Book of the History of Sculpture," p. 279.
[2] "Great American Sculptures," p. 118.

throughout the pose, and particularly in the modelling of the sensitive hands. Life and personality are here, yet withal the self-restraint
of a dignified nature.   The mass of the figure is ample and not cut
up; within its harmonious contour is a charming disposition of
drapery, which seems to be the result of the perfectly unstudied pose
of the arms.   That this effect of drapery is the reason for the pose,
is known only to the artist who planned it all with so much skill, and

FIG. 17. — PALMER: PEACE IN BONDAGE.

to the few by whom such skill is appreciated.   The right arm hangs
gracefully, the hand grasping a roll of documents.   The left hand
gathers up the official robe and rests lightly upon the hip.   The
modelling of the drapery is severe, but varied in color.   In matter of
interpretation, of charm, and of artistic integrity, nothing finer had
been done up to this time (1874) by an American sculptor. Although
previously installed in the Capitol, the " Livingston " was exhibited
at the Centennial in 1876, where it received a medal of the first class.

We are not yet converted to the Tolstoian creed, that "great works of art are great because they are accessible and comprehensible to every one," since the logical ultimate test would have to be the appreciation of the savage; but the fact that a man's art is loved of many does not necessarily disprove its admirable qualities. It may convey thoughts of universal significance, couched in terms of such beauty that all must acknowledge their appeal, and still it may conform to the demands of the severest of critics. It is a blessed privilege to be able thus to address the multitude, and when to their appreciation is added the respect of one's colleagues, an artist has certainly attained to the utmost of his dreams. It is better than to have put a pediment in the Capitol! Mr. Palmer's influence has been potent in America, interesting thousands in a beautiful art, and raising the standard of workmanship all along the line. To helpless and disappointed aspirants, grieving for Italy, his example was an encouragement as well as a rebuke. It counselled in manly tones to make the most of self, with the material at hand. The use that he made of this material and the essential ideality of the man proclaim him the most significant figure in the early development of what is now almost a national art.

Thomas Ball spent many years abroad, but has never been out of touch with his native land. He had reached middle age — at least the meridian of an average life — when he first went to Italy; he made frequent visits home; and above all he never succumbed to the enervating Italian influence. Despite his long sojourn in Florence, his art remained fundamentally his own, and therefore American. It speaks volumes for the underlying strength and rightness of his personality that from first to last, from the untutored beginnings to the masterful products of the great Florentine studio, his work has always been good sculpture and generally of the most dignified and monumental type. In the whole output of a notably industrious career there is not one hint of the meretricious or the commercial. Through all his work, as throughout his life, is found an atmosphere of cheerful earnestness and an essential nobility.

If every artist had left so trustworthy and modest a record of his life as Mr. Ball prepared for us some years ago in his autobiography,[1]

[1] "My Threescore Years and Ten." Boston, 1891.

the historian's task would not only be rendered easy, but would become a delight. The simplicity of the narrative carries one along until curiosity gives way to sincere friendliness for the handsome young man of 1857 and for the venerable patriarch of 1890 whose features are pictured on the pages of the book. It would be an injustice to attempt to paraphrase this account, and to quote is difficult; a brief summary must therefore suffice.

Mr. Ball's father was a house and sign painter of Boston, a man of more artistic temperament than his humble lot would indicate, but for some years before his early death an invalid. The son Thomas was born into this world on the third day of June, 1819, and fared well despite poverty. One of his earliest recollections is that of a visit to the State House with his father, and of his wonder at Chantrey's white-robed statue of Washington which had recently been placed there. The child grew, and after the death of his father undertook the support of the family. A position as boy-of-all-work in the old New England Museum was one of the determining steps in his progress, since it led to silhouette-cutting, the study of drawing and engraving, miniature painting, and finally full-length portraiture and even historical composition.

The young artist was well established and enjoying a modest but securely founded success when an incident turned his attention to modelling. His first bust, a small one of Jenny Lind, done from photographs, had a great vogue, as the "Swedish Nightingale" was then at the height of her fame and popularity in this country. It was followed by other "cabinet" busts, principally of musicians, with whom Mr. Ball was intimate; for the sculptor was also a vocalist of no little reputation, a participant in all of the oratorios of Boston, and the first in this country to sing the title rôle of Mendelssohn's "Elijah." Mr. Ball's earliest attempt at a life-size bust was a portrait of Daniel Webster which met with great success and led to the modelling of a statuette which grew in turn, many years later, into a large statue of Webster — the same that is now standing in Central Park, New York. The little figures found ready sale, and brought the young sculptor a gold medal from the Charitable Mechanics' Association.

In 1854 came the long-anticipated opportunity to go abroad, and

Mr. Ball, now thirty-five years of age, set sail with his bride for the
"promised land." Florence was their destination; to be a part of
that tiny but far-famed art world their ambition. Greenough had
returned to America and had died two years before; but they
were made welcome by Hart and Hiram Powers and installed in
the apartments occupied some twenty years earlier by Clevenger.
Among their associates were Thomas Buchanan Read and the

FIG. 18. — BALL: WASHINGTON, BOSTON.

painter Francis Alexander. They also made the acquaintance of
the Brownings and of many other celebrities. The first undertaking
in Florence was a study of the nude called "Pandora"; then a
"Shipwrecked ·Sailor-Boy"; a statuette of Washington Allston;
a bust of Napoleon I, and other minor works.

At the end of two years the sculptor returned to Boston, where
he remained until 1865. In spite of national disturbances he was
kept well employed during this period; at first with portrait busts

and statuettes,[1] and ultimately with one of the principal works of his life, the famous " Washington " (Fig. 18) of the Boston Public Gardens, the first equestrian group in New England, and the fourth modelled in the United States.   Mr. Ball built it up as Mr. Brown had done his a few years before, in plaster; but unlike Brown he did it all with his own hands, a task which occupied him over three years (1860–1864).   One admires the courage and the perseverance of the man, but regrets that an artist capable of producing such monuments should have spent so much time in passing that immense bulk through a " two-quart bowl," which process, as he says, gave him abundant time for meditation.   With modern methods and proper assistance the work could have been done quite as thoughtfully and more perfectly in one-third of the time, while not only Mr. Ball but the world would have been the gainers by those two other years.   However, the task was finally accomplished, and the result was a work as important in the historic annals of the country as it is in the topography of Boston, where it has been a landmark for over thirty years.

The monument has been treated with uniform respect by the critics, though Jarves, who was not always able to recognize merit, announced that it was purely " realistic."   This is just what to the modern eye it is not, though the horse was so much more true to nature than we find him in the usual pictorial representations of the time that Mr. Jarves's anxiety is readily understood.   It may be acknowledged that the attitude of the general is not so impressive as that which H. K. Brown gave him.   It is dignified, but has more the air of the everyday man, the leader looking around him sharply as he rides.   In general effect, however, of monumental distinction, as well as conscientious workmanship, Mr. Ball's achievement ranks among the finest equestrian statues of this country, and this in spite of the sculptor's handicap of inexperience and the use of a most ungrateful medium which quite prohibited charm of plastic handling. To appreciate fully the degree of Mr. Ball's success one needs but to contrast his version of the great commander with those by Clark Mills and Thomas Crawford.

[1] Among these were statuettes of Clay and Edwin Forrest and busts of Dr. Ephraim Peabody in King's Chapel, President Lord of Dartmouth, Rufus Choate, William H. Prescott, and Henry Ward Beecher.

There were no funds at the moment for casting the " Washington," so it was carefully cut into pieces by the prospective founder, and the fragments laid away for safe-keeping until a more convenient season.   This proved to be several years later, the monument being finally unveiled on July 3, 1869.   Meanwhile the sculptor returned to Florence laden with various models and commissions, among which the most important was for a marble statue of Edwin Forrest as " Coriolanus," for which he had made preliminary studies in Philadelphia.   Before beginning this important work, however, Mr. Ball was moved to execute a half life-size model of Lincoln and a kneeling slave, a work which was destined to meet with great success when executed later in heroic size.

The " Coriolanus " was ready for the marble in 1867, and is now in the Actors' Home near Philadelphia.   It has been highly praised.   Nothing could be more unique in the way of art criticism than the following paragraph gravely quoted by Clement and Hutton from Alger's " Life of Forrest " : —

" The name of Thomas Ball has acquired celebrity in art since that day, but the statue of Forrest in the character of ' Coriolanus ' will always stand as a proud landmark in his sculptured path of fame.   It was a true work of love not less than of ambition. . . . Forrest was indeed fortunate in the peaceful and time-enduring victory achieved for him by the artist in the sculptured ' Coriolanus,' whose haughty beauty and right foot, insupportably advanced with the planted weight of all imperious Rome, will speak his quality to generations yet unborn."

This was succeeded by a beautiful " Eve stepping into Life," which Mr. Ball considers his most ambitious work ; by a very popular little head called " La Petite Pensée," and by a fine bust of the musician Liszt.   A flying trip to Boston resulted in an order for a marble statue of Governor John A. Andrew, which was followed by a group for the Chickering monument in Mount Auburn Cemetery, representing the " Angel of Death lifting a Veil from the Eyes of Faith."   Figures more suggestive of the Florentine environment were " Christmas," " Saint Valentine's Morning," and " Love's Memories" ; but in spite of their " catchy " titles these are charming works of serious worth, and not mere displays of Italian handicraft.

L

Hiram Powers considered Mr. Ball's next figure, the "Saint John the Evangelist," his most perfect work. Although the subject has been represented in every church of Europe, one feels that in the rapt earnestness of this face and figure the American has added another thought and given his theme a new exaltation. There is an integrity and a genuine purity in the listening figure which one often reads into ecclesiastical sculpture only to find later naught but tantalizing disappointment; here we find soul as well as skilful

FIG. 19. — BALL: EMANCIPATION GROUP, WASHINGTON.

workmanship and the conventional attributes of holiness. The figure was made for a gentleman of Boston, and is in Forest Hills Cemetery.

An order from the Freedman's Memorial Association had the effect of expanding the little Lincoln model into the well-known "Emancipation" group of Washington, which was inaugurated in 1875 (Fig. 19). A replica was subsequently ordered for Boston (1877), where it is rather unfortunately placed in a crowded intersection of streets. Hence it has been more criticised there than at Washington. The modern connoisseur feels perhaps too strongly the inflexible surfaces of those early works. He is over-conscious of their smoothness and shine, their lack of pleasing accents. But the eye which sees in them only monotony of texture misses their chief value and shows itself lacking in a grasp of essentials. Mr. Ball's conception of Lincoln is a lofty one, which he has conveyed in a language intelligible to all and in terms as well of sculptural significance. The Lincoln monument is one of the inspired works of American sculpture: a great theme expressed with emotion by an artist of intelligence and sympathy, who felt what he was doing. It is a pity to lose sight of its nobility and power and of its simple structural beauty, merely because its surface lacks vivacity of technic. We are not wrong in prizing this quality, but there are things in art, as in life, which are more important than charm of surface. These, the fundamentals, may be found in this admirable group.

The next order was for the "Daniel Webster" of Central Park, New York, which was enlarged from the little statuette of twenty-one years before. This gigantic and imposing figure (fourteen feet in height) was cast in Munich and unveiled in 1876. In that year the sculptor and his family visited the Centennial Exposition, and returned to Florence with an order for a "Charles Sumner" for Boston. This was no sooner completed than a commission followed for a statue of Josiah Quincy. These figures are excellent works of their kind. The "Sumner" (in the Public Gardens) has a noble head, to the beauty of which the waving locks contribute not a little. The movement is spirited: that of an orator who makes a sweeping downward gesture with the right hand, while the left holds his manuscript to his breast with an abrupt bend of the elbow. The figure stands well on its feet, like all of this sculptor's men, and the drawing is everywhere adequate.

Mr. Ball's "Josiah Quincy" was erected in 1878 in the City Hall square of Boston as a pendant to the "Franklin," by Richard Greenough, and unlike the latter work is a distinctly sculptural conception. It would be untrue as well as unfair to later men of superior skill to call it a great statue, since the execution is summary. As with the "Lincoln" and others, its modelling is scarcely more refined than that of the better "staff" work of our expositions, and makes no display of technical dexterity. On the other hand, it shows a dignity of mass and a grace of line which many a sculptor of our day has sought in vain and of which many another has no conception. This figure has the qualities which lie at the foundation of great monumental art. Aside from the slightly alarmed air of the face, the general effect could hardly be improved upon.

Doubtless the big mantle has little significance to us, but it was actually worn once. The sculptor knew its value in his work and has disposed it, like the arms and hands, with great success. Indeed, our country offers but few better conceived portrait statues than this figure of Josiah Quincy. It possesses that indefinable aloofness and distinction in which modern realism often falls short, to its immeasurable loss. In a way, the very crudity of Mr. Ball's execution, the summary handling of details, serves the same purpose as the highly perfected simplification of our best sculptures of to-day.

Another " Webster " for Concord, New Hampshire, a " David " in marble, and a statue of P. T. Barnum were the principal creations of the next few years. The last named received a first-class medal in the International Exposition in Munich in 1888. Mr. Ball's seventieth birthday was spent in this country, and a few weeks later he received the most important order of his life, a commission for the Washington monument which now decorates the town of Methuen, Massachusetts. This monument had been designed many years previously for a competition in Philadelphia. It is pyramidal in form, a monolith rising from a square base of white Carrara marble. On the lower member are seated four figures in bronze: " Cincinnatus," typical of the return of peace and the laying aside of military arms; " Victory " in the shape of a beautiful woman holding a wreath, and leaning forward in an expectant attitude; " Revolution," a man of determined mien, powerful and dignified of figure and face alike; and " Oppression," a female figure, heavily chained, with drooping head and stricken aspect. In niches above are colossal portrait busts of Washington's four distinguished generals, — Lafayette, Greene, Knox, and Lincoln. Above all, crowning the work with simplicity and dignity, stands the massive figure of Washington garbed in the familiar Continental uniform and partially enveloped in a great cloak, which is caught about the neck and falls in ample folds. The right foot is somewhat advanced, and the left hand outstretched, as in benediction, gives a solemnity to the pose that is impressive.

This considerable work, undertaken by Mr. Ball at the age of threescore and ten and successfully carried through, cost him several years of unremitting labor. How well it was done may be inferred from the dignity of the principal figure, which was seen at the Columbian Exposition of 1893 — the gigantic Washington in bronze which stood in the rotunda of the Art Palace. Its majesty impressed all who entered. In conception, in expression, in pose, line, and accessories; in light and shade and, this time, even in surface handling, the figure is nobly monumental. At seventy the sculptor was at his prime. It is needless to say that the figure received the highest honors of the Exposition.

A few worthy works in sculpture had made their appearance in this country before Thomas Ball began to produce, but he set a new standard in public statuary, and the influence of such high ideals and such sincere craftsmanship as his can scarcely be overestimated. Through his own creations and those of his pupils, Milmore and Daniel C. French, he has largely shaped the monumental art of New England. Mr. French once said of him, " I respect his work and I love the man." Such is the tribute paid by all who know this grand old sculptor and his contributions to American art.

CHAPTER VIII

STORY AND RANDOLPH ROGERS

WITH the consideration of William Wetmore Story the course of American sculpture leads us again to Rome, where Mr. Story passed an unbroken residence of many years, remaining throughout that period a striking figure in the social and artistic life of the city. His eminence as a scholar and *littérateur* gave to his sculpture a somewhat exaggerated reputation, which the succeeding years have not entirely sustained. His mind, like his hand, was nimble and indefatigable; his life well rounded and fruitful. It may be confidently said that no American sculptor of his time did so much to give social standing to his profession.

Mr. Story was born in Salem, Massachusetts, Feb. 12, 1819. He graduated at Harvard College in 1844, and afterward studied law, which he never practised, though he published at least two treatises considered valuable in that profession. He published, also, in 1847, a volume of poems, a life of his father, Chief Justice Story, in 1851, and a second volume of poems in 1856. Adopting sculpture as a profession, he went, in 1851, to Rome, and opened a studio, one of his earliest works being a statue of his father, now at Mount Auburn Cemetery, in Cambridge, Massachusetts. His "Cleopatra" and his "Sibyl" were displayed at the London exhibition of 1862. The former, or rather a replica dated 1869, is now in the Metropolitan Museum of New York, where are also his "Semiramis," "Salome," "Medea," and "Polyxena." Among his other works are "Saul," "Sappho," "Delilah," "Moses," "Judith," "Infant Bacchus," "Little Red Riding-Hood," and "Jerusalem in her Desolation." He was the author of the statues of George Peabody in London and Baltimore; of Edward Everett in the Public Gardens at Boston; of William Prescott at Bunker Hill; of Chief Justice Marshall and Professor

PLATE 6. — STORY: CLEOPATRA.

Henry (Fig. 20) in Washington; and of Francis S. Key in San Francisco. Reference is found also to a portrait of Josiah Quincy, and to an equestrian statue of Colonel Shaw, for Boston. He died in Vallombrosa, Italy, Oct. 7, 1895.

Mr. Story must have been a very delightful man to know; he seems to have made a specialty of being delightful. To read his "Conversations in a Studio" (Boston, 1890), one might suspect that so much brilliancy and erudition would cloy in the end, but it was probably diluted for daily use, else this was the most extraordinary studio that the world has ever seen. Donatello and Michael Angelo certainly never listened to such accretions and aggravations of scholastic lore. No one knew Mr. Story more intimately than did his friend, Nathaniel Hawthorne, and the testimony of America's most winsome writer is valuable. We may trust the intuitions of his heart every time, even though his judgment in matters artistic is rather uncertain, as he himself frankly acknowledges.

In his journal of Feb. 14, 1858, Hawthorne writes: " William Story looks quite as vivid, in a graver way, as when I saw him last, a very young man. His perplexing variety of talents and accomplishments — he being a poet, a prose writer, a lawyer, a painter, a musician, and a sculptor — seems now to be concentrating itself into this latter vocation, and I cannot see why he should not achieve something very good. He has a beautiful statue, already finished, of Goethe's Margaret pulling a flower to pieces to discover whether Faust loves her; a very type of virginity and simplicity. The statue of Cleopatra, now only fourteen days advanced in the clay, is as wide a step from the little maidenly Margaret as any artist could take; it is a grand subject, and he is conceiving it with depth and power, and working it out with adequate skill. He certainly is sensible of some thing deeper in his art than merely to make beautiful nudities and baptize them by classic names." [1]

Elsewhere he records the charm of a summer day spent with his friend in Siena, "turning over books or talking," [2] and continues: " Mr. Story is the most variously accomplished and brilliant person, the fullest of social life and fire, whom I ever met; and without seeming to make an effort, he kept us amused and entertained the whole day

---

[1] "Italian Note-Book," Vol. I, p. 69.   [2] Ibid., Vol. II, p. 173.

long; not wearisomely entertained, neither, as we should have been if we had not let his fountain play naturally. Still, though he bubbled and brimmed over with fun, he left the impression on me that . . . there is a pain and care, bred, it may be, out of the very richness of his gifts and abundance of his outward

prosperity. Rich, in the prime of life, . . . and children budding and blossoming around him as fairly as his heart could wish, with sparkling talents, — so many, that if he choose to neglect or fling away one, or two, or three, he would still have enough left to shine with, — who should be happy if not he?"

But when it comes to a calm judgment on the sculpture of this brilliant man, it will be best to take the enthusiastic verdict of his friend with some grains of salt. Of that early portrait of Judge Story, Hawthorne wrote, "The statue of his father, his first work, is very noble, as noble and fine a portrait statue as I ever saw."[1] Tuckerman observes more temperately: "The likeness is manifestly true, and there is grace but little vigor in the work; it, however,

FIG. 20. — STORY: PROFESSOR HENRY, WASHINGTON.

was justly regarded as a successful first attempt."[2] It is a dull figure, in spite of Hawthorne; the first of a long array of seated men and women by Mr. Story, whose taste — or prudence — found slight expression in standing effigies. Judge Story is shown in his judicial robes, holding a book, and lifting his hand to attract attention. The expression is weak, the gesture obtrusive, and the modelling lamentably absent.

The one work with which the fame of Story is permanently linked, the only one which his name recalls to most memories, is his

[1] "Italian Note-Book," Vol. I, p. 70.   [2] "Book of the Artists," p. 576.

"Cleopatra." It is a little uncertain whether it was Story or Hawthorne who made "Cleopatra." At any rate it was the novelist who gave to the statue its reputation in England and America. "It is the most famous," says Clark, "not because its extraordinary merits have forced a recognition from the multitude, but because it had the good fortune to fascinate a man of rare genius, who in a sense appropriated it for his own by embodying a eulogistic description of it in one of his best known and most widely read books." [1]

It may be added that Hawthorne's "Cleopatra" was quite another than Story's. We of to-day look with amazement upon this cold, much-chiselled figure to find the regal beauty described in the "Marble Faun": "In a word, all Cleopatra — fierce, voluptuous, passionate, tender, wicked, terrible, and full of poisonous and rapturous enchantment — was kneaded into what, only a week or two before, had been a lump of wet clay from the Tiber. Soon apotheosized in an indestructible material, she would be one of the images that men keep forever, finding a heat in them that does not cool down through the centuries." Hawthorne had watched the growth of the figure almost from the "lump of wet clay." It was the wonder of this development which had fired his imagination until it far outran what his eyes beheld. Into the work he read a vast deal more than ever the sculptor was to realize, and under the magic of his words we think that we see, likewise, "all Cleopatra" in this essentially mediocre figure. By the time, however, we have walked around the marble, we need to read the description over again for new enthusiasm.

There is one view of "Cleopatra" which must have given its conscientious author great satisfaction — the one shown in our illustration (Pl. VI). Unpleasant in line and inadequate from other directions, here the composition becomes much more graceful, and we are able to discern somewhat of the majestic vision that the sculptor has tried so hard to express. But reverse the page; turn for a moment the picture upside down, and the aridity of treatment, the leanness of the drapery, become at once apparent. Reduce the "Fates" of the Parthenon to a mere decorative design by the same

[1] "Great American Sculptures," p. 88.

simple method and the difference will, as the French say, " jump at
your eyes."   It is a good lesson in the technical side of the art.   But
with all his artistic shortcomings, the sculptor had a right to claim
for himself whatever his loyal friend found in his work — and
reason to be thankful for so appreciative a critic.   The " Cleopatra "
is undoubtedly impressive when one is in the proper mood, and it
cannot be denied that it is a work of some distinction.   Into this
figure Mr. Story put his best thought and his greatest energy.
Many of his later productions were but feeble and exaggerated
variants of this theme.

The " Libyan Sibyl," which as before noted was first seen in
London in 1862, is intrinsically a more sculptural and a more impressive work.   Mr. Clark's description is enthusiastic and vivid :
" This weird woman of mystery, the child of the desert, it is true is
not a ' serpent of old Nile,' but there is about her much of that
pent-up fiery energy, threatening to burst forth at any moment to
scorch and consume, which marks the ' Cleopatra.'   The mission
of the ' Sibyl,' however, is not to lure men on to destruction — she
is the custodian of secrets, the secrets of Africa and the African
race.   And how close she keeps them, with her locked lower
limbs, her one hand pressing her chin as if to keep in the torrent
of words that threatens to burst forth, while the other grasps a
scroll covered with strange characters, which would reveal much
could we be permitted to decipher it.   On her head is the Am-
monite horn, — for she is a daughter of Jupiter Ammon, and the
keeper of his oracles, — and on her breast is the ancient symbol
of mystery, as she sits there brooding and thinking, and her breast
heaving with emotions as she thinks of what is past and what is to
come." [1]

These two figures had great success in London, where, indeed, as
Jarves states, they " placed Mr. Story, in European estimation, at
the head of American sculptors." [2]   He continues : " Profiting by
the knowledge of the old masters, and forming his tastes upon the
best styles, Story has had the independence to seek out an unused
field.   In this he confers honor on our school, and gives it an

[1] " Great American Sculptures," p. 92.
[2] Jarves, " Art Idea," p. 281.

impetus as new as it is refreshing." [1]   Was there ever a refreshing impetus so sterile of results?   Not only did Story have no followers, but he declined appreciably from year to year, falling away from his own standard, though haunted, to the point of obsession, by visions of mournful female figures, generally seated and wrapped in gloom.   It seems strange that so active a mind should dream of nothing but brooding, sinister souls, of bodies bowed in grief or tense with rage.   Never once, apparently, did there come to him a vision of buoyancy and grace, of a beauty that one could love, of good cheer and joy of very living — always those unwholesome, pouting creatures with their "heavily revolving thoughts," born of that belated Byronic romanticism in which Hawthorne himself was by no means without a share.

It was "Jerusalem in her Desolation" which came next.   The complaisant *Art Journal* of August, 1873, welcomed it to London that year with the following eulogy: "A noble female figure, clad in flowing drapery; the head, crowned with a kind of phylactery, is finely modelled, the Hebrew face having an expression of mingled distress and contempt. . . .   The general expression of the design is that of majestic sorrow, and the execution of the work throughout is most careful."   Clark, though treating Mr. Story with the utmost consideration, acknowledged in 1879 that the statue was "certainly not a pleasing one."   Proceeding, he says, "There is a stiffness and total lack of grace in the lines of the figure for which there is no reason and no excuse."   Those who have seen "Jerusalem" in the Pennsylvania Academy will consider this a very gentle criticism.   Nothing more amateurish than this figure could well be admitted to a public gallery.   Head and body alike are strangely

---

[1] Later Mr. Jarves was compelled to form a different estimate of Story's talent.   In his "Art Thoughts" he says (p. 311) : —

"For a brief moment it really appeared as if in Story we had, at last, something that savored of genius.   But a closer examination of his numerous efforts dispels this illusion. Industrious he assuredly is, possessing fancy and some skill of invention; but his strong point is his receptive faculty, which gets good from others, and strains it through his own mind. His antiquarian knowledge serves him well in the decorative part of his sculpture.   Ornaments and accessories are rightly chosen and tastefully placed, though the choice of motives appears somewhat sensational.   'Cleopatra poisoning Herself,' 'Judith having slain Holofernes,' 'Medea intending the Murder of her Children,' 'Delilah after betraying Samson,' 'Saul Mad,' and 'Sappho meditating Suicide' are hazardous topics even for genius."

deficient in construction. The arms are big but not good, and the unfortunate creature seems not to know what to do with them. How the sculptor of the "Cleopatra" could have shaped the "Jerusalem" so inadequately, is one of the mysteries of the Roman studio.

One may condone certain defects of the "Cleopatra" by laying some share of the responsibility upon the over-zealous carver; but we shall not be able to plead extenuating circumstances in regard to the "Semiramis, Queen of Assyria," in the Metropolitan Museum, a work also bearing date of 1873. To be sure, the carving is no less unpleasant than in the other examples, but in this case it has spoiled nothing excepting the beautiful stone. The figure shows no trace of sculptural inspiration. It has neither grace nor power — scarcely, indeed, a definite pose; but it makes up for these minor deficiencies through a surplusage of facial expression. The novel structure of its physiognomy is contorted by its burden of emotional display; it is fairly overlaid with it. The eyes are exaggerated, the eyebrows enormous. The hair is harshly conventionalized, and is held on the head by means of a heavy crown of clumsy workmanship. The drapery is Story's own, a sort of thin morning wrapper, as monotonous in its folds as the slats of a Venetian blind.

"Salome" is Cleopatra with arms reversed and, for variety, the legs crossed. An apology for a head seems to have been extemporized without effort, the regular-ribbed drapery was elaborated, and the thing was done. Then the trusty marble-cutter was called in and another block of snowy Carrara was doomed to take on for all time the graceless stamp of ostentatious nullity. Story's "Salome" is the uninspired product of a keen intelligence operating in a wrong direction.

The "Medea" was done with more conscience and more skill, and was greatly admired at the Centennial Exposition. The brooding brow, the sinister mouth, the conspicuous dagger — all of this very legible language of tragedy made powerful appeal to uncultivated tastes not yet prepared for subtleties and perplexities of expression. The woman seemed beautiful, and looked cross, and carried a dagger; the meaning was as obvious as in cheap melodrama. Medea's arms are awkwardly disposed and are inadequately modelled, but the figure presents a sculptural compactness, and the head is better constructed than was usual with Story. The carving likewise is far superior to that of the "Semiramis," for instance. The outer garment is simply and gracefully arranged, with an agreeable little design running around its border in dainty relief. The figure is one of Mr. Story's earlier works and is undoubtedly one of his best. His rating would be much higher if only this and the "Cleopatra" and "Sibyl" remained, along with his dignified portrait of George Peabody.

For of Mr. Story's portrait figures that of the great philanthropist is unquestionably the best. The original in London is, if memory does not err, in marble. The replica before the Peabody Institute in Baltimore is in bronze. It is not a work of great distinction, artistically speaking, — not comparing in this respect with its neighbor (in Baltimore) Rinehart's "Judge Taney," — but it shows a man of good figure and fine head sitting quietly and at ease in a large chair. The whole effect is of calm and sedateness, a comfortable impression for any statue to give. One can easily read a look of benevolence into its features, but we must not search its eyes for the gleam of a soul within, as we may the portraits by great artists. Neither shall we find here the playful handling of a plastic surface over firmly moulded masses — that charm of technic which the Paris-trained generation has taught us to admire and to demand. The "Peabody" is an arrested development, a statue well conceived and well begun; it is a pity that it was not carried further.

As much cannot be said of the oratorical "Edward Everett" of Boston. The uplifted right arm is not well adjusted to the shoulder, and would in any case become a weariness to the flesh, or at least to the sympathetic spirit. The pose is unfortunate, because untrue in effect, if for no other reason. No orator ever holds his hand above his head continuously. He makes a sweeping gesture now and then, and the power is in the movement. The rigid arm suggests a fakir of India and not an impassioned speaker. In going to the extreme of action, the artist has thwarted his own purpose and achieved paralysis.

Whatever may be said of Mr. Story's sculptural ideals and of his proficiency in his art, he was ever the cultured man of the world, and could not express himself otherwise.   On all of his portraits of men one finds his sign-manual of dignity and — excepting the " Everett " and " Prescott " — of repose.   His heroines are strangely unsympathetic, but his men have the air of gentlemen.   The " Chief Justice Marshall" (1884), who sits well down in a graceful semi-classic chair upon one of the approaches to the national Capitol, is weak in pose, but still remains impressive.   The head is intellectual and benevolent.   The gesture of the extended hand is ample and forceful, while the other arm and hand are well placed on the arm of the chair.   The drapery, likewise, is gracefully arranged ; and were it not for its unfailing sharpness of treatment, this expensive work (costing $40,000) might be considered very good.

" Professor Henry " (also dated 1884), at the entrance of the Smithsonian Institute, has the same dignified serenity.   Psychologically, the figure is well conceived.   The face and hands have life.   One is conscious of standing before a real and fine man, yet one has a curious feeling that this man is clad in a suit of corrugated iron.   The scholarly gown does not differ much from the judicial robe ; and as the figure is erect, the sculptor has been tempted beyond his strength.   An endless repetition of parallel grooves and ridges makes of this surface as painful a display as an ingenious amateur could well devise.   There is nothing like it in this country. Its only approach is in Mr. Story's other works, but in the " Professor Henry " he has been most true to his instincts.   One feels his delight in every inexorable line.   No ploughboy could have taken greater pride in the straightness of his furrows.

This satisfaction and confidence are apparent in all that Mr. Story did, and are enough to convince one of his " call."   In spite of his obvious deficiencies as an artist, there is no question of the value of his labors in the historical sequence.   In England his reputation was second only to that of Powers, whom he followed as the representative American sculptor.   His personal worth and his address gave him the regard of the cultivated, enhancing in their minds the importance of his profession, while his sculpture was no less attractive to the general public.   It must not be forgotten that "art for art's sake" touches only the few, while the "anecdote" appeals to the many. With all his brilliancy of intellect, Mr. Story talked in his sculpture a very childlike language, exactly suited to the artistic development of his days. The classic titles and costumes of his subjects were impressive, and their frowning brows and pouting lips were intelligible to the simplest.

Story's art came at the right time, and had its very powerful influence in interesting a large public.

Another sculptor who enjoyed great popularity in his day was Randolph Rogers, who was born at Waterloo, Seneca County, New York, in 1825. His youth was spent at Ann Arbor, Michigan, where, in spite of the usual artistic "symptoms," he engaged in business until the age of twenty-three. At this time he made an impromptu exhibition of his works, consisting of several figures and a bust

FIG. 21. — ROGERS: LOST PLEIAD.

of Byron. The promise of these things, coupled with the fact that the young artist had never had a lesson, nor even an opportunity to see sculpture done, led his generous employers to provide him with means to study in Rome. This was in 1848, and he went at once, spending two years under the instruction of Bartolini. Returning to America, he remained five years in New York, where the products of his short stay abroad attracted much attention and brought him many commissions. After his marriage Mr. Rogers removed, in 1855, to Rome and fixed his residence there. His later years were fully occupied by numerous monumental works of importance, but his most interesting productions are doubtless the harvest of this earlier period, when imagination and enthusiasm held sway. Best known of these are " Nydia" and the " Lost Pleiad" (Fig. 21); "Ruth" and "Isaac" followed, and a "Boy Skating" and "A Boy and a Dog." His marble statue of President John Adams was placed in Mount Auburn Cemetery in 1857. In 1858 he received the commission for the bronze doors of the Capitol. In 1861 he finished his share of the work on Crawford's Washington monument at Richmond, and in 1862 made his " Angel of the Resurrection" for the Colt monument at Hartford, Connecticut.

Notable among the larger works of Mr. Rogers are the military memorials erected at Providence in 1871 and at Detroit in 1873, with others, less elaborate in design, at Cincinnati and Worcester, Massachusetts; a bronze statue of President Lincoln, unveiled in Fairmount Park, Philadelphia, in 1871; one of W. H. Seward, placed at the junction of Broadway and Fifth Avenue, New York, in 1876; the "Genius of Connecticut," on the Capitol at Hartford (1877); and a bronze group of Indians (1881).

Rogers's "Nydia" (Fig. 22) is so well known as scarcely to require description. The figure of the blind girl is shown bent forward in the attitude of one who pauses for a moment in flight; her right hand grasps her staff; the left is lifted to her ear, while she listens before continuing her course through that darkness which is her accustomed day. The figure is graceful and intelligible, though to the sculptor or to the sensitive critic the flying drapery seems very mechanical with its parallel ribs and grooves, and the fingers and toes are monotonously rounded without characterization. A writer who was fortunately oblivious to these defects has analyzed the charm of the work with much appreciation: "The crouching attitude and the tempest-blown garments which entangle themselves in the blind girl's staff are thoroughly expressive of a hurried forward movement, or rather, of a slight pause in such a movement for the purpose of listening for some hoped-for voice to pierce the darkness and tumult. The girl's face has an expression of intense listening upon it, and the artist has increased the suggestiveness of both face and figure in this respect by the action which he has given to the left hand and arm — the arm crossing the body, and the back of the hand making a shield behind the ear to gather the sound. This movement of the hand and arm is so obvious that on looking at the statue it is difficult to think that the artist could have chosen any other to express his idea; and yet it is in just such niceties as this that the superior excellence of many of the finest works of art consists." [1]

The "Lost Pleiad" (Fig. 21) is a graceful conception of not very robust individuality, but admirably suited to the demands of its time. When a work is so pure and innocent, when it has such vogue as had this figure, with its sister, the beloved "Nydia," it is evident that there is a reason for its existence. It "fills a long-felt want," or even creates a new one, which is still more important in the progress of art. It is said that no fewer than one hundred replicas of the "Nydia" were made in marble during the author's lifetime, and possibly as many more of the "Lost Pleiad" — that sweet, wayworn traveller of the heavens. It is safe to say that they gave a vast deal of pleasure in their day, and still retain for many not a little of their pathetic charm. They may not appeal to you and to me like the "Niké," the "Venus of Milo," or the "Fates." They may seem too reminiscent of the thought of other men to thrill us; we scan them in vain for token of originality and power; but so long as our most costly homes are adorned with modern Italian carvings of laces and feathers, of silk ruffles and bathing suits, there remains a use, an educational mission even, for an art as pure and ingenuous as that of Randolph Rogers. The youthful ideals of this pioneer were both sculpturally and poetically as far above these current abominations as are the Shaw Memorial and the "Angel of Death" above any dream that ever came to him. He did his best. To-day we know the best and too often choose the worst.

Mr. Rogers's only representation in the Metropolitan Museum is a kneeling "Ruth" in marble, a graceful little figure, and in some respects the most pleasing of all his works. We are assured on excellent authority [2] that "Ruth" was Mr. Rogers's first ideal figure,

---

[1] "Great American Sculptures," p. 78.   [2] Professor Martin L. D'Ooge.

M

but Clark calls it a later production.   He describes it prettily: " The heroine of the lovely Hebrew idyl is represented as resting one knee on the ground as she gathers the gleanings in the field of Boaz.   In her lap are her gatherings, while her right hand is filled with such of the ripened grain as she has just culled from the ground.   The head is turned, as if she had glanced up a moment from her task to gaze at the figure of Boaz in the distance, and there is a peculiar expression imparted by her eager eyes and her half-opened mouth as if she was hesitating between hope and fear."[1]   The face is sensitive and pure, and the drapery less mannered than in the examples already cited.   The wheat — and the other vegetation as well — is appropriately sparse, the plants having the usual emphatic treatment with vastly tiresome details.   This figure, with the " Nydia," formed Mr. Rogers's exhibit at the Centennial Exposition of 1876.

Casts of all of these figures, as well as of many of the sculptor's later and larger works, may be seen in the art gallery of the University of Michigan, at Ann Arbor.   The life-work of any man thus gathered together and reverently preserved is bound to be impressive, and though ideals and particularly methods have changed since these figures were modelled, there is much in the group to awaken our esteem for this earnest and indefatigable sculptor of half a century ago.   From the catalogue of this collection we may be permitted to quote Professor Martin L. D'Ooge's very accurate description of the Rogers bronze doors of the rotunda of the Capitol at Washington: —

" The doors are set in a deep frame which is arched at the top. The faces of the frame are ornamented with an egg-and-dart and astragal moulding, setting off a shallow and narrow panel in which is placed a low relief which represents a series of groups of weapons, flowers, fruits, and implements more or less conventionalized, and broken at the apex of the arch by a round panel in which is placed a bust of Columbus.   The inside jambs have as decoration a raised moulding resembling a cord or band plaited and crossed.   The doors are surmounted by a sculptured lunette, at the top of which is an eagle perched upon the folds of two national flags.   The lunette contains the largest of the reliefs, which represents the scene of the

[1] " Great American Sculptures," p. 75.

landing of Columbus and of the raising of the Spanish flag upon the soil of the newly discovered world.

"This scene is the culminating point of the life of the explorer, whose story is depicted in the series of eight panels that form the body of the doors. This series begins with the lowest panel at the left hand of the spectator. In the order of the series the scenes are as follows : —

"1. Columbus presents the plan of his proposed expedition before a company of learned monks, in the monastery of Saint Stephen at Salamanca.

"2. Columbus receives the hospitality of the Convent of Saint Maria de La Rabida, near Palos, and enlists in his cause the Prior Perez, the former confessor of Queen Isabella.

"3. Columbus receives his commission as admiral from the hands of Ferdinand and Isabella at Granada.

"4. The departure of the fleet from Palos for the first voyage. (Then follows the scene in the lunette described above.)

"5. Voyages among the islands of the New World and capture of the natives.

"6. Triumphant return of Columbus and honors at Barcelona.

"7. Arrival of Columbus in chains at Cadiz after the third voyage, and in consequence of malicious reports sent to the court by his enemies.

"8. The death of Columbus at Valladolid.

"The grace and dramatic power exhibited in these reliefs, the skill with which technical difficulties have been overcome, the clearness and compactness of each scene, are qualities that cannot fail to arouse admiration. Worthy of especial notice is also the wonderful variety of ornamentations illustrative of the history of the discovery of the New World, that is used with lavish hand upon the rails that separate the panels. The stiles on each side of the panels are divided by small niches, in which are placed statuettes of symbolic figures and real personages connected with the history of the period. Europe, Asia, Africa, and America are represented by figures intended to typify the character of their respective civilizations. Among the persons represented may be named Ferdinand and Isabella, Cortez and Vespucci, John II of Portugal and Henry VI of England, Pope Alexander VII and Cardinal Mendoza. The heads of distinguished statesmen, divines, and scholars peer forth from behind the mouldings of the panels, as if eager spectators of the great event that is set forth by these pictures in sculpture."

As a rule it is seldom worth while to find fault with artists for what they have missed; we thank them gratefully or turn away with indifference, according as they have satisfied us or failed to appeal to our taste, and " no harm done "; but it is impossible to leave this important work without criticism. As has been said in the discussion of the Crawford doors, neither of these men had much instinct for the decorative treatment of sculpture. Their reliefs are made more or less interesting by their elaboration and portraiture, but they remain mere story-telling pictures without charm of composition or plastic handling. Crawford's were the freer; Rogers's the more precise. In neither was there any lack of conscience; the sculptors probably did their best. If they seem to us to have been easily satisfied, it was because of the limitations of their ideals and of their skill. The structural beauty, as well as the subtleties of the Ghiberti Gates, meant no more to them than does an intricate musical composition to a whistling schoolboy. Jarves's comments on the Rogers doors are suggestive. The sculptor would have been helpless with such a conception as he points out had it been forced upon him; but for other men and other times here is a dream of a higher standard of art in exalted places: —

" Rogers was commissioned to create doors for the Capitol at Washington. In the light of symbolic portals to a Temple of Freedom, the idea partakes of the sublime. But the American is too impatient for original inspiration, and he has no adequate conception of his opportunity for noble work. Borrowing his general ideas from Ghiberti, he hurriedly elaborates a prosaic historical composition of the ' Discovery of America by Columbus,' clever and interesting as illustration, but far beneath the requirements of creative art or the dignity of the occasion." [1]

The early death of Crawford had left a number of his works unfinished. Various sculptors residing in Rome were commissioned to carry them on to completion. To his friend Randolph Rogers

[1] Jarves, " Art Idea," p. 274.

was allotted the important Washington monument at Richmond. Crawford had supplied the equestrian group and two standing figures. To Rogers then fell the designing and execution of the four remaining portrait statues and the six allegorical figures which form the outposts of the monument and which replace as many eagles in the original design.

The front position is occupied by Crawford's spirited "Patrick Henry." Next to the right as one makes the circuit of the pile is Rogers's "Mason," succeeded by Crawford's "Jefferson"; then "Nelson," "Marshall," and "Lewis," all by Rogers. The "Mason" suggests a man of character, but is certainly not a distinguished work of art. The author of the Bill of Rights stands with an easy swing, holding the historic document — properly labelled — in one hand and his pen in the other. The figure is in colonial attire, unembarrassed by other drapery, and recalls innumerable statues in England and in Germany. The treatment throughout is formal and colorless, the hair in particular being quite without charm of handling.

The "Nelson" advances with dignified gesture and proffers a national bond. The left hand resting upon the sword suggests an alternative, but probably the movement is without significance. The pose is good; indeed, the figure stands remarkably well, but in conception and in treatment it is serenely commonplace. It was evidently done without enthusiasm. The only thing about the figure to appeal to one is its perilous position. The skittish Pegasus above has backed halfway off its pedestal directly over the unconscious financier and threatens all kinds of disaster. The "Marshall" clasps in both hands a ponderous volume inscribed "Justice." The hands are thin and sharply defined. The long robe gives to the delicate figure a somewhat effeminate look, but also affords an effective sculptural mass. One is reminded of Story's "Marshall," or even more of his "Professor Henry"; but not Rogers himself could vie with Story in matter of lean, dry treatment of drapery. "Lewis," arrayed in the picturesque garb of a trapper, is probably the best of Rogers's contributions. The figure is alert and indeed admirably conceived. Like the others it is capably constructed and stands well on its feet. Like the others, too, it is unpleasantly harsh throughout in treatment, all details being sharp and rigid. The face is expressive in an elementary way, but is guiltless of suavity of modelling. Rogers's ideals may have been high, but his technic was that of the stone mason. Were these figures actually in stone, we could extenuate their defects in part; but since the models passed through no other hands than the founder's, their execution is evidently what the sculptor intended and what he considered good art. It was the inevitable, the obligatory standard of the day.

The six little bronze women of this Washington group, who are set on pedestals directly in front of the portrait statues, were doubtless intended to enrich the work, but they do not add to its impressiveness. In reality of life-size, they look much smaller. They sit crushed into six precisely similar masses of flags, and though bearing different names are all so much alike as to become cumulatively even more uninteresting than when considered separately. Indeed, they seem to vary only in matter of pose of arms and in regard to certain accessories. "Revolution" wears a liberty cap and points sternly with her left hand at her label while lifting her sword slightly from the ground. "Bill of Rights" summons her strength and lifts the sword higher. "Independence" and "Justice" look much concerned, with appropriate gestures. "Colonial Times" is armed with an axe and holds a tomahawk in reserve. The most expressive of these quiescent, colorless figures is "Finance," beside whom the elsewhere constant cannon-end is replaced by a helmet, into which she thoughtfully drops a coin. She also holds a large book, doubtless a ledger.

Among the casts at Ann Arbor may be seen the plaster "Bill of Rights." "President John Adams" is to be found there also, just as weak and dapper as the marble at Mount Auburn, where he keeps company with Otis and Story and Winthrop in the vestibule of the new chapel. The "Angel of the Resurrection," Mr. Tuckerman tells us, is "impressive." He proceeds: "The left hand extending downward indicates an attitude of attention for the signal to blow the trumpet, which is in the right hand reposing on the bosom. The face, looking upward, is full of life. It is a figure which presents a union of loveliness and majesty."[1] We could hardly employ any of these adjectives to-day in speaking of it; the statue is too much like

[1] "Book of the Artists," p. 591.

FIG. 22.—ROGERS: NYDIA, ART INSTITUTE, CHICAGO.

the commercial gravestone images in treatment for that; the conventional head with its strange mop of hair all around it does not satisfy present-day ideas of beauty, even of celestial beauty; but the thought and the pose are certainly suggestive. The figure might become "impressive" in very fact if the right man could only work it over. Evidently Rogers appreciated its value, for he used it again in the form of a relief. An ascending female figure in high relief is less happily conceived; while a "Sonnambula," intended as a pendant to the "Nydia," is, like most "pendants," far less inspired than the first conception.

The "Genius of Connecticut," which crowns the dome of the State House at Hartford, is very unfortunate in line from all sides. Its silhouette is further marred by the weak tilt of one of the wreaths held in the extended hands. Though this was done doubtless for variety, the wreath appears to be breaking off.

On the other hand, Mr. Rogers's two important portrait statues of "Lincoln" and "Seward" are adequate. They have been spoken of with uniform respect. The "Lincoln," in Philadelphia. "is a work of very sterling qualities, and is entitled to the credit of being one of the few really successful portraits of a great man whose rather ungainly figure made him the despair of artists."[1] Regarding the "Seward," in Madison Square, New York, the *Art Journal* of London of September, 1877, said: "Although open to criticism in a few details, it is, as a whole, an excellent piece of work, worthy of its conspicuous position in one of the great centres of the metropolis."

These two seated figures are almost identical in pose and proportion, varying, like the traditional statues of the Roman emperors, only in the heads, and are characterized by painstaking finish of the old-fashioned monotonous sort, rather than by amplitude or technical grace. There is no largeness in the gesture nor freedom of attitude, though the legs are crossed unconventionally, but the facial characterization is excellent.

One would scarcely believe the great bronze "Michigan" on the military monument at Detroit to be from the same hand that made the "Genius of Connecticut." It is almost inspired; the artist has been really interested in it — an Amazon figure armed "with sword

[1] "Great American Sculptures," p. 79.

and shield, while an Indian tomahawk in the girdle and an Indian head-dress of shells and feathers symbolize the original inhabitants of the territory." She advances aggressively, and has much vigor. The unusually expressive face, the bared arms, and the sweep of the drapery contribute to make certain views very effective. Below, on successive steps, are four soldiers and four allegorical figures, interspersed with reliefs. The seated female figures are of the same character as the Richmond decorations, though rather more interesting. " Emancipation," in particular, is worthy of study; an African type, idealized and treated heroically. It is for this memorial that the sculptor did his best monumental work.

Randolph Rogers will be remembered for his industry, for the mass of his production and its dignity, rather than for original power or for skill of craftsmanship. With one or two exceptions, after " Nydia " and the " Lost Pleiad," he seems singularly stolid. For him no " impassioned personal outlook on life "! One seeks vainly in most of his work for poetry, or even for expression. His figures are of unexceptionable decorum, and one feels them incapable of anything else. The art of a Carpeaux, for instance, and that of Rogers, are as the antipodes; but Rogers and Saint Gaudens are little nearer together. Yet, "among modern sculptors, Randolph Rogers occupies a foremost place," according to his admirers, and in proof thereof it is pointed out that he was one of the three Americans selected by Lübke[1] as worthy of special mention. He was also honored in Rome by being elected as the successor of Crawford to a chair in the Academy of Saint Luke, the oldest art academy in the world.

In 1882 failing health compelled Mr. Rogers to relinquish work in his studio. He died in Rome, Jan. 15, 1892.

[1] " History of Art," Vol. II, p. 611.

CHAPTER IX

RINEHART AND JOHN ROGERS

THE name of William H. Rinehart has come again into public notice within the past few years by reason of the scholarship for which he made provision at the time of his death in 1874. The sum of money which he was able to devote to the education of American sculptors was small, but being allowed to accumulate for nearly a quarter of a century it has increased enough to become important. When, in 1895, its trustees made announcement of their choice of the first beneficiaries of the Rinehart fund, few knew more of Rinehart and his achievements than did the country at large of the two young sculptors who were to profit by his gift.

Mr. Rinehart's life seems to have been as uneventful as that of most of the brotherhood. Born in 1825, the son of a farmer of Carroll County, Maryland, his early years were those of the average farmer's boy until the opening of a quarry on the place gave further scope to his youthful energies. For some reason blasting and hammering appealed to him more than ploughing and harvesting, and in a short time the youth had become assistant to a stone-cutter and mason of the neighborhood. To most people this would appear to be but slight improvement so far as labor was concerned; but natural taste, or a blind instinct, had dictated the change, and to it we doubtless owe the fruition of this artist's life. Farmers are of small use in a city, but a stone-cutter can take care of himself there, and in 1846 the sturdy young man of twenty-one made his way to Baltimore, where he soon obtained employment and quickly demonstrated his intelligence and courage by seeking instruction in the night schools of the Maryland Institute. It is easy to see the importance of this step in the development of the artist, but few realize what heroism it represents. After working a long day of ten or possibly twelve hours at the hardest of all kinds of manual labor, it takes moral courage to devote the evening to study. On his feet continuously from seven in the morning till ten at night, day in and day out — such was the regular programme of the future sculptor.

In 1855 Mr. Rinehart was able to go abroad, and took the usual pathway straight to Italy. His stay was short, but he learned all that he could in the time, and he executed while there two bas-reliefs, "Night" and "Day." Opening a studio in Baltimore upon his return, he soon received orders for several works, among them being a fountain for the old Post-office in Washington, and figures of an "Indian" and a "Backwoodsman," which once supported the clock of the House of Representatives. Maryland was not Italy, however, and the young artist soon found that the fascinations of the Eternal City had taken a strong hold upon him. He was unhappy until he could be once more in that artist world of which Baltimore offered no hint, and he returned to Rome in 1858, there to remain until the time of his death, Oct. 28, 1874.

It is in Baltimore that one may study Mr. Rinehart's work to the best advantage. In the Peabody Institute of that city have been brought together the plaster casts of no fewer than forty-two of his most important figures, busts, and reliefs, besides three of his marbles; while but a few steps from the building is his impressive bronze statue of Chief Justice Taney. Twenty-three of these works are busts, generally bare-breasted and old-fashioned enough in air, but good professional work of their time. While these are never very intimate and can scarcely be said to make one feel acquainted with their subjects, they are well drawn and have a certain largeness of treatment, the result perhaps of this very summariness of characterization. A bust of Mrs. George S. Brown of Baltimore is superior to the average, while the head of the Hon. James M. Mason of Virginia offered a noble type which evidently inspired the sculptor.

The early reliefs of "Day" and "Night" are graceful fancies, but look very lean when compared with the casts of celebrated French decorations which stand near them in the Peabody Institute. They show the untrained hand and mind, even the first principles of relief being neglected. "Day," a little figure almost in the round, resembles Randolph Rogers's "Lost Pleiad" attached to a plaque. "Night" is

FIG. 23.— RINEHART: LATONA AND HER CHILDREN, METROPOLITAN MUSEUM.

even less happy in movement, being occupied in painting stars upon her mantle while she flies, an operation which is obviously inconvenient. A bas-relief head of the sculptor himself shows a handsome bearded man with clean-cut features. The largest cast is the seated portrait of Chief Justice Roger Brooke Taney, which, while lacking all charm of modern technic, is an admirably monumental work. One recognizes in it a fine, dignified characterization of the man, and at any distance the impressive mass makes itself felt. The original bronze is at Annapolis, Maryland, and there is a replica in Mount Vernon Square, Baltimore.

In this very complete collection of Mr. Rinehart's casts there are naturally some insignificant and unworthy works, of which mention need not be made. Others, which may be seen to better advantage in various museums, will be considered later; but there remain several graceful figures which one lingers over with pleasure. One of the earliest is a tall and beautifully proportioned nude, modelled in 1858, and entitled " Entering the Bath." " Strewing Flowers," the original of the bronze upon the grave of Mrs. W. T. Walters, in Greenmount Cemetery, is one of the most satisfying expressions of the American classic school of sculpture. A graceful standing figure, modelled in 1864 and cast in 1865, it possesses a really sculptural distinction coupled with unusual refinement. The bowed head purports to be " Greek," but is considerably tinged by the nineteenth century. The gentle mourner holds a few flowers which the extended right hand drops, one by one, upon the grave. A modification of this figure, in which a wreath of immortelles is substituted for the flowers, was made ten years later, and may be seen also in the Institute.

Another figure, a small and very earnest " Hero," in somewhat the attitude of Dannecker's " Ariadne," waits upon a rock for her lover. The pretty, conventional face wears a frown; the waves which beat around her are too tidily ruffled; but the artist's conception was a beautiful one. This little figure is in marble, well carved; a replica may be seen in the Pennsylvania Academy.

The gem of the collection, however, is the life-size marble nude of " Clytie " (Fig. 24), a work of the year 1872, which vies in distinction with the sculptor's " Latona and her Children," the marble of which is in the Metropolitan Museum. The " Clytie " gives name to a special gallery of the Peabody Institute, where it stands in well-merited prominence. A plaster cast of the figure, in the Corcoran Gallery in Washington, permits of an interesting comparison of this sweet girlish form with Powers's "Greek Slave" in the same building. In grace, in sapiency of handling, in charm of expression, there is no question of the superiority of the "Clytie." The "Greek Slave" is, technically speaking, the effort of a conscientious beginner; the "Clytie," the achievement of a skilled artist. It has its shortcomings, to be sure; the inadequacy of the head, the weakness of the left arm, the obtrusive carving of the sunflower, are sufficiently obvious; but despite all this, the modest grace and freshness of the work make it delightful: a violet would be its fitting symbol rather than the flaunting sunflower.

The Metropolitan Museum of New York contains three valuable examples of Mr. Rinehart's sculpture. The most important of these, "Latona and her Children" (Fig. 23), was carved in 1874, the year of the sculptor's death, and closed with honor a career of unusual significance. The queen mother is shown seated, bending in proud tenderness over her sleeping children. It would have been easy to lapse into sentimentality, — to have depended too much upon those "dear babies," — but the artist has guided his thoughts upon a high plane. This is more than pretty sculpture; it has a measure of breadth and bigness. It shows not only sentiment but construction, good drawing, and beautiful modelling — above all, dignity of conception and of treatment. In the nude forms there is more than a suggestion of mellowness, while even the drapery is less stiff and lean than in most works of its time. Indeed, in comparison with certain famous statues near at hand — its contemporaries — the workmanship is excellent. Accessories, too, are subordinated in such a degree that the group might almost be taken for a product of recent days. It may be added that few of our later sculptures possess the serene poetic charm of Rinehart's "Latona."

"Antigone at the Tomb of her Brother, Polynices" is perhaps the least interesting of Rinehart's larger works, although a well-constructed figure with a good "swing" and wrapped in closely studied drapery of the old school. One turns gladly to the third example of this sculptor's art, which stands near by. This is a graceful

" Rebecca," which, though of life-size, is as charming as a little Tanagra figurine. The maiden holds her pitcher in both hands, supporting it upon the knee. The dainty head is turned a little to one side as though in meditation. One observes that the chiselling of the hair is refined, and that the arms and hands are gracefully modelled. The whole conception is delicate and pure. It is one of the few works in that stately hall which one might covet. The marble is dated 1874, but the original plaster cast in Baltimore (bearing the title, " Woman of Samaria ") is inscribed with the date 1857, which would seem to be a mistake, since the figure could not have been modelled in the United States.

The Corcoran Gallery is enriched by the presence of several of Mr. Rinehart's works. He seems to have had a predilection for sleeping figures — a taste in which many another carver of stone can sympathize, since sleep offers to sculptors the double advantage of a quiescence that is plausible and does away with the necessity of the conventional eye. The closed eyelids are essentially sculptural and contribute in no small measure to the subtle, slightly veiled look of the face so precious to the accomplished modeller. Rinehart's little " Endymion " dreams peacefully in one corner of the room that is dedicated to the " Greek Slave." The less celebrated figure shows a great advance beyond the art of Powers's generation, though it reveals some unfortunate features which mark well its place in the historic sequence. Happily the couch upon which the boy reposes is less irritating to him than it is to the spectator. He is stretched upon a fleece which is quite too carefully elaborated, and the soft forms of the body and the marble wool never lose themselves together. Everywhere a strong black line of shadow separates them like the leaded figures of stained glass windows. With equal consistency the fleece holds itself well aloof from the bank upon which it has been thrown: it can be bounded like a state upon the map, and its head and legs and tail are carefully accounted for. The bank is a poverty-stricken affair, decorated with an occasional rosette of leaves — a stranded starfish on the beach — to symbolize vegetation in general. But these things are all accessories, and we have seen that no one knew how to do accessories in those days. The youthful figure is after all the important matter, and this is sculpturally

N

conceived and full of charm. Its position is easy and its lines graceful. The beautiful body is irreproachable in construction and sufficiently well modelled ; the young face, sweet without being insipid — the face of a handsome boy who sleeps well. The hair is monotonously grooved, but shows good massing. The marble-walled museum does not seem an appropriate resting-place for this little dreamer. One cannot help thinking how much more fit would be the setting of a trellised arbor or a bosquet where the amorous moonlight might steal in and caress the pale form. An Endymion amidst such surroundings would have significance. One wonders if the artist had no such vision. This figure, in bronze, forms an appropriate and touching memorial over the sculptor's grave in Greenmount Cemetery, Baltimore. The replica is in some respects much more beautiful than the marble, showing that the sharpness and severity of certain details of the latter were largely gratuitous on the part of the carver.

The same hall of the Corcoran Gallery contains a bust by Mr. Rinehart, " Penseroso," in which the family traits of the Powers heads reveal themselves. However, a second look will detect the great advance of this work beyond its prototypes by the earlier sculptor. While all of these so-called " ideal " heads resemble each other like cousins, in general effect, and even in certain specific features, such as the machine-made hair, where not a line wanders, there is here, on the other hand, a growing richness of modelling and a hint of character, an approach to personality, which the earlier men of Italian training sedulously avoided in their creations of fancy. Though not approaching the interest of Palmer's native types, the " Penseroso " has a certain charm; the profile in partic-ular is almost intelligently beautiful.

In another hall of the same building is a replica of a group of " Sleeping Children," the original of which is upon a grave in Greenmount Cemetery, Baltimore. One is reminded of Chantrey's pretty sleepers in Lichfield Cathedral. The two babies lie snug-gled together, the one with a protecting hand thrown over the other. The little couch with its comfortable mattress and pillow looks odd in sculpture; but the figures are well done, and the drapery is pleasingly arranged and carefully wrought. Such a

subject may seem trivial, but its success depends largely on its treatment. This group is certainly a work of art. Its sentiment and
its execution together make it important, like Jean Dampt's babies
and those fascinating little nestlings in the arms of Paul Dubois's
"Charity." The delightful heads and chubby arms remind one
of the latter; they are true baby heads, lovingly done, and no one
can look at them without a
feeling that the artist was
very happy in his work.

Surely, too, he must have
had a consciousness of its excellence. He must have been
aware that, whether recognized
or not, he was doing the most
beautiful sculpture that any
American had yet produced in
Italy, giving it a delicacy and
refinement unknown to his colleagues. His subjects, to be
sure, are, as a rule, the old hack-
neyed themes, — he is strictly
with his contemporaries in that
regard, — but as he looked
about him, the modest, unheralded Southerner saw no
rival in Powers and Rogers and
Story, famous though they had
become. The man who created

FIG. 24. — RINEHART: CLYTIE, PEABODY INSTITUTE.

the "Latona" and the "Endymion" need not begrudge them their
oft-repeated "Eves" and "Nydias" and "Cleopatras." These archaic
works, the puerilities of Ives, the ineptitudes of Mozier, the futile
strivings of Hart, must have amused or saddened him; but one
fancies that he did not concern himself so very much with the
question, "Who shall be greatest?" He simply toiled on with
diligence and good cheer, repaid in full by the work itself. And
now, nearly thirty years after his death, we are beginning to discover him and to think of him as one of the living men.

Rinehart was among the last of American sculptors to espouse classicism, though its traditions were continued for some time after his death by others of our artists who remained abroad. Not a few, however, of his contemporaries began early to show a tendency toward frank realism, a phase of sculpture which was destined to reach much prominence within a short time. No art could be more opposed to Rinehart's measured utterance than was the vigorously native expression of John Rogers. So abrupt is the change that it may be well to introduce the home-products by a brief reference — in the nature of comment — to work in a related field of artistic endeavor.

A generous thought was voiced by a well-known novelist of the day at an authors' dinner in London, when he told his colleagues they must face the fact that to the mass of the people literature was a blank page. In his opinion the duty of the author was to choose the audience of the highest class he was capable of reaching, and when he had chosen it, to do the best work he could. The duty of the critic was to recognize what audience the author was capable of reaching, not to take him too seriously, and not to tell him that, because he could not achieve the highest of all things, therefore he was not worth anything at all. This kindly counsel may apply with no less pertinence to other fields of criticism. Particularly in dealing with the early, half-starved art of the United States, is one impelled to follow the suggestion of that other genial critic who not long since concluded a column of keen analysis with the remorseful after-thought, " Perhaps, after all, we should praise a book [work] for what it is rather than blame it for what it is not."

To that very considerable public which has looked upon John Rogers as our greatest, if not our only sculptor, these introductory words may seem ungracious. There are to-day, however, as many more to whom a little knowledge has become a dangerous thing, and who have so far outgrown the " Rogers groups " that they do not even recognize them as sculpture. It is for the benefit of these austere critics that the above conciliatory citations are made. And for their yet further benefit it may be urged that, to the army of simple-minded admirers of " Weighing the Baby " and " Checkers on the Farm," must be joined a smaller group of thoughtful men and women

who see in Mr. Rogers's work something deeper than its indiscrimi-
nate realism and its misplaced attempts at humor. They find within
its homely oddities a hint at an indigenous art, an art inspired by the
life of our own time.

The first requisite of any artist is intelligence, and the second
sympathy; but an artist is not compounded of these two elements
alone, else we might at once pronounce John Rogers a great artist,
without further qualification. Other things are required; taste must
enter early into the artistic composition, and mastery must not tarry
far behind. Of the latter Mr. Rogers has enough for his purpose,
and for his public; but in the matter of taste he seems often very deficient. One is not disposed to blame him for his love of homely
subjects, but more beauty might well enter into his interpretation of
them. Else why do sculpture at all? Is it too much to ask that
there should be a sculptural sense and a fitness of theme to the
chosen material? Such considerations have troubled Mr. Rogers
but little; he elaborates for us a counter laden with the treasures of
a country store or a scheme involving two or three church pews, with
as much satisfaction as he shows in constructing that really monumental group, "One More Shot" (Fig. 25). Beauty, either cor-
poreal or decorative, makes slight appeal to him, and he is weakest
when he attempts such expression. It is evident, then, that his work
must be measured by other standards than those which we apply to
the achievements of Saint Gaudens and French. George Barnard
and John Rogers have at least a continent's space between them.
One is a sculptor "by first intention," the latter a story-teller who
has chosen a plastic medium for expression. But work as distinctive
and widely welcome as that of Mr. Rogers has been is not to be sum-
marily suppressed nor ignored. This interesting man has made a real
contribution to American art as well as to American history. It is
not within our power, even if we so willed, to cast the "Rogers groups"
into outer darkness.

They have been compared to chromos, but this is manifestly
unjust. Some of them, to be sure, are infinitely less artistic than
certain chromos, for a chromo may bear the design if not the color
of a masterpiece, and there is no masterpiece of designing among
Mr. Rogers's creations. These are tiny men and women, "taken

just as they come," and without thought as to how they will look
best.   But herein lies their excellence as well.   They are spontaneous and they are expressive in their straightforward way, — so
much we must acknowledge, — and these are very good things to
find in any art.

Mr. Rogers has a method of generalization all his own.   His
figures are not literal transcripts; their treatment, though precise, is
summary.   However trivial the thought, it always dominates the
execution.   Mr. Rogers is no Italian carver, in love with textures;
he corresponds more nearly to our painters, Thomas Hovenden and
J. G. Brown; he is full of his story, and insists on telling it in his
own way.   It is true that the primitive appeal of his groups is to
the uncultivated, but there is nothing flashy or exaggerated in their
sentiment.   They are as honest and as inelegant as a stable boy.
But while their stolidity is often amusing, they are alive.   The
joints of his *dramatis personæ* may creak a little, but there are no
lay figures among them.   Each character plays his part as industri-
ously and conscientiously as though the fate of the nation depended
upon it.   One understands them readily, for their mental equipment
is devoid of subtle complexities.   Their little clay brains are as free
from conflicting emotions as are their faces and clothes from suavity
of modelling.   Their smiles and frowns have been incised with the
same sharp chisel which has shaped their shoes.   But they are real
little personalities, and each one of them stands for an idea.   They
tell their story, and in spite of all their uncouthness and simplicity,
or by reason of it, they have appealed to thousands, who have found
in them their first introduction to sculpture.

Mr. Rogers was born in Salem, Massachusetts, Oct. 30, 1829.
He is of New England colonial ancestry.   His father, John Rogers
of Boston, was the son of Daniel Denison Rogers, a merchant of
that city, and his mother was the daughter of John Derby, a merchant of Salem.   He was educated in a New England common
school, and on leaving it found employment in a store.   He began
the study of civil engineering, but having strained his eyes, went, at
the age of nineteen, into a machine shop at Manchester, New Hampshire, as an apprentice.   He worked up through all the branches,
including the draughting room and office, and finally had charge of a

railroad repair shop in the West. During the first seven years of this life he remained quite unaware of his own talent. One day while in Boston he chanced to see a man modelling images in clay. The sight fired him with an ambition to experiment in the same field. He was bound to his trade during fourteen hours of the day, but in his scanty leisure he learned the use of modelling tools and materials, and soon developed an intense longing to devote himself to the fascinating art.

Finally, toward the close of 1858, he was able to make a trip to Europe in order to see and learn something of sculpture. He was absent about eight months, visiting Paris and Rome; but, as Tuckerman puts it, " Not perceiving how he could turn his style of design to account, and having no great sympathy for the classic style " (which one may well believe), he returned much disheartened, and abandoning all thought of making sculpture a profession, engaged as draughtsman in the office of the city surveyor of Chicago. The hours of work were not long, however, and the ingenious young draughtsman soon felt himself irresistibly drawn to his favorite employment, and amused himself with the construction of a group of small figures which he styled " The Checker Players." This was exhibited at a charity fair in Chicago, " where it attracted great attention and was highly praised for its faithfulness in details, which is a characteristic of all his works."

Encouraged by this success, Mr. Rogers resigned his situation, and devoted himself exclusively and enthusiastically to his new-found art. His first important work was the " Slave Auction," which he modelled in Chicago and took to New York in 1860, where it was exhibited. Owing to the excitement then prevalent over the slave question, it attracted much attention. The Civil War now brought into view a host of subjects which Mr. Rogers treated effectively and with much patriotic fervor. He hired a large attic studio at 599 Broadway, and there devoted himself zealously to the production of the groups which have given him his reputation. These were reproduced in a peculiar composition, in moulds made over bronze models. A New York journal of forty years ago tells us how these works were received : —

" All day and every day, week in and week out, there is an ever changing crowd of men, women, and children standing stationary amid the ever surging tides of Broadway, before the windows of Williams and Stevens, gazing with eager interest upon the statuettes and groups of the sculptor, John Rogers.   These works appeal to a deep popular sentiment.   They are not pretentious displays of gods, goddesses, ideal characters, or stupendous, world-compelling heroes.   They are illustrations of American domestic, and especially of American military, life — not of our great generals or our bold admirals or the men whose praises fill all the newspapers, but of the common soldier of the Union ; not of the common soldier, either, in what might be called his high heroic moods and moments, when, with waving sword and flaming eye, he dashes upon the enemy's works, but of the soldier in the ordinary moments and usual occupations of everyday camp life.   For the last year or more Mr. Rogers has been at work mainly on groups of this latter class and character.   Thus he has given us 'The Returned Volunteer, or How the Fort was Taken,' being a group of three gathered in a blacksmith's shop, the characters consisting of the blacksmith himself, standing with his right foot on the anvil-block and his big hammer in his hand, listening eagerly, with his little girl, to a soldier who sits close by on his haunches, narrating 'how the fort was taken.'   We have also another group of three, 'The Picket Guard,' spiritedly sketched, as in eager, close, and nervous search for the enemy ; the 'Sharp-shooters,' another group of three, or rather of two men and a scarecrow, illustrating a curious practice in our army of deceiving the enemy ; the 'Town Pump,' a scene in which a soldier, uniformed and accoutred, is slaking his thirst and holding blessed converse beside the pump with a pretty girl who has come for a pail of water ; the 'Union Refugees,' a pathetic and noble group, consisting of a stalwart and sad-faced east Tennesseean or Virginian, who, accompanied by his wife who leans her head upon his bosom, and by his little boy who looks up eagerly into his face, has started off from home with only his gun upon his shoulder and his powder-horn by his side to escape the tyranny of the rebels ; the 'Camp Fire, or Making Friends with the Cook,' in which a hungry soldier, seated upon an inverted basket, is reading a newspaper to an 'intelligent contraband,' who is stirring the tempting contents of a huge and ebullient pot hung over the fire; 'Wounded to the Rear, or One More Shot,' in which a soldier is represented as dressing his wounded leg, while his companion, with his left arm in a sling, is trying to load his gun to take another shot at the enemy, toward whom he looks defiantly; 'Mail Day,' which tells its own story of a speculative soldier, seated on a stone and racking his poor brains to find some ideas to transcribe upon the paper which he holds upon his knee, to be sent, perchance, to her he loves; 'The Country Postmaster, or News from the Army,' which, though a scene from civil life, tells of the anxiety of the soldier's wife or sweetheart to get tidings from the brave volunteer who is perilling his life on the battlefield; 'The Wounded Scout, or a Friend in the Swamp,' representing a soldier, torn and bleeding and far gone, rescued and raised up by a faithful and kind-souled negro, which, we think, is one of the best, if not the

FIG. 25. — ROGERS: ONE MORE SHOT.

very best of Mr. Rogers's works; and lastly, a group called 'The Home Guard, or Midnight on the Border,' in which a heroic woman, accompanied by a little girl, is represented as stepping out, pistol in hand, to confront the assailants of her humble home."

Some of these certainly were among his best; they had a reason for their existence, and an emotional as well as a sculptural unity; but in many of them, as in most of the later ones, the group is "group" only in name, the figures being scattered as upon the stage of a theatre.   Mr. Jarves once wrote high eulogies on his friend, saying among other things: "We know of no sculptor like John Rogers of New York in the Old World, and he stands alone in his chosen field, heretofore in all ages appropriated by painting" — thus noting with approval one of Mr. Rogers's weakest points and praising him for his excursions into a territory properly belonging to another art.

However, "One More Shot," "Union Refugees," and a number more are admirably sculptural in conception and, as Jarves claims, "thoroughly American in the best sense of the word." Among the later groups, "The Charity Patient" is especially notable for its tender pathos.   "The Slave's Story" and "Council of War" attracted much attention for the excellent portraits of famous men which they presented, the first including those of Whittier, Garrison, and Beecher, and the second those of Lincoln, Grant, and Stanton.

Equally good is the portrait of Joseph Jefferson in the scenes from "Rip Van Winkle," but in most of the later works the composition is hopelessly diffused and the subject of slight interest.

Mr. Rogers was made a full member of the National Academy in 1863.   He exhibited in the Paris Exposition of 1867 three groups in bronze, — "One More Shot" "Taking the Oath," and "The Wounded Scout."   At the Centennial he had no fewer than twenty-nine groups, and at the Columbian Exposition he received a gold medal for his dignified seated figure of Lincoln.   Another effort in sculpture of heroic size is his well-known equestrian statue of General John F. Reynolds, which stands before the City Hall of Philadelphia.

CHAPTER X

OTHER SCULPTORS BORN BEFORE 1830

During this middle period flourished a great number of sculptors of the second magnitude, men who were less renowned than Story and less artists than Palmer and Ball, but who are nevertheless entitled to honorable mention in any history of American sculpture. The most prominent of these names are Rimmer, Gould, Richard Greenough, Bartholomew, Akers, Jackson, and Volk.

Dr. William Rimmer achieved a unique reputation in the East, but his share in the development of American sculpture is not easily defined. His anatomical knowledge and his enthusiasm were extraordinary, and doubtless left their imprint upon many students as well as upon the public at large, which he interested to a certain degree ; but his own works, however remarkable when the method of their production is considered, were valueless as sculpture. He persisted in executing nudes, and even important monumental commissions, without models, and while he " never missed a muscle nor forgot an attachment," the results are curious rather than edifying. This interesting man was born at Liverpool, England, in 1816. His father was a French refugee, whose real name is not known. Dr. Rimmer studied and practised medicine for a time, painting portraits and religious pictures between calls. He carved in granite, in 1861, the " Head of Saint Stephen," which is now in the Boston Museum of Fine Arts, — a strange primitive conception with exaggerated muscles — and produced, soon after, the yet more archaic " Falling Gladiator." In 1864 he executed, in two weeks, the model of the much-discussed granite figure of Alexander Hamilton, on Commonwealth Avenue, Boston, thereby debarring himself from further opportunity in Boston. An " Osiris," his favorite work, followed. A "Dying Centaur" (about 1871) and a group of "Fighting Lions" complete the list of his actual works, though his projects fill a book, as his dreams peopled the entire world in which he dwelt. His "Art Anatomy," published in 1887, is a wonder of erudition, comprising the notes and illustrations of his many lectures before the Lowell Institute, Boston, the National Academy in New York, and the Boston Museum of Fine Arts. He died at South Milford, Massachusetts, in 1879.

Dr. Rimmer's services as a teacher of anatomy receive full recognition from his biographer, Mr. Truman H. Bartlett.[1] "His method of teaching was new, and would be so to-day. He drew in chalk, upon a blackboard, every bone and muscle with which the artist need be acquainted; first, as an independent fact, and then in its relations to the formation of the complete figure." Each member was drawn in turn, and finally the entire figure itself. So far as delineation and explanation could answer in a system of art education, this method sufficed. Though what it offered was "the teaching of the lecture room," rather than that "seriously discovered and applied knowledge" which serves longest and best, yet "it seemed to be precisely what was needed by the persons who attended the lectures." At any rate, they received this advantage : their instruction "came through the inspiring medium of a strong man." The same writer, in the *American Art Review* for 1880, referring to Rimmer's course of lectures at the Lowell Institute during the winter of 1863–1864, states that it "was attended by the leading artists and many of the physicians and professional men of Boston and vicinity, all of whom agreed in gladly testifying that it was the most learned and splendid exhibition of art anatomical knowledge they had ever seen."

Thomas Gould (born 1818), a merchant of refined nature and artistic inclinations, took up the study of sculpture somewhat late in life, modelling his first figure in the studio of Seth Cheney, a portrait painter of Boston, in the year 1851. The study, begun as a diversion, made strong appeal to Mr. Gould's poetic nature, and when, some years later, the war swept away his modest fortune and ended his business career, he turned without regret to art for solace and

[1] "The Art Life of William Rimmer," by Truman H. Bartlett, pp. 40, 41.

for support. We are told that he produced in rapid succession busts of John A. Andrew, Ralph Waldo Emerson (now owned by Harvard University), Michael Angelo, and the elder Booth, who, with his son Edwin, was an intimate friend of the sculptor. His colossal heads of " Christ " and " Satan " were exhibited in the Boston Athenæum in 1863, but were afterward removed to Mr. Gould's studio in Florence. Jarves pronounced the " Christ," as an opposing conception to that of " Satan," to be " one of the finest felt and conceived idealisms in modern sculpture." [1]

In 1868 Mr. Gould removed with his family to Florence, where he modelled the following year his statue of the " West Wind " (Fig. 26), probably his most celebrated work. This figure was reproduced several times in marble, and became especially prominent in 1874 through a charge that it was, with the exception of the drapery, a reproduction of Canova's " Hebe," the garment being attributed to an Italian modeller. It is pleasant to learn that while " animated newspaper correspondence followed the charge, it was proved groundless."

It would have been to the advantage of the ambitious amateur if he had followed more closely so graceful a model, for although adjudged worthy of admittance to the Centennial Exposition, the " West Wind " lacks that beauty which would give it permanent value. The thought, though slight, is pretty enough, and had it found a true sculptural expression, might have been well worth while. But this is begging the question. It is the same as saying that if the " West Wind " had been done by a real sculptor, it might have been beautiful, as it certainly would have been different. Mr. Gould, although so poetic in nature and delighting as he did in the processes of the art, was no sculptor, and never showed the sculptor's approach to any subject. Instead of seizing instinctively upon " the strongest and most statuesque aspect of a theme," he demonstrates in every line of this childish work his utter inability to conceive an artistic whole. Comparing the " West Wind " with the earliest of American sculptures, Mr. Rush's " Nymph of the Schuylkill," or even with the " Jephthah's Daughter " of the obscure wood-carver of New Haven, the latter will be found to be far more professional and more

[1] " Art Thoughts," p. 319.

beautiful. Indeed, our native art offers few examples of a more frankly helpless treatment of the human figure than is shown in the front view of the " West Wind " as it stands in the Mercantile Library of St. Louis. From the feet on tiptoe, turned at right angles to each other, up to the ill-modelled head, every form of the stiff body betrays the weakness of an untrained hand and the groping of an unclarified vision. On the side toward which the face is turned the result is not quite so bad. The deep-cut ledges and con- volutions of the drapery give a certain breeziness of effect, or a symbol of the same, further enhanced by flying ringlets, or, more properly, stringlets. The face is refined in intention, and has rather a sweet expression, showing what the artist was trying to do. Nothing could be more conclusive of the authenticity of this work than the despairing way in which the skirt is brought abruptly to an end at the waist and gathered into a belt, where the sculptor has " pinned it with a star." No Italian assistant could ever have shown such ineptitude!

Among Mr. Gould's later works of imagination were a " Cleo- patra "; a curious relief of a helmeted head, which he called the " Ghost in Hamlet "; and a " Timon of Athens." In Forest Hills Cemetery, West Roxbury, is his " Ascending Spirit." His " Ariel " is in the possession of Mrs. Grossman, the daughter of Edwin Booth, and his " Undine " is owned by the Boston Art Club. In 1875 Mr. Gould produced statues of John Hancock and of Massachusetts' war governor, John A. Andrew; the former being placed in the town hall of Lexington, Massachusetts, the latter in the cemetery at Hingham. He made also a colossal bronze of King Kamehameha I, which was erected before the government building at Honolulu, Sandwich Islands. His last order was for a " Puritan," a figure completed after his death, by his son, and now standing on Cambridge Com- mon near Harvard University.

Mr. Gould died in 1881. As may be inferred, his direct contri- bution to significant sculpture was slight, but his culture and personal worth must have had their influence in raising the moral standard of the profession and in developing that respect with which it is viewed to-day by the American public.

Richard Saltonstall Greenough, a younger brother of Horatio

FIG. 26. — GOULD: WEST WIND, MERCANTILE LIBRARY, ST. LOUIS.

Greenough, was born at Jamaica Plain, Massachusetts, in 1819, and practised his art in Paris at the beginning of his professional career. Mr. Greenough returned to the United States and lived for several years in Newport, Rhode Island, during which time he produced a number of works in bronze and marble. In 1847 he again went abroad to spend the remainder of his life in Europe. Among his works are a statue of Franklin, in the City Hall Square of Boston; the "Boy and Eagle," owned by the Boston Athenæum; a "Carthaginian Woman," "Cupid on a Tortoise," "Elaine," "Circe," and a "Psyche," which he erected as a monument to his wife in the cemetery at Rome, Italy. He was said to be "particularly successful as a sculptor of portrait busts"; but these must be in private hands, since they do not appear in the catalogues nor galleries of the art museums of the East.

Mr. Greenough's "Boy and Eagle," in the Boston Athenæum, is fairly well modelled, and has a certain picturesque value. It is sufficiently spirited to arrest the attention, though it can hardly be pronounced interesting. The exigencies of sculpture have compelled the artist to reduce the eagle to "portable" size. The youth is making gentle effort to release himself from the winged incubus which has settled upon his back. The hawk-like bird is hard to get at, and our sympathies might be mildly aroused were we sure that the boy cared very much himself. He never extorts from one the cry, "Oh, the poor man!" as did Puget's "Milo of Crotona" from the emotional Maria Theresa. It must be acknowledged that some of Richard Greenough's portrait statues are more likely to call forth such an exclamation.

His "Franklin," executed in Boston in 1855, stands in front of the City Hall, and appears to the casual observer a very commonplace work. The bronze reliefs which decorate the pedestal picture events in the life of the philosopher; two of them were modelled by Thomas Ball. Mr. Greenough's better known "Governor Winthrop" (Fig. 27) stands in Scollay Square, Boston, and a replica in marble (dated 1876) is to be found among the effigies in the sculpture gallery of the national Capitol. It is not a spirited work, although in technical merits it is above the average of its time. The figure advances with a good stride on carefully drawn legs, and

o

the disposition of the arms is happy and sculpturally massive.   The hands in particular are well placed and well modelled, the right holding the charter and great seal, the left clasping a book, probably the Bible, to the breast.   But here the excellences of the work seem to end abruptly; they are, indeed, quite lost sight of in the weakness of the total effect, a result of the characterless head which emerges as an anticlimax from the enormous ruff of the period.   The drapery has no great amount of color, but it is respectable, with a good enough figure underneath, and one finds on covering up the pathetic face that the statue has possibilities.   Between the black and the white versions there is little to choose, however, in the matter of virility.   They vie with each other in their self-depreciation, in their appeal to our sympathy.   The fact is that so mild mannered an individual would scarcely presume to stand upon his feet and to walk like a man.   It is gratifying, therefore, to discover the same subject represented in marble at Mount Auburn in a seated pose. Like the preceding, this statue has much better drawing and modelling than we are at first inclined to give it credit for, since the attitude is that of hopeless dejection, and the expression of the face is in perfect harmony therewith.   Indeed, the wan, wistful countenance, the hands clasped on the left knee, and the round shoulders suggest nothing so much as a world-weary schoolboy, the scapegoat of the class, ever prepared for the worst, and even now leaning forward in resigned expectation of the rod of the oppressor.

After such an impression one is surprised to find in the Boston Museum of Fine Arts an interesting and almost spirited figure from the same hands, the " Carthaginian Girl," a marble of about three-fourths life-size.   It represents one of the fair defenders of the doomed city, cutting her long hair, presumably for bowstrings. While it is not very well modelled, the arms in particular being strangely round, the pose is a felicitous one and the general effect good.   The expression, too, is rather noble and pathetic.   The figure comes near being attractive and even distinguished.

Edward Sheffield Bartholomew was born at Colchester, Connecticut, in 1822.   His life was most closely associated, however, with Hartford, where his " Eve " is the most important work of sculpture in the Wadsworth Athenæum.   It is almost good sculpture, judged even by the stricter canons of to-day. This figure is massive, is sculpturally conceived, and from some views is not only expressive, but really fine. The head droops despairingly, the hands lie idle in the lap. The inclination of the head, it must be acknowledged, is not quite fortunate; it gives the figure a look of uneasy equilibrium, which from certain points is weak rather than tragic. But the proportions are admirable, and parts, like the full knees, show more fleshy modelling than we have seen before in our chronological progress. The arms are full and handsome, though in construction and elaboration not quite up to the requirements of modern taste. The feet have the conventional roundness of their kind; but there is a suspicion of bones in the toes — a new feature. In the face the artist is only too faithful to the tradition of Powers and all the other compelling influences of the time. It is not devoid of expression, but one feels that the expression is only a formula for grief, and that there is no personality here — nothing that could possibly awaken sympathy.

The abundant hair is string-like and not cleverly carved. After the fashion of the day, and of Italian carvers in general, these deficiencies were supposably atoned for by the emphasis and polish expended upon other details which we prefer to see merely suggested. The fateful apple lies upon the ground, where it may not be overlooked. A tiny bite made by even incisors is turned conspicuously to the front, giving a touch of realism, an accuracy of circumstantial evidence which detracts from the poetic power of the misty old legend. The serpent's head appears under an elaborate tuft of leaves which he seems to wear like an absurd little bonnet. Beyond he winds his sinuous length around the masonry-like rock, a marvel of scaly finish. Ivy and other plants are seen here and there, cleverly carved, but so scattered, so precise, and of so many kinds as to be bewildering.

Hawthorne was not in an appreciative mood the day that he saw this figure in Rome, as the following testifies: "We have likewise been to Mr. B——'s studio, where we saw several pretty statues and busts, and among them an 'Eve,' with her wreath of fig leaves lying across her poor nudity; comely in some points, but with a frightful volume of thighs and calves. I do not see the necessity of ever

sculpturing another nakedness. Man is no longer a naked animal;
his clothes are as natural to him as his skin, and sculptors have no
more right to undress him than to flay him." [1]

Eight little reliefs inserted in the octagonal pedestal of this
statue of " Eve " give intimate glimpses of the primitive home circle.
The figures are almost in the round. Some are rather awkwardly
handled, others are exceedingly graceful. The total effect is decorative, the very naïveté of the treatment having its special appeal.
One feels enthusiasm in every touch, and behind it the inspiration
of some potent master like Della Quercia. It should be recalled
that figure and reliefs alike were carved after the sculptor's death,
and doubtless lack much that he would have given them.

In the same building are other works of Bartholomew. A rather
conventional " Sappho " rests her right arm on a convenient post, and
holds her lyre and wreath in the left hand. This figure, being in
marble, occupies a position of honor in the reading room of the
library; while a plaster " Genius of Connecticut," of far more engag-
ing charms, is set away under the backstairs. The latter is an ami-
able-looking girl with pretty face and fluttering curls, seated upon a
bale of merchandise placed in turn on blocks, apparently to keep it
dry; her plump feet are kissed by the surging waves. She holds
a flag patiently and looks gently heroic. Neither modelling nor
drapery is at all bad, but the work is cheapened by the ugly ornamented base. A relief in front shows a ship sore beset upon a
spongy sea. At the ends are dolphins and other stage properties.

Bartholomew modelled also a graceful little " Shepherd Boy of the
Campagna " and two statuettes of real beauty, " Morning Star " and
" Evening Star," conceptions of genuine charm and ideality. These,
with many others of the young sculptor's works, are pictured in a
sympathetic article published in *The Connecticut Quarterly*.[2]

Dead at thirty-six, and for most of the short years of his professional life a physical wreck, this indomitable man carved for himself a permanent if modest place in the history of American sculpture.
Without question he was fired with the divine spark. One can but
ask what such energy might not have accomplished had strength
and fit schooling and long life been vouchsafed.

[1] " Italian Note-Book," Vol. I, p. 179.   [2] Vol. II, No. 3.

FIG. 27. — R. S. GREENOUGH: GOVERNOR WINTHROP, WASHINGTON.

Another whose light failed early was Benjamin Akers — Paul Akers he was generally called, and there is a pretty tradition that the nickname was once Saint Paul, given him because of his pious character. His brief career almost exactly parallels that of his brother sculptor, Bartholomew; he was born in Maine in 1825, three years later than Bartholomew, and died in Philadelphia in 1861, at the age of thirty-five. The most noticeable feature of his childhood was his affection for his forest home and his loneliness when sent away to a school in Norwich, Connecticut. It is said that his earliest impressions of art were gained during this period of banishment by sight of a plaster cast in the house of a certain Francis Finnegan. We are told elsewhere, however, that it was a glimpse of Chantrey's "Washington" in the Massachusetts State House which first thrilled his genius into consciousness. It was in Boston, at any rate, that he subsequently (1849) learned the art of plaster-casting from one Joseph Carew, after having tried his hand at printing and various other professions, including painting. Naturally, the first step in his art education was to open a studio and practise on his sitters: such seems to have been the custom of the time. This he did in Portland, in association with a painter named Tilton. Busts of Longfellow, Samuel Appleton of Boston, Professor Cleaveland, and others gave him reputation and the means for going abroad, which he was able to do in 1852, spending a year in study in Florence. Upon his return he modelled his first figure, "Benjamin in Egypt," which was lost in the destruction by fire of the Portland Exchange. He found much employment in Washington, modelling various prominent men, including Edward Everett and sturdy Sam Houston of Texas. Once more in Europe, in 1854, he produced a series of ideal works, of which his "Una and the Lion," "Isaiah," "Diana and Endymion," "Saint Elizabeth of Hungary," and the "Pearl Diver," a beautiful figure of a drowned youth, enjoyed the greatest fame. This latter work, as well as the same artist's fine bust of Milton, was appropriated by Hawthorne, together with Story's "Cleopatra," for the furnishing of the sculptor Kenyon's imaginary studio in "The Marble Faun." [1]

[1] The reader will find further details of this singularly pure and attractive character in the last pages of Tuckerman's "Book of the Artists."

A group in the Metropolitan Museum, signed " J. A. Jackson, 1867," represents " Eve finding Abel," and gives a first impression of being excellent work.   The composition is good, though not notably original, since one recognizes in it the familiar arrangement of many Pietàs: " The mother bending with grief and wonder over the figure which rests upon her knee."   A closer examination shows that there is no real mastery here, the modelling being thin and tiresome — strangely lean, indeed, as though the horror of the moment had been long anticipated.   The expression of the mother is disagreeably overdone, reminding one of Story's sinister heroines. The work is creditable, however, as a whole, being a serious attempt in the right direction, and produces a striking effect from a distance. A bust of Wendell Phillips in the Boston Athenæum, and another of Dr. G. W. Bethune in the Sage Library at New Brunswick, New Jersey, cannot be so highly commended, since from all distances and all directions they show themselves to be rather weak work.

John Adams Jackson was born at Bath, Maine, in 1825.   Apprenticed early to a merchant of Boston, he gradually discovered his aptitude for art and studied drawing, supporting himself by portraiture in crayon and in sculpture.   He received instruction for a time in Paris under Suisse, and later opened a studio in New York. There is something not fully explained in the statement that " he was sent to Italy, commissioned to execute a statue of Dr. Kane, the Arctic explorer; but failing to carry out this commission at the time, found himself without means to return to America, and consequently remained abroad, fixing his residence at Florence."

The product of this enforced exile was the " Eve finding Abel," above mentioned.   He made a number of busts and many statuettes with fanciful names; a medallion entitled " Morning Glory " was reproduced fourteen times, and his statue " Musidora " was exhibited at the Vienna Exposition in 1873.   A Soldiers' Monument at Lynn, Massachusetts, is also his work.   He died at Pracchia, Tuscany, in 1879.

Mention may be made also of Edwin E. Brackett, who was born in Maine, in 1819.   This early sculptor began his professional career in 1838 and is remembered for his portrait busts of Bryant, Longfellow, Allston, Sumner, Choate, Butler, John Brown, Garrison, Wendell Phillips, and others.   His group " The Shipwrecked Mother," is in Mount Auburn Cemetery.   Even Jarves found something kind to say of Brackett's portraiture, praising extravagantly a certain work.

"Brackett's bust of Brown (owned by Mrs. G. Stearns of Medford), exhibiting with Olympian breadth of sentiment the intense moral heroism of the reformer, is an American type of Jove; one of those rare surprises in art, irrespective of technical finish or perfection in modelling, which shows in what high degree the artist was impressed by the soul of his sitter."

Leonard Volk, long time the only sculptor in Chicago, was born at Wellstown, New York, Nov. 7, 1828.   From a notice printed at the time of his death, August, 1895, we learn that : —

" He was given little schooling, and at the age of sixteen learned the trade of marble-cutting with his father.   As he grew older he determined to become a sculptor.   He therefore moved to St. Louis and opened a modest little studio.   It was a raw, western town, where statuary was not so much appreciated as cattle herds, and corn, and he had many obstacles to overcome.   Among his first productions was a bust in marble of Henry Clay, a copy from Hart's bust. Not long after this he was visited by Stephen A. Douglas, who was so pleased with the young sculptor's work that he offered to defray his expenses for a trip to Rome to study art.   Accordingly, Mr. Volk, leaving his wife and child in the Massachusetts home of his parents, got out and devoted himself assiduously to the study of his art for a year and a half.

" In June, 1857, he came to Chicago and opened a studio in Clark Street, opposite the Sherman House, and almost immediately he became identified with every art movement of the city.   He was one of the prime movers in the first exhibition of fine arts held in that city in 1859.   Later he assisted in founding the Academy of Design in Chicago, of which early institution he was for eight years the president.   Mr. Volk made two other visits to Europe to study, and in 1872 he ordered, at Geneva, the first shipment of Carrara marble ever made direct to Chicago."

Among Mr. Volk's more important works are the Douglas Monument in Chicago; a bust of President Lincoln, exhibited at Paris in 1867; statues of Lincoln and Douglas, in the Illinois State House, executed.from life studies; the statuary on the Soldiers' Monument for Erie County, New York, the first monument of the kind erected in this country; the Soldiers' Monument, with statues, at Rock Island, Illinois; and in the last year of his life another military memorial at Rochester, New York. His last work was a bronze figure of General Shields, presented by Illinois to the National Hall of Statuary at Washington.

Mr. Volk's contribution, aside from his efforts for art education in Chicago, was in the form of faithful portraiture. His " Faith " and " Ione," like the four seated figures around the Douglas Monument, could hardly have been considered great sculpture even in their time; but among his portrait busts of Elihu B. Washburne, David Davis, Zachariah Chandler, J. H. McVicker, and many others of prominence are to be found a number of strong types conscientiously portrayed. If without poetic grace, they are at least sturdily authentic, and therefore of great interest to succeeding generations. His bust of Lincoln is simple and dignified, while his statue in the Capitol at Springfield shows, though in a rather cramped fashion, the arrangement so successfully used by Saint Gaudens many years later, the figure of the President standing in front of the "chair of state." It is probable that Mr. Volk was the only sculptor privileged to model the features of Lincoln from life. His life mask and casts of the hands have been reproduced often, and were, of course, invaluable to later sculptors.

CHAPTER XI

ONE of the surviving "classicists," a product of the old-time Roman school, is Miss Harriet Hosmer, who is doubtless the most famous of American women sculptors. Her picturesque personality, as well as her artistic achievement, commands notice. The following account of her early life is almost in her own words.

Born in Watertown, Massachusetts, Oct. 6, 1830, the daughter of a physician, "she inherited a delicate constitution from her mother, who died of consumption; and her father encouraged her to follow a course of physical exercise such as boys only, at that period, were accustomed to take. She became expert in rowing, riding, skating, and shooting; developed powers of great endurance; scandalized the neighbors by climbing trees whenever birds' nests tempted her; filled her room, boylike, with snakes, insects, and other specimens of natural history, which she dissected or preserved; and, in a clay pit in her father's garden, modelled figures of animals. Her first instructor was a Mr. Peabody, brother-in-law of Nathaniel Hawthorne, who found it impossible to teach by his conventional methods the undisciplined child, and, in despair, returned her to her father. Mrs. Sedgwick, who had a school for young ladies at Lenox, was noted for her success in difficult cases of this kind. Harriet was placed under her care, which was exercised with such tact that the child's breezy, independent nature was disciplined almost unconsciously, and the teacher gained the love and confidence of the pupil. Three years were spent at Lenox, and then Miss Hosmer went to Boston to study drawing and modelling under an artist, Mr. Stephenson. Her sex debarred her from entering the Boston Medical School, whose course in anatomy she was anxious to take; and hearing that the medical college in St. Louis would admit her, she removed to that city. She made her home in the family of Wayman Crow, father of one of her old school friends, and from that gentleman she received her first order of a statue from Rome. Professor McDowell, of the Medical School, under whom the sculptors Powers and Clevenger had studied anatomy, was particularly kind to Miss Hosmer; and, in return, she made a medallion portrait of him after a bust by Clevenger."

After a very independent trip alone up and down the Mississippi, the young sculptor returned to her home, where she practised modelling and marble-cutting until the autumn of 1852, when with her father and Charlotte Cushman she took passage for Italy. In Rome she became the pupil of the English sculptor Gibson, with whom she remained for seven years. Her first works were ideal heads, " Daphne " and " Medusa," which were exhibited in Boston in 1853. In 1855 she had completed the commission given her by Mr. Crow, sending him her first life-size figure, " Ænone," the shepherd-wife whom Paris deserted for Helen, a marble which is now in the St. Louis Museum of Fine Arts. This is a well-conceived figure, gracefully seated and vigorously turned. If the modelling were as good as the pose, it would be an excellent work. The handling is not powerful, however, and the mournful face is uninteresting. The success of this first attempt brought immediate response, and in 1857 Miss Hosmer's " Beatrice Cenci " (Fig. 28) was ready for its destination in the Mercantile Library of St. Louis. It can hardly be claimed that this is a great work, but it has much grace, and its beauty is of a very intelligible kind. The pose is an expressive one, the fair prisoner being shown asleep on her hard couch, lying on her side with the upper part of the body turned so that the bosom rests on the pallet. The head is pillowed on the right arm, while the left, which is bare like the shoulder, has fallen, the hand resting on the floor and holding lightly a polished rosary. The right knee comes forward, and the long line of the back and of the left leg, which extends to the floor, is admirable; it could scarcely be improved. The figure is as well modelled as it is composed, and the carving of the drapery is very refined. The accessories are annoyingly pronounced; the pillow, the beads, the large ring in the stone slab, and the dainty slipper, all being too sharp and insistent for modern taste, but the conception, and in the main the execution, could hardly have been surpassed in the Roman colony of the fifties. This figure was exhibited in London and later in several cities of the United States.

Miss Hosmer's next effort was the celebrated " Puck," a work of slight importance excepting for the fact that it had an immense vogue and that the marble-cutters were kept busy night and day, so to speak, turning out replicas. Thirty of these were made, and the conscientious historians inform us that the profits amounted to

FIG. 28. — HOSMER: BEATRICE CENCI, MERCANTILE LIBRARY, ST. LOUIS.

$30,000. It is an amusing little figure, with pretty, roguish face. The short, puffy legs are drawn up on a large toadstool, and one hand holds a beetle while the other grasps a lizard. A pair of batlike wings supplement the figure; the ground is strewn with mushrooms of various species and well-defined characteristics. A companion piece, " Will-o'-the-Wisp," followed " Puck."

In the winter of 1857–1858, Miss Hosmer executed a figure reclining on a sarcophagus, a portrait of the beautiful daughter of a Madame Falconet, an English Catholic lady resident in Rome, and this work was set up as a monument in the Church of S. Andrea delle Fratte.   This was the winter that Nathaniel Hawthorne passed in Rome, and he has left us in his "Italian Notes" a vivid picture of the sculptor.   He does not seem to have been profoundly impressed by her work on his first visit, but evidently found the little lady herself most interesting.   He writes: —

"To-day we took R——, and went to see Miss ——, and as her studio seems to be mixed up with Gibson's, we had an opportunity of glancing at some of his beautiful works.   We saw a 'Venus' and a 'Cupid,' both of them tinted; and side by side with them other statues identical with these, except that the marble was left in its pure whiteness.   We found Miss —— in a little upper room.   She has a small, brisk, wide-awake figure, not ungraceful; frank, simple, straightforward, and downright.   She had on a robe, I think, but I did not look so low, my attention being chiefly drawn to a sort of man's sack of purple or plum-colored broadcloth, into the side pockets of which her hands were thrust as she came forward to greet us.   She withdrew one hand, however, and cordially presented it to my wife (whom she already knew) and to myself, without waiting for an introduction.   She had on a shirt-front, collar, and cravat like a man's, with a brooch of Etruscan gold, and on her curly head was a picturesque little cap of black velvet, and her face was as bright and merry, and as small of feature as a child's.   It looked in one aspect youthful, and yet there was something worn in it, too.   There never was anything so jaunty as her movement and action; she was very peculiar, but she seemed to be her actual self, and nothing affected or made up; so that, for my part, I gave her full leave to wear what may suit her best, and to behave as her inner woman prompts.   I don't quite see, however, what she is to do when she grows older, for the decorum of age will not be consistent with a costume that looks pretty and excusable enough in a young woman.

"Miss —— led us into a part of the extensive studio, or collection of studios, where some of her own works were to be seen: 'Beatrice Cenci,' which did not very greatly impress me ; and a monumental design, a female figure, — wholly draped, even to the stockings and shoes, — in a quiet sleep.   I liked this last.   There was also a 'Puck,' doubtless full of fun; but I had hardly time to glance at it.

Miss —— evidently has good gifts in her profession, and doubt-less she derives great advantage from her close association with a consummate artist like Gibson; nor yet does his influence seem to interfere with the originality of her own conceptions. In one way, at least, she can hardly fail to profit, — that is, by the opportunity of showing her works to the throngs of people who go to see Gibson's own; and these are just such people as an artist would most desire to meet, and might never see in a lifetime, if left to himself. I shook hands with this frank and pleasant little person, and took leave, not without purpose of seeing her again."[1]

During a visit to America Miss Hosmer conceived the idea of a figure of Zenobia, queen of Palmyra (Fig. 29), led captive through the streets of Rome, and modelled this celebrated statue in 1859, at which time Hawthorne saw the work in progress and wrote of it: —

"March 15th. — This morning, I went with my wife and Miss Hoar to Miss Hosmer's studio, to see her statue of 'Zenobia.' . . . There were but very few things in the room: two or three plaster busts, a headless cast of a plaster statue, and a cast of the 'Minerva Medica,' which perhaps she had been studying as a help towards the design of her 'Zenobia'; for, at any rate, I seemed to discern a resemblance or analogy between the two. 'Zenobia' stood in the centre of the room, as yet unfinished in the clay, but a very noble and remarkable statue indeed, full of dignity and beauty. It is wonderful that so brisk a woman could have achieved a work so quietly impressive; and there is something in 'Zenobia's' air that conveys the idea of music, uproar, and a great throng all about her; whilst she walks in the midst of it, self-sustained and kept in a sort of sanctity by her native pride. The idea of motion is attained with great success; you not only perceive that she is walking, but know at just what tranquil pace she steps amid the music of the triumph. The drapery is very fine and full; she is decked with ornaments; but the chains of her captivity hang from wrist to wrist; and her deportment — in-dicating a soul so much above her misfortune, yet not insensible to the weight of it — makes these chains a richer decoration than all her other jewels. I know not whether there be some magic in the present imperfect finish of the statue, or in the material of clay, as

[1] "Italian Note-Book," Vol. I, pp. 156–158.

being a better medium of expression than even marble ; but certainly I have seldom been more impressed by a piece of modern sculpture. Miss Hosmer showed us photographs of her ' Puck ' — which I have seen in the marble — and likewise of the ' Will-o'-the-Wisp,' both very pretty and fanciful.   It indicates much variety of power that ' Zenobia ' should be the sister of these, which would seem the more natural offspring of her quick and vivid character.   But ' Zenobia ' is a high, heroic ode." [1]

We begin to understand!   This figure was still unfinished and in the clay — plastic, palpitant, and full of promise.   The tools of the pitiless Italian carver had not yet done their work of sharpening and polishing the life out of it.   The artist's first thought was still there — a very noble and dignified thought, by the way, though not necessarily a sculptural one, — and the enthusiastic little woman was alongside to supplement the impression ; to tell what she meant to say in the work.   No wonder that Hawthorne read in its sketchy lines all that she desired!   No wonder that he was convinced that his thought was her own, and that he had found it in the haughty captive on the modelling stand!   And besides, he liked the name of Zenobia.   It is possible that another carver, one in himself an artist, could so render this figure that it might convey to us the impression of " a high, heroic ode."   As it stands to-day there is not one grateful touch, not one suggestion of half-tone and tenderness of chiselling — nothing but ridges and grooves, a lay figure draped to display an antique garb.

In 1860 Miss Hosmer was summoned home by the illness of her father, and while in this country received a commission from St. Louis for a bronze statue of Thomas H. Benton, which was modelled the following year.   It was not, however, until 1868 that this extraordinary figure was unveiled in Lafayette Park.   It has from a distance the dignity of great bulk.   Nearer approach reveals a strange, old-fashioned conception, reminding one vaguely of some effigy in Westminster Abbey.   Not only is the bent figure enveloped from head to feet in a cloak, but this garment is most perplexingly complicated.   The guessed-at body is lost in curious and unaccountable swathings from which the extremities protrude ; hands swollen

[1] " Italian Note-Book," Vol. II, p. 229.

FIG. 29.— HOSMER: ZENOBIA, METROPOLITAN MUSEUM.

and shapeless, and a remorseful face. At the back, however, all is peace, and the drapery is of the time-honored organ-pipe pattern, in perfectly straight vertical lines. One's thought in looking at the " Benton" is that it must have been very easy to do statues in those days.

In 1865 Miss Hosmer exhibited at the Dublin Exhibition her " Sleeping Faun," which was seen also at the Paris Exposition of 1867. Among other works mentioned by her biographers are a " Waking Faun"; bronze gates for the Earl of Brownlow's art gallery at Ashridge Hall; a Siren Fountain for Lady Marion Alford; a fountain representing Hylos and the nymphs; a statue of Abraham Lincoln; one of the queen of Naples, and another of Queen Isabella, for the Columbian Exposition at Chicago.

There were some other women sculptors who did work before the Centennial Exposition, — Emma Stebbins, Margaret Foley, Edmonia Lewis, Vinnie Ream, Blanche Nevin, and Elizabet Ney. As with the men, there is a certain similarity in the stories of most of these lives. We read of an early dabbling in art, then the thrilling experience of "finding one's self," followed by feverish study, and later a trip to Italy. After this a succession of "masterpieces."

Miss Stebbins, who was born in 1815 and died in 1882, took up the study of sculpture at the age of forty-two. She had previously drawn and painted for her own amusement, but upon visiting Rome in 1857 she was irresistibly attracted by the artist life and its representatives, — Miss Hosmer, Charlotte Cushman, and others. She studied sculpture with Akers and other teachers, and produced a number of works: the boy " Joseph "; a bust of her friend Charlotte Cushman; a statue of Horace Mann (1860), now in Boston ; one of Columbus, — highly praised in its day, but since lost to sight, —and a figure for a fountain, representing the " Angel of the Waters," which is now in Central Park, New York.

Miss Margaret Foley, of Vermont, exhibited at the Centennial Exposition a fountain, which was effectively placed in the Horticultural Hall. The basin was of graceful design, made apparently of overlapping leaves, underneath the protection of which were the figures of two boys and a girl at play. Miss Foley was represented also by busts of the " Prophet Jeremiah " and of " Cleopatra," the former colossal in size.   Among her other works mention may be made of a bust of Charles Sumner, which, according to Tuckerman, was "unsurpassable and beyond praise," and of bas-reliefs of Long-fellow, Bryant, and other poets.

Edmonia Lewis, a young woman of mixed Indian and African descent, won great fame for a time by a strange and rather repellant statue of the dying "Cleopatra," which she made in Rome and exhibited at the Centennial and later in various cities.   Ten or twelve years before this she had attracted attention by a bust of Colonel Shaw, which was first exhibited at the fair held in Boston during the progress of the Civil War, for the Soldiers' Relief Fund.   Her second work was the "Freedwoman," who was "represented as overcome by a conflict of emotions on receiving the tidings of her liberation." Then, after a long silence, appeared the "Cleopatra," since which time nothing more has been heard from this sculptor.

It was the misfortune of Miss Vinnie Ream (now Mrs. Hoxie) to receive from Congress, at the age of fifteen, and after a single year's study, an order for a marble statue of Lincoln.   This she executed, and it stands to-day in the rotunda of the national Capitol, a monument to the gallantry of our statesmen.   Not content with one such exhibition of its own ignorance, Congress ordered later, from the same untrained hands, a heroic statue of Farragut for the decoration of Farragut Square, Washington.   Miss Ream made also figures called "Miriam," "The West," and "The Spirit of the Carnival," and busts of various prominent personages.   This unique representative of the sculptor's art was born at Madison, Wisconsin, in 1847, and was undoubtedly as gifted as she was attractive.   With proper training and sufficient continuity of purpose, she might have won something more substantial than notoriety.   The "Lincoln" is extraordinary work for a child, and is really a far more dignified portrait than many of its neighbors in the National Hall of Statuary.   It is neither grotesque in expression nor absurd in gesture.   The bowed head gives it from a distance a serious and thoughtful air.   Closer examination reveals an absence of body within the garments, but this oversight is concealed, from certain points of view, by an abundance of somewhat irrelevant drapery.   One feels that the girl sculptor approached her subject with reverence, and, although her work is quite devoid of strength, it has its own melancholy expressiveness.

Blanche Nevin of Philadelphia was a "most promising pupil" for a time. She studied at the Pennsylvania Academy under J. A. Bailly, and made a charming little "Cinderella" as pictured in Clark's "Great American Sculptures." Mention is also made of sundry busts and of a full-length statue of "Eve" of notable merit. One would gladly know more of her career, but at this point Clark's book ends and no other takes up the story of Miss Nevin. It is hardly a kindness to refer to her insignificant "General Muhlenberg" (1887) in the national Capitol.

An honored name in the annals of culture is that of the venerable Anne Whitney of Boston. Born in 1821, she might well have received earlier mention in this record were it not for the fact that sculpture was a somewhat tardy manifestation of her talent. She was some thirty-four years of age when, having already made her mark as a poet, she took up the study of modelling, opening in 1860 a studio in Watertown, Massachusetts, her birthplace. She spent,

FIG. 30. — WHITNEY: SAMUEL ADAMS, WASHINGTON.

later, four years in Europe and established herself in Boston in 1872. Among her works are statues of Samuel Adams, Harriet Martineau, Leif Ericson (Boston and Milwaukee), "Ethiopia," "Roma," and other subjects, portrait and ideal. The "Samuel Adams" (Fig. 30), which stands in marble in Statuary Hall of the national Capitol, was executed in 1876, and represents the statesman with arms folded in a somewhat theatrical pose. Although no woman sculptor has succeeded as yet in making a male figure look convincingly like a man, this statue has a certain feminine power and is among the interesting works of the collection. A replica in bronze was made in 1880 and erected in Boston, where from a considerable elevation it surveys the busy scene with much firmness of attitude and a very positive look.

Secluded from the world in her little studio of stone, which nestles among the trees on the outskirts of Austin, Texas, still dwells and toils Elizabet Ney, one of the most interesting of characters as she is one of the best equipped of women sculptors. Nothing could be more romantic than the life history of this gifted woman, who was born in Westphalia, and was patronized by the "mad king," Ludwig II of Bavaria. That art-loving monarch was so impressed by the young girl's talent that he gave her the use of a great hall in one of his palaces as a studio, and posed for a portrait statue of himself, which was eventually put in marble and erected on the grounds of Linderhof. Her portrait busts from life of Bismarck, Liebig, Humboldt, Kaulbach, Garibaldi, and many other notables were highly esteemed in Munich. It is interesting to find in the "Century Dictionary," under "sculptress," this quotation from Zimmern's " Schopenhauer," illustrating the use of the word : " Perhaps you know the sculptress Ney ; if not, you have lost a great deal." Miss Ney left her home for political reasons, and, after a sojourn in the Madeira Islands, settled in Texas soon after the close of the Civil War.

To say that her sculpture is great, or even uniformly good, would be to use little discrimination. Her isolated life has not resulted in that growth which accompanies generous rivalry; technic is never sustained without constant reference to the best. Some of Miss Ney's recent busts lack the firm construction and the intelligent simplifications of her earlier works, while her standing figures of men are as unmasculine as such interpretations by women always have been ; but whatever their deficiencies, the results never fail to be sculpture. There are few of our statuaries who think so distinctly and invariably in the terms of their art as does Miss Ney. After seeing her works one is convinced that it would be impossible for her to trifle with the marble. The purely picturesque, the literary *motif*, the anecdotal

— these make no appeal to her. She could not conceive a subject in such fashion, even inadvertently. Hence her sketches and compositions are admirable, as are her virile, simply handled heads of the forceful sons of Texas. These busts are generally treated in the old-fashioned way, with bare shoulders and bosoms; but even thus, and with the eyes left blank, they are strangely alive. The details of the features are epitomized with great discrimination and with an easy mastery of form which is unknown to the majority of our sculptors. A memorial to General Albert Sidney Johnston, for the cemetery of Austin, shows the dead general lying upon the litter on which he was carried from the field; the flag of the Confederacy is thrown over the body and falls to the ground on either side. The conception is vivid; the touch of realism of the rude bier localizes and accentuates the drama, while the use of the simple drapery gives grace and, above all, sculptural unity — the face and hands being evolved, as it were, from a simple monumental mass. This is a work of high order, as is the promise of a sketch of Lady Macbeth, one of the most expressive and eminently sculptural conceptions among recent American ideals.

CHAPTER XII

JOHN QUINCY ADAMS WARD

THE period of fifteen years following the Civil War includes those American sculptors born between 1830 and 1845 — the group whose mature activities reached its height at the time of the Centennial Exposition. The most prominent name in this list, that of J. Q. A. Ward, is one which happily may be carried down the record to its last page. Among the early dead, who won distinction through valued work, were Launt Thompson and Martin Milmore, and that still more gifted artist, Olin L. Warner. Two men of promise, Howard Roberts and P. F. Connelly, had meteoric success, and then disappeared entirely from view. Messrs. Meade, Simmons, and Ezekiel are the last representatives of the once powerful Italianate group of American sculptors; while of those peculiarly American remaining with us Bissell and Hartley of New York and Kemeys of Washington (see Chap. XXV) form the diminished but sturdy "guard of honor."

As may be inferred from this list of names, a marked change has come over the spirit of American sculpture since the Civil War. It began at that time to show consciousness of the world about it, and to respond in some measure to the thrill of a newly guaranteed national existence. Dying Centaurs and brooding Medeas gave way to Defenders of the Flag and personifications of the Republic. The tendency was everywhere toward the monumental and the significant, and away from the graceful but somewhat meaningless products of the Roman studios. Thus, while the Centennial Exposition showed no lack of inventions purely commercial, or at least trivial, and while they seemed at that moment to be at the height of their popularity, there were already signs of a peaceful revolution in taste. Meantime Paris had been discovered, and a few of our

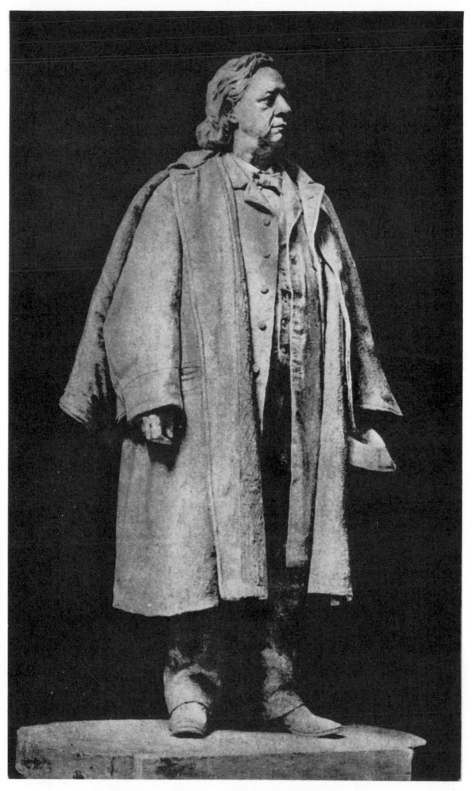

PLATE 7. — WARD: HENRY WARD BEECHER.

men, less fortunate in opportunity and perhaps less independent than Ward, sought there rather than in Italy the training which no school provided as yet in America. Such men were Warner and Roberts, who were destined to turn the whole tide of foreign quest toward France.

A critic of thirty years ago wrote of Mr. Ward's "Indian Hunter" (Fig. 31), "It is by all odds the best and most interesting statue that the [Central] Park contains," and despite the progress of American sculpture, despite the Central Park's ever increasing population of bronze effigies, the assertion may be repeated with truth to-day. To be sure, the best sculpture of New York City is not largely congregated along the asphalt walks and under the generous trees of Central Park, but Ward's earliest statue would be good anywhere. It would hold its own in much more exclusive company. Fortunate, indeed, were the Park if all of its sculptural features were up to the standard of this figure and of Mr. Ward's other contributions, — the "Shakespeare," the "Seventh Regiment Soldier," and the " Puritan." No other sculptor has so large a representation here ; no other has the same right to it. For over half a century has this gifted man plied his art in New York City, and it is not strange that we find his distinguished works on every side. They will well repay a special pilgrimage. His remarkable characterization of Horace Greeley is in front of the Tribune building. A little farther on, in Wall Street, is the noble " Washington " which bears his signature. Across the river, in Brooklyn, is his most impressive monument, the Beecher Memorial, and his latest work is the vast pedimental decoration of the new Stock Exchange. At Newport is his " Commodore Perry," at Hartford his " Israel Putnam," and at Boston his " Good Samaritan." Washington has his Garfield monument and his equestrian " General Thomas," Gettysburg his " General Reynolds," and Spartansburg, South Carolina, his " General Morgan." Cleveland, Charleston, Newburyport, and particularly Burlington, Vermont, are also fortunate in possessing important examples of his art. To these add scores of portrait busts, and not a few architectural figures and reliefs, and we have an exhibit of which any man might be proud. When it is recalled that Mr. Ward is old-fashioned enough to do his own work, and that most of these creations are not only the children of his brain, but the product throughout of his own hands, one is filled with respect for the enthusiastic consecration of their author. All this shows what may be accomplished by a man of talent who takes care not to dissipate his forces.

Mr. Ward was born in 1830, on a farm in the neighborhood of Urbana, Champaign County, Ohio. His parents named him John Quincy Adams, and encouraged him to grow up in his own way. It was a good way, for in mind and body Mr. Ward is to-day, at seventy-three, vigorous and alert, and vastly more interesting than the majority of men. Indeed, one feels after a talk with him that the average human being is half asleep. His vivid, clean-cut characterizations, his humorous reminiscences, his whole-hearted confession of artistic faith, are stimulating to both mind and body.

As a boy he played much, and later studied a little and worked more. As the seasons revolved he developed into a wiry stripling — thoughtful, but ever ready for fun. When there was riding or hunting or fishing to be done, he never faltered; always the first in the field, he did his part manfully. One day they discovered some good pottery clay on his father's farm. Young Ward was inspired to take a handful of it and model the grotesque physiognomy of an old negro of the region. Such early attempts are always pronounced "wonderful," and this was no exception. The youth did not know then that he had found his vocation. It was in the year 1849 that he first realized what he was made for. He was visiting a sister in Brooklyn when he chanced to pass the open door of H. K. Brown's old studio. The scene within appealed to him with the fascination of a world of mystery. He haunted the spot, finally found his way inside, and in some delightful fashion, almost too good to believe, was, before long, enrolled among the great sculptor's pupils.

Nothing more fortunate could have happened to him. As a critic has observed, it would have been impossible to find a better or more judicious master on this side of the Atlantic. With such opportunity, then, and an immense stock of enthusiasm, the youth made rapid strides. He remained with Mr. Brown nearly seven years, assisting him in every part of the work from kneading clay to building up frames for heroic statues. Thus he learned modelling, casting, "pointing," marble-carving, and the chasing of bronze. He had a hand in everything that was done, and more than a hand in the final product of that period, the great equestrian "Washington" of Union Square, the second equestrian statue modelled in this country.

It was during the later years of this apprenticeship that he conceived the idea of his "Indian Hunter" (Fig. 31), which he modelled first as a statuette in 1857. It was not until 1864 that he

FIG. 31. — WARD: INDIAN HUNTER, CENTRAL PARK.

executed it in large size, after a long trip among the Indians of the West and Northwest. Although he made numerous studies of the redmen, the value of this work is not in its ethnological accuracy, nor is it in its technical excellence, admirable as this evidently is; it is in something more important than these qualities, something often disregarded to-day — the fact that the artist has succeeded in conveying to us his own vivid thought. He felt the litheness and alertness of that figure. He believed intensely in what he was doing, and he has made his work "believable." Clark has well said: "The great thing is that the sculptor has undertaken to represent a man engaged in a certain act which calls all of his faculties into intense and characteristic play, and that he has succeeded in doing so. Both the dog — which fairly quivers with excitement, and which is barely stayed by the cautionary hand of his master from rushing on his prey — and the Indian who advances with stealthy step, his eye intently fixed upon the object against which he is advancing and his whole being absorbed in the eagerness of his pursuit, are instinct with an intense vitality which suggests not merely nature, but nature in one of her most interesting, because most unsophisticated, moods." [1]

But, be it noted, the "Indian Hunter" in Central Park is one of our few public statues which are suitably placed. The same group in a museum would be quite another thing. There one might wonder whether this is a real Indian, and of what tribe, and if Indians wore their clothes in that way; might compare his tense muscles with the suaver works of men of Parisian schooling. Such refinements of curiosity do not occur to one when he looks upon the original in its fortunate setting of trees and shrubs. There he is — a sudden apparition, low-bent amid the foliage. His copper glow, his preoccupation, his silence, make the illusion complete. It is a glimpse of a forgotten past evoked by the skill of a master. How much this initial work meant to the young sculptor, how much of himself he put into it, is evident when Mr. Ward talks of it to-day. His eyes gleam; he illustrates the expression — the gliding, agile step. He is as convincing as is his statue. When asked what is his favorite field of work, he always reverts to these themes of nature and of freedom, and mourns cheerily that he was not permitted to continue in that direction.

Another product of those days which seem to us so remote, a true product of the time, — and Mr. Ward has always lived in his own time, — was the "Freedman." This statuette, which appeared in 1865, is as notable for its containment as for its more technical excellences. Mr. Sturgis has pointed out that in this respect it is "curiously characteristic of the man and his whole future way of

---

[1] "Great American Sculptures," p. 115.

work; for while expressing the idea of the slave who has broken his
fetters, it represents simply a negro in an entirely natural and everyday pose — a man who has just put forth his strength and is looking
very quietly at the results; while at the same time the peculiar
characteristics of the race, as distinguished from the white man
or the red Indian, are made prominent and form a chief subject of
interest." [1]

Mr. Sturgis calls attention, also, to the fact that the sculptor
has interested himself in a truly modern fashion in the physical
peculiarities of his subject. The racial characteristics are certainly
emphasized as they had not been previously in American sculpture.
But while we of the present please ourselves in analyzing the little
figure, calmly dissecting its anatomy, it had quite a different appeal
in the days of stress and struggle which gave it birth. We read
Mr. Jarves's contemporary comments, and wonder if we have grown
callous: are we missing all that is best in these things?

"A naked slave has burst his shackles, and with uplifted face
thanks God for freedom. It symbolizes the African race of America,
the birth of a new people within the ranks of Christian civilization.
We have seen nothing in our sculpture more soul-lifting or more
comprehensively eloquent." [2]

Other times have brought other problems. Little can we of a
younger generation appreciate the emotion which was wrought into
this souvenir of the Great Rebellion. "But they wanted to glorify
heroes," said Mr. Ward, one day when in reminiscent mood, "and
they were right. It was 'good-by' to ideal subjects. From that
time to this I have never been without an order for a portrait statue
— almost always of contemporaries." The poetry was there, nevertheless, deep-bedded in the American nature, and it crops out constantly. The sympathy which gave birth to the "Freedman" enabled
the sculptor to interpret Henry Ward Beecher. The spirit of the
"Indian Hunter" reveals itself through the conventional attire of
many an athletic form; the boyhood days in the saddle are reflected
in the "General Thomas"; the uprightness and dignity of the whole
life of the sculptor leave their impress upon every portrait which he
models. Some are greater than others, but they are *men*, every one

---

[1] *Scribner's Magazine*, Vol. XXXII, p. 390.   [2] "Art Idea," p. 284.

of them.   They stand firmly on their feet and they make no weak
gestures, no self-depreciatory remarks, no attempt to win us.   " Take
me for what I am worth," each seems to say; "like me or let me
alone."   There is no restlessness, no anxiety; you feel eternity in
their attitudes, in their composure.   Their faces are grave but
serene, and one observes that there is not a vacuous countenance
among them; the sculptor has known how to endow each with an
individual intelligence.

Before the days of the " Indian Hunter " Mr. Ward had modelled
in Washington during the sessions of Congress for two winters, and
had visited Georgia to finish a bust of Alexander H. Stephens, begun
in Washington.   The year 1860 he had spent in Ohio, but he returned to New York in 1861, where he opened a studio and began
the series of works which have brought him fame and wealth.   He
was elected an associate of the National Academy of Design in
1862, academician in 1863, and president in 1874.   In 1866 he executed the large group of " The Good Samaritan " (in the Public
Gardens, Boston), in honor of the discovery of anæsthetics, and in
1867 he prepared his design for the Shakespeare statue in Central
Park, New York.

Mr. Ward's " Shakespeare " (1870) is not a great statue, but it is
a good one, and must have seemed an exceptionally good one in its
day.   The head, is not quite satisfying, but what head of Shakespeare is?   The simple, self-concentrated air of the figure commands our respect.   We could wish the statue placed even lower
that the suggestion of life might be more plausible.   Such a position would give increased significance to that attitude "of a man
deep in thought, almost pausing in a slow saunter as an idea flits
through his brain."

The " Pilgrim," which was ordered by the New England Society
of New York City, soon followed, to keep company with Mr.
Ward's other works in Central Park.   This figure has been surpassed more than once by its author, but it is a characteristic
statue.   A good opportunity for the study of the " Pilgrim " is
offered in the Art Institute of Chicago, where the original plaster
cast stands almost side by side with Mr. Saint Gaudens's " Puritan."
The individualities of the two artists are no less pronounced than

are the two types which they have portrayed. These figures illustrate precisely the attitude of the two men toward their art. Both are able sculptors, yet their points of view are widely remote. Mr. Ward, although quite capable of rich and fluent modelling (see his " General Thomas "), has elected here to interpret his subject with much austerity of detail. So definite has been his conception, so adequate and convincing his presentation, that in looking at the figure alone one asks if the " Pilgrim " could be represented in any other way. It is only when one turns to the " Deacon Chapin " that he realizes the possibility of other conceptions and other methods not less convincing.

Naturally the " Pilgrim " attracted much attention when first seen in 1885, and its promoters were warmly congratulated on the success of their effort. " It is a large and honorable achievement," wrote a critic at the time, " worthy of what it commemorates, and more than worthy of Mr. Ward's reputation and ambition as an artist. . . . It is a simple figure, heroic in measurement, of a man of perhaps forty years of age. He is standing in an easy, unconstrained attitude, one hand on the muzzle of an old Dutch wheel-lock and the other relaxed by his side. His costume is the conventional leathern jerkin of the time, loose knee-breeches, great boots of undressed leather, with wide down-turned tops; a broad buckled girdle, with powder-horn and cartridge-cases slung from his shoulder, and on his head a stiff, high-crowned, broad-brimmed hat. In the deep shadow of the last the face is lean, angular of outline, and clean shaven; the hair close-cropped; the mouth wide, thin-lipped and firmly closed; the nose strong and large, and eyes wide open, intent and steadfast. The whole impression that it conveys is that of the spirit of the New England fashioning of a man of convictions, of unbounded resolution, of unswerving loyalty to his own ideals, and surcharged with anti-liturgy and fight." There can be no doubt that Mr. Ward had a firm grasp of his subject. He has not played with it. The method is in perfect accord with the stern, inflexible repression which we associate with this manner of man.

But greater, far greater, than any of these early works are the subsequent triumphs of Mr. Ward's skill and incessant study. As already stated, these have been largely portraits of contemporaries, a field in which Mr. Ward is one of the masters of the day. Perhaps the finest of his achievements in this field is the statue of Henry Ward Beecher (1891) (Pl. VII), which stands in front of the Courthouse in Brooklyn. In it Mr. Ward has inadvertently told us much of himself. None but a big man could have grasped that character; none but a strong nature could convey to others that impression of exuberant vitality and of conscious power. The great divine stands solidly upon his feet, enveloped in a heavy overcoat and cape, his hat in hand. The pose is superbly confident; the leonine head uplifted as if in command rather than exhortation. One can imagine that the artist had in mind that crucial hour of the Liverpool address when America's fervid orator silenced a hostile audience of thousands. At either end of the oblong base Mr. Ward has introduced realistic figures which pay homage to the great man above; a youthful negress who reverently lays a palm branch at his feet, and a small boy and girl who attempt to hang a garland of oak leaves. The use of such adventitious figures is often in doubtful taste, as their realism may easily be carried beyond the bounds of good monumental art, or even of legitimate sculpture; but if they were always handled with the restraint shown here, one could not object. Though essentially unarchitectonic in conception, they have been developed with sculptural breadth and simplicity. The young negress in particular is most happily treated, both in matter of drapery and as regards the lines of the figure and of the clinging arms. The little ones on the opposite side illustrate well a combination which, though seemingly accidental, has in reality been carefully and wisely planned. The naturalness of pose and expression could scarcely be improved upon. They are close to *genre;* yet they are so winning and so closely bound to the subject through the wide, all-embracing sympathies of the man who was ever quick to respond to innocent childhood and to downtrodden helplessness alike, that there is an unusual appropriateness in their presence here. Their interpretative value will grow as the memory of the great orator becomes remote.

How consistently, one may say how inevitably, Mr. Ward has always been himself, and yet how ingenious he is withal in handling difficult subjects, is well illustrated by his " Horace Greeley " (1890). Mr. Sturgis states the case in temptingly quotable words: " The problem was, of course, to treat the odd-looking figure, the moonlike face with its loose fringe of white beard, the slovenly and queer ex- terior which attracted every one's attention in the street, in such a way as to preserve some sculpturesque interest; and at the same time to place the figure beneath a very deep arch in a thick wall and backed up in the awkwardest possible way by a huge window. The disposition of the figure in a low arm-chair, leaning forward, holding a manuscript, but looking out above it as if intently considering the subject contained in the written paper, with rounded back, with ad- vanced head; and the whole of this low and broad mass raised upon a high pedestal so as to be well out of the way of passers-by on the neighboring sidewalk — all this is managed with perfect harmony of result, with entire correspondence of means to end: with a result as fortunate as the circumstances could possibly allow." [1]

In this triumph over difficulties the sculptor has shown his mastery of his art, for the " Horace Greeley " is not only as " for- tunate as the circumstances could possibly allow," but is one of the notable successes of Mr. Ward's career. How great a success it is can scarcely be appreciated until the figure is compared with another version of the same subject still to be seen in New York. Although one of the most sculptural of all of Mr. Ward's works, the " Horace Greeley " may not appear so at first sight, for the reason that the human and personal elements are so strongly pronounced that we forget the statue; the arrangement of the figure is so happily "accidental" that we forget the sculptor.

There is no such danger with the Washington effigy which marks imposingly the spot where the first President took, in 1789, the oath of office. This figure was, as has been well said, "statuesque" from the inception, and legitimately so. Washington, in the attitude which Mr. Ward has given to Greeley, would be scarcely less absurd than a representation of the great editor in this stately pose. The Father of his Country was a monumental character in more senses than one. The traditional gravity of his bearing lends itself to the reserve of sculpture, and he has fared well at the hands of those who model

[1] *Scribner's Magazine*, Vol. XXXII, p. 391.

Q

and carve.   Foremost among the many interpretations, according to
not a few good judges, including prominent members of the profession, stands this noble figure by Mr. Ward.

A realistic treatment of the subject was by no means desirable.   Houdon gave us this, combined with a mastery of curious
skill.   Mr. Ward shows us not the intimate, domestic Washington of
Mount Vernon, nor even the actual — shall we say casual? — man seen
by the few who stood nearest at the inaugural, but the great, legendary
figure toward which the whole country turned in those days, and
which the years have further consecrated, glorifying even as they
veil.   If our very friends are largely the product of our imaginations,
how much more is a great public character but a symbol on which to
hang the attributes of our likes or our dislikes!   We owe thanks to
Mr. Ward for such a "symbol."   This quiet, impressive figure, supported by the fasces and enriched by the sweep of the great military
cloak, lifts its hand in the simple gesture which betokens authority
guided by moderation and intelligence.   It has in it the essentials of
Washington, while the peculiarities, real or imaginary, are left out.
The statue is the greater for the well-weighed omission.

Whether or not the "Lafayette" of Burlington, Vermont (1883),
illustrates its subject as he appeared when he revisited this country
in 1824–1825, no man living is prepared to say; but that it expresses
Mr. Ward there is no doubt.   He has taken a particular pleasure in
this work, and has made it very much his own.   If the "Beecher"
shows how a man of Mr. Ward's powers grapples with modern costume, and without evasion or palliation converts it into an artistic
auxiliary, it is in the "Lafayette" rather than the "Washington"
that we find him enjoying with most gusto the nearest approach to
the nude figure which modern clothing admits of, — the close-cling-
ing garments of a century ago.   Nothing simpler than the quiet pose
of this figure could be devised, the weight on the left leg, the right
advanced, as is the right arm, the hand resting on the cane, while the
left hand, brushing back the long coat, is placed lightly on the hip.
The drawing of the leg shows through the tight pantaloon, the swing
of the long coat contributes its part to the movement, and the statue's
most minor details testify to the painstaking enthusiasm of its maker,
and to his unusual gift of fitting the clothes to the person.   A more

capable and satisfactory work than this portrait few sculptors indeed
are able to imagine, much less create.

In the grounds of the Capitol at Washington rises Mr. Ward's
admirable monument to President Garfield, erected in 1887. In the
figures which adorn its base, Mr. Ward was permitted to indulge
himself once more in the luxury of modelling the nude — to do something besides portraits.   To be sure, portrait statues represent much

FIG. 32. — WARD: THE WARRIOR, WASHINGTON.

use of the model, at least in the case of figures as well constructed as
are Mr. Ward's. But the sculptor generally stops just this side of
real satisfaction. There is seldom time, and never real necessity, for
the finer passages of form-building and form-blending, which are the
joy of the experienced modeller. These figures of the "Warrior"
(Fig. 32), the "Statesman," and the "Student" were conceived, however, as nudes, for decorative purposes alone; and if the sculptor
finally covered two of them with garments, these externals are sub-

ordinated to the body instead of appearing to shape it, as does the modern costume. The "Student" is provided with the slight but appropriate accessory of a sheepskin, and is so engrossed in the perusal of a manuscript that he is quite unconscious of his scantiness of attire. This look of concentration Mr. Ward bequeathes to all the children of his studio. They are ever intent, as though they possessed clear, active minds which refuse to vegetate.

It can hardly be claimed that Mr. Ward was inspired in his treatment of the "Garfield." The figure is said to be an excellent likeness, and the pose to be characteristic; but the interest of the monument is in the three figures which recline on the radiating bases below. The graceful "Student" is a general favorite; but there is much to admire in the massive Agrippa-faced "Statesman," and yet more in the play of light and shade which gives surface charm to the powerful frame of the "Warrior," a remarkably statuesque conception.

The city of Washington is further decorated by Mr. Ward's "General Thomas" (1878), an equestrian statue of the highest value (Fig. 33). It is not enough to say that it is the finest work of its kind in Washington; it has few rivals in the country at large. It is the only equestrian work of Mr. Ward's which is yet in place, although the sculptor is engaged at the present time upon two others for the Smith Memorial in Fairmount Park, Philadelphia. The "General Thomas" suffers, like so many other statues, from being erected upon a high pedestal, but its effect is nevertheless very striking. While the charm of the modelling is lost to some extent, the contour of horse and rider against the sky is unusually expressive. Here is a horse which is nervously alive, — quite as much so as the rampant creations of the earlier sculptors, — yet subordinated in every way to the rider. The sculptor has not found it necessary to make his steed rear and cavort; he has planted the four feet firmly on the ground, yet withal the horse is one of the most spirited in modern art. Upon him, complete master of the situation, not even holding a tight rein, is the commanding form of the general. He sits easily, hat in hand, but not bowing and performing like Mills's misconceived "General Jackson." There is a power in this simplicity of pose and quietness of gesture which appeals with peculiar force to the Anglo-Saxon temperament.   It is good art as well.   Freedom shrieks in other lands and heroes brandish their swords, but such display makes little impression on us.   It is not our language.

It has been, then, Mr. Ward's great part to fix in enduring and distinguished form the ever changing apparitions about him; to immortalize the ephemeral features of his contemporaries.   Well may it be said of him, as of another, that his work has been "to exalt the present and the real . . . to teach to man the nobility of his daily walk."   That he has delighted in his task there can be no doubt. He, too, has known the "joy of power," which he has so well depicted on the face of his fine "Beecher."   But one may well ask if the sculptor of the "Indian Hunter," of the "Freedman," and of the heroic figures of the Garfield monument, has not sighed now and then for a wider field.   His very prosperity has hampered him; the success of his portraits has kept him busy all these years.   It was in 1899 that the arch for the Dewey reception in New York brought Mr. Ward his opportunity for a freer flight, and one so enticing that it was not to be neglected.   To him was awarded the crowning ornament of the great arch, a gigantic "quadriga."   Unlike the many who, having cherished a life-long ambition, find themselves in the end physically or mentally incapable of doing the work, Mr. Ward rose grandly to the occasion.   No finer, no more appropriate group could possibly have been designed for the place than that marine quadriga.

It was a time of great enthusiasm — the one supreme moment in the existence of the National Sculpture Society.   The colossal monument was to be erected in an absurdly short time.   Activity prevailed in the studios and in the great improvised workshops under the Madison Square Garden; but no one could surpass in energy the venerable president.   In all that magic work he literally led, encouraging, spurring up laggards, and setting an example of kindly aggressiveness which was infectious.   Not only did he exploit and inspire his little band during those two months of forced labor, but he designed and carried to completion this largest and finest group upon the monument, — the "Victory" in her sea chariot.   The conception was one of extraordinary beauty.   "Victory" (adapted from the Niké of Samothrace) stood with uplifted wreath upon the prow of her boat which was drawn by six sea horses.   These magnificent creatures, half emerging from the foam, were like echoes of the sublime dream of Phidias, with the rearing steeds of the sun on the one hand and the affrighted coursers of Selene on the other. Seen from afar the group was found to have carrying power and to be beautiful at any distance.   It had mass, balance, and uplift. No silhouette could be more effective than was that of the noble "Victory" dominating all that splendid confusion of tossing heads and flowing manes, of struggling Tritons and great sea waves churned to foam.   If there was any feature of the monument which convincingly and insistently called for preservation, it was this superb work of Mr. Ward's.

To the average man in the street it will be of no particular importance whether the great pediment of the New York Stock Exchange represents "The Balance of Trade" or "The Triumph of Bacchus"; whether the central figure up there is called "Freedom" or "Money," or whether it has any name at all.   What does matter is whether the sculpture makes the building look well or not.   If the culminating decoration really decorates, it will be keenly appreciated by a few; but there will be also a vague, uneasy enjoyment on the part of many who "only know what they like."   They will find themselves looking for this beautiful ornament each time they pass.   For beautiful it will be, and most effective.   It has been studied as few such problems have been in our day, and represents the mature power of a man of experience who knows what he wants, and the skill of a young man who is able to produce the result easily.   Mr. Ward and Paul Bartlett have collaborated on this important work, and the result is a very notable achievement.

Mr. Ward has had the happy inspiration to make "Integrity" the presiding genius of the group, the keynote of the composition. While the sculptor rejoices in the felicity of his lines and in the balance of light and shade of the relief, giving the while generous praise to the work of his associate, he does not seem to realize that he has here a conception as poetic as it is vital.   His keen mind has not only found means to honor the subject, — as every artistic expression must, — but has seized upon the very basic truth on which the elaborate structure of commerce and exchange is founded.

The vast triangle to be filled is over one hundred feet in length. In the centre stands, with outstretched hands, the grave impersonation of business honor, a figure some fifteen feet in height, which is disconnected from the others excepting through the gesture. The figure is given volume as well as relief by means of a large mantle, which flutters out at some distance from the body like a great shell, or like the elliptical background of the Virgin in mediæval reliefs. It is further supported by two cherubs that sit on the edges of the

FIG. 33.— WARD: GENERAL THOMAS, WASHINGTON.

dais and admirably serve their purpose of "chinking." The next measure in this really musical composition consists of two figures on either side, respectively a mechanic with his assistant and a tiller of the ground, accompanied by a small female figure. The larger figures are nude and splendidly athletic. They bend toward the centre, bowing to the inevitable cornice, and in so doing bring fine masses of shadow into the composition, the one contrasted with a broad, glistening back, the other emphasized by the heavy sack

borne by the farmer.   This burden explains his attitude, but nothing
excepting exigencies of space can reconcile to the disproportion
of the male and the female figures, the latter being a fully developed
woman, whose head would not reach her companion's shoulders
were he erect.   This is the one jarring note in the composition, and
makes one wish that the " Dairy-Maid " had been shown as a young
girl.   The outside groups down in the low corners are likewise
made up of two figures each: on the one side designers, and on the
other mining prospectors.   The first of these is especially happy in
its composition.   An adaptation of the Garfield " Student " is shown
resting on his elbow and drawing upon a sheet of paper, while he
adroitly fills that puzzlesome sharp angle with his feet.   Kneeling
toward him is his companion, who not only shows his interest in
the work, but contributes another beautiful shadow.   A sculptural
thought, good figures capably modelled, flowing, cumulative lines,
effective groupings, and charming contrasts of light and shade —
these are the elements entering into this admirable relief.   No less
important are the things left out : the superfluous details of costuming, the unintelligible piles of accessories and machinery which
cumber most pediments.   These have been swept away, or rather,
they never entered the thought of the true artist who designed
the decoration.   If not "supremely impressive," as Mr. Sturgis pro-
nounces it, the pediment of the New York Stock Exchange is at
least that rare thing, a well-understood and workmanlike production of great artistic value.   The problem has not been so ably
approached before in this country.

Such is the record of our oldest practising sculptor.   Such are
a few of the many dignified works which it has been his privilege
to contribute to the general mass of good sculpture in the United
States.   It is not to be wondered at that the entire profession delight
to do him honor.   They respect in him the upright and generous
man and the true artist.   They made him president of the National
Sculpture Society upon its incorporation in 1896, and probably will
have no other while he lives.

Mr. Ward is essentially a sculptor.   There are many in the
profession who are not.   Some of them do good work occasionally
in spite of themselves, but Mr. Ward is so much of a sculptor that

he cannot do bad work — just as he is so much of a man that he cannot conceive trifling and unworthy things. His technic may lack at times that charm of surface manipulation in which his younger colleagues excel ; but it always shows a quiet simplicity, an impressiveness of mass, which is the first element in good monumental sculpture. Over-clever men are liable at times to neglect this, but Mr. Ward could not neglect it ; it is part of his artistic personality. Whatever he does is "big" and effective, even at a distance where detail is completely obliterated. If his figures do not sparkle with coquettish accents, — if they hold themselves austerely aloof from suspicion of the painters' methods, — theirs are the fundamental virtues of a genuine sculptural conception and a structural evolution. Mr. Ward may be trusted to dignify whatever he touches.

CHAPTER XIII

A GROUP OF BUILDERS OF MONUMENTS

THE Civil War gave a great impetus to the building of public memorials, an industry which has gained in momentum with the years. As the great struggle left no hamlet without its losses, so the distribution of " soldiers' monuments " is widespread, and the end is not yet. Among the sculptors already named, Randolph Rogers and Leonard Volk were especially active in this field; others of the same period particularly identified with it have been Thompson, Meade, Bissell, Simmons, and Milmore.

Of this group none was more gifted and none more unfortunate than Launt Thompson, who was born at Abbeyleix, Queens County, Ireland, in 1833. He came with his widowed mother to America in 1847, and they found a home at Albany, New York. Chance led the boy to the office of a certain Dr. Armsby, where he began the diligent study of anatomy. As an aid in his research he made drawings of the bones and the muscles, soon discovering a rather remarkable talent. An accidental meeting with Erastus D. Palmer turned the young man's attention to sculpture, and a place was made for him in the studio. He presently became a useful assistant, and stayed with Mr. Palmer for nine years, modelling and carving under the direction of the older artist — a training which was invaluable.

In 1857 Mr. Thompson opened a studio of his own in New York, where he met with prompt recognition. His first ventures were ideal heads in relief in the style of Mr. Palmer's popular works, and showing a craftsmanship scarcely inferior to their prototypes. Soon Mr. Thompson's success with portrait busts reaffirmed his position, and finally when opportunity offered he proved himself equally a master of the entire figure. In 1868–1869 he visited Rome. From 1875 to 1887 he resided in Florence, and then returned to New York. His last years were rendered comparatively unproductive through ill health. He died at Middleton, New York, Sept. 26, 1894.

The best known of Mr. Thompson's medallions are his pretty " Morning Glory," and a portrait of General John A. Dix. Among his many busts are those of James Gordon Bennett the elder, Robert B. Minturn, Edwin Booth as Hamlet, Samuel F. B. Morse, and two of William Cullen Bryant, — one in the Metropolitan Museum, New York, and the other in the Towne Art Building, New Haven. A dignified and genial marble portrait of Dr. J. P. Thompson, also in the Yale University collection, shows excellent modern workmanship, although the bare breast gives it an old-fashioned look.

FIG. 34. — THOMPSON : NAPOLEON I, METROPOLITAN MUSEUM.

Mr. Thompson's earliest statue of importance was the remarkable " Napoleon I," now in the Metropolitan Museum (Fig. 34). This thoughtful and highly finished work was cast in bronze for a purchaser in 1889, but was modelled more than a score of years before, since it was shown along with a bust of a " Rocky Mountain Trapper " at the Paris Exposition in 1867. It is eminently characteristic of its creator. Easy in pose, yet firm on the feet, quiet and self-contained in every line, it presents a gratifying illustration of dignified monumental art. Sculpture without repose was scarcely sculpture at all to Launt Thompson. A greater vivacity of technic may be demanded to-day; but the modelling, like the drawing, of this unexpected little statue, is irreproachable. One feels that the sculptor has fairly lavished himself upon it, and that he rejoiced to work until he could do no more.

Within the precincts of Yale University stands Mr. Thompson's statue of the first president, Abraham Pierson, who guided the infant college from 1700 to 1707. This quiet cloaked figure, modelled in 1874, offers at a distance a certain family likeness to

Palmer's "Chancellor Livingston"; but nearer view discovers a lack of Palmer's refinement in both the conception and the treatment of the work. The look of the face is inflexible, and might almost be taken for sinister; but the statue as a whole is sculpturally conceived, with gratifying lines of almost architectural value.

Other examples of Mr. Thompson's portraiture are his statues of General Ambrose E. Burnside at Providence, Rhode Island (equestrian), of General John Sedgwick at West Point, of General Winfield Scott at the Soldiers' Home, Washington, and of Admiral Dupont, also in Washington. Of these, the latter although perhaps the least interesting is the best known on account of its accessibility. The admiral is shown standing with feet close together and head raised, while he grasps his spy-glass in both hands. Though the figure has a somewhat lean air of realism and a look as of standing on tip-toe, yet its workmanship is excellent. The more impressive "General Scott" stands in the pose of the "Napoleon I," as to the lower limbs, but with the right hand thrust into the coat front, and the left upon the hilt of the sword. As with all of Thompson's uniformed men, the head is bare and the hat invisible.

While lacking the finer qualities of his master, Mr. Thompson's honorable share in the elevation of his art in America is not to be denied. He was endowed with an intuitive grasp of the sculptural side of things, and with an artistic conscience, which seems the more remarkable when contrasted with his erratic life. In the gravity and perfection of his art he stood for the best that he knew, anticipating somewhat strangely the point of view of Warner. His influence, especially during his early career, was therefore extremely valuable to the cause of American monumental sculpture.

"A few years ago the good people of Brattleboro, Vermont, were startled and delighted one winter morning by the sight of a colossal snow image at the angle of two of the large avenues of the town. It wore the form of a majestic angel, crude in outline but effective and graceful. It was the wonder of the village until it melted away. Meanwhile the fact soon transpired that this marvellous creation was the work of a youth, the son of a prominent lawyer of Brattleboro."[1] In this pretty fashion does Mr. Tuckerman introduce the story of

[1] "Book of the Artists," p. 597.

Larkin G. Meade (born at Chesterfield, New Hampshire, in 1835). He continues that the incident was reported in the papers, and finally meeting the eye of good old Mr. Longworth of Cincinnati, — "a man who had a passion to cherish native art, especially sculpture," — the latter wrote to the postmaster of Brattleboro and inquired about the young impromptu artist. If the postmaster had been like some, the story might have ended right there; but luckily he replied, and so favorably, too, that Mr. Longworth was led to hold out to the boy substantial encouragement to begin the study of plastic art. He became a pupil of Henry Kirke Brown, remaining with him through the years 1853–1855, and having as his companion J. Q. A. Ward, who was five years his senior.

Mr. Meade's earliest work of importance was a statue of Ethan Allen, made from Rutland marble, and now standing in the portico of the State House at Montpelier. On the breaking out of the Civil War young Meade hastened to the Army of the Potomac, whence he sent numerous spirited and graphic illustrations of camp life and battle scenes to a New York illustrated paper. In 1862 the inevitable desire for a trip to Italy was gratified. Hiram Powers, who, it will be remembered, was a Vermonter himself, welcomed the young man to Florence and encouraged him. In a few months he had executed a pleasing statuette, " Echo," which found favor and ultimately a purchaser among his wandering countrymen. He remained in Italy for three years, pursuing his art with zeal and intelligence, and, in the words of his biographer, " finding time, notwithstanding, during a sojourn in Venice, to win and wed a fair daughter of that venerable, picturesque, and unfortunate city."

Returning to New York in 1865, he brought with him several works in marble which he exhibited to an appreciative public. He had admirably, if unconsciously, gauged the taste of his countrymen, and the reception accorded him was cordial though not always discriminating.

" These specimens of sculpture indicate both variety and scope, grasp and ideality. They consisted of four pieces: first, ' The Returned Soldier, or The Battle Story,' representing (life-size) a Union soldier with a little girl between his knees and leaning on his stalwart form in a childlike abandon, while he earnestly relates the story of the war. The attitude of both figures, as well as the expression of each, is full of life, interest, and significance; they indeed tell the story to the eye. The subject and execution of this group insured its popularity. The other pieces were 'La Contadinella,' 'The Thought of Freedom,' and 'Echo,' all attractive and effective." [1]

Abraham Lincoln had been assassinated in the preceding April, and Mr. Meade had taken care to make before leaving Florence an elaborate design in plaster for a national monument to his memory. It arrived most opportunely. It was far better than the average monumental design, and was abundantly equipped with restless sculpture. The simplicity of the massive pile, the dignity and accuracy of the Lincoln portrait, the vivacity of the subordinate groups, and the generally professional look of the sketch-model appealed to the imagination of our people. The commission was speedily awarded to the inexperienced young sculptor. The monument was destined to cost over $200,000, thus surpassing in importance all memorials which had been erected in this country. No American sculptor had ever received so large a commission. Meade's fortune was made; at least his opportunity had come, and his future was assured. His success was in a sense his country's loss, for he sailed away to Italy, never to return.

It is easier to give an order than to pay for it, and it was not until 1869 that the excavations were begun at Springfield for the monument which was destined to be also the tomb of the martyred President. The work dragged until 1874, when the pile was dedicated and the statue of Lincoln unveiled. Three years later the Infantry and Naval groups were added. The Artillery group followed in 1882, and the Cavalry group, completing the design, was put in place in 1883. The statue and the groups were modelled in Florence and shipped to Chicopee, Massachusetts, for casting. It is said that they were modelled directly in the plaster. No doubt Mr. Meade shaped the unwilling material quite as successfully as he would have handled the clay. It was suited to his precise and unrelenting touch. Conscientiously and ably he did his work. It was not his fault if he mistook "spirit" for inspiration, and substituted curious

[1] "Book of the Artists," p. 597.

Italian textures for charm of modelling.   When he designed the monument he was one of our best sculptors.   His peaceful life was thenceforth spent in Florence, quite outside the world of progress, and when, nearly twenty years later, he made his last contribution to the work, American taste had already outgrown it.   At that moment in a New York studio was developing an effigy of Lincoln which should so far eclipse the one at Springfield that the latter is scarcely remembered.

And yet Mr. Meade's " Lincoln " is by no means a bad statue. It is one of the best of many.   It stands well upon its feet.   It has dignity and seriousness, and at a distance might satisfy most eyes quite as well as does the masterpiece of Lincoln Park.   The trouble with it is elusive, yet it is a fatal one: the figure is commonplace.   The sculptor has done his best, and we honor him for his effort and for the conscientious work which he has given us; but we realize — now that we have seen a better — that he was not able to rise to the height of his theme and to do justice to his noble subject.   This bronze image, which so insistently extends to us the scroll inscribed "Proclamation," may be the very earthly counterfeit of the great Commoner.   It may have all his attributes: "the stooping shoulders, the forward inclination of the head, the manner of wearing the hair, the protruding eyebrows, the nose, the mouth, with the prominent and slightly drooping lower lip," even "the mole on the left cheek," but it gives us no thrill.   The essence of greatness is not in it.

The groups deserve more than a passing glance, because they illustrate so thoroughly the realistic ideal — if such a term may be permitted.   Their effect from a distance is not altogether sculptural, but their fault is not lack of animation.   On one side, at Lincoln's right, three figures seem to be precipitating themselves from their turret-like pedestal.   On the opposite side a dismounted cavalryman struggles to keep his horse in position.   To add to the general confusion, a glimpse of the naval group from the front shows a man crawling to the edge, apparently in distress, and a "powder-monkey " — a pretty boy — waving his arms and legs from a precarious perch on the rim of an immense mortar.   The artillerymen on the opposite corner are doing their duty, and the whole scene is one of turmoil and disorder which lacks but the actual discharge of

the "practical" guns to make pandemonium complete. Of course
this is war, and we have been told what war is. But one cannot
avoid questioning the fitness of mimic warfare over the last resting-
place of the dead. Why that prancing, frantic steed? Why these
bayonet charges and brazen shrieks of defiance? Admitting that
the representatives of the four branches of the service should occupy
their positions upon the great military tomb, it is conceivable that
they might pay a greater deference to the place and the occasion.
Interesting as may be their individual performances, the combined
effect is that of a stampede. Their sham battle, however seriously
undertaken, is irrelevant and, artistically speaking, indecorous. Not
only do they fail to enhance the impression of solemnity; they divert
and counteract. The tomb of Lincoln is forgotten in the ill-timed
vehemence of these superfluous performers.

Vermont contributed to the National Hall of Statuary in the
Capitol Mr. Meade's "Ethan Allen" (Fig. 35), one of its most
interesting figures. The arrival of the statue at Washington was
felicitously announced by a local paper of Feb. 28, 1876: "The
cost was $10,000. It represents Colonel Allen as he appeared
when demanding the surrender of Fort Ticonderoga, 'in the
name of the Great Jehovah and the Continental Congress.' The
attitude of the statue is very spirited, much more so than that of
any other in the hall."

Judged by the canons of modern Italian art, the "Ethan Allen"
is excellent sculpture. Westminster Abbey and Saint Paul's offer
few works that are so fine. America certainly possessed in 1876
not over a dozen as well done and as full of life. It must be
acknowledged that in the near neighborhood of Mr. French's
"Lewis Cass" the figure seems needlessly cut up, and despite the
Florentine carver's effort at variety of textures, the total result is
somewhat monotonous; yet if we overlook these minor details we
shall find here a vigorous and satisfying presentation of a man of
character. The pose is expressive and at the same time sufficiently
sculptural. Though the figure is very heavy set, its lines are good
from all sides, the "stand" of the leg being firm and effective ; the expression, too, of the face is frank and manly, without over-refinement
of handling. The artist has not invited Ethan Allen to a peaceful

FIG. 35. — MEADE: ETHAN ALLEN, WASHINGTON.

gathering of the great, where his deeds of valor would be sufficiently implied by his presence, but has preferred a more obvious and dramatic display of character.   This rendering is suited to the larger demand, and we need not quarrel with the artist over his choice of *motif*.   Having elected to address the general public, Mr. Meade has done so intelligibly and forcefully.   His work interests all, and conveys his meaning to all, excepting to the obtuse and to those sophisticated ones who allow harsh modelling and tiresome details to close their eyes to fundamental excellences.   Singularly enough, while the layman loves sculpture for its perforated laces, its buttons and watch-fobs and epaulettes, and its cunningly cracked bark on marble trees, the mature professional condemns a work on account of these very features.   Possibly the one over-rates the importance of such details as much as does the other.   An unnecessary display of cleverness is generally a detriment, but it should be remembered that there may be a worthy sculptural conception hidden under the hardest trappings and the most elaborated details from a modern Italian chisel.   A curious thing about a work of this character is the fact that with all its " finish " it always looks unfinished.   The sharp, undeviating lines of coat and waistcoat and boot-tops suggest a statue barely blocked out by the 'prentice, awaiting the hand of the master who shall play with these contours, soften black shadows, and enrich the surface here and there with accents and touches of charming unexpectedness.   This is France's lesson to the modern Italian sculptor, who, enamoured of his own cunning, is slow to learn.   The " Ethan Allen " and the " Lewis Cass," standing almost side by side in the National Hall of Statuary, are admirable illustrations of the two methods at their best.

It seemed a pity that amid the thronging and strident decorations of the Columbian Exposition a work of the modest worth of Mr. Meade's " Triumph of Ceres " should have been so completely lost.   No one remembers it.   No one saw it.   Yet it represented months of serious labor in the Florentine studio, and contained many graceful figures.   Of course, in a crowd where all are shouting, it is a man's own fault or misfortune if he does not make himself heard, and in the case of a decoration it is a serious defect if it does not decorate.   Undoubtedly the relief might have been missed had it been left out of the pediment of the Agricultural building, — it would have been "conspicuous by its absence," — but so far as a distinct impression is concerned, the place might have been as adequately filled by a conventional ornament or a graceful arabesque.   Better, perhaps, for precisely what was lacking in Mr. Meade's relief was line. It showed no clearly pronounced design.   Out-of-door decorations should not be in fine print.   Especially upon Exposition architecture must they be "writ large," that those who run may read.   To one who stops to examine microscopically, there will be ten thousand who give but a glance.   The one, if provided with a spy-glass, found this Thorwaldsen-like tympanum filled with disconnected beauties.   The multitude saw in it but a dim and not even graceful confusion.   The charm of color of the individual figures, their sweetness and grace, was completely lost at the only points whence the relief could be viewed.

One of Mr. Meade's most impressive works is his heroic marble statue of "The Father of Waters," a figure which he executed many years ago for a citizen of New Orleans, but which changing fortunes left upon the sculptor's hands until recently.   It portrays the Father of Waters as an old man in a half-reclining attitude, somewhat like the ancient personifications of the Nile and the Tiber.   His rocky couch represents the high shores of the river's upper course.   A spring of water is indicated flowing into the river bed beneath the left elbow.   The right hand grasps a stalk of Indian corn, from underneath which an alligator looks out, and the venerable head is crowned with a wreath of tobacco leaves intermingled with pine cones and water lilies.

Mr. Meade still lives at Florence.   He impresses all who meet him as a serious, thoughtful nature, a man of generous impulses and high ideals, who has worthily contributed his part toward the artistic advancement of the nation.   What larger rôle he might have played in American sculpture had he made his home in this country, it were futile to surmise.   He might have accomplished things of deeper significance; but the atmosphere of mediæval Tuscany seems to have fascinated him.   It is no small matter to have represented as honorably as he has done American character and American taste in the little colony of Florence.   Of the old-time brilliant group of exiles in that fair city, he is the last survivor.

In the autumn of 1902, a New York journal requested a committee of local sculptors to designate the city's six finest examples of monumental sculpture. Their task was a less difficult one than might be supposed. Their verdict, however, brought into prominence a name less well known to the country at large than to the city where George Bissell's sculpture is to be seen. Belonging, by the date of his birth, to the group now under consideration, but entering the sculptor's career somewhat tardily, Mr. Bissell escaped many of the limitations of the early days, and is so thoroughly modern in his sympathies and aspirations that, as in the case of Mr. Ward, it seems incongruous to relegate him to this early position in the chronological sequence.

Mr. Bissell was born in 1839, at New Preston, Litchfield County, Connecticut, where his father was a prosperous young quarryman and marble worker. Although showing a decided bent toward art, the boy was set to work at fourteen as a clerk in a store at Waterbury, where he remained until he was of age, when he decided to prepare for college. The war put an end to such plans, and the young man enlisted, serving until his regiment was mustered out, when he received an appointment in the United States Navy as assistant paymaster, and was ordered to the South Atlantic squadron, where he served until the close of the war. Then, joining his father and brother in the marble business, he settled at Poughkeepsie, New York. He was soon called upon to furnish designs and models for public monuments, and at the age of thirty-two received an order for a life-size statue in marble. Without study or previous experience he modelled the figure from life and cut it in marble, thus compassing in his first efforts the sculptural and mechanical processes of the art. In 1875–1876 he visited Europe, travelling and studying in Paris, Florence, and Rome. On his return he devoted himself to portrait-sculpture, modelling a great number of busts and reliefs. From 1883 to 1896 he spent much of his time in Paris, producing, among other works, the models for the Soldiers' and Sailors' Monument at Waterbury, Connecticut; a statue of Colonel John L. Chatfield for the same city; an ideal statue for a fountain at Hudson, New York; and a statue of Abraham Lincoln and a slave for a monument which he designed and placed in Edinburgh, Scotland.

During these years, when at his studio at Poughkeepsie, he modelled the statue of General Gates, now on the Saratoga battle monument at Schuylerville, New York; the "Standard Bearer" at Winsted, Connecticut; the statue of "Union" at Salisbury, Connecticut; "Chancellor John Watts" in Trinity churchyard, New York City, a bronze replica of which was exhibited at the Columbian Exposition at Chicago, and afterward placed before the Leake and Watts Orphan House at Yonkers, New York; and the statue of Chancellor James Kent, now in the new Congressional Library at Washington, D.C. His "Lycurgus" (Fig. 36) is on the Appellate Court building, New York, and his "President Arthur" in Madison Square.

FIG. 36. — BISSELL : LYCURGUS.

Among the six monuments that had the distinction of being chosen by the committee of New York sculptors was Mr. Bissell's "Colonel Abraham de Peyster," a seated figure modelled in Paris in 1896, and now decorating with much "presence" the grassy square known as Bowling Green. The first impression produced by this statue is one of flowing robes and high boots and abundant wig; but through all this ancient paraphernalia the old-time mayor and man of affairs makes himself felt as a personage of character and of authority. He sits very solidly, his right hand on his thigh, the left arm supported upon his sword as on a staff, the head turned to the left and lifted with a look of great decision. He scarcely needs the rolled charter with its pendent seal to convince us that he was once master of the situation, though his present dignity is dependent upon his remaining quietly on his pedestal.

Interesting as is this statue, it is understood that the choice of the sculptors would have fallen upon another of Mr. Bissell's works had it been eligible. His " Chancellor John Watts " (Fig. 37) was debarred from competition as a public monument because located within Trinity churchyard; but it is Mr. Bissell's finest achievement. His natural sense of fitness enables him to give to such a work an air of great dignity and composure. The ample robe of the chancellor affords mass, while its long lines lend themselves most happily to statuesque effect. Such a union of restraint with play of sculptural color is exceedingly rare, and its success speaks well for the native talent of the sculptor who, without technical training, arrived at these results. Work of this character from the hands of the untutored " gravestone man " of twenty years ago would seem incredible, were it not for the fact that Mr. Bissell has kept patiently and enthusiastically in the line of progress, visiting Paris frequently, associating with younger men of skill and attainment, and literally making each enterprise a stepping-stone and a schooling for further efforts. Deeper than all this, too, is a peculiar attitude of mind which makes this true artist keenly interested in the personality of his subjects. Be they living or dead, he imagines a vast amount of character into them. He is not satisfied to put upon them heads of merely correct proportions or even accurate features; he makes his men intensely alive, and reveals them to others as interesting as he finds or imagines them himself.

Mr. Franklin Simmons, though living abroad, is best known for his public monuments erected in various cities of the United States. He is not without imagination, and early cherished ambitions to be recognized as a sculptor of ideal statuary, but, like so many others, has gradually bowed to the demands of the period for portrait and memorial sculpture.

Born in 1839, in the town of Webster, Maine, the future artist was educated in the public schools of his native town and at Bates College, Lewiston, Maine. He was at one time employed as a runner boy in the Hill Mill of the latter place, and, while thus engaged, discovered his peculiar talent and attracted attention through his clever sketches. During his school days he delighted in modelling figures in the coarse clay from the banks of the Androscoggin River. One of his earliest attempts at sculpture was a portrait bust of Dr. Bow-ditch of Bowdoin College, which, it is said, still stands on a bracket in the Hill Mill office.   Upon graduation from college, he turned at once to his favorite employment, and met with so much success in portraiture that he was soon encouraged to follow the example of numerous other young sculptors who had hastened to Washington in search of larger opportunities.   He spent the winters of 1865 and 1866 in that city, where he was favored with sittings from Admirals Farragut and Porter, Generals Grant, Meade, Sheridan, Sherman, Thomas, Hooker, and others.   In 1868 Mr. Simmons received a com-mission for a statue of Roger Williams and went to Rome, where he has since resided.   The figure of the Rhode Island pastor was com-pleted in marble in 1870, and stands in Statuary Hall in the Capitol. It is a creditable work, which may well have ranked for years among the best in that collection.   The face is dignified and benign; the figure well understood; the drapery skilfully disposed, though some-what hard in treatment, as was the manner of the time.   This statue was joined later (1877) by Mr. Simmons's " Governor William King " of Maine, a well-posed figure, amply enveloped in a large cloak. Here, again, the head is ably suggested, though with little vivacity or charm of modelling.   The severe treatment of the drapery continues.

The same year saw the unveiling, at Providence, Rhode Island, of another statue of Roger Williams from Mr. Simmons's hand. As no authentic portrait of Williams is in existence, the artist had, as before, the privilege of expressing his own idea of the man, and produced a figure which was highly praised by contemporaries.   An impersonation of History is shown below, presumably recording the name of the worthy divine.   The use of an accessory figure of this character now so familiar, not to say *banal*, was then new to America, and was referred to at the time as follows: " This com-bination of one figure above another is altogether novel, and has been pronounced bold in the extreme." [1]   The monument had cost the sculptor four years of labor, but meantime other works had been in progress.   In the favoring atmosphere of Rome his imagi-nation had begun to expand, and he produced a series of ideal

[1] " Great American Sculptures," p. 130.

FIG. 37.—BISSELL: CHANCELLOR JOHN WATTS, NEW YORK.

statues, among which one finds the more or less familiar names of "Penelope," "Medusa," "Seraph Abdiel," "Galatea," "The Mother of Moses," and "Benjamin." Of these "The Mother of Moses," or "Jochebed," as it was first christened, was one of the earliest and a favorite. It reminds one of Mr. Story's seated figures, but is better modelled and better carved. It lacks also the exaggerated expression of his perturbed heroines, but it is, on the other hand, equally lacking in appeal. The labored carefulness of the workmanship seems to counteract the intention of the artist. The original spontaneity of the sketch has vanished. One feels that neither the mourning mother nor the crowing babe dare move lest the composition be spoiled, or the too neatly adjusted drapery disturbed. It is obvious that even the mantle thrown over the rock has been patiently arranged. In the presence of this statue, as with the "Promised Land" of the Metropolitan Museum (1874), one is reminded of the exclamation of Louis Gonse: "Alas! it is not the absence of faults which makes a masterpiece; it is flame; it is life; it is emotion; it is sincerity; it is the personal accent."

The crowning group of the Naval Monument in Washington (1878) is more persuasive in its emotional appeal. History stands, tablet in hand, ready to write the names which a mourning America confides to her. The sculptor has made no attempt to realize an ideal of national distinction, nor even of personality, in his America. It is simply a mourning figure, but the two form a good sculptural mass, and are enveloped in graceful, well-executed drapery. Below, on the western plinth, is a semi-classic Victory, supported by an infant Neptune and Mars; on the reverse a figure of Peace. These subordinate figures are like the architecture of the monument,— deficient in style and without impressiveness.

Mr. Simmons has been an indefatigable worker, having produced no less than one hundred portrait busts in marble and fifteen public monuments. His latest work of importance is the equestrian monument to General Logan in Iowa Circle, Washington, D. C., which was unveiled April 9, 1901. This elaborate memorial is unusual in being entirely of bronze, and shows a dignified conception most conscientiously and adequately wrought into form. The characterization of Logan is considered successful; the figure rides quietly, but the expression of the face and the gesture of the hand which clutches the sword mark the intrepidity of the hero. The horse is apparently in moderate movement, and is noticeable for its careful workmanship. The sides of the pedestal are filled with large reliefs, containing life-size figures of Logan and of his distinguished colleagues; while the front panel is occupied by an armed Victory, modelled almost in the round. The angles of the ornamented cornice are gracefully marked by conventional eagles with outstretched wings. These and other well-considered details give richness to a design which is exceptionally chaste in contour and effective in mass.

Martin Milmore, whose name has been immortalized by Mr. French's beautiful relief, " The Angel of Death and the Young Sculptor," deserves more than passing notice, not alone because of his early development and the rich promise which his death left unredeemed, but for the intrinsic value of much good work accomplished in the thirty-nine years of his busy life.

Mr. Milmore was born in Sligo, Ireland, in the year 1844. Upon the death of his father, a schoolmaster, in 1851, the widow and children removed to the United States, settling in Boston, where, parallel with his studies in the public school, the future sculptor made essays in wood-carving under the guidance of his elder brother, Joseph (born 1841). Experiments in modelling followed until, delighted with his own success in portraiture, the boy determined to make sculpture his work, and wisely arranged for systematic study. It was his good fortune to find a welcome in the studio of Thomas Ball, with whom he remained four years (1860–1864). His first ideal work, a high relief entitled " Phosphor," was produced during this period; it met with a kindly reception, and gained him orders for at least two replicas. Still another order followed in the same year (1863) for a statue for the Sanitary Fair, in which the artist embodied his idea of " Devotion." With great industry the boy produced a number of small works, and in 1864, when just twenty years of age, he was commissioned to execute in granite for the Boston Horticultural Hall three large decorative figures, " Ceres," " Flora," and " Pomona." There may be question as to the artistic value of these heroics of eight and twelve feet, but it is evident that in such practice there is very great advantage for the future creator of monuments.

A bust of Charles Sumner,-modelled in 1865, was presented by the legislature of Massachusetts to Mr. George William Curtis, and ultimately found its way to the Metropolitan Museum of New York. In 1867 Mr. Milmore began the first of the series of soldier monuments with which his name is principally associated. This memorial which stands in Forest Hills Cemetery, Roxbury, Massachusetts, shows a Federal soldier resting upon his gun and contemplating the graves of his fallen companions — a *motif* of far greater impressiveness than is often discovered in the more elaborate and expensive monuments with which the country abounds.

The Soldiers' and Sailors' Monument, erected on the Boston Common in 1874, was Mr. Milmore's most important work. It is the conventional military monument: a shaft with figures at the four corners of the base and crowned with a statue of Liberty, but it shows this now " stock " design at its best. Indeed, it was undoubtedly the success of Mr. Milmore's work and its intrinsic beauty which made this form of monument so popular that it has been reproduced in varying degrees of incompleteness and ineffectiveness over the whole United States. One can recall no other which has the simple, quiet dignity of the structure on Boston Common. The proportions of base and column and figures are well considered and in their relations to each other these members could scarcely be improved. The sculpture, in addition to the somewhat negative quality of being in good taste, reveals certain positive merits. The most truly sculptural feature — and therefore the best sculpture of the monument — is found in the female figures carved in relief upon the lower section of the shaft. These figures, if not distinctly poetic, are treated with a fine feeling for their architectural value, and with an intelligent deference to the material in which they are carved. Their lines are simple and chaste, yet very decorative. The conventionalization of detail rendered necessary by the unyielding granite has been managed with much skill and actually gives them a distinction which is lacking in the more subservient bronzes. Of the latter the Soldier and the Sailor were among the first ably executed figures of a realistic character used upon such monuments and are still among the best which our country has produced. Their poses are good; they stand well upon their feet, and their expressions are serious, without too great display of feeling. If " real men " must perch thus isolated upon the corners and ledges of our monuments, it might well be hoped that they should always be as decorous as these. Alternating with the two male figures are two seated females whose amiable features and well-drawn draperies are attractive, though proving in the end a little tiresome. The " Muse of History " is the more graceful of the two, but her face is strangely characterless. The crowning figure has her hands full with the flag and the ægis, and presents agreeable contours on all sides — a dignified statue, though without animation.

The bronze reliefs upon this monument are often eulogized, but they present no sculptural interest. It is strange that the artist who had handled the decorative figures above so adequately should have shown here a complete neglect of the requirements of relief. The panel of " The Sanitary Commission " shows a vast amount of work, for it is made up of portraits; but the total result is in no wise commensurate with the effort. Indeed, it is rather childish. In the " Fort Sumter " this naïveté reaches the limit. Nothing could be more unsculptural than the expanse of shiny sea with its distant fort, and then, down in the left-hand corner, occupying perhaps a sixth of the entire area of the panel, a number of tiny bronze figures in full relief.

Despite these shortcomings, the Boston monument is the best conceived and the most ably executed work of its class in this country. It does great honor not only to the brave men whom it commemorates, but to the conscience of the young artist who so faithfully wrought its every detail. Mr. Milmore did most if not all of the sculpture of this monument in Rome, and during the years of his sojourn abroad modelled, as well, a number of excellent busts, of which those of Pope Pius IX, Wendell Phillips, and Emerson may be mentioned.

Other war monuments of Milmore's designing are those at Keene, New Hampshire, at Erie, Pennsylvania, and at Charlestown and Fitchburg, Massachusetts, the last named representing " America." His statue of General Sylvanus Thayer, " Father of the United States Military Academy," is conspicuous at West Point, New York, while the great granite "Sphinx," which he executed with his brother Joseph, stands as an impressive memorial to the Union dead in Mount Auburn Cemetery, Cambridge, Massachusetts. Among other busts recorded by the chroniclers are those of George Ticknor, in the Boston Public Library, Cardinal McCloskey, General Grant, Lincoln, and Webster. The sculptor died in Boston, July 21, 1883, and was buried in Forest Hills Cemetery, where his grave is marked by Mr. French's noble tribute.

Mr. Milmore stands for good workmanship rather than for poetic expression. Few, if any, of his productions seem inspired; they never thrill. There is nothing epic in his grasp of war subjects, nothing lyric in his treatment of gentler themes; no trace of sweetness at any time. But we find throughout good honest construction, adequate modelling, and, rarest of all, a sense of the monumental in line and mass. If not always, or, indeed, if seldom, distinguished, his work was invariably restrained, without trace of flippancy or ostentation or "smartness." It possessed the fundamentals of serious, self-respecting art, and had its influence on the side of moderation and dignity.

CHAPTER XIV

NEW INFLUENCES

THE path of human progress is a zigzag route. The history of art is a record of incessant " tacking." Alongside of every successful development may be found the germs of a " new movement," destined presently to overtop its arrogant rival and to take its place until, in the fulness of time, it shall likewise have served its purpose and have made way for some fresh impulse. Thus the story of painting or of sculpture seems to be made up largely of " returns to nature," though as far as the results are concerned there is often slight evidence of a change of heart; artificiality has merely taken a new form under a fresh and persuasive leadership.

The change in American sculpture which the Centennial period ushered in was not one of name alone, but of spirit — the working of new influences now became evident. These influences were completing the exchange of a cold, impersonal classicism for an expressive and often picturesque truth, destined to attain in its highest manifestations to a new idealism. Broadly speaking, it was the substitution of the art of Saint Gaudens for that of Hiram Powers, though, of course, no transition is so abrupt as such a statement would suggest; nor could the sculpture of Hiram Powers ever have begotten unaided the sculpture of Augustus Saint Gaudens. New and various forces had been making themselves felt for some time. Though Powers died but three years before the Centennial Exposition in Philadelphia, his work was already largely discredited; that is to say, it had long since ceased to be the standard for younger men. The sturdy native works of Brown, Ward, Ball, and John Rogers, and particularly the union of familiar truth and sentiment that is found in Palmer's chaste fancies, had been exerting their powerful influence. Further, while tastes were changing at home, an artistic revolution had taken place in Italy where the native sculptors had declined to "do Greek" any longer, betaking themselves to those romantic, picturesque, and *genre* subjects and methods which have held sway ever since.   This change had been gradual, — a matter of years, — and the last American representatives of the "classic school," notably Rinehart and Miss Hosmer, showed, as has been seen, a considerable infusion of life in their ideal works; while Story, more audacious if less artistic, clung still to the ancient subjects, but treated them in a personal and exaggerated way of his own.   In 1876 Mr. Story was our most noted sculptor abroad, and Palmer the most popular at home.

Meantime others beside Richard Greenough had discovered Paris.   At least three young American sculptors had been enrolled in the École des Beaux-Arts before the Franco-Prussian War.   One of this number, Howard Roberts of Philadelphia, made his début at the Centennial Exposition, with a figure, "La Première Pose," which was so superior in technical qualities to the mass of American work that it created a sensation.   The idea, however, foreign to American experience and tastes, lent itself to a worthy sculptural rendering — a young woman, who is preparing to pose undraped for the first time in a painter's studio, and who, overcome by self-consciousness, crouches back in her chair, shrinking from observation. The figure, though beautifully proportioned and graceful, is not an altogether attractive one.   In its initial conception there is an affectation of modesty which strikes a false note.   The "shrinking" is a little too obtrusive, too professional.   A young model, who is really timid, shows it with much less effort.   The blush or paleness, the rigid pose and the startled or downcast eye, are far more convincing than all this contortion, and appeal infinitely more to the sympathy. But outside of this it must be conceded that the work is good sculpture.   It is conceived as sculpture, and it is constructed.   There is certainty in the drawing and firmness· as well as delicacy in the modelling, and finally the marble has been carved with intelligence and precision.   To some tastes the precision is indeed overdone, there being a suggestion of modern Italian handicraft in the elaborate fringe of chair and mantle and the conspicuous palette, with its running colors; but after all it is the well-modelled figure which predominates and which satisfies us through a grace extending literally to the finger-tips. Hands had not been so well done before in the history of American sculpture. Compared with the knowledge and control of the body shown in this work, many of the earlier statues look almost like examples of poor taxidermy; the features, the parts, and the superficial markings are all present, to be sure, but there is no feeling of bone and muscle underneath. With the French school-

FIG. 38. — HARTLEY: JOHN GILBERT, PLAYERS' CLUB.

ing came not only a new impulse in the spirit of American sculpture, but the demand for a comprehensive knowledge of the physical structure. Henceforth the sculptor must know his theme.

Howard Roberts was born in Philadelphia in 1843. He studied in the Pennsylvania Academy of Fine Arts, and was for some time under the instruction of J. A. Bailly. It was in 1886 that he went first to Paris, where he remained for several years as a student in the École des Beaux-Arts, in the Atelier Dumont. He also received instruction from M. Gumery. Both of these sculptors are said to have taken a lively interest in their American pupil; and while they themselves represented the old school, it is evident that he owed much to their intelligent guidance.

Returning to America, Mr. Roberts modelled several ideal busts, of which "Eleanor," in the Pennsylvania Academy, may serve as an example. This pleasing work has a pretty face, of refined type, but shows no remarkable modelling, nor a great deal of character. The hair is better handled than in most works of the time, but the drapery has a curious, wilted look. Then followed a statuette of "Hester Prynne," representing the heroine of "The Scarlet Letter" on the pillory with her babe in her arms. This meritorious work was succeeded by a series of portrait and ideal busts, and by a life-size statue of "Hypatia." Mr. Roberts returned, in 1873, to Paris with the plaster cast of this figure, presumably intending to put it in marble. He became engrossed, however, in the new theme, "La Première Pose," to the exclusion of all other interests, and the "Hypatia" was not put in marble until the artist's return to America, while "La Première Pose" was completed in time for the Centennial, where it received one of the three medals awarded to American sculptors.

A contemporaneous estimate of Mr. Roberts's "Hypatia" may be quoted, since the work was accounted a very important one in its day: "The merely technical merits of the 'Hypatia' are as great as those of the 'Première Pose,' but the subject is such a striking one, and it is treated in such a powerful and effective manner, that the statue demands to be judged on other and higher than technical grounds. This work was, after being completed in marble, put on public exhibition for a short time, and was visited by many thousands of persons. There was but one verdict in regard to it, and that was that it was the most impressive piece of sculpture that had been shown in Philadelphia for many years. This admirable statue increased the fame of Roberts even more than the 'Première Pose' did, for it appealed to a wider range of tastes, and a different order of sympathies. In it the beautiful Alexandrian Greek — the last of the pagans — is shown as turning at bay on the altar of the church into which she has been driven by the fanatical monks who are thirsting for her blood. The motion of turning is very finely expressed, — to mention one striking point of technical excellence, — and the hunted woman faces her savage pursuers with mingled indignation, disgust, and despair on her face, as with one hand she clasps her tattered draperies to her breast and with the other half supports herself by means of one of the candlesticks of the altar. Fine as this powerful performance is throughout, the face is particularly worthy of admiration. It is a purely

Greek face in type, and yet there is no Greek statue we know of that is marked by strong individuality — by what we moderns call character — to the extent that this one is." [1]

Mr. Roberts established himself in Philadelphia in 1875. Here, in a large studio which attracted many visitors, he carved his " Hypatia," and here he modelled his last ideal figure of which we have record, the " Lot's Wife." " Hypatia " is not nearly so good a figure as its companion in the Pennsylvania Academy, " La Première Pose," though it shows a vigorous thought and much clever workmanship. Its excellence is marred by exaggeration — the face is all features and frown — and by a painful insistence upon the accessories. The churchly crucifix and censer are over-prominent, fringes abound, and the carving of the hair is unpleasantly restless. The hands are remarkable for their realism, looking like plaster casts from nature.

The statuette of " Lot's Wife " is described as: " A very singular creation, which could only have been imagined by the artist in a grotesque mood. It cannot be called beautiful, but it is most original in conception and execution, and, in spite of its grotesqueness, it is full of power and impressiveness. The woman is represented in a writhing attitude, and she is not only being enveloped in the crystals of salt which are forming around her, but she is actually dissolving into salt herself. The idea of transformation is very much more perfectly expressed in this statuette than it is in Bernini's ' Daphne,' or in any attempts to represent metamorphosis that we know of. Lot's wife is really turning into a pillar of salt, and, admitting that the idea of such a transformation is a rather queer one for a sculptor to choose, we must also admit that it is expressed with remarkable skill." [2]

And here the record ends. No further notice is to be found anywhere of Mr. Roberts or of subsequent productions. Probably he felt it sufficient glory to have made us acquainted with the modern French school, and having done his work he stopped. He died in Paris, Apr. 19, 1900. [3]

---

[1] " Great American Sculptures," p. 102.   [2] Ibid., p. 103.

[3] Mr. Roberts's " Fulton " in the National Hall of Statuary is a picturesque and much-tooled figure, which shows the inventor in knee-breeches and shirt sleeves, seated in an armchair and buried in contemplation of a small model of his steamboat. The expression of the face is largely concealed by the pose of the head, and the restlessness of the technic combines with a lack of strong lines to make this an unsatisfactory work.

Another young man who won honors from the American public at the Centennial Exposition was Pierce Francis Connelly, then residing in Florence. Like Howard Roberts, his name had been quite unknown before; he enjoyed similar meteoric success, and resembled him further in the completeness of his subsequent disappearance from view. The particulars of his origin and education are to be found in no encyclopædia. Nevertheless there were many more works bearing his name at the Centennial than were exhibited by any other American sculptor, and some of these were productions of no little power. The most important of the number were a bronze group of "Honor arresting the Triumph of Death," a marble group of "Saint Martin dividing his Cloak," and marble statues of "Ophelia" and of "Thetis." Of these the "Honor and Death" is now in the Pennsylvania Academy, and the "Thetis" in the Metropolitan Museum.

Although small in dimensions, — half life-size, — the allegorical group of "Honor and Death" was among the most impressive things in the art department of the exhibition, and remains to-day a remarkable work of its time. It is composed of five figures and of a horse in vigorous action, on which Death sits revelling in slaughter, having just struck down Courage, Perseverance, and Strength, only to find himself stopped and disarmed by Honor. The thought is a fine one, and the undertaking no slight task, of which the young sculptor acquitted himself admirably in all of the main features. One scarcely knows which to admire more, the audacity of the scheme or the skill with which it has been handled. It occupied its author from 1866 to 1869, according to the inscription which it bears.

One turned with no little surprise from this turbulent product of the romantic spirit to the classic subject, "Thetis and her Son Achilles," which Mr. Connelly had completed in his Florentine studio in 1874. This work, bearing the same date as Rinehart's "Latona," is a conception of much charm, a seated figure whose every line shows the artist's sense of grace. It is unfortunate, however, in reproduction; the marble drapery is tiresome, the thin undergarment which falls over a projecting leg being especially bad, while the ornaments on the mantle are in such relief as to cut up its surface most disastrously. The " Ophelia " was yet another example of the versatility of its author, being a distinctly modern production in the Florentine style so familiar to-day. A graceful, sweet-faced figure in elaborate costume advances, offering a flower with winsome gesture. There is no trace of madness in this ideal of the unfortunate girl, and — to group incongruous thoughts — there is as slight trace of the sculpturesque in the artist's conception; but we can well believe that the fair face and the elegance of brocades and laces would more than atone with most spectators for such deficiencies. Connelly's " Ophelia " helped to confirm the growing taste for "embroidered" marbles. The tide of commercial sculpture, arrested by the Civil War and stagnant for some time afterward, now rolled in with redoubled volume.

While practically no American sculptors have established themselves of late years in Italy, a number of the older men continue there. Mr. Meade has been referred to as the last survivor in Florence, and Franklin Simmons as the dean of the diminished Roman group. Among the few others remaining must be mentioned Moses Ezekiel, who was born in Richmond, Virginia, in 1844. Mr. Ezekiel received a military education, after which he devoted himself for a time to the study of anatomy. His artistic training was obtained at the Royal Academy in Berlin. He was admitted into the Society of Artists of that city on the merits of a colossal bust of Washington, a copy of which is in the Cincinnati Museum of Fine Arts. His first important work was a marble group representing " Religious Liberty," shown at the Centennial Exposition, and remaining permanently in Fairmount Park, Philadelphia. Mr. Ezekiel has produced many portraits and no small number of ideal works, such as his " Faith," in a cemetery of Rome; " Madonna," for a church in Tivoli; "Apollo and Mercury," in Berlin; and the " Fountain of Neptune," for the town of Nettuno, Italy.

Mr. Ezekiel has a talent for exquisite carving, or at least an appreciation of it, and his *envois* to this country are always noticeable on this account in the collections where they are to be found. His " Judith " in the Cincinnati Museum is more realistic than ideal, but the skill of its workmanship cannot be denied. His "Head of Christ" in the Peabody Institute, in Baltimore, is even more trying to one's patience, if not positively offensive. It suggests vaguely the well-known bust of Caracalla — a dull, inert Caracalla. The pose and treatment, however, are striking. A rope passes twice about the body, and the drapery and hair are remarkable for their clever workmanship — so clever, indeed, are they that one quite forgets the intention of the bust while studying its surface.

In the same hall may be seen as a companion to Rinehart's "Clytie" a standing male figure by Mr. Ezekiel, entitled "Faith," presumably a replica of the one mentioned above as being in a Roman cemetery. This marble shows a handsome youth in a graceful attitude, with right hand uplifted and head thrown back. The modelling and carving of the nude forms are excellent; the effect of the figure from all sides, very pleasing.

The most important work, however, which Mr. Ezekiel has sent to this country, is his monument to Thomas Jefferson, in Louisville, Kentucky. In this somewhat whimsical conception the sculptor has placed the author of the Declaration of Independence upon the Liberty Bell, or at least has made use of a bell-shaped pedestal of bronze, surrounded by dainty decorative figures. The idea is novel and interesting, though too fanciful to be impressive. There is much beauty of modelling in various parts of the work, particularly in the subordinate figures.

Mr. Ezekiel can scarcely be called a leader in American art, but his works demand mention in this chapter rather than elsewhere, because they appeared early among the new influences which at first confused and later clarified American taste. As has been seen, his initial exhibit was made at the Centennial, where it introduced to our public the German and the new Italian methods. These schools have been neglected by the succeeding generation of American sculptors, having had few, if any, followers. Mr. Ezekiel's own art, however, so ably expressive of their methods, has been very popular, and must have contributed not a little to the downfall of the thread-bare classicism which had prevailed up to his time.

Jonathan Scott Hartley was born in Albany, New York, in September, 1846. He began working in a monumental marble yard at the age of sixteen, and had soon acquired sufficient skill to win him entrance to the studio of E. D. Palmer, for whom he carved during the years 1863 and 1864.   Soon after this he went to London, where he studied for three years in the Royal Academy, working there evenings only, however, since it was necessary that he be self-supporting.   Another year was spent in Berlin, after which he returned to this country.   He had later an opportunity to go to Italy for a few months, and concluded his long and varied student life with a year in Paris.   It was in 1875 that he finally opened a studio in New York, where he set himself at once to the task of modelling imaginative works.   The first of these was entitled " A Little Samaritan," and was exhibited at the Centennial Exposition at Philadelphia.   Mr. Hartley's professional fame was made, however, by " The Whirlwind," which appeared in 1878, and was much complimented in its day for the originality of the thought and the vigor with which it was developed.   A critic of twenty-five years ago pronounced the figure "a serious, substantial, and thoroughly artistic work, full of epic passion under self-control." Another observed : " ' The Whirlwind ' should not displease robust tastes.   The subject itself once accepted, we must acknowledge that Mr. Hartley has carried it out well, albeit a little too vigorously.   The spiral of the drapery, like a great piece of kelp, is very cleverly managed, and the general pose of the figure is good."

Mr. Hartley's first public statue was " Miles Morgan," a Puritan subject, erected in Springfield, Massachusetts, in 1882 ; his latest, produced in 1901, the figure of Rev. Thomas K. Beecher, placed at Elmira, New York.   Other public works are the Daguerre monument in Washington, D.C.; the Ericsson statue and " Alfred the Great " in New York City, the latter being one of the decorative figures which crown the Appellate Court building.   Though strongly drawn in the direction of ideal sculpture, Mr. Hartley has for some years past devoted most of his time to portrait busts, and he is now somewhat of a victim to his great reputation for this class of work. The public will not let him do anything else.   A bust by Hartley is considered by many a synonym for the most precise and authentic characterization possible.   Nothing could be more admirable than the conscience which the sculptor shows in these closely studied works.   Nothing could be more penetrating.   One submits to him with the feeling that the X-rays are to be turned on ; that not only

FIG. 39.—WARNER: DIANA, COTTIER & CO., NEW YORK.

the uttermost wrinkle will be noted, but that the innermost thought is to be revealed.   The sitter observes in the end with deep grati-tude that professional etiquette has prevailed; the sculptor has not told everything, but it has been a narrow escape — he could have done so if he had wished to.

Not that the busts of this clever man are uniformly great.   It is simply impossible to make a great work of art out of some heads; they are not made for it.   It is doubly impossible, so to speak, when the sculptor realizes this fact at the beginning of his study of a sub-ject.   His enthusiasm fails, and his clever hand is paralyzed.   At such times a man of Mr. Hartley's skill makes up on detail.   The result is that now and then there comes from his studio a head which is dry and "crummy," as the painters would say, with the skin drawn tight over the bones, the face unvivacious and unresponsive. But when Mr. Hartley is at his best he has few rivals, in this country at least, for close, intimate, unflinching characterization.   Others may generalize, giving a phase of the man, — a view that is effective and even masterful when seen in the proper lighting; but Mr. Hart-ley's searching studies present the very man himself — they will stand any light and any approach.   Take, for instance, the bust of "John Gilbert as Sir Peter Teazle" (Fig. 38), a work which was completed on Mr. Gilbert's eightieth birthday.   The bronze stands among the treasures of the Players' Club in a rather trying cross light, but it asks no favors, for it needs none.   Those shrewd eyes peer out with the keenness of an intelligence behind them.   It is almost impossible to divest one's self of a semi-conscious recognition of the face as that of a living personality.   It is one of the most real things in American art.   The modelling of soft puffy flesh and of solid bone, of wig and costume, could not be carried further.   It might be made more minute, but it would cease to be good sculp-ture, and cease as well to have the look of plastic spontaneity which is so delightful here.   One should notice how cunningly the sculptor has handled the details of the coat and of the ribbon: no hard edges anywhere, but a "touch and go," a sprinkling of accents which is a joy to the eye.   Yet what moderation does one find in all this playfulness, what control of the "whole"!   The treatment of the body is in quite another key, however, from that of the face.   The former is simplified almost to low relief handling instead of being cut up as a poorer artist might have done. It is, so to speak, " out of focus "; the head is paramount, and here the sculptor has given greater emphasis and full contrasts with the successful result which we so much admire.

We turn from this comfortable face to one of a very dissimilar type: Felix Morris as the Marquis in " A Game of Cards," a thin, amiable, and rather grotesque countenance, tinged with sadness. Here the workmanship is no less fascinating: the wrinkled cheek, still further perplexed by the aggressive collar and "choker," the sensitive, whimsical mouth, the well-modelled ear — and what a comfort it is to see an ear modelled with some respect for its individuality — the dreamy yet penetrating eye; then, after these essentials, the impetuous, sketchy massing of the hair and, once more, the softening of the outlines of the coat, which remains firm in drawing, but loses its sharp edges in grateful half-tones — these are some of the beauties of this quaint bust. It is hardly needful to say that for those who know the value of each affectionate touch in a work of art there is great satisfaction in such a performance as this.

A few portrait statues, a fountain, a half-dozen busts, and two or three score medallions — such appears at first sight the scanty achievement of one whom America's sculptors delight to honor, a man whose name stands among the highest. In one sense Olin L. Warner's life was unproductive; in another it was richly fruitful; for while it shows no long catalogue of works, everything that he signed was art and good art. Coming when he did, his influence on the side of worthy sculpture was important; had his works been more widely known during his lifetime, he might have become a recognized leader.

Olin Levi Warner was born at West Suffield, Connecticut, in 1844, the son of an itinerant Methodist preacher of long New England ancestry. The family removed from Connecticut to Amsterdam, New York, in 1846, and there the son attended the district school until his fifteenth year, when he entered an academy of Orange County. Two years after, his father's wanderings took the family to Brandon, Vermont, where the young man remained in school until he was nineteen years of age. During his childhood he had shown a decided talent for carving heads and statuettes in chalk, and now he aspired to a more serious test of his abilities — a portrait bust of his father. Unacquainted with the processes of modelling and casting, he procured a barrel of plaster, and "setting" it in one great mass, broke off the staves and attacked it with hammer and chisel. Native talent and perseverance won the day; the work was pronounced a success, and counted worthy of exhibition at the state fair. It was a turning-point in the boy's career, for it convinced him, as well as his friends, of his "call" to the sculptor's profession. It brought no aid, however, and quite dependent upon his own exertions, he set himself courageously to work to earn money with which to go abroad. He studied telegraphy, and for six years was employed at Albion and Rochester, New York, and at Augusta, Georgia. It was, therefore, not until 1869 that he was able to sail for Europe. He was now twenty-five years of age, and no time was to be lost. Good fortune directed him to Paris, where, although friendless and alone, without even letters of introduction, he soon made acquaintances of the right sort, and ultimately found safe harbor in the École des Beaux-Arts. He remained in Paris three years and a half, not only working diligently in the Atelier Jouffroy, but even assisting Carpeaux for a short time in his private studio, while making the acquaintance of such artists as Falguière and Mercié.

Meantime, other things were occurring in and around Paris. Mr. Warner's first year there was the last of the Empire, and when the Republic was proclaimed, Sept. 4, 1870, Warner, with other American residents in sympathy with the French, enlisted in the foreign legion. He remained in Paris during the siege and the occupation by the Commune of 1871, and at its termination resumed his studies. Returning to America in the fall of 1872, he took a studio in New York City, but never did an eager and expectant artist meet with more dismal reception. Warner's art was clearly ahead of his time. Always a "sculptor for sculptors," rather than for the public, his welcome was not that of those who used to bring over a "stock" from Italy, "open a studio" on Broadway, and sell out in a few weeks. For four years the sculptor hoped against hope; then, after all the sacrifices of his life, he gave up the struggle and returned for a time to his father's farm. During this dark period he had worked for manufacturers of silver and plated ware and bronze mantel ornaments. His single exhibit at the Centennial was a large medallion of Edwin Forrest, a bold and expressive work.

Restless upon the farm, Mr. Warner sought other means of livelihood, and applying to Mr. Plant, president of the Southern Express Company, was encouraged to return to his profession by an order for two portrait busts. In 1878 he met Mr. Daniel Cottier, then just opening his art rooms in New York, and was invited to exhibit his bust of Mrs. Plant. The acquaintance grew into a warm friendship, which meant much in Mr. Warner's life. A small portrait bust of Mr. Cottier is a work memorable among American sculptures, so beautiful is its craftsmanship, so genial its interpretation. Other busts followed, fascinating works of classic simplicity and extraordinary richness of modelling. Of this period likewise is a half-draped ideal figure in marble called " Twilight," a work of unusual grace. Though Mr. Warner was still unknown to the public, his position was now fully established among his colleagues; it is interesting to note that he was one of the five original members of the Society of American Artists. In 1876 he exhibited a bust of his father and some medallions; in 1879 the statue of " Twilight"; in 1880 a bust of J. Alden Weir; in 1881 a small statue of a " Dancing Nymph " and a bust of Miss Maud Morgan; in 1882 a relief of "Cupid and Psyche," and in 1883 a bust of Miss Cottier. Naturally of less refined workmanship were various Indian heads and other decorations for the Long Island Historical Society, and five colossal heads of more recent date for the Pennsylvania railway station in Philadelphia.

Late in the eighties Mr. Warner made a long tour with a party through the West. The direct harvest of this journey was a series of relief portraits of Indians, a collection of great value both ethnologically and artistically. Many of these reliefs will be found pictured in an article in the *Century Magazine*.[1] Mr. Warner's skill in relief was exceptional, and ranked with that of Mr. Saint Gaudens. His portraits of his parents, of Wyatt Eaton, of W. C.

[1] Vol. XV, p. 392.

FIG. 40. — WARNER: IMAGINATION, WASHINGTON.

Brownell, and other friends are among the choicest of our native productions in this field. His full-length portrait statues are three in number: "Governor Buckingham" of Connecticut in the state Capitol; and "William Lloyd Garrison" and "General Devens" in Boston. Of these the two first are seated; the latter is erect and very soldierly. These bronze figures, particularly the "Garrison," are among the best that our country has thus far produced. The "Governor Buckingham" is necessarily an official portrait, and bears, perhaps, a suggestion of a man sitting for his picture; but it is a fine, satisfying work of very sculptural aspect. The "Garrison" is naturally more intense, and as the interpretation of a human character in the legitimate terms of monumental art is to be rated among the great statues of America. It has something of the same quality as Mr. Saint Gaudens's "Farragut," a repose which is deceptive, and which goes far to enhance the effect of internal activity. Within the quiet, unaccentuated contours of this composition is a slumbering fire, a tension betrayed only by the clutch of the hands and the vigorous turn of the head. The sculptor has charged his work with individuality, has made it alive, aflame with energy and emotion, yet not a single stroke has carried his interpretation to excess. Garrison sits there — a pent-up volcano, a human dynamo — ready to leap to his feet, to defend, to attack, to suffer, to accomplish; and yet he is only a quiet, well-composed bronze statue in an arm-chair.

Technically we have no better sculpture than this figure. The body within the garments is "constructed"; one feels that it has been thoroughly understood, yet it is nowhere insisted upon. Like the clothed forms the details of the costume, while scrupulously exact, are never obtrusive. There is not a sharp cut nor a harsh accent in all that varied surface. It wears the light veil of subtle modelling which marks consummate sculpture; one's eye finds in it a positive satisfaction, quite apart from the significance of the work and its life-likeness. Here is where Mr. Warner never failed to show himself a master of his craft. He always remembered the "whole," never sacrificing it to a part. His almost Greek sensitiveness to form preserved him from the mistakes of the over-conscientious, or rather, the ignorantly conscientious, sculptor who insists upon every detail, who detaches every feature of face, costume, and accessory,

T

who cuts deep, underscoring, as it were, every word, not realizing that his perpetual, insistent stress is killing all effect. When such a man gets done we have the "finish" which William M. Hunt used to tell of, — "the finish which rats give to cheese." Everything is eaten up; nothing remains but fatigue for the eye and mind. With Mr. Warner, on the other hand, every touch was autographic, giving not the literal fact, but the truth adapted to sculptural ends as felt by this individual artist mind. Beauty was always present; beauty of line and that surface charm which has marked all great sculpture of the past. One finds invariably the suavity and flow of forms, the coating of atmosphere, with which a skilled artist is able to envelop his work.

Delightful in conception and exquisite in workmanship are the two figures which Mr. Warner modelled in 1888 for a fountain in Portland, Oregon; two caryatides upon either side of a pier, who assist in supporting a large basin. So beautiful are these classic maidens, so serene and graceful in pose, that they must afford keen surprise to one who discovers them in that far western city. Mr. Charles de Kay's comment is probably still true, that "there is nothing so beautiful in statuary westward from Chicago." [1] Of the same severe type of beauty is that self-contained little "Diana" (Fig. 39) which Mr. Warner modelled one winter "without hope of reward," a seated figure rousing up, though not startled, at the approach of poor Actæon. This chaste gem of classic inspiration shows Mr. Warner's mastery of the nude and makes one regret the meagreness of his opportunity. It is evident that he was capable of great expression in this, the highest field of sculpture. But united with the admirable balance of the man, with the simplicity of his purpose, was the cognate virtue, an inflexible honesty which could not be warped by the demands of a vitiated public taste. His superb workmanship was not to be diverted to unworthy ends, and as his somewhat taciturn exterior was reflected to a certain degree in the austerity of his conceptions — strange blend of New England and Hellas! — the true poet underneath was recognized by only a few men of sympathetic temperament.

The story ends all too rapidly. Mr. Warner designed for the

[1] *Century Magazine*, Vol. XV, p. 392.

Columbian Exposition the well-remembered souvenir half-dollar, and made colossal heads of various great artists for the Art Palace; he also did certain sculptures for the New York building, including busts of Governors Clinton and Flower. In 1894 he made the statue of General Devens, already referred to, and began important work for the new Congressional Library. The three bronze doors of the main entrance were to have been his, but he completed only the first. The tympanum group of five figures represents "Tradition," and the panels of the doors contain two figures of much beauty, personifying "Imagination" (Fig. 40) and "Memory." A second door was already designed and in progress when, on Aug. 14, 1896, Mr. Warner died from the effect of a fall while riding in Central Park, New York.

A unique tribute, published by the National Sculpture Society, testified to its sense of loss. Here in eloquent words Mr. W. C. Brownell recited the worth of the man and artist, bringing into relief his unusual qualities of simplicity, sincerity, and sensitiveness. His eulogy concludes as follows: —

"The potencies of beauty native to any problem were what attracted him. These once seized, he pursued their unfolding and unveiling with absolute directness. His technic, in the largest sense as well as in the minutest respect, was instinctively derivative and immediately dependent upon the character of his particular problem. He never asked himself what he could do with a conception by dressing it up or tricking it out in the execution. The conception dictated the execution. His conceptions themselves were as simple as they were fundamental. He inquired what was appropriate, not what could be made effective. The very eminent effectiveness he achieved was due to the fact that this simple and sincere way of considering a work was united with the intuitiveness and perception of a born sculptor, who, when he saw things directly, saw their sculptural side. He liked the aspect of things just in proportion as it conveys. their essence, which I take to be the true sculptor's feeling. Naturally he abhorred the meretricious, and even suspected the picturesque — the picturesque which, in sculpture, holds the ægis of its protection over so much that is superficial, empty, transitorily interesting, and thoroughly unsculptural.

He probably never in his life changed a movement or modified a plane to win Philistine favor or please a dilettante whim. . . .   He leaves his work unfinished; the best of it was undoubtedly before him, for such a nature as his, depending more on native than on acquired powers, reaches slowly the acme of its development.   But the memory of him which his friends will cherish, and which the discerning portion of the public will retain, is that of a singularly rounded and complete career."

PART III

AMERICAN SCULPTURE

CONTEMPORARY MEN, 1876–1903

PLATE 8.—SAINT GAUDENS: SHAW MEMORIAL.

CHAPTER XV

AUGUSTUS SAINT GAUDENS

WHILE influences purely local and accidental are but too often impediments in the artist's race for permanent fame, it is nevertheless a truism that the greatest men are the most perfect incorporations of their age. In this sense every artist is to some extent what Michelet called Dumas the elder, — " Not a man, but one of the forces of nature." The real, thinking, creating sculptors have in all times given visible expression to the trend of national life; their works are, intentionally or not, the records of the ideals of their day. And thus their originality is not the reward of great effort and anxious seeking, but, as has been well said, " the natural and inevitable result of a conscientious effort to express a clear conception in the clearest and completest way."

In the third period of American sculpture new influences are found at work and new characterizations become necessary. The change is quite as marked as between the first and the second periods; indeed, the mass of our sculpture produced before the Centennial seems to-day almost as old-fashioned and alien as the earliest works. A few men had opened their eyes to the world they lived in, and many had changed their themes to suit changing demands; but with most of them such apparent changes were merely superficial, our sculptors having been too generally followers rather than leaders in thought. Since 1876, however, sculpture has become a more genuine expression of feeling, the "neatness" and "correctness" of an amateur age giving way to a manifestation of true creative power. Hand in hand with an increasing perfection of form one discerns a gradual elevation of ideas. Our sculptors are learning to choose the broader and more lasting themes; the hitherto timid wings are beginning to soar.

Almost immediately after the Centennial the Italianate group became negligible as a force, and the Parisian-trained sculptors rose into a prominence which, in a short time, became domination. To-day the influence of Paris is visible in all American sculpture, but, it may be added, only on the technical side. Our art is not now French as it was once Italian.

Perhaps the most powerful influence in this general transformation is the work of a single individual, — a quiet, self-contained man who seldom speaks and never writes, and who nevertheless has accomplished wonders through the very weight and momentum of his earnest personality. Augustus Saint Gaudens was born in Dublin, Ireland, March 1, 1848. His father, Bernard Paul Ernest, a shoemaker by trade, was a native of southern France, coming from the vicinity of the town of Saint Gaudens, which is in the department of the Haute-Garonne, among the spurs of the Pyrenees. His mother, whose maiden name was Mary McGuinness, was a native of Dublin. The family came to this country while Augustus, the third child, was an infant, and after remaining three months in Boston established themselves in New York.

The boy attended school until he was thirteen, when he went to work with a cameo-cutter named Avet, and served a three years' apprenticeship. A misunderstanding led to separation at the end of the time and he found employment with a shell-cameo cutter named Le Breton, with whom he remained for another period of three years. During all the time that he was working at the wheel he studied drawing at night. During the first four years he went to the Cooper Union; the last two were spent in the life classes of the National Academy of Design.

Thus it will be seen he devoted six of the most impressionable years of his life to an employment which demands keenness of vision, delicacy of touch, and quick judgment, inviting likewise to endless refinements of manner and simplifications of method. At the age of twenty, or about the time the average educated man begins his special studies, this youth was thoroughly grounded in drawing and already a master of low relief. He was a master in the sense in which no belated beginner ever becomes a master, for with him it was both mental and physical mastery: an ability to *feel* the subject in relief, and a response in deft fingers like that of the accomplished pianist. Under favorable conditions this response becomes so immediate and so trustworthy that it seems to be spontaneous, a mere reflex of nervous energy. It was toward such perfection of physical self-possession that this double training led in the case of Augustus Saint Gaudens. The union of the two pursuits was a fortunate one; few youths delight in a systematic study of drawing for its own sake, but let them apply their acquired skill to something which interests them, and the incentive becomes great. Imagine the enthusiasm of this thoughtful boy over his first cameos, and the importance in his eyes of those evenings at the Cooper Institute, when he realized that every advance in drawing meant a proportionate improvement in his beautiful art. He was not only acquiring "discipline," but he was weaving his two pursuits into one which should gain momentum and effectiveness thereby. Not the least of the advantages of this long apprenticeship was the unforgetable lesson of systematic industry — of putting in so many hours a day at faithful work. Mr. Saint Gaudens never fell into the habit of waiting for "inspiration." He has always found enough to do between the visions, and one may even ask if his contribution of sincere, admirable, and enthusiastic toil has not as much to do with his success and with the beauty of his works as have their inherent ideas. At any rate, the inspirations have always found him "at home" and prepared to give them hospitality. He is one of those sculptors who think best with modelling tool in hand.

But neither ceaseless industry, nor clever fingers, nor keen eyes, nor a powerful mind — no, nor all of these together, will suffice to make an artist. Mr. Saint Gaudens is the master that he is to-day, not because he found these opportunities, — they existed for a hundred others, — but because the opportunities found him, a nature different from all about him. More than any other of his generation in this country he possesses that gift so rare in men of northern races, the "plastic mind." It is hardly necessary to say that the term is not employed here in the frequent and passive sense, as something impressionable, but rather in the technical meaning which the Germans have long since given it, of that innocency of vision which concerns itself with the things themselves, which delights in beauty for its own sake rather than in its symbolic or

verbal expression.   It bespeaks a mind which has an instinctive
sense of form, and sees things "in the round" with a sort of stereo-
scopic grasp, corresponding to the sensitiveness of other eyes or
minds to color, of certain ears to music.   Directed by intelligence
and strengthened by practice, such a nature may ultimately reach
the development claimed by an enthusiastic eulogist for poor Bartholomew, who was accredited with "an intuitive perception of the
strongest and most statuesque aspect of a theme."   Given this cast
of mind, every opportunity counts for progress; each new problem
means not only a new achievement, but experience and power gained
for a hundred other applications.   The only necessary boundaries of
such growth lie in the horizons of human life.

At the age of nineteen, then, or twenty, the future sculptor was
already a trained artist who, if he did not fully realize all of the
power which lay dormant within him, at least had some idea of his
own abilities, and knew clearly what he desired.   It was now his
good fortune to be able to go to Paris, where after a short period in
the preparatory school (the " Petite École") he passed to the atelier
of M. Jouffroy in the École des Beaux-Arts.   Here he had his
opportunity with the figure; one of them each week from life, in
more and more strenuous competition with others, until the facility
acquired became something almost incredible.   The certainty with
which the more advanced pupils of this school seize upon the action of a figure, the rapidity with which they swing their little clay
images into pose and proportion, the accuracy of characterization
and the perfection of finish accomplished in those six mornings, is
something astonishing.   The value of this facility is not alone a
question of time saved, — though this is of sufficient importance in
subsequent undertakings when the young artist is paying the model
himself, — but lies even more in the mental grasp of the human figure
resulting from much acquaintance.   Its various significant poses
are like the letters of an alphabet with which one is to spell out
words and write sentences.   It is better to have them in the mind
than to be obliged to look them up each time in the primer.   Saint
Gaudens had his alphabet well learned when his student days ended
in Paris.

It was now 1870 and he had been in the school three years.

During this time he had had as companions such brilliant French-men as Mercié and Bastien-Lepage, men of genius, whose lives were wrapped up in their art. It was an inspiring atmosphere. Mercié had received the *Prix de Rome;* and Saint Gaudens decided that it was time to follow him to Italy. He spent another three years in that home of beauty, seeing and profiting as one may who has already formed a standard of judgment. There is no evidence in his work from first to latest that he was ever swayed by the meretricious art of any land. Such art seems to have had no appeal for him. With extraordinary poise and independence of mind, with unerring taste, he selected and assimilated what his mature judgment recognized as worthy, and it became part of him. Canova and Thorwaldsen meant little to a modern of his temperament; the deco-rative sense was too strongly developed within him, the love of refinement and

FIG. 41.—SAINT GAUDENS: ADMIRAL FARRAGUT, NEW YORK.

truth too vital to allow him to enjoy their lean compositions and their bald generalizations of surface. Deeper than this, how-ever, was the inherent honesty of the man which recognized the insignificance and superficiality of an art founded upon imitation. Far different was the appeal of the early Italians. Their spontaneity, their sincerity, their frank delight in their work, took hold of him and fascinated his imagination as their rare decorative effects grati-fied his artistic sense. Even more than his French colleagues did he comprehend them, for he was more nearly akin to them. Mercié

was inspired, no doubt, by Donatello and wrought his beautiful
" David " on lines suggested by the elder teacher. Consciously or
otherwise, it was an imitation. Saint Gaudens, on the other hand,
proved himself yet more directly of the inheritance, not by copying
and by professing, but by treating the subjects about him in the
very spirit of artistic comprehension which we recognize in the masters of the early Renaissance. In other words, he has been of his
time as they were of theirs, taking the themes of current life, the
portraits and memorials as they have come to him, and making of
them works of enduring value. Thus his kinship with the men of
the fifteenth century is established through family traits rather than
by means of a garb which may be put on or off; and these evidences
of the birthright extend, as we have seen, to the qualifications of a
refined, decorative sense and to the still rarer capacity for taking
infinite pains.

During the three years in Rome, Mr. Saint Gaudens executed
two statues, entitled " Hiawatha " and " Silence "; the former was
bought by Governor Morgan of New York. Returning in 1874 to
the United States, his first work was the execution in marble of a
bust of William M. Evarts. Somewhat later he received an order
for a large decorative relief for Saint Thomas's Church, New York.
His style, like his technic, was already formed, and this work
revealed not only a remarkable felicity of touch, but a delicacy of
invention full of promise for the future.[1]

In 1878 came the important commissions for statues of Admiral
Farragut (Fig. 41) and Robert R. Randall, and the sculptor sailed at
once for Paris, where he modelled them, exhibiting the " Admiral
Farragut " in the Salon of 1880. He also served as a member of the
International Jury for Fine Arts at the Paris Exposition of 1878.

Returning with his two statues, Mr. Saint Gaudens spent much
time in collaboration with the eminent architect, Stanford White;

---

[1] An appreciative reference to this, his first public undertaking, will be found in an article
by Clarence Cook on " Church Decoration," in *Scribner's Magazine* of February, 1878, where is
pictured a fragment of the relief, showing many angels in the act of adoration of the cross.
Of this beautiful panel the critic writes : —

" The charm of Saint Gaudens's work is not easy to express. It is, as near as words can
give tongue to our thinking, its harmonious interweaving of deep, childlike religious fervor
with a strong buoyant sense of delight in living and loving."

together they designed and perfected an appropriate pedestal for the " Admiral Farragut." At one time there was a possibility of the withdrawal of the figure, since the Park Commissioners of New York had enacted a labor-saving rule that all pedestals should be alike. The sculptor naturally protested, insisting upon the use of the novel design which he had elaborated, and the matter was finally compromised by " permitting " its erection.

Thus it was not until May, 1881, that Mr. Saint Gaudens made himself known as a sculptor to the people of the United States. With the appearance of the " Admiral Farragut " he became a public character and took his place at the head of American sculpture — the position which he has retained ever since. His thorough technical equipment, combined with a remarkable grasp of the subject, had resulted in a figure which was a revelation to our critics. Fortunately for our national art there were men here of sufficient taste and discernment to appreciate such a truly fine work. From the day that the " Admiral Farragut " was set upon its worthy pedestal in Madison Square, American monumental art has been colored by the dominant influence of Saint Gaudens. Entirely apart from the obvious and inevitable plagiarisms, — the brood of younger Farraguts and Lincolns which look like distorted casts from his models, — the general results of his example have been a higher conception of sculptural form, a far more perfect craftsmanship, and a vast infusion of vitality into our public memorials.

These claims require no demonstration, but the last point may be made clearer. Eschewing in his works the much-sought illusion of life, Saint Gaudens is rewarded for his voluntary sacrifice by a pervading animation which can scarcely be defined in words. There had been reactions before from the calm and complacent deadness of our public effigies. No doubt Clark Mills felt that in his " General Jackson" he was uttering a noteworthy and convincing protest against the moribund statues of his day. Meade adorned his Lincoln monument at Springfield, Illinois, with agitated groups of soldiers who threaten to jump from their pedestals. But such paroxysmal displays, such uneasiness and unbalance, are not thoroughly satisfying in sculpture. They are not convincing, and even those who have no formulated confession of faith regarding the statuary's art soon

find such effort disagreeable to look upon.   Perhaps this assertion
should be limited to the standpoint of American taste; the modern
Italians seem to like restless sculpture, and so also, to a certain
degree, do the French.

Up to the time of Saint Gaudens and the "Admiral Farragut"
we have seen but few examples of a happy medium between the conventional, petrified men of our early national art and the galvanized
athletes, foredoomed to eternal toil, who succeeded them.   Of the
two kinds one instinctively prefers the former.   They are evidently
and decently dead, and have the good grace to recognize the fact.
They move not, nor ever could.   The others irritate.   They are
tiring themselves so unnecessarily!   It is not life, but Powers's
clockwork which has gotten into them.   If you do not sympathize
with them, you at least sympathize with yourself.   You come to hate
their insistent stress and wish them consigned to some distant limbo
along with the "advertising novelties" which they so much resemble.

The admiral stands perfectly still.   His hands are not raised in
gesture; his mouth is not open.   But he is so much a man that he
holds one's attention instantly, and he is so quiet that he seems to
move.   In the first place, the artist has mastered his subject and
conceived the very soul of the man.   He has worked from this outward.   He has thought of Farragut as a natural leader, born to
command, therefore strong and tranquil.   He knew him to be a
cultivated gentleman, a man of character, unostentatious, alert, and
keen, and all of this he has realized in gesture and expression.   He
has planted him firmly upon his two feet, and these well apart, as in
Donatello's "St. George"— the attitude of a man who accommodates
himself to an unstable basis, like the farmer erect in his jolting
wagon, or the sailor on the swaying deck of a vessel.   The right
arm is dropped by the side in perfect repose, the left hand raised
almost to the belt, holding thus suspended the traditional spy-glass.
The long line of the one arm and the angle of the other are the combination which Donatello so delighted in, and which Michael Angelo
appreciated.   More particularly, however, does the modelling of the
virile face remind us of the art of those modest men of the early
Renaissance who found their joy in the expression of personality.
What pleasure there must have been in shaping that fine, strong

head, in developing those clear-cut masterful features! It has been done in no perfunctory spirit; the artist has been full of it. He has fairly lived with his subject and in his work. He has taken no liberties, made no attempt to display his cleverness, but with a noble deference has sunken his own personality out of sight in his desire to do honor to his hero. In so doing he has shown himself as great as his handicraft proves him skilful.

The sweeping lines and the quiet, well-modelled surfaces lead the eye agreeably and inevitably to the fine head. In that serene countenance, in those steady eyes, in the unfrowning brow, in the firm, unexaggerated mouth, is an intensity of life, a positiveness of being which will be found in no American statue of an earlier date. This is a man of no other land nor time than our own, and the sculptor has revealed him to us as he was, epitomizing into one quiet comprehensive attitude and expression the whole character and energy of the great admiral. The secret is in the reserve force, the look of potential power. The figure does not move, but it is ready to do so. The arms are not gesticulating, but they are alive, and we half expect to see the telescope lifted. The head is slightly turned; the eyes peer into distance; the mouth might speak. By his very restraint the artist has succeeded in making this statue almost quiver with pulsating life.

The figure presented a perfection of workmanship new to our people. For the first time they saw the fluent ease of handling of the modern French school combined with a severity of outline befitting the subject. It is interesting to notice how this severity is again modified by the breezy touch of the fluttering coat. It is sufficient to put the whole work into an unusual key — to suggest out of doors and salt sea winds.

The pedestal was as pronounced a success in its way as was the statue. Nothing like it had been seen before in this country, and it still remains one of the most perfect examples of monumental architecture. Mr. Saint Gaudens has shown from the first a realization that the effect produced by a work of art depends largely upon the way in which it is approached. Treat it with disrespect, and it is robbed of its power; enshrine it appropriately, and its gain is remarkable. His monuments are in almost every case object lessons in fitness of setting. This pedestal was the prototype of the numerous exedras which have since been scattered over the country. Its tranquil lines seemed very novel in those days and contrasted strangely with the many-membered bases and ill-proportioned blocks upon which our bronze worthies had hitherto been placed. Of distinctly architectural mass, its members are suavely united into a coherent whole. There are no heavy mouldings and no sharp edges; the contour flows with an easy sweep; the surfaces are large, strong, and restful to the eye. The reliefs and the inscriptions are unobtrusive, but so eminently decorative, so happily simplified, and withal so original, that they impress a sculptor almost as much as does the statue itself. Yet at a distance of a few yards they are indistinguishable from the bulk of the gray granite. The artist has appreciated his material and its object: he has sketched those delightful figures with a few vigorous strokes; has incised a conventional ripple here to suggest the deep, a sword there, in just the right place; has bent sporting fishes into arms for the seat, and set a crab in the pavement, as his fancy has dictated, playing with the rock, but never cutting it up nor weakening it even in appearance.

These touches are distinctly, happily, his own. It is perhaps conceivable that the " Farragut " might have been modelled by some other sculptor — by one of the best of the Frenchmen; but these embellishments could have been conceived by no other mind, could have been executed by no other hand than that of Saint Gaudens. Upon this, his earliest monumental work, he put his seal and sign-manual with as much firmness as he has upon his latest. His artistic character was fully pronounced from the beginning.

The monument has grown smaller as the cliff-like walls of vast business houses have climbed steadily higher around it; but it has not diminished in value. It remains to-day one of our greatest and most perfect public memorials, celebrating with dignity a worthy man and marking a notable day — the beginning of a new era — in American sculpture.[1]

[1] It is interesting to turn back to the article in *Scribner's Magazine* of June, 1881, in which Mr. Richard Watson Gilder eulogized this monument — an article which deserves to become historic because of its sympathetic comprehension and its bold claims for the newly discovered master. Time has justified these claims; but who can say how long a period might have

FIG. 42.—SAINT GAUDENS: AMOR CARITAS, LUXEMBOURG GALLERY, PARIS.

When, in 1887, Mr. Saint Gaudens's "Lincoln" (Frontispiece) was unveiled in Lincoln Park, Chicago, it was hailed as the greatest portrait statue in the United States. It has remained so. From its exalted conception of the man to the last detail of its simple accessories it is a masterpiece. The sculptor's idea was a novel one, which may have been suggested by Mr. Volk's "Lincoln" at Springfield, Illinois. He introduces the striking adjunct of a large chair, from which the President is supposed to have risen. Before it stands the gaunt figure with bowed head, as though lost in thought, or preparing to address a multitude. The left foot is well advanced; the left hand grasps the lapel of the coat in a familiar gesture. The right is behind the back, affording an agreeable but inconspicuous counter-balance to the droop of the head, It has been pointed out that the bent left arm gives interest to the lengthy front and at the same time suggests an arrested movement of the hand to the brow, thus reënforcing the idea of concentration of mind.

But it is the expression of that strange, almost grotesquely plain, yet beautiful face, crowned with tumbled locks, which arrests and holds the gaze. In it is revealed the massive but many-sided personality of Lincoln with a concreteness and a serene adequacy which has discredited all other attempts and, indeed, with the "Admiral Farragut," has "brought about a new scale of values" in our portrait art. It has been Saint Gaudens's rare talent to give life without realism, to offer us "a suggestion of reality shrouded in poetry and grace." For even this gnarled form has a grace all its own — the "inward grace" which a profound master has apprehended and made visible.

"The pose is simple, natural, individually characteristic — as far

been required had not the modest sculptor found such champions to vouch for him and for his unfamiliar art. Mr. Gilder's appreciative description of statue and pedestal alike would illumine these pages; but quotation must be limited to a minor paragraph. It is sufficient to show the author's prophetic insight : —

"The manner in which Saint Gaudens has handled the lettering is a matter worthy of consideration. Should it be popularly considered successful, we are likely before long to find any number of more or less fortunate imitations."

Mr. Saint Gaudens's inscriptions *were* popularly considered successful, and have revolutionized lettering upon works of art in the United States. The old-time "scare-heads" of various fonts have disappeared, and although no one has learned to make of inscriptions so beautiful and organic a decoration as does Mr. Saint Gaudens, there has been a marvellous change in the direction of refinement and even of charm.

removed from the conventionally dramatic or 'sculpturesque' as from the baldly commonplace. Neither physical facts nor facts of costume are palliated or adorned . . . and the figure is idealized only by refinement and breadth and vigor in treatment. . . . This 'Lincoln,' with his firmly planted feet, his erect body, and his squared shoulders, stands as a man accustomed to face the people and sway them at his will, while the slightly drooped head and the quiet, yet not passive, hands express the meditativeness, the self-control, the conscientiousness of the philosopher who reflected well before he spoke, of the moralist who realized to the full the responsibilities of utterance. The dignity of the man and his simplicity; his strength, his inflexibility and his tenderness; his goodness and his courage; his intellectual confidence and his humility of soul; the poetic cast of his thought, the homely rigor of his manner, and the underlying sadness of his spirit, — all these may be read in the wonderfully real yet ideal portrait which the sculptor has created."[1]

The sculptor and the architect, Mr. Stanford White, worked together here as architect and sculptor always should, with an eye to effects at various distances. The statue has the immense advantage of a generous and dignified setting, far from the confusion of downtown streets. Paths sweep gracefully toward the broad structure, which is upon a slight rise of ground and is backed by trees. The width of the great exedra is sixty feet and its depth thirty. It is flanked by large globes of bronze. The walls bear appropriate inscriptions in the lettering which is so constant a feature of Mr. Saint Gaudens's decorations. One reads: "With malice toward none, with charity for all, with firmness in the right as God gives us to know the right, let us strive on." The opposite wall bears the quotation, also taken from the Cooper Union speech of 1860: "Let us have faith that right makes might, and in that faith let us to the end dare to do our duty as we understand it."

The massive block on which the figure rests is raised so little above the height of the wall that at a distance the various members work together for a solidity of effect, one might almost say an inevitableness of structure, which is rare indeed in the monumental architecture of this country. From the side the bold separation of figure and chair

[1] Mrs. Schuyler Van Rensselaer, in the *Century Magazine*, Vol. XIII, p. 39.

may appear at first odd and even unpleasant, but one soon becomes accustomed to it. From the front, the coöperation of the mass and lines of the chair is very grateful to the eye, especially at a distance where the silhouette of the slender unaided statue would be meagre. It gives the volume and the "color" which the old-time sculptors sought to gain by hanging cloaks on their figures and by piling improbable accessories about them. Upon nearer approach the chair fades out of focus; the magnificent head holds the entire attention.

It seems almost sacrilege to put a mental microscope to our eyes in order to examine such a work technically, inch by inch. It may be said, however, for the benefit of the student, that its greatness is not alone in the idea which gave it birth, nor yet in the controlling lines of its pose and the broad planes in which it has been handled. Its mastery lies, after all, in no small measure, in those same square inches of honest workmanship, each one of which bears the imprint of its creator. Every part has been done as well as the sculptor knew how, yet has been kept subordinate to the whole. The effect is charmingly plastic throughout, as if the clay had never been allowed to dry and grow unresponsive. However true the physique to its ungainly prototype, there is no leanness in its modelling; all of the forms are enveloped, and all staring details modified, until the surface is as harmonious as a bas-relief, yet without weakness. One could not have believed it possible to treat the modern costume with so much grace. The sculptor has wrought a wonder; he has actually made coat and trousers decorative, and thus taken away the last excuse of the mediocre sculptor who pleads their artistic hopelessness.

The value of so high an example of the monumental art can scarcely be overestimated. Its workmanship will be a canon and a guide for generations of sculptors to come, and the serene dignity of the conception has already had its marked influence on the side of gravity and distinction in public works. Strange, is it not, that this quiet figure which lifts not a hand nor even looks at you, should have within it a power to thrill which is denied the most dramatic works planned expressly for emotional appeal!

CHAPTER XVI

AUGUSTUS SAINT GAUDENS (CONTINUED)

THE three earliest statues, the " Farragut," the " Randall," and the " Lincoln," are notably quiet in pose.   In his next figure, the "Deacon Chapin " (Fig. 43) of Springfield, Massachusetts, the sculptor showed his imaginative freedom by representing the grim-visaged old Puritan striding sturdily to or from the meeting-house, " clasping his Bible as Moses clasped the tables of the law, and holding his peaceful walking-stick with as firm a grip as the handle of a sword." [1]

The figure is clad in the picturesque costume of three hundred years ago — full knee-breeches, a long pointed jacket of many buttons, and an immense cloak thrown widely open by the gesture of the arms and the breeze which he arouses in his progress.   The treatment of all these details is a joy to the eye; the flow and hang of surfaces, the variety of textures, the looseness and freedom extending even to the high conical hat which crowns this self-contained but energetic personage.   How convincing he is!   One feels in that austere presence that here is not only Puritanism incarnate, but a very real and personal human being.   Even down to the puffy hands there is every proof that this is "somebody in particular"; yet we know that the sculptor began with only a name and has evolved and perfected this more than plausible individual around it as he built up and perfected his clay figure around the skeleton irons.   The old Greeks took men and made from them noble abstractions; the modern master poses an abstraction and develops it into a living man. At least such is the gift of Saint Gaudens.

But Mr. Saint Gaudens is not only the most skilful of our sculptors; he is also the most versatile.   He can do more kinds of things well than can any other, and likewise he has a wider range of practical

---

[1] Kenyon Cox, in the *Century Magazine*, Vol. XIII, p. 30.

ideals.   In his memorials to Dr. McCosh and Dr. Bellows, he introduced a form of portraiture which has won the admiration of artists
and public alike.   The full-length figures stand in comparatively
high relief against a lettered and delicately decorated background.
The portrait is, of course, excellent in each instance, yet the effect is
less realistic than in the case of a statue.   One has a sense of the
relationship between figure and background, between draperies and
legend and ornament.
The " McCosh," with
its direct front view
and vertical lines, its
desk and authoritative
gesture, is the more
vivid of the two.   The
" Bellows," in ample
robes, stands turned, a
" three-quarter " view,
and is a triumph
of sculptural arrange-
ment and sapient
handling.   The Re-
naissance ornament
which surrounds it
and which, along with
the inscription, plays
over the background,
is as unobtrusive as a
far-away recessional.

FIG. 43. — SAINT GAUDENS: DEACON CHAPIN.

Its notes are sweet and
restfully harmonious.   These memorials give one the ever quickening
satisfaction found only in genuine works of art.   To the first glance
they tell their story distinctly yet with an elegant composure; then
with inexhaustible resource do they show themselves worthy of much
study and of many visits, revealing new beauties at each inspection.
        Other work of a still more ideal nature had been hinted at in the
angel relief of Saint Thomas's Church, which stands in the relation of
a sweet prologue or " argument " to the sustained achievement of

Saint Gaudens's poet-life. Since that day the sculptor has produced a number of the most admirable angel forms known to modern
art. Three of these figures, a celestial choir at the foot of a cross,
were intended for the decoration of the Morgan monument at Hartford, Connecticut, and were unfortunately destroyed by fire. A modification of one of them has become the gracious " Amor Caritas "
(Fig. 42), of which a bronze copy has been added to the collection of
the Luxembourg, along with a number of Mr. Saint Gaudens's low reliefs. Yet others, wingless, but evidently of the same heavenly brood,
are the caryatides of a mantel in one of the Vanderbilt residences.[1]
Nothing more beautiful than these figures has been conceived in
this country. It will be observed, even without the side-lights of Mr.
Kenyon Cox's article in the *Century Magazine*, that the exquisite
creature there pictured is not an impersonal figure, built up by
formula and culminating in a conventional head. It is more individual and more fascinating with its vague air of portraiture than
any purely extemporized head could be; it possesses something of
the subtlety and illusiveness of real womanhood. One cannot love
a diagram nor a lay-figure, however graceful; but one could easily
fall in love with this flower of fairest womankind, even though we
know her to be but a sculptor's dream.

It will be remembered that Saint Gaudens's early tutelage was
entirely in low relief. It is not strange, then, that he remains
to-day our leader in this fascinating but perplexing department of
sculpture, nor that he delights in turning his hand to it from time to
time. His eminence in this field may be inferred from his generous representation in the museum of the Luxembourg. These
plaques are little jewels, or rather, precious pictures fashioned with
delicate use of light and dark, and always with thought of the effect
of the whole rather than of the imitation of any particular detail.
They are unusually rich in "color," and the skill with which the drawing and planes are lost and found is extraordinary. It not only grati-
fies the sensitive eye, but confers an air of absolute spontaneity.
With Mr. Saint Gaudens this quality never degenerates into mere
picturesqueness; firmness is never wanting as a foil; an emphatic
plane, a powerful stroke now and then, marks the underlying struc-

[1] See illustration in the *Century Magazine*, of November, 1887.

ture and gives one an unconscious sense of security, a feeling which
is very real and grateful, however unanalyzed.

Such methods naturally struck certain of the veterans as revolutionary, or at least as strangely heterodox, and Mr. Saint Gaudens's
reliefs have occasioned no little rubbing of eyes. Their charm is
incontestable, however, and they have won the day for plasticity and
freedom. Among the most noted of his achievements in this refined
art may be mentioned the well-known tributes to his friends, Bastien-
Lepage and Robert Louis Stevenson, the delightful portraits of the
children of Prescott Hall Butler and of Jacob H. Schiff, portraits of
Miss Violet Sargent, of Mrs. Schuyler Van Rensselaer, of William
D. Howells and his daughter, and many others, not forgetting the
medal of the World's Columbian Exposition.

In Rock Creek Cemetery, Washington, D. C., is one of Mr.
Saint Gaudens's most beautiful and least known works, the strange
figure called variously " Grief " and " Death," and sometimes, more
fitly, " The Peace of God " (Fig. 44). It is a memorial to a Mrs.
Adams, a woman who lived and died, — and the monument says no
more. Indeed, not even that, since it bears no inscription of any
kind. For once even the delicate lettering in which Saint Gaudens
delights is omitted as superfluous. This memorial speaks a language of its own, which leaps directly to the soul and requires no
halting translation into sounds articulate.

No statue could be more effectively placed, although it has to be
discovered by each visitor. No path, no guide-board, leads to it.
One wanders among the white slabs and truncated columns and
draped urns until finally his search is rewarded by the sight of a
mass of evergreens — a circle without gateway. Pressing through
a rift in this wall he finds himself within an enclosure of dense
foliage and face to face with a bronze figure which seems to be
alive, whose deep-shadowed countenance photographs itself at once
upon the memory for all time.

The monument, primarily a great slab of polished granite, forms
one side of a hexagonal plot of perhaps twenty feet in diameter.
Against this slab and facing the centre leans the unearthly genius
of the place. Opposite and occupying three sides of the hexagon is
a massive stone bench. Outside of the wall of green rise forest

trees of considerable height, extending their long, thin arms over
the sacred earth. In this little space one is completely isolated
from the world. Above is the blue sky; all around, the rustling
screen; before one, that figure. The unknown dreamer, with head
half hidden in drapery and listless hands, sits like one of the old-
time fateful Three — a sibyl peering through closed eyes into
futurity. Or shall we call her rather the modern expression of
Nirvana — a soul returned upon itself, "petrified by the sentiment
of the infinite," reposing in measureless peace?

Just what he has meant the great artist has carefully abstained
from telling us, but that he has charged the figure with significance,
at least with the appearance of meaning, cannot be gainsaid. It is as
perplexing as the look of Leonardo's " Mona Lisa." Some one has
written of it despairingly : " It appears to know all there is to know,
and is a positive and negative to every sentiment one can suggest
concerning the unknown." Baffled, but ever fascinated, one lingers
there, indifferent to the flight of time, dimly conscious of the song of
birds overhead and of the shadows of leaves trembling upon the
Silent One opposite. Strangers who stroll in speak to one another
in subdued tones and move away softly. The bronze figure with
closed eyes compels it; one is awed into reverence. You may recognize beautifully proportioned mouldings on the granite background, or may perceive that the shrouded form is seated upon a
boulder of different material; that the modelling of the drapery is
very broad and coarse in texture; but these things seem to mean
very little in this presence. One feels no concern in trifles when
confronting eternity. And that is where one finds himself when
under the spell of this amazing work.

Like an uncrowned king or a prophet of old sits Peter Cooper
in bronze, before the building which is his monument, the Cooper
Institute in New York City. Here, as always, the sculptor has done
something more than to place an effigy upon a pedestal, like a man
caught up from the crowded street and forced into momentary, unwilling prominence. He not only makes his subject worthy of our
homage through his dignified generalization, but he enhances this
dignity many fold by its surroundings. One does not " happen
upon " this statue of the great philanthropist; one approaches it

FIG. 44.— SAINT GAUDENS: ADAMS MEMORIAL, WASHINGTON.

and is conscious of the approach.   In its classic niche, with a background and adjuncts of admirably proportioned architecture, the
figure becomes more than human, a monumental apparition, a veritable presence, majestic in its kindly serenity.

It cannot be claimed that Mr. Saint Gaudens is equally inspired
at all times; no man of genius can be.   Aside from its excellent
workmanship the Garfield Memorial in Fairmount Park, Philadelphia, — a bust of the President and a standing figure of the Republic,
— is interesting because of its maker rather than because of its
poetry, and even more markedly does the Logan statue of Chicago
show the result of a somewhat unsympathetic treatment.   To be
sure, it is one of the finest equestrian statues in this country, and it
would be rash to attempt to name a sculptor who could have treated
the subject better or with more of the *bravura* which was deemed
essential.   The point is that *bravura* is not Saint Gaudens's natural
expression; he has acted it well, but in the Shaw Memorial and the
" Sherman " he is more truly himself, and therefore vastly more convincing.

The gallant Logan is shown bareheaded, grasping a flag which
he has seized from a falling color-bearer; the horse, a splendid
animal, is powerfully reined in and paws the ground with nervous
impatience.   The motive of the work is thoroughly martial.   The
sculptor himself has said of it: " To that end I concentrated my
energies, and everything else was subordinated to that idea.   I
wished to present a figure that would embody the highest type of
the warrior — one of fierce, indomitable energy and fiery patriotism,
such as General Logan is known to have been.   If I have achieved
that end, it is that I have produced those characteristics of General
Logan which were brought out in striking effect in the incident
before Atlanta which is illustrated in the subject."

In spite of our suspicion that this enthusiasm is a little factitious,
the effect of the statue is masterly.   It offers a remarkable union of
the dash and impetuosity of the subject with the inexorable limitations of monumental art.   Vitality and self-restraint are harmonized
in perfect balance.   Nearer approach brings the same æsthetic
pleasure which we find in Saint Gaudens's smallest relief.   Each
stroke is as it should be.   Nothing is neglected, yet nothing is over-

insistent, detail being subordinated to the general result. Even the brazen wreaths about the base, so admirably decorative, do not cry out for recognition.

To many the greatest and most original of all of Mr. Saint Gaudens's works is the Shaw Memorial in Boston (Pl. VIII). Colonel Robert Gould Shaw was a gallant young officer selected by the governor of Massachusetts to lead the first regiment of colored troops organized in that state. The commission was an unusually perilous one. There was a memorable departure from Boston on May 28, 1863, and before the summer was half passed the wires brought the tidings of an attack upon Fort Wagner, and of the death and burial of Colonel Shaw among scores of his dusky followers. Such was the story which the monument was intended to commemorate. It was not to be raised to one man alone, but to the memory of all who shared in this episode of the Rebellion. The artist has been able to lift it to a still higher significance while ably, poignantly recalling the specific incident.

The first thought was an equestrian statue, but this was soon discarded as limiting the honor to one man. The idea of an equestrian figure, backed by a column of marching soldiers in low relief, next presented itself, and was put in execution only to be remodelled subsequently in much higher relief. For twelve years the project grew, not only in the sculptor's mind, but in tangible form, with radical changes and improvements from year to year, the while other works of simpler *motif* were being finished and leaving the studio. Well was the artist rewarded for his seeking, and the committee for their waiting. The relief, when inaugurated on Decoration Day, 1897, and when shown in plaster at the French Exposition of 1900, received the plaudits of those best capable of appreciating noble work. It is one of the most impressive monuments of modern times — one of the masterpieces of the nineteenth century. While it speaks an unusual language, the Shaw Memorial is notable for being distinctively American. It would be difficult to trace its ancestry outside of our country. There is nothing like it, or even suggestive of it, in the annals of art.

A very large relief in bronze, perhaps fifteen by eleven feet in dimensions, containing many figures of soldiers who march across the narrow stage, the foreground occupied largely by a young officer on horseback; above and vague, like a cloud, a floating female form which points onward — this is what appears at first glance, this and an impression of many shouldered muskets cutting sharp and inexorable athwart the metal sky; a feature almost as striking as the forest of lances in Velasquez's picture, the "Surrender at Breda." Nearer view reveals new beauties. The scene is evidently the departure of the colored troops; the leader a young man of noble mien who recognizes the significance of the fateful day. With head square set upon the broad shoulders and sad eyes unflinching, he rides steadily to his fate. The fiery horse is a splendid sculptural achievement, clean cut and magnificently wrought, but, conspicuous as he is, easily dominated by the presence of the silent rider. Then, behind and across the entire background, march with swinging tread the black men, their muskets over shoulders which bend under the burdensome knapsacks. They are equipped for a long journey from which not many will return. The movement of this great composition is extraordinary. We almost hear the roll of the drums and the shuffle of the heavy shoes. It makes the day of that brave departure very real again.

Mr. William Howe Downes calls attention to the effect produced on the mind by this suggestion of unbroken movement, picturing the vision evoked by its endless, irresistible sequence: —

"And the black rank and file! With what a wonderful sense of human pathos, of fateful forward movement; with what wavelike rhythmic momentum, as of marching legions tramping southward; with what a suggestion of the slow but irresistible grinding of the mills of God, has the artist clothed these humble, united, obedient, devoted, doomed men! Are they not exalted by this deep, serious art to a plane of Egyptian dignity? Does not the martyrdom which overhangs them ennoble them? Unutterable sadness, sublime resignation, and an invincible determination is visible in all these set countenances, all facing the same way, all looking toward the South, all intent on a great final business and a glorious death. The impression is not so much that of a group of individuals as of a whole army, a vast, endless, countless host, moving like a huge human tide, hardly of its own volition, unhasting but not to be stayed short of the goal, a mere complex instrument in the hands of Providence, rolling on like a mighty flood."[1]

Such is the orchestral accompaniment of this great work, the murmurous undertone which is awakened in one's mind when even a mere reproduction of the relief is seen. What is it that gives this power to a bronze panel? Why should it bring dimness to the eyes and a grip to the heart? On what ground do men call it the highest expression of American art? Certainly it is not because of the workmanship alone; muskets and trousers and varied African types, however perfectly modelled, could not thrill us thus; neither could the splendid steed nor even the physical presence of the hero who rides.

After all, it is the largeness of the man behind the work, of the artist-mind which saw more in that scene than uniforms and accoutrements, or types of human kind, who felt the greater import of it; who bore it for twelve years upon his mind and heart, studying, dreaming, living with its great idea until it was purged of all mere accidents of the moment, all qualifying phrases, and finally rose spiritualized and perfected above the earth, the fit and adequate expression of America's new-born patriotism.

Mr. Saint Gaudens modelled from life many years ago the " General Sherman," which stands to-day in the Pennsylvania Academy of Fine Arts. It is an astonishing work; an unexpected meeting with it is like suddenly coming face to face with a real man of powerful and impressive personality. The sculptor made some sacrifice in order to convey this look of intense life. The bust has little of his usual suavity of handling, which he evidently found inconsistent with the character of the nervous, restless old general. The touch is all "staccato." The chin is aggressive, the tight mouth defiant, the nose inquiring, the eye like an eagle's; the beard is short and stubbly, the hair writhes and twists from very virility; the coat lapels are angular and stand out sharply; even the buttons seem proud of their relationship. Quite in harmony with these features is the play of vivid lights and shadows. They are restless and keen, abrupt to picturesqueness. If ever there were excuse for deserting the traditions of classic art and italicizing a character,— for punctuating with

[1] "Twelve Great Artists," Boston, 1900.

FIG. 45. — SAINT GAUDENS: SHERMAN, CENTRAL PARK, NEW YORK.

hammer strokes its individuality, — it was in the case of this intense, irrepressible, "driving," nineteenth-century American.

Out of this study grew that more recent work, the Sherman Memorial (Fig. 45), which was unveiled in Central Park, New York, on Decoration Day, 1903. Thanks to his knowledge of his subject, the sculptor was able to present the rugged warrior with convincing faithfulness of portraiture; but beyond its accuracy of feature and even the more elusive "air" of the man, this remarkable group has a poetic inspiration which is most distinctly embodied in its winged "Victory," but which permeates the whole achievement. Mr. Saint Gaudens has revised his work critically and made various changes since it was first shown at the Paris Exposition of 1900, but such modifications were necessitated by the author's temperament rather than by any evident defects in modelling. The Parisian artists acknowledged with enthusiasm the beauty and distinction which raised the "Sherman" far above the entire category of equestrian statues there, excepting that gem of modern French art, the "Joan of Arc" by Paul Dubois.

Indeed, the sculptor's conception has a spiritual quality which enters into few works of this era. It follows naturally that the feeling of flesh does not predominate; the only criticism that one heard passed upon the group in Paris was that it seemed to some a little "lean." It is not lean, but is intentionally and consistently slender in its elements. The aggregate presents, nevertheless, an imposing mass. The "Victory" is not related to those ample demoiselles who thrive and bloom so unstintedly upon the average French monument. She is not a real woman, who takes the field with Gallic enthusiasm for the picturesque; she is a spirit presence, the personification of a force, rather than an individual. Within the lines of a definite sculptural mass the artist has created the miracle of an ethereal form. She is necessarily in human shape; one sees her, yet the impression is rather of a presence felt. With extraordinary delicacy the artist has known how to suggest and to develop this conception within our minds. One of the secrets of this power is the fact that there is no display of physical peculiarities forced upon our attention. Saint Gaudens's "Victory" differs from the deep-chested, generous-limbed "Niké" of Samothrace as our conception of a spirit differs from the Greek ideals of the immortal gods. She is an expression of our race and time. Saint Gaudens is unsurpassed and unique in this form of expression. The " Victory " is but another phase of that haunting ideal of his which first revealed itself in the angel choir of Saint Thomas's Church, and which reached its hitherto highest expression in the " Amor Caritas." Such an ideal is the artist's rarest gift. One might even say that it is of greater value than knowledge or skill, were it possible to disassociate thought from the means of expression. But there is no feeling of inadequacy in the structure of this figure. If there were, it would thwart its purpose; one would think of the body. The sculptor has known how to give it strength and yet entirely to subordinate the physical. No detail strikes one with emphasis; one sees and remembers only the earnest, inspired look, the outstretched arm which seems to command, the majestic wings, and the beauty of long, sweeping folds of drapery. What the costume, the manner of coiffure, the kind of shoes — these things one does not notice. The particulars make no impression. One only knows that here is a noble being which leads on and ever on to triumphs ever new, but under her guidance inevitable.

General Sherman's tall figure is partially enveloped in his military cloak, which is filled out by the breeze. They are advancing. He leans forward, his head bare, hat in hand. His face is serenely confident, almost smiling. Why should he not be confident when led by Victory! The general's horse is built like himself, of structure spare but strong. It is a real horse, a serviceable horse, with an individuality as distinct as that of his rider. The entire group is exquisitely modelled. Every touch is significant and gives proof of Saint Gaudens's artistic conscience. The work was executed in Paris, whither the sculptor went in 1897 for a protracted visit. With the Shaw Memorial, the " Amor Caritas," and a collection of low reliefs, it won for its author the highest award of the exposition.

It was first seen in this country at the Pan-American Exposition of 1901, where, most fortunately placed, its effect was even more impressive than in Paris. In the Palais des Beaux-Arts it rose above a forest of plastic creations, competing necessarily with thousands of other attractions. At Buffalo, on the other hand, it was

given an ideal location. Facing the Art building, but at a considerable distance from all structures, with a glassy lake and billows
of green foliage as a background, it formed the natural centre of a
great picture. Its pedestal was at the head of the stairs which led
to a boat landing. The line of large trees which border the lake
being interrupted at this point, descended gently through gradations of shrubbery of diminishing height, forming a wide notch
or bow in which the group seemed suspended. Beyond this was
the mirror of smiling waters, then the distant bank, and finally
the arch of blue sky, against which was silhouetted the great
white mass. The effect was indescribably fine. No one could
see that monument as it stood in the Buffalo park without realizing how much the beauty of even a masterpiece is enhanced by
fit surroundings.

Posterity may select the Shaw Memorial as Saint Gaudens's
greatest work. In some ways it is the most original thing that
he has done; but repeated views of the "Sherman" confirm and
strengthen one's first impression that it will rank among the
sculptor's highest achievements. The suspicion of leanness of
modelling which troubled a little in the cutting light of the exposition palace has quite disappeared. In the diffused illumination
of outdoor daylight, and even in the direct rays of the sun, horse
and rider and winged guide are all like a splendid vision in which
is nothing mean or trifling.

CHAPTER XVII

DANIEL CHESTER FRENCH

THE boy-life of Daniel Chester French was a fortunate one. Every influence of family and of environment was favorable to the development of a sensitive, poetic nature. As his years have not been accentuated with notes of stress and hardship, so his art is genial, sympathetic, dignified; above all, serene. It expresses admirably his character.

Mr. French was born in Exeter, New Hampshire, Apr. 20, 1850. His parents, Henry Flagg and Anne (Richardson) French, were of substantial New England families, connected with those of Daniel Webster and John G. Whittier. One of his grandfathers was chief justice, the other attorney-general, of New Hampshire, and his father was a lawyer, a judge, and assistant secretary of the United States Treasury. He was one of the founders of the public library at Exeter, and took the lead in planting the town with trees. His artistic instinct showed itself in a love of poetry and a taste for landscape gardening. His descendants testify with pride that "he beautified every place in which he lived."

The youth showed no special taste for sculpture, and made no display of artistic ability until he had reached his nineteenth year. Early friends remember him as a handsome and gentle child, of sunny disposition, bright and witty, like all of the family, but by no means decided as to his future work. His most pronounced taste was a liking for birds and for the art of the taxidermist. It was not until he had spent a year of study in the Institute of Technology and a period of work upon his father's farm that he found his true vocation. One day he emerged from his room with a grotesque figure of a frog in clothes, which he had carved from a turnip. His discerning stepmother is said to have exclaimed upon seeing it,

PLATE 9.—FRENCH: DEATH AND THE YOUNG SCULPTOR.

" Daniel, there is your career." His father was not less appreciative, and thenceforth the future sculptor never lacked for encouragement. Miss May Alcott, the Amy of " Little Women," and the artist of her family, was at that time teaching drawing in Boston, and as she and Daniel's father travelled to and fro upon the cars, they conversed upon the future of the young artist. She saw his work, was much interested in it, and offered to lend him tools for modelling. The French family lived on a farm near Concord; and the evening when Daniel was bidden by his father to harness the horse and to go and bring from the village Miss Alcott's materials is still a memorable one in their annals. Upon his return the family gathered around the dining table, and all had an evening of modelling, Daniel making a dog's head. It is a curious fact that he who now employs another to make the animals of his groups began his own artistic career with the modelling of dogs, birds, and other animals.

Now followed enthusiastic study, wild flights of fancy, and ofttimes the crushing defeats of untutored genius. The horizons of youth are, in one sense, so narrow, its moments of failure seem so final and irrevocable! Poetic natures do not always expend themselves in yearning, however; they may be sensible and wholesome. It was fortunate that Daniel French did not begin with Venuses and Apollos, that he delighted rather in humbler subjects. Best of his youthful works was a very amusing pair of love-sick owls, which has been reproduced in many lands. One remembers also a Rogers-like " Dolly Varden" group, elaborated to the last degree. Presently the young artist turned his new-found skill to portraits — busts and reliefs of members of the household, and of accommodating neighbors. When nineteen years of age he made a visit to relatives in Brooklyn, and had the good fortune to gain access to the studio of J. Q. A. Ward. Here he worked for a month, and thus began a life-long friendship with that eminent sculptor. Slight indeed was the schooling which prepared Mr. French for his remarkable career. There was no possibility of study from nature, and Boston had no classes, even casts from the antique being scarce. For instruction the young sculptor had to content himself with Dr. Rimmer's courses in artistic anatomy, and an occasional view of the statuary of the Athenæum and the few public monuments. In

1870 he was in Chicago on a visit to his brother, Mr. W. M. R. French, now director of the Art Institute of that city, at which time he received his first paid order, one for a bas-relief portrait. It was also in Chicago, in the old Crosby Opera House, that he made his first public exhibition — a bas-relief of his sister Sarah.

Mr. French was but twenty-three years of age when he received his first really important commission, that of the " Minute-Man." This figure is sufficiently noteworthy to repay our attention. A small sum of money had been left by a former citizen of Concord for a monument to be placed upon the exact spot where the militia and the minute-men had fought in 1775. The site had been acquired, and all things were now in readiness. The sculptor proved to be close at hand. With the advice and under the direction of his father, young French submitted a design for the monument, — which had previously passed the ordeal of family criticism, — to the town meeting, in March, 1873. At the same time he offered to make the statue in plaster, of heroic size, and if the authorities would appropriate $400 for expenses, he would deliver the statue to the town; if it chose to pay an additional sum for his work, he would be grateful, and if not he would endeavor to be content. This modest proposition was seconded by Ralph Waldo Emerson, Judge Hoar, and others, with the result that the favored sculptor was soon enthusiastically engaged upon the work in the Studio building in Boston.

All the American world knows of the successful completion of the statue; but when it was unveiled, on April 19, 1875, the artist, who had put his best endeavor into it, was not present, having already sailed for Italy. It was a pity that he should have missed that historic occasion in which the dedication of his work was so prominent and essential a part. Emerson made a brief speech, Lowell read the poem, and George William Curtis, who that day pronounced the statue " masterly," delivered the oration to a great and distinguished assembly.

When it is recalled that up to this time Mr. French had had no instruction beyond the month in Mr. Ward's studio and the anatomy lectures, his triumph is seen to be an extraordinary one. It is interesting to note what the figure, so alert and so American in character, owes to its senior colleague, the " Apollo Belvedere." It would never

FIG. 46. — FRENCH: GALLAUDET GROUP, WASHINGTON.

be suspected, but a large cast of the "Apollo" was Mr. French's sole model. He made good use of it, although the poses are not identical. It speaks well for the untutored young artist that he was able to impress upon his very first work so much of his own personality and so much of the spirit required that he completely concealed his classic model. How sensible and contained he was in it all, one can best appreciate by contrasting his stern, tense embodiment of patriotism with the usual exuberant productions of beginners. The "Minute-Man" has nothing of their artistic lawlessness; neither does it show aught of that other failing of inexperience—the timid clinging to another man's work. Mr. French had definite notions even at the beginning of his career, and on all occasions took a decided and straightforward course. He had the intelligence to appreciate his subject, the imagination to conceive it vividly and simply, and the skill—or perhaps we should rather say, considering his youth, the ingenuity—to express it in adequate terms.

While the movement of the two figures is essentially the same, a number of changes were necessary to convert the sun-god into an "embattled farmer" of 1775. The level left arm of the "Apollo" was judiciously lowered that the hand might rest upon the plough which it is about to relinquish. The right hand grasps a long flint-lock rifle. The rather meagre sleeves are rolled up to the elbows, showing arms not over ample in their modelling. The fine head is turned, Apollo-wise, to the left. The expression is strong yet unexaggerated, a striking instance of moderation in a young artist, who is generally tempted to over-emphasize. The picturesque effect is much enhanced by the long hair in a queue and the broad-brimmed hat turned up on one side. The high, well-wrinkled boots contribute their effective note, and a coat, or cloak, thrown over the deserted plough, adds to the volume of the mass. On the whole it was and is a figure to be enthusiastic about. The applause which went up on its unveiling was not the usual perfunctory hurrah. Daniel French's first statue was done with conviction and charged with emotion. Possibly he has never shown quite so much feeling since.

During his sojourn of a year in Florence Mr. French lived with the family of Mr. Preston Powers, but most of his work was done in the studio of Thomas Ball, for whose dignified art he has always expressed great regard. Excepting this brief study-time in Italy, Mr. French is self-trained, having gained a great amount of practice during the following years in the execution of large decorative works for various public buildings. Among these were figures and pedimental groups for the St. Louis Custom House (1877), the Philadelphia Court House (1883), and Boston Post Office (1885). The advantages of such experience with large problems can scarcely be overestimated. It was an opportune time, and the knowledge acquired through those practical experiments has counted in everything which the artist has since undertaken.

It is not quite just to overlook a " Sleeping Endymion," a perfectly legitimate and, in style, inevitable product of the Florentine year. This muscular youth, with his conventionally classic head, his carefully arranged limbs and sharp-cut drapery, is not so good as Rinehart's, but it is better than the average product of American skill and enthusiasm in combination with Florentine methods. It must be acknowledged that it is quite the most uninteresting of the sculptor's works, a woeful falling off in inspiration from the virile, original power of the " Minute-Man." If the Italian atmosphere was thus disastrous to an individuality as sincere and authentic as that of Daniel French, what was to be expected when weak, colorless natures were immersed in it? Is it any wonder that the invertebrates of art have found there a vast burying-ground of all their ambitions? Mr. French's good angel, or good sense, or mayhap a mere instinct of self-preservation, brought him back safely and promptly to these shores, to the very great advantage of American art.

In 1879 it was the sculptor's privilege to model from life a bust of Ralph Waldo Emerson. The work was done in Mr. Emerson's study, and Mr. French favors us with a short account of this interesting occasion: " I think it is very seldom that a face combines such vigor and strength in the general form with such exceeding delicacy and sensitiveness in the details. James speaks somewhere of 'the over-modelled American face.' No face was ever more modelled than Mr. Emerson's; there was nothing slurred, nothing accidental, but it was like the perfection of detail in great sculpture — it did not interfere with the grand scheme. Neither did it interfere with an almost childlike mobility that admitted of an infinite variety of expression and made possible that wonderful lighting up of the face so often spoken of by those who knew him. It was the attempt to catch that glorifying expression that made me despair of my bust. When the work was approaching completion, Mr. Emerson looked at it after one of the sittings and said, 'The trouble is, the more it resembles me, the worse it looks.'" It will be remembered, however, that the sage finally gave the bust his unqualified approval in the oft-quoted remark, " That is the face that I shave."

Mr. French's heads are invariably fine, intellectual, and commanding. His exceptional privilege of intimacy with the choicest spirits and noblest types of our country has given him a great advantage over many artists. It provides him a mental gallery, as it were, of all that is best. The portraits of Emerson and Alcott are singularly delicate and appreciative studies. They bear the look of elevation which we attribute to such as climb the heights, yet they are intensely human. Mr. French, in his use of the portrait bust for monumental purposes, with subordinate decorative figures, as in the John Boyle O'Reilly Memorial and the Richard M. Hunt Memorial, has solved with distinguished success one of the most difficult problems of modern sculpture. The bust gives us the essential, the intellectual side of the man, with its personal interest, while there is an actual gain in concentration through the absence of the insistent details of coat and pantaloons, seams and buttonholes, shoes and shoestrings — things which one scarcely notices upon the living, moving man, but which fairly clamor for attention upon the surface of the petrified effigy.

The ideal-portrait statue of John Harvard at Cambridge was executed in 1882, and may be called the last of Mr. French's early works; at least from this point we find the suaver touch of a matured artist. The slight angularity, the artistic severity of this figure, do not seem out of place in such a subject. One feels the Puritan inheritance in its very contours, yet the ascetic face is sweet and winning. If the artist had not made this statue for John Harvard, he might have called it "John Milton," and we should have been satisfied, so refined is the ideal, yet withal so intense and so personal. The deficiencies of execution, if we may thus characterize the consistent leanness of its drapery and the general tightness of drawing, are merely superficial; the "Harvard" is a distinctly sculptural conception. The pose of the head is admirably expressed; the arms, and particularly the sensitive hands, could not have been better placed. There is nothing shrinking or lean about their lines. They have been as carefully arranged as were those of the "Endymion"; but here one is not aware of the effort. Conception, composition, construction, every step has been "right."

FIG. 47. — FRENCH: O'REILLY MONUMENT, BOSTON.

In the summer of 1888 Mr. French went to Paris to model his important statue of General Cass of Michigan, the marble of which now stands in the National Hall of Statuary at Washington. Like a man who knows what he wants, and is not dazzled by the merely superficial, Mr. French set about assimilating the best that is in modern Parisian art. He had not come too soon; his artistic character was already formed and had asserted itself strongly in many original productions. Neither did he stay too long. He is, and ever will be, American to the core.   But he learned there, in that one piece of work, and during those few months of observation, what was destined to influence and perfect everything which was to follow. Knowing his own needs, he obtained more in that brief period than it is possible to acquire in years of immature strivings.

The " General Cass " did not altogether please some of the Paris sculptors.   Mr. French has related how M. Aizelin criticised its ponderous and solid pose, with the weight carried equally on the two legs.   He adds with a smile that the eminent sculptor evidently thought that he " did not know any better."   But like Saint Gaudens with his " Farragut," Mr. French had a sturdy subject to deal with, and selected the position best suited to express the character of the man.   With all its solidity the artist treated so well the surface and made the flesh so mellow and the drapery so crisp and full of color that the figure easily takes its place among the best portrait statues of the country.   It unites admirable characterization with no less attractive technic.   The first quality the artist had already shown ; the second was the result of the Parisian experience.   This figure is one of the few good things in that extraordinary collection of the Capitol.   Among its hard, conventional companions it stands almost alone.   It has an individuality, an equipoise, and a technical perfection undreamed of by the earlier generation of American sculptors.

From that day we have a succession of notable achievements from Mr. French.   Subjects permitting of more poetic expression than the " General Cass " have since come to him.   The next one of importance was the Gallaudet group, one of the most pleasing portrait monuments of our time (Fig. 46).   It was modelled in the year 1888, and now decorates the Columbian Institution for Deaf Mutes in Washington.   The famous teacher of the deaf and dumb is shown seated in a chair with a little girl of eight or ten years standing beside him.   It was the good doctor's interest in this child, Alice Cogswell, which led him to devote his life to the education of deaf-mutes and to the introduction into our country of new methods of teaching.   In the group the teacher is shown bending toward his pupil with sympathetic look ; she, with outstretched arm, closes her little hand, thus shaping a letter of the new language which he has given her. Her eyes look the gratitude of the pent-up soul. The artist's conception is as beautiful as a strain of music. The execution of the group is no less satisfying, the composition of line and mass being very successful, though novel. The sweep of the child's simple dress is happily employed; the straight little arm offers just enough contrast to the other graceful but less significant lines. It concentrates attention, leading the eye back finally to the wistful, pleading face and to the reassuring smile of the teacher. Among all of the sculptures which America has produced one recalls few indeed approaching either the originality or the tender, poetic charm of this exquisite work.

At the Columbian Exposition, surrounded by the extravagances of the Italian carvers and the clever plastic jokes of the Spanish modellers, Mr. French's relief of "The Angel of Death and the Young Sculptor" rose superb — the expression of a self-respecting master of a noble art (Pl. IX). Putting aside the actual signifi-cance of the idea, which appeals to all, though so variously, one finds in the handling of this memorial to Martin Milmore some new and interesting features. The artist has attempted no por-traiture. The young sculptor is not Milmore, though Mr. French was reminded, after the sphinx was introduced, turned around and remodelled, that Milmore had actually carved one of these weird creatures for the Mount Auburn Cemetery. In a way the *motif* of the relief suggests Watts's "Love and Death"; but how much more beautiful and impressive this mysterious angel form than the grisly, threatening *something* which presses, silent and irresistible, upon the figure of Love in the famous painting! It is, to be sure, only a question of point of view. Mr. French's angel may be looked upon as a friend, even a benefactress; one of our eloquent clergymen has so interpreted it in a suggestive sermon.

The manner in which the artist simplified and etherealized the face of the angel is very interesting. One feels firm modelling underneath it all, but a skilful blending of the forms avoids sharp-ness and angularity. The overshadowing mass of drapery cuts off all direct light, and shrouds the noble face in a dim half-tone. By these ingenious and happy devices the sculptor has succeeded to a remarkable degree in escaping the aggressive realism which spoils so many of the would-be ideal works of this period.   This face has mystery; it is impressive and grand.   It speaks to every imagination.

The universality of this appeal proves, in a way, the greatness of the work; the sympathetic response which it evokes is the highest tribute possible.   All human kind, from the ignorant, the uncouth, even the flippant, to the most refined and the most spiritual, show a quick flash of recognition when introduced to this truly great thought. It stirs the sluggish, prosaic mind; it arrests the frivolous.   It calms the work-weary and tempest-tossed; it is big enough in grasp for the philosopher and the seer.   Strange it sounds to speak of a gravestone as "popular," yet were the word not so abused by the companionship of the meretricious, it could well be employed in this connection. Photographs of this relief are to be seen in every picture store; they hang in thousands of homes.   One finds them in offices and upon the desks of men of business.   It is a wonderful thing, a very great privilege, to be able to talk thus to one's countrymen.   And to do it in a language so exalted, with an eloquence so sustained — how rare!

To revert for a moment to the technical execution of the group, there is a great lesson for sculptors in the treatment of those admirable wings.   Their masterly simplicity was emphasized by the neighboring Florentine angels at the Columbian Exposition.   The Italians verily cannot stay the hand until every feather is ruffled into unrest. Feathers are hardly enough; they delight in marking even the striæ with a fine-toothed comb.   Very different is Mr. French's treatment. Much is eliminated to begin with; the great feathers are reduced to three or four.   Then broad surfaces are left quite undisturbed or are blended together into simple masses, with here and there an occasional accent.   But this accent is quite enough — far more effective, indeed, than a monotonous teasing of the entire surface.

Other beautiful angels of later date from the hand of Mr. French are the little reliefs of kneeling figures decorating the Clarke monument, Forest Hills, Boston; the impressive creation for the White Memorial, also in Forest Hills Cemetery, and the dreamy little vase-bearer of the Chapman Memorial in Milwaukee.

To continue the catalogue of Mr. French's works, we turn again to the Columbian Exposition, where, amid the endless array of sculp-

Y

tural decorations, the work of this masterful artist stood preëminent.
It is unnecessary to explain that this was not alone because of the
enormous size of the figure of the "Republic." That crowning
feature of the Fair was more than a big feature; it was a great one.
Some did not like it, but that was their misfortune; it was not
Mr. French's problem to make a merely pretty thing. He took his
commission more seriously. His the task to represent something
more enduring than the exposition, and to embody it in a form
which should enter into an architectural scheme of classic spirit. It
was to be seen from a distance, in connection with those buildings;
it must be a monument as well as a statue. Hence its symmetry and
balance. Hence the straight, severe lines of the lower portion of
the figure. Its archaic severity was not accidental. The artist
studied long on his problem, eliminating and simplifying until the
monument stood reduced to its lowest terms, a triumph of intelligent
selection. No doubt Mr. French could have made his "Republic"
graceful as a Hebe, as sinuous as Bernini's contorted divinities;
but he knew better. Those long lines and broad masses fairly
insisted upon leading the eye up to the arms and head. One could
not avoid the countenance — that "stern, sweet face" which realized
Lowell's vision. Such a union of personality with sculptural generalization is rare. To convey the impression of a soul so great yet
so far removed is a remarkable achievement. To realize the magnitude of Mr. French's success one need only compare a good photograph of the "Republic" with such other immense creations as
Schwanthaler's "Bavaria," Schilling's "Germany," and Bartholdi's
"Liberty."

Of this time also were those first important collaborations with
Edward C. Potter, the well-known sculptor of animals, a former
pupil of Mr. French. Every one remembers the spirited "Columbus
Quadriga" which crowned the so-called Peristyle, and those most successful decorative groups of the Court of Honor, in which appeared
"The Teamster," "The Farmer," "The Indian Girl," and that other
unnamed, classic beauty, all so effectively combined with Mr. Potter's
noble horses and oxen.

The success of the Milmore Memorial brought now from Boston
a second order of similar character, that for the John Boyle O'Reilly

FIG. 48. — FRENCH AND POTTER: WASHINGTON, PARIS.

monument (Fig. 47). This fine work, dedicated in 1896, is most
happily situated in the region known as the Back Bay Fens, and is
well worthy of a special pilgrimage. The scheme is primarily a
massive stone of Celtic design, against one face of which is placed
a bust of the poet; on the other side is a bronze group. The idea
of this group is not a complex one, — the day for sculptural rebuses
is gone by, — but its significance is enhanced by its very simplicity.
The figure of Erin, a presence of rare beauty, sits twining in mournful pride a wreath of laurel. She is supported on the one hand by
the personification of Patriotism and on the other by Poesy, a beautiful youth who, with outstretched hand, offers leaves for the wreath.
These three do not sit there upright and politely ignoring one another,
like self-conscious strangers, but are closely bound together in thought
and in composition. The subordinate figures are shown as supplying
the material of the wreath and following its growth with sympathetic
interest. There is nothing theatrical in the composition; all is calm
and reverent. Yet one is responsive to an undercurrent of exaltation, a service of gratitude as well as of sorrow. Erin rejoices in the
memory of her gifted son even while she mourns her loss.[1] There
are certain great qualities which we always expect in the work of
Mr. French which might, however, escape the unpractised eye of the
non-professional — the sculptural compactness which he has given
to the group as a whole, and the " color," or play of light and shade,
with which he has enlivened these surfaces. The apparently unstudied swerve of the figures has been most delicately planned to
produce undulation, advance, and retreat of masses. The total effect
is one of gentle dignity — a combination of tenderness and reserve.

Mr. French has produced in collaboration with Mr. Potter, three
equestrian statues of high value; the "General Grant," which was
unveiled in Fairmount Park, Philadelphia, on the 27th of April, 1899;
the " Washington " (Fig. 48) presented to France by the Daughters
of the Revolution, and formally dedicated on July 4, 1900; and the
" General Joseph Hooker," inaugurated in Boston on June 25, 1903.

No better descriptions of the two former works have been written
than those found in an article on Mr. French by Mr. William A.
Coffin, published in the *Century Magazine.*

[1] Described in *Century Magazine*, Vol. XXX, p. 158.

"Washington, in Mr. French's statue, is represented as taking command of the army at Cambridge, dedicating his sword to the service of his country, and appealing to Heaven for the justice of his cause. With the head thrown slightly backward, the figure holds with the left hand and arm the military hat and the bridle reins, and, the other arm being extended perpendicularly, the right hand holds the sword exactly upright. The pose is heroic and dramatic. The spirit of the motive is admirably expressed in the action of the figure, and the head is noble and commanding in aspect. The horse, with arched neck and showing splendid lines of construction and action, is imposing, and holds its proper place in the work, which is, as a whole, superlatively excellent in style. The pedestal was designed by Mr. Charles F. McKim. The total height from the ground to the head of the figure is about thirty feet.

"The figure of General Grant is in complete repose. The body is firmly erect, and the head, facing directly forward, is fixed and steady. The hands are resting, one upon the other, on the pommel of the saddle; and an army cloak, hanging from the shoulders, falls on the hips and the back of the horse. The face looks out from under the brim of the stiff-crowned hat with a meditative, calm expression, beneath which quiet exterior one feels there is concealed a vast amount of determination and force. When looked at closely, the eyes are seen to be turned a little to one side. The figure expresses immobility and watchfulness. Captain and horse seem to be one in this uncompromising attitude, and the horse is so unobtrusive as part of the group, and yet so thoroughly in character with his rider, that a special meed of praise is due to Mr. Potter for understanding so well the needs of the subject, and expressing them so finely in his part of the work. This brief description of the two statues is sufficient to show that Mr. French is endowed with a faculty of the greatest importance in the arts of sculpture and painting — that of expression, not only by fidelity of detail, but also by the composition of a work as a whole, the character of the subject, and of causing the beholder to receive in a general view an impression corresponding to the artist's conception. He decides that his Washington shall be heroic and striking and dramatic (but of course

FIG. 49.— FRENCH : ALMA MATER, COLUMBIA UNIVERSITY.

not theatrical), and he produces just this impression on the spectator by the large style of his means; while his detail, when the time comes to take note of it, is seen to be in harmony with the trend of his great lines and masses. He conceives his Grant as a great captain who showed the least emotion under the mightiest strain, the greatest exterior calm in the most acute and trying situations, and consistently develops a figure whose posture may not be inaptly likened to that of a sentinel in a shower of rain which causes the passers-by to hurry to shelter, but leaves him standing unmoved in the steady drenching. There is no sensitiveness to merely annoying conditions, but an alert readiness to judge quickly what to do if the occasion comes for action. The feet are stuck into the stirrups, the body is straight and at rest, the head is as steady as a sign-post; but one feels that his head might turn in an instant and the body swing round while an order was briefly given, and that the figure might then resume its position, every line in it expressing quiet deliberation and coolness in the face of danger." [1]

The more recent equestrian statue of General Hooker in Boston has been placed at the Park Street end of the State House grounds. It shows both the commander and the noble horse at rest. The whole effect is quiet but impressive while not lacking in decorative value at even a considerable distance. Its character is as distinctly pronounced as that of either the "Washington" or the "Grant," neither of which it resembles excepting in the perfection of its workmanship.

Among Mr. French's works not already mentioned are portrait statues of Thomas Starr King in San Francisco (1890); Rufus Choate, Boston (1898); Governor John I. Pillsbury, Minneapolis (1901); Commodore George H. Perkins, Concord, New Hampshire (1902); General William F. Bartlett and Governor Wolcott, for the State House of Boston; and a group for the new Chamber of Commerce, New York, containing a portrait statue of De Witt Clinton, supported by two allegorical figures. His memorial to Richard M. Hunt, previously referred to, stands upon Fifth Avenue in New York, near Seventieth Street, and is notable for its happy union of sculpture and architecture, which are indeed personified here in bronze figures at either end of a stately exedra. These presiding

[1] *Century Magazine*, Vol. XXXVII, p. 871.

geniuses are treated with fitting formality; but within the severe outlines of their classic garments is much richness of plastic hand-ling, while their heads show new and gracious types, being among the most beautiful of Mr. French's creations. The dignified bust of the great architect is virile and animated — in every way worthy of its conspicuous position.

Mr. French has had in his studio for several years three pairs of doors destined for the Boston Public Library. They differ from the usual bronze doors of many panels, being simply large reliefs of separate figures. The subjects are: Music and Poetry; Knowledge and Wisdom; Truth and Inspiration. These allegoric figures, en-veloped in much graceful drapery, are treated in very low relief, and will rank among our choicest examples of that elusive form of sculpture. It is recognized that low-relief work is one of the final tests of a sculptor's skill. In the importunate and most difficult problems of composition, foreshortening, and draping, reduced al-most to the ethereal, Mr. French has shown his skill to be quite equal to his refined taste.

Mr. French devoted a large portion of the years 1902 and 1903 to the elaboration of his imposing "Alma Mater" (Fig. 49), which now adorns the approach to the Library of Columbia University, New York. The figure is of heroic dimensions, seated in a curule chair, her elbows resting on its arms. It has been well said of Mr. French that whether he does a thing in the "large" or as a figurine, he always does it largely, and his smallest creations have dignity and force, just as his most grandiose have tenderness and refinement. This figure, though very commanding, has the grace which one would willingly attribute to a subject so beloved. The sculptor has given definite and gratifying form to the intangible but cherished dream-mother of all college men. "Alma Mater" suggests not a little the sculptor's "Republic," now seated and at her ease; but this figure is more winning and more personal — "Alma Mater" in-vites not only the reverence but the love of all her children.

This figure may be said to epitomize, as well as any one work can do so, the general character of Mr. French's art. In it one rec-ognizes a refined and poetic thought combined with a singular purity of technic. Grace and plastic charm are qualities inherent in almost everything that Mr. French has done, giving a distinct value to whatever he fashions, quite aside from its primary significance. He conceives his works in a large and sympathetic way and delights in every step of the processes which externalize his thought. It is his great distinction to have created good sculpture which the people could love; works which reveal their beauty to the most primitively informed in art, and which nevertheless are gratifying to the brother craftsmen. In this respect as well as in many others Mr. French is truly a leader. No one has a greater following and yet, most agreeable paradox! no one has done better work.

That this should have been done without some concession to popular taste is remarkable, yet it may be asserted that Mr. French's art is not only far removed from the theatrical, but is, on the contrary, notably reticent and self-contained. Sculpture is not with him a " passional expression," but the outward symbol of a serene, or at least a highly controlled, nature. Indeed, it may be said that abstract serenity is the most uniform characteristic of his productions. How far this is a matter of temperament, and how far it is due to personal theories of the legitimate scope of sculpture, it would be interesting to know; but as such theories are largely the result of the "personal equation," it is probable that the answer is not far to seek. Since Mr. French is the best known and the most highly appreciated of our native sculptors, his work becomes doubly interesting as a demonstration of the artistic possibilities of our race and as an indication of present-day tastes and tendencies. That such men as Mr. French and Mr. Saint Gaudens are known and admired by the general public is a most encouraging sign; that sculpture so noble and so original as that of Mr. French should be produced by an American and a New Englander is not less significant.

CHAPTER XVIII

FREDERICK MACMONNIES

In more than one respect Frederick MacMonnies is an extraordinary artist. For sheer dexterity of manipulation there is no American sculptor to be compared with him. His eminence is not limited, however, to the skill of the hand. In invention he is prolific to a remarkable degree, and if his work never reaches the exquisite higher notes of his master, Saint Gaudens, nor traverses the gamut to the depths of feeling of George Barnard, it extends over a wide range — a range equalled by few living sculptors. He has done many things, but has yet to record a failure. From the " Bacchante " to the " Shakespeare," from the irresistible " Donatello " babies to the military groups of Brooklyn, he has shown in all his mastery of his art. Some sculptors avoid failures by attempting only commonplaces; but Mr. MacMonnies cannot be accused of undue caution. He is audacious. He experiments. He tries all fields known and unknown. We can quite believe his comment that every one of his important works has been " born of a great enthusiasm "; but each has been developed under a firm hand, guided by a reasoning mind.

The result of these various unusual qualities is a capacity for production almost without parallel in the art world of to-day. During the ten years of his greatest activity, Mr. MacMonnies not only created more good sculpture than did any contemporary, but more than most sculptors produce in a lifetime. Indeed, as one recalls the story of the past, it does not seem a stretch of fancy to claim that in all likelihood no sculptor ever accomplished the same amount of good work in the same brief period.

There are not lacking, of course, those to mourn that he did not "attempt less and put more thought into it"; but it may well be questioned if greater deliberation would have produced more

PLATE 10. — MacMONNIES: NATHAN HALE.

remarkable results. Mr. MacMonnies may not be a profound thinker; and then again he may be — so profound as to realize that art should not attempt to compass the entire horizon of philosophy. Whether he could have felt things any more strongly or expressed them any more vividly by "taking thought" is doubtful. He is not of the brooding kind. He exults in accomplishment, and his ardor increases with the progress of the work instead of burning out and leaving us but cold ashes.

What could we spare from all his array of beautiful creations? What would you wish him to have spent more time upon? Some are wrought with the caressing finish of the mediæval goldsmith; others are enveloped in a plastic suavity of surface which seems to have "come of itself," so little look of labor is there in it; but each treatment is suited to its object, and there is not one thing in all the list which has been neglected. There is not a figure which does not stand well on its feet, not a fold of drapery which has not been considered. The American conscience is sometimes said to be over-developed. It must be confessed that in matters artistic there are examples within reach where it seems to preponderate to the exclusion of other desirable qualities. In the work of Mr. MacMonnies one feels the just balance. You infer the conscience from the results. A good man does not spend his days in incessant prating about duty. He does not obtrude his conscience, but lives it. So Mr. MacMonnies lives his art, expressing himself in it to his best ability. He thinks in terms of sculpture, and therefore his art is spontaneous, vital, and convincing.

For all his sophistication Mr. MacMonnies is, like his master, much nearer in his sympathies to Donatello than to Michael Angelo. His art is essentially plastic rather than glyptic. He has no leaning toward the stone-cutter's massive generalizations. One recalls but a single work of his translated into the marble, the "Venus and Adonis," and for this the sculptor perversely chose a red granulated stone full of streaks and blemishes. Perhaps it was Mr. MacMonnies's early study of painting which turned him from the white and developed the color sense that he has gratified in later years by a temporary change of profession. It is more likely, however, that it was the taste which preceded and led to the youthful revels in color. At any rate it is evident that with all his industry Mr. MacMonnies has little love for the painful process of the pointing instrument, the mallet, and chisel. His art is a joyous one, which must find playful and swift expression. He delights in the "feel" of the clay and handles it like a magician, astonishing even himself with the results. And when the effect is obtained, when his dream is realized, then he is done with it. It must be preserved exactly as his fingers have left it. He knows that no other hand could reproduce his touch in marble. He would chafe under the restraint of doing it himself, and, besides, he has something else to do; he is already aflame with a new idea. Even more inevitably than with Saint Gaudens, his compositions are conceived for the bronze alone. Certain of the elder sculptor's works could be put into marble successfully; there are few, if any, of Mr. MacMonnies's that would not lose all appropriateness through the change.

Mr. MacMonnies was born in Brooklyn, New York, Sept. 28, 1863. His father, William MacMonnies, of Clan Menzies in Scotland, came to New York at the age of eighteen and in the grain business laid the foundation of a considerable fortune which, however, was swept away during the Civil War. The artistic temperament was an inheritance from the mother, Juliana Eudora West, a niece of Benjamin West. The boy's talent revealed itself early, and developed in the face of many difficulties. Though obliged to leave school while still a child and to earn his living as clerk in a jewelry store, he nevertheless found time to pursue his favorite study, and at the age of sixteen attracted the attention of Mr. Saint Gaudens, who received him as an apprentice in his studio. Delighted as the youth must have been, he could not have realized at that time the full significance of his good fortune. During the next five years he received the best possible training in the fundamental principles of his art. He was an industrious and eager student, not confining his efforts to the studio, but working at night in the life-classes of the Academy of Design and the Art Students' League; and when, in 1884, he was enabled to go abroad, he went equipped with a knowledge of modelling which made him ready to reap the whole benefit from the foreign schools. It is safe to say that no young American sculptor had ever journeyed to Europe so well prepared to profit immediately by the privileges there offered. During those formative years he had enjoyed the priceless advantage of frequent and familiar association with the greatest artists of the country. Our leading painters, architects, and writers, as well as the brother sculptors, made Mr. Saint Gaudens's studio a sort of rendezvous in those days. Their late-afternoon chats and discussions must have opened new worlds to the eager mind of the youth. He seldom spoke, but was always within ear-shot.

Mr. MacMonnies went direct to Paris and was promptly enrolled in the École des Beaux-Arts. While most of the American students of that day had made their little start at home without instruction, and had not known enough to build up a figure upon their arrival in the school, this young man of twenty stepped into place with perfect confidence and at once showed his companions that he could swing his weekly *bonhomme* into shape with the cleverest of them. The cholera broke out that year in Paris, and in deference to the wishes of his parents the young sculptor packed up and moved on to Munich, where he spent some months in painting. Then followed a glorious tramp through the Alps and the return to Paris, but he was scarcely re-installed when he received word that he was needed in Mr. Saint Gaudens's studio. He left at once for New York, where he remained one year. He was in Paris again in 1885, and once more in the school, toiling with feverish intensity and making great strides. In the *concours d'atelier* at the end of this year, the highest competition open to foreigners, he took the prize away from all of the *anciens* of the studio.

After a couple of years the slender purse was quite exhausted, and half regretfully Mr. MacMonnies went back to the New York studio to work and to replenish his fund. Within a year he was in Paris again, full of projects and ambitions. The school had grown distasteful. M. Falguière counselled him to take a studio and strike out for himself, at the same time offering to employ him occasionally in his own private studio. This was, of course, a high compliment as well as a piece of good fortune. But a dream which the young artist had been cherishing of a majestic " Diana " drove out presently all other thoughts, and he gave himself up completely to this fascinating study. Though a remarkably rapid worker, Mr. MacMonnies is also a most persistent and critical one. For the space of an entire year he toiled, making the figure as perfect in construction and as rich in surface modelling as possible.   A story is told of a visit which his professor made him while it was in progress.   Falguière, it will be remembered, was something of a specialist in Dianas.   The great sculptor of flesh viewed the work from all sides, and then began to make suggestions.   Growing interested, he ventured a slight touch here and there.   Before long he had quite forgotten the young artist's presence, forgotten that the little model was not his own, forgotten everything but the problem before him, which he was solving in his own way; and while his reverent but very much worried pupil looked on with bulging eyes, the old sculptor twisted and punched the figure into an entirely new pose. " *Voilà*," he cried, as he gave it a final caress, "*j'aime mieux ça !*" Perhaps our friend was pale with excitement as he bowed his amiable visitor out, endeavoring the while to express a gratitude which somehow did not well up quite spontaneously at the moment. When he went back he sought in a portfolio a photograph of Falguière's famous running " Nymphe," and compared it with the present state of his model.

The movement was exactly the same!   Unconsciously the master had fallen into " the line of the least resistance."   Having posed one limb " thus," the other naturally went " so," and without suspecting it he had re-invented his own statue.   It is needless to say that the clay figure got another twisting before the sun went down, and under those impatient fingers was soon restored to its original pose.   Diana emerged radiant and superb, and won for her creator his first honor at the Salon, a " Mention."   This was in 1889, and the same year brought him his first commission, an order for three life-size figures of angels in bronze, for Saint Paul's Church, New York City.

The angels proved very successful, and his all-powerful friend and master felt justified in turning in his direction various other orders of increasing importance.   In 1889 it was the " Nathan Hale" (Pl. X), and in 1890 the remarkable portrait statue of James L. T. Stranahan of Brooklyn.   These were exhibited at the Salon of 1891, where they won for Mr. MacMonnies a " second medal " — the first and only time that an American sculptor has been so honored at

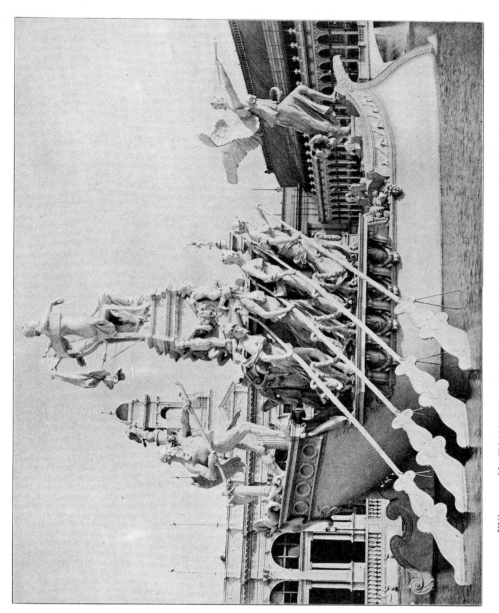

FIG. 50.—MACMONNIES : COLUMBIAN FOUNTAIN, COLUMBIAN EXPOSITION.

the Salon.   There are not a few intelligent people who have found in his figure of Nathan Hale a greater satisfaction than in any other portrait statue of this country.   To be sure it is not strictly a portrait at all, since there were no data to work from, but this makes small difference.   The artist has realized the character that we desire.   This might well be the young patriot; it satisfies perhaps even better than might the authentic face and figure.   Its first appearance was greeted with enthusiastic applause, and time has wrought no change in the public attitude of admiration excepting to intensify it.   The work is one of our few public sculptures which have not lost in the transition from the studio light to their pedestals.   It is finer there in the City Hall Park of New York than in the best of the photographs, beautiful as they are.

The artist chose the supreme moment of the patriot's life.   He has shown him pinioned, with arms close bound to his sides and ankles fettered, standing proudly but without the defiance with which a lesser hero would have posed before the world and with which a lesser artist would have disfigured his work.   The face is exalted with the emotion of the hour.   The lips seem to speak the memorable words, " I only regret that I have but one life to lose for my country."   Expression and sentiment were never more perfectly in accord.   The hero realizes the sacrifice, and makes it gladly.   No modern work better illustrates the effectiveness of composure.   It is so easy to overdo the heroic and to make it absurd or repugnant. Any conspicuous display of feeling which the mind cannot follow sympathetically begins at once to antagonize.   The calm, the sincerity, and the entire lack of " pose " of the " Nathan Hale " win us at once.   Even the casual passer-by feels, if only for the instant, a recognition of lofty sentiment which may never have come within his ken before, but may haply be repeated until it shall find an abiding place in his soul.   This is what the sculptor desired.   While he has given us one of the most artistic figures in our country, it represents more than " art for art's sake."   In conversation upon this subject one day MacMonnies said earnestly: " I wanted to make something that would set the boot-blacks and little clerks around there thinking — something that would make them want to be somebody and find life worth living."

The order for the "Stranahan" was a peculiarly welcome one. The statue was destined to an important position in Brooklyn, and upon it the artist put his most enthusiastic work. He had the unusual privilege of modelling the figure during the life of his subject, and both as a portrait and as a faithful rendering Mr. MacMonnies still finds in it a satisfaction which his most inspired works of fancy fail to give him. Nothing truer has been done in our day. While there is a sculptural bigness in the arrangement as a whole and an unconventional freedom throughout, one is struck above all with the incisive characterization ; the personality of the man is the first and last impression. You forget everything else. He is real. He is alive.

Few will be able to recall another portrait statue of our time in which the sculptor has ventured to complete the costume with the high silk hat. The benevolent-looking old gentleman holds it in his right hand; in his left, which is gloved, is his sturdy cane; on his arm, an overcoat. Nothing could be simpler nor more natural and logical, yet it was left for this young beginner to overcome the difficulties of modern costume by facing them squarely. The result is completely successful and we wonder why others have not done it before. They must have thought of it, — one hardly thinks of a man out of doors without his hat, — and, excepting the soldiers, those called to the honor of sculptural representation are generally of the class that wears silk hats. But possibly Mr. MacMonnies would say we are paying too much attention to that high hat, which was a matter of course with him, and that we are losing the better part. He would tell us that if the figure is valuable for all time, it is because it is true to our time. It has its own place and significance as a historic document, artistically rendered. It will inspire confidence in other days, and men of other centuries will look into its face with the little thrill of recognition which we feel in approaching a bust from the hand of Mino da Fiesole, or a portrait by one of the great Dutch masters.

Between his more important undertakings Mr. MacMonnies has made a practice of amusing himself by the creation of fanciful figures of slight import but of great technical charm. Their very irresponsibility is no doubt one of their most bewitching graces. They are evidently done for amusement, and it is no small comfort to see

now and then a piece of good sculpture unfreighted with a cargo of
deep moral significance. Beyond their compelling good humor is
the perfection of their workmanship. This perfection seems to be
inherent, not all upon the surface. Its completeness unfolds upon
acquaintance, and there is a particular and delicate pleasure in the
progressive discovery.

The so-called " Pan of Rohallion " was the first of these many
fancies which the young artist has wrought out with so much zest.
It is a decorative bit, a fountain figure of a boy standing upon a
globe in a mock heroic attitude, and laughing as he plays upon a
double reed. The pose is symmetrical throughout, the weight resting equally upon the legs, and the arms are lifted alike. To accuse
this jovial little fellow of "theatricality," as some have done, is to lay
entirely too much stress upon the *motif*. It is the antic of a merry
child striking a pose and making music to himself. Nothing could
be more spontaneous and buoyant. The globe upon which the mischievous little chap poises a-tiptoe is in turn supported by eight
able-bodied fishes which stand upon their tails and spout water with
commendable diligence. The other slight accessories, the wreath
on the head, and the fluttering scarf, are indefinite but effective,
being enough, along with the smile, to transform an excellent
" academy " into a real work of art.

Up to the summer of 1893 Mr. MacMonnies's name was known
to comparatively few of his countrymen. Suddenly, as it were in a
day, it was upon the tongues of thousands, and his skill was the
common possession and pride of all America. This prompt and
widespread popularity is without parallel in the history of our art.
If the early enthusiasms over Powers and Crawford were somewhat
similar, let it be recalled how meagre was their public as compared
with the multitudes who visited Jackson Park during the season of
the Columbian Exposition.

The story of the Columbian fountain (Fig. 50), better known
as the " MacMonnies Fountain," is interesting. Mr. Saint Gaudens,
serving upon the advisory board of the Exposition, had counselled a
liberal use of sculpture and suggested many of the features which
were so happily incorporated into the general scheme. Most important among these were the giant figure of the " Republic " and the

great fountain of the Court of Honor. The former had been awarded
to Mr. French. Who should do the fountain? Who could do it
adequately? There were many more capable sculptors in the
country than either the directors or the general public suspected at
the time, and some of these were destined to make their débuts in
the work of the Exposition; but at the moment, with Saint Gaudens
and French out of the question, it must have looked hopeless to
attempt to find among American sculptors a man equal to this enormous undertaking — a man who could conceive a majestic affair in
the style of the French exposition sculpture. A fountain was demanded whose lines should "carry" to a great distance, and whose
details should possess "style"; in short, a work which would be a
real ornament to the grounds from all directions and all distances.

When the subject was brought up for final settlement, Mr. Saint
Gaudens offered the name of Frederick MacMonnies as an artist
equal to the occasion, and, upon the request of the directorate,
presented him to them. Solely upon the recommendation of his
friend and teacher the commission was awarded to him, with
$50,000 to carry it out. The preliminaries being settled, the young
man — he was then but twenty-seven years of age — exultant, but
burdened with his great responsibility, hastened back to Paris to
begin the vast work.

The fountain was intended to be, and was, the finest sculpture
on the grounds. The artist saw at once that it would be useless to
attempt to compete with the enormous buildings which were to sur-
round it; he could not make it look big. So he wisely chose the
better part, elaborating a wonderfully chiselled jewel instead. Between its easy mastery and the amateurish scratches and vague
details which characterized so much of the work about it, there was
a great gulf. This imposing composition, with its twenty-seven
colossal figures, was as well done as the "Stranahan" or the "Boy
with Heron." It was no more troublesome to its author than the
little "Pan." He managed it from start to finish with perfect ease
and perfect success. It may be noted, also, that the artist grudged
money as little as work in his effort for perfection. He made no
attempt to save, but spent freely upon it every dollar of the large
sum given him.

The design was a definite and happy one, suggested no doubt by the fountain of the Paris Exposition of 1889, but a notable improvement as far as clean lines and elegance were concerned. The central mass was a great white ship of charming design, upon which, loftily enthroned, sat Columbia in regal grace. On the prow of the vessel was the tall, exultant figure of Fame with uplifted trumpet. On the high stern an athletic Father Time had general

FIG. 51.— MacMonnies : Soldiers' and Sailors' Memorial, Brooklyn.

supervision of the progress of the bark, whose motive power consisted of eight strong-armed sisters of great beauty, standing figures purporting to represent the arts and industries. They were too much preoccupied with their work to display their professional attributes, but we were told that those on one side represented Sculpture, Architecture, Painting, and Music, and their colleagues on the other side, Agriculture, Science, Industry, and Commerce.

To many the "Columbia" was the least satisfying portion of the design, — a misfortune, since this figure was supposed to be the centre and culmination of the entire scheme. Elegant in line and modelling, she sat there in almost the identical position of Mac-Monnies's first-prize figure of the Paris *concours* of 1885. The pose was a proud and a sculptural one, but not a few found the nudity of the figure repellent or at least undignified, while to others the type of the face seemed unworthy. It is probable, however, that Mr. MacMonnies had no ambition to satisfy all ideals of the Republic, leaving to Mr. French the more serious task of adequately typifying the nation. This was to be merely a beautiful figure playing its part in an elaborate composition, perfectly satisfying to the eye if not to the mind. The keynote of the entire conception was a pageant, a tableau, something gayly ephemeral, rendered doubly impressive by reason of its short tenure of life.

The pedestal supporting the throne was exquisite. There was nothing more beautiful in all the park than those kneeling cherubs which served as picturesque caryatides. The groups of oarswomen made superb masses on either side. The eye was led to them unconsciously by the long, firm lines of the decorative oars. They were well together, so that distance gave them a surprising unity; but within that simple grouping there was a no less remarkable diversity. The graceful figures were clad in light garments, which seemed actually to flutter in the gentle breeze. So adroitly varied were the forms, so skilfully lost and found, that they rendered the very charm if not the illusion of thin drapery in motion. Perhaps the daughters of Niobe suggested this treatment, but their rigid mechanical lines from Roman chisels are far inferior to those which Mr. MacMonnies gave us. One must turn to the "Niké" of Samothrace to find the true inspiration of these rare effects.

Mr. Will Low points out with particular emphasis the beauty of the "admirable decorative ship" and of its accessories, the garlands and various emblems, "all exceedingly well distributed, chosen, and executed."[1] Bands of charming detail formed the rich borders of the great untroubled surfaces of the ship. Athwart these restful zones extended the oars, connecting the vessel still more intimately with the water and with the scattered satellites of the composition,

[1] *Scribner's Magazine*, Vol. XVII, p. 620.

the great sea-horses, the dolphins, and their semi-human companions. The latter were as sportive as were serious the fair sisters above in their make-believe rowing. What cared these revellers for the "Progress of Civilization," for the trumpet blasts of Fame, or the struggles of long-bearded Kronos to keep things going straight! But every one of the twenty-seven great figures, from the star-eyed goddess up there against the sky to the least of those graceful gymnasts of the deep, had its part to play in the impressive and splendid whole. So fine was the result, so free from effort, that we took it all for granted, as a matter of course, as we do the marvels of woods and fields, the glories of dawn and sunset. In our enjoyment we often forgot to give credit to the mind which had conceived and the hands which had shaped this vision of beauty. Its perfection had been built up thoughtfully and consistently. Such successes as the Columbian fountain do not "happen."

The "Sir Henry Vane" of the Boston Public Library is an airy work in which the artist has delightfully embodied his idea of the man and of the life of his day. Mr. MacMonnies's interpretation of the subject is presented so lightly and seems to have been wrought so easily that one gives no heed at first to the sincere effort underneath it. Art has concealed art — and labor, too — so well. How personal and real and vivacious he is! No stern old Deacon Chapin he, no vengeful Cotton Mather. In the swing of the body, the turn of the head, the easy movement of the arm, indeed, in the very trifling import of the gesture — the buttoning of a glove — there is a subtle expression of character which shows the artist's taste. He has attempted nothing imposing. He disdains even to impress you, unless you feel so disposed.

Sir Henry is evidently a gentleman, accomplished, serene, and adequate. We know that he was forceful and not lacking in strong religious convictions. The artist tells us only as much as he sees fit of all this, giving his subject the poise and imperturbability of a man of the world. Sculpturally, the movement of the figure is an admirable one. It turns the body enough to give variety to its larger planes, putting vigor into the shoulders and their relation to the head; it also increases the simplicity of contours, while the diagonal sweep of the arm adds an effective line and much play of light and shade. Its value has long been appreciated and, the wide world over, warriors of bronze and heroes of stone are represented tugging at their swords with this same movement. But Sir Henry had no occasion to unsheath his sword, so he does the next best thing—he buttons his gloves.

Even while we analyze and find good reasons for the gesture, there remains a lurking suspicion that the act is trivial and a little unworthy of perpetuation. We recognize in it the refuge of the hapless illustrators of fashionable society. Their ephemeral heroes and heroines hide their feelings incessantly —and most thoroughly, be it acknowledged—in this graceful preoccupation. But bronze is a different matter, and one shrinks a little from the thought of a man—a man of heroic size—spending an eternity in buttoning his gloves. We are offered here, however, the charm of beautiful modelling, to be enjoyed without stint. The undulation and color of the flowing surfaces, their piquancy and lightness of treatment, are all strangely bewildering qualities to those who know only the unhappy creations that stand, in the manner of Saint Simeon Stylites, above our eastern cities. The visitor in Boston, happening upon the figure in the Public Library after a ramble among the older monuments, will be struck by the contrast. They are indeed "come down to us from a former generation," those black, brazen worthies of the round trouser-legs and shining hardware coats! After their oppressive

FIG. 52.—MacMonnies : Shakespeare,
Congressional Library.

heaviness the "Sir Henry Vane" seems playful, as though the artist had not taken his work seriously; yet with all this grace and vivacity, all this legerdemain of the technician, we find that the construction is there — the body is within the clothes. Yes, and fashioned with a truth, an accuracy and — could we see it — a firmness never dreamed of by those who wrought the old-time effigies. The figure before us is a young athlete on dress parade, his strength concealed beneath his caparison; the others, too many of them, are but gigantic examples of the steam-fitter's art, rigidly jointed yet ponderously weak.

The famous "Bacchante" (Fig. 53) was produced in 1894, while the following year saw the completion of the "Shakespeare" of the Congressional Library. These two works, which were carried on side by side, were begotten of very different moods and serve to emphasize the versatility of their author. They also mark, according to some, his highest expression, — Mr. Saint Gaudens in particular considering them his pupil's best work.

The "Bacchante" is an extraordinary combination of realism and ideality. It is evidently a faithful portrait of an individual, but it is also the product of the artist's imagination; no mere patient copying of a model's body could have tenanted a figure thus with the very spirit of "sun-burned mirth." It is endowed with an atmosphere of physical exultation and conscious adequacy rare indeed in modern sculpture. The joy of animal existence — the joy of grassy fields and arching woods — could scarcely find more convincing expression. A work of this character seems even less at home within the marble hall of the Metropolitan Museum than it would in the narrow court of the Boston Public Library, where at least it might have been bathed in sunlight. It needs the open, without hint of prison walls. However, one is grateful for an opportunity to approach it, since the modelling of the "Bacchante" and of the whimsically veracious infant will repay the closest study. To make anatomy so true and yet to simplify it enough to convey the illusion of motion is one of the most difficult of problems. In contemplating this modern triumph one appreciates Mr. MacMonnies's rather pitying comment on contemporary art: "It is in the air to try to do things in the easiest way; to avoid difficulties." Mr. MacMonnies's sculpture looks "easy," but it is the product of infinite patience and painstaking, which the sculptor has had the art to conceal.

The "Shakespeare" (Fig. 52) has been approached in a reverent spirit, but is sufficiently mystifying to many. In following the bust at Stratford and the Droeshout portrait, approved by Ben Jonson, Mr. MacMonnies has given to his statue a rather austere and archaic look, which surprises one at first, though it is quite as satisfying in the end as the intimately imagined but markedly inadequate types evolved by other sculptors. Curiously enough he has taken pleasure in clothing this thoughtful figure in a costume of much bulk, covered with elaborate embroidery the details of which would confuse the attention were it not for their extremely low relief. In some ways the "Shakespeare" is the most original of all of Mr. MacMonnies's works, the most removed from one's range of experience. It is so seriously conceived and so evidently a work of conscience that it makes instant appeal to one's respect, and, however unwinning at first, gradually replaces in the mind all other representations of the great poet.

The Congressional Library has other works from Mr. MacMonnies's hands; indeed, almost the first things to attract the visitor's attention, the decorations of the central door, are of his design. Two figures in low relief are supposed to personify respectively "The Humanities" and "The Intellect"; while in the tympanum above, "Minerva," flanked by owl and printing-press and aided by winged messengers, distributes improving literature to the waiting world.

Another product of those busy years, 1894 and 1895, was the "Victory" of West Point, a winged figure of much amplitude. Its fine effect in position demonstrates the sculptor's instinct for mass as well as for line and for light and shade. The model when seen near at hand appeared heavy and somewhat lacking in grace, but so justly had its author estimated the encroachment of the atmosphere — which seems to gnaw upon contours — that the figure when raised upon its lofty shaft was at once transformed, growing light and poising airily as though ready to float away with the clouds.

Mr. MacMonnies's largest works are connected with Prospect Park, Brooklyn. Of these the most important by far are the deco-

FIG. 53. — MACMONNIES: BACCHANTE, METROPOLITAN MUSEUM.

rations of the Brooklyn Memorial Arch (Fig. 51), consisting of three enormous groups in bronze, two of which, "The Army" and "The Navy," decorating the piers, are treated as reliefs, although the figures are largely in the round. The third group is a quadriga surmounting the arch. Of "The Army" it is not too much to say that nothing finer has been done on similar lines since Rude carved "Le Départ." That the group recalls that mighty achievement is at once its distinction and its misfortune. No doubt the one suggested the other; but the critic will be surprised upon examining the two compositions to find that there is no tangible point of resemblance. Their only similarity is in the initial impulse which inspired and permeates them both, their irresistible *élan*. They move, and they carry one with them.

The rush, the fire of the group, are tremendous. It is difficult to realize fully how much a man must expend in conceiving a work like this; how he must keep up his nervous force through months of toil, during all the laborious evolution of his thought. A high-pressure enthusiasm under complete control is the rare endowment demanded of a sculptor in this field. He must be at "concert pitch" all of the time. Indeed, these forms which he has called into being stand before him like an orchestra under the guidance of its leader. He can make confusion by letting them run away with him; he may produce discord; he may evolve only weakness and insipidity; or he may build up with singleness of purpose and infinite delicacy and variety of means a rendition of the composer's thought in which each instrument shall have its just share: advancing, retreating, asserting, deprecating, or dying away, as the common cause may demand. The sculptor is both composer and leader, the two in one; but the vigor, the instant effectiveness of the man who wields the baton illustrates best the tense activity of the sculptor in the presence of a great unformed composition.

"The Army" is symbolized by a group of soldiers in active combat. An officer with uplifted sword furnishes the long dominating lines of the composition. His fallen horse gives the solidity of a large mass to the lower portion of the work, while a trumpeting Bellona on a magnificent winged steed crowns it, filling the upper third with a rich play of lights and shadows. The contour is agitated, bayonets bristling on every side. Mr. MacMonnies says that he conceived the group as an "explosion"; a mass hurled against a stone wall and which, bursting in all directions, has been petrified as it flew.

In this group Mr. MacMonnies, beyond challenge, has again proved himself a master of his art. No other American has as yet demonstrated on a large scale what he has successfully shown here — the ability to weld a tumultuous, picturesque mass into a harmonious whole. The secret, apart from the lines of the composition, which speak for themselves, rests largely in simplifications and in binding parts together. One must preserve constantly a sense of the whole. The artist realizes that accents are not accents at all if they occur too frequently. It is the occasional, carefully considered emphasis which counts in expression. So, while conspicuous forms must be treated with precision, even with insistence, many others may be quite obliterated to good advantage. In the lights such details as buttons, accoutrements, and folds of drapery play their part infinitely better when subtly blended. This is not slurring the work; the forms must be there first. It will take two or three times as long to "envelop" them as it would to make them cheaply imitative — to put on real buttons! — but it is worth while. It is the difference between sculpture and waxwork.

In the shadowed depths even greater liberties must be taken. There are no black holes in good sculpture. The caverns must be filled, plausibly or otherwise; not to the brim, of course, — else our sculptured mass would become as uninteresting in form as a worn bar of soap, — but sufficiently to produce luminous shadows within their depths. Especially must their boundaries slope off with easy transition on one side, at least, carrying the light by insensible degrees down into the darks. Some sculptors, like MacMonnies, seem to possess an intuitive sense of beauty in modelling. Others acquire skill in that direction through laborious and costly experience; while certain ones, possibly men of marked power in other phases of their art, seem to be serenely unconscious of its existence. It is very rare that the work of a beginner possesses this quality; he always begins with literal imitation.

In "The Navy," on the other hand, Mr. MacMonnies has produced a very different kind of composition; one's first thought, indeed, is that this group of men, standing quietly shoulder to shoulder, is not a "composition" at all. We find, however, a compactness of placing and of handling, a sweep of gesture on one side and the apparent accident of a kneeling figure on the other which serve to bind the group together, quite independent of that sentiment pervading the whole which is perhaps its most potent bond of unity. For it was the sculptor's thought to show these men as standing upon the deck of a sinking vessel quietly awaiting their fate. Whether he has made this clear, or ever could, by legitimate sculptural means, may be questioned; but the spectator acquainted with his intention will find the group most dramatic in its very reserve. It becomes easy to persuade one's self that the vessel is sinking. Seen from below, the square platoon rounds into effective composition, while the men build up in sculptural array, their quiet poses showing a stanchness and solidity like that of tree-trunks in the forest at twilight. Marvellously, too, does the strange figure above them improve with distance. She has lost the look of cheapness and vulgarity which irritated us at the Exposition of 1900. She is ample and strong, but seems no longer gross, while the face that we see is so far away that we imagine it whatever we please. It certainly has been purified; the veil of atmosphere does its part.

The spacious circle which forms the vestibule to Prospect Park makes an admirable setting for the completed monument. The whole scene reminds one agreeably of Paris. The arch, while much smaller than the Arc de Triomphe, looms up very stately and imposing. Chaste in contour and rich in the sculptural color of these two masses of bronze, it is fitly crowned by its great quadriga, which, in the early morning and at sunset, glows against the deep blue of the sky, a ruddy apotheosis of the Republic in a chariot of fire. Bearing aloft her oriflamme and heralded by winged victories whose trumpets are almost vibrant, "America" surveys content the busy but peaceful land spread out before her. The brave spirits of the past have done their work well, but it is not useless that their deeds of valor should be thus rehearsed in bronze and stone. For centuries, it may be, these sculptured heroes will tell their story of the price of our national existence and shout their appeal to drowsing loyalty.

2 A

Within their breasts of metal the artist has imprisoned the very essence of patriotism and the unconquerable spirit of war. The Brooklyn Memorial Arch offers a gratifying example of a great sculptural idea, nobly inspired and effectively carried out.

Of quite different mood are the gigantic " Horse Tamers " (Fig. 54), which adorn another entrance to Prospect Park and which also formed part of Mr. MacMonnies's remarkable exhibit at the Ex-

FIG. 54. — MACMONNIES: HORSE TAMERS, BROOKLYN.

position of 1900. These fantastic works show enormous decorative chargers which play tricks and take astonishing poses in order to make picturesque sculptural compositions of themselves. In audacious enterprises of this sort Mr. MacMonnies has all the cleverness of the French. His unruly steeds are reminiscent of Regnault's picture of " Automedon with the Horses of Achilles," rather than of the sculptured " Chevaux de Marly " on the Champs Élysées, there being two horses in each group; but the diminutive groom rides the one while training the other.   All do their part well; one does not see how they could be improved upon, if it is "color" and restlessness that one desires.

Before ceasing from his labors and thus bringing to a close the first cycle of his artistic career, Mr. MacMonnies executed during 1900 and 1901 an admirable standing figure of his friend and patron, General Woodward of Brooklyn, and a spirited equestrian statue of General Slocum for the same city.   These, with a considerable number of medallions, reliefs, and statuettes, round out the almost unprecedented achievement of thirteen years.

Mr. MacMonnies has been criticised for lack of spirituality, of depth, and beside certain of our sculptors this deficiency is evident enough; but it is almost as unreasonable to find fault with him for what he lacks as it is to reproach him for his facility, though even this has been done by lovers of conscientious and obvious toil.   To learn to appreciate his sincere contribution is better business.   After all, a work of art is for the individual who responds to it.   One who is enamoured of the naïveté of the early Florentines may not relish the modernity of Mr. MacMonnies.   If he be eclectic enough to enjoy both, so much the better for him.   Certain it is that Mr. MacMonnies has made a notable contribution which cannot help but raise the standard of American sculpture in the future as it has already done in his own time.

CHAPTER XIX

GEORGE GREY BARNARD

Mr. Barnard is a Westerner, although he chanced to be born in Bellefonte, Pennsylvania, where his parents were temporarily residing in 1863. The sculptor's father is a clergyman, and the fortunes of the ministry afterward led him to Chicago, and thence to Muscatine, Iowa, where the son passed his boyhood. An old friend writes of Barnard's youth: " One of his first boyish passions was for birds and animals, and he made many solitary excursions in the woods across the Mississippi River from his home. As a result of these wanderings he surrounded himself with a remarkable collection of living and stuffed creatures. In a short time he became a self-taught but expert taxidermist and brought together a collection of hundreds of fine specimens. His menagerie and museum occupied the barn and the attic of the parsonage. He was always 'trying his hand' at some new thing, testing his latent resources. In the native clay he began modelling birds and animals, and his success finally led him to attempt a more ambitious task in this new line of effort, a portrait of his small sister. The likeness which he obtained was so faithful that it aroused the admiration of the entire village. However, the good, 'practical' people of the town felt that so great a skill of hand and eye should be turned into a means of gaining him a certain livelihood, and he entered the local jewelry store as an apprentice. In this trade, and particularly as an engraver and letterer, he soon became an expert. The longing for an art career was by this time thoroughly awakened in him, and he came to Chicago. This move was ostensibly to pursue his trade and to bring himself to a higher degree of proficiency therein — a plan which he took steps to carry out immediately upon his arrival.

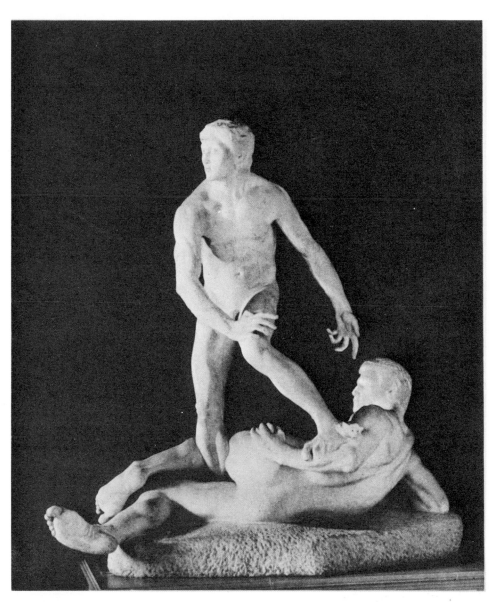

PLATE 11.—BARNARD: THE TWO NATURES.

"He had not, however, been long at work under one of the best engravers in the city when the desire to become a sculptor got the upper hand of him. For several months the boy waged a constant battle of deliberation between his art ambitions and his trade. By means of the latter he could earn what was then a very handsome salary for a young craftsman, as he was recognized as a workman of superior abilities. On the other hand, if he chose to learn how to model it was equally certain that he could earn, for the time being, at least, practically nothing. On the one hand he was assured comfort; on the other unknown privations."

Mr. Barnard decided to study sculpture and entered the Art Institute of Chicago, where he remained about a year and a half, when an order for a bust of a little girl brought him the sum of $350. On this meagre allowance he set off for Paris in November, 1883. He soon became known as the hardest worker among the Americans there, having neither money nor the disposition to join in the student diversions. Few, if any, knew him intimately, but all respected him. He remained for three years and a half in the Atelier Cavelier of the Beaux-Arts, working with a fiery diligence and laying up the stores of knowledge and skill with which he has since astonished the art world. No day was allowed to pass without paying tribute. It is given to few sane men to take life so seriously.

The first year in Paris cost Mr. Barnard just $89. One can readily understand that life might wear a serious look under such circumstances. But no imagination can fully picture the ever present sense of privation, the constant reminder of things desired only to be denied, the tantalizing memories of abundant home life. It is remarkable that the student escaped with his health. Evidently he used good sense in his enforced economies. Perhaps he was already immune. At any rate, he emerged from his various experiments in dieting with one of the finest physiques to be found among all the brotherhood. To see him at work one feels that the chisel belongs by right in his powerful hands. He is the ideal hewer of marble.

It would be a mistake to imagine that the young sculptor was morose, or bore his trials with an air of martyrdom. He was not

of that kind. There were plenty of others ready to pour their
woes into sympathetic ears, but Barnard never complained; these
conditions were a matter of course — things of his own choosing.
Later he grew to be even more of a recluse, shutting himself up
persistently in his studio, emerging only at night, when he walked
the streets of Paris, lost in the dreams of ambition. It was a
trying period of incubation and brooding, but out of it came
great things. It made his exhibit of 1894 possible. It gave him
his standing to-day in the world of art.

The first of his noteworthy productions was the " Boy," which
he began long before his school training was over and which he
finished in marble in 1885. In this conception of a crouching
child, with a bowed head, he shows as plainly as in his latest works
his feeling for an art essentially glyptic in character. The figure
is not merely a boy carved in marble, but a figure conceived for
the marble and expressed in purely sculptural terms. It has a
restful, self-supporting completeness about it, an arrangement which
is satisfying to the eye, regardless of its significance. Not a few
noted sculptors professedly working for the marble miss this constantly. They do not have that intuitive sense of the material
which Mr. Barnard never fails to illustrate. Where he acquired
this peculiar instinct no man knows. It antedates the instruction
of venerable M. Cavelier, whose art suggests cabinet-making in
marble. It could not have been derived from his training as an
engraver, nor from stuffing birds. One does not find in his
father's sermons more plausible explanation than in his gentle
mother's practice upon the " first piano in Chicago." But the gift
he has, and in a more marked degree than any other sculptor of
America. With it he possesses the training to make it available.
One perceives also that in the exquisite modelling of this " Boy "
and in the delicate blending of its contours with the rugged rock
surfaces the artist shows the same qualities which we shall find
giving charm to his later works. He was already himself — even
before he began. What a saving of time!

In 1886 Mr. Barnard modelled a heroic-sized statue of " Cain,"
which he afterward destroyed, and in 1887, having received an order
from a Norwegian for a tombstone, he conceived and wrought out

his poetic symbol of "Brotherly Love," a strange, massive block, in which two nude figures are shown but partially detached. The faces are concealed, but their powerful frames are full of character and individuality. Of this memorial Mr. W. A. Coffin has written appreciatively: "The 'Brotherly Love' violates some of our traditions, but it is beautiful and possesses a weird, indescribable charm. It is a group intended for a tomb, and shows the figures of two nude young men whose heads are partly buried in the roughly hewn marble which forms the bulk of the monument, and whose hands seem to have forced their way through it and to be searching each other's grasp. I suppose that the marble mass may typify rock or darkness, or eternity, or something else tangible or intangible, and that the brothers are groping through it to join each other after death." [1]

It has been said that a poet is entitled to credit for anything that his poems suggest. If the same applies to sculpture, Mr. Barnard may claim on this work a bountiful royalty, for it has been interpreted in many ways: "Life drawn unto Death," "Life reclaimed by Relentless Matter — Earth," "For now we see through a glass, darkly; but then face to face," "Sympathy," and the like. The original idea of the artist was, however, "The Unseen Giver," one who extends a helping hand without hope of recognition or reward.

It would seem that only a superficial or prejudiced critic could object to the rough rock background when, as here, it forms an essential feature of the *motif*. But so vital an issue is art in France, and so virulent its wars, that those who are arrayed against the towering genius of Rodin never fail to hit at anything which smacks of his influence. Hence we find here and there in the mass of French writing on Mr. Barnard's achievements such querulous expressions as these: "Like a second Rodin he has the cleverness of handling to catch the public, such as in leaving, at times, the statues half in the rough. Mr. Barnard ought to leave this last mannerism to those who possess less talent. . . . The experiment of leaving the rough background we do not think worthy of his talent." Just why a sculptor should not be permitted to increase his range of effect by this means is not clear. It can be readily overdone, of course, and

[1] *Century Magazine* Vol. XXXI, p. 879.

in many cases might be most inappropriate, but judiciously used the
rough-hewn background is an effective foil to the carefully modelled
surface.   It is legitimate, because logical in the development of the
work ; there is nothing adventitious about it, nothing dragged in ; the
sculptor has merely stayed his hand at this point, elaborating, insisting upon such things only as he deems worthy of first place.   A
master does not play his composition straight through, with the
relentlessness of a music-box.   Whether upon the organ or the block
of white stone, he accentuates and shades, using on the one hand
chisels and rasps and "points," as on the other stops and pedals.
Furthermore, in sculpture at least, there is created a singular psychological impression of force and mastery where the steps of the work
are boldly recorded.   Here, the perfection of sinuous modelling
and softly blended light and shade ; there, the rough quarry marks.
From the amorphous boulder to the all but palpitating flesh — behold
the whole gamut of nature and art.

Now followed the heroic group which is the best known of Mr.
Barnard's works, and which occupies, in marble and in plaster, prominent positions in the Metropolitan Museum of New York and the
Art Institute of Chicago.   "The Two Natures" (Pl. XI) was
suggested by a line of one of Victor Hugo's poems, "*Je sens deux
hommes en moi.*"   The group was begun in 1888, finished in clay
in 1890, and completed in marble during the winter of 1894.
Two figures are shown : a victor, half erect, half bending over a
prostrate foe.   The bodies are nude, considerably larger than life,
and powerfully modelled.   The attitudes are notably original ; the
treatment throughout consistently that of the marble.   Consistent is
this strange work, however, in more ways than one.   It is consistently perplexing from its very name and intention all the way down
to the last touches on its curiously wrought extremities.   "I feel
Two Natures struggling within me" is its full title — the artist's
point of departure.   And depart at once he does.   He shows the
two natures, and the struggle, or at least the end of a vigorous round,
which leaves the momentary triumph by no means in doubt.   But
here our sculptor is tantalizing ; he never deigns to tell us "which
is which."   The inscrutable faces are those of twin brothers, — they
might have been cast in the same mould, — and to tell the truth they

are not prepossessing. Docs Mr. Barnard belong to the good old school of art where right always triumphs in the last act? Or does he view life with the eye of the hopeless modern " veritist," calmly persuaded that "whatever is, is wrong"? Probably he is doing the most modern thing of all — leaving us to guess the riddle as we will. And believing in our heart of hearts that right will conquer in the end, we read this meaning into the group before us and are pleased at our own cleverness in having fathomed the artist's intention without his telling us anything.

Beyond this the work is not winning. It aims no more at grace of line than at charm of expression. In the conventional sense it is not even a good composition, for it looks more like an accidental grouping than like a carefully adjusted harmony of lines. Perhaps it is this very lack of convention which fascinates one against his will, which draws and holds, though it may not persuade. Mr. Barnard's thought is too powerful, his expression too original, to strike responsive chords at once. How could it? What is there within us to respond to such notes as these? — what in our daily humdrum lives to bring us into tune with such Titanic dreams of struggle? And yet there is something of the force — shall we say the uncouthness? — of nature about this work which is irresistible. It is unique and reminds one of no other; nor can one in its presence look at aught else until he has made the circuit of all its extraordinary views. It is the manly and not less artistic expression of conflict, in form so new and yet so intelligible that its primary significance cannot be mistaken nor its intensity ignored. It is the work of a man who is first of all a sculptor. In our admiration for whittling and for clever joinery most of us have not yet learned what sculpture is.

As for the "repose" and "balance" which we are wont to demand of great works of art, it is evident that the intuition of genius could hardly have found a moment better fitted than this for the purposes of vital sculpture. With all its rugged unrest of line, the group offers absolute repose, though indeed it is the feverish repose of breathless men who must stop for an instant or suffocate. The shadow of the struggle is over them still; the fearful embrace again so near at hand that we do not at once recognize the absolute immobility of the moment. In its every member the composition shows the fervid fancy of a strong man who has *felt* the whole scene.   It is almost superfluous to point out the poetical advantage of this quiescent moment over any incident of the actual struggle.   To have re-created " The Wrestlers " of antiquity, the usual " Jacob and the Angel," or those bloodthirsty men of Copenhagen, would have been to remove the whole thing from the realm of spiritual interest and to have made of it a prize fight.   It would have been an error almost as fatal as to transform this impressive group into a conventionally unified and balanced composition with its comfortable dénouement assured by every well-established line.

But there is a balance here as well — the " balance of power." Not the solid symmetry of a pyramidal design, but the fluctuating equilibrium of the scales.   In its very incompleteness, in the lack of finality of composition, the artist has made appeal to our emotions.   He leaves us in suspense.   The uncertainty of the outcome is written in the fundamental lines of the group.   The issue, as with each of us, is unknown to the end.   Herein lies much of the universality of its significance and the potency of its appeal.

Another extraordinary product of this period was a " Norwegian Stove " (1891).   A stove in those northern lands is very different from our cast-iron affairs, and this important work is far more than a mere happy adaptation of design to industrial purposes.   Barnard's stove, or lofty fireplace, is monumental in size and in conception, illustrating in relief various episodes of the wars of man and the elements, such as are sung in the old Scandinavian sagas.   In one portion man is seen struggling with the sea, typified by the formidable serpent Hidhœgur.   The combat is a terrible one.   Man is but half disengaged from matter, and the serpent is winding itself around him, strangling him in its folds.

With all the intensity of the subject the artist gives us here a fine illustration of a master playing with his materials.   Parts are so fanciful that they might have been suggested by the accidental combinations of unfinished clay figures wrapped in their damp swathings and half seen at twilight.   The treatment is superbly plastic; some of the forms are only hinted at, but others are wrought with tragic earnestness and carried to the last degree of effective finish.   The sculptor draws the line where he will; he elaborates only what he

FIG. 55. — BARNARD: THE HEWER.

desires to emphasize. The subtly modelled bodies emerge from a mass of rough-hewn stone with an astonishing variety of treatment and play of light and shade. The effect of the pile from a distance is almost Japanese in its capricious outline; near at hand one finds such workmanship as is learned in Paris alone, and such original use of this skill as is found only in the works of reactionaries of the modern French school. Mr. Barnard has since united several fragments of this composition in a sumptuous clock, carved in oak. It is one of the most spontaneously artistic products of American sculpture, so beautifully decorative are its massings and lines, so fine is the sensuous charm of the modelling, and withal — and not to be forgotten amid its excellences — so completely convincing is its air of painless creation, of easy control.

Two of the figures from the stove Mr. Barnard carved in marble in 1892. The following year is not accounted for, but was doubtless spent largely upon the marble of " The Two Natures." In 1894 he also made a reduction of the " Brotherly Love," and a bust of a lady.

It was in the Salon of the Champ de Mars of 1894 that Mr. Barnard made his long-anticipated début. The result was an even greater success than he could have hoped for. To make such an impression in artistic Paris is the tantalizing dream of every sculptor and painter. Artists and critics united in proclaiming his work the sensation of the year; and the sculptor, now famous, was fêted and entertained by the great art patrons of Paris. The newspapers were loud in their applause. The *Figaro* said: " Mr. Barnard is possessed of very great qualities, the first of which is the freshness of eternal youth. We feel the warmth of life itself in all his sculpture, especially in his large group;" the *Patrie* declared that Mr. Barnard was "represented with the most éclat"; the *Liberté* thought that " one must have an extraordinary heroism to attack such marbles as these and bring them to completion."

The verdict was unanimous, and M. Thiébault-Sisson, the thoughtful art critic of the *Temps*, quite went out of his way to say: " We have a newcomer, George Grey Barnard, who possesses all the qualities of a great master. He belongs to that young and virile America, whose efforts are manifested in various forms, for the most part unexpected. He demonstrates with a singular power his

contempt for conventional methods, and his passionate longing for
the new and creative in art manifests itself in everything he puts his
hand to.   To him all nature is new, and he has great breadth of conception.   The heroic alone seems capable of attracting him, but an
heroic special in its kind; — special also in his manner of treating it.
He does not show us one man battling with another; his conception
has a far deeper meaning and lesson : man struggling with the elements; man fighting with the inner man, with the baser instincts
of his nature.   He has witnessed the overthrow and fall of the
noblest in life; the highest aspiration toward good, stifled by the
meanest brute force in humanity; and it has been his desire to embody in a colossal group one phase of these innumerable struggles.
Full on the fallen moral being, instinct plants a triumphant foot; but
the victory is doubtful, the victim of an hour revolts; he trembles,
he suffers in expiation of his fault, but he will rise again stronger
and wiser for the contest.

" In the realization of this conception the artist has exhibited a
fire and given proof of a knowledge which place him very high in
his art.   Possibly the composition may lack a little of that precision
and clearness which conventional allegory requires, but in spite of that
the group has movement and life, and the execution is as bold as it
is finely shaded.   All is said with majestic energy that knows its
power and scorns useless details.   Study these sculptures attentively,
and you will find them to be works of astonishing genius.   If the
artist has started from principles found in the French masters,
he has developed all that is essentially his own, and that with an
extraordinary power.   Unless I am greatly mistaken, Mr. Barnard
is destined to make no small stir in the world."

Returning to the United States in 1896 Mr. Barnard's first enterprise was to make a public display of his works, which was done
in the autumn of that year in the Logerot Gardens, New York.
The singular exhibition was visited by many people and was widely
discussed in art circles, but did not receive much appreciative
comment from the press, doubtless because the press did not know
what to say.   The artists, however, were of one accord in their
recognition of Mr. Barnard's power, and some of them, as Mr. Coffin
tells us, spoke in superlative terms.

Mr. Brownell has remarked somewhere: " The French sculptor may draw his inspirations from the sources of originality itself; his audience will measure the result by conventions." Oddly enough, however, while the French critics were practically unanimous in praise of an artistic talent to which no one can deny an astonishing originality, — recognizing its greatness even when mystified by its novelty and qualifying their approval of some of its means of expression, — the writers of America have been very conservative in their acceptance of Mr. Barnard's point of view. In his own country he has received a courteous but far from cordial welcome. We are too timid; not sure enough of ourselves. We are afraid that this may not be good art. It does not look like things which we have seen before. We do not know what to do with it. There has been nobody just like George Barnard, so he has not been classified yet. He must stand in suspense, like the animals of the Garden of Eden, waiting to be named. So much for being a new individual upon the face of the earth. Our American sculptors do so little ideal work, make so few nude figures, that it is not strange that Mr. Barnard's art fails to be appreciated here as it is appreciated in Europe. Mr. Coffin observes only too truly: " He is perhaps just a little out of the perspective of modern days. We have too much talent, conventional and tranquil and adaptive in its tendencies, to calmly accept a man of striking originality and divergence."

Having come home with the avowed object of assisting in the development of a " national art," Mr. Barnard must have been rather bewildered to find himself promptly engaged upon a large statue of the " Great God Pan," intended to surmount a rustic fountain within the court of an apartment building. It never reached its destination, but was called higher, to the adornment of Central Park. In common with each of Mr. Barnard's works in turn, it has been pronounced " one of the strangest and most original things yet done by an American sculptor." Its whimsical novelty is as marked as the skill of its execution, — an execution no less cleverly adapted to bronze than is most of Mr. Barnard's sculpture to stone. One wonders how he ever happened to make this monstrous creature. What inspiration could the sculptor of the " Two Natures " find in such a subject? Probably some moss-stained fountain figure of classic Italy gave him the idea, and he overlooked its anachronism in his love of muscular modelling, and of nature in general, which Pan may still be permitted to typify. The subject is not very interesting, however; the head is too powerfully grotesque, and the misshapen legs are unpleasant.   The transition of the latter from the human to the brutish form should have been made more plausible.   Frémiet, with far less felicity of surface handling, could have made those legs convincing.   The venerable master would have made us feel sure that if ever there had been such monstrosities, they must have been just as he saw fit to fashion them.

In his New York studio Mr. Barnard has had for some years a strikingly novel composition, a sketch model of an enormous group, in comparison to which the " Two Natures " is mere child's play. The latter was, indeed, but a stepping-stone, leading the imagination of the young untrammelled genius to more remarkable excursions. Never before has a scene like this been embodied in sculptural form.   The idea was suggested, doubtless, by those misty legends of the North, over which Mr. Barnard pored with the delight of a discoverer during the progress of his Norwegian reliefs.   A great vessel of prehistoric form is seen attacked by a monster of the deep. The dread sea-serpent has gathered two or three of the sailors into his slimy coils, and, with awful head upraised, threatens the entire bark.   Upon the shore are other men and women in attitudes of dismay and defence.   It is a " landscape with figures," in sculpture, and not even in relief.   But there is nothing of the merely pictu-resque nor of the trivial in this vast vision of tempestuous struggle. To say that it is sculptural in its entirety is more than one would venture, for there is nothing in the world with which to compare it. But that its elements are inherently monumental cannot be gainsaid. Every pose, every group is admirable in line and rich in possibilities. The work as a whole, however, is overpowering in its audacity.

As though in acceptance of the challenge of those wingless imaginations which, clinging to the ground, deride all who seek loftier flight, Mr. Barnard has demonstrated his ability to realize this gran-diose conception, by modelling and carving one of its twenty figures. " The Hewer " (Fig. 55), which was finished in 1902 in marble, would stand some ten feet high if erect, and with all its perfection of detail occupied the sculptor many months in the doing. It makes no appeal beyond its magnificent craftsmanship, yet there is in that superb physique something which almost awes. This giant ancestor of ours chops wood; to many he may say nothing, but to an artist his forms are eloquent. Kneeling and breaking the twigs, with a stone hatchet clutched in the upraised right hand, his attitude is full of strength without strain. The swing of the mighty arm brings into play all the powerful muscles of the shoulder and chest. The figure shows not only sculptural "bigness,"—that breadth of treatment which is essential in great art,—but reveals an unusual emphasis in the matter of straight lines and planes, which give it remarkable carrying power. Close at hand some of these planes may appear a trifle arbitrary, but at a distance their value is felt in the assurance of structural strength and adequacy which merely rounded bulk never conveys. In his use of these firm surfaces, as in his knowledge of construction and his subtle and varied model-ling, Mr. Barnard has reaffirmed his position as a master. It is safe to say that no other nude figure of the strength of " The Hewer " has up to this time been done or even conceived in America.

Of recent years, a new and tenderer element has entered into Mr. Barnard's work, revealing itself in a memorial figure, the " Rose Maiden," and again in the more recent "Maidenhood." The first of these, which is shut from public view in a mortuary vault at Muscatine, Iowa, shows a dreamy girl with bowed head and downcast eyes — a conception as different as possible from the pro-digious works which we have discussed. The figure is a poem of sweetness and mystery and grace, fragrant with the dew of spring mornings. She stands with her apron filled with blossoms, regard-ing them as though their short, radiant lives were prophetic of her own. In this statue the artist has created a work of marked origi-nality, the more notable because of the familiarity of the thought. He has wrought it out *con amore*, and it shows the perfection of skill and painstaking. Yet for all the delicate details of its work-manship, there is no suggestion, in either the elaborately simple drapery or the flowers, of fatigue of hand or mind. All remains as spontaneously fresh in effect as when the clay received the last caress — a rare virtue in sculpture. Then, as if loath to part with

2 B

his fair white vision, desiring to pay her yet further tribute, the artist carved a pedestal also, overgrown, as it were, with wild roses, and bearing many lines of sympathetic verse. The pitfalls of dry, monotonous lettering and of Italian realistic carving of flowers he avoids without suggestion of danger. The experiment which in most hands would mean failure is here a distinct triumph. The

FIG. 56. — BARNARD: MAIDENHOOD.

snowy statue in the chill burial-vault of the western river-town is a poem of light-winged spring, rapt and bound and forever shrouded by untimely frost.

One day a fair model suggested another beautiful figure, a nymph, perhaps, sitting upon the seashore and twining her hair, all unconscious of her chaste nudity, radiant like Venus rising from the white sea-foam. The artist has succeeded in transferring his thought to the marble, and of conveying to us the pleasure which he has felt. Such sweetness and grace of rich feminine forms, such purity of line, — and of inspiration as well, — such nobility of countenance combined with appealing personality, one finds in few modern works. In it are united the heritages of two antiquities: the joy of life and the glory of the body which we were taught by old Hellas, and the soul which entered with Christianity (Fig. 56).

It is not the purpose of this work to make comparison between contemporaries; our object is to appreciate and when necessary to criticise. The relative value of men and their contributions will take care of itself; no living soul can foresee the final rating. So when we attribute to Mr. Barnard the largest measure of inspiration for the purely glyptic art, it is quite another thing from claiming that he is destined to be our greatest sculptor. This is for others to decide — a hundred years from now. The more plastic art which expresses itself by preference in bronze is no less honorably sculpture. The magic skill of MacMonnies, the profoundly sympathetic art of Saint Gaudens, the thoughtful serenity of Daniel French, — not to name others, — make in turn their appeal to us. We do not have to choose; it is our privilege to enjoy them all.

Like these men Mr. Barnard has a pronounced artistic conscience. He is working for all time; he will not be hurried. More than once he has occasioned comment by declining important orders because of the time-limit set upon them. The fact that he does much of his marble-cutting himself reveals his attitude toward his work. He has endless capacity for taking pains. But he loves the chisel; the marble is his native element, and he would repel in wonder the charge of being "patient." It requires no patience, no heroism, to do the things that one most enjoys.

Beyond its cachet of individuality, above its virility and veiling even its extraordinary craftsmanship, another quality already alluded to appears in much of Mr. Barnard's work — that touch of the universal which is the essence of the highest art. Not only has he the vital force to detach and "fix the momentary eminence" of his theme so that it holds us "the tyrant of the hour," but he sees in it and makes us feel, vaguely at least, a larger meaning. He charges it with significance, causing the simple symbol before us to stand for the whole world, the common experience of humanity. In a work like the Seidel Memorial Urn with its reliefs of the cycle of life we

read the "sweet and smart of personal relations, of beating hearts
and meeting eyes, of poverty and necessity, and hope and fear."
The constant presence of this larger, almost mystical quality in the
work of Mr. Barnard calls to mind Professor Barrett Wendell's
remarks on Emerson: "A dangerous feat, this. Any one may
attempt it, but most of us would surely fail, uttering mere jargon
wherein others could discern little beyond our several limitations.
As we contemplate Emerson, then, our own several infirmities slowly
reveal to us more and more clearly how true a seer he was. With
more strenuous vision than is granted to common men, he really
perceived in the eternities those living facts and lasting thoughts
which, with all" —   But the rest of the paragraph does not apply!
Mr. Barnard's attitude is not one of "careless serenity" nor of "intellectual insolence," but of proud humanity, reverent alike to the
mysteries above and to those incarnate mysteries here below with
which we live and hold halting converse. To his ardent imagination has been added the patience and precision of utterance of one
who knows his message to be valuable.

Mr. Barnard's story of hardship and struggle has an old-fashioned
and almost improbable ending; the newspapers of August, 1902, contained the following paragraph: —

"George Grey Barnard has been selected to execute all of the
sculpture to adorn the new Capitol building for the state of Pennsylvania. The plan provides for an elaborate series of groups in four
general divisions, to cost $300,000. The chief work will be a colos-
sal bronze group, 'The Apotheosis of Labor,' to stand before the
base of the dome. The group will be thirty-five feet high, and will
include three horses. The rest of the sculpture will be of marble.
The second division will consist of four pairs of caryatides supporting
this last group. They will represent miners, ironworkers, lumbermen,
and farmers, the typical forms of labor that have combined to build
up the state. The third division will comprise two groups of primitive men, women, and children, to be placed at either side of the main
entrance. The fourth division is to include four groups to flank the
subordinate front entrances in the wings. These will portray the four
classes of people who have made the state what it is, — the Quakers,
the Scotch-Irish, the English, and the Pennsylvania Dutch."

PLATE 12. — BARTLETT: MICHAEL ANGELO.

CHAPTER XX

PAUL WAYLAND BARTLETT was born at New Haven, Connecticut, in 1865, the son of Truman H. Bartlett of Boston, art critic and sculptor. The mother and son went to Paris many years ago to reside, and in that vast and perennial exposition of the fine arts the boy soon found his vocation. At the early age of fifteen he entered the École des Beaux-Arts, where he rapidly became proficient in modelling. Mr. Bartlett is, and always has been, a worker, making his own living from boyhood, and thereby gaining such a mastery over the details of his art in all its branches as is possessed by very few, even of the French sculptors. In addition to the regular routine of the atelier, he managed to attend the course on animal sculpture directed by M. Frémiet at the Jardin des Plantes, and in consequence was able to serve in various studios as an animal specialist, thus earning money with which to carry on his own studies. He relates that he and M. Gardet used to go about like peripatetic cobblers or harvesters, "doing animals" for whomsoever they found in need of their services; and among the important embellishments of Paris may be picked out not a few bits shaped by his boyish hands. There is a certain lion, "fierce and terrible," among the modernized decorations of the Porte St. Denis, which he modelled, and a three-headed dog of his best make is attached to an "Orpheus" in the Luxembourg. At the Exposition of Amsterdam was a gigantic elephant, whose nameless creator did not work on that occasion for glory, but had great amusement with it, none the less.

Young Bartlett's home was in a quaint little street or passage off from the Rue de Vaugirard, a pretty nook, as secluded as though in the woods. Here he had a small, vine-covered studio, where he began, while still in school, an important work for the Salon, the group of the "Bohemian Bear Trainer." After spending a year upon it, he became dissatisfied with the composition and made changes involving another year's work. His skill in the modelling of animal forms is shown in the delightfully clumsy bear cubs of the group in question. The original plaster cast of this early effort stands in the Chicago Art Institute; the bronze is in the Metropolitan Museum of New York. If not a great intellectual triumph, it is at least a novel and interesting work of real sculptural quality.

It gives way in perfection of modelling, however, to the strange "Ghost Dancer" (Fig. 57) which was shown at the Columbian Exposition, a vicious-looking savage, quite unclothed excepting for an imaginary coat of paint. He hops in the loose-jointed way characteristic of the Indian dancer, though quite without the ceremonial solemnity which always marks this most significant of aboriginal dances. The brutal head is shaved and decorated with a feather, the mouth wide open, the hands hanging like a prairie dog's paws on the outstretched arms. In construction and in plastic treatment of flesh the "Ghost Dancer" was not surpassed by any piece of sculpture in the Art Palace, but one was inclined to ask why the artist had made it. As in certain of Frémiet's works, the interest was ethnological rather than artistic. In one way it was doubtless at the time the best American Indian that had been modelled; from another point of view it was not even a good Indian. It was like a plaster cast from nature put into a difficult pose; infinitely skilful in workmanship, but without inspiration or reason.

Since that time Mr. Bartlett's artistic sense has overtaken his manual dexterity, and he has produced more gratifying works. His "Dying Lion," though not widely known, is one of the most original of them all. The fallen monarch lies low, prone upon the earth, the massive head raised upon the upward slant of a rocky ledge, which forms his death-bed. The eyes are closed, but the claws still seek support and clamp themselves like springs of steel upon the stony pillow. It is doubtful if Barye himself ever did anything of greater dramatic power, while the perfection of the workmanship shows a knowledge and skill which establish Mr. Bartlett's position among the best of the living sculptors of animals. This tense body is no mere catalogue of bones and muscles, but a beautiful harmony of expressive forms.   If we can trace in it the dissected frame-work, with everything accounted for and in the right place, there is on the other hand such charm of modelling, such delicacy of touch and flow of surface within the bolder masses, that the play of light and shade is exquisitely tender and decorative.   It possesses another quality,

strangely rare in works of our time — a perfect fitness of method to the material employed or in view.   This almost Assyrian epitome of the lion is not a direct imitation of nature; it is an adaptation.   It is not realistic, not a petrified lion, but a distinct creation.   It is, first of all, "sculptural."

Mr. Bartlett made, in the Salon of 1895, an extraordinary display of small bronzes: beetles, fishes, reptiles, and crustaceans.   In

FIG. 57. — BARTLETT: THE GHOST DANCER, PENNSYLVANIA ACADEMY.

them his profound study of bronze-casting in its most difficult forms, and his skill with patinas (coloring of bronzes), shows to great advantage.   His beetles and reptiles were tiny masses of modelled metal of such wealth of color as one could scarcely believe possible outside of the realm of precious stones, — rich golden browns and greens, iridescent and brilliant in the light and intense and deep in their shadows, effects as of metallic jasper and beryl and agate and of vibrant blue, like azurite; the mimicry of the work of centuries.   It was apropos of Mr. Bartlett's studies in this field that the late Jean Carriès, France's remarkable potter-sculptor, expressed himself: —

" He reminds me of one of those artisans of the Renaissance who had nothing but art in view and in mind — of those artists who, jealous of the perfection of their work, would not think of leaving anything of it, however menial, to be done by other hands; who were masters of a foundry as well as a studio, and to whom the smallest details to ennoble a work of art were as important as the conception. Unfortunately the majority of the artists of to-day are not sufficient artisans. In ancient times it was thought natural for an artist to be an architect and at the same time a sculptor, as the Gothics were; then for artists to sculpture in marble and stone and be able to cast in bronze like Donatello, or be a jeweler, sculptor, and founder, like Benvenuto Cellini. Nor were they satisfied to be chisellers in stone and precious metal; most of them were past masters in the art of painting, and they painted their pictures scientifically; they themselves preparing their colors, and oftentimes inventing them in secret. To-day we have great artists, but no masters. Very few modern works combine taste and execution. We French have a great reputation for taste; but, unfortunately, we are in too great a hurry, and we leave the execution to practitioners, and nothing could be more fatal to works of real art. Execution in sculpture is as important as in painting, and the rules must be practised according to the material employed. It stands to reason that modelling in soft clay is very different from chiselling in stone, and as stone is the material in which the model will finally be made, sculptors ought to see the importance, as did the ancients, of working it themselves.

" Bartlett spends his days in his studio, in his foundry, not only giving life to his conceptions and modelling them in clay, but after the selection of the material it is he who cuts and chisels. He works like the ancient artisan who spent days locked up in his studio to discover an artistic effect, which to the casual observer may pass unnoticed; but which, to future connoisseurs, may establish not only the lasting reputation of the artist, but elevate national art. When his mind is fatigued with working at some grand piece of sculpture, he seeks relief in modelling curious reptiles, small objects of art, and he himself casts them *à cire perdue;* then comes the most fascinating of his occupations, the making of patinas. Paul Bartlett's patinas vie with those of the old Japanese artists; they are simply most admirable."

In studying the circle of bronze effigies which decorate the rotunda of the Congressional Library it may be thought that Mr. Bartlett was, in the allotment of subjects, the most fortunate of all the sculptors employed. Be that as it may, he distinguished himself there as did few of his colleagues. Some of our best artists made but commonplace returns in this friendly rivalry. Though most of the sixteen figures are sufficiently well modelled for their elevated position, the poses are as a rule feeble and uninteresting. The lines do not "carry." Mr. Bartlett's "Columbus" (Fig. 59) has a distinct thought, and here, as in his "Michael Angelo" the handling is vigorous and definite enough to mean something at a distance. One questions if a figure with uplifted face is quite suited to an elevation where it can be seen only from directly below, but the face invisible is better than one which means nothing, upon a body without action. At any rate, the "Columbus," among all these figures, stands out clear in memory as an original and spontaneous conception. It shows us the discoverer in a new light; no longer the gentle dreamer, the eloquent pleader, the enthusiast, nor yet the silent victim in chains, but a hero of might and confidence hurling proud defiance at his calumniators.

He is standing, perhaps, in the presence of the sovereigns to whom he has given a new realm. We may imagine him interrupted in his account by one of those persistent enemies who surrounded him here to belittle his triumph as they once gathered to thwart his project. He pauses in his story, and crushing the maps in his left hand, throws his head back like a creature at bay. Do his eyes seek the throne in wrathful inquiry, demanding protection? or is he looking to a higher power for the vindication which only the centuries may bring?

The novelty of the *motif* interests at once, and the sculptor's large treatment of lines and surfaces is found to be consistently adequate. The eyes are deep set, the nose and chin strongly pronounced; the hair falls in bushy masses around the powerful neck. In the handling of the costume Mr. Bartlett is no less successful. He is one of the few who know how to retain in the finished work

the freshness and "color" of a sketch.   All details are sufficiently
emphasized to give the effect of completeness; there is no sense of
neglect, and yet nothing is treated literally.   Along with infinite
variety of plastic manipulation, little accidents of surface freshen
and keep alive the firmly modelled planes.   Here and there forms
are eliminated; edges particularly must be lost sometimes in order
that the work may gain the higher truth of variety and movement.
Just how to compass this is Mr. Bartlett's secret.   No sculptor of a
generation ago had guessed these possibilities of the material.   Such
zest of handling is distinctly of to-day.   Notice, for instance, the
maps which the great discoverer crumples in his vehement grasp;
they have in them all the technical charm of modern art.   Sheets of
paper or of vellum are sharp and thin; as treated by the earlier men,
nothing could be more unsculptural; but here they contribute in no
small measure to the beauty as well as the significance of the statue.
How ingeniously, how easily it has been managed!   The slightly
separated sheets form a solid mass, as the eye would see them at a
distance.   This mass appears firm and distinct in outline, yet is
cleverly broken up and filled with light and shade.   The traditional
tinlike sculptured map, if inserted here, would change the character
of the whole work.

The same felicity of surface handling characterizes the sombre
"Michael Angelo" (Pl. XII).   The skin-tight nether garments and
the broad surface of the heavy apron caught up under one arm
contrast effectively with the lighter material of the sleeves.   The
hands are heavy-veined; the face is deep-furrowed yet fittingly plastic.   But to speak first of the technic of this extraordinary work is
to show disrespect to its author, who has subordinated every touch,
every detail, to the building up here of a distinct and lofty personality; who has succeeded in conveying a vivid notion of the character of his subject.   The short, gnomelike figure with stumpy legs;
the big, powerful hands; the stern face, rough-hewn, with its frown
and tight lips — all these conspire to make of this at first sight an
unwinning presentment of the great artist; but it has the quality
which will outlive all others, excepting that portrait which we would
readily believe the master once painted of himself and which has
evidently inspired this statue.

FIG. 58.—BARTLETT: LAFAYETTE, PARIS.

The adequacy of Mr. Bartlett's characterization of these two men goes far to prove his own largeness as an artist. He has not made his subjects attractive, but he has shown them powerful, sufficient, and therefore convincing. He has appreciated them and has risen, for the moment at least, to their height. Marshalling in memory the various Italian conceptions of Michael Angelo — of the girl-boy Michaels carving the satyr face, of the inane youths, of the suave and picturesque gentlemen toying with mallets — which have libelled his immortal name, one rejoices that it was left to an American sculptor to grasp thus nobly his character and to create the one worthy representation of the mighty Florentine. *This* man might have carved the "Moses," might have toiled alone for years on the scaffolding of the Sistine Chapel, might have lived "the tragedy of the Tomb," might have withstood the arrogant Julius, might have bowed in proud humility to the reproaches of an ungrateful and fault-finding father, might have wept over unhappy Florence, and have exulted with a fierce joy in the downfall of her enemies. Such a man one finds in the "Michael Angelo" of Paul Bartlett; such a man is found in no other effigy of the great master.

With works like these already accomplished, yet more may be safely predicted. The sculptor is a growing man, and his greatest achievements are still to come. We may count upon his excelling in the weighty undertaking which now occupies his mind and hand. His equestrian figure of Lafayette (Fig. 58) will stand in one of the most coveted sites in all Paris; it is to be erected in the Place du Carrousel, within the court of the Tuileries. In allowing Mr. Bartlett to aspire to the decoration of this square — the very jewel-case of the palace demesne — the present architect of the Louvre pays a remarkable compliment to the taste and ability of the young American sculptor. A work for such a place of honor in Paris must possess more than negative qualifications. It is not enough that it should be inoffensive; it must be strikingly good. It must have great qualities of style and it must disclose mastery of every sculptural problem. It must be just right in size and in perfect harmony with its surroundings, for it cannot be seen apart from them. Whatever its inspiration, it must be decorative in effect; it is part of an architectural scheme. The silhouette must be carefully studied, for while few look closely at an equestrian statue, all get an impression of it. Thousands will see the " Lafayette " from the windows of the palace, to one who approaches its pedestal. Therefore its lines must be monumental, strong, and legible, its action and significance so simple as to be gathered at a glance. The sculptor has described the work and his intention as follows: " Lafayette is represented in the statue as a fact and a symbol, offering his sword and services to the American colonists in the cause of liberty. He is shown sitting firmly on his horse, which he holds vigorously. He is attired in the rich embroidered costume of a noble officer. His Flemish steed is represented with its mane knotted and tail dressed in the style of the time. Lafayette's youthful face is turned toward the west, his sheathed sword being slightly uplifted and delicately offered. He appears as the emblem of the aristocratic and enthusiastic sympathy shown by France to our forefathers. His youth, his distinction, his noble bearing, the richness of his costume and of the trappings of his horse — everything serves to emphasize the difference of his race and his education. An equestrian statue of Lafayette is appropriate, for, after landing in South Carolina, he rode from Charleston to Philadelphia on horseback, and there offered his services to Congress."

In a secluded studio at St. Leu, a village some fifteen miles to the north of Paris, Mr. Bartlett lived almost a hermit's life throughout the winter of 1899, working upon the model of this statue like a day laborer from early dawn until the light failed at sunset. Here he studied his favorite horse, a beautiful creature; here he developed his idea of the young Lafayette, and familiarized himself with all the elaborate details of costume and equine accessories of a century and a third ago. He gave himself up to this work with a concentration and a singleness of purpose which guaranteed success. The customary steps were made with unusual precision. First, the preliminary sketch, a few inches in height, was doubled in size. This more careful study was then reproduced, with many alterations, in still larger form — a figure somewhat over one-half life-size, upon which the artist put a great amount of labor. The statue was desired for the 4th of July, 1900, but the order was given so tardily that it was impossible to have the bronze ready. Indeed, the one-third size model was completed but six weeks before the date of unveiling. A colossal plaster model was therefore prepared and used upon the occasion. That even this could be accomplished in six weeks is remarkable, but the French are at home in such problems. The "working model" was sawed into pieces and distributed in several establishments in Paris; thus the horse and rider developed in various parts of the city at the same time. The legs and lower part of the horse were built up in a large studio on the Rue de Vaugirard. In another atelier, at Montrouge, the upper part and head emerged rapidly from chaos; while over on the other side of the town, at the works of the famous Barbedienne, the aristocratic rider was carved into shape. These scattered fragments were brought together only a day or two before the ceremony, but fitted perfectly. The completed group looked down upon a very brilliant scene, and Mr. Bartlett's great work was applauded by thousands.

In his fountain, "The Genius of Man," at the Pan-American Exposition, Mr. Bartlett showed his easy mastery of large decorative problems. It was his first opportunity, and there was an air of exhilaration about the result which gave it a particular charm among not a few perfunctory works by those who have seemingly passed the age of great enthusiasms. The subject of the fountain was sufficiently banal, and the architectural necessities of its intended position controlled largely the form of the low-lying groups; but within their lines Mr. Bartlett produced a vast sketch of much intrinsic beauty and of still greater promise. Unable to execute personally the large work, or even to superintend the "pointing up," he was obliged to abandon it to the tender mercies of the plaster-workers. It lost, of course, a great deal in the process of enlargement; of the plastic piquancy of the artist's sketch models little remained. And when later it was found impracticable to turn off the water in order to put the fountain in its rightful place and it was left stranded upon a grassy bank near the Art Palace, the sculptor may well have felt that he was faring badly. However, the environment might have been worse. The chariot and sea-horses rose proudly out of rippling waves of verdure, and the ruffled fishes and unruffled water-babies sported together in the hot sunlight, quite unaware that they were not afloat in their natural element.   The leading lines of the composition were there, and great masses of fluttering drapery; even in the crude rendering of the plaster-builders there remained a great deal of sculptural color.   The outriders were admirable; those great sea-horses in detached groups seemed to be every whit as finely conceived as the noble creatures which disport themselves in the fountain of the Observatory, in Paris.   Delightful satellites to these were the cor-

FIG. 59.—BARTLETT: COLUMBUS, CONGRESSIONAL LIBRARY.

rugated fishes with their baby companions. Possibly the fishes were the most artistic features of all. With them the artist could be fantastic and playful, while his abundant knowledge of the humbler forms of animal life safeguarded him from any absurdities. He had learned his lesson and had had his practice in Paris upon the little bronzes; now he could take liberties as one who knows what he is doing. These were no cheap imitations of any particular fish, but logical, decorative syntheses of all that their creator had learned about fishes.

Since doing this work Mr. Bartlett has spent a year in New York, collaborating with Mr. Ward upon the pedimental group of the New York Stock Exchange. This important and very successful composition has already been discussed elsewhere, but it is only just to repeat that while the design is Mr. Ward's, the actual modelling of the figures has been entirely the work of Mr. Bartlett. The execution is worthy of the design, and the details of "the most formidable piece of combined sculpture yet undertaken in America" owe to Mr. Bartlett's skill a beauty of treatment as unfamiliar as it is effective.

Upon the completion of the models of this group, Mr. Bartlett returned to Paris, where he has resumed work upon various unfinished orders, among them being the "Lafayette," an equestrian "McClellan" for Philadelphia, and a "General Warren" for Boston. In these and in the works to follow one may count with reasonable certainty upon dignified yet vivid renderings of the problems in hand. We may even expect surprises, for the man who created the "Michael Angelo" and the "Columbus" has not told all that he knows nor all that he feels. But whether or not he puts the same dramatic intensity into his future achievements, Mr. Bartlett will always give us good sculpture. His art is essentially monumental, with a happy balance between the austere and the more picturesque or plastic tendencies; it may, indeed, be characterized as a union of the better qualities of the two. He conceives things simply and fundamentally; he gives them form in legitimate sculptural terms; and to these rare virtues he adds the more intimate charm of a delightfully varied yet unobtrusive technic. No man is better equipped for his work than is Mr. Bartlett, and we have the right to expect from him works of preëminent value.

In sculpture, though the productions of the specialist are eagerly sought, it is perhaps fortunate that the requirements of study and the exigencies of professional life widen the general scope rather than develop any particular line of work. The opportunities which come are seldom exactly what the practitioner would himself have chosen, and even when an artist is granted absolute choice, he not infrequently mistakes his own powers — as he may have done in his original choice of a profession. With chances thus moderate the average sculptor is content to work out his own salvation on such lines as offer, trusting for reward in the calmer joys of the studio rather than in an exalted reputation.

Occasionally, however, there is a happy concurrence of aptitude, training and opportunity leading to distinct and unusual achievement. In Mr. Herbert Adams the whole fraternity recognizes a master almost unequalled in a certain form of sculpture as rare as it is exquisite — the creation of beautiful busts of women. If

2 C

attention is directed particularly to these works rather than to **Mr. Adams's** other productions, it is not because the latter are to be depreciated or can be. He is an accomplished sculptor and knows every branch of his art, but there is nothing so distinctive in his figures of men. His " Professor Henry " and his " Channing," for instance, might have been done equally well by any one of twenty sculptors, whereas in these female heads he transcends almost every one we know in modern sculpture, not only being without rivals in this country, but being unsurpassed in France. Indeed, a retrospect of the history of sculpture brings to light but few busts approaching in elegance the works of Herbert Adams.

Mr. Adams was born at West Concord, Vermont, on Jan. 28, 1858. He received his general education in the grammar and high schools of Fitchburg, Massachusetts, where his boyhood was passed, and his special education at the Worcester Institute of Technology and at the Massachusetts Normal Art School. This was followed by five years of study in Paris, where in 1887 he modelled his first notable bust, a portrait of Miss Adeline V. Pond, who afterward became his wife. It was in Paris also that his earliest work with the figure was produced — a fountain for Fitchburg, Massachusetts, showing a bronze group of two boys at play with some turtles, modelled in 1888 and cast by the *cire perdue* process in Brussels.

On his return to America, in 1890, Mr. Adams was engaged as an instructor in the Art School of Pratt Institute, Brooklyn, where he criticised the modelling for eight years. During this time he produced, besides a number of busts, the Pratt Memorial Angel for the Baptist Emmanuel Church, Brooklyn; the Hoyt Memorial in the Judson Memorial Church, New York; a number of works for the Congressional Library, including the bronze statue of Professor Joseph Henry in the rotunda, and the bronze doors representing " Writing," the commission for which had been given originally to Olin Warner, but which was intrusted after his death to Mr. Adams. Following these came the Welch Memorial, a work in marble for the Auburn Theological Seminary; the Jonathan Edwards Memorial, a bronze relief for the church at Northampton; the Bulfinch Memorial tablets in bronze for the Boston State House; the bronze statue of the type founder, Richard Smith of Philadelphia; the statue of

William Ellery Channing erected in 1902 in Boston; and a pair of bronze doors for the Vanderbilt Memorial, Saint Bartholomew's Church, New York. Nor should we forget such beautiful though ephemeral works as the colossal nude, " Light," which crowned the electric tower at the Buffalo Exhibition, and the graceful " Victories " which lined the approach to the so-called " Dewey Arch " in New York.

Mr. Adams's early portrait of Miss Pond (Fig. 60) still remains in some sense unsurpassed by his later achievement; he has never done another quite so sympathetically. Despite the time put upon it, this bust has an air of unusual spontaneity and seems to have been the result of mere toying with the clay. For although executed in marble, the effect is of such perfect mastery that the face and neck, at least, appear plastic, as if responsive like wax to the pressure of the artist's thumb. The conception had a certain quaintness which accords well with the piquancy of the thoughtful face. In harmony with it the hair was arranged in a fashion somewhat out of date, high on the back of the head and partially covering the ears with its flowing tresses — quite different, however, from the hood-like coiffures of our grandmothers. The costume is admirably adapted to sculptural expression. There are moderately puffed sleeves which lose themselves in the square base, and the tight-fitting bodice and shoulders are covered with a filmy kerchief which is in reality but little more than a change in the direction of the chisel strokes.

For, be it understood, this is not one of those time-honored busts from Italy, " finished " all over with impartial file and sand-paper, and cut off abruptly to suit the purchaser. Mr. Adams's busts are conceived as works of art, complete in themselves, as bust-portraits are conceived by good painters. The face is emphasized as the centre of interest, and other parts accentuated with diminish-ing force according to their distance from this focal point. This particular face lent itself unusually well to sculptural treatment, for it shows both beauty of form and character. The eyes are large and alert — wonderfully has the sculptor suggested them; the straight nose is distinguished, and the mouth is of the kind that artists seek, with lips of full rich curves sinking into shadowy corners, wherein are sensibility and strength as well as kindliness;

the chin is that of a New England maiden who knows her mind and is able to express it.   Every inch of this surface is exquisite; every stroke of the chisel has been firm and yet so tender.   The solid structure is not only clothed in softly rounded flesh, but is enveloped in "atmosphere."   No part is quite so distinct as it is actually in nature, because the effect would be unreal.   We seldom scrutinize one another closely, and this veil is just enough to give the illusion of life and movement, the equivalent of the composite impressions which come in everyday intercourse.   Here it is the response of one who listens intently.   The lifted eyebrows and wide open eyelids have a question in them, and somewhat of the wonder of a child looking out upon a strange world.   How far is the look of their shadowy depths removed from the blankness of the old-time orbs!   There is mystery in these and a charm that we have found nowhere else.   But with all their illusiveness they do not lack good drawing; the cheeks are not only well-rounded, but are perfect in form; the delicate mouth is as true as it is subtle.   The perfection of the hair — perfect because incomplete — has proved a revelation to the best of our sculptors.   It is not machine-grooved, nor even insistent upon fact; but the magic touch is there, with the playful lights and shadows which give truth of effect.   We have here the acme of modern marble-cutting in the contrast between the delicately accentuated features and the airy freedom of these irrepressible locks. How the sculptor has delighted in their doing and in their undoing! The neck and bosom show as profound study as does the face, and as easily expressed, without thought of labor.   The shoulders slope gracefully, as women's shoulders have since the beginning of time, and are lightly covered; that is, we accept as thin drapery these fascinating strokes of the chisel which trace the imaginary kerchief and pin it under the bosom.   There is a delightfully human touch about the unfinished base where the artist had outlined mouldings and begun his perfunctory "eggs and darts," then, wearying, threw across them a sprig of spring buds and ceased his labors.

This bust was shown at the Columbian Exposition with another in marble called "Primavera," and a beautiful colored bust of "Saint Agnes" which attracted much notice.   Succeeding exhibitions have been adorned by various works of the same exquisite character, like

FIG. 60. — ADAMS: PORTRAIT BUST.

the "Portrait of a Young Lady" in tinted marble with bronze decorations; the "Rabbi's Daughter," in pink marble, with dress and ample widespread sleeves in wood, with gold decorations; and the portrait of Miss Julia Marlowe, — all of which were seen at the Pan-American Exposition of 1901. All show the qualities of the first, and demonstrate the truly artistic temperament of their author. It is in his choice and treatment of these heads that Mr. Adams reveals his true personality. It is as impossible for him to represent what is ungracious and unrefined as it is for him to be crude in workmanship. No man could hold such lofty ideals as are his unless he were of the most sensitive and sympathetic fibre. No man could devise and carry through such a decorative scheme as, for instance, that presented by the "Rabbi's Daughter," with its elaborate wood-carving and metal fashioning, unless he sincerely loved the details of the work and delighted in the very feeling of the materials. In this respect Mr. Adams is closely akin to M. Dampt and M. Rivière-Théodore, the French sculptors, not to go farther back in the history of the art.

As has been shown, these heads form but a small part of Mr. Adams's productions, and we may look for the same qualities in his larger works. The figures in relief of the Hoyt Memorial were of singular charm, winning the applause of all at the exhibition of the National Sculpture Society in 1895. Of a graver note is the Welch Memorial, a marble triptych in which the deceased minister is pictured half length, as seen in the pulpit, upon the central panel, while kneeling figures are shown bearing churchly attributes upon either side. The perils and pitfalls of low relief have been avoided with consummate skill, and the result is a joy to the eye as well as to the intelligence. One of these kneeling women is among the gems of American sculpture. The standing angel of the Pratt Memorial is likewise a work of gratifying purity and elevation.

The bronze doors for St. Bartholomew's Church, New York, are elaborately decorated with Scripture subjects in high relief. Above them a semicircular tympanum (Fig. 61), the model of which was seen at the 1902 exhibit of the Sculpture Society, pictures the Madonna and Child within a wreath held by two kneeling maidens. The inspiration of this relief, which is a work of great

delicacy and tenderness, will be traced by many to Luca della
Robbia, because we are familiar with reliefs of this form attributed
to him, but beyond the roundel of fruit the suggestion is rather of
Desiderio.   This smiling Madonna and Child and their sweet-faced
attendants, though so simply treated as to be almost classic, have
more complex mentalities than we ever find in Della Robbia's
glorified peasants.   Though physically naïve, they have not only

FIG. 61.— ADAMS: TYMPANUM, SAINT BARTHOLOMEW'S CHURCH, NEW YORK.

souls but a fair share of worldly wisdom behind their placid features.   Indeed, in amiable intelligence they approach the expressiveness of the drooping-eyed Madonna and Child of the famous
tomb of the Cardinal of Portugal.   The attendant figures are much
less agitated, however, than are those of Rossellino's masterpiece.
They take their places quietly, with a thoughtful regard for architectural conditions that further enhances our respect for their
graces of mind.   It is hard to be naïf "to order," and Mr. Adams
has prudently compromised with the advance of civilization.   He
has created something beautiful on old-time lines; he has even kept
the fragrance of the fifteenth century; but he has been wise
enough to acknowledge that this is a tableau, a dream, — something akin to Abbott Thayer's " Modern Virgin Enthroned," — and
not the reality.   His honesty, which may have been inevitable,
disarms criticism, and we can enjoy without stint the grace, the

tenderness, and the very real if unobtrusive originality of the relief which lies to so great an extent in the personal note of its workmanship. In suggesting that this frank modernity was inevitable, we would not set bounds to Mr. Adams's skill, for he knows how to model a Florentine relief that would deceive the very elect; but with his artistic temperament he could not bring himself to sacrifice his own identity in any work. Sympathetic as he is with the early Italians, he is nevertheless quite of his own time, and, consciously or not, impresses the seal of his own vision upon all that he does. In these faces, in particular, Mr. Adams shows again the cherished ideal which is his distinctive possession.

CHAPTER XXI

NIEHAUS AND BOYLE

CHARLES NIEHAUS has never done anything finer than his earliest public monument, the "Garfield" of Cincinnati (Fig. 62). It was his first commission, and, just home from study abroad, the sculptor put into it all of the enthusiasm of ambitious youth animated by love of the work and reënforced by the lure of a reputation to be won.

Mr. Niehaus was fortunate from the outset. His conception of the man was adequate. The figure has dignity, distinction, and personality. It is one of the few oratorical statues which do not antagonize at first sight. An uplifted arm is usually a danger signal — a warning of an impotent and inexpressive work; but this silent speaker is eloquent. We do not resent his gesture as we do that of Story's "Edward Everett" in Boston. With that figure the swing of the arm is everything; here there is something more; the moderate gesture is part of the man, and the whole man is behind it. The "Garfield" shows more charm of modelling than any of Mr. Niehaus's subsequent works. The treatment is firm, the drawing admirable, and to those fundamental qualities the sculptor has added a delightful play of textures. The drapery is varied and full of color; the head is delightful in its plastic freedom — a freedom which is lacking in the "Hahnemann" and in the bust of Mr. Ward. The "Garfield" has as good construction as these; it has in addition the quality which means delight — the give and take of happy workmanship.

This artist's great talent is distinctly in the line of monumental sculpture. One need not look to him for the expression of the gentler graces, nor for a deep emotional cry. Herbert Adams's dainty busts are as far outside his scope and his sympathies as are Barnard's soul-burdened strugglers. He employs a great variety of methods, — his collective works look as though they had come from a dozen different hands, — but whatever the style of technic which circumstances or momentary whim may dictate, one quality runs through all of the vast array of monuments, figures, and reliefs; — every one of them is conceived and bodied forth in the legitimate terms of sculpture, and generally, be it said, in sculpture of a very high standard. It is a standard of severe probity of line which never deigns to be either playful or tender; never adds to itself the grace of picturesqueness, nor offers the piquancy of a surprise, but relying upon its own intrinsic dignity, its self-respecting reserve and calm, speaks to us with the compelling force of a monumental character who would seem to say, " I am a man."

This is Mr. Niehaus at his best. When he nods there always remains the saving grace of the sculptural conception. He could scarcely make a bad sketch. The finished work may prove a disappointment, but the little model is generally irresistible, not alone for the fine detail which beguiles all committees alike, but for the rarer and more precious qualities of good composition and artistic grasp of the material. Mr. Niehaus is not the only sculptor whose work looks better in the sketch than when completed. Few indeed are the masters who do not offer us this disappointment over and over again. If it is more noticeable in the work of Mr. Niehaus than with some others, this may be due in part to the extraordinary merit of the sketch models, whose promise is so tantalizing when it just misses fulfilment, and not less to the abundant output of his studio. However industrious and however clever, an artist cannot be at his best all of the time. When statues are produced by wholesale, certain of them are likely to miss the "loving touch" which counts so potently in the personal appeal of a work of art. Not that Mr. Niehaus, or any other prosperous New York sculptor, intentionally slights his work. He is an honorable man, as are they all, and spares no pains. But this, if one were inclined to fault-finding, is too often the trouble; the " pains " are there, but not the pleasure. The weary artist substitutes faithfulness of detail for the inward spirit. He " has not time to be brief," for to summarize means profound study, while " putting in wrinkles " is only a question of patience.

Take the "Hahnemann" (Fig. 63) as an illustration, because it does illustrate so well. Nothing finer in the way of monumental portraiture has been conceived in this country for many years. The little sketch model, in the Cincinnati Museum, gives a thrill of pleasure whenever seen. One can hardly say too much in its praise. It unites within itself the qualities of a convincing realism and a pervasive ideality — a combination extremely rare. The great scholar is pictured to us lost in thought, wrapped in meditation as in the great garment which so admirably conceals the artificial accidents of modern costume. The masses are big and simple, the lines most felicitous, though apparently unsought. Such was the promise of the sketch. But there is an appreciable falling off in the completed work; little indeed that one can point out specifically, but a general sense of loss and disappointment. The sculptor has produced a fine figure and one of the most effective monuments in Washington. Doubtless we should be grateful to discover anything so good in the city of tiresome monuments, instead of demanding the impossible. But it is the penalty of such genuine talent as Mr. Niehaus possesses; he has suggested the very finest thing and then given us less.

Perhaps, some day, "when the hurly-burly's done," and the fierce competition of the artist life in New York has calmed down, the sculptor may return to this noble conception and add to its strength the visible grace of suave, masterful modelling, — wiping out some of those dry wrinkles in the face, modifying the literalness of the hand, refreshing the great arid patches of drapery, replacing its acute edges with significant planes, and filling these with charming color. He knows how; he has done it more than once. And when he shall have gone over the figure thus and allowed himself to enjoy it for a while, we shall be ready to enjoy it with him; there will be nothing finer, nothing more impressive, in sculptural portraiture in this country.

It may be added that, whatever the changes over-critical admirers may suggest for the sculpture, alteration could scarcely be made to advantage in the architectural features of this monument — a beautiful example of the Greek exedra type. The statue occupies the centre of the stone platform, which is approached from the front by four steps, and at the back of which rises the superstructure

FIG. 62.—NIEHAUS: GARFIELD, CINCINNATI.

which is elliptical in form. The central portion, forming the background of the statue, is composed of four columns supporting an entablature. Above this rises what is known as an attic, bearing the principal inscription, " Hahnemann." Between the two front columns is a niche, which is also elliptical in form, and which terminates in a semicircular arch. Along the base of the wall are stone seats, above which are bronze reliefs picturing the life of the great physician.

For the following facts regarding Mr. Niehaus we are indebted to a brochure written by Miss Regina Armstrong in 1902, and embellished by many examples of the sculptor's productions: —

" Charles Henry Niehaus, the sculptor, is a Western man, being a native of Cincinnati, Ohio, where he passed the formative years of his life. His parents were of German birth, and the artist son, with the usual German thrift, was put to making his own living at an early age. But fate seems to have directed his earliest efforts toward the career he is now identified with, for he successively engaged in wood-engraving, stone-cutting, and carving in marble. As a boy he was a capable draughtsman, and when chance put some clay into his hands, he realized that it was through its medium that his future work must be expressed. He became a student at the McMicken School of Design in Cincinnati, and there won a first prize in drawing and modelling. Then, with little equipment and small means, but with a full stock of enthusiasm and determination, he made his way to Munich, entering the Royal Academy, and quickly winning his way to honors and commissions. Among the former was the distinction of obtaining, at the time of his matriculation, a first prize, medal, and diploma for a composition entitled ' Fleeting Time.' He then set out to see the sculpture of the Old World. . . .

" His return to America and to his native city of Cincinnati was almost contemporaneous with the death of President Garfield, and sentiment, following the tragic event, provided for memorials to his memory. The state of Ohio appropriated funds for a statue of Garfield to be placed in the rotunda of the Capitol at Washington, and public subscription erected the one now on Race Street, Cincinnati. Both of these commissions were given to the young sculptor who had returned to his native state with honors won abroad, and a further commission naturally followed in the statue of William Allen, the gift of the state of Ohio to the rotunda of the Capitol, known as Statuary Hall. With these substantial successes, and the friends and alliances they brought, Mr. Niehaus did not seek further advantage, but returned to Italy for the opportunities it afforded to the artist in study and experimentation. He established a studio in Rome in the Villa Strohl-Fern adjoining the Villa Borghese, just outside the Porta del Popolo, and there modelled those things that every artist delights in doing just for the pure love of the work. His associations at this time could but lend aspect to the subjects he chose, and it was admiration of the ancients that moved his inspiration and set the body of his conceptions in the antique form. The most of these studies were destroyed, being in perishable material, but three of them have been preserved, and are in this country. They are 'The Scraper; or, Greek Athlete using a Strigil,' 'Cæstus,' and 'Silenus.' The former justified its survival by an Italian recognition at the time, by reason of which Mr. Niehaus was made a Fellow of L' Associazione della Artistica Internazionale di Roma, and through later exhibitions by honors received at different times, among them that at the World's Columbian Exposition, where it had the distinction of being recommended for a special medal. Mr. Niehaus has been a resident of New York City since 1885, and during that time has executed a number of the important awards of sculpture in this country."[1]

Mr. Niehaus has a pronounced leaning toward classic subjects, which he treats with a classic simplicity of line, enlivened, however, with many accents of modern realism. "The Greek Athlete using a Strigil," above mentioned, has been considered — until recently at least — his best study of the nude. It is well known to the artist world under the title of "The Scraper," and is undoubtedly one of the few good nude figures in American sculpture. Morally or emotionally considered, the figure is without appeal; it is as though its author had scrupulously avoided even the suspicion of any motive other than good modelling and the artist's frank delight in a symmetrically developed body. Ideality as such is subordinated to literal truth, but truth conveyed so simply, in so large and master-

[1] "Charles Niehaus, Sculptor," by Regina Armstrong, New York, 1902.

ful a way, that for very unfamiliarity it becomes in turn a form of imaginative expression. This realistic-classic figure makes a unique note in American sculpture, and was the early guarantee of a remarkable talent unusually well equipped for its work. The " Cæstus " of the same period is another faithful rendering of the male figure, quite as admirably constructed as " The Scraper." To a sculptor of Mr. Niehaus's temperament, the very way in which this figure is planted on its sturdy legs is reason enough for the doing. To one of another temperament these athletes might possibly appear to be but " conscientious nudes," hardly to be mentioned among the mature achievements of an artist.

The marble "Garfield" of the Capitol is possibly as good a likeness as its twin brother, the bronze of Cincinnati, but it seems very tame in comparison, and is not one of the interesting statues in the motley collection of Statuary Hall. Its companion, however, another work of those initiatory years, is a very striking figure of William Allen of Ohio. This tall form, in its long, unbuttoned overcoat, is an acute characterization and still ranks among Niehaus's best portraits.

Not less successful were the " Hooker " and " Davenport " for the State House of Connecticut. Although in a sense but architectural decorations, these two statues have been treated with manifest respect. Distinctly conceived and faithfully wrought, they are models of intelligent sincerity. The " Davenport," in particular, is a vivid rendering of a man of vast earnestness and power. Placed, likewise, at a considerable height upon this curiously elaborate building are several tympanums of vigorous relief — good illustrative works picturing incidents in the history of early Connecticut. Possibly their success brought the sculptor his important order for a pair of the Astor Memorial doors for Trinity Church, New York City. This commission, like Ghiberti's of old, was won through competition. In this work Mr. Niehaus has employed an unusual method — a high-low relief, if it may be so expressed. The figures are kept very flat and are modelled with much refinement as in low relief, yet those in the foreground are permitted to project quite as much as in high relief. They are sharply undercut, and from the side the panels have an odd, laminated look, but from a proper position the effect is very pleasing.

2 D

Mr. Niehaus's contribution to the Congressional Library was important, consisting of two figures, — " Moses " and " Gibbon," — and three charming tympanums carved in wood. The " Moses " is from certain directions strangely impressive. The " Gibbon," however, betrays no touch of Mr. Niehaus's genius. It is commonplace, a graceful figure without significance or personality, the careful workmanship of a clever, uninspired modeller. In the multitude of his commis-

FIG. 63.—NIEHAUS: HAHNEMANN, WASHINGTON.

sions and their attendant problems it is not strange that the artist has occasionally wearied of profound search for inspiration; that he has contented himself with familiar *motifs*. As one turns the pages of the booklet which brings them together, it is interesting to note, for example, the similarity of pose between the " Morton " of the Capitol and its vis-a-vis, Mr. French's " General Cass." The unconscious resemblance is a fortunate one, making the " Morton " one of the most striking figures there. Mr. Niehaus's " Farragut," at

Muskegon, Michigan, might readily be mistaken at first glance for Saint Gaudens's famous work; the "Lincoln," at the same place, seems oddly familiar, while the reliefs — "Memory" and "Grief" — on the Drake monument recall instantly their prototypes by the lamented Warner. Upon close comparison these resemblances disappear, only to come back teasingly when the attention is withdrawn from superficial detail to the general air of the work. It is better employment to turn to the faithful, almost fanatical accuracy of exterior in the busts of J. Q. A. Ward, Rabbi Gottheil, President McKinley, and others; to the beauty of the calling woman in the group entitled "Story of Gold," — a figure of rare inspiration, — at the Pan-American Exposition; and, above all, to the array of monumental designs in which Mr. Niehaus shows his distinctive talent. Here are no failures and no plagiarisms. Not only the Hahnemann and the Drake memorials, but competitive models for a "Sherman," a "Lee," and a "William the Silent," must be mentioned; — all these, whether executed or not, are among the best monumental projects that American art has produced. In his equestrian statue of General Forrest, for Forrest Park, Memphis, Tennessee, Mr. Niehaus has shown us how adequate is his talent for this form of sculptural expression. The figures of rider and steed alike have been highly praised for their truth and vigor. A photograph of the model gives promise of one of the best equestrian statues in the country.

This sculptor's group, "The Triumphant Return," a decoration for the ephemeral arch of the Dewey celebration, was a very effective work. While recognizing the success of the other participants — the vigorous realism of Mr. Bitter's "War" and the tenderness of Mr. French's "Peace" — one found the Niehaus group imbued with a calm dignity quite peculiarly its own. The serene aloofness of that uplifted image of Athena victorious, was strangely impressive. The artist's conception was a noble one, considered from either the pictorial or the poetic side. The introduction of the archaic figure provided a new and striking note in the composition, a note of effective value, marking by its severity of treatment a profound contrast with the realism of the group below, and also in a larger sense vastly increasing the range of suggestion. It symbolized a higher power as no addition of figures merely graceful could possibly do. Our faith has become so sadly shorn of symbols that we are obliged to have recourse to a pagan religion for visible forms of expression, but here the symbol served its purpose and became universally intelligible. There was nothing absurd or incongruous in the presence of that rigid Athena as the eidolon, present if unobserved, giving significance to the rejoicings of those who return from war.

Mr. Niehaus's latest undertakings are the "General Forrest," already referred to, and the large nude figure, "The Driller," shown at the exhibition of the National Sculpture Society in November, 1902. This statue is the important feature of a monument at Titusville, Pennsylvania, to the memory of Colonel Edwin L. Drake, who sank the first oil well in Pennsylvania, in 1859. "The Driller," which is intended to symbolize the energy of labor, shows a nude figure of powerful build in a kneeling position, with uplifted hammer, in the act of driving the drill into the rock. The face is sternly in earnest, though somewhat impersonal; the action vigorous and convincing. The workmanship is so admirably broad, yet precise, that each new point of view increases our respect for the patience and conscience, or shall we rather say the enthusiasm, of the man who has wrought so well. Such work does us good. Of it Mr. Russell Sturgis has recently written: "It is, as an adaptation of the heroic in size and in character to strictly modern requirements of design, a piece of immense value."[1]

Although very different from Mr. Niehaus in many ways, John J. Boyle is a sculptor of no less pronounced individuality. Bluff, hearty, and genuine, he transmits these qualities unfailingly to his work. It is done with a zest which testifies to the sturdy character of the man and the irresistible momentum of his impulses. No languid interest his; no "primrose path of dalliance"! He feels things strongly; his likes and dislikes have in them something elemental. Each work seems to him vastly important and full of opportunity.

His most valuable contribution to our national art is undoubtedly in his favorite field of aboriginal subjects. He has done many things, and some of them remarkably well, but one feels that in these primitive themes he is at his best. Some of the younger men may excel him in "finesse," in subtlety of modelling and charm of line; but for

[1] *The World To-day*, Vol. IV, p. 262.

FIG. 64.—BOYLE: THE STONE AGE, FAIRMOUNT PARK, PHILADELPHIA.

the expression of power, for monumental simplicity and integrity of conception, his groups, " The Alarm," in Lincoln Park, Chicago, and " The Stone Age " (Fig. 64), in Fairmount Park, Philadelphia, have not been surpassed. In their very deficiencies they err on the right side, and one may even question if a certain harshness, a crudity of handling here and there noticeable, does not positively contribute to the impression of force. At any rate, it removes them far from the class of exquisitely finished and exquisitely foolish Indians of the jewelry stores, with which not a few public works have a close relationship.

The first group, " The Alarm," was modelled in Philadelphia, and was intended to commemorate the Ottawa tribe of Indians, with whom the pioneer donor — Mr. Martin Ryerson — had held for years most friendly relations. The title is rather a misnomer, for the " alarm " is expressed merely by a look of concentrated attention in the face of the great male figure, who stands otherwise at ease, with his robe drawn loosely about him and his long pipe in hand. His squaw rests quietly at his feet, her round face a triumph of placid vacuity. The papoose in its little cradle seems likewise in perfect accord with the environment, sharing its mother's grateful torpidity of mind, quite untroubled by dreams of lurking foe. The shaggy dog is on the alert, however, and makes an uncompromising feature in the group.

Even this dignified work has its amusing side. In order that the much-admired bronze should be given its full value, a massive pedestal was planned, a square of polished granite with classic mouldings; and, as if to emphasize the incongruity and fix it without possibility of evasion, large Greek triglyphs were deeply incised upon its surface. Perched high upon this imposing structure, the figures are conspicuous, but have lost the charm of illusion. Nature and art alike have given way to artificiality. Imagine this admirable group upon a rough-hewn boulder of irregular form, half concealed amid shrubbery, where one might come upon the dusky household as unexpectedly as in those already legendary days when similar statuesque figures made our forests even more darkly silent by their mysterious presence. How delightful such a surprise might be made in one of our formal, showy parks! How much more the group would mean to us, and how much it would gain in artistic value! Then, too, the pedestal might be made curious with signifi- cant aboriginal carvings, adding their suggestiveness to the scene, or at least providing a tinge of local color. But we are the "heirs of the ages," and we insist upon jumbling and flaunting our posses- sions.

In the installation of the second group, in Fairmount Park, Mr. Boyle evidently had his own way and made no attempt to quote Greek; the result, if not notably artistic, is at least incon- spicuous. As to the group itself, however, the artist used to com- plain bitterly that he had not been left free. He had sketched a fine thing, an Indian woman of mighty physique defending her children from a powerful eagle, — a western Rizpah, as it were. The children were living ones, however, and clung to their mother's skirts, as far as possible from the vanquished bird, which lay upon its back claw- ing the air and apparently shrieking defiance in impotent rage. The great outspread wings offered beautiful lines, and their shadowy concaves set off the figures most effectively. The sculptor was pleased with his work, and when he had the full-sized model well advanced he called in a photographer, that the committee at home might note his progress.

The answer came, and all too soon, for it urged with sufficient emphasis that it would never do to treat the national bird so igno- miniously, and would the sculptor not kindly substitute some other creature? He did so. It is perhaps as well that there is no record of his half-murmured observations as he cut off those magnificent wings and painfully converted the Bird of Freedom into a bear cub! It lies there to this day — very dead. The squaw still clasps her baby to her breast and clutches her stone hatchet, looking out from under dishevelled locks, scanning the horizon for signs of a more formidable foe, the while the naked papoose on the ground — care- fully studied from a bright-eyed Italian child — sits quietly and looks about with interest. Despite his restrictions, Mr. Boyle made of this group a valuable contribution to our native art, a work of sculptural beauty and of great significance. One quite agrees with the report of the Fairmount Association in its claim that " The group is among the most masterly works which have been added to the decorations of the Park, and Mr. Boyle is undoubtedly the first sculptor who has adequately presented the Indian's case in American art."

The sculptor has done much work since the unveiling of "The Stone Age," in 1888, and good work, too, but unfortunately little of it has been in this field, where he stands preëminent. We had another glimpse of his possibilities at the Pan-American Exposition at Buffalo, where his two massive groups, "The Savage Age," were among the very best of the sculptural decorations. It is safe to say that no other American sculptor could have treated the subject better. The groups showed, even after the devastating process of mechanical enlargement, more than a remnant of sturdy strength and of primitive simplicity. Though the tendency of the pointing machine and its human allies was to efface the touches that express individuality and to reduce the productions of a score of men to the same dead level, they did not succeed in eliminating the personal quality in Mr. Boyle's work. As for the conception, it was unmistakably his; the very twist of the figures, their massive construction, even their unexpected combinations, — all bore the seal of the mind which had evolved "The Alarm" and "The Stone Age." The swing and movement of the later groups showed a practised hand and a matured imagination. Above all, in the great amount of "color" infused into a very simple coherent mass, did they prove the essential sculpturesque attitude of the artist's mind. The result is a combination of vigor and restraint which is good to see and good to feel. Indeed, these groups were too valuable to lose. They well merited more careful execution and reproduction in bronze or stone.

Among Mr. Boyle's other achievements may be mentioned the decorations of the Transportation building of the Columbian Exposition; a charming little bronze, "Tired Out," which won a medal there; a very attenuated "Bacon" in the Congressional Library; and particularly the heroic "Franklin" presented to Philadelphia by a prominent citizen in 1900. Into this well-constructed figure Mr. Boyle has succeeded in putting no small amount of individuality. His statue seems very much alive, and very convincing as well. One does not believe in those "Franklins" of the city of Washington, nor in any other excepting the Houdon bust; but this creation seems adequate, giving us the quiet, thoughtful, humorous, and, above all, sane man of perfect balance. The face is benign, showing the kindly smile of one who has mental "collateral" and can smile without looking foolish. If the figure is not altogether distinguished in treatment, it may be because the sculptor has chosen to allow *bonhomie* to predominate over dignity, and ease in a measure to supplant elegance. This is not saying, however, that Mr. Boyle's "Franklin" is either undignified or inelegant; we would merely point out that these attributes are subordinated to the very grateful expression of an amiable personality. The Philadelphia "Franklin" may not be imposing, but it is winning.

Mr. Boyle was born in New York City in 1851, but his youth was spent in Philadelphia. His education was derived from the public schools of that city and from the Pennsylvania Academy of Fine Arts, where his artistic promise was sufficient to justify the journey to Paris and several years' study in the École des Beaux-Arts. Here his talent and faithful effort won him substantial recognition, as did in turn his first important exhibit in the Salon. He practised his art for a number of years in Philadelphia, removing in 1902 to New York.

CHAPTER XXII

OTHER NEW YORK SCULPTORS

ALTHOUGH New York has produced comparatively few sculptors, the city has attracted a great many gifted men from every part of the country. Even to catalogue them all here is impossible; but in this chapter a few of the more important names remaining may be considered — men of American birth who have been established for some time in the metropolis.

One of the best known of this number is Frank Edwin Elwell, who was born at Concord, Massachusetts, in 1858. Left an orphan at the age of four, he grew up with his grandfather Farrar, who was descended from the earliest settlers of the township. Mr. Elwell received his first artistic impulse from Miss May Alcott in the little drawing class at Concord, in 1876, and continued his studies in the Boston Museum of Fine Arts. He went abroad in 1881, studying first in the École des Beaux-Arts in Paris, and later privately with M. Falguière. He returned to this country in 1885, establishing himself at once in New York.

Mr. Elwell's principal works and their locations are included in the following list: "Death of Strength," in the cathedral garden at Edam, Holland; bust of Mr. Peter Esselmont, Lord Provost of Aberdeen, Aberdeen, Scotland; "Diana and the Lion," Art Institute of Chicago, 1893; "Egypt Awaking" bought at the Paris Salon of 1896 by M. Gabriel Goupillat of Paris; "Dickens and Little Nell," bought by the Fairmount Park Art Association of Philadelphia, Pennsylvania; memorial to Edwin Booth, Mount Auburn, Cambridge, Massachusetts; equestrian statue of General Winfield Scott Hancock, on the battlefield of Gettysburg, Pennsylvania, 1896; "New Life," Lowell cemetery, Lowell, Massachusetts, property of Hon. Charles Sumner Lilley, called the "Bonney Memorial," 1899 (plas-

ter in Pennsylvania Academy of Fine Arts); "Orchid," owned by
Mr. Theodore B. Starr, New York City, 1899; "Aqua Viva," prop-
erty of the Metropolitan Museum of Art, New York City; Andrew
McMillan Memorial, Utica, New York; "Kronos," Pan-American
fountain, 1901; "Intelligence," in front of New York state building,
Pan-American Exposition, Buffalo, New York, 1901; "Elihu Yale,"
Yale Club, New York City, 1901; and busts of Vice-Presidents
Morton and Hobart, Senate Chamber, Washington.

As the list testifies, Mr. Elwell has done much work in the years
which have slipped away since his return — much work and much
thinking. It may be safely affirmed that he has put an idea into
each thing that he has created. This is a more unusual claim than
at first appears, for few realize how small a number of concepts are
made to do service in all the annual output of statuary. One new
thought a year, per man, is a high average, while many a thrifty
artist is able to run his entire course on a single idea and its variations. Further, when we come to examine these products of Mr.
Elwell's fertile fancy, we shall find that a very large proportion of
them are legitimately sculptural ideas. As has been elsewhere
remarked, there are not a few respectable sculptors who never have
had a sculptural idea. Mr. Elwell's execution varies much with his
moods, and his drawing is not impeccable, but he always has something to say, and says it in a manner so original, so different from
the expression of others, that he is almost invariably interesting;
which is one way of stating that his utterance is intensely personal.
This is true, though not always obvious. While his work is so much
his own that there is never hint of imitation, it is on the other hand
bewilderingly diverse. His approach to his various subjects is as
novel as are the ideas themselves, and as impossible of classification.
We set him down as a devotee of Egyptian art, of the massive, the
rigid, the petrified; and in the next exhibit we find from him a
flowerlike creation, with fluttering robes, poising lightly on one
foot. We turn from the strange chimera, "Kronos," to Charles
Dickens, chatting in unaffected familiarity with Little Nell, then
back to the essentially monumental figure of the "New Life,"
which certainly shows slight family resemblance to the realistic "Water Carrier" of the Metropolitan Museum. Have we

FIG. 65. — ELWELL: EGYPT AWAKING, PARIS.

another sculptor who has so many phases, who speaks so many languages?

Mr. Elwell's "Egypt Awaking" (Fig. 65) is fine in thought and developed with skill. A seated female figure, of Egyptian simplicity and stiffness in its lower members, is shown coming to life. The bosom swells, and the arms are lifted in the wide exultant sweep of one who stretches the limbs after much slumber. The head is raised, and in its unfamiliar features is a strange commingling of wonder and of confidence. It is an intelligence that is keen, and trained, suddenly confronted with new and extraordinary conditions. Such is the internal value of the work; its sculptural expression is not less interesting. In the contrast between the vague yet adequate generalization of the lower limbs of a Nefert, for instance, and the carefully modelled torso and arms pulsating with life, there dwells an effect as striking as ever Rodin has attained through contrasting technics. The rigidity of the legs, bound to their support, is the simplest expression of glyptic art; the bilateral symmetry of the pose contributes its sculptural impression, and the large significant gesture, particularly in such contrast, is strangely monumental. Mr. Elwell has made of "Egypt" a new Galatea or an imprisoned Daphne upon whom the gods have taken pity. It is not to be wondered at that so original a work should have found prompt appreciation and purchase in Paris. There, as in Athens of old, many go about seeking to learn of some new thing. In that great centre of artistic effort, if anywhere, a poetic sculptural idea is recognized and valued.

In his "Dickens and Little Nell" the sculptor has given us that rare thing, — a portrait statue which makes an emotional appeal. To be sure, its dramatic power is due to a secondary figure, as is the case in Mr. French's "Gallaudet," but the use of such a figure is legitimate when it detracts nothing from the effect of the principal, but rather enhances it, and when it is in itself as charming in conception as is Mr. Elwell's "Little Nell." Strictly speaking, the Dickens group — if such it may be called — is a tableau and not a monument. The novelist is shown in a too accidental and familiar guise to satisfy the requirements of great sculpture. Not that we would ask him to pose with assumed majesty, consciously "sitting for a picture." The object of a monument is neither to exaggerate nor to minimize the importance of a subject, but to give the truth in as large and simple a way as possible. The highest ideal of a statue of Charles Dickens is not one which suggests his veritable every-day presence, graciously accommodating himself for a moment to this public seat, as at an author's reading, and exchanging amiable glances with the pass-ers-by, but one which shows the essential man withdrawn a pace and protected by an invisible barrier of dignity and distinc-tion. Theoretically, then, and judging the work from the ideal standard of a severely monumental art, the sweet child figure which so intimately connects the effigy with ourselves is a solecism. Practically, we would not have it otherwise than it is. Its absence would not make the easy-

FIG. 66. — ELWELL: THE NEW LIFE, LOWELL, MASS.

going "Dickens" any more impressive, and would be a distinct loss to the art beloved of the people.

Mr. Elwell's "General Hancock," on the battlefield of Gettys-burg, is a striking memorial, but hardly justifies Professor Goodyear's characterization of it as "one of the most important equestrian monu-ments in modern history."[1] The sculptor's mortuary relief, "The New Life" (Fig. 66), will be recognized as another very origi-nal work, fearlessly conceived and evolved with much sincerity. The gesture of the arms is a favorite one with the sculptor, and has

[1] "Renaissance and Modern Art," p. 264.

in it a keynote of largeness. In this somewhat mystical conception it possesses peculiar significance. The face is of a fine type, though in view of the theme one could imagine it more radiant, but Mr. Elwell probably realized how easily this might be overdone, and wisely kept himself in restraint. Perhaps the same explanation may be made for the rather summary treatment of the drapery; the arms, however, and shoulders are well elaborated in a broad sculptural way. The total effect of this work, in place, is dignified and impressive.

To view another of the products of Mr. Elwell's untrammelled fancy one should return in thought to the beautiful esplanade of the Pan-American Exposition. In the large sunken basin at its western extremity stood two strangely imposing figures surrounded, the one by curious web-footed sea horses, the other by still more remarkable amphibious elk. The figures themselves, "Ceres" and "Kronos," were the most novel decorations on the grounds. Furthermore, they were true decorations and not merely transcripts of actuality, like so much exposition work. Amid groups of plaster men who hammered and ploughed and ran machinery, these images rose more impressive because frankly sculpture. Their neighbors were too often like untrained supernumeraries, hastily huddled into a tableau; these rough-hewn colossi seemed of all time, rooted there like the rocks. In pose they were archaic, without superficial grace. Their arms were wide extended and lifted a little above the horizontal. The rear view of "Kronos," in particular, was most extraordinary, resembling some gigantic insect with outstretched *elytra*, and the thinner wings just unfolding. Both figures were sculptural, however, from every point of view, and the "Kronos," at least, was weirdly effective, with his veiled face thrown far back, his enormous physique, and the great Egyptian wings symbolic of the swiftness of time. The massive legs rose, however, from the back of a turtle, significant of a Time that does not always "amble withal." The outstretched hands, scarcely disengaged from the wings, supported globes. The whole conception was symbolic, yet so skilfully and so powerfully conveyed that it seemed reasonable in itself. One was conscious of a strong artistic personality behind these prodigious apparitions — a power which made of them something foreign to

2 E

their surroundings. They seemed to speak a language all their own
as they stood, aloof and alien, facing each other across the sheet
of water where, though disconnected, they were bound together by
mysterious ties. One could easily imagine their sombre spirits
communicating with each other in some ancient code of wireless
telegraphy over the heads of their restless and commonplace associates.

It is this imaginative freedom and above all this flavor of the
artist's personality,—so happily illustrated in his own work,—which
Mr. Elwell considers the most precious qualities in art. He believes,
heart and soul, that the greatest thing in the world is for a man to
know that he is his own, and that the great end in art is the discovery
of the self of the artist. For such freedom he makes battle in season
and out of season; sometimes, as it seems, with unnecessary strenu-
ousness, since after all, as he himself acknowledges, " It is nothing
but good art that counts in the end." The artist with something to
say will say it, while the man with no song cannot possibly be made
to sing, however great his freedom and however pressing the solicita-
tion. Literally and metaphorically, Mr. Elwell always has something
to say, and knows how to say it well. In his present position of
Curator of Sculpture in the Metropolitan Museum he has done
valuable service for the cause in several ways: in the admirable
arrangement of the new galleries, in the dignity with which he has
invested the earlier American works of intrinsic worth, in the com-
pilation of an enormous amount of data regarding our sculptors,
and in the many kindly acts which his position has enabled him to
show to brother-artists. But for all this one grudges every hour
that Mr. Elwell spends in the routine of this work. A man of his
originality should not cease to produce.

Among the more recent accessions to the artistic ranks of New
York is Mr. William Couper, who was for twenty years a resident of
Florence. Although Mr. Couper is well known in Europe, and has
a growing reputation in the East, he may require introduction in
other parts of the United States. Born in Norfolk, Virginia, in 1853,
his professional education was gained largely at Cooper Institute, New
York. In 1874 he went to Munich, where he entered both the
Academy of Fine Arts and the Royal College of Surgery. At the

FIG. 67.—COUPER: BEAUTY'S WREATH FOR VALOR'S BROW.

end of 1875 he was obliged to leave for Italy on account of ill health. While in Florence, Mr. Thomas Ball invited him to study under him, giving him place in his own studio. This offer was gladly accepted, and thenceforth the young sculptor's time was devoted principally to portraiture and works of an ideal nature. Among the latter may be mentioned " Mother's Love," a group in marble; " Psyche," a life-size figure in marble; two large sphinxes for Governor Stanford; a life-size figure in marble entitled, "Coming Spring"; a portrait statue for Governor Routt (Denver, Colorado); " Falconer," a running figure; and a life-size marble statue called " Beauty's Wreath for Valor's Brow."

Returning to the United States in 1897, Mr. Couper established himself in New York, and the list of his works has since been extended as follows: an allegorical relief, " Repose," bronze; heroic marble statue, " Moses," Appellate Court building, New York City; " Recording Angel," heroic, bronze, placed in cemetery at Norfolk, Virginia; heroic angel for a tower in Methuen, Massachusetts (for Mr. E. F. Searles); two figures on a sarcophagus for McKim, Mead, and White; heroic portrait of Professor Thomas Eggleston, bronze, for Columbia College; " Angel of the Resurrection," life-size, marble, Chicago; tablet to the Rev. James Mulcahey, St. Paul's Church, Broadway, New York City; drinking fountain for Mr. Howard Willets, White Plains, New York; relief on east side of Dewey Arch, " Protection of our Country." A reduction of this relief has since been made and cast in bronze for Colonel William Lamb, Norfolk, Virginia. Also a heroic portrait bust of President William McKinley; a bronze group, " Headed for Goal"; " Te Deum Laudamus"; portrait of Dr. William S. Hubble; portrait of Henry Maurer; " Rural Industry."

Mr. Couper's art is essentially Italian in manner, or at least so tinged with the Florentine accent that it has a rather unfamiliar look in our exhibitions, where, for many years, almost everything sculptural has reflected in greater or less degree the Parisian school. Those who have seen the results of Italian influence upon our earlier sculptors might infer that Mr. Couper was a belated Powers or Crawford; but they will discover that fashions have changed in Florence and Rome quite as much as in America. The modern Italian is as far from Canova as is Saint Gaudens or Ward — but on the opposite side. The poverty and reserve of the pseudo-classic school have given way to a riot of cleverness and a wealth of detail. In the more familiar examples marvellously carved accessories take the place of sculptural line, of expression, of emotion, of everything which a trained taste requires in a worthy work of art. This is not — could not be — the case in the work of a man of Mr. Couper's innate refinement; but, as with even the greatest of living Italian sculptors, his art is necessarily colored by the predominant influences of his surroundings. Its one defect is a somewhat irritating insistence upon details, and conversely a neglect of powerful lines and planes. If this slight criticism seems somewhat ungraciously obtruded at this point, it is that we may be done with it. It applies to all of Mr. Couper's work, just as the sign of sharp or flat at the beginning of a piece of music extends its sway to the end, and just as the "personal equation" enters into every act of our lives; but, despite differences of method, no sculptor of catholic tastes can fail to recognize the beauty of Mr. Couper's art.

For he is a poet and a man of intelligence as well. The emotional and the reflective sides are both developed within him and sustain each other. He never begins a work without a definite and worthy idea, while his cunning craftsmanship proves his enthusiasm and his power of concentration. He is not only a good sculptor, but an exceedingly skilful one. He delights, as every true artist must, in the processes of his work, and, as hinted, sometimes idolizes it into a decline. One feels a suspicion of this in the essentially noble figure of "Moses," on the Appellate Court building. It is a magnificent conception, and justly admired; its only weakness is over-elaboration. Here the "loving touch" has lost its potency, because it is seen everywhere. It would seem that for that elevation a severe architectural treatment would be more effective; planes rather than veins in the arms, a more conventional and massive drapery, a little less breaking up of the surface — but that is all that can be said against the figure. These things are superficial; within the statue is that rare thing in art — a soul. None but a man of Mr. Couper's imagination and grasp could put into a head so much dignity, so obvious a fitness to lead. His "Moses" has the intellectual strength and fire of the old-time prophets. It is not "the meekest man," but rather that other Moses who, in his righteous indignation, broke the tablets of stone.

Mr. Couper has made particular and sympathetic study of winged figures. For those whose tastes have outgrown the conventional and rudimentary images of our graveyards, the "curly chirping angels spruce as birds," Mr. Couper's heavenly host make fascinating appeal. There are few if any American sculptors who know

how to model angels so generally acceptable as are his. They are not merely pretty, but they are beautiful, radiant creations, gracefully conceived, carefully drawn, and exquisitely carved. If they are sometimes tangled in billows of realistic drapery, they are all the more winning on this account. Thus the angel of Methuen, Massachusetts, might possibly be criticised for its too great abundance of this world's goods, but as to the figure itself there can be no reproach; it is imbued with rare tenderness and delicacy. The severe treatment of the great wings does

Fig. 68. — COUPER: TE DEUM LAUDAMUS.

much to counter-balance the floridity of the robe, which, it must be acknowledged, is to many minds one of the great attractions of the work. As a study in drapery it is certainly remarkable and worthy of all praise, alike for its grace of line and its sculptural color. The relief is high but without background, the bronze figure being attached directly to the wall of a stone tower. If it has not the commanding majesty of Mr. French's Angel of Death, in the Milmore Memorial, it has a sweet beauty of its own, in which all its elements are gracefully harmonized.

Although Mr. Couper's fame will probably rest on these foundations, he has treated many other themes. One of his most important works is the seated figure entitled "Beauty's Wreath for Valor's Brow" (Fig. 67), a tender and poetic creation. The movement of the body, the turn of the lovely arms, the bowed head, are all sculpturally beautiful, and win the applause of those to whom the minute elaboration of the drapery and accessories makes less appeal. A graceful idea is conveyed in the low relief "Te Deum Laudamus" (Fig. 68), a bust portrait in profile of the sculptor's son. Very angelic he looks with bowed head and the suggestion of a bass viol, the strings of which his fingers press. The modelling of the youthful face is sensitively pure; the hair is a lesson in plastic handling, and the slight drapery over the shoulder is what sculptured drapery ought to be. There is hardly a touch in this relief which one could desire altered.

Mr. Couper has had the good fortune to win a competition over twenty-two other sculptors for the important memorial to be erected at Pittsburg, Pennsylvania, in honor of Colonel Hawkins. The sculptural portion of this monument is to be a statue in bronze, eight feet high, portraying the soldier in field uniform, including overcoat and cape. His hat is pulled well down over his brow, and his cloak thrown back from his arms. He stands in an easy attitude with one foot advanced and his hands resting upon his sword, which is held in front of him, the point resting on the ground. A reproduction of the sketch model shows a chaste architectural design of the exedra type with ingenious modifications, and a figure which even in tiny size gives promise of large monumental qualities, of simplicity and repose and distinction.

A unique place among American sculptors is that held to-day by Mr. Frederick Wellington Ruckstuhl. A man of intense nature and great activity, he has made his mark in two distinct departments, not only producing much work as a sculptor, but doing perhaps even more notable service as the organizer and in some sense the leading spirit of the National Sculpture Society, of which he was for several years the secretary. To this association he has consecrated his best energies with a devotion and an executive ability which alone have safeguarded its existence and made it the power that it is. It is more than likely that the combined efforts of the fraternity — efforts which have already organized five important exhibitions and which culminated in 1899 in the so-called " Dewey Arch " — would have been impossible without the self-sacrificing labor of this public-spirited man. There may be room for individual opinion in regard to the policy of the National Sculpture Society and in regard to its methods, but the fact remains indisputable that it is a significant expression of conditions to-day, that it fairly represents the men who constitute its membership, and that it has done much to keep the claims of the profession before a rather apathetic public. It was Mr. Ruckstuhl who was able to solidify the vaporous and often futile sentiment of his brother sculptors, to bring them together and to teach them to voice their needs and their qualifications in other language than the inarticulate terms of their art.

The sculptural decoration of the Appellate Court building in New York City, though the work of many hands, is a monument to Mr. Ruckstuhl's disinterested efforts. Like the beginnings of things everywhere, it has its crudities and is overdone, while lacking the harmony of perfectly concerted effort ; but it was worth the doing, not alone for visible results, but for the mere practice, and for its perpetual suggestion to the public. A great art, like that of France, for instance, does not come in a day, but is the slow product of years of experiment and of failures as well as of successes. The skill of to-day is the sum-total of all the influences which have gone before, to which each generation has added its modicum of energy. Parallel with this slow accretion of physical aptitude, and mysteriously mingled with it, has been the mental development of artists and public alike ; the growth of that general æsthetic sentiment which is so noticeable in France and which has been so conspicuously absent in the United States : the ability to *look at* a work of art, to form a reasonable judgment as to its value ; in short, to enjoy it intelligently. In the service of so desirable an evolution of taste a concrete object lesson like that presented by the much-decorated Appellate Court building is of infinite value. The very weaknesses of the scheme are possibly of greater utility to us to-day than would be a perfection that could not be criticised. Appreciation is not intuitive, and discussion is often the first step toward it — at least it prepares the foundation of mental standards. To this aroused attitude of mind, which promises so much at the present hour, Mr. Ruckstuhl's personal effort has contributed more than is generally known.

Without question Mr. Ruckstuhl's most beautiful work is his marble figure of "Evening" (Fig. 69) which he modelled in Paris, and which won him an honorable mention at the Salon of 1888 and a medal at the Columbian Exposition. It is a poetic conception, very simply expressed in a pose of unusual grace, and reveals a close study of nature. It well deserves its prominent place in the Metropolitan Museum, where it marks an interesting contrast with early American sculpture of a less fluent character. The dreamy face is not of to-day, however; nor indeed is the treatment of the body altogether akin to that which appears in its contemporaries and neighbors, the "Bacchante" of MacMonnies and Stewardson's "Bather." Mr. Ruckstuhl has a lingering sympathy for modern classicism; at least he subordinates personal peculiarities more than do most of his colleagues. Unlike the "Bacchante," for instance, his "Evening" does not reproduce undeviatingly the model who posed for it, nor does it suggest a nude model at all. The figure is essentially, and by intention, a statue; it has been modified and, in a sense, conventionalized to that end; herein is its particular beauty and power.

Mr. Ruckstuhl varies his methods, however, with the problem before him. In his bust of John Russell Young he has carried observation and precision of rendering to a remarkable point while preserving a treatment which is large, suave, and decidedly fleshy. Other well-known works of his are the novel "Mercury teasing the Eagle of Jupiter," in St. Louis; "Solon," in the Congressional Library, and the two seated figures of marble, "Wisdom" and "Force," which guard the entrance of the Appellate Court in New York City. Exceptionally spirited in a legitimate way is his equestrian statue of General John F. Hartranft, at Harrisburg, Pennsylvania. This group Mr. Ruckstuhl modelled at St. Leu, near Paris, after much preparation in the way of visits to many European capitals. He has pictured his subject riding quietly, cap in hand, and

FIG. 69.—RUCKSTUHL: EVENING, METROPOLITAN MUSEUM.

the right arm well back, as though acknowledging the salutations of those who welcome the brave soldier home. The figure shows dignity and self-containment; the horse is of the Colleoni type, in modern guise. It is not an imitation, but was evidently inspired by the Venetian masterpiece, sharing its irresistible momentum and gratifying the eye with clear-cut lines and a very modern vivacity of treatment of head and mane.

Another successful work is the "Victory," which Mr. Ruckstuhl made for the Soldiers' and Sailors' Monument at Jamaica, Long Island, a winged figure which offers a palm and a laurel wreath with an imposing gesture. The carefully studied drapery and the effective simplification of the powerful wings are especially noteworthy. A natural development of this idea is shown in the sculptor's latest and most popular work, "The Spirit of the Confederacy," a strongly modelled group of two figures, in which the "Victory" becomes a personification of the Lost Cause, and gathers in her arm a falling soldier of the Confederate army. The thought is that of Mercié's "Gloria Victis," but the arrangement of the group suggests rather the "Quand Même" of the same gifted sculptor. The treatment is, however, Mr. Ruckstuhl's own, and despite his somewhat whimsical protests against "individuality" in art, the sculptor's methods of thought and execution are so definitely pronounced that his personal style is written in every fold of the drapery, in the admirably decorative wings, and not less in certain mannerisms of treatment of the face and hair. The conception, so far removed from the uninspired realism of most of our military memorials, has a poetic strain, and is sculpturally significant as well; the execution is that of an experienced and conscientious master of the monumental art. The total effect when the group is reared at its proper height cannot be other than impressive.

A sculptor who has rendered valuable service to the cause of art by means of his lectures and his writings, as well as through his more concrete expression in marble and bronze, is William Ordway Partridge. He is the author of various works on art — "Art for America," "The Song-Life of a Sculptor," "The Technique of Sculpture," "The Angel of Clay" — besides numerous magazine

articles, and he has given courses of lectures on sculpture at Columbia University and the Brooklyn Institute.

Mr. Partridge's professional work shows a responsive imagination
and versatility of method. His general culture has broadened the
range of his interests, and one is not surprised to find him at his
best in picturing the great poets. His rendering of their physiog-
nomies is sympathetic, and most of his busts show a charming

FIG. 70. — PARTRIDGE: TENNYSON.

variety of technic, from the
nervously emphasized features
to the sketchy accessories and
the simply massed shoulders
and base. In such works Mr.
Partridge is as interesting as
his good taste is unfailing.
The expressions of his "Shel-
ley," "Tennyson" (Fig. 70),
"Burns," "Whittier," etc., are
those of inherent refinement,
not untouched with the deeper
glow of creative fire. His
"Shakespeare," in Lincoln
Park, Chicago, a seated figure, is admirably conceived; a
graceful work of pronounced
sculptural quality, massed in
a large simple way and pleasingly and adequately modelled.
His "Hamilton," in Brooklyn,
has won astonishing eulogies. Professor Goodyear, says of it: "As
the ideal of an orator, it appears to me the most successful work in
modern art."[1] The figure is well drawn and has much life and intensity, being especially pleasing when viewed from the side; from
the front the peculiar spread of the arms gives an unfortunate suggestion of a man balancing himself upon a precarious support.

In later works Mr. Partridge seems to have allowed his love for
"sketchiness" to run away with his discretion. His recent "Nathan

[1] "Renaissance and Modern Art," p. 264.

Hale," for instance, is well conceived, the face showing refinement and not a little exaltation; but the sculptor, in his desire to oppose to this focal point the contrast of a masterly generalization, has deprived the figure to a certain degree of that treatment which is somewhat arbitrarily termed "modelling." Portions are left barely outlined. With increasing distance from the head, on which we are supposed to concentrate attention, the treatment becomes more and more summary, so much so, indeed, as to waive anatomical truth. Thus the legs of the "Nathan Hale" are merely suggested by straight lines, which contrast strikingly with the well-rounded limbs of the "Hamilton."

Mr. Partridge's equestrian "Grant" in Brooklyn is a happy embodiment of the silent hero, and as a sketch would be considered of great interest and promise. But these are the days of specialists, and the horses of Potter and Proctor, not to mention the achievements of Frémiet and of the sublimely patient Paul Dubois, have taught us to demand a perfection of both organic structure and of surface handling unknown to the art of fifty years ago. In the face of such demands Mr. Partridge's more recent experiments in a loose technic and an impressionistic effect are likely to provoke discussion. To not a few who appreciate thoroughly the artist's mental grasp of his themes, this recent change of methods is an unwelcome one. That it is sustained, on the other hand, by the sculptor's personal conviction, there can be no doubt.

The versatile Irish have found in America a favorable field for artistic development; transplanted to this spacious land not a few of the race have revealed an unusual gift for sculptural expression. The promise of Thomas Crawford's brief life has been repeated in the case of several others during the years which have followed. Martin Milmore, Launt Thompson, and John Donoghue were all men of exceptional talent, whose careers were cut short prematurely. Mr. Donoghue, whose death by his own hand in July, 1903, sealed the tragedy of his life, was doubtless the most richly endowed of the three. Born in Chicago, in 1853, of very humble parentage, his vocation revealed itself to him even amidst his routine duties as an employee in the county clerk's office. A short period of schooling at the old Academy of Design of Chicago was so well rewarded that

the young sculptor felt justified in going abroad.   He studied for a
time with Jouffroy at the École des Beaux-Arts, exhibiting a head,
" Phædra," in the Salon of 1880, at which time he returned to
Chicago.   Oscar Wilde, during his visit to America in 1882, called
attention to Donoghue's artistic promise, and he was enabled to return to Europe the following year.   This time he established himself in Rome, where he produced a number of remarkable works: a
relief, "Seraphim" (Salon of 1884); "Young Sophocles," his masterpiece (Fig. 71), in 1885; and a "Hunting Nymph" in 1886.   Among
his later works were a voluptuous Venus, shown at the Columbian
Exposition under the title of "Kypros"; a "Boxer"; a colossal figure called "The Spirit," modelled for the Columbian Exposition,
but which never reached its destination, and is now lost; and a
"Saint Paul" in the rotunda of the new Congressional Library.
The "Young Sophocles leading the Chorus after the Battle of
Salamis" was undoubtedly Mr. Donoghue's highest inspiration, and
stands among the most perfect examples of ideal sculpture yet produced by an American.   Its handling is plastic, yet shows singular
restraint.   Its large simplicity, due to the elimination of all unworthy
detail, is remarkable.   The meaning of the figure is as fine as its
form; it was conceived upon a very noble plane.   The exuberance
of the young sculptor's first ideal enhances the contrasts of his
career.   The journey from the exaltation which produced the
"Young Sophocles," down to the gloom of his desperate undoing,
is one of the most pitiful descents recorded in the annals of art.

The Metropolitan Museum contains an old bust of Robert Burns,
by Charles Calverley, an interesting contrast in style with this veteran sculptor's incisive portrait of himself shown at the exhibition of
the National Sculpture Society in 1895.   Mr. Calverley's permanent
reputation will rest largely upon his medallions, which, in their precision and firmness of construction, are among the admirable products of the art.   A forceful characterization of aged Louis Menand
is especially noteworthy.

James Wilson Alexander McDonald has long been a picturesque figure in the world of monumental art, and has done much
creditable work.   William R. O'Donovan is best known for his portrait busts, and has also produced a number of refined reliefs.   The

FIG. 71. — DONOGHUE: YOUNG SOPHOCLES, ART INSTITUTE, CHICAGO.

reliefs of James E. Kelly are essentially illustrations in bronze, but, like his statuette, "Sheridan," they are full of spirit and often excellent in portraiture. Mr. Kelly's "General Buford" stands on the battlefield of Gettysburg, where is also his monument to the 6th regiment of New York Cavalry. "The Call to Arms," a figure of Columbia, some seventeen feet in height, crowns a soldier's monument at Troy, New York.

Others who have made something of a specialty of military figures are Frederick Moynihan, Alexander Doyle, and William Clark Noble. Mr. Noble has also done considerable portraiture, his statue of Channing, at Newport, Rhode Island, being one of his most successful works. George T. Brewster, likewise, has a reputation for vigorous military figures. His "Defence of the Flag" is at Athens, Pennsylvania. Mr. Brewster's early "David," was hailed as a work of much promise. His "Indiana," on the Indiana state Soldiers' and Sailors' Monument, is said to be the largest bronze figure in the country. His "Fountain of Nature" was conspicuous at the Pan-American Exposition, and, while appropriately far less restrained than its distant pendant, Mr. Grafly's "Fountain of Man," showed certain admirably plastic features.

Frederick E. Triebel, a sculptor of German parentage, from Peoria, Illinois, made his début at the Columbian Exposition with a considerable number of small marbles, the harvest of a prolonged stay in Florence. Best remembered of these works is the elaborate "Love knows no Caste," in which two well-modelled but unrelated figures are shown separated not only by their presumable social stations, but also by much architectural detail and a wealth of cunningly carved accessories. The sculptor's unquestioned talent has been better applied since then upon subjects of legitimate sculptural form, most prominent among these works being a military monument in his native city.

Another excellent memorial of similar character is the Soldiers' Monument at Milwaukee, Wisconsin, which likewise pictures vividly the climax of a struggle around a standard bearer. This realistic group of several figures is the work of John S. Conway, who studied painting in Paris, and more recently in Rome has devoted himself to sculpture. Another American sculptor who continues to prefer

Rome as a residence is Waldo Story, son of William Wetmore Story.

Louis Saint Gaudens has been rather lost sight of in his brother's fame, but is a sculptor of talent and excellent training in every phase of the art. His lions in the vestibule of the Boston Public Library are well known. His " Faun " at the Pan-American Exposition was counted worthy of a silver medal. He will have larger opportunity at the St. Louis Exposition, where he is to be represented in part by a colossal seated figure of " Painting," one of the permanent decorations of the Art Palace.

Thomas Shields Clarke is by instinct and by training an artist. Born at Pittsburg, Pennsylvania, in 1860, a graduate of Princeton in 1882, he devoted himself early to the study of drawing and painting, first at the Art Students' League, and later in Paris under various masters. His excellent achievements on canvas have brought him honors at home and abroad; but a course in modelling under Chapu diverted his attention to sculpture. One of his earliest efforts was that serious but somewhat unwieldy and but slightly decorative conception for a fountain, " The Cider Press," which was exhibited at the Columbian Exposition, and finally found a resting place in Golden Gate Park, San Francisco. This work showed a vigorous and well-constructed nude figure turning with much effort the screw of a cider press, — a somewhat tantalizing motive for a drinking fountain. Four caryatides on the Appellate Court building in New York show a more refined decorative sense. The subjects, " The Seasons," are charmingly presented with an intelligent regard for the material; " Winter," in particular, is a work of much poetic and sculptural grace. Mr. Clarke's tribute to " Alma Mater," a work for the campus at Princeton, is a dignified, impersonal presentation of the theme — a seated female figure in classic drapery, to whom a nude athlete offers homage.

Another well-known painter, William Sergeant Kendall, has also shown a decided aptitude for sculpture, his " Head of a Breton Girl " receiving an honorable mention at the Pan-American Exposition.

CHAPTER XXIII

THE YOUNGER GENERATION IN NEW YORK

THE opening twentieth century brings before us a group of young sculptors equipped by nature and by training as in the past few Americans have been. With a skill that would have bewildered our masters of twenty-five years ago, they stand ready to execute prodigies. In many cases their delicacy of taste, their fertility of imagination, — in short their personal value, — remains to be established. Some have had opportunity to reveal themselves in part.

One of the most promising of this number is Hermon A. MacNeil. Born in Massachusetts in 1866, he showed early the usual artistic instinct for drawing. He began his studies in Boston schools and was graduated with the highest honors at the Massachusetts Normal Art School, whence he was called to the position of instructor in drawing at Cornell University. In 1888 he went to Paris and in 1890 exhibited a bust in the Salon. Returning to America, he was invited by Mr. Martiny to aid him in the preparation of his sketch models for the Columbian Exposition. In Chicago, later, he did effective original work on the Electricity building, and as other opportunities soon followed, he decided to make that city his permanent home.

Well equipped with the training which the Parisian studios give, Mr. MacNeil was early discontented with the banality of modern sculptural themes. The makeshift subjects of his comrades seemed to him unworthy. He wanted to do things more original and more truly expressive. Western life and the Indian had for him a great appeal, and he made several trips to the redman's reservations north and west, in order to study what he considered the most sculptural *motifs* which America offers. His reliefs over the doors of the Marquette building in Chicago — scenes of the life and death

437

of Père Marquette — show to what good use he put his material. He was wont to talk of the artistic possibilities of the Indian in sculpture with an enthusiasm that was eloquent if not always convincing.   To him they were as fine as Greek warriors and as worthy to be immortalized.

It was in the autumn of 1895 that the first award of the Rinehart scholarship was made, and two young sculptors were selected to

FIG. 72. — MacNEIL: AGNESE.

enjoy its privileges abroad for four years.   The first men to be thus honored were Mr. MacNeil and Mr. Proctor, the animal sculptor. In many ways they must have been ideal — those days in Rome. Four years of them with three hundred and sixty-five days in each year! To live in the Villa dell'Aurora, to work upon subjects of one's own choice, with no care and all expenses paid — what better could an artist ask for?   The only requirements made by the trustees were " satisfying evidences of industry," to be attested in the form of " a life-size figure at the end of the second year, a relief containing two life-size figures before the close of the third year, and during the fourth year a life-size group of two or more figures in the round." These Mr. MacNeil set himself to creating, with a statuette or so and some remarkable busts added thereto, as it were, for good measure; the while his gifted wife modelled dainty little figures, adjuncts for teapots and inkstands, and all sorts of pretty household bronzes.

Meantime Mr. MacNeil's friends at home wondered what would be the effect of this long sojourn so near the heart of the old-time classic life. The young sculptor must appreciate the Greek the more; would he admire the Indian the less? Would the physical vigor of the wild man, his picturesqueness and his barbaric trappings, sink into a second place in his estimation as the ideals of youth gave way to others, loftier and more profound? He answered the question in the four successive works which he created in the studio in the Villa dell'Aurora. A glance at them will repay attention, not only because of their interest, but because this remarkable series of student efforts — in an unusual sense public property — illustrates so well the evolution of an artist's nature.

The first was "The Moqui Runner," a naked Indian speeding through cactus growth, his face aflame with fanatic zeal, his hair streaming in the wind, and in his hands a loathsome tangle of serpents. It is savagery personified. The little figure looks as though it would rush by and out of sight, so animated is the pose; but it is modelled very closely, with a seriousness of treatment and of expression befitting its religious significance. Of course painstaking accuracy of detail is not best suited to convey the impression of the flashing light and shade of a human projectile; but this thought opens another subject, and a discussion of the appropriateness of violent movement for sculptural representation might lead too far afield. As may be imagined, this figure appeals to the same restricted clientèle which would enjoy Mr. Bartlett's "Ghost Dancer." Its beauty is that of good construction and admirable modelling. While poetically delinquent and void of ideality, the figure might also possess an ethnological interest if it bore the characteristics of the race which it purports to represent. The Moquis are, however, a slender, delicate race of gentle mien and regular features, —

almost Japanese in suggestion, — while this creature has the build of a young Hercules and the face of an amiable demon. Perhaps it was done at too long range — Rome is far from Arizona.

The next figure, "A Primitive Chant," possesses every technical quality of good sculpture. While the idea of an Indian making strange noises by blowing or shouting in the crook of his arm awakens no responsive thrill of imagination, this is nevertheless a powerful work. Its triumph is all the more marked since our surrender is, in a sense, an unwilling one. We are not prejudiced in favor of this tuneful creature, who, unlike a Hector or an Achilles, brings to his aid no emotional backing of poetry, no prestige of three thousand years' success upon the "boards." This is sculpture pure and simple, — beauty of form, strength with refinement of modelling, compactness, breadth. The figure kneels, taking hold of the earth with powerful limbs; the hands are clasped, the right elbow tight across the body, the arm raised at a right angle, concealing largely the savage face. The expanded chest and powerful back have fascinated the sculptor; he has shaped them superbly.

That these are adequate reasons for the statue one is hardly prepared to say, though such beauty of modelling is almost a sufficient excuse. The trouble is that with nine persons out of ten, nay, with ninety-nine out of the hundred, beautiful modelling is not interesting nor a *raison d'être;* and with the more thoughtful the very fact of such costly elaboration enhances the perplexity. Why so much labor and so much time expended upon a thing unbeautiful in idea? With all its masterful workmanship, and even its sculptural pose, it remains but an illustration of an incident, a custom; curious it may be, and even to some persons moderately interesting, but possessing for none a deep significance. Where does the emotion come in — the poetic thrill which we are told is fundamental in the genesis of every great work of art, and which in turn a truly great work must convey in some fashion and some degree to men and women of taste? We are obliged to admit that in the lack of any supplementary hint at a deeper import — as of mourning or of love-making, of solitude, or of worship — the only response awakened by the action of the figure is a rather unsympathetic query regarding the nature of the "music" produced in so outlandish a fashion!

FIG. 73.—MACNEIL: THE SUN VOW, OWNED BY HOWARD SHAW, ESQ., CHICAGO.

The next year Mr. MacNeil reached the problem of the relief, — "a relief containing two life-size figures"; but the sculptor was ambitious and spurned all restraint. He set himself to devising a large composition on the theme, "From Chaos came Light." It is made up of many figures, that is to say of four or five almost complete, and numerous others suggested by heads and hands emerging from vaporous billows. A large high relief in form, it shows a swirl of these powerfully modelled bodies, emerging, reaching, ever ascending, as they struggle from their cerements of mist and darkness into the light. With faces that aspire and yearn, with hands that cling, they press forward, led by a form of rare beauty, which, already in the upper world, raises pure eyes to the fountain of light. Later, certain defects creep into view; — slight things that tend to moderate a trifle one's first enthusiasm, but which by no means spoil the brave work: jawbones of exaggerated length, an uncertain leg, a head unaccounted for, and others that count for too much. Above all, the culminating figure, while beautiful, is unduly realistic and her face is not quite equal to the demands of the situation. But the relief was a remarkable undertaking for a student, and promised fine things to follow.

The "Sun Vow" (Fig. 73), the most perfect of Mr. MacNeil's productions, is an enlargement of a sketch which he made in Chicago. An old Indian, seated, watches the effort of a boy who shoots an arrow toward the sun. The group is of life-size, compact, and admirably sculptural from every point of view. The modelling is careful, yet never dry. There are few American sculptors who manipulate the clay as charmingly as does Mr. MacNeil. His work is full of delightful touches and felicitous passages, yet the firm construction is never sacrificed to the superficial graces. He stops short of over-elegance, but even where he simplifies arbitrarily for purpose of subordination, as in the detail of the war-bonnet, the charm of handling is still apparent, — indeed, so apparent that one wonders if these bits of still life have not been done with even more zest than the figures themselves. Every part is elaborated in the same manner, — moccasins, robe, braided hair; but the elaboration of detail has always the subtle charm of low-relief work, the surfaces flowing together most suavely, without jarring edges or black holes. The artist has taken full advantage of the opportunity presented by his subject for contrasting physiques. One notes the consistent character of the two figures in their slightest detail; it tells of the sincerity of a skilled man, delighted with his theme and his models, full of the exhilaration of discovery and of the pleasure of doing. The expressions of the two faces are remarkably

good, the old man's earnest squinting in the light being extremely realistic; while the pose of the youth, savage though he be, has in it something very winning. The figures are bound together in sentiment as well as in composition, a sentiment which any one can understand and with which any one can sympathize. The group is so satisfying, especially in the beautiful harmonious bronze, that one could scarcely find a serious defect to criticise, from whatever point of view. No one grudges the young artist the honors which this work has brought him: a silver medal at the Paris Exposition of 1900, and a gold medal at the Pan-American.

FIG. 74.—LUKEMAN: MANU, APPELLATE COURT, NEW YORK.

Even were his career to be cut short to-day, this group, like Stewardson's "Bather," or Donoghue's "Young Sophocles," is good enough and important enough to assure its author a permanent place in the history of American art.

Mr. MacNeil became restive at last in quiet Rome and, forsaking that miniature "mesa" from which the Villa dell' Aurora dominates the Italian capital, he betook himself in 1899 to Paris, where there was work to be done in the decoration of the United States building at the Exposition. Since his return to America he has found plenty

of orders to occupy his time and talent. A pediment for the An-
thropological building, the massive and impressive group " Despot-
ism," and the medal of award of the Exposition were Mr. MacNeil's
share in Buffalo's great artistic enterprise. Two busts of women
modelled by him are among the finest works yet produced by an
American. Herbert Adams alone has surpassed the " Agnese "
(Fig. 72), which was done in Rome from a patrician beauty, and exhibited at Buffalo in 1901. " Beatrice," a later work, is no less beautiful in execution, though somewhat strained in pose. These busts
illustrate the artistic conscience of the sculptor, his delight as well
as his skill in pure modelling. Earnest and industrious, he is blessed
with a continuity of energy which counts for more than paroxysms of
effort. Mr. MacNeil is now engaged upon the great " Fountain of
Liberty " for the St. Louis Exposition. He is also designing the
sculpture for a large memorial arch in honor of President McKinley,
to be erected at Columbus, Ohio, and has just finished an important
group of Indians for Portland, Oregon.

Roland Hinton Perry is an exception among the New York
sculptors in being a native of that city. He was born in 1870, and,
as his numerous achievements attest, he found his vocation early.
Entering the Art Students' League at sixteen, he studied drawing
and painting for three years, when he went to Paris. He was with
Gérome for a year, then exchanged the brush for the modelling tool,
studying with Chapu, and later with Puech. He is one of the few
American sculptors whose art may be described as florid. He
delights in restless surfaces and exaggeration of muscle, and in
his early work, like " Siegfried and the Dragon," the immaturity of
his style was very evident, but likewise the promise of great vigor and
of considerable skill. His " Thor struggling with the Midgard Serpent " showed a decided advance and has won much favorable comment. Mr. Perry's first important commission was for the " Fountain
of Neptune " before the Congressional Library. This spectacular
work, involving five figures, two sea-horses, and several humbler
denizens of the deep, was accomplished easily in a year and a half.
It is regrettable that the time was so short, for with all their vigor
and audacity the figures lack the beauty which comes from careful,
appreciative study of nature. They are effective at a distance, as

stage scenery is effective, but are less interesting on nearer approach. Mr. Perry's giant " Elk " for Portland, Oregon, showed a more docile dependence upon nature.   His " Circe " and " Lion Amoureux " illustrate his skill with the female figure, while certain of his portrait busts have been handled with much charm.   His most recent works are a series of decorative figures for the New Amsterdam Theatre.

FIG. 75. — LOPEZ: THE SPRINTER.

The year 1870 saw the birth of more than one American sculptor, for Henry Augustus Lukeman was born in Richmond, Virginia, at that time.   He spent his boyhood in New York, early giving proof of his love for the art of sculpture, and entering when ten years of age a modelling class held in a boys' club.   Three years later he became a pupil of Launt Thompson, in whose studio he remained for a number of years, devoting his evenings to the study of drawing at the National Academy of Design and at the Cooper Union.   After Mr. Thompson's death, Mr. Lukeman found employment as a modeller, executing ornamental and architectural designs for public buildings, until the preparations for the Columbian Exposition attracted him to Chicago. There he made the acquaintance of Daniel C. French, whom he assisted in the enlargement of the colossal statue of " The Republic," which stood in the Court of Honor. Later he visited Paris and was for six months a pupil at the École des Beaux-Arts under Falguière. On his return to America he became a pupil of Daniel C. French, and later his assistant. For some years he has been executing independent commissions. Although so young, Mr. Lukeman has produced many works: portraits, busts, bas-reliefs, memorials, and monuments. His best known works are his remarkable and architecturally effective statue of " Manu, the Lawgiver of India" (Fig. 74) for the Appellate Court building, New York, and his statue of President McKinley for Adams, Massachusetts.

Still another who counts his years from 1870 is Charles A. Lopez, who was born at Matamoras, Mexico, but came early to New York. His art education was begun in the studio of J. Q. A. Ward, and was continued in Paris with Falguière. Mr. Lopez is accounted one of the most skilful of the younger men. His interesting work at the Charleston Exhibition has been surpassed by his " Sprinter " (Fig. 75), an admirable study of the nude figure in action, or, rather, in the tense moment that precedes action. His " Mohammcd " is one of the decorations on the Appellate Court building, New York. A relief, " Maternity " (Fig. 76), shows an ingenious and original handling. Mr. Lopez has been commissioned to erect an important monument in memory of President McKinley at Philadelphia.

Andrew O'Connor, a pupil of Daniel C. French, received a bronze medal at the Pan-American Exposition for a portrait bust of notable workmanship. Since that time he has been employed principally upon some bronze doors which complete, with those of Messrs. Adams and Martiny, the Vanderbilt Memorial for St. Bartholomew's Church. Mr. O'Connor's reliefs have been pronounced by some the finest of all. At any rate, they show remarkable aptitude for composition in many figures, and an exceptional felicity of handling. To this young artist has been intrusted one of the most important of the sculptural decorations at the St. Louis Exposition, namely, the crowning figure, in bronze, of the permanent Art Palace, a seated statue of " Inspiration."

Another interesting sculptor is Jerome Conner, who was connected for some time with the Roycroft establishment at East Aurora, New York, but who has since removed to Syracuse. Mr. Conner exhibited at Philadelphia, in 1903, a number of studies which give him claim upon the respect of his colleagues. His special field is the interpretation of the life of the workingman — an office that he performs with remarkable directness and sympathy.

Many other sculptors remain to be mentioned. John H. Roudebush, was awarded a bronze medal at the Paris Exposition of 1900, and a silver medal at Buffalo in 1901, for his group, " The Wrestlers." At the latter exhibition, as at Paris, the preceding year, the reliefs of John Flanagan and those of Victor D. Brenner, a pupil of

FIG. 76. — LOPEZ : MATERNITY.

Roty, were particularly admired. The former received silver medals at the two expositions; the latter, medals of bronze. Mr. Flanagan, who began his work with Mr. Truman H. Bartlett of Boston, studied later with Saint Gaudens, and in Paris with Chapu and Falguière. He has spent much time upon the sculpture of an elaborate clock for the Congressional Library. Amory C. Simons, who was born in 1869 at Charleston, South Carolina, and who was a pupil of the Pennsylvania Academy and of Dampt and Puech in Paris, won an honorable mention at the Salon, and again at the Pan-American Exposition for his ingenious " Surprise." Edward Berge received at the Pan-American Exposition a bronze medal for his " Muse finding the Head of Orpheus," and Charles R. Harley was equally honored for his " Pierrot " and " Mother of Sorrows." " The Snake Charmer " of Louis Potter attracted favorable comment at the same exhibition; while his later busts, especially those of " A Tunisian Jewess " and a

"Young Bedouin," are worthy of high praise. A figure of "Lake Superior," by Carl E. Tefft, was particularly noticeable among the decorations of the electric tower at Buffalo. Its grace of line and careful modelling distinguished this work from the majority of its companions. The Director of Sculpture at the Pan-American and the St. Louis fairs has been able to offer, at the latter exposition, still more generous opportunities to young sculptors to show their power. Among those who, through this admirable policy, are coming into prominence, are: James E. Fraser, pupil of the Art Institute of Chicago and of Saint Gaudens, sculptor of "Cherokee Chief"; Gustave Gerlach, a pupil of Karl Bitter, and sculptor of the colossal personification of "Minnesota"; Carl Heber, sculptor of "Indian Territory," and of an admirable nude, entitled "Pastoral"; L. O. Lawrie, pupil of Martiny and Saint Gaudens, sculptor of "South Dakota"; Frank H. Packer, pupil of Martiny and Saint Gaudens, sculptor of "Nebraska"; Antonin Skodik, pupil of Art Students' League, sculptor of "Montana" and two figures for the Varied Industries building; Adolph Weinmann, pupil of Saint Gaudens and Charles Niehaus, sculptor of "Kansas," the group "Destiny of the Red Man," and two figures with shield, for Machinery building; and Bruno Louis Zimm, pupil of Karl Bitter, and sculptor of "North Dakota."

A novel note has been contributed to American sculpture by the "figurines" of Mrs. Bessie Potter Vonnoh, which, though slight, possess a significance quite disproportionate to their size and number. The prompt and cordial recognition which they won from the artist world was a greater surprise to the modest girl who had made them "for fun" than it was to those who had watched her progress. While their analogy to the figurines of Tanagra has often been pointed out, no one traced them to their true inspiration, the tiny bronzes sent to the Columbian Exposition by Prince Paul Troubetskoy, which were exhibited in the Italian section. These remarkable plastic sketches quite captivated Miss Potter, and she forthwith set about "doing Troubetskoys," as she termed her new diversion. Her skill and her artistic independence were sufficient to insure complete originality. The works of the Russian gave the suggestion merely, and the little figures and groups which sprang up in the

2 G

Chicago studio were as much Miss Potter's personal expression as they were indisputably American and of the day. The first tentative experiments were naturally efforts at portraiture — miniature studies of willing friends. Presently these fashionable-looking little personages were compelled to give way to such freer conceptions as " The Duet," " A Girl Dancing," and the very delightful little " Reader."

FIG. 77. — VONNOH: MOTHER AND BABE.

The artist struck a still deeper note in her first " Mother and Babe," and in such themes of tenderness and in the portraits of children she has done her most valuable work. The " Mother and Babe," herewith illustrated (Fig. 77), is a dainty portrait study, a recent production.

Several other women sculptors of New York received their preliminary education at the Art Institute of Chicago. Mrs. Hermon A. MacNeil has done interesting work in ideal subjects as well as in applied sculpture. Her " Foolish Virgin " has deserved the praise which it has received. Miss Helen Mears, for some time Mr. Saint Gaudens's assistant, is now engaged upon a marble figure of Miss Frances E. Willard for the sculpture gallery of the national Capitol. Miss Janet Scudder, whose work reflects Mr. MacMonnies's influence, has been signally honored in Paris, two of her medallion portraits having been purchased by the government for the Luxembourg Gallery. Miss Evelyn Longman, the most recent of these talented women from the West to seek fortune in New York, has enjoyed the benefits of Mr. French's instruction, and will have opportunity to display her skill upon a winged figure of " Victory," which is to surmount the Varied Industries building at the St. Louis Exposition.

Other work is being done for the same exposition by Miss Elsie Ward of Denver, a pupil of Saint Gaudens, and by Miss Enid Yandell of Louisville, Kentucky, who has had considerable experience in such undertakings. At Chicago, in 1893, Miss Yandell was represented by the caryatides of the Women's building and much more worthily by a clever figure of Daniel Boone. At Nashville, in 1897, Miss Yandell was awarded the contract for a colossal " Athena," which stood in front of the Art Palace; and at the Pan-American Exposition she showed the plaster cast of her elaborate " Carrie Brown Memorial Fountain," erected in Providence, Rhode Island, the product of a considerable stay in Paris. In this important work she tried the difficult experiment of a combination of figures of various scales. The result is confusing, but certain features of the struggling group are very fine indeed. There is a back of a noble, Amazon-like woman which would do honor to any of our sculptors. Miss Yandell has made many small figures with admirable skill, and abounds in happy inventions. In this diminutive work and its application to household embellishment Mrs. Clio Bracken has also shown considerable taste. Her " Omar Khayyam Punch Bowl " is said to be very ingeniously conceived.

CHAPTER XXIV

DECORATIVE SCULPTORS AND MEN OF FOREIGN BIRTH

It is a curious fact that the list of architectural sculptors in the United States is made up almost exclusively of men of foreign birth. This is not without its significance and would seem to indicate, not that our sculptors are necessarily more ambitious than their brothers from over the sea, but that they are less endowed with the decorative sense. It is here particularly that inheritance and precedent count for much. In sculpture we have them not, and must look to the children of France and Germany, of Austria and Italy, for the more "musical" expression of the sculptor's art — for such is decoration. From the earliest efforts of Greenough and Powers down to the present time most of our sculpture has been bare and austere, lacking in rhythm and grace of movement as well as in that playfulness of surface treatment which is called sculptural "color," and which is the *fioritura* of the art. When it has been attempted the results have shown, as a rule, no structural development, but rather a veneer of borrowed ornament, through the crudity and inappropriateness of which the plagiarism makes itself but too evident. Latterly a change has been observable; already a few of our sculptors have decked their solid virtues with these external graces, — which are, however, from within, — and it is gratifying to note that these men are not all of foreign birth. Those, however, who make a profession of decorative sculpture, who practise with success the delicate art of beautifying architecture with sculptural adjuncts, are almost without exception men from over the sea, with the schooling of the centuries in their clever hands and fertile brains.

Take, for example, Mr. Philip Martiny, perhaps the most brilliant technician of the group. Mr. Martiny was born in Alsace, France, in 1858, and claims lineal descent from Simone di Martino, an Italian

painter of the Sienese school, who lived in the thirteenth and fourteenth centuries. Beginning his career in the studios of France,
where he worked as a boy, studying under Eugene Dock, Mr. Martiny received the most careful training in the fundamental principles
of his art, and that almost incessant practice which counts for so
much in the mastery of any profession.   Later, coming to the United
States, he became an assistant in the studio of Augustus Saint
Gaudens, where his
native exuberance was
doubtless directed for
a time into paths of
exceptional sobriety.

Mr. Martiny works
with incredible rapid
ity and apparently
with little reflection,
yet with such an in-
stinct for the right
thing, decoratively
considered, that he
seldom fails to pro-
duce a beautiful re-
sult.   His decorations
on the Agricultural
building of the Colum-
bian Exposition made
him known to the
country at large, and
will be recalled with

FIG. 78. — MARTINY: FOUNTAIN OF ABUNDANCE,
PAN-AMERICAN EXPOSITION.

pleasure by all who saw them.   They could scarcely have been
surpassed, and gave to decorative sculpture a higher standard
than it had held before in this country.   Those caryatides and
" Abundances " which, near at hand, seemed made of sharp
grooves and wooden visages, were so admirably adapted to their
positions that they became delightful ornaments when interspersed
among the broad surfaces of the lofty façades.   The vast tympani
at either end of the building were filled merely with two colossal

figures of great beauty of line, and instantly intelligible to the eye.
It was upon the terminal decorations of the roof, however, that Mr.
Martiny's fancy had freest rein.   Perhaps there was overmuch
sculpture there, but which of those groups could one have wished
to spare ?   The ingenious paraphrase of Carpeaux's " Four Quarters
of the Globe " will be remembered for its graceful nude figures, surprisingly simple yet rich in modelling; and the immense groups, which
included horses and cattle, were no less decorative.   But perhaps
most beautiful of all were the very original and yet formal " Seasons "
— draped figures seated back to back, with uplifted arms from which
depended garlands.   From a distance these four figures united to
form a symmetrical bouquet of rich lights and shades, an exquisite
ornament for the pavilions of the great white palace.

Mr. Martiny also did certain decorations of a severer type for the
Columbian Art Palace and for the Art Institute of Chicago.   The
sculpture of the grand staircase in the Library of Congress is his,
and at the Pan-American Exposition of 1901 his " Fountain of
Abundance " (Fig. 78) was one of the most conspicuous decorations.   Slight as is the facial beauty of its central figure, the effect
of the whole from a sufficient distance was charming.   Who but
Martiny could have improvised such a composition so easily!
The arms, it is said, were casts hanging in his studio; they were
attached *sans façon* to the little figure, which was quickly enveloped
in Mr. Martiny's special style of papery drapery.   The head evidently
took no time; then garlands of flowers and garlands of babies were
hung about, and this spontaneous work was complete — at least it
seems as though it must have sprung into being in some such magi-
cal fashion.

Mr. Martiny's novel and very chaste Soldiers' and Sailors' Monument was unveiled in Jersey City in 1899, and consists of a seated
female figure in classic costume, with helmet and sword, offering an
olive branch with outstretched hand.   The abundant drapery is fine,
the pedestal most harmonious, and the total effect of the monument,
though unusual, is strangely impressive.   Among other works of
importance executed by this sculptor are eight figures and a fountain for the residence in New York of Senator William A. Clark of
Montana; two groups for the new Chamber of Commerce, New

York, the central figures of which represent John Jay and Alexander Hamilton; statuary for the Carnegie Library at Washington, D.C.; figures for the Courthouse at Elizabeth, New Jersey; statuary on the Appellate Court building, New York; medallion portraits of Generals Alexander Webb, Hancock, etc., at West Point (Cullom Memorial); statuary and group for the Kunhardt Memorial in the Moravian Cemetery, Grant City, Staten Island; the caryatides for the residence of Charles T. Yerkes, New York; the tympanum over the doors of the memorial chapel in memory of Elliot F. Shepherd, at Scarboro-on-the-Hudson; and a set of bronze doors of elaborate workmanship for Saint Bartholomew's Church, New York, a portion of the Vanderbilt Memorial in which Messrs. Adams and O'Connor have also participated.

FIG. 79. — MARTINY: VICTORY.

Of late Mr. Martiny has given more attention to monumental statuary. His excellent figure of Vice-President Hobart was erected in Paterson, New Jersey, in 1902, and he is now engaged upon a statue of President McKinley for Springfield, Massachusetts. One of his most pleasing designs is his project for a monument to Admiral de Ternay and his men, to be erected at Newport, Rhode Island (Fig. 79). In front of an obelisk a winged figure upon a decorative prow lifts the victor's wreath. In her left hand she holds a trumpet. The movement is powerful yet full of grace; the head is more seriously considered than in most of Mr. Martiny's works; the wind-blown drapery is charmingly effective, — the complete design a union of dignity and decorative elegance.

As a whole Mr. Martiny's work, however spontaneous, is far removed from the emotional. Its value does not depend upon its

deeper significance.   He is not an interpreter nor a devotee of
"character"; he is neither a mystic nor a moralist, and to express
in terms of sculpture the "meaning of life" is no part of his programme.   He is first and last a decorator, a decorator not by chance
or circumstance, but by instinct.   Hence his art, while appealing
little to the imagination, serves its legitimate purpose in delighting
the eye and mind through the poetry of light and shadow and line.
At his best he, of all our sculptors, shows the most highly developed
decorative sense and the most astonishing skill in its expression.
He brings us what we as a nation lack, the gift which France possesses in such prodigal abundance.

Mr. Karl Bitter's contribution to art has been so large that,
although by birth and education a foreigner, he has earned a
high place among American sculptors.   His connection with three
World's Fairs, as the most conspicuous decorator of the first and
the official director of sculpture at the two succeeding ones, — including the Louisiana Purchase Exhibition, in St. Louis, in 1904, —
is in itself enough to emphasize his activity and genius for organization.   He was born in 1867 in Vienna.   At the gymnasium he
absorbed Latin and Greek, and at the Academy of Fine Arts he
found his forte in the study of sculpture.   From the age of sixteen
he made every effort to come to America, but did not receive the
consent of his parents until 1889, when he sailed for New York.
With no other equipment than his technical education, he arrived in the strange land, applied for citizenship, and set to work
as an assistant with a firm of house decorators.   He had neither
friends nor relatives in this country, but soon made the acquaintance of Mr. Richard M. Hunt, the architect, who at once took an
interest in the homeless youth, and later opened to him the door
of opportunity.   However, the young Austrian was by no means
unable to look out for himself.   The very first year of his stay it
was his privilege to compete for one of the gates of Trinity Church,
New York, and, unknown and practically friendless, to win the order
on the merits of his skilful work.   This commission enabled him to
open a small studio in Thirteenth Street, New York, which was soon
exchanged for more commodious quarters farther up-town.   Then
came the Columbian Exposition and Mr. Bitter's larger opportunity.

It will be remembered that the stately Administration building was the work of Mr. Hunt, who, by this time convinced of the young artist's talent, invited him to design the elaborate sculptural decorations which were to embellish its every available space. Mr. Bitter was fully equal to the task and knew it; nor did he hesitate to add to this great undertaking the further responsibility of decorating the Liberal Arts building at the urgent request of its designer, Mr. George B. Post.

Mr. Bitter's work in Chicago was his first introduction to the general public. To most of us those great lawless compositions on the Administration building were curious rather than beautiful, though all recognized the fertility of invention and the skill of the audacious foreigner who threatened to overwhelm the structure with his lightly conceived giants of plaster. He pictured the " Elements Controlled " and the " Elements Uncontrolled," and the zest which he put into these themes, — the latter in particular, — revealed a temperament of singular power and intrepidity, if not a mature taste. The Administration building of the most orderly and carefully considered of all expositions was " enlivened " with cataracts of contorted figures wild as the dreams of Bernini or Puget, — though more immediately related to the nymphs of the Opera House of Vienna, — whose appropriate abode should have been nothing more formal than an aquarium or a grotto at Versailles. The massive groups above were more satisfactory, if less picturesque, while the winged trumpeters fringing the base of the dome had an air of well-ordered elation harmonious with the time and place. With all our natural resourcefulness there were but two, or at most three, native Americans who could have "swung" such work with the easy mastery, the professional *bravura*, that Mr. Bitter showed in nearly every sketch and to a certain extent in the final groups, — those enormous constructions of timber and staff, built up of excelsior and fibre dipped in plaster and chopped into form *à la hachette*.

Later came various notable works and a great mass of decorative material turned out with a rapidity and a profusion which invites the use of the term "commercial." Probably Mr. Bitter would claim no other classification for the larger portion of this copious output, only insisting that it has been good work of its kind. This is cheerfully conceded, nor is there any doubt that much of this wholesale and impersonal production is not only very excellent technically, but of great decorative charm.   If in detail it is of too superficial a character to hold our attention long, being conceived in a lighter mood and designed for another purpose; if it seems too purely a product of intuition and dexterity to merit serious study,—it becomes in mass of the highest importance as a quiet, persistent influence toward the elevation of the standard of American workmanship, and of no less importance in the cultivation of American tatse through familiarity with admirable examples.

FIG. 80.—BITTER: STANDARD BEARER, PAN-AMERICAN EXPOSITION.

A catalogue at hand of Mr. Bitter's works offers material sufficient to fill many pages.   In it are named figures and figure reliefs (some of the latter thirty and forty feet long) for "Biltmore" and other residences of the Vanderbilts, for the homes of C. P. Huntington, John Jacob Astor, and many others.   But still more numerous are his decorations for public buildings, libraries, churches, stores, etc., in most of our principal cities.   Notable among these are the enormous reliefs for the Broad Street station of the Pennsylvania Railroad, at Philadelphia.   The pediment is adorned with a group some fifty feet in length, representing "Mercury and Athena advancing in the Chariot of Civilization."   Below, in the waiting-room, is another vast allegory picturing "The Triumph of Civilization."   Works of such size and intricacy would represent years of toil for the average plodder, even were it possible to imagine his arriving at the suavity and cleverness, the grace and elegance, of these gigantic panels.   It is a part of Mr. Bitter's gift to be able to design for a shopful of assistants and to direct the execution of many things at once.   The sculptural result may not be profound, it may not take hold of one like an individual appeal, it certainly never can clutch at one's heart as do certain works of much less suavity and elegance and grace; but it is a gift indeed to be able to create spontaneously, unweary-ingly, these beautiful things.   To make such a contribution to the charm of our cities is as worthy a work as the other.   After all, the finest thing in the world is to make use of one's special, distinctive gifts to the best advantage.   We should feel grateful to Mr. Bitter for every one of those delightful mantelpieces and friezes, for all the spandrels and cartouches, for the whole army of graceful stone men and women, be they caryatides, evangelists, or bacchantes!

Mr. Bitter has taken an active part in the affairs of the National Sculpture Society, having been for some time a member of the Board of Directors.   When the commissioners of the Pan-Ameri-can Exposition applied for a director of sculpture, he was nomi-nated to that position by the Society.   His administration was an artistic and a financial success.   The total amount expended approached a quarter of a million dollars, which sum kept about thirty-five American artists and over a hundred assistants busy for more than a year.   What is more to the point, it enriched the buildings and grounds of the " City of Light " with a wealth of effective statuary, admirably suited to its purpose.

Whatever criticisms may have been applied to the individual sculptures at Buffalo, there were certain conspicuous features so evidently appropriate, so perfectly adapted to their position, that not a syllable has been uttered against them.   Mr. Bitter's personal contri-bution, the enormous " Standard Bearers " (Fig. 80) of the great py-lons, were among the finest things ever devised for any exposition. One does not require of festal decorations that reserve and inevita-bleness which we demand in permanent monuments.   A rearing horse is an abomination under a portrait figure, yet in these fanciful works the very instability of the pose delighted us.   Mr. Bitter stood his horses almost on end; they fairly sat on their haunches and threw out their feet for balance.   Like the fluttering banner above them, their exuberance filled the spectator with elation; they gave the note of joy to which the whole gala scene was attuned. The construction of these handsome monsters — forty feet in height — was masterful, and they showed a selection of just such details as would be most valuable, and of absolutely no more. It may not be amiss to point out that, for all their restlessness, the fiery steeds did not threaten to walk off their pedestals. While they spurned the ground and seemed ready to mount skyward, like Pegasus, their poise and balance were so perfect that they suggested no catastrophe. They were of a different breed from the imperilled charger of Richmond and Jackson's performing horse in Washington.

In the building of the arch for the Dewey reception in New York Mr. Bitter was one of the leading spirits. Of the four groups on the piers his realistic composition was generally the favorite. It was a stirring conception, a vivid epitome of naval warfare.

We have saved something for the last, as indeed has Mr. Bitter himself — a glimpse of another phase of character and of other aspirations than have been previously attributed to this popular artist. At the second exhibition of the National Sculpture Society, in 1895, Mr. Bitter's bust of Dr. Pepper, provost of the University of Pennsylvania, and his sketch model of a seated figure of the same subject, sounded a new note, a more dignified self-containment and a deeper analysis of character than this sculptor had hitherto attempted. The completed statue, of heroic size, is a gratifying success, and shows beyond its admirable workmanship a subtle union of kindliness and reserve which make it a convincing expression of individuality. It was at the Sculpture Society's exhibition at Madison Square Garden, in November, 1902, however, that Mr. Bitter's deeper nature made most striking revelation of itself. His exhibit consisted of two figures to be placed over a doorway of the Chamber of Commerce of New York, fine plastic forms of great distinction, and — what concerns us more particularly at this point — two very original memorials. These works were not only beautifully modelled, as was to be expected, but had about them an atmosphere of poetic gravity and of pathos quite unfamiliar in Mr. Bitter's sculpture. The Villard Memorial (Fig. 81), the larger of the two, is in the form of a high relief, or, to be more exact, a figure in the round against a large and curiously decorated background. The figure is nude, a powerful, athletic young man reposing beside an anvil and grasping lightly the handle of a sledge-hammer. The head is thrown far back, the lips are parted, as with one who listens to distant music or who falls asleep. The whole attitude is one of complete relaxation after toil. Is it death, or sleep, or merely day-dreaming? The artist has been kind enough not to tell us. He

FIG. 81. — BITTER: VILLARD MEMORIAL.

has conveyed a part of his idea forcibly and without danger of error; he has left to us the privilege of sup-plying the rest, and thereby he has pre-served for us the poetry of his first in-spiration.

A few feet away stood the Hubbard Memorial, inscribed "Thanatos." Again a seated figure lean-ing against a slab of stone, again the head thrown back, the lips parted. But here the resemblance ceases; instead of a nude form, this figure of mysterious mien is amply clothed. Is it a weary mortal who draws the draperies of his couch about him, a panting soul that sweeps off the cerements of life, or a symbol of resurrection — a Lazarus who begs mutely to be "loosed"? The breathlessness, the swaying arms, the grip of the hand, the press-ure of the feet, the tangle of the enveloping shroud give this figure another kind of impressiveness from the awful calm of Saint Gaudens's sibyl. Mr. Bitter's conception is less majestic, but has an intensity which grows upon one. This unknown being, wrapped in its mantle as in one of Vedder's swirls, this groping, unseeing creature, has in its make-up something of the ideal, of the large and the deep, by virtue of which it seems full of significance.   The sculptor must have meant something by it.   What its meaning, each must read for himself.

Another man who has contributed much to the beautifying of our cities is J. Massey Rhind.   While his work is largely architectural, and therefore in a measure foreign to the purpose of this book, he has done several monuments of importance, and not a few of his decorations rise above the level of commercial sculpture.

Mr. Rhind is a Scotchman, and was born in Edinburgh.   He comes of an artistic lineage, both his father and his grandfather having been sculptors, and his brothers still continuing the family tradition in the old country.   The advantages of such early and familiar contact with the profession are easily demonstrable, and it is not surprising to find in Mr. Rhind's earliest works a facility of modelling which might well be the envy of veteran practitioners. Some of this skill was inherited, and much, no doubt, came from the sympathetic training of M. Dalou, the great French sculptor under whom he studied for several years in London and later in Paris. After two years in the latter city he returned to England, where he found immediately an abundance of work; but seeking a larger field, he came to America in 1889, the same year that brought Karl Bitter.

It was exactly the right moment.   Up to that time there had been but little employment for the decorative sculptor in this country; but, with increasing wealth and the knowledge gained from much intercourse with Europe, a change was just then making itself manifest in the character of our buildings, both public and private.   Besides, talents like those possessed by Mr. Rhind and Mr. Bitter create their own demand.   It would be hard to estimate the value of the service of these men and of Mr. Martiny to this country.   Within a few years their labors have elevated most incredibly the standard of architectural sculpture in our chief city and to a certain extent throughout the entire country.

Like Mr. Bitter, Mr. Rhind found his first success in connection with the Astor memorial doors for Trinity Church.   To him was awarded one of the three, on the strength of a beautifully modelled panel depicting the expulsion of Adam and Eve from Paradise. The work was carried through with painstaking enthusiasm and is recognized as a worthy companion to the Niehaus and Bitter portals. Next followed the unique memorial fountain in Albany erected in honor of Senator Rufus King. There may be mentioned also the decorations of the American Surety Company, Broadway and Pine Street, New York, where Mr. Rhind coöperated most happily with the architect, Mr. Bruce Price. The architects, with whom Mr. Rhind is deservedly popular, assert that no one knows better than he how to make sculpture an integral part of the whole design. Mr. Rhind has given this problem particular study, realizing that his own work gains by the harmony. An example of such felicitous union of structure and embellishment is found in the elaborate front of the Alexander Commencement Hall at Princeton, a work which occupied the sculptor some three years.

Other noteworthy examples of Mr. Rhind's art are the bronze doors of the chapel of the General Theological Seminary in Chelsea Square, New York; the "Henry Hudson," "Peter Stuyvesant," "General Wolfe," and "DeWitt Clinton," on the Exchange Court building, Broadway; the "Corning Fountain" at Hartford, Connecticut; a nude figure, "Progress lighting the Way of Commerce," upon the tower of the Montgomery Ward building in Chicago; and, especially noteworthy, the sculptural frieze of the Farmer's Deposit National Bank of Pittsburg, Pennsylvania. He has also produced several statues of public men, among them a "Robert Burns" at Pittsburg, a gigantic "Calhoun" for the South, and portraits of Generals Grant and Sherman at Muskegon, Michigan, of ex-Speaker David B. Henderson at Clermont, Iowa, of H. H. Houston in Fairmount Park, Philadelphia, and of Stephen Girard, also at Philadelphia. The latter figure is one of more than ordinary interest, since it unites with pleasing technic an unusual incisiveness of characterization.

Mr. Isidore Konti came to us, like Mr. Bitter, from Vienna, where he was born in 1862. His preliminary art education was acquired in the Imperial Academy of that city, where these two future Americans worked side by side. Later a fortunate scholarship enabled him to spend two more years in study in Italy. He came to this country in 1892, and worked on the sculpture for the

World's Fair in Chicago, after which, settling in New York, he made a specialty of decorative sculpture for private and public buildings.

Among these works are: a relief on the door of Grace Church, in East Fourteenth Street; two spandrels on the Home Life Insurance building; the interior work in the residence of Elbridge T. Gerry; the group "West Indies" and the spandrels, the "North River" and "East River," for the Naval Arch; and work for the Pan-American Exposition, consisting of four groups for the Temple of Music, — "Heroic Music," "Lyric Music," "Sacred Music," and "Dance Music," — a group, "The Despotic Age," for the esplanade, and different groups of playing children for the Court of Fountains and the Temple of Music. Among Mr. Konti's ideal works may be mentioned the figures, "Inspiration" and "Orpheus," the groups "Pan and Cupid," "Awakening of Spring," and a fountain symboliz-ing "The Brook." The last-named possesses an unusual charm and was one of the few works of pure ideality shown in the exhibition of the National Sculpture Society in 1902. Mr. Konti is always refined, but this coy figure is a veritable embodiment of sinuous grace. Care-fully studying from nature, the artist had nevertheless the exceeding good taste to "cover his tracks," eliminating all offensive realism, all accidents of the individual body, and permitting the figure to stand for just what it is, a beautifully sculptured form. The relation of the statue to its pedestal is delicately adjusted with a sense of line and propor-tion which cannot fail to give pleasure to every eye, and finally the plinth is decorated with what is perhaps the most artistic feature of the entire work, a high relief of swimming babies mixed up with a flotilla of formidable geese. The idea is sufficiently amusing, and the execution is delightful. The little plump bodies and the aggres-sive fowls are not pasted upon the plinth, but grow out of it, and the union is lost in subtle half-tones. From the crown of the fair Undine's pretty head to the water-line of the pedestal, the treatment of the fountain is consistently sculptural. It bespeaks the marble, and its realization in the ultimate material is assured, since the foun-tain was sold on the first day of the exhibition.

It was Mr. Konti's work at the Pan-American Exposition, however, which first attracted particular attention. Though placed so high

above the cornice of the Temple of Music and obscured by heavy gilding, his four groups of "Music" won for the poet-sculptor many friends.
All were massive, but ingeniously composed of several figures in graceful attitudes. "Dance Music" showed a seated youth of lengthy
limb playing the pipes for a maiden and child who danced. "Heroic
Music" was conceived fitly in a large spirit, and represented blind
Homer striking the lyre under the inspiration of a winged muse
who floated serenely above him. Apollo with attendant figures is
probably the most felicitous in arrangement, but "Sacred Music"
(Fig. 82) gives a good idea of the sweetness and charm of Mr. Konti's
imaginings. The upper figure is unfortunately cut off, and is criticised by the violinists as not holding her instrument according to
any earthly method; but the composition as a whole is admirable in
line and in "color," while the sentiment which it breathes is rare
indeed in public decorations of any kind.

Then, as though to defend himself against any charge of effem-
inacy, of over-sweetness, Mr. Konti proceeded to show in another
more monumental work on the esplanade of the Exposition a different
phase of his mental make-up. "The Despotic Age" was as forbid-
ding in sentiment as were those other works delightful. It was just
as good — perhaps better — sculpture, but it breathed a spirit of inexorable domination. Unlike Mr. MacNeil's treatment of the same
subject, this group showed no crowding, no confusion and tumult.
Its very repression made it the more intense. The manner of execution harmonized with the thought. There was power in the lines
and a mute rigidity throughout. Heartless, unbending mastery
was personified by a stern-visaged Cæsar to whose chariot were
yoked three humble captives. A winged fury lashed the trembling forms; the monarch saw them not, nor heeded the plaints of
others chained to the chariot's tail. The conception was most
dramatic, and the group received much applause from Mr. Konti's
colleagues.

A sculptor whose refined art deserves a wider fame than has
come to it is Henry Linder of New York. With a graceful and
sometimes whimsical fancy, he imparts to all that he does a peculiar
charm, distinctly his own, and of genuinely decorative quality.
Whatever he makes, from andirons to sweet-faced Madonnas, bears

2 H

the stamp of his intensely personal point of view ; though expressed with all sorts of captivating circumlocutions and elaborations, it arrives without fail at a very definite decorative effect.   His dainty little busts, the sitting figure, " Music," and " Spring," a project for a small fountain, seen some years ago at one of the exhibitions of the National Sculpture Society, were among the choicest things there,

FIG. 82. — KONTI: SACRED MUSIC, PAN-AMERICAN EXPOSITION.

showing not only invention, but a fine sense of sculptural proprieties. Another German, Rudolph Schwarz, now settled in Indianapolis, does work of a very different character.   Though a comparatively recent arrival, he has devoted himself to the creation of American soldiers.   The groups which he has added to the Indiana State Soldiers' and Sailors' Monument are picturesque and spirited.   Mr. Schwarz won in 1902 the competition for a statue of Governor Pingree of Michigan, for Detroit.   He is also to be represented in the decorations of the St. Louis Exposition.

Other sculptors of foreign birth who, if not exactly making history, are doing their share toward commemorating it, are Louis Amateis and George Zolnay. Their realistic military figures are to be seen in many places, particularly in the South, where they are most popular. Professor Amateis — of the Columbian University, Washington, D.C. — will be remembered as the designer of the monument to the defenders of the Alamo, in Austin, Texas, of a large military memorial at Galveston, Texas, and of the group " El Caney," at the Pan-American Exposition. Mr. Zolnay's name is associated with the statue of Jefferson Davis and with the graceful angel which bends over the tomb of Miss Winnie Davis in Hollywood Cemetery, Richmond, Virginia.

Messrs. Fjelde, Rohl-Smith, and Gelert have ably represented the land of Thorwaldsen in our artistic Congress of Nations. Of these three only John Gelert remains. Mr. Jakob Fjelde was identified with Minneapolis, but died before opportunity came for notable achievement. Mr. Carl Rohl-Smith practised his art successfully in Louisville, Chicago, and Washington. His poorly paid Soldiers' Monument at Des Moines, Iowa, is a gravely grotesque design which was dictated to him by a committee, and his share in it was a long-drawn-out martyrdom, unfortunately perpetuated in bronze. His striking group commemorative of the Fort Dearborn massacre stands in Chicago upon the scene of the bloody event; but his last undertaking, the important Sherman statue, in Washington, was destined to be completed by other hands than his own. It is one of the ironies of fate, that after such hard-fought battles he should have fallen just as victory was in sight. Mr. Gelert's contributions have been largely in the form of architectural adjuncts, as seen at the various expositions. Though he was kept busy for several years in Chicago, peopling parks and squares with Old World celebrities, he has also been prolific in imaginative works. Doubtless the most spontaneous and charming of these was that early group of two nude children playing in the sand, christened " The Little Architects." This pleasing marble has won plaudits and prizes in not a few exhibitions. Other conceptions of a graver nature are, " Thor wrestling with a Bull," " The Struggle for Work," and " Resurrection."

A young Scandinavian whose work gives promise of being interesting is Hendrick Christian Andersen.   His first bust, " The Con-
cierge's Daughter," an essay in tinted sculpture, has a quaint charm
which has been highly appreciated.   Mr. Andersen has done a number
of portraits, two groups, " Serenity " and " Fellowship," and a strange
equestrian statue, executed apparently without models.[1]

Among the best-known of the many clever Italians who ply
their traditional arts in America is the house of Piccirilli, a family of
sculptors and marble-cutters who lead in modern New York the life
of a Florentine household of the Quattrocento.   The great dining
room of the establishment is like an old-time refectory, where five
stalwart sons with their wives and children gather around a kindly,
keen-eyed patriarch.   In the large studios adjoining much work is
completed in marble for various American sculptors; but one of the
sons, Attilio Piccirilli, is already well known in the profession as
the successful competitor for the monument to the dead soldiers and
sailors of the *Maine*, which promises to be one of our best military
memorials.   Mr. Piccirilli has done several well-modelled and exquisitely carved figures, like the " Young Faun " and the " Dancing
Faun," which brought him a silver medal at the Pan-American.   A
younger brother, Furio, has also exhibited a relief portrait of a sister,
carved with much delicacy.

A newcomer, Vicenzo Alfano, a Neapolitan, displayed at the
exhibition of the Sculpture Society of 1902 a fascinating little work
" Tout danse devant le Grand Perturbateur."   The signature was
hardly necessary to demonstrate that it was from a foreign hand.   No
sculptor of American birth has yet attained to the " chic " and dainty
charm of that fantastic relief, in which humanity is shown brought
captive and dancing for the amusement of mischievous, all-powerful
King Eros.   Unlike Mr. Alfano's " Cicerone," also shown at the same
exhibition, this panel made no pretence to monumental gravity, but
in both design and execution it was a *chef d'œuvre* of grace.

Other names of foreign flavor on the roll of the National Sculpture Society or in the catalogues of recent exhibitions, are those of
Henry Baerer, Theodor Bauer, Gutzon Borglum; Caspar Buberl

[1] "A New Sculptor," by Mrs. Schuyler Van Rensselaer, in *Century Magazine*, Vol. LXI,
p. 17.

(deceased); Victor A. Ciani; Louis A. Gudebrod, director of sculpture at the Charleston exhibition; Charles F. Hamann; Albert Jaegers, author of many clever reliefs and excellent busts; Frederic R. Kaldenberg, Paul N. Lachenmeyer, Oscar Lenz, Herman Matzen, Max Mauch, Kasper Mayer, Fernando Miranda, Domingo Mora, Giuseppe Moretti, Maximilian Schwarzott; Joseph Sibbel, sculptor of ecclesiastical statuary; Michael Tonetti, who, aided by his wife, — formerly Miss Mary Lawrence, — made the groups, "Birth of Venus" and "Birth of Athena," at the Pan-American Exposition; Gaetano Trentanove; Albert Weinert, who modelled the group of General Johnson and King Hendrick, in the State Park at Lake George, New York; and Emil Wuertz, whose career was cut short by his untimely death at sea in the tragedy of the *Bourgogne.*

CHAPTER XXV

SCULPTORS OF ANIMALS

In a country as rich in native fauna as the United States it would be strange indeed if a certain number of men should not combine the instincts of the hunter with some form of artistic expression. Such has been the case, and America's group of animal sculptors is worthy of more than passing notice. Aside from the many who have undertaken equestrian statues with varying degrees of success, at least a half-dozen men have shown remarkable aptitude in a more varied field. These are Edward Kemeys, Edward C. Potter, A. Phimister Proctor, Solon H. Borglum, Eli Harvey, and Henry M. Shrady. Paul Bartlett also has done work which puts him in the front rank of our sculptors of animals.

Mr. Kemeys leads the list, not only chronologically, but by virtue of his achievements. No American has done more to record the life of mountain and plain, and his works have justly enjoyed a great popularity. He was born in Savannah, Georgia, in 1843. His parents, who were Northerners, removed soon after to New York City, where he received his education. His natural gift for art was not at first granted an opportunity to develop, and on leaving school he went to work in the iron business. This he relinquished at the outbreak of the Civil War, to enlist in the Federal army, and while hostilities continued he saw constant duty. His intelligent service was rewarded by successive promotions, bringing him ultimately to the rank of captain of artillery. He took part in the engagements before Richmond in 1862. At the close of the war he was employed on the civil engineering corps of Central Park, New York, and while there made his début as a sculptor. He made a specialty of Indians and American wild animals, spending much time in the West studying them from life. In 1878 he exhibited at

FIG. 83. — KEMEYS: PANTHER AND CUBS.

the Paris Salon his group, " Bison and Wolves." Returning to New York the following year, he produced in rapid succession his well-known works: the " Still Hunt," in Central Park, New York; the " Wolves," Fairmount Park, Philadelphia; " Panther and Deer," " Raven and Coyote." In 1887 he modelled the colossal head of a bison for the new Omaha Bridge of the Union Pacific Railroad. In 1892 he went to Chicago, executing there a number of large groups for the Columbian Exposition. During his residence of eight years in Chicago he modelled the large bronze lions in front of the Chicago Art Institute building, an Indian figure for Champaign, Illinois, and numerous small bronzes for private collections.

Self-trained as he is and indifferent to the methods of other men, Mr. Kemeys makes no pretence of clever technic. One scrutinizes his work in vain for those passages of beautiful modelling which form the secondary charm of Barye's little masterpieces. He seems to have found a fierce pleasure in giving us the bare facts, and in stopping abruptly when his story is told. He loses much thereby, since his interpretations of nature do not always win one back in search of new discoveries; but, on the other hand, this summary, impressionistic treatment has its own particular appeal. It conveys with an element of rugged forcefulness a sense of movement which none but a master can express by means of careful modelling. Mr. Kemeys knows his subjects thoroughly — one is almost tempted to say instinctively. He has studied them alive and dead, and has dissected every kind of four-footed creature. He is too much the artist, however, too intense a lover of life, to sacrifice, even to science, the larger truth. Hence he has avoided that danger which Ruskin points out, of "substituting in our thoughts the neatness of mechanical contrivance for the pleasure of the animal." "The moment," continues Mr. Ruskin, "we reduce enjoyment to ingenuity and volition to leverage, that instant all sense of beauty ceases." This mistake Mr. Kemeys has never made. It is safe to say that no American artist has more truly epitomized the spirit of the animal. Particularly in rendering the moods of creatures of the cat tribe is he almost epigrammatic (Fig. 83), while his bears, their "vast limbs crooked with power," are in more senses than one irresistible, whether pictured in the serious occupations of their existence, or enlivened with that "touch of terrific comedy" which they take on so readily.

In a most appreciative article, written as long ago as 1884, Mr. Julian Hawthorne expressed admirably the significance of Mr. Kemeys's art, in which one finds, "not merely, nor chiefly, the accurate representation of the animal's external aspect, but what is vastly more difficult to seize and portray — the essential animal character or temperament which controls and actuates the animal's movements and behavior. Each one of Mr. Kemeys's figures gives not only the form and proportions of the animal according to the nicest anatomical studies and measurements, but is the speaking embodiment of profound insight into that animal's nature, and knowledge of its habits. . . . Here is an artist who understands how to translate pose into meaning, and action into utterance, and to select those poses and actions which convey the broadest and most comprehensive idea of the subject's prevailing traits."[1] If we put ourselves back in the time when this was written, eliminating all that has been done in American sculpture since that year, we can begin to realize how much Mr. Kemeys's sturdy art has meant in the national evolution. Apparently, outside of equestrian statues,

[1] "American Wild Animals in Art," *Century Magazine*, Vol. VI, p. 214.

there is record of just two native animals sculptured in the United States before Mr. Kemeys began his work, the one being the panther in Henry K. Brown's early group, the "Indian and Panther," and the other the dog which Mr. Brown's pupil, J. Q. A. Ward, modelled, some years later, as a travelling companion for his "Indian Hunter." Hence Mr. Kemeys's contribution has not only the twofold value of

Fig. 84. — POTTER: FARM HORSE, COLUMBIAN EXPOSITION.

its own intrinsic worth and of historical record, preserving, as Mr. Hawthorne says, in permanent and beautiful form the vivid figures of a wild fauna which is destined within a few years to vanish altogether, but it has a third significance of perhaps greater import than either of these in the slow unfolding of a national art: he was one of the first to see and appreciate the immediate world about him, to recognize the artistic possibilities of our own land and time. By this keen intuition and the use he has made of it Mr. Kemeys has shown himself a true artist.

It is probable that no American sculptor knows the horse quite so well, structurally, as does Mr. Edward C. Potter, born November 26, 1859, at New London, Connecticut. Several have shown great aptitude for equestrian statuary: Brown, Ward, Saint Gaudens, Mac-Monnies, and Niehaus — to name but a few of the successful designers of large works ; but most experienced of all in this particular field is Mr. French's old-time pupil and all-time colleague.

Mr. Potter's first prominence was due to his collaborations with Mr. French at Chicago in 1893, where their Columbus Quadriga and other groups were among the most admired of the many decorations. No more beautiful quadriga has been sculptured in modern times than the imposing group called the "Apotheosis of Columbus," which crowned the great colonnade misnamed the "Peristyle." The noble horses were led, two and two, by maidens whose flying draperies contributed movement and color, while the decorative effect, as well as the originality of the work, was accentuated by youthful standard-bearers, who served as outriders. In these latter features Mr. Potter showed his ability with the human figure as well as with the horse; the picturesque little squires rode well and had genuine charm. However, to most visitors the colossal quadriga, lifted sixty feet in the eastern sky, was but an "effect," — a small fraction of vaster effects which bewildered the eyes from all sides. Far more intimate and more readily appreciated were the great four-footed creatures which, with their attendant figures, formed the immediate decorations of the lagoon within the Court of Honor (Fig. 84). Here were draught horses of massive build and oxen of tremendous girth, sculptured as such animals never had been done before in this country. The accompanying figures, representing a farmer, a negro teamster, an Indian woman, and a classical version of America, were the work of Mr. French, and it may be said that two men have seldom joined forces more harmoniously for a common artistic result. The evident truth of these imposing groups, coupled with their simplicity and dignity, made them great favorites. The surging crowds may not have realized how good they were as sculpture, but their intrinsic beauty appealed to all.

Since the days of the World's Fair Mr. Potter has been kept busy, most of the time in collaboration with Mr. French. Their

" General Grant" in Fairmount Park, Philadelphia, their " Washing-ton "(Fig. 48), in Paris and Chicago, and their " General Hooker" in Boston have been described elsewhere. Mr. Potter has not re-stricted himself, however, to animal sculpture nor to partnership enterprises. His delightful little " Sleeping Faun" (Fig. 85) is in the Art Institute of Chicago. A well-conceived " Fulton" bears his signature in the circle of bronze dignitaries of the Congressional Library dome, and his " Governor Blair" of Michigan stands in admirable repose before the state Capitol at Lansing, a model of sober portraiture, on a pedestal no less deserving of mention. Mr. Potter's equestrian statue of General Slocum on the battlefield of Gettysburg, appearing coincidently with Mr. MacMonnies's inter-pretation of the same commander, serves to illustrate the different points of view of two skilful men. Mr. Potter's " General Slocum" is considered a striking portrait. The soldier sits at rest on his charger in an easy, well-poised attitude, both horse and rider being quiet but alert, as if awaiting the moment of action. There is no more impressive sculpture upon the famous battlefield.

Among the gifted men who found their way to Chicago during the busy days of the building of the World's Fair was Mr. Phimister Proctor, who was at that time quite unknown to fame. Full of enthusiasm, he did his best and won prompt recognition, which led to his sharing with Hermon A. MacNeil the initial scholarship of the Rinehart fund. This scholarship, which was at first supposed to represent a single year's stay abroad, proved to be for an indetermi-nate period, and the one year was lengthened into a second and then into two more, since which time Mr. Proctor has followed his pro-fession in New York.

Mr. Proctor's father is a Highland Scotchman and his mother a native of New York State. Their son was born in Ontario, Canada, in 1862. He had reached the age of five when the family removed to Des Moines, Iowa, where they remained for several years. Like many another, the future artist showed his bent and ability while still a mere child. There in Des Moines, almost without guidance, he began drawing and made his earliest essays in modelling. From the first he had a definite idea of becoming an artist. The removal of his family to Denver gave the deciding impetus to his life. Here he had his first opportunity of climbing the mountains and seeing wild animals in their rocky fastnesses. This life had a wonderful attraction for him, and many a day did he spend in hunting and in making studies of animals, living and dead. Practice soon developed him into a good marksman. He was thirteen years of age when he killed his first deer, but the great day of his youth was when, at sixteen, while hunting entirely alone, he encountered and despatched successively a large grizzly bear and a bull elk. This was enough to give him great local renown, as well as to confirm his passion for the chase. With his rifle and his no less inseparable sketch-book, he spent all of his vacations in these profitable wanderings. For weeks at a time he would lose himself in the forests and amid the peaks of the Rockies, seeing no human being, but driven out by a wild enthusiasm and learning by heart the mountains'

FIG. 85. — POTTER: SLEEPING FAUN, ART INSTITUTE, CHICAGO.

fauna. No place in the world has to him quite the attraction of those scenes of his youth. In Chicago, in New York, and even in Paris, he is ever sighing for his " happy hunting-grounds."

In 1887 Mr. Proctor had made so much advance in his art that he realized his need of better training. He believed then, as now, that in order to model wild animals one must study them in their native haunts, but he also appreciated the fact that no great artist was ever entirely " self-made." There is too much to learn, and even genius needs guidance. Happily the way was open. There was a convenient ranch to sell, and also an interest in a mine. With the proceeds Mr. Proctor went to New York and was speedily enrolled in the classes of the National Academy of Design. Here, and later in the Art Students' League, he worked with an earnestness which won the respect of comrades and teachers alike. It was the huntsman's ardor harnessed down and concentrated. The keen eye and ready hand with which " grizzly " and cougar had coped in vain were equal to the new task.

It was the Columbian Exposition which brought Mr. Proctor into prominence. His excellent training had been just in time. How well he executed the important decorations intrusted to him will be long remembered. Few things, indeed, in the entire Exposition were more interesting and impressive than those great motionless creatures, the native American animals as sculptured by Proctor and Kemeys. After the close of the World's Fair Mr. Proctor moved to New York, where he did a number of fascinating little bronzes. His time, however, was largely taken up in work for other sculptors, the horse for Saint Gaudens's " Logan " being in great part the young sculptor's production.

Then came the unexpected and very flattering award of the Rinehart scholarship, and the voyage to Europe. While Mr. MacNeil was sent to Rome, Mr. Proctor elected to go to Paris, where he remained for five years studying, not with an " animalist," as might have been expected, but with Puech and Injalbert. Mr. Proctor knew exactly what he needed. It was not animal structure and comparative anatomy as taught at the Jardin des Plantes, but the charm and variety of technic, which these other men have at their finger-tips. Moreover, Mr. Proctor had no idea of being classified as merely a sculptor of animals. He has never failed to " decorate " his groups with human figures whenever possible, sometimes with problematic success, it must be acknowledged, but later with an easy mastery born of sincere and intelligent study.

The " Indian Warrior " (Fig. 86) proves that he is now fully equal to the difficult problem of the human body. This admirable group is the most important of the small bronzes which he has given us. His " Bison " shows evidence of the sculptor's close observation and acute sense of the animal character. Contrasting with it is his timid " Fawn " — a product of the World's Fair period — and distinctly humorous is his jolly little bear frightened by the sudden apparition of a tiny, long-eared rabbit. These last two, though so small, are really distinguished in their expressive workmanship. The " Striding Panther " (Fig. 87) is a powerful work, which reveals throughout its sinuous length the knowledge and research of its creator.

Mr. Proctor ended his term of scholarship rather abruptly in order to undertake an important though ephemeral work, that of the great quadriga which crowned the portico of the United States pavilion at the Paris Exposition of 1900. The subject chosen was " The Goddess of Liberty on the Chariot of Progress." Of course it did not make very much difference what the name of the figure was, so that she looked stately and that her steeds were picturesque and fiery! All of this was admirably accomplished. It is not easy to make anything very original out of a quadriga, but Mr. Proctor succeeded in varying the well-worn theme with figures of running youths on either side of his rampant horses. This offered a novel and decorative silhouette and, above all, was full of life and motion. The effect from the river was very fine, and likewise from the Pont des Invalides, as far as it could be seen ; but it may be remembered that just as one approached near enough to enjoy the details an imperti- nent projection of the Turkish building shut off the view. The group was counted so successful that it was brought to this country and happily employed — four times over — in the decoration of the pediments of the Ethnological building at Buffalo.

The American exhibit of sculpture at the Paris Exposition of 1900 was in evidence from the moment one walked through that singular main entrance on the Place de la Concorde. For there, keeping guard at the gate, stood the outposts of Mr. Proctor's menagerie, his well-known panthers, of Prospect Park, Brooklyn. These great crea- tures stand with heads high lifted and are almost Egyptian in their impressiveness. In them the sculptor has done justice to one of our most beautiful quadrupeds, while the increase in size adds majesty to grace. The strangeness of the pose gives one a little shock at first, as do all artistic treatments which are " original "; but we are speedily converted to the sculptor's way of thinking. These mighty felines of the uplifted heads give another proof of Mr. Proctor's thorough knowledge of his subject, for he tells us that the attitude is one which he has often seen the wild animal take when startled. One cannot but feel a real gratitude for these new contributions to American art, contributions as novel and personal as they are powerful.

An interesting member of this group of nature worshippers is Mr. Solon H. Borglum, a genuine product of the West, who unites in his creations the untamed freedom of the frontier with the tender-

FIG. 86. — PROCTOR: INDIAN WARRIOR.

ness of a true artist. Mr. Borglum's groups have sometimes the accidental look of fragments of rock or of twisted ingots of melted metal, but they are sure to reveal somewhere the caressing touches of a trained and intelligent hand. They are a new and enthusiastic manifestation of the myriad-sided life of this vast country, significant and important, and couched in terms so sculptural as to seem at first uncouth, yet having by birthright more of nature and more of art than it is often given to a sculptor to put into similar efforts.

Born in Ogden, Utah, in 1868, — the son of a one-time wood-carver of Denmark, transformed into an American physician, — Mr. Borglum's youth was spent in the neighborhood of Fremont, Nebraska, where his father's practice led him over a wide stretch of prairie country among scattered whites and Indian villages. Thus in these long excursions which he often shared, and later in the more serious business of a cattle ranch, the boy's life was spent largely in the saddle; his schooling was that of the great "out doors." When a mere child he was as much at home on his pony as most boys are on their feet, and could throw the lasso with skill. He was "an integral part of the rough life around him," but yet an artist at heart. The visit of an elder brother, a painter of some prominence, turned his thoughts in the direction of his future unknown work, but he was already twenty-six years of age when this suggestion suddenly appealed to him with irresistible force. Without instruction he had drawn a little, as the work of the ranch permitted, his favorite subjects being the cattle and horses about him — the principal features of life in that part of the world. He sold his ranch, and, instead of going east, rather oddly drifted westward to the home of another brother in the Sierra Madre Mountains of California. Later he painted a portrait, and studied horses on a ranch near Los Angeles, then opened a "studio" in Santa Ana, where he taught painting one day in each week, roaming the mountains the rest of the time. Later it occurred to him to seek an art school, and arriving in Cincinnati, in the autumn of 1895, with a capital of $64, an oil stove, and a blanket, he established himself for study. The little room which he hired was like a prison to him, but he found light and air in a large livery stable near by, and there he spent most of his time outside of school hours. His work in the drawing classes

21

of the Museum school was faithful; that in the stable was more rapid and enthusiastic, for he modelled there a statuette of a horse pawing a dead companion, supposably lying on the plains, which won him a special prize. The following year a scholarship and prize were easily won by his unique display of seventeen different studies of horses, and in 1897 he was enabled to go to Paris. However homesick the

FIG. 87. — PROCTOR: STRIDING PANTHER.

traveller may be in a foreign land, equine language is everywhere the same, and Mr. Borglum solaced his lonely hours with a study, " Lassoing Wild Horses," which he made in one of the large stables of the city. This group and another horse formed his exhibit at the Salon. The following year he undertook his most ambitious work, a large group, " Stampede of Wild Horses," which, with " The Lame Horse," brought him an honorable mention at the Salon of 1899, and was afterward placed in the centre of the United States pavilion at the Paris Exposition of 1900, where his work brought him a silver medal. A similar recompense was his at Buffalo in 1901 for a re-markable exhibit of twelve little bronzes and marbles, including the two herewith illustrated.

It cannot be claimed that all of Mr. Borglum's ideas are as artistic as these here presented. He is not infallible in his intui-tions; several of his groups show a mistaken effort to depict rapid motion, and some are far from beautiful in line or composition. But all have significance; all have a rude primitive strength and a kind of impressionistic generalization which subordinates details to the intense expression of the artist's one thought. In such work as " The Last Round-up," " Our Slave," and " On the Border of White Man's Land " (Fig. 88), Mr. Borglum has hit upon a very large and impressive treatment which is distinctly sculptural in its inspiration; while in the tiny "Burial on the Plains" (Fig. 89) there is a mysterious emotional note which has been touched by few indeed of our sculptors, a sentiment that might easily have been dissipated by a more insistent technic. Mr. Borglum's work is only begun, but it gives promise of a new and virile interpretation of the magnificent "epic of the West"; of an art of national flavor, yet distinctly individual, which will be enjoyed long after the cowboys have followed the wild red men over the "long trail" into the dim land of legend and song.

In the nature of things the lives of our sculptors of animals have been more varied and picturesque than those of most men of the profession; the large number of these specialists are Westerners by birth or adoption, and many are still comparatively young men. The youngest, however, of the group, a man of thirty-two years, has never been a hunter nor even visited the "high country," has had no training outside of the "Zoo," nor even a struggle for recognition; yet his life offers the most dramatic career of them all. Mr. Henry M. Shrady, who recently won the government competition for the $250,000 monument at Washington, was in 1899 an employé of the Central Match Company of New York, without thought of becoming a sculptor. Born in 1871, the son of a physician of artistic bent, the young man's life was that of the well-to-do; his preparation for a business career was completed by a college course at Columbia University, where he graduated in 1894. His office work allowed him some leisure, and on his way home afternoons he had a habit of stopping before a fancier's window and making sketches in a note-book of the dogs and cats he saw there. He also taught himself to paint, and a portrait of a fox-terrier, submitted without his knowledge, was accepted and hung at an exhibition of the National Academy of Design. Turning to modelling and working from memory of his saddle horse, Mr. Shrady next constructed his panoramic little group of "Artillery going into Action," an ingenious work composed of six horses and as many soldiers in spirited movement. This first attempt found favor in the eyes of a dealer in Russian bronzes, who reproduced it and suggested further work to the amateur sculptor for their mutual benefit. Two small bronzes, a "Moose" and a "Buffalo," the result of numerous visits to the Zoölogical Garden in Bronx Park, attracted the attention of Mr. Karl Bitter, who proposed their enlargement for the Pan-American Exhibition at Buffalo. The older sculptor offered Mr. Shrady a part of his studio, and helped him over the difficulties of an unknown process so effectively that the two animals, nine and eight feet high, were completed in staff in six weeks. They were counted very successful, and were reproduced several times for the embellishment of various bridges on the Exposition grounds.

Meantime Mr. Shrady's later effort, " The Empty Saddle," had attracted attention, and on the strength of it he was invited to participate in a competition for a statue of Washington for Brooklyn. Mr. Shrady's model was the successful one. The statue is good sculpture though tending toward the picturesque. It is a question whether an accidental effect suggestive of wintry blasts is not better suited to a statuette than to a work of monumental importance. " Washington at Valley Forge," wrapped in a storm-swept overcoat, would have its local significance if placed on the site of the historic camping-ground, but it is rather too specific to give the larger view of the great general. One cannot help thinking that there will be certain days in July and August when the shivering hero will be something of a solecism. But this is not the sculptor's fault; he has produced an admirable version of the allotted theme, a model of broad, simple handling, in which the subject dominates its every part.

Apparently it was written that this sane, industrious young man should know nothing but success, though attempting the most audacious and improbable things. He now entered seriously the competition for the Grant monument to be erected opposite the White House, the most expensive sculptural work which the government has thus far undertaken. Mr. Shrady stood first in the preliminary test, and was invited, with Mr. Niehaus, to enlarge his model for further consideration. In the end his design — made in collaboration with Mr. Edward Pearce Casey, architect — was accepted with enthusiasm, not only by the military men, but by the sculptors, Messrs. Saint Gaudens and French, who were consulted by the monument commission. So far as one can judge from the reproductions, their choice will give popular satisfaction. If Mr. Shrady

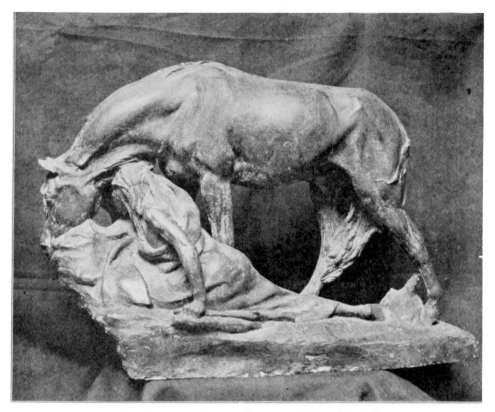

FIG. 88. — BORGLUM: ON THE BORDER OF WHITE MAN'S LAND.

succeeds in preserving in the larger work the monumental qualities of his study (the repose and unconventionality of his Grant, who sits his vigorous steed as if reviewing an endless column of troops) he will achieve a notable triumph. The long stone terrace from which the massive pedestal rises is actually to be employed as a reviewing stand, and there is something which appeals to one's imagination in the thought of that towering effigy presiding on such occasions. Large pedestals at either end of the terrace will support colossal groups, showing cavalry and artillery in action. Here again Mr. Shrady will confront certain of the most difficult problems in sculpture. In his sketch model of " Artillery coming to a Halt," he has chosen the best possible moment, and avoided with fine taste the two pitfalls of bald realism and unintelligible generalization. The evolution of this important work will be watched with keen interest.

Mr. Eli Harvey devotes himself almost exclusively to animals of the cat tribe. His " Rampant Jaguar," modelled at the Jardin des Plantes in Paris, was seen at the Salon of 1898 and later at the Pan-American Exposition, where the sculptor exhibited also a "Lion Roaring," "Lion Cubs," and bas-reliefs. At the exhibit of the National Sculpture Society of 1902 Mr. Harvey was represented by certain of the foregoing, and still more prominently by two "Sentinel Lions," adaptations for architectural purposes. Mr. Harvey was born in Ogden, Ohio, in 1860, and studied at the Cincinnati Museum and later with Frémiet.

An attempt to classify our American sculptors is difficult and must appear somewhat arbitrary. Most of these animal sculptors are well-trained modellers of the human figure, and they are put here merely because of distinguished success in a more limited field. Mr. H. K. Bush-Brown practises all forms of sculpture, being as well known for his decorations as for his portraits; but so decided is his penchant for animal sculpture, so conspicuous his superiority in this department — perhaps a taste derived from his uncle, Henry Kirke Brown — that he may well be considered in this chapter. He was born in Ogdensburg, New York, in 1857, and educated at Suglar's School, Newburgh, New York. He studied drawing at the National Academy of Design, and modelling with his sculptor-uncle, after which he spent the years from 1886 to 1890 in Paris and Italy. He first made himself known to the larger public through his group, "The Buffalo Hunt," exhibited at the Columbian Exposition. This was a realistic representation of one of the tragedies of the plains, and showed, not only a precise knowledge of the two — or shall we not say, three — animals involved, but a considerable amount of creative energy and sustained effort. Less picturesque and illustrative and more sculptural are Mr. Bush-Brown's later works: his equestrian statues of General George S. Meade and of General John F. Reynolds, both at Gettysburg. As to the thoroughness of the sculptor's knowledge of animal anatomy and his mastery of technic, photographs are insufficient data; but these figures show satisfactory proportions and significant attitudes, while the "General Meade," at least, has an air of distinction and of monumental dignity. Our country offers few equestrian statues more happily conceived than this of the quiet, resourceful commander. Other works from this artist's hands are: a statue of Justinian on the Appellate Court building, New York; "Commander Hall," on the Naval Arch; a group representing "Truth," at the Pan-American Exposition; a large memorial tablet for the Union League Club of Philadelphia (a bronze relief some eight by twelve feet in size, showing the departure of the troops presided over by a winged figure); sculptural decorations for the Court of Records, New York; and many busts and reliefs. Mr. Bush-Brown has also done good service in the cause of munici-

pal art, having written and lectured frequently upon this and kindred subjects.

Many others have made interesting excursions into the field of animal sculpture. One of the most gifted of the number is Mr. Frederick G. Roth, whose work at the Pan-American Exposition attracted much favorable notice. Mr. Roth is a young man, born in Brooklyn in 1872. He enjoyed the somewhat exceptional advantages of Vienna, having studied there for a time with Professor Hellmer. His

FIG. 89. — BORGLUM: BURIAL ON THE PLAINS.

contribution to the art exhibit proper at Buffalo was slight, consisting merely of his ingenious little bronze of the "Elephant and Trainer." He was represented on the grounds, however, by three groups of excellent craftsmanship: "Resting Buffaloes," "Stallion and Groom," and, more notably, by that unusual work so readily recalled, the "Roman Chariot Race," a quadriga in violent motion, the flying steeds swinging around the sharp curve of the "meta," the chariot wheels in the air. Whether so tumultuous a motive is a fit theme for sculpture is a question apart; it is certain that Mr. Roth handled

the problem in a masterful way and produced a result that, from
many points of view, was interesting and even impressive.   From a
man of such originality and technical skill much may be expected.
Mr. Roth is at present engaged, like so many of the younger men,
upon decorative groups for the St. Louis Exposition.

Mr. Frederic Remington has also been tempted to carry certain of
his illustrations over into another medium, and it must be confessed
that, while they remain illustrations, this clever artist seems as
much at home in one form of expression as in the other.   Mr.
Remington is not an interpreter, nor is he likely ever to conceive
a theme sculpturally; but his dashing compositions not only picture
with much skill the machinery and paraphernalia of four-footed loco-
motion, but occasionally suggest somewhat of the spirit of the
centaur life of the West.   His " Broncho Buster " and "Wounded
Bunkie" were exhibited at the Pan-American Exposition.

CHAPTER XXVI

PRESENT–DAY SCULPTORS OF BOSTON AND PHILADELPHIA

THE withdrawal of Thomas Ball from Boston, in 1865, made way for his young pupil, Martin Milmore, whose early death left the field in turn to the versatile Dr. Rimmer and Truman H. Bartlett. Neither of these interesting men made large contribution to monumental sculpture, but both did much to quicken the artistic life of the city. Mr. Bartlett has held a high ideal of his profession, and his work as a teacher has had a wide influence which his writings and lectures have still further extended. He has done considerable decorative modelling for reproduction in terra-cotta. His most important public work is his "Horace Wells" in the State House grounds at Hartford, Connecticut. The Boston Museum of Fine Arts contains a few works by Francis Dengler, a young sculptor who was born in Cincinnati in 1853, and died in Boston in 1879. After some study abroad he was called to the Museum School as a teacher, where, although death came so early, he left a record of great usefulness. His group of playing children, entitled "Caught," is not only cleverly modelled, but shows a genuine apprehension of the requirements of sculptural grouping. Another name long associated with the artistic and intellectual life of Boston was that of Cyrus Cobb, a cultivated gentleman who possessed some talent for sculpture. Daniel C. French was likewise associated for a period with Boston, since his home and studio were for several years at Concord.

Longest established in Boston of the younger generation of sculptors is Henry Hudson Kitson, who was born at Huddersfield, England, in 1865. Mr. Kitson's art education was acquired to some extent in the studio of his elder brother, Samuel J. Kitson, also of Boston, and in the École des Beaux-Arts, Paris. Continuous bad health has limited Mr. Kitson's direct production, but he is the author of a number of important works, while his influence is felt through the achievements of several talented pupils. His delightful bronze, "The Music of the Sea" (Fig. 90), was modelled in Paris in 1883, and gives proof of the early talent of its author. It is an unusually happy conception, wrought with charming spontaneity, and nevertheless kept well within the bounds of legitimate sculpture. Among Mr. Kitson's public works are the "Minute-Man" at Lex-

ington, Massachusetts, a military figure at Framingham in the same state, and a "Farragut" in Boston. He has received a number of medals and decorations.

Mrs. Kitson, formerly Miss Theo Ruggles, was the most gifted of Mr. Kitson's pupils. Her first exhibits of importance were at the Columbian Exposition, where she showed four works, — two busts and two small studies of the nude. She received an honorable mention at the Paris Exposition of 1889, and a similar distinction at the Salon of the follow-

FIG. 90. — KITSON: MUSIC OF THE SEA,
BOSTON MUSEUM OF FINE ARTS.

ing year. Mrs. Kitson is one of the three women members of the National Sculpture Society. Her talent is robust, and she attacks fearlessly the problems of monumental statuary. Her "Volunteer," erected in 1902 as a soldiers' monument at Newburyport, Massachusetts, has been justly applauded, and will be reproduced as the Massachusetts monument upon the battlefield of Vicksburg. In the presence of this spirited and ably composed work one is almost compelled to qualify the somewhat sweeping assertion that no woman has as yet modelled the male figure to look like a man.   If not a powerful man, the " Volunteer " is at least a most satisfactory representation of adolescent youth.   Mrs. Kitson's statue of Esek Hopkins, the first admiral of the American navy, may be seen at Providence, Rhode Island, and is a simple and forceful interpretation of the subject.

Another member of the group of young men who serve the cause in a double capacity is Bela L. Pratt, sculptor and teacher in the Boston Museum School of Fine Arts.   Since he is less known to fame than some of his metropolitan colleagues, it might be surmised that his whole energy has been concentrated in the fulfilment of his duties as an instructor — a field in which he has met with gratifying success.   But the saying that "the busiest people have the most time to do things" has more of logic than of paradox in it, and Mr. Pratt's professional achievement needs no apology.   Despite the demands of the school upon his time and his strength, the list of works accomplished by his unaided hands in the ten years from 1893 to the present time is a long one.   Few have been large or spectacular, but all have been wrought with skill and with conscience; and the sum total is one that the young sculptor may well review with satisfaction.

Mr. Pratt was born at Norwich, Connecticut, in 1867.   He may be counted a representative New England product, since his ancestors have lived in that region for two hundred years.   He modelled and drew at home when a child, and at the age of sixteen entered the Yale School of Fine Arts, where he studied under Professors Niemeyer and Weir.   In 1887 he entered the Art Students' League of New York, continuing there his studies under Saint Gaudens, Elwell, Chase, and Kenyon Cox.   Mr. Pratt enjoyed for a time the privilege of working in Saint Gaudens's studio, and upon his advice went, in 1890, to Paris, where he studied under Chapu and Falguière.   He had the gratifying and remarkable experience of entering the same year the Ecole des Beaux-Arts at the head of his class.   While in school he received three medals and two prizes. Returning to the United States in 1892, Mr. Pratt busied himself at once with important decorations for the World's Fair.

The commission for two colossal groups on the Water Gate of the so-called Peristyle, at Chicago, gave Mr. Pratt his first opportunity, and in the sketch models he struck perhaps his highest note. They showed a sense of mass, of sculptural fitness, and likewise of color, which suggested the influence of Michael Angelo, but it was an inspiration only, and the models were as distinctly personal as they were sustained. That the ultimate works were less effective is readily comprehensible by those acquainted with the rapid and sometimes unintelligent methods of execution employed in the emer-

FIG. 91. — PRATT : BISHOP BROOKS.

gencies of such vast enterprises. It was no fault of Mr. Pratt's if the groups which the public saw had lost something of the initial spirit which had so impressed the artists upon first view of the small models.

Mr. Pratt's record of industry in Boston begins with a medallion in low relief — the first of a long series of similar works, all very cleverly handled, and generally of great charm of composition. In 1895 and 1896 he was kept busy with his share of the decorations of the new Congressional Library: a figure, "Philosophy," in the rotunda, six large spandrel figures over the main entrance, and four medallions, representing the "Four Seasons," in the ceiling of one of the large halls. In the reliefs particularly was Mr. Pratt's contribution of great value, the "Seasons" being among the most interesting of all the sculptured decorations of the Library. The year 1896 saw also the birth of an ideal "Victory" for the battleship *Massachusetts* and the achievement of two excellent busts. The following year was devoted in large measure to the modelling and execution in marble of a recumbent figure of Dr. Coit of St. Paul's School, Concord, New Hampshire. This work was given an honorable mention at the Paris Salon of 1897, where it was followed the next year by a graceful if somewhat Gallic "Orpheus mourning Eurydice," which Mr. Pratt modelled in Paris under the guidance of M. Falguière. In 1899 he made the Brown memorial tablet for Cornell University and the bronze portrait bust of Phillips Brooks for Brooks House, Harvard University (Fig. 91), an admirable representation of the great divine's massive and unique personality. In 1900 he produced a portrait bust of Dr. Shattuck for St. Paul's School, Concord, New Hampshire; the Avery memorial bust for Groton, Connecticut; a bronze group for the United States battleship *Alabama*, and the marble study of a young girl, to which reference will be made later.

Mr. Pratt's contributions to the Pan-American Exposition were numerous, and certain of them of great beauty. A winged figure in particular, for the Liberal Arts building, was one of the most graceful works on the grounds. The groups, however, on the same building, lacked mass, and the two large, detached groups of Floral Wealth, "Blossom" and "Fruition," showed deficiencies in sculptural conception which were disappointing to those who remembered Mr. Pratt's achievements at a former exposition. These shortcomings could scarcely be laid to the charge of the machine modellers who did the enlarging; they were inherent in the composition. The misfortune lay largely in the subject. One is at a loss to know how an impressive sculptural mass can be built around so light and ephemeral a *motif* as a flower. More flowers are worse. The only bulk possible consists of garlands and baskets of bloom bound into some kind of coherence. In relief, low or high, the problem is a much simpler one, and the flowers afford grateful accents of sculptural color. One recalls with pleasure a minor feature of those scattering groups with their horseless chariots and their windy drapery: this was the "team" of little capering cupids which led the way so gleefully. They showed great beauty of modelling, and the attitude of two of them with outstretched legs was irresistibly amusing.

But it was in the Art Palace that Mr. Pratt was most satisfactorily represented, though by a single work, and this a statuette. It was only a little figure, of perhaps half life-size — a nude girl seated on the ground, supporting herself with her arms behind her, and her sensitive face bowed; but that little marble was worth more, artistically, than nine-tenths of the plaster giants outside. It had an æsthetic reason for existence; it was born of an emotion. Firmly and flexibly modelled, the young body was truth itself, yet truth plus the charm of "the general." It was the grace of young maidenhood stripped of all that is accidental and unimportant, or even too minutely personal.

Mr. Pratt's two latest works of importance show conceptions of great diversity, though bound together by a strain of martial sentiment. The one is a heroic figure of a soldier for St. Paul's School, Concord, New Hampshire, erected in honor of one hundred and twenty of St. Paul's boys who fought in the Spanish-American War. The other is a very original memorial to General Benjamin F. Butler, for Lowell, Massachusetts. The first is one of the most satisfactory military figures in the country, an ideal — possibly a composite — soldier of noble seriousness who stands at his ease and looks his admirable, intrepid manhood not only from his fine face but from every line. The statue is sculpturally conceived. This is its great advantage, that all of the study and painstaking detail has been put upon something that started out to be good sculpture to begin with. It is possible to make realism and picturesqueness and all sorts of things look like sculpture by dint of much elaboration, but this *is* sculpture.

The Butler Memorial (Fig. 92) represents more thought and labor than the casual observer would imagine. Mr. Pratt has spent much time upon it, but such effort is never lost. It is appreciated by those at least whose appreciation the artist most covets. This work is in form a large relief of bronze showing " Peace " and " War," personified by two female figures. " War," with sad, foreboding face, stands prepared to draw the sword, but halts irresolute because of the pleading of sweet-visaged " Peace." The heads are perhaps a trifle conventional — how to avoid this and to escape, on the other hand, portraiture of one's favorite model is a problem. However, the type is not lacking in its national and even local accent. The long, narrow face of " War " would contrast interestingly with Schilling's " Germania," for instance. " Peace," while equally impersonal, shows great beauty of feature and of sentiment. The richness of modelling in her face, throat, and shoulders is noteworthy. The delicacy of the profile obtains effective contrast through the dark shadows behind it cast by the veil. This drapery sweeps downward and over the extended arm, and with the arm and shoulder of " War " completes a very distinct oval — a frame, as it were, for the heads and busts. Below this line the

FIG. 92. — PRATT: BUTLER MEMORIAL.

sculptor has introduced no striking accents with the exception of the hands and certain shadow notes on the edge of the composition, the lower limbs being lost in the flowing drapery, and the latter in turn being carefully thrown out of focus by means of very subtle modelling.

It is this refinement of modelling which gives great artistic value to the relief. It floats over all like an impalpable veil, very evident below, less obliterative where the beautiful arms and busts reveal themselves like the undulation of a fair landscape through lifting curtains of mist, closing down again upon the shadowy " Peace " and swept away in part but never completely from "War's" troubled countenance. So intangible, so unobtrusive are certain of the virtues of this sterling work, that one might overlook them at first. Fortunately it invites many returns, and, like a worthy friend, reveals new beauties upon each approach. The drapery offers several masterly passages of sculptural simplification, and it is rare that one meets in monumental art anything so fine as the union of tenderness and strength in the left arm and hand of " Peace." From the clinging fingers the eye travels with pleasure to the massive elbow upon which the hand is laid and takes notes of its planes, of the firm modelling of bone and muscle, the while the mind responds to the significance of the gesture.

Cyrus E. Dallin is of the West, but studied in Boston, where, after many wanderings, he has established himself again. He holds the position of instructor in modelling in the Massachusetts Normal Art School. In studying the record of Mr. Dallin's life one is struck with the preëminent value of two of his works. A man of intellect as well as of skill, he has tried many things and met with good success in all, but without rising above the high average of numerous clever colleagues. In his equestrian Indians, however, he has produced something striking and distinctive. " The Signal of Peace " is worth a score of " Paul Reveres " and " Shermans " and " Reynoldses "; and " The Medicine Man " (Fig. 93) is appreciably finer than even its predecessor. We have no one who does these " Wild West " subjects with the impressive gravity which Mr. Dallin puts into them. His possible rivals are few: Mr. Borglum has not yet demonstrated his ability with large groups; Mr. MacNeil, like Mr. Boyle, has yet to essay the horse, and Mr. Proctor threatens to become, like Mr. MacNeil, almost too clever to be convincingly savage. By reason of excessive refinement of modelling, their works, while undeniably beautiful sculpture, have lost something of the sturdy, solid virtues of the aboriginal man. Their surfaces hold our attention. Mr. Dallin knows the horse and he knows the Indian, he also knows how to model; but whether less expert than these two colleagues of his, or less enamoured of the clay, or, as one likes to think, merely intent upon expressing his thought in the simplest and most straightforward manner, he omits some portion of that delightful and dis-

FIG. 93.—DALLIN: THE MEDICINE MAN, FAIRMOUNT PARK, PHILADELPHIA.

tracting elaboration which distinguishes their work, and gives us a result unique in its impressiveness.

His knowledge of the horse is the result of studies begun at a very early age on the farm in Utah where he first saw the light in 1861; and as for acquaintance with the Indians, he tells us that his earliest home was surrounded by an adobe wall ten feet in height to prevent undue familiarity on their part. There were other red neighbors, however, who were not to be feared, and with these the future sculptor became well acquainted, addressing them in their own tongue and learning not a few of their ways. At the age of eighteen he went to work at one of his father's mines, first as a cook and then at sorting ore, which he combined with the recreation of "driving" a wheelbarrow. One fateful morning the miners struck a bed of soft, white clay, and its consistency was too inviting to be neglected. The boy forgot his wheelbarrow and modelled two life-size heads — and his fate was sealed. How he got to Boston and how he began study with Mr. Truman Bartlett may be read elsewhere;[1] likewise the story of his professional struggles, his somewhat tardy trip to Paris in the autumn of 1888, and the result of Chapu's training plus the inspiration of "Buffalo Bill," who came to Paris with his show the following year. The Indians seemed to strike a responsive chord, and led the thoughts of the Westerner away for a time from such themes as "Apollo and Hyacinthus" and "The Awakening of Spring." "The Signal of Peace" began to take form in his mind, and was completed, full-size, in time for the Salon of 1890, where it received an honorable mention. Brought later to America, it was seen at the Columbian Exposition, where it was awarded a medal. The subject is a Sioux chief attired in moccasins, breech-clout, and feathered war bonnet only. One hand rests on the neck of his pony, and with the other he raises aloft his feathered spear, the point upward, a recognized signal among the Indians. The pony's ears are directed forward, and all four feet are planted on the ground.

"The Signal of Peace" remained in Chicago, being now one of the adornments of Lincoln Park in that city. It was nearly ten years before Mr. Dallin's other work permitted him to return to his

---

[1] "Cyrus E. Dallin, Sculptor," by William Howe Downes, *Brush and Pencil*, Vol. V, p. 1.

favorite and most successful field. His greatest achievement, " The Medicine Man," was begun in April, 1898, and occupied just a year, being ready for exhibition at the Salon of 1899. The poses of both horse and rider are almost identical with those of " The Signal of Peace," yet the general expression is entirely changed, and the technical qualities are vastly improved. As before, the horse is per- fectly quiet, yet intent upon some distant object; the Indian's left hand, removed from the pony's neck, now rests upon the thigh with a firm pressure which gives solidity to the whole composition. The right hand no longer extends the spear, but is lifted in a gesture of authority, with fingers slightly spread, as if commanding silence. The head, weirdly adorned with buffalo horns and feathers, has an awe-inspiring look. With open mouth and frowning brow this rep- resentative of the mysteries commands not only the respect of his followers but the startled attention of every passer-by. Mr. Dallin has succeeded in putting great intensity into his work, and in mak- ing it convincingly real, although so far removed from our experi- ence. It possesses a sort of hieratic majesty, and seems to voice the message of one who practises dark arts, imposing them abso- lutely upon superstitious men. The priests of Osiris and of Baal must have lifted the hand thus. " The Medicine Man " is one of the most notable and significant products of American sculpture. It was purchased by the Fairmount Park Association in 1900, and is a conspicuous ornament of Philadelphia's great pleasure-ground.

Other works by Mr. Dallin are an excellent marble bust of a young lady, shown in the Salon of 1898, his " Newton " in the rotunda of the Library of Congress, and a fantastic little " Don Quixote " on horseback, an angular conception made up of armor and bones. In this work Mr. William H. Downes has found much to admire. " It is conceived in an absolutely ideal spirit, and is enveloped in an atmosphere of romance which is completely in harmony with that of Cervantes. The character of Don Quixote, moreover, is taken seri- ously, and with a proper appreciation of its intrinsic nobility and pathos. The type is that of the nervous, melancholic, and imagina- tive man, and his traits are reflected in the gaunt and bony physique. The knight holds in his right hand a long spear, and in his left hand the slack reins. He wears a full suit of armor, except that the helmet is without a visor. The face is exceedingly expressive. The eyes are set deep in their sockets, the nose is aquiline, the cheek-bones are salient, the form of the jaws and the pointed beard accentuate the idea of length and emaciation. The eyebrows almost meet in a single arch; but the vertical wrinkles between them, and the piercing, sustained, and dreamy gaze of the sad eyes well bear out the conception of a solemn, cranky, and romantic old gentleman, somewhat out of date, but eminently imposing, dignified, and even lovable. He sits his horse well, and has a noble bearing. The Rosinante is positively a creation of genius, nothing less. The long, lean, osseous head of this prehistoric wreck of a nag, and the dismal droop of the ears, convey a whole world of mournful equine biography." [1]

Another sculptor connected with Boston, by education at least, is Mr. Richard E. Brooks, who has made his home for some years past in Paris. Mr. Brooks was born at Braintree, Massachusetts, in 1865, but spent his youth in the vicinity of the granite quarries of Quincy. He began to model and carve when a mere boy, and was permitted to gratify his taste through employment in the works of a terra-cotta company. He finally established a business for himself, doing all kinds of commercial sculpture, but steadfastly seizing every opportunity for study and self-improvement. His clever modelling attracted attention, and he received an order for a bust of Governor Russell, which gave him his first opportunity to work from life. The result was so satisfactory that Mr. Brooks was encouraged to go to Paris, where he put himself under the instruction of M. Aubé. Like most artists sojourning in Paris, he made early quest for a " Salon subject." The " Chant de la Vague " was the result, a graceful nude female figure presumably seated on the shore of some nameless but sounding sea. The work was counted very promising, and received an honorable mention; but with this success the sculptor's excursions into the domain of the ideal seem to have abruptly terminated. His next important exhibit was the " Colonel Thomas Cass" (Fig. 94), which now stands in the Public Gardens of Boston, one of the finest examples of a quiet, soldierly figure that American art has thus far produced. With its folded arms and steady gaze it is sufficiently removed from the accidental poses of warfare to justify its prominence

[1] *Brush and Pencil*, Vol. V, p. 16.

and permanency. It is one of those motionless figures which seem strangely endowed with life, while its technic could hardly be surpassed for that rarest of qualities, — precise generalization. Mr. Brooks was honored with a gold medal for this figure at the Paris Exposition of 1900, and received at Buffalo in 1901 a gold medal for an exhibit consisting of the "Colonel Cass," two portrait busts, a number of medals, and two interesting examples of applied art, — a curious candlestick and a necklace. His latest works have been bronze statues ordered by the state of Maryland, the "John Hanson" and the "Charles Carroll," which were installed in 1903 in the National Sculpture Gallery at Washington. Mr. Brooks is at present occupied with a statue of Robert Treat Paine, to be erected in one of the public squares of Taunton, Massachusetts.

Other names connected with the plastic art in Boston are those of Samuel Kitson and Max Bachman, architectural sculptors; Robert Kraus, deceased, sculptor of the Crispus Attucks monument; and Miss Anna Vaughn Hyatt, of Cambridge, a pupil of Henry H. Kitson, who has done some effective work in animal sculpture.

In Hartford, Mr. Carl Conrads, a German of good training, has identified himself with sculpture in granite and has done much creditable work, well adapted to the requirements of that ungrateful material. Karl Gerhardt also at one time produced a rapid succession of bronze figures, of which the "Nathan Hale," in the Connecticut State House, is worthy of mention.

In New Haven one finds not only several works of historic interest, but an artist who has made at least two important essays in monumental statuary. Yale University has received embellishment from the hands of its long-time professor of art, John G. Weir. To say that Professor Weir's statues of Professor Silliman and of President Woolsey are great sculptures, would be extravagant, for the workmanship is labored and the treatment heavy. But even with the achievements of our masters in mind one views these efforts with great respect. They are the conceptions of a grave, thoughtful man capable of appreciating the dignity of his subjects, and in the more recent "President Woolsey" one feels as well a comprehension of the demands of the material employed. This bowed figure of the aged scholar is no trifling work, but

FIG. 94.— BROOKS: COLONEL THOMAS CASS, PUBLIC GARDENS, BOSTON.

one which the younger world about it may well regard with veneration.

In Philadelphia the early sculptural traditions were continued before the days of Howard Roberts and of the Centennial by various wanderers, among whom were Hugh Cannon, an Irishman, and Isaac Broome, a Canadian, who carved Crawford's pediment on the Capitol at Washington. Most prominent, however, of those coming from afar, was Joseph A. Bailly, a Frenchman (born in Paris in 1825), who settled in Philadelphia in 1850, and built up a considerable business in portraits and clever specimens of commercial art. Mr. Bailly had a number of private pupils and also taught for a time in the Pennsylvania Academy, where are to be seen two of his works, companion groups in marble, entitled "The First Prayer" and "The Expulsion." These rather childish conceptions are expressed with considerable facility and suggest good academic training. This sculptor is represented further in Philadelphia by a "Washington" (1869), in front of Independence Hall, and a "Witherspoon" in Fairmount Park. At the Centennial Exposition his model for an equestrian statue of President Guzman Blanco of Venezuela was the conspicuous if somewhat inappropriate central ornament of the rotunda of Memorial Hall. Bailly died in 1883.

Among the pupils of Bailly was Albert E. Harnisch, a Philadelphian of German parentage, who went to Italy and sent home a number of works of which the titles, "Love in Idleness," "The Little Protector," and "Boy robbing an Eagle's Nest," give some indication. Henry J. Haseltine, a native of Philadelphia, went abroad after serving in the Civil War, and opened in 1867 a studio in Rome. Among his earlier productions were "Excelsior," "Autumn Leaves," "Liberty," "New Wine," "Religion," and "Superstition." He sent to the Centennial Exposition three figures: "Spring Flowers," "Captivity," and "Lucretia." Other names connected with public works in Philadelphia are those of Henry Jackson Ellicott, who modelled an equestrian "General McClellan," and Alexander Milne Calder, who furnished most of the sculptural decorations of the enormous City Hall, as well as a "General Meade" in Fairmount Park.

Coming now to the active sculptors of to-day in Philadelphia, we find two names of prominence, — Charles Grafly and Stirling A. Calder. Mr. Grafly is of Quaker lineage and was born in Philadelphia in 1862; he has known no other home and belongs emphatically to this environment. He is a product thereof and appreciates its needs. His development has been logical and symmetrical by steps of genuine, hard-won advancement. He attended school until seventeen years of age, when he entered a stone-carving establishment in order

FIG. 95. — GRAFLY : SYMBOL OF LIFE.

to gain practical knowledge of the sculptor's craft. He remained there for five years, reproducing in marble a number of figures. During this time he attended the art schools of the Spring Garden Institution. In 1884 he was admitted to the Academy, where he studied modelling and painting under Thomas Eakins, a training which bespoke much devotion to anatomical research and practical dissection. In 1888 he went to Paris, studying at first at the Académie Julien, where he was under the inspiring influence of Chapu in the department of sculpture, and of no less famous professors in drawing. He turned later to the École des Beaux-Arts, remaining there until the spring of 1890. At the Salon of that year he made his début with two heads, "Dædalus" and "St. John." The "Dædalus" was afterward exhibited in Philadelphia, awarded honorable mention by the Temple Trust Fund, purchased and cast in bronze by the Pennsylvania Academy, and placed in its permanent collection.

A busy summer in this country was followed by a return to Paris in the autumn. The product of the winter of 1890–1891 was a life-size nude female figure, "Mauvais Présage," which was accorded honorable mention in the Salon of 1891. This figure is now in the possession of the Detroit Museum of Art. About this time Mr. Grafly received his call to the chair of sculpture in the Pennsylvania Academy and also in Drexel Institute. By way of preparation he visited the chief art centres and schools of Europe before returning to America. In 1893 his exhibition of the above mentioned works at the Columbian Exposition won him a medal, and in 1895 his admirable portrait bust of his mother, modelled in 1892, brought him a similar recompense in Atlanta. The result of a fourth winter in Paris (1895–1896) was the "Vulture of War." Since that time he has resided in Philadelphia, occupied largely with his teaching and the execution of various commissions.

Mr. Grafly has made himself known to the artistic public largely by means of certain small groups in bronze which he has shown in the art museums of various cities of America, as well as at the Paris Exposition of 1900, where he received for his collective exhibit the high honor of a gold medal. Perhaps the most original of these diminutive works is "The Symbol of Life" (Fig. 95). Though small, the two nude figures, male and female, which stand side by side, taking step together, are "big" in handling. Their faces are grave, and there is dignity, almost solemnity, in their carriage. The woman holds in her hand a globe of ivory, from which springs a stalk of wheat. The man leans upon a primitive scythe. There is enough of symbolism here to give significance to the work, but it requires no such appeal in order to win our respect. The modelling of those superb bodies is a language sufficiently intelligible. One can hardly pass the group without walking around it and around again, so masterful and satisfying is the workmanship. We may not know why the sculptor made the Juno-like woman larger than her companion; we may not know why he gave her that mannish stride, except that they may keep step; we can only guess at the significance of the globe of ivory and the stalk of wheat, but we can enjoy the sculptor's pleasure in the construction of these two figures. Their bigness of handling, the feeling of the flesh firm upon the bones, the sinuous flow of the surface, so contrasting in the two, the power and the subtlety of modelling of all things essential, and the noble disregard of impertinent and importunate details, must appeal to one who knows sculpture at all.   The very way in which the nails are *not* done is refreshing to one wearied with monotonous, non-significant technic.

Not less remarkable in its modelling is that later group, " From Generation to Generation."   Though it is even more cut up in mass than the preceding, the figures in themselves are simple and every way admirable.   Again they are two, a youth and a decrepit old man, standing as it were at the parting of the ways, before a large winged dial.   The aged one, a nude figure of extraordinary thinness, bends under the burden of years and clutches a full distaff.   The youth, advancing with buoyant step and head elate, prepares to spin the uncertain thread of life.   Again one may pardon the leaning toward symbolism; it is but a faint flavor here, and we are rather glad to discover it, because it enables us to recognize the artist in his work. It is Grafly and no other.

Our sculptors are producing few works of imagination in these days, and to undertake one without a commission is counted foolhardy; but Mr. Grafly is an exception and persists in developing these strange fancies of his in spite of their considerable cost.   He seems to think that this is what sculpture is for, — the expression of one's ideas in form, — and he protests that he does it because he " must."   Smaller men excuse themselves for mediocre and slovenly work with the same plea, but it is almost bewildering to hear an artist acknowledge that work of this high order is done under stress of necessity.   The reward of such artistic conscience lies not only in the achievement of the moment, but in the strengthening of the artistic character.   When opportunity comes, and with it demand for a man's highest abilities, he who has always done his best has himself well in hand.   Such an opportunity came to Mr. Grafly at the Pan-American Exposition.   While the sculptural decorations of that most charming of fairs were as a rule well suited to their purpose, and contributed much to its beauty, there were few features of striking originality.   The one which stands out in memory as of permanent value, as a lasting contribution to the art of this country,

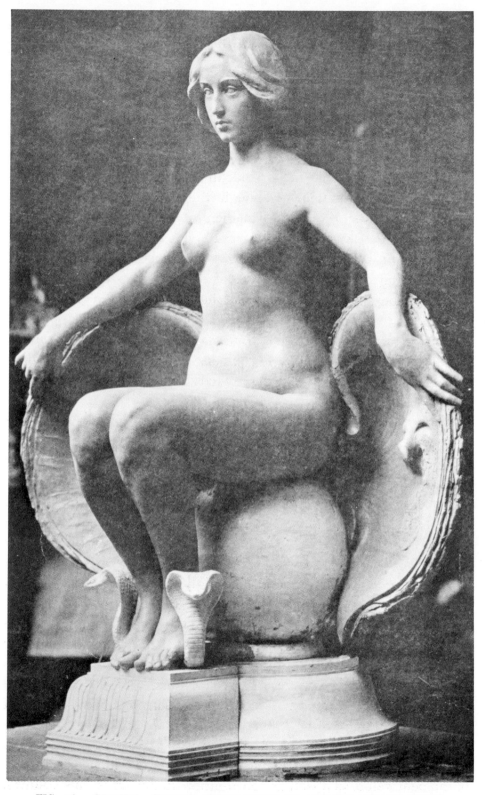

FIG. 96.—GRAFLY : TRUTH, DECORATION OF ART PALACE, ST. LOUIS.

is Mr. Grafly's " Fountain of Man " (Fig. 97). The first glimpse of this worthily sculptural conception showed that the sculptor had approached his subject with respect and had risen admirably to the occasion. The chaste architectural lines, the compact masses of the figures with their richness of modelling, and their contrasts one with another, made the *ensemble* a joy to the eye long before closer study revealed the significance of parts.

The official explanation of the fountain was as follows: " Its subject is ' Man.' The crowning figure, which is double, so that the same effect is produced upon either side, represents that being, so mysterious in his origin and destiny; whose powers are so incalculable, while he is yet so impotent; who though wrapped about with the shadow of the unknown as a garment, looks out upon life with courage and a resolute will. ' Man ' is upheld by a group of five figures clasping one another's hands and moving slowly upon a circular plinth. They have bowed heads, and they represent the five senses working in unison and in subjection to him. In the figures the sculptor has aimed to express the characteristics of each sense. The fountain has a basin . . . supported by four groups of crouching figures, a male and female figure in each, representing the struggling emotions."

Mr. Grafly's symbolism, always a little annoying to some tastes, became exasperating in the crowning figure of this work. A double-faced, double-bodied monstrosity like this " Man " is not man at all, but a *lusus naturæ*. A pure, wholesome, reasonable art does not take such liberties with nature, even in order to convey a psychological idea. The Greeks repudiated the grotesque and the deformed with unerring good taste. Mr. Grafly lost himself for the time in Egyptian mysticism, and the consequence is an Egyptian chimera. It was the double man as seen in profile which was objectionable, however; the one man viewed from either front was admirable and a great achievement. To make one's work impressive is among the most difficult problems in art, and Mr. Grafly succeeded. This figure possessed a strange, almost hypnotic power, which absolute realism could never have produced. The artist devised a peculiar, all-enveloping garment which lent itself to the effect of mystery. From its parted veil the strong, inscrutable face peered out as might the eyes of death from a shroud. The long folds were handled in broad planes, as if blocked out in stone, producing an effect massive and architectonic, yet not crude. The artist knew just where to stop in his simplification. Anything harsher would have broken the spell, for the eye would have been irritated. On the other hand, a more caressingly realistic treatment would have banished the spiritual quality, the sense of unreality, which was the power of this singular statue. We should then have looked upon a man up there — an individual in clothes — and not " Man."

FIG. 97. — GRAFLY: FRAGMENT OF FOUNTAIN OF MAN, PAN-AMERICAN EXPOSITION.

The five figures of " The Senses," which circled around the central shaft as uneasy caryatides supporting the upper basin, were frankly realistic in their proportions, being more robust than elegant. The artist was too much in earnest to be elegant. He told his story forcefully throughout. But if these were no languid Goujon nymphs, they were superb in their strength. They, too, were " carved "; ample and mellow in modelling, they stopped just this side of lusciousness, for here and there was a firm broad plane as of the simplifying chisel, giving their forms not only an increase of carrying power, but warning the curious and the indiscreet that these were not women and men but sculptured creations.

Showing the same " color " sense and well-constructed throughout were the four groups of crouching figures which supported the lower basin. Simple and compact, " so that they might be rolled down hill without breaking," yet varied in composition and infinitely rich in light and shade, they came close to the ideal of glyptic art. They had in them the qualities of Sinding's " Captive Mother " and "A Man and a Woman," of Lefevre's " Bonheur," of Rodin's " Le Baiser."   If not "great " sculpture, they were near to it.   Their vague suggestion of "those strange figures which peer out from under the stage of the theatre of Dionysos at Athens" has been noted,[1] but these were no Greek conceptions. While they were elemental and trembled with the passions of all time, their faces were those of our own brothers and sisters of to-day.

Mr. Grafly's later works include several busts, as well as a " General Reynolds " for the Smith Memorial in Fairmount Park ; " In Much Learning," a nude female figure of extraordinary beauty of technic, and " Truth " (Fig. 96), a nude seated figure for the permanent art building of the St. Louis Exposition.   No better illustration could be offered of what may be called mellowness of modelling than is shown by this exquisite work.   As was suggested regarding Story's " Cleopatra," a reversal of the page will analyze its decorative value.   It will be found that the lights and shades which play over the rich form of the "Truth " are no less beautiful when the page is viewed upside down.

Less known to the public, but highly esteemed by brother artists, is the work of Alexander Stirling Calder.   Mr. Calder, who is still a young man, -- he was born in Philadelphia in 1870, — may be said to have inherited his profession, since he follows in the footsteps of his father, A. M. Calder.   He studied four years in the Academy of Pennsylvania and two years in Paris under Chapu and Falguière, and since his return has been connected with the Philadelphia School of Industrial Art, a field where his decorative sense and sympathies find congenial employment.   However, his work in other forms of sculpture is by no means inconsiderable.   His first commission was for a statue of Dr. Samuel D. Gross, which now stands in front of the Army and Medical Museum in Washington. This statue, though offering certain eccentricities of pose, is one of the most workmanlike examples of modelling in the capital city. It shows a large simplification of forms, and the handling of the modern costume is admirably done, while the characterization of head and hands is no less gratifying.   Among later works

[1] Mrs. Cyrus E. Dallin in *New England Magazine*, vol. XXV, p. 228.

2 L

by Mr. Calder are the six figures of heroic size which give meaning
to the exterior of the Witherspoon building in Philadelphia. These
six representative Presbyterians are as follows: Dr. John McMillan, Rev. Francis MacKenzie, Dr. Marcus Whitman, Rev. Dr.
Samuel Davies, Rev. James Caldwell, and John Witherspoon, D.D.
Even at the height imposed by the architectural scheme the rugged
figures show much individuality. In his treatment of the material,
as in his grasp of subjects, Mr. Calder is plain and straightforward.
Even his decorative inventions are remarkably free from complexity.
His fountain for the class of 1892 of the University of Pennsylvania
is an excellent illustration of his style. Among more ideal themes
are such interesting works as " The Man Cub," " Child Playing,"
" Mother and Baby," " The Dozing Hercules," a study for " Momus,"
" The Miner," " Narcissus," and " Primal Discontent," the latter a
notably powerful study of the nude. His sketch model for a monument to Matthias W. Baldwin is one of the best designs for a figure
and pedestal yet produced in this country.

Samuel Murray, a pupil of Thomas Eakins, has produced few
large works, being best known for his statuettes, notably a " Boxer,"
and for his busts, which are well constructed and very carefully
modelled. Mention should also be made of Charles Brinton Cox
who models animals as well as men, and of Miss Katherine Cohen,
who has produced a considerable number of decorative figures and
reliefs.

It is quite possible that the fame of all of these artists might
have been overshadowed by the talent of another Philadelphian,
had fate permitted him to fulfil the promise of his young manhood. Edmund Austin Stewardson left only one work, " The
Bather" (Fig. 98), but this figure is so masterly in every respect
that, in bronze and in marble, it is counted among the chief treasures
of the Pennsylvania Academy and of the Metropolitan Museum.
It is impossible for a figure so well conceived and so ably treated
as this ever to be considered other than good sculpture. As a first
effort, it naturally expresses but the unfolding of an artistic character. It is not an ambitious work, nor one of deep significance, and
the sculptor would doubtless have developed higher ideals, freeing
himself from the limitations of the model; but as an example of

FIG. 98. — STEWARDSON : THE BATHER, METROPOLITAN MUSEUM.

accurate knowledge, of technical skill, and of good taste, " The Bather " is justly ranked among the finest products of American art. Mr. Stewardson was born in Philadelphia in 1860, studied at the Pennsylvania Academy, and later at the Ecole des Beaux-Arts, as well as under Allar and Chapu, modelled " The Bather " in 1890, and was drowned while boating, at Newport, Rhode Island, July 3, 1892.

CHAPTER XXVII

SCULPTORS OF THE SOUTH AND WEST: CONCLUSION

WHILE nine-tenths of our sculptors are gathered in New York City, working together with more or less harmony, or at least, as Hawthorne said of the early colony in Rome, keeping each other warm by animal heat, it has been the fortune of a few to be assigned by fate to picket duty on a somewhat bleak frontier. Each of our secondary cities has its sculptor, called to the lonely task of upholding the standard of art in a community without artistic traditions and very much engrossed in other concerns. Were he nothing but an artist — in the familiar restricted sense of the word — such an isolation would soon become intolerable, like that of the signal-service officials in the mountains. Fortunately, most of our sculptors are not only artists, but robust, thinking men, and keenly alive to the interest of their surroundings. Unlike so many of the earlier generation, those who are now at work are very much of their own time and country, believing in them and interpreting them with a zest which is one of the most hopeful features of this period.

But the position of the isolated sculptor is a peculiar one. In some ways he is related to the pioneers of the forties and fifties. If there is more visible art to-day, the artist is, on the other hand, quite as dependent upon himself for initiative and momentum. They had enthusiasm at least in those primitive times! Powers and Hart, Brown, Clevenger, and all the rest, were objects of interest to their countrymen. They were able, also, to make profitable circuits, gathering rich harvests of busts to be carved abroad. The elevated standard of to-day has its own drawbacks; our wealthy people have so much theoretical knowledge that the majority patronize home art not at all. The result is that the young sculptor has an exceedingly precarious foothold. Busts have "gone out"; they are no longer necessities of the home, for the home itself is on castors and must be kept in light marching order. Public monuments are furnished by the granite companies, and the department stores offer "a complete line" of alabaster statuary at prices which would not repay a sculptor for conceiving the figures, let alone modelling and carving them!

So the sculptor, from necessity, "teaches"; and of this necessity has come one of the greatest factors in the rapid progress of recent years. If there is anything that is indisputably "worth while," it lies in helping others to help themselves; above all in leading young talent to the fields of usefulness for which it is particularly adapted. No mortal is without his gift; but comparatively few are situated where they may do their best, and many never discover their own abilities. Our most intimate circles contain their "mute inglorious Miltons," who are often quite as unconscious of their powers as they are of their deficiencies. The teacher cannot make sculptors, but he can point the way and afford opportunity. Of the many who come to him none is likely to be injured by a little knowledge of the processes of sculpture, and among them is an occasional "genius." It would surprise the reader to learn what numbers attempt this fascinating art. Each of our cities of five hundred thousand or more inhabitants has its school of art, and in the larger ones modelling is generally a prominent feature. In the Art Institute of Chicago, for instance, no fewer than one hundred adults receive each year some instruction in sculpture. The Saturday juvenile classes in modelling contain perhaps as many more school children. Few, indeed, of this great number will become professional sculptors. Among them are wood-carvers and marble-cutters, decorators, school-teachers, and future instructors in the various arts, as well as many young women soon to be called to the high responsibilities of home-making. Throughout the West this quiet influence is spreading until already there is scarcely a neighborhood without its centre of artistic taste and refinement. It may be but a modest home; generally it is a group of women who study about art, and whose ultimate ambition is to provide their community with an art collection and a school of design.

Then there are the pupils of exceptional talent. In a sense our schools are for them, the many providing the means that the few may go farther. After the home school come New York and Paris, and after Paris generally New York again; but a few professionals return to their own cities to carry on the work. Among those who have in turn become teachers and are serving the cause in this capacity as well as in their studios, are Messrs. MacNeil in New York; Dallin, Kitson, and Pratt in Boston; Grafly and Calder in Philadelphia; Keyser in Baltimore; Barnhorn in Cincinnati; Mulligan in Chicago; Bringhurst in St. Louis; and Tilden and Aitkin in San Francisco. Enthusiastic instructors, all of them, — like Saint

FIG. 99. — BARNHORN: MAGDALEN, ART MUSEUM, CINCINNATI.

Gaudens, Adams, and Barnard in the past, — these men are not teachers alone, but, as their records show, busy sculptors as well. If thus grouped here, it is to emphasize their locations and the peculiar conditions under which they work, as well as to explain their relatively small output. It should be remembered that not only do these sculptors give from one to three days of each week to their classes, but that their productions are almost entirely the work of their own hands. The shop system of New York does not extend to the provinces. A certain amount of assistance is not only legitimate but almost indispensable in the handling of large work, but the isolated sculptor seldom requires it in the execution of his

modest commissions. When the emergency does come, he is generally obliged to depend upon the inexperience of young pupils.
It is evident, then, that where a sculptor is compelled to do individually all parts of the work, from building up armatures to making the
cast, not to speak of carving the marble and chasing the bronze, he
can hardly compete in productivity with an "establishment."

With the exception of Edward Kemeys no sculptor of distinction
has come as yet from the Southern states, — at least from the states
below Virginia, — a fact which seems strange when one considers
the culture of the South and its old-time wealth.   That the artistic
instinct is not lacking in that part of the country is demonstrated by
the fact that a number of our excellent painters and architects were
born in the region of the Gulf of Mexico; but thus far it has produced no sculptors. While Maryland and Virginia have given birth
to several sculptors, the leading cities of these two states can boast
to-day of only one each.   The lone representative of the plastic arts
in Baltimore is Ephraim Keyser, who was born in that city in 1852.
Mr. Keyser studied in the Royal Art Academy of Munich from
1872 to 1876, under Professor Widmann, and enjoyed later, in
Berlin, the instruction of Professor Albert Wolff.   Here his life-size
figure of " Psyche," now in the Cincinnati Museum, won for him
not only the silver medal of the Academy, but the " Michael
Beerche prize," with the privilege of one year's study in Rome at
government expense.   His best known achievement is the memorial to Chester A. Arthur in Albany Rural Cemetery, Albany, New
York, a graceful and expressive work.   An angel with drooping
wings and sorrowful visage stands beside the sarcophagus, upon
which she lays a palm branch.   Even more satisfying is Mr. Keyser's
" Stein Memorial " in the Hebrew Cemetery of Baltimore.   Within
a massive die is a seated, winged figure in comparatively low relief,
so harmoniously composed and modelled that it shows neither discord of line nor disagreeable spots of shadow.   The mourner, with
bowed head supported by the hands, is framed in by the great wings
which form an irregular oval.   The admirable qualities of this relief
testify to the artist's equipment for his work as well as to his poetic
imagination.   Another product of Mr. Keyser's skill to be seen in
Baltimore is a bust of a man, in the Peabody Institute.   This frown-

ing portrait could hardly be surpassed for incisive characterization. Like the relief just mentioned, it is carved with "atmosphere" — to use the painter's term once more — and demonstrates the all-round training of the sculptor.

Edward Valentine was born in Richmond, in 1838, and his name and works have been very closely associated with his native city. He made early choice of the profession of sculpture, taking a course in anatomy when scarcely more than a boy.   After exhausting the resources of the local artists, he went abroad in 1859, studying for a time in Paris with Couture, then journeying to Italy, where he spent a year among monuments and museums.   At length he found himself in Berlin, where he became the pupil of Kiss, with whom he remained until the death of the aged sculptor.   Returning to Richmond in 1865, a time of hopeless depression, he was introduced to his public through a statuette of General Lee, which he had already exhibited in London.   No commissions came to him in those dark days, but he did a number of ideal heads; among others " The Samaritan Woman," " The Penitent Thief," and — more significantly local — " The Nation's Ward," a laughing darky boy.   Another study of the African, somewhat akin to the contemporaneous " Rogers groups," was entitled " Knowledge is Power," and showed a negro boy, clothed in tatters, who has fallen asleep with his dog-eared book dropping from a very limp hand.   An order of importance finally came to the expectant sculptor.   Upon the death of General Lee, in 1870, he was commissioned to execute a memorial to be placed in the Washington and Lee University at Lexington, Virginia.   He represented his subject as stretched upon a narrow soldier's bed, in his uniform of a general.   One hand is placed on the breast, the other lies by the side, resting upon the sword.   The likeness is said to be excellent.   Other orders have come to the sculptor in the form of numerous portraits, including bronzes of General T. J. Jackson and General W. C. Wickham and a marble statue of Thomas Jefferson in the Hotel Jefferson, all at Richmond. His most serious ideal work is his group " Andromache and Astyanax," the moment represented being that just after Hector's farewell, when the mourning wife sits unconscious even of the child upon her knee.

In Cincinnati, John Frankenstein, an almost unknown sculptor, has left slight but interesting traces. A number of casts of heads, hidden away in the studio of a venerable painter, show masterly handling of the clay, a gift which seems never to have been recognized, or at least never to have been encouraged. Louis T. Rebisso, who taught modelling for many years in the Art Academy of Cincinnati, was not a great sculptor. His equestrian

FIG. 100. — DUVENECK: TOMB OF MRS. DUVENECK, ENGLISH CEMETERY, FLORENCE.

statues appear to have been in much demand, since they are found in several cities, but they are uniformly commonplace, not good enough to be considered seriously from an artistic standpoint, nor bad enough to be picturesque. His "General McPherson" is in Washington, "General Harrison" in Cincinnati, and "General Grant" in Chicago. Mr. Rebisso's most valuable contribution was, therefore, in the capacity of a teacher; in his encouragement and guidance of such men as Niehaus, Barnhorn, and Borglum he did good service.

Cincinnati's remaining sculptor is Clement J. Barnhorn, who was born in that city in 1857. Mr. Barnhorn obtained his general education in Saint Xavier's College, and after leaving this institution began as a carver in wood; but the career seeming at the time badly chosen, he turned to marble work, at which he remained for seven years. Later he went back to wood-carving with Henry L. Fry, an old English carver, who had worked on the House of Parliament in London, a remarkable man, who showed the artist in everything he did. Mr. Barnhorn writes: "His stories of his youth and trials as a carver were to me most interesting. He had worked in shops in England when men still wore long queues, unbuckled their swords, and hung them beside their bench before beginning work. I was greatly fascinated with this man, and as he was an artist, I profited much by his instruction." During all this time Mr. Barnhorn had been engaged in night study at the Cincinnati Art Academy, where he was for eleven years under the instruction of Louis T. Rebisso. At the end of this period he had shown such convincing proofs of talent that the Art Museum of Cincinnati, on behalf of the Academy, sent him abroad for a further period of study. He remained in Europe for three years, spending most of the time in Paris, but including six months in Italy. The visible result of this sojourn in the great art centre, where he studied sculpture with Puech and Mercié and drawing at Julien's, was an ideal figure, " Magdalen " (Fig. 99), which won an honorable mention at the Salon of 1895 and a bronze medal at the Exposition of 1900. Mr. Barnhorn had the unusual good fortune to receive a second bronze medal at this exposition — the " Art Nouveau " medal for the designing and carving of a remarkable piano. At the Buffalo Exposition also he was awarded a bronze medal for a bust of a baby.

The " Magdalen," a recumbent, mourning figure now in the Cincinnati Museum, is good sculpture, definitely conceived and beautifully modelled. It is an old, old subject, but artists of personality know how to renew ancient themes by the manner in which they present them, and Mr. Barnhorn has given us a new Magdalen, which appeals to us as much through its style and purity of lines as by reason of its undoubted emotional significance. This admirable nude has in it a promise which the sculptor's present environment may do little to bring to fruition, for the call for "ideal" statuary is very slight in our Western cities. Beyond giving such works house-room in the museums, public responsibility ceases. However, Mr. Barnhorn cannot complain of lack of appreciation at home, and has fared exceptionally well. Not only was he provided with the means for study abroad, but his talent has been constantly employed ever since his return in the designing and execution of a series of public memo-

rials and of many portraits. In these he shows the thorough training of the crafts-man who knows his art and more. A charming wall-fountain for an Indianapolis high school, shown at the Madison Square Garden exhibition of 1902, gave an idea of his inventive ingenuity on semi-architectural lines. Still more interesting is the beautiful relief, "Mænads," a bronze panel ordered by the Queen City Club of Cincinnati for

FIG. 101.— MULLIGAN: MINER AND CHILD.

the decoration of a mantel. In it the artist has shown a fine perception of the requirements of such design, — the interlacing of graceful lines, the balance of light and shade, and the subtler graces of movement and allure. If here and there the drawing is cursory and the captious eye may discover details which annoy, the effect as a whole is all that could be desired, especially in the rich bronze which glows through an exquisite velvety patina.

A name intimately associated with Cincinnati may be included here, that of the gifted painter, Frank Duveneck, whose one essay in sculpture is a work of such significance and beauty that it cannot be overlooked (Fig. 100).   As will be seen from the illustration, it is a memorial to the artist's wife, who died in Florence and was buried in the English cemetery of that city.   There, against its sombre background of cypress trees, the tomb is an object of pathetic interest to all visitors.   So exquisite is its sentiment, so worthy its execution that even the plaster cast, when shown in an exhibition of the National Sculpture Society at New York, in 1898, seemed to convert its surroundings into a memorial chapel.

In Chicago the promise of the Columbian Exposition has had scanty fulfilment.   A considerable number of the sculptors, brought thither by the great fair, tarried after its close to reap a further harvest; but the financial unsettlement of the country affected the over-built city of the West with peculiar severity, and the disappointed sculptors and decorators withdrew with one accord to a more congenial environment.   Architectural sculpture, so auspiciously introduced, had failed to take root.   Among those who remained for a longer or shorter period were Messrs. Kemeys, MacNeil, Proctor, Gelert, Rohl-Smith, and Wuertz, all of whom migrated in the course of time.   In spite of this discouraging exodus several sculptors are to be found in Chicago to-day.   Among the names most frequently met in the catalogues of local exhibits are those of Richard Bock, Julia Bracken, Leopold Bracony, Alice Cooper, Leonard Crunelle, Will LaFavor, Max Mauch, Lou Wall Moore, Charles J. Mulligan, and Erwald Perry.

Mr. Bock is known for his architectural decorations and military memorials.   By all odds the most valuable of his works is the strange " Boulder Man," which he designed and modelled to crown a heavy gate-post.   This compact mass, a powerful body apparently half buried in the earth or struggling like one of the sons of the Dragon's Teeth to emerge from the soil, is a work of unique originality.   Though treated in a summary manner, it is impressive from every view; one feels it to be sculpture.

Mr. Crunelle has a novel specialty.   Although born of a line of colliers, and himself through youth a worker in the mines, he has a style of marked delicacy and grace which finds fitting expression in portraits of children.   " Crunelle's babies " have been seen at various exhibitions in the East as well as at Chicago, and never fail to attract by their sympathetic rendering of the various infantile emotions. The wondering look, the mystery and the unconscious helplessness of infancy, he interprets with fascinating truth and a very skilful touch. Mr. Crunelle received a silver medal at the Atlanta Exposition for his bust of " Marguerite."

Mr. Charles J. Mulligan has demonstrated his right to a place among the men of promise in American sculpture. His " Digger," shown at the Pan-American Exposition, and the four figures of workingmen which he produced in rapid succession for the Illinois building at the same fair, had an individual quality, a convincing robustness and dignity, which removed them far from the usual stop-gaps of architectural sculpture. In his " Miner and Child " (Fig. 101), Mr. Mulligan has taken another step, replacing realism with a broader generalization, and presenting in a simple sculptural mass a remark-able union of strength and tenderness, — a blend of these two ele-ments as pleasing to the fancy as is the composition to the critical sense. Mr. Mulligan seems to have a distinct gift in this direction. He may be destined to become the prophet of hopeful, cheerful labor. His heart is in it; he knows his subjects thoroughly, and his strong right hand has within its grasp the delicacy and precision which come from long and patient training.

[Lorado Taft, the author of this " History of Sculpture," was born in Elmwood, Peoria County, Illinois, in 1860. His father, Don Carlos Taft, was a professor in the State University at Cham-paign, Illinois, and there Mr. Taft was graduated in 1879. He went abroad in 1880 and studied for three years in the École des Beaux-Arts. After a visit home he returned to Paris for another period of two years. In 1886 he established himself in Chicago, where he soon took charge of the classes in modelling at the Art Institute. He has taught there ever since, besides giving many courses of public lectures, both at the Institute and in the extension depart-ment of the University of Chicago. His professional work has been largely in portraiture and military monuments. He contributed to the Columbian Exposition the groups, " The Sleep of the Flowers " and " The Awakening of the Flowers," on the Horticultural building. Among his more recent works are, " Despair," 1898 ; " The Solitude

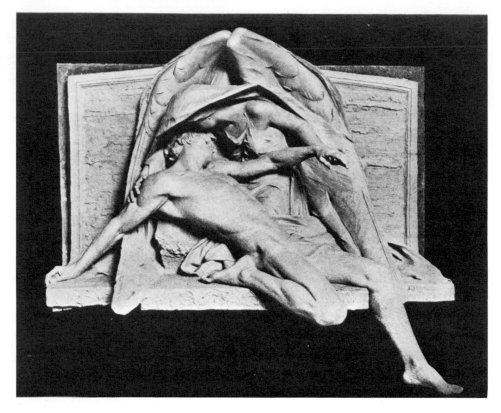

FIG. 102. — BRINGHURST: THE KISS OF ETERNITY.

of the Soul," 1900; "Knowledge," 1902; and the "Fountain of the
Lakes," 1903. A military group for Jackson, Michigan, was also
done in 1903. — EDITOR.]

Miss Bracken is the leader of the women sculptors of the West.
She has abundant ingenuity and a well-characterized style of her
own, recognizable for its decorative grace. Miss Bracken has done
considerable work of a high quality, not limiting herself to the usual
processes and materials, but carving in wood and marble with equal
facility. Her clever reliefs of Ibsen, Carlyle, and others are well
known through reproductions; her portraits are strong characterizations, while her works of fancy are rich in unexpected charms; a tiny
Japanese mother and baby, for instance, has not been surpassed in
this country for dainty grace. Her stately "Illinois welcoming the
Nations," a souvenir of the Columbian Exposition, stands in bronze
in the capitol at Springfield. Miss Cooper, who comes from Denver,
Colorado, has shown her skill in a number of interesting works.

Her "Summer Breeze," "Dancing Nymph," and "Frog Girl" are charming conceits which reveal much originality. Mrs. Moore has likewise a nimble fancy; her ingenious little figures and busts and her carefully considered reliefs make one wish to see larger and more adequate expressions of a nature essentially artistic.

The year 1903 finds the eyes of all the fraternity directed toward St. Louis on account of the coming Exposition, but in normal times that city has only a temperate appetite for sculpture, supporting as it does a single representative of the profession. Mr. Robert P. Bringhurst has practised his art there alone since 1885, when he was called to take charge of the classes in sculpture of the local art school. Born in Jersey County, Illinois, in 1855, Mr. Bringhurst was obliged to assist early in the support of a widowed mother and younger brothers, and turned to the marble business, which he followed for some time in the neighboring town of Jerseyville. He became a clever carver; the usual progress from lettering to weeping willows and ultimately to lambs and pointing hands, was made rapidly, but left the ambitious workman unsatisfied. He visited the St. Louis School of Fine Arts, and as it chanced that some kind of instruction was then given in modelling, he arranged for a term's study, which lengthened into several. Finally the most stringent economy made a trip to Paris feasible, and there, in the Atelier Dumont of the École des Beaux-Arts, the young man had his first experience in modelling from life. The sojourn was all too short, but was resumed a year or two later, and enabled the eager student to gain the knowledge which he so coveted and which has stood him in good stead as sculptor and teacher in his adopted city. The habits of industry of his youth have continued. The walls of his commodious studio, opposite the Art Museum, are lined with his works; its shelves groan under their burdens of sketch models; while few of the public buildings of St. Louis are without their record of his skill in the form of portrait busts or memorial tablets. His decorations of the Art Palace at the Omaha Exposition were works of much beauty, and his important sculptures for the Educational building at the St. Louis Exposition promise to be even more successful. Mr. Bringhurst received a medal at the Columbian Exposition for his "Faun" and his "Awak-

2 M

ening of Spring," a graceful figure of a young girl, modelled in Paris and now in the Art Institute of Chicago. His tastes lie in the direction of poetic themes of this character. The studies and compositions which he produces incessantly show many beautiful fancies. "The Kiss of Eternity" (Fig. 102) is a good example of his style.

From St. Louis one must travel far afield before coming to another centre of artistic activity. Denver has produced some sculptors, but no sculpture; her gifted children find it necessary to descend to a less attenuated atmosphere in order to create. It is not until we reach San Francisco that we find the sculptor's art practised with enthusiasm. In that isolated but opulent region, which its inhabitants term the "right hand" of the continent, the conditions are somewhat similar to those of the East of fifty years ago. Somewhat, but not entirely. Like our ancestors — and theirs — of the Atlantic shore, these stalwart men of the sunny slope are without artistic training, but avid for "art." Their wealth, their instincts, and their pride demand it, and they indulge their tastes without stint, but thus far, it would seem, without great discrimination. They build memorial arches embroidered with ludicrous sculptures, and set up statues which cause pain in the Eastern foundries where they are cast. They ask no counsel from artist or critic.

Herein is the very great difference between the two sections of the country. The East, intrepid in business and fertile in invention, was long exceedingly timid in matters æsthetic, clinging closely to the traditions of Europe, seeking a precedent for every step, doing only what was being done abroad. The Western coast in its self-sufficiency seems more typical of America, showing an attitude which might have been expected everywhere in this land of independence. Having nothing, it proceeds to create in its own way sculpture and paintings, as it has already — and brilliantly — created its own literature. Where there are no restrictions the products must necessarily be in large measure formless and uncouth; but be they amusing or pathetic, they will disclose a quality of freedom and spontaneity, of that delight in doing which is the very soul of art. In time this soul will find itself a body; not an amorphous hulk of giant size, but a symmetrical organism which may convey nobly the

FIG. 103.—TILDEN: FOOTBALL PLAYERS.

dignity and grandeur of the creator's conceptions. In the East the "body" was builded first, laboriously, conscientiously, with many a measurement and reference to authority — and its soul has but begun to make itself felt. The ardent, exuberant West must perforce do its work in its own way, and its individual expression promises to be vastly interesting.

For the present, however, this young soul, so buoyant and self-confident, is somewhat naïf. It is not yet developed, and, like vigorous youth everywhere, cares more for the pleasure of doing than for what is done. The physical grasp predominates over the mental. Hence the traveller in California is startled now and then by such absurdities as the sculptured frieze on the Stanford Arch, such crudities as the Lick monument, and such extravagances as the "Mechanics' Fountain" (Fig. 104). The latter work differs, however, from the others in being the production of an accomplished artist, who has allowed the intoxicating atmosphere of his native state to affect his judgment. Unexpected as is such work from a man of Mr. Tilden's training, it is easy to trace through all of his earlier productions that love of physical strength — of the body for its own sake — which here fairly runs riot. It is seldom that our art shows this wholesome athletic tendency, and even the "Mechanics' Fountain" has its refreshing side.

Douglas Tilden, the most eminent sculptor of the Western coast, comes of an old and highly respected family, derived originally from Maryland. He was born in 1860, and at the age of five had the misfortune to lose his hearing as the result of scarlet fever. He was educated at the Institute for the Deaf and Dumb at Berkeley, and later entered the University of California, but, being offered a position as teacher in the Institute, abandoned his ambition for a collegiate education. He had always drawn, but had not modelled, nor thought of sculpture, until he was twenty-three years of age, when, upon seeing a brother's experiment with the clay, he resolved to try it himself. Delighted with the result, he sought instruction, and, after taking a few lessons, practised by himself throughout the four years of his connection with the Institute. In 1885 his first work, a statuette entitled "The Tired Wrestler," won for him the privilege of further study abroad. After seven months in the

Academy of Design in New York, he sailed for Paris, where **he** put himself under the tutelage of M. Paul Chopin, a deaf-mute sculptor of high standing. His first exhibit at the Salon was "The Baseball Player," a realistic representation of a "pitcher," on the point of throwing the ball. The following year, 1889, the sculptor exhibited the bronze reproduction of this figure, which now stands in Golden Gate Park, San Francisco, and a new work, "The Tired Boxer." The latter, reproduced in bronze, was accorded an honorable mention at the Salon of 1890. In 1892 Mr. Tilden exhibited a large and tumultuous group, "The Bear Hunt," representing a struggle between two Indians and an enormous monster standing on its hind legs. There is much science and much savagery in this study, but it is melodramatic; the result is unpleasant and hardly worthy of sculpture. All of these important works, and a small bronze called "The Young Acrobat," were seen at the Columbian Exposition, where they would undoubtedly have brought the sculptor a medal had this honor not been anticipated by his appointment on the jury. His last work in Paris, closing his long stay of seven years, was the admirable group of "The Football Players" (Fig. 103). This group shows in both modelling and composition the progress of those seven earnest years, and is the most scholarly expression of Mr. Tilden's robust art.

Arriving in San Francisco in 1894, his first important commission was for the "Native Sons' Fountain," the elements of which are a well-proportioned column, embellished by two figures: a miner at its base, who waves a flag with animated gesture, and a graceful winged figure poised airily upon the capital and holding above her head a tablet. The order for the "Mechanics' Fountain" followed, a memorial in honor of Peter Donahue, a pioneer ship and railroad builder. The sculptor made various more or less conventional designs, with which he could not satisfy himself, until in passing one day a machine shop he caught a glimpse of workmen operating a large lever punch. This gave him a *motif*, which he expanded into the strange design since realized in bronze and granite. While bizarre and restless beyond the proper limitations of monumental art, it is made up of admirable factors, and the whole work breathes an audacity and enthusiasm which are almost convincing. Unacademic

as is the artist's approach, certain aspects of the composition are sufficiently sculptural, and almost all views could be used happily in relief,
where the rigid outlines of the machine might be somewhat veiled.
The figures suspended upon the arm of the lever have the improba-
bility and the zest of demons.   By the terms of the contract the completed work was due at the foundry in six months from its beginning.

FIG. 104. — TILDEN: MECHANICS' FOUNTAIN, SAN FRANCISCO.

There was no time for weariness of mind and for reconsideration.
In one half-year those seven tons of clay were converted into what
may fairly be termed the most unconventional work of sculpture in
the United States.   Its merits are evident; "its faults are those
that belong to the land of sun and harvest" where it grew.   We
may look upon its lawless composition and its ragged contour with
the eye of criticism, but we can feel only admiration for the ardent
and intrepid sculptor who wrought this wonder in those brief

months.   As Pitt said of a speech by Fox, " Don't disparage it;
nobody could have made it but himself."   Not only could no one
but Mr. Tilden have made the " Mechanics' Fountain," but it could
have been done in no other city than San Francisco.   In allowing
himself " full swing," the sculptor of the Pacific slope has given us a
historic document, full of significance of time and place.

The most conspicuous of Mr. Tilden's pupils is Robert I. Aitkin,
who has succeeded him as instructor at the Mark Hopkins Institute.
Mr. Aitkin appears to share his teacher's energy and already, in
some degree, his skill.   Though scarcely more than a youth, he has
done several important works, the most noteworthy of which are a
mortuary relief, " The Gates of Silence"; the McKinley monuments
for St. Helena, California, and for San Francisco; and the decorations of the Dewey Monument in the latter city.   The colossal
" Victory," which crowns the shaft of this memorial, one hundred
feet from the ground, has been highly praised by those who have
seen it in place.

Others who received their first inspiration from Mr. Tilden are
Edgar Walter, who has exhibited at six successive Salons works
of increasing power and interest, and Earl Cummings, who has also
won honors abroad.   Frank Happersburger has a large and permanent place in the sculpture of the Pacific coast.   His " Garfield "
he made in Europe, but the sculpture of the Lick monument was
modelled and cast in San Francisco.   In this enormous work the
designer has pictured various scenes of Western activity, as well as
a portion of the animal life of California.   He was assisted in his undertaking by V. Guglielmo, a skilful Italian modeller.   Mr. Marion
F. Wells, the sculptor of the giant figure of " Progress " which crowns
the dome of the San Francisco City Hall, and of a statue of James
Marshall, the discoverer of gold, died in 1903.

The slight artistic impulse of a hundred years ago has grown
strong and has extended over a vast territory.   With increasing
definiteness, as well as growing momentum, it has attained even to
our far western limits.   What was at first the mere groping of an
untaught instinct, destitute of message or appeal, has gradually
developed a character, a fundamental sincerity, and remarkable gifts

of utterance.   Where once was indecision and a timid leaning on the past, there exists to-day a valuable nucleus of artistic conscious-ness.   The American sculptor no longer puts himself deliberately out of touch with his time, but endeavors to be a part of the life about him.   He realizes that, in order to exert an influence, his art must speak no alien tongue, but must follow the vernacular of his day and race.   He must keep close to the people — close to them, but a little ahead, drawing them forward in appreciation step by step. If he recognizes the hour's peculiar problems, and if, in conjunction with his fellows, he expresses himself frankly and adequately, the national flavor will follow.

In this bewildering period of American history, elements new, varied, and contradictory are pouring into the national crucible; doubtless the solvent will be adequate to reduce all these to a condi-tion of homogeneity, but no man can say just what the ultimate product will be.   The American character is not yet fully formed; the very features are restless upon our unsettled faces.   If Herbert Spencer is right in his prediction that the eventual mixture of the allied varieties of the Aryan race "will produce a finer type of man than has hitherto existed," and that ours is to be "a civilization grander than any that the world has known," we may look forward confidently to a remarkable artistic expression founded upon what has gone before, yet the logical product of new and generously favor-able conditions.   The story of American Sculpture is but begun.

SUPPLEMENTARY CHAPTER: 1923

TWENTY years have passed since the foregoing was written, twenty years freighted with events of vast significance in our national life. To claim that American art has kept pace with our material development would be to jest. The recent expansion of industry and commerce within our borders has no parallel in the history of the human race. It is not strange if our rather meager showing in the refinements of life seems, by contrast, conspicuously pitiful. It should be noted also that the World War, which, thanks to our safe isolation, contributed an enormous impetus to American manufactures, did not fail to paralyze for a time our "non-essential" fine arts almost as completely as was the case in the stricken lands of Europe. Hence if some of the prophecies of this book have come true, many of them have not. A number of our most prominent sculptors have died, leaving slight record. Among the survivors the creative impulse has not always persisted. Some have frankly given up the job; others have diminished their output to the point where it is negligible. However, new men have appeared, men of just as convincing talent and ever-increasing skill. The world grows old and grows young again!

Erastus D. Palmer (1817–1904) and Thomas Ball (1819–1911) lived into the new century. These patriarchs departed literally "full of years" and well-earned honors, beloved by all who knew them. John Rogers, born in 1829 and famed for his sturdily American "groups," lived likewise until 1904. Others whose persistent exile made their careers almost legendary were Larkin G. Meade (1835–1910), Franklin Simmons (1839–1913), and Moses Ezekiel (1844–1917), all of whom the enchantment of Italy held to the end. George E. Bissell (1839–1920), affectionately called "Père Bissell" by his protégés; Jonathan S. Hartley (1846–1912), a gentle nature of moderate creative gift; Charles Calverley (1833–1914), a craftsman of sterling worth; Edward Kemeys (1843–1907), almost great as an animal sculptor, self-trained and amazingly informed in the lore of wild life — these also were some of the older men to pass on during this period.

John Quincy Adams Ward (1830–1910), who reached a ripe old age, was for many years the honored dean of the profession. The last work associated with his name was the pediment of the New York Stock Exchange (1903), in the modelling of which he was happily reënforced by Paul Bartlett. This tympanum is distinguished not only for its fine decorative quality but for its profound thought, glorifying Integrity as the foundation stone of Commerce. Among Mr. Ward's later works, largely completed by younger hands, were: Soldiers' and Sailors' Monument, Syracuse, N. Y., 1907; "General Hancock," Philadelphia, 1908; "General Sheridan," Washington, D. C., 1908.

When, in 1907, Augustus Saint Gaudens's slow martyrdom was mercifully ended, American art sustained a greater loss than was realized. Highly as he was appreciated by his colleagues, his true position and influence are better understood to-day. From 1900 onward the master's hand had gradually lost its power; certain of his later works, however nobly conceived, show a more faltering touch or the irrelevancies of the assistant. This decline is not apparent in his second "Lincoln," that grave seated figure, made, like its predecessor, for Chicago, and the prototype of so many admirable "Lincolns" by younger men, but it is all too evident in the Phillips Brooks Memorial of Boston and in the caryatides for the Albright Gallery of Buffalo. Although physical weakness had the final word, the master lives in a score of America's choicest treasures; sixteen years have passed since his death, yet how few works of sculpture have been created in that time which one could think of naming in the same breath with them.

Louis Saint Gaudens (born 1854) survived his brother by only six years.

The brilliant career of Karl Bitter was abruptly closed in 1915. He was still young and full of vigor, physical and mental; his interest in experiment, in conquering difficulties, marked him to the end as one of the most adventurous of our group. It was his delight to expend himself in colossal enterprises like the embellishment of

great expositions.   Those of Buffalo and St. Louis had his personal
direction, while San Francisco benefited by his counsel.   He loved
the very labor of his profession: the demands of an intricate architectural composition, the silent challenge of a reluctant stone, he
met in turn with eager joy.   His pediment for the Wisconsin State
Capitol is one of the finest in America; the Carl Schurz Memorial
in New York City and the Lowry Memorial in Minneapolis are triumphant solutions of new and exacting problems.   What a far cry from
the tumultuous groups of the Columbian Administration Building
and the exuberance of the Broad Street relief, to these impressive
works!   Karl Bitter had learned to endow his art with the "hint of
eternity."   His memory is an inspiration.[1]

John J. Boyle (1852–1917), whose sturdy interpretations of the
redman were all too few, will be remembered likewise for his "Franklin" in Philadelphia and Paris, and his "Commodore Barry" in
Washington.   Richard E. Brooks (1865–1919), a sculptor of much
skill, from whom more was due; Frank E. Elwell (1858–1922),
whose agitated career reveals a wistful blend of noble dreams and
inadequate workmanship; Henry Linder (1854–1910), a little known
master of a delightfully decorative art — all of these were men of
talent who were denied full utterance.   One fated to be taken while
very young was Charles Albert Lopez (1870–1906), whose brief
workday was full of promise.   Charles J. Mulligan (1866–1916), of
Chicago, ever hearty and unconventional, was called to an heroic
but losing battle; much work he did, but never sufficiently recom-
pensed to permit of adequate study.

Quite other was the record of Henry M. Shrady (1871–1922),
whose name will be forever associated with one great achievement,
the U. S. Grant Memorial in the city of Washington.   Mr. Shrady
put his best into this great enterprise, devoting no less than nineteen years to its completion.   If its subordinate groups, representing
the Cavalry and the Artillery branches of the army, seem at the
present moment too vehement and too realistic, they nevertheless
have the respect of every sincere craftsman.   Their vivid detail
affords an effective foil for the stern simplicity of the principal fea-

[1] For a more detailed appreciation of Karl Bitter's art see Professor Schevill's "Karl
Bitter — A Biography" and the writer's "Modern Tendencies in Sculpture."

ture, a very large equestrian portrait of the taciturn general. In this, as in his "Washington" at Brooklyn, N. Y., Mr. Shrady earned for himself a place among the greatest sculptors of equestrian statues of modern times. His death just upon the eve of the dedication of his life work was lamentably tragic.

Bela Pratt (1864–1917) as sculptor and teacher won generous recognition in his home city of Boston. Strangely enough this sad-eyed son of the Puritans was at his best in modelling youthful girlish forms. He made many portraits, some of them admirable as his "Phillips Brooks." Some of his later works, the seated "Hawthorne" for Salem, Mass., and "Alexander Hamilton," Chicago, were touched with the weariness which in the end was to master him.

Another whose untimely passing we still mourn was Solon Borglum (1868–1922), one of nature's noblemen, an artist of unusual originality, as modest and unassuming as he was talented. These later years added much to the tale of his achievements. Among his more important works are: equestrian statues of General John B. Gordon, Atlanta, Ga., and "'Bucky' O'Neil," Prescott, Ariz.; a statue of Hon. Jacob Leisler, New Rochelle, N. Y., and the Shieren Memorial, Brooklyn, N. Y. Not the least of Mr. Borglum's services to our nation's art was the founding of an "American School of Sculpture" for practical instruction. This school it is proposed to perpetuate as a memorial to one of America's most beloved sculptors.

Henry Dickinson Thrasher (born in 1883, killed in France in 1918) was an artist of undoubted ability whose gifts held great promise for the future. It was his misfortune to be called just when he was ready to give expression to his slowly maturing ideals. François M. L. Tonetti (1863–1920) was another who had a real talent which was never permanently put on record. Cartaino di Sciarrino Pietro (1886–1918) will be remembered for his sympathetic portraiture of his friend John Burroughs.

If many are hampered by poverty, Charles Cary Rumsey (1879–1922) suffered, on the contrary, from the handicap of wealth. Despite his prowess at polo he attained to considerable distinction in his art, being particularly interested in horses. He designed the frieze on the arch of the Manhattan Bridge, a Soldier and Sailor

Memorial in the Brownsville section of Brooklyn, and received at the Panama-Pacific Exposition a medal for his striking equestrian statue of Pizarro.

Among the elder sisters of the guild whose peaceful lives extended into the twentieth century were Miss Harriet Hosmer (1830–1908) and Miss Anne Whitney (1821–1915), both of the "Roman tradition." Of a very different school was Mrs. Edith Woodman Burroughs (1871–1918), one of the few women sculptors — or, one might better say, one of the few American sculptors — who have attained to a distinctive personal expression. Her untimely death came at the moment of her greatest promise, as evidenced by her "Fountain of Youth," at San Francisco, her notable portrait of John La Farge and certain quaint renderings in terra cotta of themes from the Arabian Nights. Another whose early summons brought grief to her colleagues was Miss Helen Mears (1876–1916), a favorite pupil of Saint Gaudens. Miss Mears did important work for her native state, Wisconsin, and modelled the portrait of Frances E. Willard in the National Sculpture Gallery, Washington, D. C. The latest loss to the profession is the departure of Elsie Ward Hering, who was born in Howard County, Missouri, in 1871, and died on January 12, 1923.

Daniel Chester French, the present dean of American sculptors, has set a fine example of diligence and of artistic uprightness. His performance in the last twenty years is monumental in quantity as well as quality. To name but the most important works, we have: the Quadriga and other decorations of the Minnesota State House, St. Paul; Parkman Memorial, Boston; Melvin Memorial, Concord, Mass., and Governor Oglethorpe Monument, Savannah — the two latter in 1910; "Memory," Marshall Field Memorial, Chicago, 1911; statue of General William Draper, Milford, Mass., and "Lincoln," Lincoln, Neb., 1912; Longfellow Memorial, Cambridge, Mass., and statue of Emerson, Concord, Mass., 1914. The year 1915 produced the "Genius of Creation" for the Panama-Pacific Exposition, the figure "Sculpture" for the St. Louis Art Museum, and the Spencer Trask Memorial at Saratoga Springs, N. Y. The groups "Brooklyn" and "Manhattan" for the Manhattan Bridge, and the Lafayette Memorial, Brooklyn, were executed in 1918, while the great "Lincoln" for Washington occupied the sculptor during 1918 and 1919. A "Lafayette" was made for Lafayette College, Easton, Pa., in 1921; "The Weaver" for Brooklyn, a military memorial for Exeter, N. H., and the Dupont Fountain, Washington, D. C., in 1922. In the Metropolitan Museum one finds a recent nude, "Memory," and the sculptor's latest creation is an idyllic group in marble.

The uniformly high excellence of these works and the exquisite beauty of many of the number make one thankful indeed that Mr. French has been spared so long to toil with a truly youthful ardor and undiminished skill for the glory of American art. In such a catalogue there are subjects of restricted appeal, but Mr. French seems to find everything in the world interesting, and through his enthusiasm, his invention, and his genial modelling he almost always carries us with him. Certain themes and treatments stand out from the array with particular vividness. The highest note in sculptural expression is found in such richly massive forms as the Melvin "Victory" and the personified "Sculpture." When, however, one considers the fragile grace of the "Spirit of Life" of the Trask Memorial, the classic purity of the Palmer Memorial, the physical loveliness of the Metropolitan nude, the spiritual consecration of the "Washington," and the impressiveness of the great "Lincoln," one recognizes that Mr. French's genius "speaks a various language." Our loss would have been great had he been restricted to a single form of utterance.

In spite of generous contribution of his time to public affairs Herbert Adams — twice president of the National Sculpture Society and later president of the National Academy of Design — has to his credit many new achievements, varying from architectural sculpture, as his four figures on the Brooklyn Museum, to the sensitive tinted heads which will always be associated with his name. In the latter delicate art his hand has not lost its cunning; recent examples are "Primavera" (Fig. 105) and a portrait bust of Miss De Fanti, two of the most vivid and delightful of a long series. Particularly fine are Mr. Adams's seated portraits of John Marshall and Rufus Ranney, of the Cleveland Court House, and the historic figures of Stephen Langton and Simon de Montfort, which decorate the same building.   His dignified "William Cullen Bryant" of Bryant Park, New York City, is more widely known, while the graceful group of the McMillan Fountain (Washington, D. C.) and a sister nymph in a garden of Cooperstown, N. Y., are universally admired.   Beyond these it must suffice to enumerate the bronze statues of General

FIG. 105. — HERBERT ADAMS: PRIMAVERA.

A. A. Humphreys, Fredericksburg, Va. (1909); Colonel Loammi Baldwin, Woburn, Mass. (1917); Matthias Baldwin, Philadelphia, and Jerome Wheelock, Grafton, Mass. (1906); the colossal granite monument erected by the state of Michigan at Vicksburg; the Tevis Memorial, San Francisco; the Welch Monument, Auburn, N. Y.; the Mrs. Woodrow Wilson Memorial, Rome, Georgia; the General Hawley bronze relief in the Hartford Capitol, and the relief of Joseph Choate for the Union League Club of New York City.

George Barnard's grandiose dream of decoration for the Pennsylvania Capitol was to be but partially realized. The scandalous history of the building left his name unsmirched, but the promised opportunity faded away until naught remained except the two groups of the main entrance: " Burden of Life " and " Work and Brotherhood." These enormous compositions, containing thirty-two figures of heroic size, represent a labor of several years amid heartrending difficulties, balanced, however, by a rare enthusiasm. Some of the figures are among the finest things in American sculpture; the total result is vastly impressive to those who appreciate exalted ideals and masterly craftsmanship. Fragments of the groups are to be found in various museums, as the " Father and Son " in the Carnegie Institute, Pittsburgh. They are always recognizable from their power and their distinctly individual character. Barnard has not ceased

FIG. 106. — BARNARD: WOMAN, METROPOLITAN MUSEUM.

to dream; his projects become every day more intricate and overpowering. Among his recent works, actually carried out, are the much discussed " Lincoln " of Cincinnati and Manchester, England; " Adam and Eve," a marble group at Tarrytown, N. Y., and the admirable " Woman " (Fig. 106) of the Metropolitan Museum.

Frederick MacMonnies has continued with untiring industry his magnificent achievement. Novel, surprising, exotic, anachronistic as may seem to many his ideas and ideals, there runs through his output one constant factor, more precious, more needed in American art than any other, and that is perfection of workmanship. MacMonnies's aim is to make each work "a classic." When all is

summed up it will be found that no American has made a greater
contribution to the development of the art of sculpture in this land.
If one emphasizes the technical side of MacMonnies's works, it is
because this is so exceptional, so rarely possible in this country.
The Pioneer Fountain at Denver reveals new beauties upon every
visit.   Its groups are massive, yet delightfully varied; their fundamental precision is concealed under the suavity of incomparable
modelling.   The same marvellous quality is found in the Princeton
Battle Monument, a masterpiece of luminous expressive modelling.
The conception of this majestic group is worthy of all the loving
toil expended upon it.   The " Washington " which crowns it is one
of the most appealing thus far created.   MacMonnies's ideal of
" Civic Virtue " may not be yours or mine.   Neither was his
" America " of the Columbian Exposition; but what of the " Mac-
Monnies Fountain " as a whole?   What modern creation has equalled
it in splendor?   Chicago allowed it to perish because it was not
understood that it could be saved.   May its glory again grace the
earth !   The masterly " Civic Virtue " is but a part of an unusually
fine fountain whose every detail is exquisitely wrought.   Some day
it will be seen as a whole and appreciated, as must be the " Inspiration " and " Truth " of the New York Public Library.

Compared with some, Paul Wayland Bartlett's list is a short
one; but if his progeny be few, each is a " lion."   The item " Pediment on House Wing of National Capitol — Washington," occupies
little space upon a page, but what an amount of painstaking toil
of head and hand went into that enormous composition !   The choice
of artist was justified; the distance which separates Crawford's
naïf essay over the Senate entrance from Bartlett's triumphant
achievement is not alone one of years but vividly registers the
entire progress of American sculpture.   The story of the " Lafayette "
of Paris, acceptably completed in 1900 but unsatisfactory to the
sculptor, who gave it twelve more years, is characteristic of Paul
Bartlett, who works for eternity.   His statue of General Joseph
Warren in Roxbury, Mass., and his friendly " Franklin " in Waterbury, Conn., testify to the same conscience· and reveal the same
perfection of technique.   Calumet, Mich., has his " Agassiz " and
Philadelphia his " Philip Morris."   Always an experimenter, Mr.

Bartlett's statues of the " Puritans " on the Capitol at Hartford and the decorative figures upon the Public Library of New York present contrasts as notable in treatment as in subject. Those of the Library are like white blossoms hung upon the marble façade. A statue of " Patriotism " in red granite, a novel effort in an unusual material, is greatly treasured in Duluth.

A veteran of vast achievement and solid worth is Charles H. Niehaus (born, Cincinnati, 1855), winner of numberless competitions and indefatigable builder of monuments. His record speaks for itself. The dates have not been provided, but here are some of the highlights: the colossal equestrian statue of General Forrest, Memphis, Tenn. (one of the best of its kind in the United States); statue of Hon. J. J. Ingalls, Statuary Hall, National Capitol; McKinley Statue, Canton, Ohio; Benjamin Harrison Monument, Indianapolis, Ind.; Beardsley Monument, Bridgeport, Conn.; two statues of Governor Goebel and the notably fine pediment of the State Capitol, at Frankfort, Ky.; John Paul Jones Monument, Washington, D. C.; Commodore Perry Monument, Buffalo, N. Y.; statues of Zachariah Chandler and General Click, National Capitol; " Hernandez Cortez," Panama-Pacific Exposition; Francis Scott Key Memorial, Baltimore, Md. (1922); World War Memorial representing Embarkation and Debarkation, Hoboken, N. J. (1922); World War Memorial, Newark, N. J. In addition to these major works are numerous tablets and busts, including two portraits of Charles H. Hackley, Muskegon, Mich.; Robert Blum, Art Museum, Cincinnati, Ohio, and the Reverend Dr. Collier, Cooper Union, New York City.

The vast output of J. Massey Rhind (born, 1860) is difficult to classify, as it is impossible to recapitulate. The children of his studio are like the sons of Deucalion; they spring up about him numerous as the progeny of the dragon's teeth. In New York, New Haven, Providence, Philadelphia, Washington, Pittsburgh, Indianapolis, Memphis, and one knows not how many other places, they sit upon the front steps of great buildings or look down from tympanum or cornice. There is something friendly and familiar in their appearance; you feel that you have met them before. They are generic rather than individual — of good mass and always decorous. Perhaps more should not be asked of decorative art. Mr.

Rhind does not limit himself, however, to architectural sculpture; among his subjects are the Colt Memorial, Hartford, Conn., 1905; a statue of Andrew Carnegie, Carnegie Institute, Pittsburgh; equestrian statue of Washington, Newark, N. J., 1912; Soldiers' and Sailors' Monument, Girard College, Philadelphia, 1913; Peter Stuyvesant Monument, Jersey City, N. J., 1913; Robert Burns Monument, Pittsburgh, 1914; Statue of General Alexander S. Webb, College of the City of New York, 1916, etc., etc. The McKinley Birthplace Memorial at Niles, Ohio, has become a museum of sculpture through Mr. Rhind's industry, and is not yet complete. A large alto-relief, "Over the Top," to decorate the exterior of the 106th Infantry Armory, Brooklyn, shows unusually vigorous modelling.

Isidore Konti's themes run a wide gamut from sportive founta'n figures to imposing funereal piles. He is of the same exuberant school as was exemplified in Karl Bitter's early art, and it is in the joyous creations of his fancy that one finds him most himself. The titles, "Illusion," "Orpheus," "Wood Nymph," bring back graceful forms, half-remembered; "Genius of Immortality," "Solace," and "Dying Melodies" strike a deeper note. The exquisite "Mother and Child" of the Metropolitan Museum would make a perfect fountain group. The Gumbel and Hyam Memorial fountains are in New Orleans. Mr. Konti's sepulchral monuments have great distinction, as the recumbent figure of the Reverend Dr. Morgan Dix in Trinity Church, New York, and the memorial to Bishop Horatio Potter in the Cathedral of St. John the Divine. Amid many happy decorations for world's fairs Mr. Konti's frieze for the "Column of Progress" in San Francisco stands out as particularly beautiful. An impressive memorial to the heroes of the World War at Yonkers, N. Y., brings the record to date, although scores of busts and smaller works are necessarily omitted.

Carl Ethan Akeley was born in Orleans County, N. Y., in 1864. He was associated with the Field Museum, Chicago, from 1895 to 1909, and has been with the American Museum of Natural History since that time. Mr. Akeley has made taxidermy a sculptural art, but has also done much work in the sculptor's medium, as testify his two animal studies in Brooklyn Institute, numerous groups in the

American Museum of Natural History, and particularly his impressive project for a memorial to Theodore Roosevelt.

Whether or not John Flanagan (born, Newark, N. J., 1865) had any choice in the matter, the public has apparently decided that he should consecrate his life to the refined art of the medallist. If he preferred to make statues — and he does them well — he should not have shown himself so completely the master of low relief. A group of Mr. Flanagan's medals and plaques is like an exquisite musical composition written in a single key but full of delightful and surprising variations. From the trained hands of this master have come no fewer than thirty bronze portrait plaquettes and fifteen medals, the latter series culminating in the admirable " Medaille de Verdun," commissioned by the War Department and struck in 1921. Realizing that the designing and elaboration of a good medal represents as much study as the making of a statue, one is able to form an idea of the painstaking toil which has gone into this aggregation. It is a life's work, so concentrated that it might be carried about in a handbag, but precious as jewels. How few there are who leave so much! Among other sculptures by Mr. Flanagan we note a high relief, " Antique Education " (1903), over the entrance of the famous Free Public Library of Newark, N. J.; a statue of Professor Joseph Henry, Albany, N. Y.; " The Philosopher " and " The Missionary " for the Panama-Pacific Exposition; a portrait medallion of Samuel Pierpont Langley, in the Smithsonian Institution; a large memorial in bronze and marble to the founder of the Ætna Life Insurance Company in Hartford, Conn., and a number of excellent busts.

The twenty years in question have been busy ones for Hermon A. MacNeil. Following the " Great Cascade " of the St. Louis Exposition, he next occupied himself with " The Coming of the White Man," the well-known group of City Park, Portland, Oregon. The McKinley Memorial of Columbus, Ohio, is justly admired as one of our best monuments; the proposed triumphal arch became finally a large exedra with portrait statue and, at the ends, handsome bronze groups. Perhaps the finest monumental work that Mr. MacNeil has done is his Soldiers' and Sailors' Memorial in Washington Park, Albany, N. Y., dedicated in 1912. It includes a majestic figure of " America " in bronze, backed by a large rectangular block of stone which is enriched with a frieze of marching soldiers. Messrs. MacNeil and Calder made the two companion relief-portraits of George Washington which embellish the north side of the Washington Arch at the foot of Fifth Avenue, New York City. "The Adventurous Bowman" on the high "Column of Progress" was one of the best of many decorations of the Panama-Pacific Exposition. Then followed two large groups in bronze for the Patton Gymnasium of Northwestern University, Evanston, Ill.; these portray respectively "Physical" and "Intellectual Development." For the giant Soldiers' and Sailors' pylons of the Parkway, Philadelphia, were modelled in 1921 certain fine groups and reliefs, not yet placed. Mr. MacNeil has made four historical figures for the State Capitol at Hartford, Conn.; portraits of Oliver Wolcott, Colonel David Humphreys, Judge Ellsworth, and General David Wooster. There are also busts a-plenty, such as the monumental portrait of John Stewart Kennedy, in the New York Public Library; and we must not forget that it is to Mr. MacNeil that we owe the useful as well as artistic quarter-dollar now current. His present preoccupation is an important Marquette group for Chicago.

Gutzon Borglum was born in Idaho in 1867, of Danish parents. His early history, like that of his brother Solon, is one of eager study and toil. His irrepressible energy continues without sign of abatement. Among the many products of the period which we are considering must be mentioned his equestrian "General Phil Sheridan," at Washington, D. C.; twelve apostles in the Cathedral of St. John the Divine, New York; colossal head of Abraham Lincoln, rotunda of Capitol, Washington, D. C.; "Mares of Diomedes," Metropolitan Museum, New York; "The Aviator," Charlottesville, Va.; Governor William Dempster Hoard Monument, Madison, Wis.; John Mackay Monument, Carson City, Nev. Mr. Borglum is now producing a group of forty-two heroic figures in bronze, "Wars of America," for Newark, N. J.; a colossal bronze equestrian statue of General Phil Sheridan for Chicago; the Governor Aycock Monument, for Raleigh, N. C.; a monument to Collis P. Huntington; and finally the extraordinary relief, "seven hundred feet by one hundred feet on the face of Stone Mountain, near Atlanta, Ga., involving several hundred figures, a memorial to the Confederate Army."

The work of Edmond T. Quinn always shows taste and conscience. He does not indulge in "mass production," and there is a quality in his art which is not found in the output of the factory-studios. Mr. Quinn was born in 1868 in Philadelphia, and his professional work begins with a statue of John Howard at Williamsport, Pa., erected in 1905. In 1908 he completed reliefs for the Battle Monument at King's Mountain, S. C.; in 1909 he was occupied with a series of decorative figures in relief for the Pittsburgh Athletic Club, and also the statue of Zoroaster on the Brooklyn Museum. Omitting several busy years, we come in 1917 to the statue of General Pemberton in the National Cemetery at Vicksburg, Miss. The next year saw the completion of the well-known and much admired "Edwin Booth as Hamlet," in Gramercy Park, New York City. Mr. Quinn made in 1921 a fine "Victory" for the World War Memorial at New Rochelle, N. Y. He has modelled many busts, among them the striking head of Edgar Allan Poe in Poe Park, New York City; characterizations of Professor Franklin Hooper and the Reverend Father Sylvester Malone, both in the Brooklyn Institute Museum (1922), and excellent portraits of such notable subjects as Edwin Markham, Vincente Blasco-Ibáñez, and Eugene O'Neill.

A sculptor whose product is invariably sculpture is Albert Jaegers, born in Elberfeld, Germany, 1868. His monumental conceptions appeal to his brothers of the craft. One is not surprised to learn that his noble "Arkansas" at the St. Louis Exposition especially interested Saint Gaudens, while his winning design for the Von Steuben Memorial had the enthusiastic support of that master. It could not be otherwise; the Von Steuben (1910) portrait and attendant groups, combined with admirable architecture, form one of the finest monuments in the nation's capital, and therefore in the United States. In 1913 Mr. Jaegers began work upon his elaborate and impressive Pioneer Monument (Fig. 107) for Germantown, Pa. This memorial, finished in 1920, stands some thirty-three feet in height and includes three large bas-reliefs and a group, and is crowned by a colossal seated figure of "Light-Bearing Civilization." Upon its completion the sculptor indulged for a brief period in developing long cherished fancies for garden decorations. The Monsignor Stein Memorial for Paterson, N. J., is a recent work, while his very striking equestrian statue representing " America Upholding the Flag " will soon be added to the artistic assets of Orange, N. J.

Royal Cortissoz wrote of Saint Gaudens: " I do not know how

FIG. 107. — ALBERT JAEGERS: PIONEER MONUMENT, GERMANTOWN, PA.

better to express the ideal that he stood for than to say that from the Saint Gaudens point of view the doing of a scamped or insincere piece of work was a fairly shameful performance, a kind of moral wrong." No one has exemplified this influence more conscientiously than his pupil, Adolph A. Weinman, who was born in Karlsruhe, Germany, in 1870. Mr. Weinman first attracted widespread interest through his large group, " The Destiny of the Red Man," a decoration of the Louisiana Purchase Exposition which was not fated to be forgotten like its ephemeral companions; indeed one of its figures — a blanketed warrior — was so arrestingly impressive that the younger men still reproduce it. The next conspicuous work was the admirable "General Alexander Macomb" of Detroit (1906), followed by the Maryland Union Soldiers' and Sailors' Monument at Baltimore (1907), a highly successful bronze group which likewise finds its echo in the work of other men. Meantime Mr. Weinman has produced a series of fine reliefs and, in particular, much decorative sculpture for the Pennsylvania Railway Terminal in New York City, culminating in the dignified bronze statue of Alexander J. Cassatt (1909). The same year saw the completion of his much admired seated "Lincoln" for Lincoln's birthplace, Hodgensville, Ky. (A replica is to be found at the University of Wisconsin.) Two years later he made a standing "Lincoln" for the Kentucky capitol. The year 1911 also saw the adornment of another state capitol at his hands, the Senate pediment at Madison, Wis. Monuments to Lieut. Col. William F. Vilas at Vicksburg and Mayor William Maybury at Detroit followed in 1912. Mr. Weinman's contribution to the Panama–Pacific Exposition was greatly appreciated; his fountains of "The Rising Sun" and "The Setting Sun" gave pleasure to all. Various monuments of high quality continue to add to the sculptor's reputation. Among them may be mentioned war memorials for a school chapel in Pomfret, Conn., for Forest Hills, New York, and for Pottstown, Pa. A good medal is recognized among sculptors as the final test in artistry; in this field Mr. Weinman has had a series of successes, for he it was who made the medals of the Louisiana Purchase Exposition, the Institute of American Architects, the National Institute of Arts and Letters, the J. Sanford Saltus Award Medal of the American Numismatic Society, and finally the well-known dime and half dollar of this great American Republic.

It is surprising how much good sculpture some of these modest men have been permitted to accomplish without notoriety. Augustus Lukeman is an artist who can be depended upon to do quietly and well his job, whether in the studio or on committees. He has no press agent and the Sunday supplement is not for him, but behold what he has created in the years which have elapsed since this book was written: in 1905 the " Columbus " of the U. S. Customs House, New York City; in 1907 four statues for the Royal Bank Building, Montreal; 1908, the Soldiers' Monument of Somerville, Mass.; 1909, four statues for the Brooklyn Institute of Arts and Sciences; 1910, the equestrian statue, " Kit Carson," Trinidad, Col. (horse by Roth); 1911, U. S. Grant Memorial, San Diego, Cal.; 1912, group, " Women of the Confederacy," Raleigh, N. C.; 1913, statue, " Franklin Pierce," Concord, N. H.; 1914, the graceful Straus Memorial Fountain, New York City; 1917, statue of General William Shepard, West-field, Mass.; 1919, " Honor Roll," Soldiers' Monument, Prospect Park, Brooklyn; 1920, Soldiers' Monument, Red Hook Park, Brook-lyn; 1921, equestrian statue of Francis Asbury, Washington, D. C.; 1922, equestrian statue of General David McM. Gregg, Reading, Pa.

For a man who once upon a time had to go to California for his health, Alexander Stirling Calder is astonishingly productive. Merely to name what he has done since 1903 would fill the page. His " Fountain of Energy " at the Panama–Pacific Exposition was characteristic of the man, exultant and irrepressible — disconcert-ingly so to those whose ideal of sculpture is serenity and "the integrity of the mass "! Other vast groups of his begetting were the spectacular " Nations of the East " and " Nations of the West," in which he literally replenished the earth, to the delight of all who saw those enormous compositions. As might be expected, his works are scattered from Pasadena to Vancouver, from Maine to Florida. They are in various museums, but, better yet, rejoice many a park and garden. Who can see the Depew Memorial Fountain in In-dianapolis without thankfulness that Karl Bitter's playful thought found such sympathetic realization? In his small works Mr. Calder often shows a remarkable gift for simplification, a selection of the essential, which is as rare as it is enviable. His " Naiad with Mask " (1918), Montclair, N. J., is a pleasing example; the " Last Dryad " is equally characteristic. Perhaps he has never surpassed in poetic beauty his distinguished Lea Memorial, Laurel Hill Cemetery, Philadelphia (1910).

In his Schenley Memorial Fountain (1919) for Pittsburgh, Victor David Brenner (born, Shavely, Russia, 1871) made an interesting excursion into the domain of decorative sculpture, but his popularity as a medallist is likely to grant him little time for such adventures. Aside from a host of beautiful medals and seals, may be named these important works: a marble bust of Professor Charles Eliot Norton, Fogg Museum, Cambridge, Mass. (1903); John Paul Jones plaquette, American Numismatic Society, New York City (1905); tablet portrait of Spencer Trask, National Arts Club, New York (1907); Panama Canal Employees medal (1908); tablet portrait of Professor William H. Welch, Johns Hopkins Hospital, Baltimore (1910), one of several reliefs in that institution; bronze bust, Samuel P. Avery, Brooklyn Museum of Art (1912); Lincoln Tablet, Washington Irving High School, New York City (1914), and tablet portrait of Professor Hutton, Engineers' Club, New York (1919). It is a matter of congratulation that America has men so skilled in this delicate and exigent art as are Victor Brenner and John Flanagan; others have turned upon occasion to the making of medals and coins; one recalls the successes of Aitken, MacNeil, Manship, and Weinman.

Willard D. Paddock (born, Brooklyn, N. Y., 1873) is an artist whose versatility leads him to a wide range of expression — from whimsical little bronzes to the austerely impressive Noah Webster Memorial at Amherst.

Charles Keck (born, 1874) is perhaps most widely known for his gracious figure of " America," the principal piece of sculpture of the elaborate Allegheny County Soldiers' Memorial, in Pittsburgh. He has exhibited many fine things since his return from the American Academy in Rome, notably a portrait bust of Elihu Vedder. A monument presented by the American people to Brazil on the first centennial of that country's independence contains portrait statues of Washington and Lincoln and of two Brazilian statesmen and is crowned by a classic figure of " Friendship." More recent is a colorful group of " Lewis and Clark " for Charlottesville, Va.

Carl Heber was born at Stuttgart, Germany, in 1874, but grew up in Dundee, Ill. He supplemented his course at the Art Institute of Chicago with a protracted stay in Paris, where he learned many things. The earliest public demonstration of his artistry was the recumbent figure, " Pastoral " (1904), now in the St. Louis Museum of Fine Arts. Returning to America, the young sculptor found his first opportunity in a Schiller Monument for Rochester, N. Y. (1905), often referred to as an example of "good work fortunately placed." Mr. Heber always "makes good" and each order brings another, as the following partial list would indicate: statue of Benjamin Franklin, Princeton University, and "Roman Epic Poetry," Brooklyn Museum of Fine Arts (1907); Champlain Memorial, Plattsburg, N. Y., and Light House Memorial, Crown Point, N. Y. (both 1910); two groups for the Manhattan Bridge approaches, New York City (1912); "Bondage," San Francisco Museum of Fine Arts (1913); Kane County Memorial, Geneva, Ill. (1914); Everett Memorial, Goshen, N. Y. (1915); Husted Memorial, Peekskill, N. Y., and sculptural decorations for mansion of Charles M. Schwab, Loretto, Pa. (1916); Civil War Memorial, Ellsworth Park, Union Hill, N. J. (1917); Wausau County Memorial, Wausau, Wis. (1922).

Henry Hering (born, New York City, 1874) enjoyed for several years the privileges of Saint Gaudens's studio and is equipped for any form of sculpture. He has chosen to specialize in architectural art, and the "strait and narrow way" is opening to a very opulent reward. Among his larger achievements — most of which represent many carefully modelled figures — we find the reliefs of the impressive Civil War Memorial for Yale University (1913); the Robert Collyer Memorial, Church of the Messiah, 34th Street, New York City (1915); sculpture of the Field Museum of Natural History, Chicago — a score of classic figures of great beauty (1917) — and finally the sculptural decorations of three Federal Reserve Banks, namely, of Dallas, Kansas City, and Cleveland. Mr. Hering has also done his quota of fountains, tablets, and busts; his contribution, unusually widespread, is of particular significance to this country.

James Earle Fraser was born in 1876 at Winona, Minn. He studied for several years at the Art Institute of Chicago. Later, at the "League" in New York, he made the acquaintance of Saint Gaudens, whom he assisted for some time in this country and in Paris, notably upon the "General Sherman." Mr. Fraser's talent, his industry, and his fair-mindedness have won him a high place in the esteem of his colleagues. His skill is great, but this is not what most impresses the admirers of his varied works; it is the good taste, the sanity, and the sculptural import of all that he conceives. One recalls with pleasure the Harriman Fountain at Arden, N. Y. (1910); the recumbent figure of Bishop Potter in the Cathedral of St. John the Divine (1912); the reliefs of the Harry Payne Whitney children (1912) — that classic of true Saint Gaudens tradi-

tion, and the massive and original John Hay Memorial in Cleveland (1914). A recent group, " The Journey through Life" (1920), in Rock Creek Cemetery, Washington, D. C., is a work of appealing beauty (Fig. 108). Nor can we forget " The End of the Trail," that poignantly expressive climax of the Panama-Pacific Exposition. The "present writing" — so soon to become ancient history — finds Mr. Fraser's studio crowded with important works: an heroic " Alexander Hamilton" just unveiled before the Treasury Building,

FIG. 108. — JAMES EARLE FRASER: DETAIL, KEEP MEMORIAL, WASHINGTON, D.C.

Washington, D. C.; the Ericsson Monument for the same city; an ideal figure for a war memorial in the Bank of Montreal, Canada, and an important war memorial for Winnipeg. Mr. Fraser has also added over forty excellent portraits to our country's artistic wealth, besides designing the nickel five-cent piece with Indian head and buffalo (1919), the medal of the American Academy of Arts and Letters, and several others.

Lee Lawrie was born in Rixdorf, Germany, in 1877, and studied with Saint Gaudens. He is one of the few American sculptors who have consistently followed the profession in the spirit of the mediæval craftsmen.   He writes: " Nearly all of my work and most of my interest have been in building decoration; not the kind of work where the architect's drawings are copied or even interpreted, but the kind that allows my own selection of the subject and character of both ornament and figure."   From 1906 to 1908 inclusive Mr. Lawrie was occupied with the general ornamentation of the new buildings at West Point.   A bronze figure, " Peace," known as the Forsythe Monument, in Forest Hills Cemetery, Boston, and a bronze relief of Josiah Willard Gibbs for Yale University, date from 1910; in 1916 we find — to note only the most important — a group and various decorations for Saint Vincent Ferrer Church, New York City, followed in 1917 by a statue of the Virgin and Child in alabaster and onyx for the same church.   The years 1917 and 1918 were largely devoted to the modelling of fifty-seven figures and most of the ornament of the reredos in Saint Thomas's Church, New York, said to be the largest and most elaborate ecclesiastical sculpture in the world.   For this magnificent labor of love and triumph of consecrated skill, Mr. Lawrie and Mr. Goodhue were both given gold medals by the American Institute of Architects.   In 1919–1921 Mr. Lawrie made for the tower of the Harkness Memorial Quadrangle at Yale University thirty-two statues and much ornamentation. Here is a record to be proud of.   America is vastly richer for it.

In spite of the fact that Mahroni M. Young (born Salt Lake City, Utah, 1877) is an instructor in the Art Students' League, a painter and illustrator, he has produced much interesting and virile sculpture.   Best known are " The Man with Pick," Metropolitan Museum of Art, New York; Hopi and Apache groups, American Museum of Natural History, New York; bronzes, " A Laborer," " The Rigger," Free Public Library, Newark, N. J., and the "Sea Gull Monument," Salt Lake City, Utah.

Few have quite so long a list of important works executed in the last twenty years as has Robert Aitken (born 1878).   Apparently no one toils quite so feverishly and persistently.   Mr. Aitken's native city of San Francisco possesses his " Victory " on its monument to the American Navy; also his McKinley Memorial; and it was for the Panama-Pacific Exposition of that city that he later created his

FIG. 109.—EDWARD McCARTAN: DIANA, METROPOLITAN MUSEUM

notable " Fountain of the Earth," with its vast amount of rich detail. He was in Paris from 1905 to 1907, producing there a number of ideal works which were exhibited at the Salon. Returning to America, he made a series of admirable busts, including among his sitters: Augustus Thomas, David Warfield, Willard Metcalf, George Bellows, William Howard Taft, Nathaniel S. Shaler, and Henry Arthur Jones. These and certain well-known statuettes, like " The Flame" and " Dancing Faun," brought recognition and ever increasing patronage. Since that time Mr. Aitken has never been without important commissions. One recalls certain impressive bronze doors for tombs, the Elihu Burritt Memorial at New Britain, Conn., the Bliss Memorial in Woodlawn Cemetery, New York City, the dramatic George Rogers Clark Monument at the University of Virginia, the martial vigor of the Camp Merritt Memorial. His garden figures are among the best yet made in this country — happy combinations of strength and grace. Mr. Aitken served for nearly two years in the World War as captain of a machine-gun company. Since his return to America he has designed and executed a number of war memorials; the great one for Kansas City upon which he is now engaged in collaboration with H. Van Buren Magonigle, architect, provides a magnificent opportunity for his powers. He has also modelled several excellent coins and medals, including the Watrous Medal for Sculpture awarded by the National Academy of Design and the Marshal Foch medal issued by the American Numismatic Society.

In his " Golden Hour," Rudulph Evans, almost unheralded, produced one of the finest things in American sculpture. This embodiment of the charm of young girlhood is a rare combination of delicacy and strength, of frankness and reticence. Reproductions of Mr. Vanderlip's treasure have been welcomed in the Metropolitan Museum and in the Luxembourg. Mr. Evans was born in Washington, D. C., in 1878, studied in New York and Paris, and is favorably known for his portraits, as well as ideal subjects. His " Boy and Panther" was one of the most attractive groups in the sculpture exhibition of 1923.

Edward McCartan was born in Albany, N. Y., in 1878. His name is associated with grace and charm. He does not " turn out" sculpture, but labors deliberately, and each new carefully-studied work brings its reward of appreciation from the discriminating public. His garden figure, "Spirit of the Woods," received the Widener Memorial Medal in 1916 and is now in the garden of Mr. Harold I. Pratt, Glen Cove, L. I. "Girl Drinking from a Shell" — "Youth" — "Pan" — "Nymph and Goat" — ("in its light gayety as inspiring

FIG. 110. — SHERRY FRY: MODESTY.

as a decoration by Clodian") — "Nymph and Satyr" — each name recalls a distinct pleasure. The imaginative and appealing Eugene Field Memorial was dedicated in Chicago in 1922. Perhaps most beautiful of all is the "Diana" (Fig. 109) recently bought by the Metropolitan Museum.

Another Westerner who has made good in the East is Sherry Fry, who was born in 1879, at Creston, Iowa, studied sculpture at the Art Institute of Chicago and the " League," and in 1908 won the American " Prix de Rome."   Whether he strikes the now official archaistic note of the Roman Academy or merely models well, Mr. Fry's work is invariably interesting, and his execution never hasty — least of all in such treatments as he has shown us in " Modesty" (Fig. 110), which was first called an " Unfinished Figure."   His list begins with the well-known " Mahaska " of Oskaloosa, Iowa, which received a medal at the Salon of 1908, and includes many garden and fountain creations of great charm, culminating in the twelve graceful figures for Festival Hall at the Pan- ama-Pacific Exposition.   A notable achievement is his " Peace " at St. George, Staten Island, a happy adaptation of the Apollo of the west pedi- ment at Olympia.   Mr. Fry has made a number of dig- nified portraits, as the " Ira Allen " (1920), for the Uni- versity of Vermont, and the statue of Monsignor Cloeric (1922), also in Burlington.   He

FIG. 111. — JOHN GREGORY : PHILOMELA, MANHAS- SET, L. I.

has designed two good pediments for sumptuous residences, but it is in simpler works like his " Modesty" and " Mother and Child " that his personality becomes most eloquent.   His experiments in "pale " sculpture will be watched with keen interest by his brothers of the studio.

John Gregory is by birth an Englishman (born in London, 1879). His years in the American Academy in Rome have left a pleasant but not overwhelming impress upon him.   He introduced himself to us through his sufficiently archaic " Venus," a marble over-mantel panel for Mr. Meredith Hare, of Huntington, L. I.; " Bacchante " and " Wood Nymph " are life-size marble figures in the garden of Mr. H. P. Whitney at Roslyn, L. I.; " Orpheus and Dancing Leopard" is a bronze group of heroic size in the garden of Mr. Charles M. Schwab, Loretto, Pa.; "Philomela" (Fig. 111), perhaps the most exquisite of Mr. Gregory's works, is in the Bird Garden of Mr. Payne Whitney, Manhasset, L. I. "The Voyage" is a vast circular relief on the floor of the office of the Cunard Line, Broadway, New York City. "Toy Venus" is a three-fourths life-size marble, and other fancies beautiful and whimsical are taking form.

FIG. 112. — MANSHIP: LITTLE BROTHER.

Chester Beach is one of the talented sons of California (born in San Francisco, 1881). It has been his enviable privilege to devote his time almost exclusively to ideal subjects. From the days when he found himself a fortunate pensionnaire of the American Academy in Rome he has been "seeing things" in blocks of marble and — unlike many of his colleagues — he has been able to reveal his dreams to others. Conceptions like "The Sacred Fire" in the new home of the Academy of Arts and Letters, New York, a recent noble reredos in marble for Saint Mark's-in-the-Bowerie, and a very beautiful head of Mrs. Beach in the Art Institute of Chicago, have given this sculptor a high place in contemporary art.

Paul Manship was born in St. Paul, Minn., in 1885. He studied at the St. Paul Institute of Art and the Pennsylvania Academy, winning there the Prix de Rome, and spending the years 1909–1912 at the American Academy in Rome. Mr. Manship's skill and the novelty of his archaistic inventions have made his work welcome in many art collections. One notes " Centaur and Nymph," Metropolitan Museum of Art; "Centaur and Dryad" and " Flight of Night," Detroit Institute of Art; " Indian and Pronghorn Antelope" and "Dancing Girl and Fauns," Art Institute, Chicago; " Playfulness," Minneapolis Institute of Art; " Dancer and Gazelles," Cleveland Museum, also Luxembourg, Paris, and Corcoran Art Gallery, Washington; J. P. Morgan Memorial, Metropolitan Museum; also " Pauline," a remarkable portrait of the sculptor's infant child; the delightful " Little Brother" (Fig. 112); the reliefs of the " Elements" for the Telephone and Telegraph Building, New York City, and many quaint medals.

Leo Friedlander, another of the well-trained brotherhood of the Roman Academy, was born in New York City in 1889. His works are already many; of them we may note the sculptures on Washington Memorial Arch, Valley Forge; figures on altar of St. Thomas's Church, Frankfort, Pa.; Bacchante friezes, private home, Hillcrest, L. I.; figures over main entrance, Masonic Temple, Detroit; bronze equestrian group, " Potential America"; garden figure, Belvidere, N. J.; " From the Land of the Hyperboreans," equestrian statue (sketch); and, best known of all, the strange but powerful " Mother and Infant Hercules."

Carl Paul Jennewein came to us from Stuttgart, Germany, where he was born in 1890. He began his study of sculpture at the Art Students' League. Although but recently returned from the Academy in Rome he offers the following list of works: Dudley Memorial Gate, Harvard University; Darlington Memorial Fountain, Washington, D. C.; Caruso Tablet, Metropolitan Opera House, New York; sculptural decorations on the Cunard Building, New York; the Eastman School of Music, Rochester, N. Y. Mr. Jennewein is best known for his delightful " Cupid and Gazelle" in the Metropolitan Museum.

Georg J. Lober, who was born in Chicago in 1892, is one of the coming men. Each new work from his hand shows progress and confirms the faith of his colleagues. Examples are a " Kneeling Nude," and the " Eve" of the exhibition of 1923. Still better known are the sturdy " American Fighting Man," and the bust of genial

Frank Bacon, of "Lightnin'" fame. Paul Fjelde, the son of the Norwegian sculptor Jacob Fjelde, was born in Minneapolis, Minn., in 1892. His reliefs and medals have found favor in New York exhibitions as well as in the West, while his admirable bust of Lincoln was welcomed in Christiania, Norway. Allan Clark was born in Missoula, Mont., in 1896. He had at the sculpture exhibit of 1923 a well-modelled bust of Mme. Galli-Curci; "Italian Tones" in polychrome, and bronze figures, "Satyr" and "Nymph" — "the lovely dancing Nymph of Allan Clark," as Royal Cortissoz proclaimed it.

Our sculptors of animals have made notable advance in the last twenty years. Mr. Proctor has fulfilled the promise of earlier days, creating a host of admirable works, among which one recalls with especial pleasure the massive lions of the McKinley Monument in Buffalo and the superb "Princeton Tiger." Of late Mr. Proctor has subordinated his animals to the human figure, and in such works as his "Indian Drinking," for Saratoga Springs, and the "Pioneer" of the University of Oregon (Eugene, Ore.) the animals are omitted. Denver's Civic Center has two of Mr. Proctor's equestrian subjects: an incredibly active "Broncho Buster" and the fine Indian "On the Warpath." Portland, Ore., has recently welcomed his mounted "Roosevelt the Roughrider." Edward C. Potter (born, New London, Conn., 1859) collaborated with Mr. French for several years, as recorded elsewhere. Among his more recent works are the Lions of the Public Library, New York City; the equestrian "General Phil Kearny" of Washington, D. C., and his distinguished "General Custer" at Monroe, Mich. Frederick C. R. Roth has had all the honors and has earned them. His group, "Polar Bears," is one of the classics of American sculpture; his horses, seals, and "Highland Bull" are no less fine. Eli Harvey's "Lioness and Cubs," his clean-cut greyhounds, and his official "Elk" have given him greater fame than have his excellent portraits of many distinguished men. The brilliant promise of Arthur Putnam (born, Waveland, Miss., 1873) was interrupted by ill health, but not before his vivid bronzes had found their way from California into our best collections. Amory C. Simons delights in the horse and is at his best in such subjects as the "New York Fire-Engine Horses,"

"The Storm, New York Police," and "Colonel Cody." Eugene Morahan makes a specialty of small bronzes. Edward Field Sanford (born, New York City, 1886) may demur at being classed among the animalists, since he has done much commemorative and decorative sculpture, but his "Great Dane" has brought him wider renown than all these. Edwin M. Deming (born, Ashland, Ohio, 1860) is too versatile to be classified, but has made some most interesting groups and figures of wild life. The achievements of Miss Hyatt, Mr. Laessle, and others are referred to elsewhere.

FIG. 113. — FURIO PICCIRILLI: PIERRE GAUTIER DE LA VARENNE, WINNIPEG.

Known to every sculptor of America is the "Bottega Piccirilli," that big New York shop where this family of industrious and gifted brothers model for themselves and carve for other less skilful artists. Attilio Piccirilli's work on the well-known Monument to the Maine extended from 1901 to 1913, and resulted in some very beautiful sculpture. Of the same period is that powerful and tragic nude, "The Outcast." "A Soul" (1909) is another study of the nude, an exquisite female form. A "Mater Consolatrice" followed in 1914. A fine pediment, in granite, for the Wisconsin State House is one of Mr. Piccirilli's greatest achievements. He was represented at the exhibit of 1923 by "A Boy of the Piave" and "Fragilina," both excellent nudes.

Furio Piccirilli has been no less busy.   His groups for the " Court of the Four Seasons" were much admired at San Francisco.   In 1920 he carried out the entire sculptural decoration of the Parliament House at Winnipeg.   If all of its features reach the standard of the " Pierre Gautier de La Varenne " (Fig. 113) — pictured in the *American Magazine of Art*, July, 1921 — Canada possesses one of the gems of this continent; we have no finer architectural sculpture than this figure.

At a recent meeting of the National Sculpture Society there were four candidates for membership — all Italians.   On another occasion, among ten candidates four again were Italians.   The catalogue of the great sculpture exhibit of 1923 seems to be half Italian.   Masters of the solid attainments of the Piccirillis, the wizardry of Lentelli, and the imagination of Billotti, Salvatore, and Scarpitta enliven exhibitions of the Academy and make their valuable contribution.   This brilliant group of Latins gathered together in New York represents, like the rest of us, various degrees of culture and of artistic conscience.   Some are among our best sculptors ; others are frankly commercial, reaping immense harvests, particularly in the South. One even boasted awhile back that in the sixteen years of his happy sojourn among us he had made and sold " twenty-seven public monuments, sixteen portrait statues, and seventy-five busts," an achievement several times greater than the entire life work of Augustus Saint Gaudens!   On the whole, however, the presence of this army of traditional sculptors is one of the most potent factors in America's artistic development.

Leo Lentelli comes from Bologna, Italy, where he was born in 1879.   He was formerly instructor in the California School of Fine Arts, and at present holds the same position in the Art Students' League, New York.   His fluent decorations are to be found in churches and theatres in many cities, including San Francisco, Denver, St. Louis, and New York.   He received in 1922 the medal of the Architectural League.

The medals of Anthony de Francisci merit particular notice — the " Almighty Dollar " is sure of it.   Antonio Salemme and Vincent Salerno have won fame through their portraits, while Benjamin Bufano has made his distinct impression on the Western coast.

Mario Korbel (born, Osik, Bohemia, 1882) has added some exquisite things to our spiritual possessions: busts of fair women, reliefs, slender fountains with bewitching little sprites high-perched, fascinating nudes on tiptoe, elegant to the fingertips of their uplifted hands — these are some of the contributions for which we thank this dreamer of beautiful dreams. Cecil de Blaquière Howard was born in Clifton, Canada, in 1888. He studied under James Earle Fraser in Buffalo, and later in Paris. He has two war monuments in towns on the Normandy coast, but is best known for his nudes, carved directly in the marble. Despite the efforts of a too eager press, Jo Davidson's real talent, coupled with extraordinary industry, is winning the respect of his colleagues. His series of vivid portrait busts of scores of notables of the World War is a remarkable achievement.

Frederick W. Ruckstull, as he now spells the name (born, Alsace, 1853), after making a great number of Confederate memorials has devoted himself for some time to literature and editorship. In both skill and industry J. Otto Schweizer (born, Zurich, 1865) does honor to his name. Sometimes his facility almost runs away with him, but in portraiture he is sure and convincing, rising when his subject permits to great nobility, as in his " General Muhlenberg " in Philadelphia, and his " Lincoln," grouped with admirable portraits of Generals Pleasanton and Gregg, in the Pennsylvania State Memorial at Gettysburg. Other interesting works are " Von Steuben," Ithaca, N. Y., and Valley Forge, Pa.; portraits of Generals Humphreys, Geary, and Hays; Molly Pitcher Monument for the state of Pennsylvania at Carlisle, Pa.; " Lincoln " statue and several relief portraits in the Union League of Philadelphia.

Frederick Ernst Triebel (born, Peoria, Ill., 1865) has designed various state memorials for battlefields and has made many portraits, as the " Robert G. Ingersoll " in Peoria; " Senator Henry M. Rice " and " Senator George L. Shoup " in the National Hall of Statuary.

Henry Hudson Kitson's list is long; among his portraits and memorials one notes statues of General N. P. Brooks and Patrick A. Collins and the William M. Hunt and Robert Burns Memorials, all in Boston; " General Lloyd Tilghmore," Paducah, Ky.; " General Lee," Vicksburg, Miss., etc.

William Couper, having completed a long array of well-modelled busts, the fine " Longfellow " in Washington, D. C., and the Colonel Alexander Hawkins Memorial in Pittsburgh, is now resting from his labors. George T. Brewster (born, Kingston, Mass., 1862) has done yeoman's service as a teacher, first at the Art Students' League and later at Cooper Union. He made the equestrian statue of W. P. Hussy at Danvers, Mass., " Greek Statesman " and " Greek Drama " on the Brooklyn Institute Museum, and a Soldiers' Monument at Malden, Mass. Ernest Wise Keyser (born in Baltimore, 1876) has done his generous share of portraits and monuments, as the Enoch Pratt Memorial, Baltimore, Md.; bronze figure, " Sir Galahad," Harper Memorial, Ottawa, Canada; Peter Fenelon Collier Memorial, New York City; Leith Memorial, Deal, N. J.; Isaac L. Rice Memorial, Pelham Bay Park, N. Y.

Charles Louis Hinton (born, Ithaca, N. Y., 1869) is a mural painter who likes to model. His small bronzes are in various collections and are often very delightful, as the happy " Fountain Figure " shown at the sculpture exhibit of 1923. A graceful pendant, " Boy with Fish," was the contribution of R. Hinton Perry, who, although likewise a painter, has produced a surprising number of facile portrait statues and handsome garden decorations.

Allen G. Newman (born, New York, 1875) created some years ago for Staten Island a military figure, " The Hiker," which has been pronounced by more than one critic " the best bronze soldier in America." Be this as it may, Mr. Newman has knowledge and skill and puts a vast amount of vitality into his work. His monuments are widely scattered: " The Pioneer " is in Salem, Ore.; " Women of the South " in Jacksonville, Fla.; " Doughboy," Pittsburgh; Henry Hudson Monument, New York City; and a " Lord Harris " in far-away Caracas, Venezuela. Another who knows how to make a convincing soldier is Finn H. Frolich. No American sculptor, however, has surpassed the compelling power which John A. Wilson put into his steady, motionless " Pennsylvania Volunteer." Carl E. Tefft made a strikingly original " Battle Monument " for Fort Lee, N. J. Burr C. Miller set his animated " General Herkimer," likewise, upon a boulder. Bruno Louis Zimm has adorned many cities with his graceful figures and many public buildings with his tasteful tablets.

Others to whom their colleagues have given a vote of confidence in the form of full membership in the National Sculpture Society are: John M. Bateman, Henry Crenier, Gleb Derujinsky, C. Percival Dietsch, Ralph Goddard, Louis A. Gudebrod, C. F. Hamann, C. H. Humphriss, Augustus Jaegers, F. Lynn Jenkins, F. R. Kaldenberg, Ephraim Keyser, Lawrence Maldarelli, Eli Nadelman, F. H. Packer, Ulysses Ricci, Anton Schaff, M. M. Schwarzott, Theodore Spicer-Simson, Louis St. Lanne, Edgar Walter, and Albert Weinert.

Most widely known perhaps of our women sculptors is Janet Scudder (born, Terre Haute, Ind., 1873), who has filled the years with a joyous brood of fountain figures. Her elfish children might be truants from the Florentine "Cantoria," and yet they are always delightfully her own. Long may they continue to multiply upon the face of the earth! Miss Scudder's reliefs are well known, early finding their way into the Museum of the Luxembourg as well as to numerous art collections of America.

Another eager spirit out of the West is Bessie Potter Vonnoh, whose little bronzes are welcomed the world over. Like Miss Scudder she received her first impetus from the Columbian Exposition. Her point of view has been admirably worded by a writer in the *International Studio* as "a glad and unpremeditated attempt to catch the lovely minuteness of life, rather than to labor at a conventional dignity of mere bulk. Her dominant note, the note to which I find myself most sympathetic, is her rendering of a sort of delicate domesticity. One feels that the touch which has evoked the nursery in the placid permanence of sculpture has been moved by that degree of tenderness with which it would caress a living thing."

Abastenia St. Leger Eberle was born in Webster City, Iowa, in 1878, and studied at the "League" under George Grey Barnard. Miss Eberle has made a real contribution to American art through her plastic snapshots of door-step and pavement — those arresting glimpses of the humbler life of a great city. Her small bronzes are sympathetic but unfailingly sculptural in conception and handling, even when the theme is dancing and skating children. "Little Mother," "The Windy Doorstep," and "The Rag-Picker" are little classics.

To no one has the great city been kinder than to Evelyn Beatrice Longman. Born in Winchester, Ohio, in 1874, she at one time spent two years in Olivet College, Mich., and later gained the fundamentals of her craft at the Art Institute of Chicago. Her first work of importance was a male " Victory " for the Festival Hall of the St. Louis Exposition. Miss Longman's bronze doors for the chapel of the Naval Academy at Annapolis were the result of a competition of thirty-three sculptors. Beyond these doors were other doors — those of the library of Wellesley College; then the colossal " Electricity " on the tower of the Telephone and Telegraph Building, New York City; next came another important competition and another success: the Senator Allison Memorial for Des Moines, Iowa. Now follow memorials without number: one to Gwendolen Sedgwick Batchelder at Windsor, Conn. (1919); the Peck Memorial, Waterbury, Conn. (1920); a war memorial at Naugatuck, Conn. (1920); Schmidlapp Memorial, Cincinnati (1921); Williams Memorial, All Souls' Church, New York City (1923). Add to these selections two beautiful nudes, " The Future " and " Nature," several notably refined busts, various medals, and a number of purely decorative works, — here is indeed an array of which to be proud.

Laura Gardin is in private life Mrs. James E. Fraser, but professionally is quite able to stand alone. Like all the preceding she came from afar. Born in Chicago in 1889 she studied modelling at the Art Students' League. Her work is unusually original. Her " Satyr and Nymph " of the Metropolitan Museum is representative; a most difficult problem, her conception and handling of this weird group are worthy of the highest praise. From a note so elemental to the subtler art of the medallist is an enormous span, yet we find her no less assured and successful in her miniature reliefs. A beautiful example is the medal " Better Babies."

Anna Vaughn Hyatt is one of our foremost sculptors of animals. The daughter of Alpheus Hyatt, a professor at Harvard, Miss Hyatt has inherited the scholarly attitude of mind; her art is as profound as it is externally pleasing. Her recent achievement, the majestic " Joan of Arc " (Fig. 114) on Riverside Drive, New York, places her securely among the recognized leaders. What living sculptor could have done it better? Her " Great Danes " in blue Italian marble are a

FIG. 114.—ANNA VAUGHN HYATT: JOAN OF ARC, NEW YORK CITY.

noble pair; her " Colts in a Snow-Storm " are almost tragic in their new-found woe; but one remembers perhaps most vividly those " Reaching Jaguars," which their author has planned for two gate posts. They are among the most original things in American art.

New York's group of women sculptors is large. It is impossible even to name them all. In addition to the above, the National Sculpture Society has honored with membership the following: Mrs. Gail Sherman Corbett, whose monumental work is dignified and impressive; Harriet W. Frishmuth, a clever artist of unusual skill in modelling of the nude; Grace Mott Johnson, proficient in animal sculpture, ranging in subject from chimpanzees and elephants to calves, colts, and kittens; Mrs. Carol Brooks MacNeil — wife of the sculptor — abounding in quaint fancies of rare charm; Enid Yandell, whose activities within and outside the studio have made her well known. In the recently acquired collection of American sculpture in the Metropolitan Museum one finds the graceful marble reliefs of singing girls by Frances Grimes and interesting work by Brenda Putnam, the gifted, all-round artist whose sundial-baby took the George D. Widener Gold Medal of the Pennsylvania Academy in 1923. Mrs. H. H. Kitson of Boston and Nellie V. Walker of Chicago are also members of the organization.

Associate members of the Society are: Mrs. Clio Bracken; Malvina Hoffman, whose spirited groups fascinate one in spite of personal theories regarding sculpture as the static art; Edith Howland; Mrs. Louise Allen and Mrs. Anna Coleman Ladd of Boston; Mrs. Jess M. Lawson-Peacey; Eleanor M. Mellon; Mrs. Edith Baretto Parsons, whose joyous " Duck Girl " made her famous, but has been surpassed by a delightful "Springtime"; Mrs. Lucy Perkins Ripley; Eugenie F. Shonnard, who revealed to us the decorative possibilities of " His Majesty the Heron"; Mrs. Lindsey Morris Sterling; Alice Morgan Wright, whose tiny sketches are frequently the most interesting things in an exhibition; and Mrs. Gertrude V. Whitney, who has shown originality in such works as her Aztec Fountain in the Pan-American Building, Washington, D. C., and the ephemeral El Dorado Fountain of the Panama-Pacific Exposition, and whose art becomes personal and impressive in the Titanic

Memorial — not yet placed — and in the figure of a young soldier entitled "Honorably Discharged."

There are other women sculptors in New York — a hundred of them — mostly gathered from distant places. Caroline Peddle Ball was born in Terre Haute, Ind. Her exhibits are few, but are always of interest to the craftsman. Mabel Conkling is from Maine; her fountains, sundials, and medallions reflect her superior training under Saint Gaudens and MacMonnies. Isabel Moore Kimball was born in Iowa and is best known through her admirable "Winonah" of Winona, Minn. Annetta Johnson Saint Gaudens came from Ohio. From Albany comes Gertrude Lathrop, whose young goat, "Nancy Lee," has just bounded into popularity. Belle Kinney is from Nashville, and has expressed in her Memorial to the Women of the Confederacy the unforgettable sacrifice of the South. Nor can we overlook the intrepid Mrs. Sally James Farnham, who, self-taught, "without master or tradition," undertakes equestrian statues like her "General Bolivar," and does them well enough to please the New York Municipal Art Commission. Lillian Link, on the other hand, triumphs in tiny impressionistic baby forms as dainty as apple blossoms. Margaret French Cresson makes refined and distinguished portraits.

Probably nine-tenths of our sculptors are huddled in New York. Other cities sustain from one to a half dozen each, perhaps as curiosities. In connection with Boston one thinks first of Cyrus E. Dallin. Mr. Dallin seems to have been "called" to make a distinctive and invaluable contribution, alike to American art and to American history. Exceptionally equipped by early environment, he has been able to trace his pathway with complete certitude. His mounted Indians are among the most interesting public monuments in this country; one recalls with growing satisfaction "The Signal of Peace" in Lincoln Park, Chicago (1894); "The Scout," a striking silhouette upon a hill-top in Kansas City; the weird "Medicine Man" in Philadelphia, and particularly the majestic "Appeal to the Great Spirit" (1909) before the Boston Museum of Art. Other well-known works of Mr. Dallin are: a marble relief of Julia Ward Howe, Museum of Fine Arts, Boston (1909); "The Hunter," Arlington, Mass. (1915); "Alma Mater," Mary Institute, St. Louis, Mo. (1916);

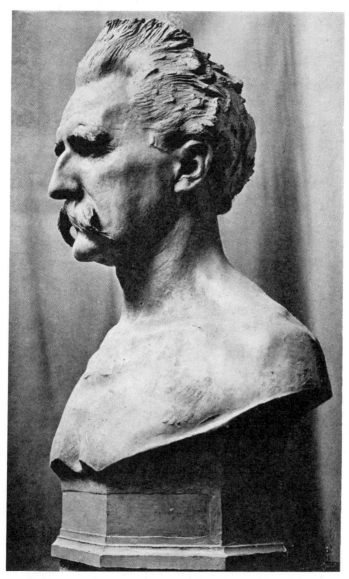

FIG. 115. — CHARLES GRAFLY: BUST OF HERMANN
KOTSZCHMAR, PORTLAND, ME.

" Massasoit," Plymouth, Mass. (1921); " Anne Hutchinson," State House, Boston; the Provincetown Memorial, " Signing the Compact" (1922); " The Last Arrow " (1923).

Less familiar is the name of Albert H. Atkins of Boston and Providence, whose interesting work — ideal and architectural — appears too infrequently in our exhibitions. Richard Recchia is one of several young Italian sculptors of Boston who are doing good work. Mrs. Theo Alice Ruggles Kitson has produced a great amount of meritorious sculpture, largely military memorials. The vigor and genuine craftsmanship which she puts into her regiments of soldiers and countless busts (as at Vicksburg) have won the appreciation of the entire sculptural guild. Mrs. Anna Coleman Ladd has followed a different path; her imagination supplies a numerous round of sprightly Pucks and fairies to make glad the fountains of pleasant gardens.

Andrew O'Connor lives in the neighborhood of Worcester, Mass., where he was born in 1874. May be mentioned his fine " General Lawton" of Indianapolis; "General Lew Wallace," in the National Hall of Statuary, Washington; Governor Johnson Memorial at St. Paul, Minn., and Lincoln of Springfield, Ill.[1]

In Philadelphia Charles Grafly still rules the destinies of the young sculptors. To be known as America's best teacher is a sufficiently proud distinction, but to be recognized as our greatest master of portraiture is likewise Mr. Grafly's due. Each head that he models is an artistic triumph, its completion an event. Dates are lacking, but the following come readily to memory: portraits of Dr. Joseph Price, Frank Duveneck, Thomas Anschutz, Elmer Schofield, William Paxton, Edward Redfield, Hermann Kotszchmar (Fig. 115), George C. Thomas, and Paul W. Bartlett. Like John Sargent, Mr. Grafly is unwilling to confine himself to the field which has made him famous; he has produced of late a number of monumental works, among them the " Pioneer Mother" of San Francisco, and more recently the elaborate General Meade Memorial for Washington, D. C., a happy combination of realism and allegory upon which the sculptor has expended much thought and a vast amount of conscientious labor.

[1] Illustrations of a number of Mr. O'Connor's works will be found in the writer's " Modern Tendencies in Sculpture."

One of Mr. Grafly's best known pupils has chosen a very unusual pathway.   Mr. Albert Laessle (born, Philadelphia, 1877) reveals to us, with extraordinary research and unfailing skill, the grotesque humor of animal life.   No one can make a toad more appealing nor portray the home life of a lobster with a tenderer sentiment.   Mr.

FIG. 116. — ALBERT LAESSLE: VICTORY, METROPOLITAN MUSEUM.

Laessle's bronzes are in a class by themselves, unsurpassed by the cunning artificers of China and Japan (Fig. 116).   Among Mr. Grafly's students are many Italians.   The Pennsylvania Academy exhibitions are enriched by their clever contributions, while that amazing place, the Graphic Sketch Club, is a crowded museum of their achievements.   Prominent among them is Giuseppe Donato, well known alike for admirable portraiture and ideal works.   Other names not to be overlooked are Louis Millione and Aurelius Renzetti. Beatrice Fenton has won many honors, and in works like her " Seaweed Fountain " shows happy invention.

Dr. R. Tait McKenzie is a Canadian by birth (Almonte, Ontario, 1867), but has been for many years a director of physical education in the University of Pennsylvania, a unique opportunity for a sculptor. His artistic development has been like the progress of the Greeks, beginning with the creation of simple figures of young athletes. On this solid basis of unemotional, scientific study he has evolved a personal expression which grows stronger with every utterance. His "Whitefield" (1919) is eloquent and convincing. His "Captain Drummond" (1918) and particularly the English "Homecoming" — the Cambridge Memorial — (1922) have a thrill-conveying quality seldom attained in our military monuments.

Henry Lewis Raul lives in Easton, Pa., where he was born in 1887. His works include the handsome Northampton County Monument to the martyrs of the *Maine;* and the spirited Soldiers' Monument at West Chester, Pa.; along with such lighter themes as "Sunlight on the Wave," "Mermaid Playing," and "The Hour of Twilight."

At the memorable exhibition of the National Sculpture Society which was held in 1907 in a great armory of Baltimore, that city discovered that it possessed several gifted and well-equipped young sculptors. They have since found their opportunity.

Hans Schuler (born, 1874, in Alsace-Lorraine) won in 1900 the Rinehart Scholarship in Paris, and upon his return exhibited a fluent "Ariadne" and an unusually successful group, "Paradise Lost." Since then his list shows several portrait statues, a number of busts, and a multitude of reliefs and medallions. Among his memorials are the Buchanan Memorial, Washington, D. C., the Johns Hopkins Memorial, Baltimore, and the Fiske Memorial, Ashland, Ky.

Edward Berge (born, Baltimore, 1876) is most widely known for his charming little garden figures. He has, however, done many monuments for his city: Watson; Tattersall; Latrobe and Armistead; while his ideal works are widely scattered, as " Pietà," St. Patrick's Church, Washington, D. C. (1910); Group, "The Scalp," Honolulu (1915); Garden figure — Mme. Melba, Melbourne (1915); Ryals Tomb, Savannah, Ga. (1916); Soldiers' and Sailors' Memorial, Prince George, Md. (1920); Fountain figure, Ardsley-on-Hudson (1920). Mr. Berge's medallions are exceptionally fine.

J. Maxwell Miller (born, Baltimore, 1877) enjoyed the privileges of the G. A. Rinehart travelling scholarship from 1900 to 1905, and has produced much good work, notably: " Ishmael," St. Louis Museum (1902); " Separation of Orpheus and Eurydice," Peabody Library, Baltimore (1904); " The Poets," Peabody Concert Hall, Baltimore (1908); Portrait of Young Lady, Walters Gallery, Baltimore (1909); the very fine James Cardinal Gibbons Jubilee Medal (1911); Monument to French Soldiers and Sailors buried at Annapolis (1911); Latrobe Monument (in collaboration), Baltimore (1913); School Children's Monument, Baltimore (1914); Monument to the Confederate Women of Maryland, Baltimore (1918); Monument to those who died in the Great War, Wilmington, N. C. (1921); Daniel Coit Gilman Memorial, Johns Hopkins University, Baltimore (1923).

Turning to the Nation's capital, we find Henry K. Bush-Brown (born, Ogdensburg, N. Y., 1857) continuing his thoughtful work. Mr. Bush-Brown has a penchant for heroic equestrian statues — like his " General Anthony Wayne," Valley Forge, and his "General John Sedgwick " of Gettysburg — which he seems to produce as easily as Mr. Dunbar makes busts. The latter (Ulric S. J. Dunbar, born London, Ont., 1862) has scores of portraits to his credit, while his well-known "' Boss' Shepherd," on Pennsylvania Avenue, proves his ability with the figure. George Julian Zolnay (1863), after a prolonged sojourn in St. Louis, has returned to Washington. His sketchy bronzes are abundant in the South. Among his successful works one notes the gigantic lions of University City, Mo., the dramatic Laclede Memorial of St. Louis, and the Industrial Memorial, New Bedford, Mass. He has recently completed a large war memorial for Nashville, Tenn.

In Cincinnati Clement J. Barnhorn continues to make his valuable contribution, not only as an able sculptor, but as an exceptional teacher. His pupils are found in many lands. Mr. Barnhorn's best-known statue is his " Theodore Thomas," in the Cincinnati Music Hall. Several of his fountains, designed in the spirit of the *Cinquecento*, have been admirably translated into faïence by the Rookwood Pottery. Among his many religious sculptures are the " Madonna and Child " of the cathedral of Covington, Ky., and the Wetterer Memorial in Cincinnati, both beautiful examples of sincerity and faith.

A similar pioneer service has been performed for Cleveland by Herman N. Matzen (born, Denmark, 1861), who has made many decorations for the court houses of Cleveland and Akron, Ohio, statues of Richard Wagner and Tom L. Johnson, and interesting mausoleums and memorials. At the Ohio State University, Columbus, Bruce W. Saville (born, Quincy, Mass., 1893) is now instructor in sculpture, while doing much professional work.

In Indianapolis one finds Mrs. Myra Richards, whose originality reveals itself in a wealth of fancies ranging from mischievous sprites to impressive memorials, and including such sympathetic portraiture as her statue of James Whitcomb Riley at Greenfield, Ind.

In Chicago Albin Polásek, who succeeded Charles J. Mulligan as instructor at the Art Institute, has not only developed unusual qualities as a teacher, but through his able craftsmanship has won the place of leader in the West. Born in Frenstat, Moravia, in 1879, Mr. Polásek came at an early age to the United States. A pupil of the Pennsylvania Academy, he gained in 1910 the Prix de Rome. Among his most prominent works are busts of Frank D. Millet, Charles F. McKim, J. P. Morgan, Charles L. Hutchinson, Frank Logan, and Charles W. Hawthorne. The three last named are in the Art Institute of Chicago, where is also " The Sower." A statue of Governor Richard Yates was recently finished for Springfield, Ill. Mr. Polásek is now engaged upon a major work, his memorial to Theodore Thomas for Grant Park, Chicago. Fountains spring up wherever this gifted artist wanders, and the fashioning of small bronzes is his recreation. Several of his pupils are on the verge of "making history" and doubtless will be recorded in the next edition of this book.

Leonard Crunelle, who was born in 1872 in a coal-mining village near Lens, France, is spiritually allied to the Florentines of the early Renaissance. His is a soul kinship to Benedetto and Desiderio. Circumstances compel him to model soldier memorials and dead governors in " Prince Albert " coats. He does them well, but is at his best in his caressing tributes to childhood. Among his best-known works are the "Squirrel Boy" and various decorations in Chicago parks; Hixon Memorial, LaCrosse, Wis.; Military Memorial,

Jacksonville, Ill.; statue of Governor Oglesby, Chicago; and Governor Palmer, Springfield, Ill.; many busts, tablets, and medals.

A visitor in Hannibal, Mo., will be shown not only the boyhood home of " Mark Twain," but an excellent statue of the great author, the work of another son of that region.   Frederick C. Hibbard (born, Canton, Mo., 1881), long resident in Chicago, has been very industrious since he left the Art Institute.   Among his portraits distributed through fifteen states, are " Carter Harrison " in Chicago, " General Lawton " in Fort Wayne, Ind., and the " Mark Twain." Of his military memorials the one erected in Shiloh National Park by the United Daughters of the Confederacy is the most important as well as the most beautiful.

Nellie V. Walker is well known not only for her appealing group entitled " Her Son " in the Art Institute of Chicago, but for numerous monuments in several states.   Prominent among these is the noble " Keokuk " in the Iowa city of that name.

Emil Zettler by practice and precept upholds the mediæval standards of craftsmanship.   His carvings in wood and stone are especially interesting.   Richard Bock puts the flavor of the Old World into his quaint and original conceptions.   Hester Bremer is a newcomer of strong individual expression, as shown in her " Mother and Baby" fountain.   Kathleen Wheeler is likewise from abroad.   Her English training has been unusually thorough ; in her chosen field — small bronzes of domestic animals — she has few equals in this country.   Emory Seidel models children's heads with much skill and taste.   "The Torreys" (Fred and Mabel) delight in similar subjects. Mrs. Torrey's happy fountain, " Wynken, Blynken, and Nod," in Denver, is her most important work.   Agnes Fromen, with her charming baby heads and her ingenious small fountains, has done much to enrich Chicago, while the tinted reliefs of Mary Parker Adelsperger brighten many a home.   George Ganière takes pleasure in making ideal figures " out of his head."   The public understands better his " Lincoln," and his well-composed " General Anthony Wayne," at Fort Wayne, Ind.   Sidney Bedore is equipped for serious undertakings, as is proved by his admirable standing " Roosevelt " of Benton Harbor, Mich.   A group of three striking figures from the early annals of his native city, Green Bay, Wis., promises to be a notable monument. Gilbert Riswold has extraordinary facility, and in his "Stephen A. Douglas" of Springfield, Ill., achieved success with unpromising material. He is finding his great opportunity in a large military memorial for Salt Lake City. John Paulding does much thoughtful work of considerable variety. Sigvald Asbjörnsen and Charles Haag are not to be overlooked. Leon Francis Hermant is of the Parisian "Beaux-Arts" tradition and is exceptionally prepared for important work.

Varied and strangely exotic are the offerings of such men as Alfeo Faggi — whose masterly busts of Tagore and Yone Noguchi testify that his distortions of the human figure are wilful; Stanislaus, Szukalski, clever and fantastic; Alfonso Ianelli, a painter and decorator as well as an able sculptor; and G. Arcila-Uribe, who comes from Bogotá, Colombia, — all of these intensely personal notes add to the joy of our exhibitions, where Marcello Rebechini, John David Brcin, and Samuel Klastorner represent the younger generation.

The writer has of late devoted himself to the creation of fountains, as: "The Great Lakes" (1913) and the "Fountain of Time" (1922), both in Chicago; the sculpture of the Columbus Memorial Fountain, Washington, D. C. (1912); the "Trotter," "Paducah," and "Thatcher Memorial" fountains, respectively in Bloomington, Ill., Paducah, Ky., and Denver, Col. Also a "Washington" (1909) in Seattle, Wash., and "Blackhawk" (1911) in Oregon, Ill.

Victor S. Holm (born Copenhagen, 1876), instructor in the St. Louis School of Fine Arts, has a rugged talent plus certain decorative graces acquired through prolonged association with Philip Martiny. His Missouri Monument in the National Cemetery at Vicksburg, his "Governor Thomas Carlin" of Carrollton, Ill., and a recent memorial to the students of Washington University, St. Louis, who died in the World War are good examples. Other sculptors of St. Louis are the veteran Robert P. Brinkhurst, and three women of talent: Adele Schulenburg (Gleason), Caroline Risque (Janis), and Nancy Coonsman (Hahn). The latter completed in 1922 a Memorial to Missouri Soldiers dead in France.

A nude "Aviator" for Topeka, Kan., happily introduces a young sculptor of Kansas City, Robert M. Gage. The profession is worthily represented in Minneapolis by John K. Daniels, whose

"General Sanborn" and "Colonel Wilkins" are in the State Capitol, St. Paul, and whose soldiers are to be seen at Shiloh, Andersonville, Memphis, and elsewhere.   He has a figure of "Memory" at Nashville, Tenn., and many portrait busts throughout the Northwest.

Denver has done much in recent years in the way of civic adornment; the presence in that enterprising and beautiful city of a number of young sculptors, including Clara Sorensen Dieman and Robert Garrison, promises increased activity on artistic lines.   Alice Cooper Hubbard, likewise of Denver, made in 1905 an admirable "Sacajawea" for Portland, Ore.

Avard Tennyson Fairbanks, perhaps the only "Professor of Sculpture" in America, is endeavoring to carry the message of art into remote corners of the West.   The enthusiasm which would put the same bronze doughboy into every county seat of Oregon is a little bewildering, but the figure is a vigorous one!

While California's gifted sons, like Aitken and Beach, find profitable recognition in the East, the indefatigable Armenian sculptor, Haig Patigian, has identified himself with San Francisco, where he creates public monuments and decorations with joyous prodigality. Edgar Walter's interesting work ranges from "Primitive Man" and "Nymph and Bears" to his thoughtful decorations for Leland Stanford University.

The sculptors of Los Angeles, under the leadership of David Edstrom, made in 1922 a notable exhibition which revealed much unsuspected talent in that part of the world.   Julia Bracken Wendt has a long-established and well-merited reputation, but among the discoveries was the work of Kathleen Robinson Ingels of Toronto, and, more recently, of Chicago, where her marble group, "Inspiration" is a prized possession, of the Art Institute.   Another welcome arrival in the Western colony is Miss Clyde Chandler, formerly of Dallas, Tex.   Miss Chandler's early works were full of whimsical witchery; later she expended herself upon the elaborate Sidney Smith Memorial Fountain for Dallas, Tex., a creation of much imaginative beauty.   Miss Ella Buchanan has made a number of pieces of a hortatory nature.   Frank C. Wamsley's nymphs, on the other hand, betray small interest in social problems; they are satisfied to stretch their graceful limbs in the California sunshine!

Professor Post in his monumental history of sculpture [1] finds little encouragement in the present outlook in America — indeed, according to him, Manship's clever echoes of Olympia and Pompeii are the only hopeful signs that he is able to discern. In spite of the comprehensiveness of his book one is persuaded that the field has not been completely scanned nor have certain promising tendencies been given full recognition. The last twenty years have seen a great production of excellent work in America, amazing in amount as in quality. Sculpture is at last taking root. With this increasing abundance comes familiarity and ultimately appreciation.

Architectural sculpture has been the foundation of great art in all periods. There could be no more hopeful symptoms to-day than the fact that men like Hering, Lawrie, and Weinman have given a large part of their time to the embellishment of worthy buildings, public and private, while many others have made important contributions in the same field. This is as it should be; America is the gainer by it. Consider for instance the subject of fountains. How arid was the chronicle of the last century; but since 1902, beginning with the spectacular cascade of the St. Louis Exposition, see how they have burst forth! Our gardens and public places are brightened by their sparkle and humanized by their graceful forms. Our best sculptors delight in making them; one recalls charming efforts in this line by Adams, Aitken, Bitter, Calder, French, Fry, Konti, Lukeman, MacMonnies, Manship, McCarten, and scores of others. All of our women sculptors find a natural and happy expression in this field, creating beauty in numberless playful works.

There is no use in reproaching our ancestors, but beyond question the one thing which shadows the future of American sculpture is our lack of an æsthetic past. The absence of cultural tradition and the diminishing importance of the handicrafts in our daily life are factors which make development difficult and slow. The mass of our people, so intelligent upon many subjects, possess naught of the appreciation which comes from doing skilful things with their own hands. What with standardized production and the attendant humiliation of the workman, the whole social trend is away from

[1] "A History of European and American Sculpture from the Early Christian Period to the Present Day," by Chandler Rathfon Post, Harvard University Press, 1921.

such worthy achievement and pride in it. "Study hard, my boy, so that you will not have to work when you are grown up," is the tacit implication in most of our schools. We shall not have a great national art until we once more count it honorable to work with the hands — until thousands of craftsmen are doing their best and hundreds of thousands are acclaiming their triumphs of skill and ingenuity. Young Donatello was but one of a group of dexterous workmen; when he surpassed them they knew it and each enthusiastically accorded him the position which he had earned. We are not making Donatellos to-day; who would recognize them if through some fortunate accident they were to appear?

On the other hand — and there is another hand — there are certain hopeful signs. One has been named — the indisputable fact that good sculpture is being done. Another is the inexplicable but constant factor of natural aptitude. Call it atavism, a miracle, or what you will, even the "best families" produce now and then a child so instinct with creative power that he *must* draw or paint or write or model. Traditions and surroundings count for nothing; self-expression is all-compelling — another artist has appeared!

GENERAL BIBLIOGRAPHY

BENJAMIN, S. G. W.   Art in America.   New York, 1880.

CAFFIN, CHARLES H.   American Masters of Sculpture.   New York, 1903.

CLARK, WILLIAM J., JR.   Great American Sculptures.   Philadelphia, 1877.

CLEMENT AND HUTTON.   Artists of the Nineteenth Century.   Boston, 1880.

DOWNES, WILLIAM HOWE.   Twelve Great Artists.   Boston, 1900.

DUNLAP, WILLIAM.   History of the Rise and Progress of the Arts of Design in the United States.   New York, 1834.

ELLET, MRS. E. F.   Women Artists in All Ages and Countries.   London, 1858.

FRENCH, H. W.   Art and Artists of Connecticut.   Boston, 1879. ✓ *WARNER,*

GOODYEAR, W. H.   Renaissance and Modern Art.   New York, 1899.   *PRATT*

HARTMANN, SADAKICHI.   A History of American Art.   2 vols.   Boston, 1902.   *BARTLETT*

—— Modern American Sculpture.   Plates.   Edited by Sadakichi Hartmann.   New York.

HAWTHORNE, NATHANIEL.   The French and Italian Note-books.   Boston, 1858.

JARVES, JAMES JACKSON.   The Art Idea.   New York, 1877.

—— Art Thoughts.   Boston, 1879.

MARQUAND AND FROTHINGHAM.   A Text-book of the History of Sculpture.   New York, 1899.

PARTRIDGE, WILLIAM ORDWAY.   The American School of Sculpture.   The Arena, Vol. 7, p. 641. ✓

RADCLIFFE, A. G.   Schools and Masters of Sculpture.   New York, 1894.

STURGIS, RUSSELL.   Sculpture.   Forum, Vol. 34, p. 248.

—— Exhibition of the National Sculpture Society.   The World Today, Vol. 4, p. 261.

TAFT, LORADO.   American Sculpture and Sculptors.   The Chautauquan, Vol. 22, p. 387, No. 4.

—— Sculpture of the Nineteenth Century : American Sculpture.   Progress, p. 322.   Same in Current Encyclopædia, p. 1061.

TUCKERMAN, HENRY T.   Book of the Artists.   New York, 1867.

VIARDOT, LOUIS.   Wonders of Sculpture.   New York, 1873.

SPECIAL BOOKS AND ARTICLES

ANDERSEN.   A New Sculptor, by Mrs. Schuyler Van Rensselaer, Century, Vol. 61, p. 17.

BALL.   My Three Score Years and Ten, by Thomas Ball.   Boston, 1891.
   Thomas Ball, by William Ordway Partridge, New England Magazine (N. S.), Vol. 12, p. 291. ✓

BARNARD. A New American Sculptor, by William A. Coffin, Century, Vol. 31, p. 877.

A Great American Sculptor, by L. C. Dennis, Review of Reviews, Vol. 19, p. 49.

The Sculptor of Pan, by Regina Armstrong, Critic, Vol. 33, p. 354.

Barnard's Pan, by Charles de Kay, Art Interchange, Vol. 41, p. 5.

George Grey Barnard, by Regina Armstrong Hilliard, Munsey's, Vol. 20, p. 456.

George Grey Barnard, Sculptor, by Alexander Blair Thaw, The World's Work, December, 1902, p. 2837.

BARTLETT. Some American Artists in Paris, by Frances Keyzer, Studio, Vol. 13, p. 246.

The Statue of Michelangelo in the Congressional Library, Scribner's, Vol. 25, p. 381. ✓

BORGLUM. S. Borglum and His Work, by W. G. Bowdoin, Art Interchange, Vol. 46, p. 2.

The Frontier in Sculpture, by Arthur Goodrich, The World's Work, Vol. 3, p. 1857.

BROWERE. Unknown Life Masks of Great Americans, by Charles H. Hart, McClure's, Vol. 9, p. 1053.

Life Masks of Great Americans, by Charles H. Hart, McClure's, Vol. 12, p. 337.

CALDER. Alexander Stirling Calder, by L. R. E. Paulin, House and Garden, Vol. 3, p. 316.

CLARKE. Thomas Shields Clarke, by Arthur Hoeber, Brush and Pencil, Vol. 6, p. 193.

CONNER. A Sculptor of the People, by Francis B. Sheafer, Booklovers Magazine, Vol. 1, p. 623.

CRAWFORD. Crawford and Sculpture, by Henry T. Tuckerman, Atlantic, Vol. 2, p. 64.

Thomas Crawford : A Eulogy, by G. S. Hillard, Atlantic, Vol. 24, p. 40.

Thomas Crawford (unsigned), Living Age, Vol. 56, p. 274.

DALLIN. Cyrus E. Dallin, Sculptor, by William H. Downes, Brush and Pencil, Vol. 5, p. 1.   Same in New England Magazine (N. S.), Vol. 21, p. 196.

DONOGHUE. John Donoghue, by W. Lewis Fraser, Century, Vol. 35, p. 957.

The Young Sophokles by Donoghue, by Charles de Kay, Art Review, Vol. 1, No. 4.

The Career of John Donoghue, Sculptor, by J. C. McCord, Brush and Pencil, Vol. 12, p. 364.

FRENCH. The Sculptor French, by William A. Coffin, Century, Vol. 37, p. 871.

New Figures in Literature and Art, by Royal Cortissoz, Atlantic Monthly, Vol. 75, p. 223.

Daniel Chester French, by Mrs. H. B. Emerson, New England Magazine, Vol. 16, p. 259.

Daniel Chester French, American Sculptor, by J. P. Coughlan, Magazine of Art (London), Vol. 25, p. 311.

Daniel Chester French, Sculptor, by Lorado Taft, Brush and Pencil, Vol. 5, p. 145.

French's O'Reilly Group, by John C. Van Dyke, Century, Vol. 30, p. 158.

Daniel French's Summer Studio, by John J. A'Becket, Art Interchange, Vol. 49, p. 132.

Daniel Chester French, Sculptor (unsigned), Munsey's, Vol. 19, p. 234.

Recent Work by Daniel Chester French, by Nelson R. Abbott, Brush and Pencil, Vol. 8, p. 43.

GRAFLY. Charles Grafly's Work, by Victoria C. Dallin, New England Magazine (N. S.), Vol. 25, p. 228.

Charles Grafly, Sculptor, by Lorado Taft, Brush and Pencil, Vol. 3, p. 343.

GRAFLY. Charles Grafly, Sculptor, by Helen W. Henderson, The Booklovers Magazine, Vol. 2, p. 499.

HART. The Old Masters of the Blue Grass, by General Samuel Woodson Price. Louisville, Kentucky, 1902.

HARTLEY. Mr. Hartley's Sculpture (unsigned), Art Amateur, Vol. 39, p. 71.

HOSMER. Harriet Hosmer, by L. M. Child, Living Age, Vol. 56, p. 697.
Harriet Hosmer, by W. H. Bidwell, Eclectic Magazine, Vol. 77, p. 245.

KELLEY. A Sculptor of American History, by Anna Leach, Munsey's, Vol. 14, p. 446.

KEMEYS. American Wild Animals in Art, by Julian Hawthorne, Century, Vol. 6, p. 213.
Edward Kemeys, A Sculptor of Frontier Life and Wild Animals, by Hamlin Garland, McClure's, Vol. 5, p. 120.

MACMONNIES. Frederick MacMonnies, by Will H. Low, Scribner's, Vol. 18, p. 617.
An American Sculptor, by Royal Cortissoz, The Studio (London), Vol. 6, p. 17.
Frederick MacMonnies, Sculptor, by H. H. Greer, Brush and Pencil, Vol. 10, p. 1.

NIEHAUS. The Sculpture of Charles Henry Niehaus, by Regina Armstrong. New York, 1902.

O'DONOVAN. Grant and Lincoln in Bronze, by Cleveland Moffett, Munsey's, Vol. 5, p. 419.

PARTRIDGE. Sculptor and Student, by Charles Chapin Sargent, Jr., Munsey's, Vol. 19, p. 436.

POTTER (Mrs. Vonnoh). Bessie Potter, by Lucy Munroe, Brush and Pencil, Vol. 2, p. 29.
A New Note in American Sculpture, by Arthur Hoeber, Century, Vol. 32, p. 732.
Miss Bessie Potter's Figurines, Scribner's, Vol. 19, p. 126.
The Work of Miss Bessie Potter, by Helen Zimmern, Magazine of Art, Vol. 24, p. 522.

POWERS. Hiram Powers, the Sculptor, by Edward Everett, Living Age, Vol. 15, p. 95.
Hiram Powers, the Sculptor, by Samuel Y. Atlee, Living Age, Vol. 42, p. 569.
Hiram Powers (unsigned), Eclectic Magazine, Vol. 71, p. 1028.
Hiram Powers, by Henry Boynton, New England Magazine (N. S.). Vol. 20, p. 519.

PRATT. The Work of Bela L. Pratt, Sculptor, by William H. Downes, New England Magazine, Vol. 27, p. 760.

PROCTOR. A. Phimister Proctor, by Lorado Taft, Brush and Pencil, Vol. 2, p. 241.

RHIND. A Scotch-American Sculptor, by John A'Becket, Art Interchange, Vol. 48, p. 84.
A Genius of the Chisel, by N. MacDonald, Munsey's, Vol. 14, p. 671.
Kindred Spirits After All, by Elizabeth E. Newport, Art Interchange, Vol. 41, p. 50.

RIMMER. Dr. Rimmer (unsigned), Atlantic, Vol. 51, p. 263.
The Art Life of William Rimmer, by Truman H. Bartlett. Boston, 1882.
The Art Life of William Rimmer, by C. H. Moore, Nation, Vol. 35, p. 557.
Dr. William Rimmer, by T. H. Bartlett, American Art Review, Vol. 1, pp. 461 and 509.

ROGERS. John Rogers, by William Ordway Partridge, New England Magazine (N.S.), Vol. 13, p. 705.

RUCKSTUHL. F. Wellington Ruckstuhl, Sculptor, by Elizabeth Graham, Metropolitan Magazine, Vol. 10, p. 489.

RUCKSTUHL. Frederick Wellington Ruckstuhl, Sculptor, by Richard Ladegast, New England Magazine (N. S.), Vol. 25, p. 615.

The Spirit of the Confederacy, by Charles de Kay, Outlook, Vol. 71, p. 645.

Mr. Ruckstuhl's Solon (unsigned), Art Interchange, Vol. 37, p. 116.

RUSH. William Rush, by E. L. Gilliams, Lippincott's, Vol. 52, p. 249.

SAINT GAUDENS. Augustus Saint Gaudens, by Kenyon Cox, Century, Vol. 13, p. 28.

Saint Gaudens's Lincoln, by M. G. Van Rensselaer, Century, Vol. 13, p. 37.

The Shaw Memorial and the Sculptor Saint Gaudens, by William A. Coffin, Century, Vol. 32, p. 179.

SHRADY. The New American Sculptor, by Charles H. Garrett, Munsey's, Vol. 29, p. 546.

STORY. William Wetmore Story and His Friends, by Henry James. Boston, 1903.

William Wetmore Story, by Mrs. Lew Wallace, Cosmopolitan, Vol. 21, p. 404.

William Wetmore Story (unsigned), Magazine of Art, Vol. 2, p. 272.

TILDEN. Douglas Tilden, Sculptor, by William Dallam Armes, Overland Monthly (N. S.), Vol. 31, p. 142.

A California Sculptor, by Elizabeth K. Tompkins, Munsey's, Vol. 19, p. 914.

VALENTINE. Edward Virginius Valentine, by Mrs. Margaret J. Preston, American Art Review, Vol. 1, p. 277.

WARD. J. Q. A. Ward, the Sculptor, by G. W. Sheldon, Harper's, Vol. 57, p. 62.

The Work of J. Q. A. Ward, by Russell Sturgis, Scribner's, Vol. 32, p. 385.

WARNER. Notes on an American Sculptor, by Ripley Hitchcock, Art Review, Vol. 1, No. 5.

Olin Warner, Sculptor, by Henry Eckford (Charles de Kay), Century, Vol. 15, p. 392.

The Sculpture of Olin Warner, by W. C. Brownell, Scribner's, Vol. 20, p. 429.

Famous Indians, by C. E. S. Wood, Century, Vol. 24, p. 436.

WUERTZ. Emil H. Wuertz, an Appreciation, by James Spencer Dickerson, Brush and Pencil, Vol. 3, p. 107.

YANDELL. Enid Yandell, the Sculptor, by Richard Ladegast, Outlook, Vol. 70, p. 81.

SUPPLEMENTARY BIBLIOGRAPHY

The Spirit of American Sculpture, by Adeline Adams. The National Sculpture Society, 1923.

Sculpture of Today, by Kineton Parkes. Chapman and Hall, Ltd., 1921 (Vol. 1).

A History of European and American Sculpture. From the Early Christian Period to the Present Day, by Chandler Rathfon Post, Harvard University Press, 1921 (Vol. 2).

Modern Tendencies in Sculpture, by Lorado Taft. University of Chicago Press, 1921.

Karl Bitter, by Ferdinand Schevill, University of Chicago Press, 1917.

Harriet Goodhue Hosmer, by Cornelia Carr. Moffat, Yard & Co., 1912.

Augustus Saint Gaudens, by Royal Cortissoz. Houghton Mifflin & Co., 1907.

Augustus Saint Gaudens, by C. Lewis Hind. John Lane Co., 1908.

The Reminiscences of Augustus Saint Gaudens, 2 vols. Century Co., 1913.

Paul Manship, by A. E. Gallatin. John Lane Co., 1917.

John Quincy Adams Ward, An Appreciation, by Adeline Adams. The National Sculpture Society, 1912.

MAGAZINE ARTICLES

ADAMS. Herbert Adams, Sculptor (unsigned), Bul. Pan Am. Union, Vol. 45, p. 93.
   Sculpture of Herbert Adams, by E. Peixotto, Am. Mag. of Art, Vol. 12, p. 151.
AITKEN. Robert I. Aitken, American Sculptor, by A. Hoeber, Int. Studio, Vol. 50,
   sup. 3.
   Art of Robert Aitken, Sculptor, by E. A. Semple, Overland (N. S.), Vol. 61,
   p. 218.
   Sculpture of Robert Aitken, by A. Hoeber, Int. Studio, Vol. 54, sup. 15.
   Robert I. Aitken (unsigned), Bul. Pan Am. Union, Vol. 47, p. 562.
BALL. Caroline Peddle Ball, Interpreter of Childhood, by M. Edson, Arts and Dec.,
   Vol. 1, p. 484.
BARNARD. George Grey Barnard, by J. N. Laurvik, Int. Studio, Vol. 36, sup. 39.
   Spirit of the New World in Sculpture, by K. M. Roof, Craftsman, Vol. 15, p.
   270.
   Great Sculptor Whose Work Has Reached the People, by M. Twombly, World's
   Work, Vol. 17, p. 11256.
   Sculptures of Barnard, by F. W. Coburn, World Today, Vol. 16, p. 273.
   Virile American Sculptor, by E. Knaufft, Rev. of Rev., Vol. 38, p. 689.
   Barnard's Mighty Sculptures for the Pennsylvania Capitol (unsigned), Cur.
   Lit., Vol. 49, p. 206.
   Petrified Emotion, by C. II. Meltzer, Cosmop., Vol. 49, p. 667.
   Barnard's Lincoln Once More (unsigned), Art World, Vol. 3, p. 190.
   Cloisters of George Grey Barnard, by E. F. Baldwin, Outlook, Vol. 109, p. 198.
   Mistake in Bronze; Barnard's Statue of Lincoln (unsigned), Art World, Vol. 2,
   p. 210.
   A Word for Barnard's Statue of Lincoln, by I. Tarbell, Touchstone, Vol. 2,
   p. 224.
BARNHORN. Decorative Designs by Clement J. Barnhorn, by C. H. Caffin, Int.
   Studio, Vol. 20, sup. 141.
   Clement J. Barnhorn, by E. B. Haswell, Int. Studio, Vol. 55, sup. 43.
BARTLETT. Paul Bartlett: American Sculptor, by E. S. Bartlett, New Eng. Mag.
   (N. S.), Vol. 33, p. 369.
   Evolution of an Equestrian Statue, by C. N. Flagg, Scribner's, Vol. 45, p. 309.
   Sculptor Who is also a Craftsman, by K. E. Chapman, Craftsman, Vol. 16,
   p. 437.
   Bartlett's Pediment for the House of Representatives, Washington, D. C., by
   W. Walton, Scribner's, Vol. 48, p. 125.

Recent Work of Paul W. Bartlett, by W. Walton, Scribner's, Vol. 54, p. 527.

Bartlett's Sculpture for the House Wing of the Federal Capitol, by G. Brown, Art World, Vol. 1, p. 39.

Paul Bartlett's Decorative Sculptures for the New York Public Library, by M. Carroll, Art and Archæol., Vol. 1, p. 163.

Paul W. Bartlett's Latest Sculpture, by J. J. Klaber, Arch. Rec., Vol. 39, p. 265.

Paul Wayland Bartlett (unsigned), Bul. Pan Am. Union, Vol. 45, p. 351.

BEACH.   Studies of Human Emotions in the Sculpture of Chester Beach (unsigned), Craftsman, Vol. 30, p. 350.

BERGE.   Edward Berge, Sculptor, by W. W. Brown, Int. Studio, Vol. 56, sup. 58.

BISSELL.   The Elton Memorial Vase, by George E. Bissell (unsigned), Int. Studio, Vol. 28, sup. 43.

BITTER.   Karl Bitter, by O. G. Villard, Survey, Vol. 34, p. 112.

Karl Bitter and his work, by E. Brush, and Others, Art and Progress, Vol. 6, p. 295.

Work of Karl Bitter, Sculptor, by H. H. Greer, Brush and Pencil, Vol. 13, p. 466.

Karl Bitter — Decorative Sculptor, by J. N. Laurvik, Sketch Book, Vol. 6, p. 1.

BORGLUMS.   Gutzon Borglum, Painter and Sculptor, by L. Mechlin, Int. Studio, Vol. 28, sup. 35.

Versatile Talent of Gutzon Borglum (unsigned), Cur. Lit., Vol. 40, p. 499.

Confederate Memorial by Gutzon Borglum (unsigned), World's Work, Vol. 34, p. 437.

Work of Gutzon Borglum (unsigned), Bul. Pan Am. Union, Vol. 44, p. 479.

Gutzon Borglum, by A. von Ende, Am.-Scand. Rev., Vol. 7, p. 353.

Gutzon Borglum and His Stone Mountain Plan, by R. V. S. Berry, Art and Archæol., Vol. 15, p. 228.

Solon H. Borglum, Sculptor, by C. H. Caffin, Int. Studio, Vol. 19, sup. 127.

Sculptor of the Prairie, Solon H. Borglum, by F. Sewall, Century, Vol. 68, p. 247.

Solon H. Borglum, Sculptor of American Life, by S. A. Armstrong, Craftsman, Vol. 12, p. 382.

Solon H. Borglum, by Gutzon Borglum, Am. Mag. of Art, Vol. 13, p. 471.

In Recognition of an American Sculptor, by Louise Eberle, Scribner's, Vol. 72, p. 379.

BRACKEN.   Woman Sculptor and Symbolist of the New Art, by M. A. Fanton, Craftsman, Vol. 8, p. 472.

BRENNER.   Designer of Coins and Sculptor of American Culture (unsigned), Cur. Opinion, Vol. 60, p. 50.

Two New Worlds and a Sculptor's Clay, by P. U. Kellogg, Survey, Vol. 35, p. 19.

CALDER.   Calder — a "Various" Sculptor, by A. Hoeber, World's Work, Vol. 20, p. 13377.

Stirling Calder, Sculptor, by H. R. Poore, Int. Studio, Vol. 67, sup. 37.

America, Sculpture and War: an Interview with A. Stirling Calder (unsigned), Touchstone, Vol. 1, p. 22.

CRUNELLE. Leonard Crunelle, Sculptor of Children, by I. MacDougall, Craftsman, Vol. 15, p. 26.

DALLIN. Work of Cyrus E. Dallin, by M. S. May, New Eng. Mag. (N. S.), Vol. 48, p. 408.

An American Sculptor: Cyrus E. Dallin, by A. Seaton-Schmidt, Int. Studio, Vol. 58, p. 109.

Dallin's Indian Sculptures, by W. H. Downes, Scribner's, Vol. 57, p. 779.

Cyrus E. Dallin and His Indian Sculpture, by J. S. Dickerson, Mon. News, Vol. 21, p. 679.

DAVIDSON. American Creator of the New Statuary (unsigned), Cur. Lit., Vol. 52, p. 99.

Jo Davidson, Sculptor, by H. F. Griffin, World's Work, Vol. 22, p. 14746.

Jo Davidson's Portrait Busts, by E. Anderson, Am. Mag. of Art, Vol. 11, p. 469.

A New Message in Sculpture, by R. Wyer, Fine Arts Journal, Vol. 26, p. 263.

Jo Davidson, by G. P. du Bois, Int. Studio, Vol. 76, p. 177.

EBERLE. Two Women Who Collaborate in Sculpture, by B. H. Smith, Craftsman, Vol. 8, p. 623.

New Bottles for New Wine, by C. Merriman, Survey, Vol. 30, p. 196.

Babies in Bronze, by D. Wilhelm, Illus. World, Vol. 24, p. 328.

EDSTROM. David Edstrom, American Sculptor, by G. R. Brigham, Art and Archæol., Vol. 9, p. 231.

David Edstrom, Sculptor, by M. Christie, Int. Studio, Vol. 69, sup. 87.

David Edstrom's Masterpiece, "Man Triumphant," by M. Carroll, Art and Archæol., Vol. 14, p. 50.

ELWELL. Life and Art of F. Edwin Elwell, by B. O. Flower, Arena, Vol. 39, p. 259.

EVANS. Sculpture of Rudulph Evans, by H. C. Candee, Int. Studio, Vol. 55, sup. 84.

EZEKIEL. American Sculptor in Rome, by K. H. Wrenshall, World's Work, Vol. 19, p. 12255.

New Statue of Edgar Allan Poe, by Ezekiel, by Mrs. L. Turnbull, Art and Archæol., Vol. 5, p. 306.

Sir Moses Ezekiel: American Sculptor, by H. K. Bush-Brown, Art and Archæol., Vol. 11, p. 226.

FAGGI. Alfeo Faggi, Sculptor, by G. C. Eglington, Int. Studio, Vol. 73, sup. 40.

Alfeo Faggi, by S. Rubinstein, Art in America, Vol. 9, p. 192.

Alfeo Faggi, Sculptor, by R. Offner, The Arts, Vol. 1, p. 3.

FAIRBANKS. Remarkable Boy Sculptor, by L. E. Zeh, Tech. World, Vol. 17, p. 294.

What One Boy Is Doing, by A. H. Seaman, St. Nicholas, Vol. 39, p. 14.

FJELDES. Two American Sculptors: Fjelde — Father and Son, Am.-Scand. Rev., Vol. 10, p. 467.

FLANAGAN. John Flanagan, Sculptor and Medalist, by F. O. Payne, Int. Studio, Vol. 75, p. 114.

FRASER. James Earle Fraser, Sculptor, by E. A. Semple, Century, Vol. 79, p. 929.

James Earle Fraser and His Work (unsigned), Bul. Pan Am. Union, Vol. 46, p. 648.

Fraser Bust of Roosevelt, by L. Eberle, Scribner's, Vol. 68, p. 427.

James Earle Fraser, by E. Seachrest, Am. Mag. of Art, Vol. 8, p. 276.

Fraser, Sculptor of People and Ideals (unsigned), Touchstone, Vol. 7, p. 87.

FRENCH. French's Bronze Doors for the Boston Public Library, by R. Sturgis, Scribner's, Vol. 36, p. 765.

Daniel Chester French, Sculptor, by C. H. Caffin, Int. Studio, Vol. 20, sup. 133.

Work of Daniel Chester French, by N. II. Moore, Chautauquan, Vol. 38, p. 141.

French's Groups of the Continents, by C. de Kay, Century, Vol. 71, p. 419.

An American Sculptor, Daniel Chester French, by S. Brinton, Int. Studio, Vol. 46, p. 210.

Daniel Chester French, by E. A. Rockwell, Int. Studio, Vol. 41, sup. 55.

Later work of Daniel Chester French, by W. Walton, Scribner's, Vol. 52, p. 637.

Daniel C. French (unsigned), Bul. Pan Am. Union, Vol. 44, p. 66.

Recent Sculpture of Daniel Chester French, by S. Brinton, Int. Studio, Vol. 59, p. 17.

How French's Lincoln Was Put into Marble, by W. M. Berger, Scribner's, Vol. 66, p. 424.

Daniel Chester French, Sculptor, by A. Seaton-Schmidt, Am. Mag. of Art, Vol. 13, p. 3.

GRAFLY. Charles Grafly in His Summer Home, by A. Seaton-Schmidt, Am. Mag. of Art, Vol. 10, p. 52.

HAAG. Charles Haag, Immigrant Sculptor of his Kind, by C. Eastman, Chautauquan, Vol. 48, p. 249.

Charles Haag, Sculptor of Toil, by J. Spargo, Craftsman, Vol. 10, p. 432.

Wood Carvings and Bronzes by Charles Haag, by E. I. Colley, Fine Arts Journal, Vol. 34, p. 181.

HARVEY. Impressions in the Studio of an Animal Sculptor, by J. Lemont, Int. Studio, Vol. 51, sup. 106.

HERING. Work of Henry Hering, by G. P. du Bois, Arch. Rec., Vol. 32, p. 510.

Henry Hering's Sculpture for the Field Museum in Chicago, by C. O. Cornelius, Arch. Rec., Vol. 44, p. 430.

HOSMER. Life and Works of Harriet Hosmer, American Sculptor, by R. A. Bradford, New Eng. Mag. (N. S.), Vol. 45, p. 265.

HYATT. Two Women who Collaborate in Sculpture, by B. H. Smith, Craftsman, Vol. 8, p. 623.

Anna Vaughn Hyatt's Statue of Jeanne d'Arc, by G. Humphrey, Int. Studio, Vol. 57, sup. 47.

Miss Hyatt's Statue of Joan of Arc, by C. H. Caffin, Century, Vol. 92, p. 308.

Artist-patriot; a Sketch of Anna Vaughn Hyatt, by C. Morrow, Touchstone, Vol. 5, p. 286.

JENKINS. F. Lynn Jenkins: His Decorative Sculpture, His Methods, by M. H. Spielman, Mag. of Art, Vol. 25, p. 294.

JOHNSON. Grace Mott Johnson, A Sculptor of Animals, by I. Moore, Am. Mag. of Art, Vol. 14, p. 59.

KECK. Salient Characteristics of Keck's Work, by A. G. Byne, Arch. Rec., Vol. 32, p. 120.

KEMEYS.   Edward Kemeys, an Appreciation, by L. Mechlin, Int. Studio, Vol. 26,
    sup. 10.

KONTI.   Hungarian Sculptor in America, by A. S. Levetus, Int. Studio, Vol. 45,
    p. 197.

LADD.   Anna Coleman Ladd: Sculptor, by A. Seaton-Schmidt, Art and Progress,
    Vol. 2, p. 251.

LAWRIE.   Lee Lawrie, Architectural Sculptor, by H. Tachau, Int. Studio, Vol. 75,
    p. 394.

LINDER.   Henry Linder: His Life and Work, by G. F. Kunz, Int. Studio, Vol. 53,
    sup. 21.

    Work of Harry Linder, Sculptor, by S. Howe, House B., Vol. 35, p. 20.

    How Henry Linder Brightened Homes, by C. de Kay, Arts and Dec., Vol. 3,
    p. 127.

LINK.   Children that will Never Grow Old (unsigned), Craftsman, Vol. 30, p. 547.

LONGMAN.   Evelyn B. Longman: a National Figure in Sculpture, by J. S. Dicker-
    son, World Today, Vol. 14, p. 526.

    Evelyn Beatrice Longman, by J. A. Rawson, Jr., Int. Studio, Vol. 45, p. 99.

LUKEMAN.   Lukeman, a Representative American Sculptor, by R. M. Furniss,
    Arch. Rec., Vol. 35, p. 414.

    Augustus Lukeman's Equestrian Statue of Francis Asbury, by M. E. Fenton,
    Am. Mag. of Art, Vol. 13, p. 476.

MCKENZIE.   Robert Tait McKenzie, American Sculptor, by R. Barr, Outlook, Vol.
    79, p. 556.

    Canadian Celebrities: Robert Tait McKenzie, by T. B. Donaldson, Canadian
    Mag., Vol. 25, p. 110.

    R. Tait McKenzie, Sculptor and Anatomist, by H. S. Morris, Int. Studio, Vol. 41,
    sup. 11.

    McKenzie, A Molder of Clay — and of Men, by W. Adler, Outing, Vol. 65,
    p. 586.

    R. Tait McKenzie, — Physician and Sculptor, by H. D. Eberlein, Century,
    Vol. 97, p. 249.

    Revival of Athletic Sculpture, by E. N. Gardiner, Int. Studio, Vol. 72,
    p. 133.

    Scientific Sculptor of the American Athlete, Cur. Opinion, Vol. 69, p. 378.

MACMONNIES.   Career of F. W. MacMonnies, by F. Strother, World's Work, Vol.
    11, p. 6965.

    Frederick MacMonnies, Portrait Painter, by E. Pettit, Int. Studio, Vol. 29,
    p. 319.

    Frederick MacMonnies, Sculptor, by C. H. Meltzer, Cosmop., Vol. 53, p. 207.

MACNEILS.   Sculptors MacNeil, by J. S. Halden, World's Work, Vol. 14, p. 9403.

MANSHIP.   Pauline — Mr. Manship's Portrait of His Daughter at the Age of Three
    Weeks, by M. G. Van Rensselaer, Scribner's, Vol. 60, p. 772.

    Two Amazing Portraits by Paul Manship, by F. O. Payne, Int. Studio, Vol.
    71, sup. 74.

    Sculpture by Paul Manship (unsigned), Fine Arts Journal, Vol. 33, p. 429.

    Paul Manship and His Work, by A. E. Gallatin, Studio, Vol. 82, p. 137.

MILLER.   Recent Memorial by Joseph Maxwell Miller, by W. W. Brown, Int. Studio, Vol. 68, sup. 29.

NADELMAN.   Breaking Loose from the Rodin Spell (unsigned), Cur. Opinion, Vol. 62, p. 206.

Eli Nadelman, by M. Birnbaum, Int. Studio, Vol. 57, sup. 53.

NIEHAUS.   Charles Henry Niehaus, American Sculptor (unsigned), Int. Studio, Vol. 29, p. 104.

Lincoln as Pictured by Niehaus, by F. O. Payne, Int. Studio, Vol. 58, sup. 40.

O'CONNOR.   Andrew O'Connor, Sculptor, by W. Walton, Scribner's, Vol. 45, p. 637.

Work of Andrew O'Connor, by R. Cortissoz, Art and Progress, Vol. 1, p. 343.

PADDOCK.   Recent work by Willard Dryden Paddock (unsigned), Int. Studio, Vol. 46, sup. 66.

Willard Dryden Paddock: Idealist, by A. L. Wangeman, Am. Mag. of Art, Vol. 7, p. 328.

PERRY.   Shakesperean Scenes in Bas-relief (unsigned), Cur. Lit., Vol. 40, p. 265.

PICCIRILLIS.   A Family of Sculptors, by A. Adams, Am. Mag. of Art, Vol. 12, p. 223.

PIETRO.   Art of C. S. Pietro, by J. Lemont, Int. Studio, Vol. 51, sup. 115.

Statuary of C. S. Pietro, by M. Morgan, Art and Archæol., Vol. 7, p. 313.

POLÁSEK.   Work of Albin Polásek, by A. G. Richards, Fine Arts Journal, Vol. 35, p. 122.

POTTER.   Sculpture of Edward Clark Potter, by H. W. Lanier, World's Work, Vol. 12, p. 7968.

PRATT.   Work of Pratt, Sculptor, by W. H. Downes, Int. Studio, Vol. 38, sup. 3.

Bela Pratt, Eminent New England Sculptor, by C. H. Dorr, Arch. Rec., Vol. 35, p. 508.

Bela Lyon Pratt, Appreciation, by L. M. Bryant, Int. Studio, Vol. 57, sup. 121.

Bela Lyon Pratt (unsigned), Bul. Pan Am. Union, Vol. 44, p. 778.

Americanism in Sculpture, by F. W. Coburn, Pal. and Bench, Vol. 2, pp. 95, 127.

PROCTOR.   Wild Beasts Sculptured by A. P. Proctor, by R. Cortissoz, Scribner's, Vol. 48, p. 637.

Phimister Proctor: Canadian Sculptor, by W. H. de B. Nelson, Canadian Mag., Vol. 44, p. 495.

Sculptor of the West, by E. Peixotto, Scribner's, Vol. 68, p. 266.

An Animal Sculptor, by E. H. Brush, Arts and Dec., Vol. 1, p. 392.

QUINN.   Edmond T. Quinn: Sculptor, by A. Sterner, Int. Studio, Vol. 55, sup. 10.

RIPLEY.   Lucy Perkins Ripley, Sculptor, by L. Merrick, Int. Studio, Vol. 75, p. 14.

ROGERS.   John Rogers: Sculptor, by C. H. Israels, Arch. Rec., Vol. 16, p. 483.

Catching up to John Rogers, by W. P. Eaton, Am. Mag. of Art, Vol. 11, p. 392.

ROTH.   Animal and Other Sculpture of Frederick G. R. Roth (unsigned), Art World, Vol. 9, p. 346.

F. G. R. Roth, Interpreter of Animals, by G. T. Wells, Arts and Dec., Vol. 2, p. 222.

SAINT GAUDENS.   Work of Saint Gaudens, by R. Cortissoz, North Am. Rev., Vol. 177, p. 725.

Work of Saint Gaudens, by C. H. Caffin, World's Work, Vol. 7, p. 4403.

Augustus Saint Gaudens, by T. Williams, Int. Studio, Vol. 33, sup. 123.

WARD. Work of a Veteran Sculptor, by M. Schuyler, Putnam's, Vol. 6, p. 643.
     John Quincy Adams Ward, First of American Sculptors (unsigned), Cur. Lit.,
         Vol. 48, p. 667.
     Work of John Quincy Adams Ward, by W. Walton, Int. Studio, Vol. 40, sup. 81.
WEINMAN.   A. A. Weinman, Sculptor of Monumental Architecture, by C. H. Dorr,
         Arch. Rec., Vol. 33, p. 518.
     Work of Adolph Alexander Weinman (unsigned), Bul. Pan Am. Union, Vol.
         45, p. 775.
WENDT.   Art of Julia Bracken Wendt, by E. C. Maxwell, Fine Arts Journal, Vol.
         23, p. 271.
WHITNEY.   Sculpture of War, the Work of Gertrude V. Whitney (unsigned), Touch-
         stone, Vol. 6, p. 188.
     Mrs. Whitney's Journey in Art, by G. P. du Bois, Int. Studio, Vol. 76, p. 351.
YANDELL.   Enid Yandell, the Sculptor, by R. Ladegast, Outlook, Vol. 70, p. 81.
YOUNG.   Bronzes of Mahroni Young, by J. L. Lewine, Int. Studio, Vol. 47, sup. 55.
     Life as Mahroni Young Sees It (unsigned), Touchstone, Vol. 4, p. 8.
     A Sculptor and a Painter of Utah, by J. P. Wilson, Fine Arts Journal, Vol. 24,
         p. 96.
     An Etching Sculptor: Mahroni Young, by F. Weitenkampf, Am. Mag. of Art,
         Vol. 13, p. 109.
ZOLNAY.   Sculptor Zolnay, by R. Douglas, World Today, Vol. 20, p. 450.
     Sculpture of George Julian Zolnay, by R. Douglas, Fine Arts Journal, Vol. 24,
         p. 295.
     Zolnay's Central High School Frieze (Washington), by R. Douglas, Art and
         Archæol., Vol. 3, p. 289.

ABBREVIATIONS OF MAGAZINES

Am. Mag. of Art	American Magazine of Art
Am.-Scand. Rev.	American-Scandinavian Review
Arch. Rec.	Architectural Record
Arts and Dec.	Arts and Decoration
Bul. Pan Am. Union	Bulletin of Pan American Union
Canadian Mag.	Canadian Magazine
Cosmop.	Cosmopolitan
Cur. Lit.	Current Literature
Cur. Opinion	Current Opinion
House B.	House Beautiful
Illus. World	Illustrated World
Int. Studio	International Studio
Mag. of Art	Magazine of Art
Mon. News	Monumental News
New Eng. Mag.	New England Magazine
Pal. and Bench	Palette and Bench
Rev. of Rev.	Review of Reviews
Tech. World	Technical World

INDEX OF SCULPTORS' NAMES

INDEX TO SUPPLEMENTARY CHAPTER